H O L T

Economics

CONTENT REVIEWERS

Donald G. Fell
Florida Council on Economic Education
Economics

Unit 1

John Tribble
Russell Sage College
Economics

Unit 2

John Clow
State University of New York, Oneonta
Microeconomics

Unit 3

Robert Reinke
University of South Dakota
Microeconomics and environmental economics

Warren Matthews
Houston Baptist University
Economics

Unit 4

W. F. Mackara
East Tennessee State University
Economics

Unit 5

Gerald F. Draayer
Boise State University
Macroeconomics

Unit 6

Gail Tamaribuchi
University of Hawaii, Manoa
Economic education

EDUCATIONAL REVIEWERS

Don Bender
Shaler Area Senior High School
Pittsburgh, Pennsylvania

Sharon Cruse
Central Hardin High School
Cecilia, Kentucky

Rachel Gragg
Clear Creek High School
League City, Texas

Richard Sipe
West Albany High School
Albany, Oregon

James G. Slenker
Liverpool High School
Liverpool, New York

Field Test Reviewers

Nicholas D. Confalone
Mansfield Senior High School
Mansfield, Ohio

Sharon Cruse
Central Hardin High School
Cecilia, Kentucky

George Dillow
Troy High School
Troy, Ohio

Alton Dale Gilmore
Tate High School
Gonzalez, Florida

Wayne Lechlitner
Venice High School
Venice, Florida

Christina B. Monroe
Chattanooga School of Arts and Science
Chattanooga, Tennessee

R. Kraig Rittenhouse
Warren Central High School
Vicksburg, Mississippi

Julia M. Sargent
George County High School
Lucedale, Mississippi

Richard Sipe
West Albany High School
Albany, Oregon

H O L T
Economics

R O B E R T   L .   P E N N I N G T O N

HOLT, RINEHART AND WINSTON

Harcourt Brace & Company

Austin • New York • Orlando • Atlanta • San Francisco • Boston • Dallas • Toronto • London

About the Author

Dr. Robert L. Pennington is the Assistant Dean of the College of Business Administration at the University of Central Florida and an Associate Professor of Economics. He also is the director of the University of Central Florida Center for Economic Education. Additionally, Dr. Pennington is a member of the American Economic Association, the National Association of Economic Educators, the Association for Private Enterprise Education, the Southern Economics Association, and the Western Economics Association.

Dr. Pennington received his Ph.D. from Texas A&M University. He has written, edited, and reviewed numerous books and articles dealing with economics and economic education.

Executive Editor

Sue Miller

Managing Editor

Jim Eckel

Editorial Staff

Diana Holman Walker, Senior Editor
Katharine Graydon, Project Editor
E. Shannon Barker, Associate Editor
Joni Wackwitz, Editor
Tracy C. Wilson, Editor
Kevin N. Christensen, Associate Editor
Bob Fullilove, Editor
Nancy Katapodis Hicks, Copy Editor
Joseph S. Schofield IV, Copy Editor
Carmen Saegert, Administrative Assistant

Editorial Permissions

Ann B. Farrar

Book Design

Diane Motz, Art Director
Katie Kwun
Tonia Klingensmith
Sonya Mendeke
Teresa Carrera-Paprota
Jane Dixon

Image Services

Greg Geisler, Art Director
Debra Schorn
Elaine Tate
Linda Richey

Photo Research

Peggy Cooper, Photo Research Manager
Tim Taylor
Kristin Hay

Cover Design

The Quarasan Group, Inc.

New Media Design

Carey Smith, Design Manager

New Media

Randy Merriman, Vice President, New Media
Ken Whiteside, Senior Technology Projects Editor

Production

Gene Rumann, Production Manager
Rosa Mayo Degollado, Production Coordinator
Leanna Ford, Production Assistant

Media Production

Kim Anderson
Belinda Barboza
Nancy Hargis

Manufacturing

Jenine Street

H O L T
Economics

CONTENTS

Introduction to Economics 1

Chapter 1

WHAT IS ECONOMICS? **2**

Chapter 2

ECONOMIC SYSTEMS **22**

UNIT 2

→ Elements of Microeconomics 48

UNIT 3

⋯⋯▸ Free Enterprise at Work   142

UNIT 4

⋯⋯▶ Elements of Macroeconomics 226

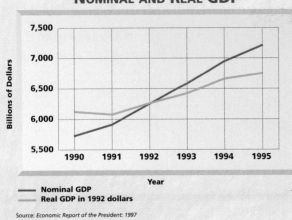

NOMINAL AND REAL GDP

Billions of Dollars

7,500
7,000
6,500
6,000
5,500

1990 1991 1992 1993 1994 1995

Year

— Nominal GDP
— Real GDP in 1992 dollars

Source: *Economic Report of the President: 1997*

Chapter 10

UNIT 5

Government and the Economy 276

Chapter 12

ROLE OF GOVERNMENT   278

Reference Section 454

Features

Careers in Economics

Case Study

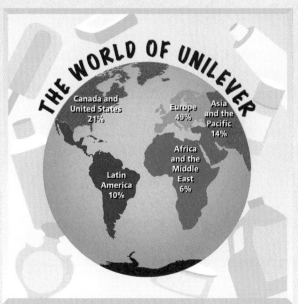

MULTINATIONAL CORPORATION: UNILEVER'S 1996 SALES

THE WORLD OF UNILEVER

Canada and
United States
21%

Europe
49%

Asia
and the
Pacific
14%

Africa
and the
Middle
East
6%

Latin
America
10%

Economics in Action

Global Exchange

Linking Economics and

Tables, Charts, and Graphs

DECREASE IN DEMAND

Price per Car Stereo

$600
$500
$400
$300
$200
$100
0

D1

D3

0 1 2 3 4 5 6 7

Quantity Demanded (in thousands)

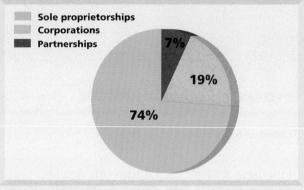

ABSOLUTE AND COMPARATIVE ADVANTAGE

Domestic Pretrade Product Ratios

1 lb. coffee
1 lb. coffee
1 lb. coffee
1 lb. coffee
1 lb. coffee

Costa Rica 5:1

1 lb. coffee
1 lb. coffee
1 lb. coffee

Panama 3:1

Costa Rica–Panama

1 lb. coffee
1 lb. coffee
1 lb. coffee
1 lb. coffee

Trade Ratio   4:1

STOCK MARKET PERFORMANCE

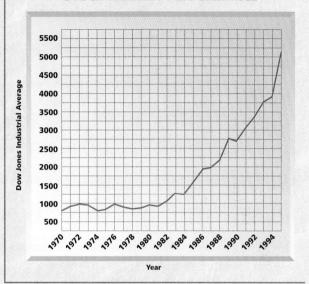

New Business Incorporations and Business Failures, 1993

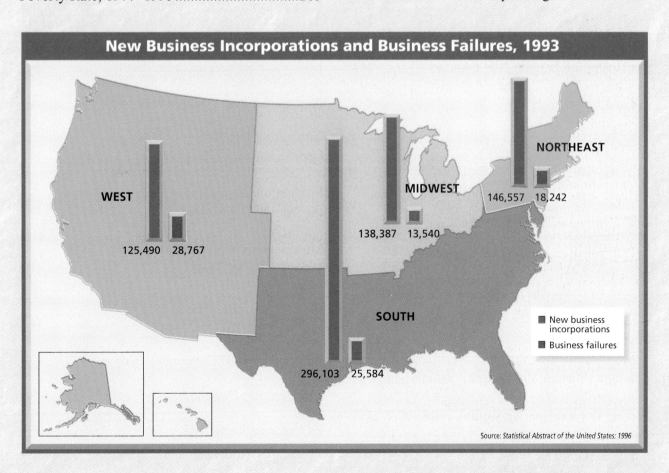

Source: *Statistical Abstract of the United States: 1996*

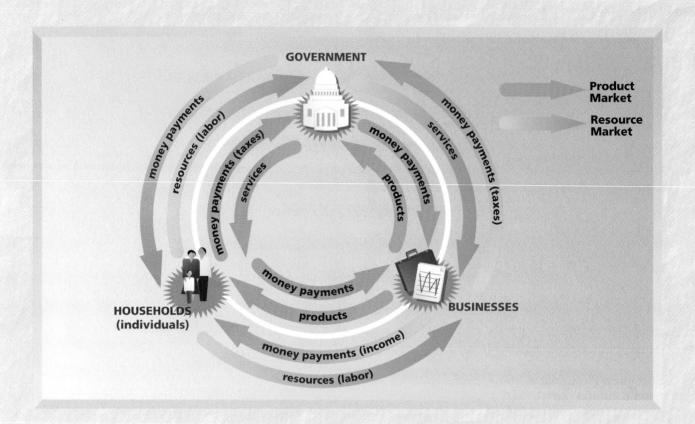

Maps

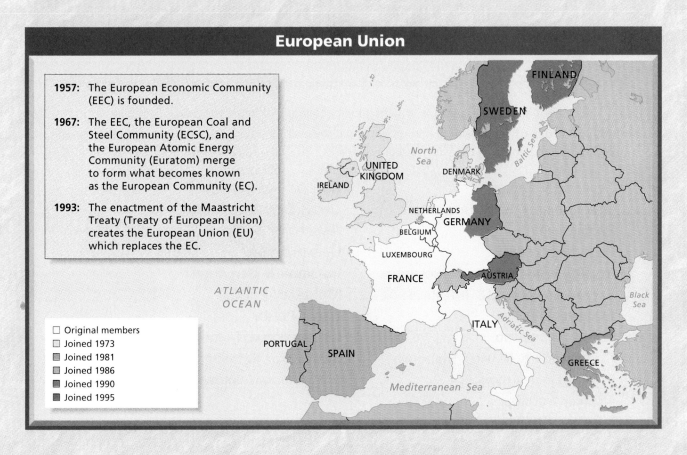

THEMES IN ECONOMICS

Holt Economics examines the way in which economics affects the lives of individuals and how individuals, through their economic choices, shape their world. You will notice several recurrent themes in the study of economics.

SCARCITY & CHOICE

OPPORTUNITY COST & TRADE-OFFS

PRODUCTIVITY

ECONOMIC SYSTEMS

ECONOMIC INSTITUTIONS & INCENTIVES

EXCHANGE, MONEY, & INTERDEPENDENCE

MARKETS & PRICES

SUPPLY & DEMAND

COMPETITION & MARKET STRUCTURE

INCOME DISTRIBUTION

MARKET FAILURES

ROLE OF GOVERNMENT

GROSS DOMESTIC PRODUCT

AGGREGATE SUPPLY & AGGREGATE DEMAND

UNEMPLOYMENT

INFLATION & DEFLATION

MONETARY POLICY

FISCAL POLICY

INTERNATIONAL TRADE

BALANCE OF PAYMENTS

INTERNATIONAL GROWTH & STABILITY

CRITICAL THINKING AND THE STUDY OF ECONOMICS

Throughout *Holt Economics*, you are asked to think critically about the events and processes that shape your global, national and local economy. Critical thinking is the reasoned judgment of information and ideas. People who think critically study information to determine its accuracy. They evaluate arguments and analyze conclusions before accepting their validity. Critical thinkers are able to recognize and define problems and develop strategies for resolving them.

The development of critical thinking skills is essential to effective economic habits. Such skills empower you to make informed economic choices. For example, critical thinking skills enable you to evaluate information you hear in news reports. In addition, critical thinking about economics enables you to be a skilled consumer and improves your ability to make wise decisions about budgeting, spending, and investing.

Helping you develop critical thinking skills is an important tool of *Holt Economics*. Using the following 12 critical thinking skills will help you better understand the concepts and forces involved in economics. Additional skills to help you understand economic concepts and processes can be found in the Skills Handbook, which begins on p. xxiv.

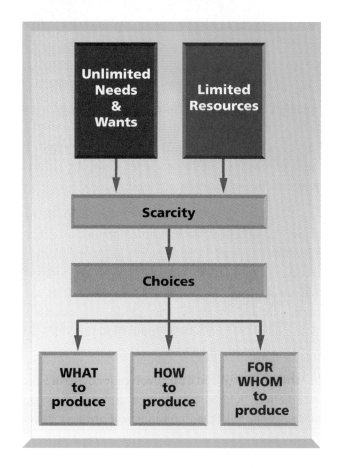

1. Recognizing Point of View involves identifying the factors that color the outlook of a person or group. Someone's point of view includes beliefs and attitudes that are shaped by factors such as age, sex, religion, race, and economic status. This thinking skill helps us examine why people see things as they do, and reinforces the realization that people's views may change over time, or with a change in circumstances. A point of view that is highly personal or based on unreasoned judgment, is said to be *biased*.

2. Comparing and Contrasting involves examining events, situations, or points of view for their similarities and differences. *Comparing* focuses on both the similarities and the differences. *Contrasting* focuses only on the differences. For example, by comparing capitalism and democratic socialism you might note that although these economic systems have different levels of government control, they both are mixed economies. By contrasting, on the other hand, you might note that capitalism involves limited government control over the economy and democratic socialism involves moderate government control.

3. Analyzing
is the process of breaking something down into its parts and examining the relationships among them. An *analysis* of something's parts enables you to better understand the whole. For example, to analyze the government's role in the economy, you might study taxation, the federal budget, and fiscal policy strategies.

4. Assessing Consequences
means studying an action, an event, or a trend to predict or determine its long-term effects and to judge their desirability. *Consequences* are effects that are indirect and unintended. They may appear long after the event that led to them. One could, for example, assess the consequences of higher interest rates on consumer spending habits.

5. Identifying Values
involves recognizing the core beliefs held by a person or group. *Values* are more deeply held than opinions and are less likely to change. Values commonly concern matters of right and wrong and may be viewed as desirable in and of themselves. In a capitalist economy, for example, individual freedom of choice is highly valued.

6. Hypothesizing
is forming a possible explanation for an event, a situation, or a problem. A *hypothesis* is not a proven fact. Rather, it is an educated guess based on available evidence and tested against new evidence. An economist, for example, might hypothesize that government intervention in the economy inhibits economic growth. The economist would then organize the evidence to support this hypothesis and challenge other explanations of poor economic growth.

7. Synthesizing
involves combining information and ideas from several sources or points in time to gain a new understanding of a topic or an event. Much of the narrative writing in this textbook is a synthesis. *Holt Economics* pulls together data from many sources to create an explanation of global, national and local economies. Synthesizing the history of the Great Depression, for example, might involve studying photographs and economic statistics from the 1930s. It might also involve studying

interviews with people from all parts of the world who lived through the period.

8. Problem Solving is the process of reviewing a situation, determining its troublesome elements, and then making recommendations for improving or correcting them. Before determining solutions, however, the problem must be identified and stated. For instance, in seeking a solution to the problems caused by the national debt, you might state the issue in terms of the relationship between the national debt and high interest rates. You would then propose and evaluate possible solutions or courses of action, selecting the one you think is best and giving the reasons for your choice.

9. Evaluating is assessing the significance or overall importance of something, such as the success of a tax cut or the impact of a trade deficit on economic growth. You should base your judgment on standards that others will understand and are likely to think important. An evaluation of a price increase for a particular product, for example, would assess the quantity of the product supplied by producers and the quantity demanded by consumers.

10. Taking a Stand involves identifying an issue, deciding what you think about the issue, and per-

suasively expressing your position on it. Your stand should be based on specific information. In taking a stand, even on a controversial issue such as labor unions, state your position clearly and give reasons to support it.

11. Studying Contemporary Issues and Problems involves identifying a current topic frequently discussed in the media, reading several sources of information on the topic, and evaluating that information. Finding space for all the waste a society creates, for example, is a contemporary problem you may be familiar with. You might feel the effects of it through recycling programs in your community or school. By studying this issue, you will be able to understand the cause of excess waste and evaluate solutions others have developed to ease the problem.

12. Applying a Model involves depicting something in its ideal state and evaluating how well a specific example matches the ideal. A model of an ideal capitalist economic system, for example, might be applied to the economy of Brazil. By evaluating how well each element of Brazil's economic system matches each element of a model capitalist system, you can determine whether or not Brazil has a capitalist economy or how close it matches an ideal system.

COMPARING ECONOMIC SYSTEMS

		Ownership of Natural Resources and Capital	
		Private	**Government**
Allocation Choices	**Private**	**Market Capitalism** Examples: United States, Western Europe, Japan	**Market Socialism** Examples: Yugoslavia, China
	Government	**Command Capitalism** Examples: many nations in Latin America, Africa, and the Middle East	**Command Socialism** Examples: Soviet Union, Cuba, North Korea

ECONOMICS SKILLS HANDBOOK

Economics is a part of almost every aspect of our daily lives. To grasp this relationship, you will need to understand the forces that shape economics. The skills covered in this handbook will enable you to analyze economic concepts and processes. The handbook will also introduce you to key sources of economic information that can be presented in a variety of forms. Your understanding and appreciation of economics will grow as your study skills improve. Your study of economics also will provide you with opportunities to sharpen your research, writing, and test-taking abilities.

1 IDENTIFYING THE MAIN IDEA

In the study of economics, significant events and concepts sometimes get lost among surrounding issues. The ability to identify central elements is a key to understanding any complex issue. This book is designed to help you focus on the most important concepts in economics. The focus questions at the beginning of each section are intended to guide your reading and the chapter summary reinforces the main ideas presented. But not everything you read is structured this way. Applying these general guidelines will help you identify the main ideas in what you read.

How to Identify the Main Idea

Read any introductory material. Read the title and the introduction, if there is one, which may point out the material's main ideas.

Have questions in mind. Formulate questions about the subject that you think might be answered by the material. Having such questions in mind will focus your reading.

Note the outline of ideas. Pay attention to any headings or subheadings, which may provide a basic outline of the major ideas.

Distinguish supporting details. As you read, distinguish sentences providing additional details from the general statements they support. A trail of facts, for instance, may lead to a conclusion that expresses a main idea.

WORLD'S CLASSICS

ADAM SMITH
WEALTH OF NATIONS

Applying Your Skill

Read the paragraph below, from the Chapter 6 subsection "Era of Big Business," to identify its main idea.

"At first the U.S. government did not interfere with the trusts [huge monopolies]. Most economists and policy-makers at the time believed firmly in a laissez-faire economic philosophy. This philosophy states that economic systems prosper when the government does not interfere with the market in any way. (Laissez-faire is a French term meaning 'let people do [as they will].') Thus, the federal government initially favored leaving the market and the trusts alone."

As the lead sentence indicates, the paragraph focuses on the nature of government involvement in the U.S. economy at a specific point in time. Details about economic philosophy are included to provide background and a more complete understanding of the government's actions. The main idea is clearly stated in the final sentence.

Practicing Your Skill

Now read the third paragraph of the subsection on page 130 and answer the following questions.

1. What is the paragraph's main idea? How does the writer support that idea?
2. What is the relationship between the main ideas in this paragraph and the one excerpted above? Combine them into one statement that summarizes both paragraphs.

2 IDENTIFYING CAUSE AND EFFECT

Identifying and understanding cause-and-effect relationships is fundamental to interpreting economic concepts. A *cause* is any action that leads to an event; the outcome of that action is an *effect*. To investigate both why an economic event took place and what happened as a result of that event, economists ask questions such as What is the immediate activity that triggered the event? and What is the background leading up to the event? Your task is simpler than the economist's: to trace what he or she has already determined or theorized about the web of actions and outcomes.

How to Identify Cause and Effect

Look for clues. Certain words and phrases are immediate clues to the existence of a cause-and-effect relationship.

Cause & Effect Clues	
as a result of	aftermath of
because	as a consequence of
brought about	depended on
inspired	gave rise to
led to	originated from
produced	outcome
provoked	outgrowth
the reason for	proceeded from
spurred	resulted in

Identify the relationship. Read carefully to identify how events are related. Writers do not always directly state the link between cause and effect. Sometimes a reader has to *infer,* or determine, the cause or the effect from the information.

Check for complex connections. Beyond the immediate, or superficial, cause and effect, check for other, more complex connections. Note, for example, whether (1) there were additional causes of a given effect; (2) a cause had multiple effects; and (3) these effects in turn caused any additional effects.

Applying Your Skill

The diagram below presents an important cause-and-effect relationship in the concept of demand. The diagram below describes the effects of price ceilings. Note how an effect may in turn become a cause.

Cause
Rental costs for apartments and houses become too high for many people.

Effect/Cause
The government introduces a price ceiling on rental properties.

Effect
The quantity of rental properties supplied decreases as landlords are unable to raise rents to cover expenses.

Practicing Your Skill

Think about your own economic activities, such as holding a part-time job or buying a concert ticket. Show how cause and effect have played a role in your choices. Draw a chart showing the relationships between the actions and the outcomes. Then write a paragraph that explains the connections.

The ability to distinguish facts from opinions is essential in judging the soundness of an argument or the reliability of an economic analysis. A fact can be proved or observed; an opinion, on the other hand, is a personal belief or conclusion. One often hears facts and opinions mixed in everyday conversation—as well as in advertising, political debate, and government policy statements. Thus, in an argument, opinions do not carry as much weight as facts, although some opinions can be supported by facts.

How to Distinguish Fact from Opinion

Identify the facts.
Begin by asking yourself whether the statement at hand can be proven. Determine whether the idea can be checked for accuracy in a source such as an almanac or encyclopedia. If so, it is probably factual. If not, it probably contains an opinion.

Identify the opinions.
Look for clues that signal a statement of opinion—for example: phrases such as *I think* or *I believe*. Comparative words like *greatest* or *more important* and value-laden words like *extremely* or *ridiculous* imply a judgment, and thus an opinion.

Applying Your Skill

Economic policy reflects the opinions of decision makers. For example, read the following excerpt from President Franklin D. Roosevelt's first inaugural address.

"Values have shrunken to fantastic levels; taxes have risen; our ability to pay has fallen; government of all kinds is faced by serious curtailment [shortening] of income; the means of exchange are frozen in the currents of trade; the withered leaves of industrial enterprise lie on every side; farmers find no markets for their produce; the savings of many years in thousands of families are gone. . . .

"Our greatest primary task is to put people to work. This is no unsolvable problem if we face it wisely and courageously. It can be accomplished in part by direct recruiting by the government itself, treating the task as we would treat the emergency of war, but at the same time, through this employment, accomplishing greatly needed projects to stimulate and reorganize the use of our natural resources. . . ."

While the first paragraph in this excerpt presents facts that can be proven or disproven, the second paragraph presents Roosevelt's opinion of how the government should respond to the Great Depression.

Reprinted with permission, "Star Tribune", Minneapolis

STEVE SACK
Courtesy Minneapolis Star-Tribune

Practicing Your Skill

The excerpt that follows is from Andrew Carnegie's essay "The Gospel of Wealth." Read the excerpt and answer the questions on the next page.

"This, then, is held to be the duty of the man of wealth: To set an example of modest . . . living, shunning display or extravagance; to provide moderately [reasonably] for the legitimate [proper] wants of those dependent upon him; and, after doing so, to consider all surplus revenues which come to him simply as trust funds, which he is called upon to administer . . . as a matter of duty in the manner which, in his judgment, is best calculated to produce the most beneficial results for the community—the man of wealth thus becoming the mere trustee and agent for his poorer brethren, bringing to their service his superior wisdom, experience, and ability to administer, doing for them better than they would or could do for themselves. . . ."

1. Is this excerpt a statement of fact or a statement of opinion?
2. What words does Carnegie use to describe why the wealthy should support those with more limited finances?
3. Which words provide clues to Carnegie's opinion of the wealthy?

 # BUILDING VOCABULARY

The study of economics may challenge your reading comprehension. You will probably encounter many new and unfamiliar words. But with regular effort you can master them and turn reading economics into an opportunity to enlarge your vocabulary. Following the steps outlined below will assist you in this endeavor.

How to Build Vocabulary

Identify unusual words. As you read, be aware of words that you cannot pronounce or define. Keep a list of these words. Words that are somewhat familiar are the easiest to learn.

Study context clues. Study the sentence and paragraph carefully where you find each new term.

This *context*, or setting, may give you clues to the word's meaning. The word may be defined by either an example or another, more familiar word that means the same thing.

Use the dictionary. Use a dictionary to help you pronounce and define the words on your list. Review new vocabulary. Look for ways to use the new words—in homework assignments, conversation, or classroom discussions. The best way to master a new word is to use it.

Practicing Your Skill

1. What is context? How can it provide clues to a word's meaning?
2. As you read a chapter, list any unusual words that you find. Write down what you think each word means, and then check your definitions against those that you find in a dictionary.

 # CONDUCTING RESEARCH

To complete research papers or special projects, you may need to use resources beyond this textbook. For example, you may want to research specific subjects or business organizations not discussed here, or to learn additional information about a certain topic. Doing such research typically involves using the resources available in a library.

The general theory of employment, interest, and money
by John Maynard Keynes.
San Diego : Harcourt, Brace, Jovanovich, 1964 [1991 printing]
xii, 403 p. : ill. ; 21 cm.
Originally published: 1953.
"A Harvest/HBJ book."
Includes bibliographical references and index.
Subjects:
   Economics.
   Money.
   Monetary policy.
   Interest.
Search for other works by:
   Keynes, John Maynard, 1883-1946.

Language	Call Number	LCCN	Dewey Decimal	ISBN/ISSN
English (eng)	HB99.7 .K378 1964	91006533 //r91	330.15/6	0156347113 : $8.95

How to Find Information

To find a particular book, you need to know how libraries organize their materials. Books of fiction are alphabetized according to the last name of the author. To classify nonfiction books, libraries use the Dewey decimal system and the Library of Congress system. Both systems assign each book a *call number* that tells you where it is shelved.

To find a particular book's call number, look in the library's *card catalog*. The catalog lists books by author, by title, and by subject. If you know the author or title of the book, finding it is simple. If you do not know this information, or if you just want to find any book about a general subject, look under an applicable subject heading. Many libraries have computerized card catalogs. These catalogs generally contain the same information as a traditional card catalog, but take up less space and are easier to update and to access.

Librarians can assist you in using the card catalog and direct you to a book's location. They also can suggest additional resources. Many libraries now rely on computerized resources and have access to the Internet. Specialized CD–ROMs such as the *Holt Researcher CD–ROM: Economics and Government* also provide access to statistics and other government information.

How to Use Resources

In a library's reference section, you will find encyclopedias, specialized dictionaries, atlases, almanacs, and indexes to material in magazines and newspapers. *Encyclopedias* often will be your best resource. Encyclopedias include economic, political, and geographic data on individual nations, states, and cities, as well as biographical sketches of important historical figures. Entries often include cross-references to related articles.

Specialized dictionaries exist for almost every field. For example, an economics dictionary will focus on defining economic concepts.

To find up-to-date facts about a subject, you can use almanacs, yearbooks, and periodical indexes. References like *The World Almanac and Book of Facts* include economic information and a variety of statistics about population, the environment, sports, and so on. Encyclopedia yearbooks keep up with recent, significant developments not fully covered in encyclopedia articles.

Periodical indexes, particularly *Readers' Guide to Periodical Literature*, can help you locate informative, current articles published in magazines. The *New York Times Index* catalogs the news stories published in the *Times*—the U.S. daily newspaper with perhaps the most in-depth coverage of national and world events.

Practicing Your Skill

1. In what two ways are nonfiction books classified?

2. What kinds of references contain information about economics?

3. Where would you look to find the most recent coverage of a political or social issue?

⑥ ANALYZING PRIMARY SOURCES

There are many sources of firsthand economic information, including editorials, policy statements, and legal documents. All of these are primary sources. Newspaper reports and editorial cartoons also are considered to be primary sources, although they are generally written after the fact. Because they permit a close-up look at a given topic—and often a chance to get inside people's minds—primary sources are valuable analytical tools.

Secondary sources are descriptions or interpretations of events that are written after the events have occurred and by persons who did not participate in the events describe. Books such as *Holt Economics*, biographies, encyclopedias, and other reference works are secondary sources.

How to Analyze Primary Sources
1. Study the material carefully. Consider the nature of the material. Is it verbal or visual? Is it

based on firsthand information or on the accounts of others? Note the major ideas and supporting details.

2. Consider the audience. Ask yourself: For whom was this message originally meant? Whether a message was intended, for instance, for the general public or for a specific, private audience may have shaped its style or content.

3. Check for bias. Watch for words or phrases that present a one-sided view of a person or situation. Determine if the information represents fact or opinion.

4. When possible, compare sources. Study more than one source on a topic. Comparing sources gives you a more complete, balanced account of the topic.

Practicing Your Skill

1. What distinguishes secondary sources from primary sources?

2. What advantage do secondary sources have over primary sources?

3. Of the following, identify which are primary and which are secondary sources: a newspaper, a biography, an editorial cartoon, a deed to property, a snapshot of a family vacation, a magazine article about the economics of Thailand. How might some of these sources prove to be both primary and secondary sources?

7 WRITING ABOUT ECONOMICS

Holt Economics presents several writing opportunities in the Section Reviews, Chapter Reviews, and Unit Labs. Following these guidelines will improve your writing about economics as well as other subjects.

How to Write with a Purpose

Always keep your purpose for writing in mind. That purpose might be to analyze, evaluate, synthesize, inform, persuade, hypothesize, or take a stand. As you begin, your purpose will determine the

most appropriate approach to take and when you are done, it will help you evaluate your success.

Each purpose for writing requires its own form, tone, and content. The point of view you are adopting will shape what you write, as will your intended audience: whoever will be reading what you write.

Some writing assignments in *Holt Economics* ask you to create a specific type of writing, such as a newspaper editorial or an advertisement.

▶ A newspaper *editorial* is a public statement of an opinion or a viewpoint. It takes a stand on an issue and gives reasons for that stand.

▶ An *advertisement* is an announcement to promote a product or an event. Effective ads are direct and to the point, and use memorable language, such as jingles and slogans, to highlight important features.

How to Write a Paper or an Essay

Each writing opportunity will have specific directions about what and how to write. Regardless of the particular topic you choose, you should follow certain basic steps.

There are five major stages to writing a paper or essay: prewriting, creating an outline, writing a first draft, evaluating and revising your draft to eliminate any awkward passages, and proofreading and producing a final draft of your paper for presentation. Each of these stages can be further divided into more specific steps and tasks. The guidelines outlined below can help you improve your writing abilities.

Prewriting

Choose a topic. Select a topic for your paper. Take care to narrow your subject so that you will be able to develop and support a clear argument.

Identify your purpose for writing the essay or paper. Read the directions carefully to identify the purpose for your writing. Keep that purpose in mind as you plan and write your paper.

Determine your audience. When writing for a specific audience, choose the tone and style that will best communicate your message.

Collect information. Write down your ideas and the information you already know about your topic, and do additional research if necessary. Your writing will be more effective if you have many details at hand.

```
                Communism in the Soviet Union
  I.  Political philosophies of Marx
 II.  Rise of communism
      A. War communism
         1. Private property abolished
         2. Land redistributed
         3. Factories brought under government control
      B. New Economic Policy
         1. Some private incentives restored
         2. Larger enterprises controlled by government
      C. Stalin's rule
         1. Introduced Five-Year Plans
         2. Emphasized heavy industries
         3. Began system of collectivization
      D. Central planning
      E. Production
         1. Shift toward more consumer goods after Stalin's death
         2. Low agricultural output necessitated food imports
      F. Soviet problems
III.  Beginnings of reform
      A. Collapse of the Soviet Union
         1. Dissatisfaction with standard of living
         2. Perestroika introduced by Gorbachev
         3. Price hikes failed to correct shortages
         4. Republics of Soviet Union declare independence
      B. Russian reform
         1. Yeltsin begins transition to market capitalism
         2. Prices and production largely free of government control
         3. Many state-owned firms privatized
```

How to Create an Outline

Think and plan before you begin writing your first draft. Organize themes, main ideas, and supporting details into an outline.

Order your material. Decide what information you want to emphasize or focus on. Order or classify your material with that in mind. Determine what information belongs in an introduction, what should make up the body of your paper, and what to leave for the conclusion.

Identify main ideas. Identify the main ideas to be highlighted in each section. Make these your outline's main headings.

List supporting details. Determine the important details or facts that support each main idea. Rank and list them as subheadings, using additional levels of subheadings as necessary. Never break a category into subheadings unless there at least two: no As without Bs, no 1s without 2s.

Put your outline to use. Structure your essay or report according to your outline. Each main heading, for instance, might form the basis for a topic sentence to begin a paragraph. Subheadings would then make up the content of the paragraph. In a more lengthy paper, each subheading might be the main idea of a paragraph.

Writing the Draft

In your first draft, remember to use your outline as a guide. Each paragraph should express a single main idea or set of related ideas, with details for support. Be careful to show the relationships between ideas and to use proper *transitions*— sentences that build connections between paragraphs.

Evaluating and Revising the Draft

Review and edit. Revise and reorganize your draft as needed to make your points. Improve sentences by adding appropriate adjectives and adverbs. Omit words, sentences, or paragraphs that are unnecessary or unrelated to a main idea. Check your work to make sure you have covered all details.

Evaluate your writing style. Make your writing clearer by varying the sentence length and rephrasing awkward sentences. Replace inexact wording with more precise word choices.

Proofreading

Proofread your paper carefully. Check for proper spelling, punctuation, and grammar.

Write your final version. Prepare a neat and clean final version. Appearance is important; it may not affect the quality of your writing itself, but it can affect the way your writing is perceived and understood.

Practicing Your Skill

1. What factor—more than any other—should affect how and what you write? Why?
2. Why is it important to consider the audience for your writing?
3. What is involved in the editing of a first draft?

8 LEARNING FROM VISUALS

Visuals are graphic images which can provide information about culture and society. These clues are available in a broad range of formats, including photographs, paintings, television, web sites, and political cartoons. Visual images record a large amount of diverse data. To extract this data, you must carefully examine the details in the image.

Courtesy of the "Chattanooga Times"

How to Study Visuals

Identify the subject. Look at the content of the picture. What is the main focus? For example, is it a group of people, a building, or a particular event? Who is the intended audience? What do you think the creator of the image is trying to convey? Read the title, captions or listen to the dialogue to pick up clues to its subject matter.

Examine the details. Gather subtle information from the image. Are there clues about time or place? Look at details such as clothing style, architecture, and the arrangement of the image's components to further evaluate its effect and meaning.

Identify the tone. Most people think that visuals present only facts. A visual image, however, also exposes feelings about a subject. What do the images reveal about peoples' feelings? How do you feel when you look at the picture? Does it make you laugh, or feel sad or angry? Try to identify what specific elements in the image evoke this feeling.

Put the data to use. Combine the information you gathered from the visual images and written or spoken words to analyze a particular subject.

Practicing Your Skill

1. What is the subject of the cartoon on this page?
2. What symbols and images does the cartoonist use to convey his message?
3. What is the cartoonist's opinion about Greenspan's economic policy? Do you agree? Explain your answer.

9 UNDERSTANDING MEASUREMENT CONCEPTS AND METHODS

Measurements can give us information about the magnitude, amount, or size of a particular item. Measurements usually are presented in the form of numbers. Finding the information you need from these numbers however, may be difficult unless you know what to look for. Understanding measurement methods and learning to read the results of measurements is key to learning about economics and many other subjects.

Many measurements in *Holt Economics* are statistics. These are facts presented in the form of numbers and are typically arranged to show applicable information about a subject. Statistics often are presented in the form of percentages or ratios.

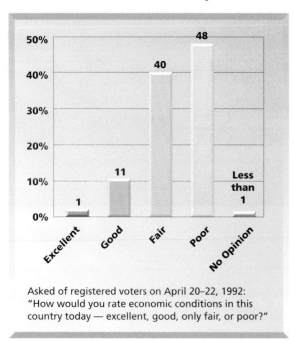

PUBLIC OPINION POLL, 1992

Asked of registered voters on April 20–22, 1992: "How would you rate economic conditions in this country today — excellent, good, only fair, or poor?"

Source: *The Gallup Poll 1992*

Measurements can provide a wide variety of information. For example, you might read measurements that tell you how many people in your state agree with raising the speed limits or what the rate of inflation was over the past year.

How to Read Measurements

Look for clues.   Use the information presented with measurements to help you understand their significance. If the measurements appear in a chart or graph, read the title or labels to find clues. If the numbers appear in the text, read the paragraph surrounding them to gain more information.

Identify form.   What form is the measurement in? Is it expressed as a percentage? a ratio?

Evaluate the method and purpose of measurement.   How was the data collected—through a poll, government census, or price analysis? Why was this information collected and who will use it?

Put the data to use.   Use the information in the measurement to build a mental picture of the data or group described. Draw conclusions from the information presented.

Practicing the Skill

1. What is the subject of this data?
2. Why do you think the data is presented in the form of percentages?
3. What conclusions can be drawn from the data?

10 UNDERSTANDING CHARTS AND GRAPHS

Charts and graphs are means of organizing and presenting information visually. They categorize and display data in a variety of ways, depending on their subject. Several types of charts and graphs are used in this textbook.

Charts

Charts commonly used in economics include tables, flowcharts, and organizational charts. A *table* lists and categorizes information. A *flowchart* shows a sequence of events or the steps in a

CIRCULAR FLOW MODEL OF GOODS AND SERVICES

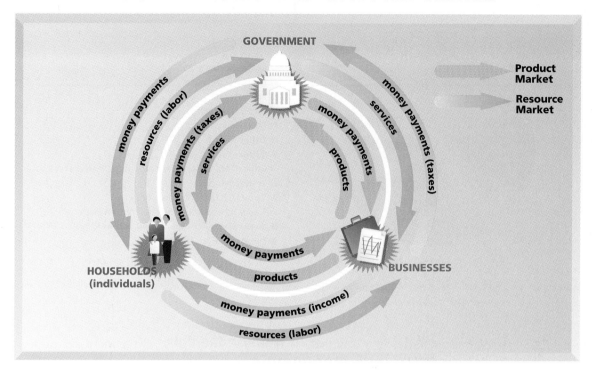

process. Cause-and-effect relationships are often shown by flowcharts. For example, see the Circular Flow Model of Goods and Services chart. An *organizational chart* displays the structure of an organization, indicating the ranking or function of its internal parts and the relationships among them.

How to Read a Chart

Read the title. Read the title to identify the focus or purpose of the chart.

Study the chart's element. Read the chart's headings, subheadings, and labels to identify the categories used and the specific data given for each category.

Analyze the details. When reading quantities, note increases or decreases in amounts. When reading dates, note intervals of time. When viewing an organizational or flowchart, follow directional arrows or lines.

Put the data to use. Form generalizations or draw conclusions based on the data.

Graphs

There are several types of graphs, each of which is well suited for a particular purpose. A *line graph* plots information by dots connected by a line. This line also can be called a *curve*. A line graph such as the one below shows changes or trends. A *bar*

PRODUCTION CURVE

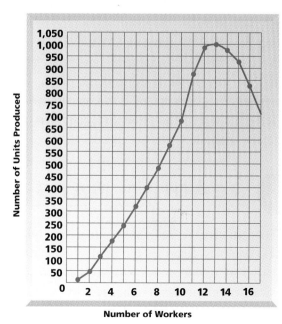

FEDERAL BUDGET, 1996

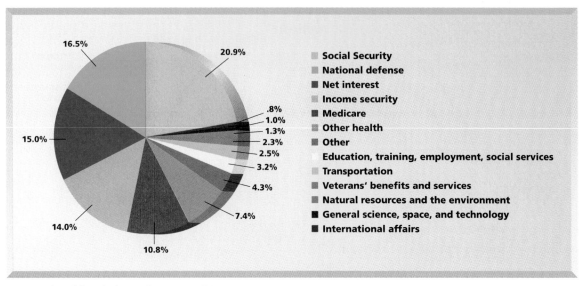

Source: *Budget of the United States Government: 1996*

graph displays amounts or quantities in a way that makes comparisons easy. A *pie graph*, or *circle graph*, such as the one above, displays proportions by showing sections of a whole as if they were slices of a pie.

How to Read a Graph

Read the title. Read the title to identify the subject and purpose of the graph. Note the kind of graph it is, remembering what each kind is designed to emphasize.

Study the labels. To identify the type of information presented in the graph, read the label for each axis. The *horizontal axis* runs from left to right, generally at the bottom of the graph, while the *vertical axis* runs up and down, generally along the left-hand side. In addition, note the intervals of any dates or amounts that are listed.

Analyze the data. Note increases or decreases in quantities. Look for trends, relationships, and changes in the data.

Put the data to use. Use the results of your analysis to form generalizations and draw conclusions.

Applying Your Skill

Study the pie graph above. You can see how the federal government plans expenditures.

Practicing Your Skill

Use the line graph "Production Curve" on page xxxiii to answer the following questions:

1. Describe the type of data illustrated and the intervals used for (a) the horizontal axis and (b) the vertical axis.
2. What generalizations or conclusions can you draw from the information in this graph?

11 READING MAPS

Economics and geography often are related. Economics describes the production and consumption of resources. Geography describes how physical environments (composed of resources) affect human events and how people influence the environment around them. Geographers have developed five themes—location, place, region, movement, and human-environment interaction—to organize this information into a format that is useful for everyone.

Geographic information for all five themes—can be presented in text or represented visually in maps. Maps convey a wealth of varied information through colors, lines, symbols, and labels. To read and interpret maps, you must understand their language and symbols.

Types of Maps

A map is an illustration drawn to scale of all or part of the earth's surface. Types of maps include physical maps, political maps, and special-purpose maps. *Physical maps* illustrate the natural landscape of an area. *Physical maps* often use shading to show relief—the rises and falls in the surface of the land—and colors to show elevation, or height above sea level.

Political maps illustrate political units such as states and nations, by employing color variations, lines to mark boundaries, dots for major cities, and stars or stars within circles for capitals. Political maps show information such as territorial changes or military alliances. See the map on page xxxvi.

Special-purpose maps present specific information such as the routes of explorers, the outcome of an election, regional economic activity, or population density. The map shown below is a special-purpose map.

Many maps combine various features of the types listed above. For example, a map may combine information from a political and a special-purpose map by showing national boundaries as well as trade routes.

Map Features

Most maps have a number of features in common. Familiarity with these basic elements makes reading any map easier.

Titles, legends, and labels A map's *title* tells you what the map is about, what area is shown, and usually, what time period is being represented. The *legend*, or key, explains symbols, colors, or shadings used on the map. *Labels* designate political and geographic place-names as well as physical features like mountain ranges, oceans, and rivers.

The global grid The *absolute location* of any place on the earth is given in terms of *latitude* (degrees north or south of the equator) and *longitude* (degrees east or west of the prime meridian). The symbol for a degree is °. Degrees are divided into 60 equal parts called minutes, which are represented by the symbol '. The global grid is created by the intersecting lines of latitude (parallels) and lines of longitude (meridians). Lines of latitude and

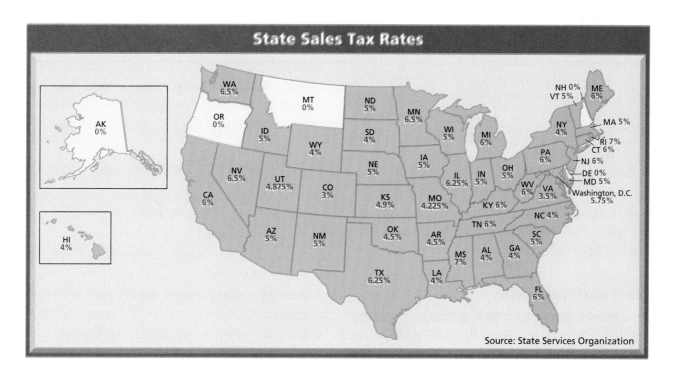

State Sales Tax Rates

Source: State Services Organization

Independent Nations Formed from the Soviet Union

longitude may sometimes be indicated by tick marks near the edge of the map or by lines across an entire map. Many maps also have locator maps, which show the subject area's location in relation to a larger area, such as a continent or the world.

Directions and distances   Most maps in this textbook have a *compass rose*, or *directional indicator*. The compass rose indicates the four cardinal or primary points—using N for north, S for south, E for east, and W for west. You can also find intermediate directions—northeast, southeast, southwest, and northwest—using the compass rose. These directions are helpful in describing the relative location of a place. (If a map has no compass rose, assume that north is at the top, east is to the right, and so on.)

Many maps include a *scale*, showing both miles and kilometers, to help you relate distances on the map to actual distances on the earth's surface. You can use a scale to find the true distance between any two points on the map.

How to Read a Map
Determine the focus of the map.   Read the title and labels to determine the map's focus—its subject and the geographic area it covers.

Study the map legend. Read the legend and become familiar with any special symbols, lines, colors, and shadings used in the map.

Check directions and distances.   Use the directional indicator and scale as needed to determine direction, location, and distance.

Check the grid lines.   Refer to lines of latitude and longitude, or to a locator map, to fix the location in relation larger area.

Study the map.   Study the map's basic features and details, keeping its purpose in mind. If it is a special-purpose map, study the specific information being presented.

Practicing Your Skill

For the map shown above, answer the following questions.

1. What is the special focus of the map?
2. How is a map helpful in presenting this information?
3. What special symbols, if any, are used in the map?
4. What do the color variations and different lines indicate?

12 TAKING A TEST

When it comes to taking a test, for economics or any other subject, nothing can take the place of preparation. A good night's sleep added to consistent study habits give you a much better chance for success than hours of late-night, last-minute cramming. By preparing well, you will be better able to ignore distractions while you are taking the test.

But keeping your mind focused on the test and free from distractions is not all you can do to improve your test scores. Mastering some basic test-taking skills also can help. Keeping up with daily reading assignments and taking careful notes as you read can turn taking a test into a mere matter of review. Before taking a test, reviewing material that you already know takes less time—and causes less stress—than trying to learn something new under pressure.

You will face several basic types of questions on economics tests—for example, fill-in-the-blank, short answer, multiple choice, matching, and essay. In answering multiple-choice questions, eliminate any answers that you know are wrong, in order to narrow your field of choice. When completing a matching exercise, first go through the entire list, matching those that you are confident that you know. Then study any that remain.

Read essay questions carefully so that you know exactly what you are being asked to write. Make an outline of the main ideas and supporting details that you plan to include in your essay. Keep your answer clear and brief, but cover all necessary points.

How to Take a Test

Prepare beforehand. This all-important step involves not only studying and reviewing the material prior to the test. It also means being physically rested and mentally focused on the day of the test.

Follow directions. Read instructions carefully. Listen closely if the directions are oral.

Preview the test. Skim through the entire test to determine how much time you have for each section. Try to anticipate which areas will be the most difficult for you.

Concentrate on the test. Do not watch the clock, but stay aware of the time. If you do not know an answer, move on to the next question. It is best to answer as many questions as you can within the time limit.

Review your answers. If you have time, return to questions that you skipped or were unsure of, and work on them. Review your essays to catch and correct any mistakes in spelling, punctuation, or grammar.

Practicing Your Skill

1. How can you improve your chances on multiple-choice questions?

2. Why is it important to skim through an entire test before you begin?

3. Name three things that can help you in taking a test.

UNIT
1

CHAPTER 1

WHAT IS ECONOMICS?

CHAPTER 2

ECONOMIC SYSTEMS

Economics Lab

How would you go about choosing an economic system for a new society? Find out by reading this unit and taking the Economics Lab challenge on pages 44-47.

INTRODUCTION TO ECONOMICS

WHAT IS ECONOMICS?

Why do designer jeans cost more than "no-name" jeans? Why are there so many brands of soft drinks? Why do you have to pay sales tax on compact discs (CDs)? Why does the restaurant you work for not pay you $100 an hour?

For the answers to all these questions you must turn to economics. In fact, economics touches every aspect of your life—every time you make a choice.

You might think of economics as the study of choices—the food you eat, the clothes you wear, the movies you see, and the music you buy. By studying your choices as well as the choices of others, you will see how economics shapes the world around you and, in turn, how you can shape your world.

Economics Notebook

In your Economics Notebook, list your daily activities. How does choice influence your activities? Which activities would you describe as "economic"?

SECTION 1

AN ECONOMIC WAY OF THINKING

Economics Dictionary

economics
economist
microeconomics
macroeconomics
consumer
producer
good
service
resource
factor of production
natural resource
human resource
capital resource
capital good
consumer good
technology
entrepreneurship
entrepreneur

Objectives

▶ What is economics?
▶ What are the factors of production?
▶ What is the goal of entrepreneurship?

How do you decide what food to eat, what clothes to wear, and what movies to see? The study of the choices that people make to satisfy their needs and wants is called **economics**. A person who studies these economic choices is called an **economist**.

Economists generally classify economic actions into two categories: microeconomics and macroeconomics. **Microeconomics** is the study of the choices made by economic actors such as households, companies, and individual markets. Although the term *micro* means "small," microeconomics can focus on large participants in the economy. For example, the production at one company—even one as large as Exxon Corporation, whose total output exceeds that of some nations—is considered a microeconomic topic because only a single economic actor is involved.

Macroeconomics, on the other hand, examines the behavior of entire economies. For example, unemployment in the United States is a macroeconomic topic.

What can you learn from economics? By examining the economic choices you make, you can take advantage of the opportunities available to you—from choosing where to eat lunch to deciding whether to go to college, from buying a pair of jeans to choosing a career.

The first step in examining the economic choices you make is to develop an economic way of thinking. As you will see, you already understand many economic concepts, even if you think of economics as an unfamiliar subject. Whether you realize it or not, you take economic action every day. Now you must expand your understanding and think economically.

Economic Decisions

How does an economist view the world? Economists pay attention to economic decisions, observing not only who makes them, but also how those decisions are made.

Who Makes Decisions? You do! You may choose to buy concert tickets or to start a tutoring business. The people around you also make decisions, as do people around the world.

In economic terms, there are two large groups of economic decision makers. The people who decide to buy things are called **consumers**. The people who make the things that satisfy consumers' needs and wants are called **producers**. Consumers choose what to buy, and producers choose what to provide and how to provide it. This network of decisions is the basis of all economic systems. Every society around the world

You make decisions every day based on your needs and wants. **What goods and services do you need and want during an average day?**

has an economic system, whether that society consists of a neighborhood or a nation.

How Do You Make Decisions?
You make economic choices based on your needs and wants, which reflect your desires for certain goods and services. Economists generally classify as needs those goods and services that are necessary for survival, such as food, clothing, and shelter. Wants are those goods and services that people consume beyond what is necessary for survival, such as magazines, television sets, and car washes.

As you can see, the economic decisions you make also focus on goods and services. In economic terms, **goods** are physical objects that can be purchased. A pizza, a bicycle, and a pair of tennis shoes are examples of goods. **Services** are actions or activities that are performed for a fee. Lawyers, plumbers, teachers, and taxicab drivers perform services. The term *product* often refers to both goods and services.

Economic Resources

Economists also are interested in the environment in which people make decisions. What do you see when you look around you? People, cars, trees, buildings? An economist sees these same things as economic resources. A **resource** is anything that people use to make or obtain what they need or want.

Resources that can be used to produce goods and services are called **factors of production**. Economists usually divide these factors of production into four categories:

- natural resources,
- human resources,
- capital resources, and
- entrepreneurship.

Natural Resources Items provided by nature that can be used to produce goods and to provide services are called **natural resources**. Natural resources can be found on or in the Earth, or in the Earth's atmosphere. Examples of natural resources on or in the Earth are farmland in California, trout-filled rivers in Montana, oil fields in Oklahoma, and coal mines in West Virginia. Atmospheric resources include sunlight, wind, and rain.

A natural resource is considered a factor of production only when it is scarce and some payment is necessary for its use. For example, the air you breathe on the beach is not a factor of production because it is not scarce and you do not

Economic resources that are used to produce goods and services are called factors of production. **Of which factor of production is this attorney an example?**

Careers

in Economics

Economist

How many potential car buyers live in Savannah, Georgia? How much are people willing to pay for a pair of in-line skates? What goods and services does the United States export to other countries? How does the income of an orchard owner in Oregon compare to the income of an orchard owner in Virginia? Economists answer these—and many other questions—on a daily basis.

Economists collect information on many aspects of the economy. They can determine how a society such as that of the United States uses its land, labor, raw materials, and machinery. Economists also try to identify why producers choose to provide certain goods and services, as well as the costs and benefits of consuming those products.

How can you become an economist? Generally you will need a college degree in economics. Additionally, courses in mathematics, government, international relations, and other social sciences can help you understand how economic developments affect individuals and societies. Computer skills also are critical, because economists rely on computers to help collect, sort, and interpret data. Some economists also earn a master's degree or doctorate.

As an economist, you might be employed by a private company such as a research firm, management-consulting firm, bank, or insurance company. Economists also work for federal, state, and local governments. For example, economists at the Federal Trade Commission (FTC) analyze industries to help enforce fair business practices. Economists in the Department of Commerce study production, distribution, and consumption of goods and services.

Dr. Alice Rivlin is a well-known government economist. In addition to publishing several books, she was the founding director of the Congressional Budget Office and was appointed by President Clinton to the Board of Governors of the Federal Reserve.

have to pay to use it. If you go scuba diving, however, you have to pay for the bottled air in the scuba tanks.

Human Resources Any human effort exerted during production is considered a **human resource**. The effort can be either physical or intellectual. Assembly-line workers, ministers, and store clerks all are human resources.

Capital Resources The manufactured materials used to create products are called **capital resources**. Capital resources include capital goods and the money used to purchase them. **Capital goods** are the buildings, structures, machinery, and tools used in the production process. Department stores, factories, dams, computers, and hammers are examples of capital goods.

Ecotourism

You may have read news stories describing the harmful effects of tourism on the environment. Hotel construction can disturb the habitats of native animals and plants. Speedboats can frighten and sometimes injure—or even kill—aquatic animals. Litter can disrupt habitats and the food chain.

At the same time, however, tourism provides income for many regions. How can this economic need be balanced with the need to preserve the environment and respect local traditions? Some countries hope to find the answer in ecotourism.

In its ideal form, ecotourism is travel to natural areas in a way that conserves the environment and sustains the well-being of the local people. The country of Costa Rica, for example, relies on ecotourism in its efforts to preserve the rain forest.

The construction of an aerial tramway in the canopy (treetop level) of the rain forest is an example of the potential for a mutually beneficial relationship between nature and the economy. Using a converted ski lift along a one-mile course near Braulio Carrillo National Park, biologists offer a 90-minute tour that allows visitors to see one of the most diverse populations of plants and animals on Earth. Although the tram attracts nearly 100 people a day, its operators have tried to minimize its impact on the environment. Each car carries only five people and is spaced at a considerable distance from other cars on the cable.

Construction materials for the tramway were brought in by helicopter, eliminating the need to build a road beneath. Whenever possible, trees were pulled out of the way of the cable with ropes to avoid cutting them down. Development of the tramway has preserved an ecological sanctuary and provides the region with a steady source of income.

Despite the fact that ecotourism is the fastest-growing segment of the travel industry, many environmentalists argue that the word itself has no meaning. In the United States alone, more than 200 outfitters offer excursions termed "eco-tours." A 1995 *U.S. News & World Report* investigation, however, determined that many ecotours do not give environmental concerns a high priority. In the Galápagos Islands, for example, all the tour boats dump sewage directly into the ocean.

In addition to environmental concerns, some people argue that ecotourism has fallen short of its economic goals. Tour profits often do not find their way into local businesses and salaries. Most profits go to the tour companies, usually based in other countries.

Despite these shortcomings, supporters argue that ecotourism has worked in many areas. Many governments now are trying to improve ecotourism programs through a combination of educational efforts and regulation.

How does Costa Rica reconcile the often conflicting demands of tourism and environmental protection?

What Do You Think?

1. Is it possible to meet both economic and environmental demands at these special tourist destinations? Explain your answer.

2. What are the possible long-term effects of ecotourism on a region's economy?

Capital goods are the manufactured resources that are used in making finished products. These finished products—the goods and services that people buy—are called **consumer goods**.

Some products can be either capital goods or consumer goods, depending on how they are used. A bicycle purchased for personal use is a consumer good. The same bicycle will be classified as a capital good, however, when it is purchased by a New York City messenger service for use in making deliveries.

Technology is the use of technical knowledge and methods to create new products or make existing products more efficiently. For example, advances in computer technology have dramatically changed how work is done. In some highly automated plants, computers direct production by issuing electronic instructions to robots on assembly lines.

Entrepreneurship The organizational abilities and risk taking involved in starting a new business or introducing a new product are called **entrepreneurship**. The goal of entrepreneurship is to develop a new combination of the other factors of production, creating something of value. An **entrepreneur** is a person who attempts to start a new business or introduce a new product—risking economic failure in return for the possibility of financial gain.

Many entrepreneurs begin their businesses by finding answers to their own questions. Michael Dell grew up tinkering with computers and noticed that salespeople frequently were not able to answer his questions. Convinced that computer stores did not provide enough services, he decided to go into business for himself. One year after starting college, Dell had earned more than $700,000.

In 1985 Dell also developed a clone, or copy, of the IBM personal computer (PC). Believing that stores could not meet customers' needs, his company—known as Dell Computer Corporation—sold computers by telephone or mail order. Because Dell computers were priced as much as a third below IBM computers, many consumers found them more affordable than the "name-brand" model. By 1996 Dell Computer Corporation's annual sales had reached more than $5 billion.

SECTION 1 — REVIEW

1. Define the following terms: economics, economist, microeconomics, macroeconomics, consumer, producer, good, service, resource, factor of production, natural resource, human resource, capital resource, capital good, consumer good, technology, entrepreneurship, entrepreneur.

2. What are the key influences on your daily economic decisions?

3. Consider the factors of production and give one example not listed in the text of each of the following: natural resources, human resources, and capital resources.

4. Why might a person become an entrepreneur? What characteristics might someone need to be a successful entrepreneur?

5. **Thinking and Writing Critically** You use the factors of production every day. For example, you use a human resource—your own effort—to finish your homework. What other factors of production do you use in your daily activities?

6. **Applying** SCARCITY & CHOICE Explain how technology is used to create new capital goods. Provide an example from your own experience.

SCARCITY AND CHOICE

Economics Dictionary

scarcity
allocate
productivity
efficiency
division of labor
specialization

Objectives

▶ Why does scarcity exist?

▶ What issues must producers address to distribute resources?

▶ Why do producers study productivity?

You have learned that economists study the decisions that people make about using a variety of resources. Why do people need to make these decisions?

Consider an economic decision you may have faced many times: how to spend a limited amount of money from an allowance, a birthday gift, or your paycheck. You can use the money to buy several compact discs (CDs), movie tickets for your friends, or a new outfit for school. But you cannot buy all these things. Because your resources (money) are limited, you are forced to make an economic decision—to choose how you will spend the money. Such limitations on resources—and how people respond to them—are a part of every aspect of economics.

Scarcity

All resources are limited. People's wants, however, are unlimited. This combination of limited economic resources and unlimited wants results in a condition known as **scarcity**. Scarcity is the most basic problem of economics, because it forces people to make decisions about how to use resources effectively (see Figure 1.1).

Many factors contribute to scarcity. Low amounts of rainfall, for example, may lead to poor harvests and therefore to a scarcity of fruits and vegetables at grocery stores. During World War II silk and nylon were used to make parachutes—creating a scarcity of women's stockings, which had been produced from those materials during peacetime.

Identifying Economic Questions

How do you—and other people—respond to scarcity? Limited amounts of products require people to make decisions. People decide how to **allocate**, or distribute, resources in order to satisfy the greatest number of needs and wants. To allocate resources effectively, an economic

SCARCITY & CHOICE *Scarcity is the most basic problem of economics.* **How does recycling allow for a more effective use of scarce resources?**

system or a society must address three basic economic questions:

▶ what to produce,
▶ how to produce, and
▶ for whom to produce.

The answers to these questions help a society determine the best distribution of resources to meet its needs and wants.

What to Produce A society's needs and wants can never be met completely. Therefore, the society's economic system must determine the urgency of those needs and wants. Suppose that a large number of people decide to move to a particular city, and that many of them have school-age children. Should the city build a new school to accommodate these students, or should more money be spent on school buses and drivers so that more students can attend existing schools? What if a new school *and* additional buses are necessary? The city must decide what resources will be allocated for construction and what resources will be allocated for transportation.

How to Produce A society can allocate resources in many different ways. During construction of the new school, for example, the builder must decide how the roof will be built. Suppose that a worker can attach shingles using either a hammer and nails or a nail gun. Either method will result in a stable, well-made roof. A worker using a nail gun will work faster—and tire more slowly—than a worker using a hammer. How does the builder choose a method of production? If unemployment is high, the builder may decide that hiring additional workers is less expensive than investing in equipment. If workers demand high wages, the builder may decide to hire fewer workers and provide them with equipment that increases their speed.

For Whom to Produce A society must determine how to distribute the goods and services that it produces. For example, who will attend the new school? Will any students at existing schools be transferred to the new school? How will city

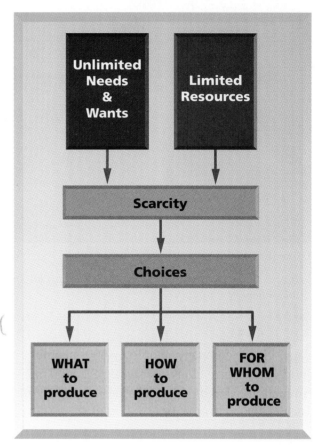

FIGURE 1.1 The combination of unlimited needs and wants and limited resources results in a condition called scarcity. **What three economic decisions does scarcity force a society to make?**

residents pay for construction? To allocate resources effectively, a society must consider who will consume goods and services.

Productivity

After choosing what, how, and for whom to produce, a society must carry out these decisions. In doing so, the society tries to make sure that its resources are used as effectively as possible. Remember, the problem of scarcity forces people to make wise use of resources.

People determine if resources are being used wisely by studying productivity. **Productivity** is the level of output that results from a given level of input. For example, suppose that the Sleepy

PRODUCTIVITY *Workers on an assembly line demonstrate the concept of specialization.* **How does specialization benefit a producer?**

improve **efficiency**, which is the use of the smallest amount of resources to produce the greatest amount of output.

One option might be for the factory to introduce a **division of labor**, assigning a small number of tasks to each worker. For example, one worker might attach the clock face, and another might install the power switch. Because these steps are performed repeatedly, workers gain expertise in the assigned tasks. This focus on one activity is known as **specialization**. The process of specialization allows each employee to work faster and produce a greater number of alarm clocks. Introducing division of labor would enable the Sleepy Time company to increase production to 5,000 alarm clocks per week.

On the other hand, the Sleepy Time company might decide to increase efficiency by finding shortcuts that allow workers to construct clocks more quickly. Now only 25 employees would be needed to produce 1,000 clocks per week. Although the company produces the same number of clocks, productivity increases because input—the number of workers—is reduced.

A third option might involve mechanization. Some of the workers might be replaced by machines that work faster and longer—and therefore at a lower cost per unit—than employees.

Time clock company employs 100 people to build 1,000 alarm clocks per week. Sleepy Time's productivity thus is 10 clocks per employee per week (1,000 ÷ 100 = 10).

Now imagine that the company president decides that productivity is too low and asks staff members to suggest improvements. The finance manager for Sleepy Time points out that each worker builds an entire clock from start to finish. She suggests that the company find ways to

SECTION 2 — REVIEW

1. Define the following terms: scarcity, allocate, productivity, efficiency, division of labor, specialization.

2. Why do people need to make choices about distributing resources?

3. What three questions must all economic systems address?

4. Why is productivity important to a society?

5. **Thinking and Writing Critically** How do you decide to distribute your limited time and effort in your studies? Explain how you answer the three main production questions when studying for your classes.

6. **Applying** **PRODUCTIVITY** How do division of labor and specialization affect productivity in your classroom or in your home? Could you improve efficiency to increase productivity? Explain your answer.

SECTION 3

OPPORTUNITY COSTS

Economics Dictionary

trade-off
opportunity cost
production possibilities curve

Objectives

▶ Why is sacrifice an important element of economic choice?

▶ What assumptions are involved in creating a production possibilities curve?

▶ Why might future production possibilities differ from current production possibilities?

As you have learned, scarcity requires producers and consumers to make choices. Similarly, a society must answer the three economic questions of what to produce, how to produce, and for whom to produce. What are the results of these economic decisions?

Trade-Offs and Opportunity Costs

Choosing among alternative uses for available resources forces people to make choices. If a resource is used to produce or consume one good, that same resource cannot be used to produce or consume something else. One good is sacrificed for another. In economic terms this sacrifice is called a **trade-off**. The cost of this trade-off—the value of the next best alternative given up to obtain that item—is called the **opportunity cost**.

People face trade-offs and opportunity costs every day. Consider the following example. Michelle Tanabe has two events she would like to attend in the same week—a concert and an ice hockey game. Tickets for the concert and the hockey game cost the same amount. Unfortunately, Michelle has only enough money to purchase one ticket. She must make a trade-off because she cannot afford to buy both tickets. If she spends money on a ticket to the concert, the alternative choice—the ticket to the hockey game—is the opportunity cost of buying the concert ticket.

The above example is a simple, two-item choice. Most choices, however, involve many more trade-offs (see Figure 1.2). When resources are used to build a factory, the trade-off is not between the factory and one other use of the resources. All of the workers, equipment, and financial input used to construct the factory could be used to build many combinations of homes, offices, and shopping centers. These factors of production might also be used in fields

KEVIN'S DECISION-MAKING GRID

ALTERNATIVES	CRITERIA			
	Cost Within Budget?	Acceptable to Parents?	Lasting Benefit?	Entertaining?
Go to Choir Practice	yes	yes	yes	yes
Go out to Dinner	no	no	no	yes
Watch Television	yes	possibly	no	yes
Do Homework	yes	yes	yes	no
Go to Football Game	yes	no	no	yes

FIGURE 1.2 Kevin has $10 left from his allowance. **Based on his decision-making grid, what is his best choice for a Friday-night activity? What are the trade-offs? What is the opportunity cost?**

other than construction. For example, investors might decide to deposit their money in savings accounts, or the land might be used as a park.

Although many trade-offs may be possible within a set of choices, only one of these—the next best choice—is considered the opportunity cost. For example, suppose that you are deciding how to spend your Saturday afternoon. You can choose between a trip to the beach, a visit to a carnival, and a hike in a nearby park. After some thought you decide that you are not interested in going on a hike, and that although the carnival would be fun, you would prefer to go to the beach. Both the carnival and the hike are considered trade-offs. However, only your *second-best* choice—the carnival—is considered an opportunity cost of going to the beach.

Undamming the Deerfield

OPPORTUNITY COST & TRADE-OFFS Across the country the effects of dam construction on rivers are being reconsidered. Rivers have long provided power to turn machinery in mills and to run electric generators. In fact, the federal government has licensed hundreds of dams in order to advance the nation's industrial development. Although both industry and consumers have benefited from this development, the rivers and the communities along them have often been harmed in some unexpected economic ways.

For example, the Deerfield River, which runs through Vermont and Massachusetts, has a series of 10 dams that were built along its course during the World War I era. At the time, government officials and many residents believed that the benefits of building the dams to generate hydroelectric power outweighed the interruption of the river's natural flow. Today, however, this trade-off is being re-evaluated. Why?

The dams affected the environment of the river's fish species including salmon, which could no longer return upstream to spawn. As a result, the area's fishing industry suffered. Likewise, the dams limited the river's potential as a site for water sports. Finally, the local ecosystem was jeopardized by the presence of the dams. Wildlife and water quality declined.

As a result, in 1995 New England Power, owner of nine of the dams, agreed to adapt their water usage to meet these economic and environmental concerns. As more water is released from the dams, dry stretches of river are once again able to support life. The construction of fish runs is expected to allow salmon to travel along the river for the first time in decades. Additionally, periodic water releases from one of the dams have created one of the country's most exciting whitewater kayak runs.

This re-evaluation of water use along the Deerfield River shows how trade-offs and opportunity costs can change over time. By periodically reviewing these types of decisions, producers and consumers can make the best trade-offs and limit the effects of opportunity costs.

Production Possibilities

Trade-offs and opportunity costs can be illustrated using a production possibilities curve. A **production possibilities curve** shows all of the possible combinations of two goods or services that can be produced within a stated time period, given two important assumptions. First, it is assumed that the amount of available resources

OPPORTUNITY COST & TRADE-OFFS *Re-evaluation of public use of New England's Deerfield River has created new opportunities to kayak its whitewater rapids.* **What are the trade-offs of recreational use of the river?**

and technology will not change during the period being studied. Second, it is assumed that all of the natural, human, and capital resources are being used in the most efficient manner possible.

The above assumptions are important because they determine which production combinations will fall on the curve and which will not. All of the combinations on the curve meet these assumptions. Combinations that lie inside (below) the curve, on the other hand, represent an inefficient use of existing resources. Combinations that lie outside (above) the curve represent production impossibilities, given existing technology. Each production combination is measured in terms of opportunity costs. That is, more of one good can be produced only by making less of the other good.

Keep in mind that a production possibilities curve is a model, or a simplified version of reality based on specific assumptions. Models are useful tools that help people understand how the real world works. Because the production possibilities curve is based on assumptions relating to current conditions, it is a helpful model.

Current Production Possibilities

Figure 1.3 shows the possible production options that would be available to the U.S. automotive industry if it concentrated its current resources on the production of only two types of cars: economy and luxury. Like all production possibilities curves, this curve is based on the assumptions that the amount of resources—raw materials, labor, and capital goods—will not change and that those resources will be used efficiently.

The curve that connects points A through E shows the production combinations that meet the stated assumptions. At point A, all resources are devoted to the production of luxury cars. Point E represents the other extreme—all resources are devoted to the production of economy cars. In these two extreme cases (points A and E), the opportunity cost of producing one class of cars is the entire production capacity of the other class of cars.

Consumers are interested in purchasing a variety of cars, however, so automobile compa-

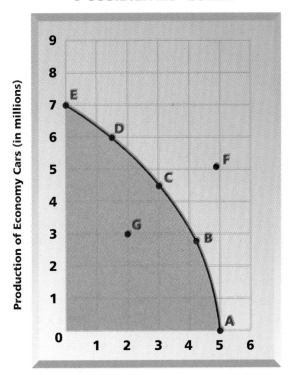

THE PRODUCTION POSSIBILITIES CURVE

Production of Economy Cars (in millions)

Production of Luxury Cars (in millions)

FIGURE 1.3 The production possibilities curve is a helpful model for understanding efficient use of resources. **What two assumptions must be considered when studying a production possibilities curve?**

nies probably would not choose to limit production to either luxury or economy cars. Instead, automobile companies would most likely produce some combination of the two classes of cars. These combinations are represented by points B, C, and D on the curve. The opportunity cost of producing a certain number of one class of cars would be the number of cars of the other class that could not be produced. For example, the production of 5 million economy cars would limit the production of luxury cars to 2.5 million.

Two additional points, F and G, are included in the graph. Point F, which lies outside the curve, is a production impossibility given the current levels of technology and other resources. No matter how the automotive industry mixes the existing factors of production, it cannot produce

SHIFTING PRODUCTION POSSIBILITIES CURVE

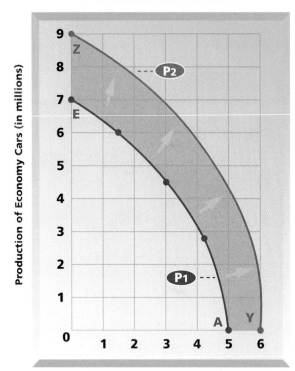

Production of Economy Cars (in millions) (vertical axis, 0–9)

Points labeled: Z, P2, E, P1, A, Y

Production of Luxury Cars (in millions) (horizontal axis, 1–6)

FIGURE 1.4 A shift of the production possibilities curve to the right indicates that improvements in technology have occurred or that new resources are available. **What conditions would cause the curve to shift to the left?**

at this high a level. Point G, which lies inside the curve, represents an inefficient use of resources. If the existing factors of production were used more efficiently, the industry should be able to produce at a level represented by one of the points on the production possibilities curve, instead of at the level of point G.

Future Production Possibilities In the real world, technology and the factors of production do not remain constant. When improvements in technology occur or new resources become available, the entire production possibilities curve changes. A new curve is formed to the right of the old curve. Economists say that the curve has "shifted to the right."

The production possibilities curve in Figure 1.4 shows a shift to the right. The new curve, which connects points Y and Z, represents the expanded production that results from advances in technology or the introduction of new resources. The new curve, like the old one, makes the standard assumptions of fixed resources and efficiency. If the assumptions change—if new technology or resources become available—the curve again shifts to the right. The curve may also shift to the left if resources become unavailable.

SECTION 3 — REVIEW

1. Define the following terms: trade-off, opportunity cost, production possibilities curve.

2. What assumptions determine the production possibilities curve?

3. What condition is represented by a point lying inside, or below, the production possibilities curve?

4. How can an increase in available resources affect the production possibilities curve?

5. **Thinking and Writing Critically**
   From your own experience, describe a recent choice you have made. What trade-offs were involved in this choice? What was the opportunity cost?

6. **Applying** OPPORTUNITY COST & TRADE-OFFS
   Explain how a current event in national politics or economics reflects the concepts of opportunity cost and trade-offs. Do you agree with the choice that was made? Explain your answer.

SECTION 4

EXCHANGE

Economics Dictionary
exchange
barter
money
credit
value
utility
self-sufficiency
interdependence

Objectives
▶ What are the difficulties associated with barter?
▶ Why is true self-sufficiency rare?
▶ What are the economic benefits of interdependence?

How do producers find out if they indeed have determined the most efficient and productive method of using resources? If consumers purchase more calculators from Texas Instruments than from Radio Shack, Texas Instruments knows that it made the correct economic decisions. Producers gain this information through a process called an **exchange**, in which producers and consumers agree to provide one type of item in return for another.

Forms of Exchange

The principle of exchange has existed throughout history. Exchange can take one of three forms: barter, money, and credit.

Barter Many societies—today and in the past—exchanged one set of goods for another. This direct trade is known as **barter**. Barter relies on bargaining and often results in complicated

transactions. Suppose that two students agree to trade lunches. One student may offer a turkey sandwich in exchange for a carton of chocolate milk. The student who has the milk, however, may only be willing to trade for an apple. For the exchange to be completed, therefore, the student with the turkey sandwich must find a *third* person who has an apple—and hope that this person is willing to participate in the lunchtime trade.

Money The difficulties of barter commonly lead to the development of a standardized means of exchange. This means of exchange is called money. **Money** is any item that is readily accepted by people in return for goods and services. When you think of money, you probably

EXCHANGE, MONEY, & INTERDEPENDENCE *Traders from throughout the former Soviet Union flock to the border town of Pogranichni, Russia, to barter goods with Chinese businesspeople.* **What are some of the difficulties associated with barter?**

Year-Round Produce

Have you ever wondered why you can buy fresh tomatoes or peaches all year long, even though these fruits generally grow only in the summer? Perhaps you have noticed kiwi fruit from New Zealand or grapes from Chile available at your local supermarket in the winter. Although you probably have grown accustomed to fresh produce year-round, this luxury has not always been available to consumers.

What makes it possible for you to enjoy fresh produce anytime you want? Relatively recent technological developments permit fresh produce to be transported from countries around the world to your local store.

For example, in 1995 British Airways World Cargo announced the opening of a new warehouse devoted to perishable cargo, such as fresh flowers and produce. Trained specialists oversee shipping and storage and rely on equipment such as blast chillers and ethylene scrubbers to ensure that the warehouse remains a safe environment for fresh produce.

These and other developments in rapid shipping and advanced refrigeration equipment mean that distant countries can supply their produce to U.S. markets. Chile, for example, grows most of its produce between October and April, because its location south of the equator makes these the warmest months of the year. "Reversed" seasons in Southern Hemisphere countries such as Chile and New Zealand complement the growing season in the Northern Hemisphere and extend the season for fresh products and produce.

imagine bills and coins such as dollars, pesos, lire, shekels, and yen. In various societies many other items have been used as money, however, including precious metals, salt, beads, and cocoa beans.

Money has three functions. It serves as

- a standardized item that is generally traded for goods or services,
- a measure of value that allows both producers and consumers to determine and express worth, and
- a store of value that can be saved and used to purchase items at a later date.

Credit A third form of exchange, called **credit**, allows consumers to use items before completing payment for the merchandise. Credit allows consumers to pay for an item over a specified period of time. For example, you may decide to buy a portable stereo priced at $200. You do not have $200 at the moment, however, so you arrange to pay for the stereo over a period of six months. The use of credit allows you to take your stereo home today—even though you have not made all of your payments.

Consumers who fail to make the necessary credit payments, however, may be required to return the merchandise for which they are paying. They also risk losing future opportunities to receive credit.

Many societies combine different forms of exchange within their economies. For example, both money and credit are important to the U.S. economy as a whole, while individuals within the U.S. economy sometimes may rely on barter. A plumber, for example, may agree to fix his neighbor's clogged drain in exchange for help building a covered patio. You will learn more about credit and other common forms of exchange in later chapters.

Value

How do consumers and producers determine the worth of items in an exchange? In order to avoid the problems of barter, goods and services are assigned a **value** that can be expressed as an amount of money, or a price. Suppose, for example, that Craig Patterson collects stamps. The value of his collection is determined by how much another collector would be willing to pay for the stamps.

Which do you think are more likely to carry higher values—needs or wants? Many needs, such as water, have low monetary values. Water is necessary to life, but it is not expensive. A want such as a diamond necklace, on the other hand, is very expensive even though it is not a necessity.

Why do many wants carry higher values than many needs? In the example described above, consider the availability of each item. Diamonds are extremely rare, while water is plentiful in most regions of the world. Scarcity, therefore, can create value.

Value is also determined by the degree to which a product has **utility**, or usefulness to a person. Utility can be more difficult to determine than scarcity, because one person may find a product useful while another finds the product to be of no use at all. Do diamonds and water have utility? Yes, both are useful. Water is necessary to life, and diamonds are both a popular gemstone and an important tool in some industries.

Water, therefore, has utility but is not scarce, while diamonds have both utility and scarcity. This combination of utility and scarcity forms the basis for determining value.

The determination of value allows producers and consumers to decide the relative worth of goods and services in an exchange. Consider again the case of Craig Patterson. Some of the stamps in his collection are very rare, while others are not. Additionally, other stamp collectors are likely to feel that his collection has a high utility, while noncollectors may disagree. The value of Craig's collection, therefore, depends on the scarcity and the utility of the stamps.

Interdependence

Why would you participate in an exchange? For an exchange to be successful, each participant must be able to provide goods and services that the other wants but does not possess. If both people are satisfied with the goods and services they already have, an exchange will not take place. The principle of exchange depends on unmet needs and wants.

Are you able to produce all of the goods and services you need? People—or a society—demonstrate **self-sufficiency** when they can fulfill all of their needs without outside assistance. True self-sufficiency is rare, however, because resources are limited. To produce everything you need would require a tremendous supply of tools, equipment, and raw materials. In addition, self-sufficiency demands extensive skills and knowledge in a variety of fields.

Instead of being self-sufficient, people tend to specialize in certain areas of production and rely

EXCHANGE, MONEY, & INTERDEPENDENCE *Amish settlements, located primarily in Ohio and Pennsylvania, attempt to be completely self-sufficient by fulfilling all their residents' needs without outside assistance.* **Why do most societies fulfill wants and needs through interdependence?**

on others for additional goods and services. For example, a landowner in the Rio Grande Valley of Texas is more likely to cultivate grapefruit than to fish for Atlantic cod, because the region's soil and climate are well suited to citrus crops—and because Texas is a long way from the North Atlantic. The landowner in Texas must rely on fishing companies in the New England states to provide cod, just as fishing-boat captains who want grapefruit must rely on citrus farmers in Texas and other states with appropriate soil and climate conditions.

This reliance among economic actors is known as interdependence. **Interdependence** means that events or developments in one region of the world or sector of the economy influence events or developments in other regions or sectors. Increased home construction may encourage a paint company to expand production and hire additional workers. Bad weather in Oregon and Washington may lead to a poor apple crop, which in turn can increase the price of apple juice and frozen apple turnovers.

Interdependence encourages individuals, industries, and regions to meet particular needs and wants. If you know that you can purchase clothing at a nearby store, you do not need your own loom. Sometimes, however, interdependence

EXCHANGE, MONEY, & INTERDEPENDENCE *Societies can specialize in the production of certain goods and services when they practice interdependence.*

can present challenges if the good or service becomes unavailable. For example, in 1990 Iraq invaded Kuwait, a small, oil-rich country. Many people feared that a stoppage of oil production and shipments would weaken the economies of the countries that received their oil supplies from Kuwait. Although interdependence offers many benefits, it also can pose the threat of economic vulnerability.

SECTION 4 — REVIEW

1. Define the following terms: exchange, barter, money, credit, value, utility, self-sufficiency, interdependence.

2. How do problems associated with barter contribute to the use of money as a form of exchange?

3. What are the benefits and liabilities of credit?

4. Describe the benefits and risks of interdependence.

5. Thinking and Writing Critically
How do forms of interaction within your school demonstrate interdependence? For example, do math teachers also teach English classes? Does the librarian also work in the school office?

6. Applying EXCHANGE, MONEY, & INTERDEPENDENCE
Identify three goods and services that are exchanged on the Internet. How do these exchanges reflect the concept of interdependence?

SECTION 1 Economics is the study of the choices that people make to satisfy their needs and wants. A need is anything that is necessary for survival, such as food, clothing, and shelter. Wants are goods and services that people consume beyond what is necessary for survival. Goods are physical objects that can be purchased, and services are actions or activities performed for a fee. People who supply goods and services are called producers, and people who purchase goods and services are called consumers.

Economic decisions involve resources. A resource is anything that can be used to satisfy a consumer's want or need. Resources that can be used to produce goods and services are known as factors of production. Economists generally recognize four categories of resources: natural resources, human resources, capital resources, and entrepreneurship.

SECTION 2 Scarcity is the basic fact of economic life. Human needs and wants are always greater than the resources available to satisfy them. Thus, choices must be made concerning how to best use the limited resources available. To make these choices, an economic system or society must answer the three basic economic questions of what to produce, how to produce, and for whom to produce.

Once an economic system has answered the questions of what, how, and for whom to produce, production must be carried out as effectively as possible. To reach the highest possible levels of productivity, producers may rely on division of labor and specialization.

SECTION 3 Scarcity requires choice. Economists call the sacrifice of one choice for another a trade-off and the next best choice an opportunity cost. The production possibilities curve can be used to analyze the trade-offs and opportunity costs involved in producing specific combinations of goods and services. A production possibilities curve assumes that the amount of available resources and the state of technology will not change during the period being studied, and that resources are used as efficiently as possible. Changes in resources or technology result in a shift of the entire production possibilities curve either to the right or the left.

SECTION 4 Producers and consumers distribute goods and services through a system of exchange. Forms of exchange include barter, money, and credit.

In an exchange, goods and services are assigned a value, or a worth that can be expressed in terms of money. This price is determined by the product's scarcity and utility. Utility, or usefulness, can vary from person to person.

Exchange reduces self-sufficiency and encourages interdependence, linking different regions and economic actors. Interdependence, in turn, encourages specialization, as individuals, industries, and regions concentrate on producing specific goods and services to meet particular needs and wants.

Economics Notebook

Review what you wrote about your economic activities in your Economics Notebook at the beginning of this chapter. Now that you have studied this chapter, would you change your evaluation? Why or why not? Record your answer in your Notebook.

REVIEW

REVIEWING CONCEPTS

1. What is the difference between microeconomics and macroeconomics?

2. Why is scarcity important in economics?

3. What three production issues must an economic system address?

4. How can division of labor and specialization increase productivity?

5. Identify the assumptions on which the production possibilities curve is based.

6. Why might future production possibilities differ from current production possibilities?

THINKING AND WRITING CRITICALLY

1. **SCARCITY & CHOICE** Explain how entrepreneurship and technology relate to natural, human, and capital resources.

2. **OPPORTUNITY COST & TRADE-OFFS** Determine whether the following products are capital goods or consumer goods: tennis shoes, motion picture projectors, forklifts. Explain your answers.

3. **SCARCITY & CHOICE** Consider the resources that are available in your classroom, such as reference books, chalk, and display areas. How do these resources reflect the principle of scarcity?

4. **OPPORTUNITY COST & TRADE-OFFS** Suppose that you are a member of the school band and have been asked to participate in a Saturday car wash to raise money for new uniforms. A group of friends invites you to play basketball the same afternoon as the fund-raiser. What are the trade-offs if you choose to work at the fund-raiser? to play basketball?

YOUR LOCAL ECONOMY

How does your school utilize the factors of production? Develop a chart that lists each factor of production—natural resources, human resources, capital resources, and entrepreneurship—and describes the role of that factor in your school. For example, how does your school affect and rely on natural resources? What human resources does it use?

COOPERATIVE PORTFOLIO PROJECT

With your group, develop an idea for a new study aid. Respond to the three production questions of what to produce, how to produce, and for whom to produce. Assign members of the group to work as researchers, copywriters, and artists. Create an advertisement that makes the answers to these three questions clear by describing what the product is, how it is made, and the audience it targets.

PRACTICING SKILLS: UNDERSTANDING CHARTS AND GRAPHS

You have been given $50 and need to decide how best to spend the money. After some thought, you have narrowed your choices to the following list: a pair of jeans, movie tickets for you and several friends, and a baseball glove. Create a decision-making grid that lists these choices along the side. Across the top, label five columns with the following headers: *Is Cost Within Range?*, *Acceptable to Parents?*, *Lasting Use?*, *No Additional Costs*, and *Few Limitations on Use*. For each choice, respond to the column headers by placing check marks in the appropriate boxes. Then answer the questions on page 21.

1. Based on the table, which choice satisfies the greatest number of criteria?

2. What is the opportunity cost of this choice?

3. Is the decision-making grid a useful tool in making economic choices? Explain your answer.

THE INTERNET: LEARNING ONLINE

Search the Internet to learn about the economy in your community. Specifically, look for information about your city or state chamber of commerce by typing in search words such as *chamber of commerce* and the name of your city or state. What can you learn about the purpose of the chamber of commerce you have selected? Who belongs to the chamber of commerce you are investigating? Using e-mail, contact the chamber of commerce and ask for more information about the services it provides to members and the community.

ANALYZING PRIMARY SOURCES

Principles of Economics

Alfred Marshall (1842–1924) was a noted English economist and mathematician. In his 1890 book *Principles of Economics*, Marshall examined the nature of economics and economic laws. Read the excerpt below and answer the questions that follow.

"Economics is a study of men as they live and move and think in the ordinary business of life. But it concerns itself chiefly with those motives which affect, most powerfully and most steadily, man's conduct in the business part of his life. . . .

"The steadiest motive to ordinary business work is the desire for the pay which is the material reward of work. The pay may be on its way to be spent selfishly or unselfishly, for noble or base [low] ends; and here the variety of human nature comes into play. But the motive is supplied by a definite amount of money: and it is this definite and exact money measurement of the steadiest motives in business life, which has enabled economics far to outrun every other branch of the study of man.

"Just as the chemist's fine balance has made chemistry more exact than most other physical sciences; so this economist's balance, rough and imperfect as it is, has made economics more exact than any other branch of social science. But of course economics cannot be compared with the exact physical sciences: for it deals with the ever changing and subtle forces of human nature. . . .

"The laws of economics are to be compared with the laws of the tides, rather than with the simple and exact law of gravitation. For the actions of men are so various and uncertain, that the best statement of tendencies, which we can make in a science of human conduct, must needs be inexact and faulty.

"The term 'law' means then nothing more than a general proposition or statement of tendencies, more or less certain, more or less definite. . . .

"Thus a law of social science, or a Social Law, is a statement of social tendencies; that is, a statement that a certain course of action may be expected under certain conditions from the members of a social group.

"*Economic laws* . . . are those social laws which relate to branches of conduct in which the strength of the motives chiefly concerned can be measured by a money price.

"There is thus no hard and sharp line of division between those social laws which are, and those which are not, to be regarded also as economic laws. For there is a continuous gradation [progression] from social laws concerned almost exclusively with motives that can be measured by price, to social laws in which such motives have little place; and which are therefore generally as much less precise and exact than economic laws."

1. What is Alfred Marshall's definition of economics?

2. Why does Marshall consider economics to be more "exact" than other social sciences?

3. Why does Marshall consider economics to be less exact than physical sciences such as chemistry?

4. According to Marshall, what is the difference between the terms *social law* and *economic law*?

CHAPTER 2
⌐ ECONOMIC SYSTEMS

As you have learned, there are three basic economic questions: what to produce, how to produce, and for whom to produce. Like individuals, societies also must answer these basic production questions, and they do so in different ways. For example, in some societies the government makes the production decisions, while in others these decisions are made by business owners. In all societies, however, production decisions are designed to meet people's needs and wants. The decisions form an interlocking network of production and consumption, and are the basis of all economic systems.

In this chapter you will learn how different societies make production decisions. You also will learn about the U.S. economy—what it is supposed to do and how it affects you.

✎ Economics Notebook

In your Economics Notebook, list your personal economic goals. For example, you may want to buy a new jacket or take a trip. Which of your economic goals are short-term, and which are long-term? Explain your answers.

TYPES OF ECONOMIC SYSTEMS

Economics Dictionary

traditional economy
command economy
market economy
market
self-interest
incentive
mixed economy
authoritarian socialism
communism
capitalism
democratic socialism

Objectives

▶ How are the three basic economic questions answered in traditional, command, and market economies?

▶ What are the roles of self-interest and incentives in a market economy?

▶ What types of mixed economies exist today?

You know that scarcity affects all aspects of economics and that it requires economic actors—individuals, businesses, and governments—to make choices. You, for example, have a limited amount of money and time. This scarcity forces you to make choices among ways to spend your money and your time.

Nations also must make choices in order to use their natural, human, capital, and entrepreneurial resources efficiently. A nation—or, more directly, its leaders—must address the three basic economic questions: what to produce, how to produce, and for whom to produce.

A nation's responses to these questions are determined by its economic system. An economic system reflects the process a nation—or any society—follows to produce goods and services. There are four types of economic systems:

▶ traditional,
▶ command,
▶ market, and
▶ mixed.

In truth, all economies are mixed. Pure traditional, pure command, and pure market systems are models that do not exist in the world today. A few mixed economies are closest to the pure traditional model and are classified as traditional economies. Mixed economies that are closest to the pure command model are classified as command economies. Similarly, mixed economies that are closest to the pure market model are classified as market economies. See Figure 2.1 on page 26 for a summary of types of economic systems.

ECONOMIC SYSTEMS *In a traditional economy, children—such as this Navajo girl—often carry on the economic roles played by their parents.*

Traditional Economies

As you might guess, a **traditional economy** is based on custom and tradition. In other words, the answers to the three economic questions are found in the past. Contemporary economic activities are based on the collection of rituals, habits, laws, and religious beliefs developed by the group's ancestors.

In a traditional economy, children often carry on the economic roles played by their parents. This means that tradition determines in large part what is produced. For example, if you lived in a society with a traditional economy and one of your parents earned a living by catching fish in the nearby river, you would earn your living in the same way. Tradition decides what you produce—fish. Note also that traditional economic roles generally are passed down from father to son and from mother to daughter, because in traditional economies men and women often perform distinct tasks.

Custom determines how items will be produced in a traditional economy. For example, hundreds of years ago some American Indian tribes planted corn when oak leaves grew to the size of a squirrel's ear. This timing was based on traditional agricultural practices rather than individual decisions.

For whom are goods produced in a traditional economy? Economic activities tend to be centered around traditional family and social units such as a tribe. The goods and services that are produced are distributed among the group's members. By sharing products, members of a traditional economy work to maintain the entire group rather than just themselves. For example, members of Inuit tribes in Canada share equally in the results of a hunt. When a seal or other large animal is killed, the meat is divided among the members of the hunting party. Hunters then share their meat with family members in an effort to help the entire community survive the harsh winter.

Traditional economic systems still exist in parts of North America, Latin America, Asia, Africa, and Southwest Asia. For example, the Dinka of central Africa herd cattle and grow crops on the southern plains of the Sudan as their ancestors have done for centuries. Other traditional economies include the San of the Kalahari Desert and the Aborigines of Australia. The Mbuti of central Africa are also organized into a traditional economic system.

CASE STUDY

The Mbuti of Central Africa

ECONOMIC SYSTEMS The Mbuti are inhabitants of the Ituri Forest in the central African Democratic Republic of Congo. The 35,000 Mbuti live, work, and travel in bands, or small groups, of 30 people or less, and members of a band view themselves as a family. Because the Mbuti have a traditional economy, they rely on long-standing customs to answer the three basic economic issues of what, how, and for whom to produce.

The main duty of all band members is to provide food, and the Ituri Forest offers an abundance of natural resources. The Mbuti are hunter-gatherers. They collect roots, mushrooms, fruits, berries, and nuts. In addition, they hunt for wild game using nets, spears, bows, and arrows, which sometimes are dipped in poison. The men hunt, and the women and children

ECONOMIC SYSTEMS *In the Mbuti tribe's economy, tradition determines which tasks will be done by men, women, and children.* **For whom do the Mbuti produce?**

gather and prepare the food. Tradition dictates which jobs will be done by men and which will be done by women, as well as what duties children will perform.

Although members of traditional economies generally resist change, the Mbuti have adopted new tools in recent years. Neighboring tribes produce metal machetes and knives. The Mbuti trade for these items because they do not have the necessary resources and skills to produce metal tools.

Command Economies

While a traditional economy relies on the past, a pure **command economy** relies on government officials to answer the three basic economic questions. The officials—sometimes called central planners—have the power to decide what products will be made and how these products will be produced. These planners also decide who will receive the products once they are completed. Command economies may also be called planned economies.

Because central planners make decisions about what, how, and for whom to produce, individuals in a command economy have little or no say in economic choices. The government maintains complete control over the factors of production.

Although pure command economies no longer exist, they were quite common in the past. For example, during the Old Kingdom period of Egyptian history (2700–2200 B.C.), the pharaoh, or monarch, ruled both the economy and the government of Egypt. The monarch owned the land, controlled all trade, collected taxes, and supervised the building of the kingdom's pyramids, dams, canals, and granaries.

During the Zhou Dynasty (1122–221 B.C.) in China, emperors were able to control resources by distributing land to supporters called vassals. The vassals pledged their military and political loyalty to the emperor in return for the land grants.

A similar system existed in Western Europe during the Middle Ages. Monarchs and other feudal lords granted resources such as land—called fiefs—to vassals in exchange for loyalty, military support, and payment. These vassals granted

ECONOMIC SYSTEMS *Egyptians, such as those shown posting taxes on the Old Kingdom tomb above, lived in a command economy.* **Who controls production in a command economy?**

peasants the right to work the lands in exchange for money, crops, or livestock. The lord had absolute control over the use of human, natural, and capital resources on the manor and therefore made all decisions about what, how, and for whom to produce.

Market Economies

In a pure **market economy**, individuals answer the three basic economic questions. The government has no say in what, how, and for whom goods are produced, and the factors of production are owned by individuals. People can buy, sell, and produce anything they want.

This free exchange of goods and services is referred to as the **market**. The market—which is sometimes called the marketplace—provides the only form of control over what goods and services are bought and sold.

Self-Interest How does the market regulate economic activity? One of the first people to explain this process of market regulation was Adam Smith (1723–1790), a Scottish economist and philosopher. In 1776 Smith published his ideas in the book *An Inquiry into the Nature and*

Causes of the Wealth of Nations.

Adam Smith

He contended that when the government is not involved in the economy, the market is driven purely by **self-interest**—the impulse that encourages people to fulfill their needs and wants.

Although some people believe that self-interest leads individuals to ignore the needs of others, Smith argued that self-interest benefits all of society by helping the economy grow. According to Smith, in a market exchange each person attempts to gain the greatest possible advantage from the transaction. While individuals work to meet their own needs and wants, however, self-interest acts as an "invisible hand" that also leads them to do what is best for society—even if they are unaware of how their actions may benefit others.

How can self-interest benefit others? Suppose that you have a job as a newspaper carrier. Why did you accept this job?

(a) You believe that everyone deserves a newspaper.

(b) It is a good newspaper, and more people should read it.

(c) You are paid to deliver the newspaper.

Probably your answer is *c*. You deliver newspapers because you are paid to do so. At the same time, however, newspaper delivery makes it easier for people to learn about world and community events. Thus, your self-interest benefits other members of society.

Smith believed that government involvement in the economy conflicts with self-interest and limits the ability of the "invisible hand" to regulate the market. Suppose that the government set a limit on how many newspapers you could be paid to deliver each day. Would you try to sell newspaper subscriptions to people who moved into houses along your route? Probably not, because once you reach the maximum number of deliveries, additional subscriptions would offer you no personal benefit and would not be in your self-interest. The government policy, therefore, effectively would have limited newspaper circulation, reducing the benefits to you and to society as a whole.

TYPES OF ECONOMIC SYSTEMS

Economic Systems	WHAT to Produce	HOW to Produce	FOR WHOM to Produce	Examples
TRADITIONAL	• determined by tradition • economic roles often passed from generation to generation	• determined by custom	• usually centered around traditional family and social units such as a tribe	• Aborigines of Australia • Mbuti of Central Africa • Inuit of Canada
COMMAND	• determined by government officials	• determined by government officials	• determined by government officials	• Old Kingdom Egypt • Middle Ages in Europe • Zhou Dynasty in China
MARKET	• determined by individuals	• determined by individuals	• determined by individuals	• United States • Canada • Australia

FIGURE 2.1 Economic systems are defined by the way they answer the three basic economic questions. **How does the U.S. economic system differ from that of Australian Aborigines?**

Incentives In a market economy, how do you decide what economic choices are in your self-interest? You—and other individuals in the economy—respond to incentives. An **incentive** is something that encourages you to behave in a particular way.

For example, the newspaper may offer you a bonus for every 50 new subscribers you sign up. This financial reward acts as an incentive, encouraging you to sell as many subscriptions as there are customers who want to buy them.

Incentives also can take the form of penalties. The newspaper may, for example, have a policy that financially penalizes its carriers if they do not sell at least 10 subscriptions per month: $2 is deducted from a carrier's monthly paycheck for each of the 10 subscriptions the carrier fails to sell. This penalty, like the bonus, acts as an incentive and encourages carriers to sell subscriptions. Negative incentives, however, can have additional consequences. As a carrier, you might become angry at the newspaper for docking your wages and decide to quit.

Mixed Economies

A **mixed economy** combines elements of traditional, market, and command economic models to answer the three basic economic questions. Because each nation's economy is a different blend of these three economic models, economists classify them according to the degree of government control. The three main categories of mixed economies are

▶ authoritarian socialism,
▶ capitalism, and
▶ democratic socialism.

Authoritarian Socialism Mixed economies that are closest to the pure command model are said to practice **authoritarian socialism**, which is also known as **communism**. In these economies the government owns or controls nearly all the factors of production.

How does a nation practicing authoritarian socialism answer the basic questions of what,

ECONOMIC SYSTEMS *Top to bottom: a Cuban worker cutting sugarcane in an authoritarian socialist economy; U.S. soldiers training in a capitalist economy; a government-owned airplane being built during France's democratic socialist era.*

how, and for whom to produce? For example, government officials in Cuba develop long-term plans outlining how the nation's resources will be used. This long-range planning serves to limit the decision-making power of individuals.

Capitalism While economies closest to the command model are said to practice authoritarian socialism, those closest to the market model are said to practice capitalism. In an economy based on **capitalism**, individuals own the factors of production and answer the basic economic questions. The economies of the United States, Canada, Mexico, Japan, and Taiwan are classified as capitalist.

For example, you can decide what to produce when you select a career. Your decision to be an electrician, an engineer, a reporter, or a fashion designer determines what is produced. This choice is not based on the jobs held by your parents and grandparents, or on the national goals of a central planner, but on your interests and skills as an individual.

Although the government of a capitalist nation may enact some regulations, its involvement in the economy is relatively limited. What is the government's role in a capitalist economy?

Taxation and spending policies enable the government to provide a variety of services, including education, social welfare programs, and national defense. The government also may regulate health and safety standards in the workplace. In spite of this government activity, however, private ownership and free choice—rather than central planning—remain the basis of capitalism.

Democratic Socialism The third type of mixed economy falls between authoritarian socialism and capitalism. In this type of mixed economy, called **democratic socialism**, the government owns some of the factors of production. In most cases, government ownership is limited to key industries such as electrical utilities and telephone networks, which are of national concern. Individuals are able to influence economic planning through the election of government officials.

The economies of many European nations, including Sweden, Poland, and France, have included elements of democratic socialism. In addition, the economies of many of the world's less industrialized countries, such as Tanzania, Angola, and Mozambique, have been classified as democratic socialist.

SECTION 1 — REVIEW

1. Define the following terms: traditional economy, command economy, market economy, market, self-interest, incentive, mixed economy, authoritarian socialism, communism, capitalism, democratic socialism.

2. How do traditional and command economies differ?

3. Who answers the three basic economic questions in a market economy? Why are self-interest and incentives important in this economic system?

4. What are the three types of mixed economies? Describe the extent of government involvement in each economic system.

5. **Thinking and Writing Critically**
Consider your economic actions and decisions during the past month. How has your self-interest benefited others?

6. **Applying** ECONOMIC INSTITUTIONS & INCENTIVES
What incentives do you experience at home, school, or work? Identify whether these incentives are positive or negative.

SECTION 2

FEATURES OF THE U.S. ECONOMY

Economics Dictionary

free enterprise
private property
contract
competition
product market
resource market
income

Objectives

▶ What are the main features of free enterprise in the United States?

▶ What are the two markets of the circular flow model?

▶ How does the circular flow model reflect exchange?

Y ou have learned that nations have different economic systems. Why does a nation develop a particular economic system? Why might national leaders decide to pursue capitalism instead of democratic socialism? The answer is that nations, like individuals, make choices that will satisfy needs and wants. Therefore, a nation will develop the economic system that it believes is most likely to meet the needs of its citizens.

As you know, the United States has a capitalist economy and leans toward the market model, which is driven by individuals. This means that individuals in the United States are free to exchange their goods and services, seek jobs of their own choosing, use their resources as they wish, and own and operate businesses.

In fact, individuals in the United States have a great number of economic freedoms. Because of these freedoms, the capitalist economy of the United States is sometimes called a free-enterprise

system. Enterprise is simply another word for business. Thus, **free enterprise** is a system under which business can be conducted freely with little government intervention.

Free Enterprise in the United States

The free-enterprise system of the United States is based on five main features. In the United States, individuals have the right to

▶ own private property and enter into contracts,
▶ make individual choices,
▶ engage in economic competition,
▶ make decisions based on self-interest, and
▶ participate in the economy with limited government involvement and regulation.

The final feature—limited government intervention and regulation—is what separates the U.S. economy from the pure market model.

Private Property and Contracts Goods that are owned by individuals and by businesses, rather than by the government, are considered **private property**. Your own private property might include clothes, compact discs (CDs), and

ECONOMIC SYSTEMS *The U.S. economy is based on the market model, which is driven by individuals.* **Which of the five main features of a free-enterprise system separate the U.S. economy from the pure market model?**

BABY BLUES reprinted with special permission of King Features Syndicate, Inc.

ECONOMIC SYSTEMS *In the United States, individuals have the right to own private property.* **What are the other four features of free enterprise in the United States?**

books. A business's private property might include a factory, office building, machinery, and other equipment, as well as the land on which the factory and office buildings are located.

Individuals and business owners can use their property or dispose of it as they wish. They can buy as much private property as they can afford. They also can sell as much as they wish, so long as a buyer is willing and able to purchase the property. For example, you can choose to give or sell your clothes, CDs, and books to friends.

Individuals also have the right to enter into agreements with one another to buy and sell goods and services. These agreements are called **contracts**. If Peter Donnelly agree to sell a CD to his friend Adam Barker for $10, they have a contract. Peter agrees to supply the CD, and Adam agrees to supply $10 in exchange.

A contract can be either oral or written, but regardless of its form, it is legally binding. If any person fails to fulfill the terms of the contract, the issue may be taken to court in order to ensure that the agreement is carried out or that a satisfactory compromise is reached. Although Peter and Adam are unlikely to take legal action over a $10 CD, their agreement is nonetheless considered a contract.

Individual Choice Property owners, laborers, producers, and consumers in the United States enjoy freedom of choice. This freedom of choice

is closely linked to the right to own private property and to enter into contracts. Property owners are free to use or dispose of their private property as they choose. Laborers are free to pursue job opportunities. Producers are free to make whatever goods and services they wish. Consumers are free to buy those goods and services that best meet their needs and wants.

Suppose Toussaint Waller owns several acres of undeveloped land. He is free to choose how to use the land. He may live on the land himself, or he may sell it to a developer for construction of homes and businesses. Perhaps Toussaint will

ECONOMIC SYSTEMS *In a free-enterprise system, property owners are free to use their property as they wish.* **What economic choices might this couple make about the use of their house?**

give the land to the city for use as a park, or perhaps he will leave the land undeveloped, thus providing a space for plants and wildlife.

Suppose that Toussaint sells the land to the BuildQuik development company, which constructs a small shopping center and parking lot on the property. These two initial individual choices—Toussaint's decision to sell the land and BuildQuick's decision to use the land for a shopping center—will set off a series of other economic choices and opportunities. Construction workers may choose whether to pursue a job with BuildQuik. The new stores will provide others with a choice of sales and management positions. BuildQuik also may decide to hire security guards to patrol the parking lot, and

Careers in Economics

Real Estate Agent

Think about your dream home. How might you look for it? You might visit every home in the city or town of your choice. Perhaps you might call people on the phone and ask if their homes are for sale. Neither of these is a practical approach—you would simply waste time and money. Instead, you would probably rely on an efficient method with proven results—hiring a real estate agent.

A real estate agent lists new properties for sale and shows them to potential buyers. Real estate agents have to be part salesperson and part private detective. Your real estate agent will need to find out what type of neighborhood you want to live in, what kind of house you would like, and how much you can afford to pay, to match your needs to the seller's product.

Once a match is made, agents help both parties negotiate a price and help buyers find financing. In addition, agents make sure that all conditions of the purchase, such as inspections, are carried out before the sale is final. Because these responsibilities involve working with people, real estate agents need excellent interpersonal and communication skills.

Most real estate agents are associated with brokers or agencies but are responsible for building their own client base. Although no standard formal training is required to sell real estate, agents must obtain a state broker's license. In addition, most agents take courses sponsored by the National Board of Realtors. College-level courses in economics, marketing, and finance also are helpful because agents often are required to put together—and explain—complicated mortgage packages for home buyers.

Why do people become real estate agents? Flexibility, potential for profits, and opportunities to work with the public make real estate agent a popular occupation.

Real estate agents match the needs and wants of home buyers with those of home sellers.

maintenance workers to repair plumbing and electrical problems in the shops. Laborers in many careers therefore are free to pursue these job opportunities.

Producers, like property owners and laborers, are able to make choices. The new shopping center provides space for a number of businesses. Why might a business owner decide to rent space in a new shopping center? Perhaps the business owner believes that many people in the area around the shopping center would be interested in a particular good or service. For example, the owner of the Good Food supermarket chain may feel that the shopping center is a prime location for a grocery store because of the number of consumers living in the area.

Consumers also make choices. The shops constructed by BuildQuik at the new Waller Shopping Center provide goods and services. Consumers can decide to buy those goods and services that best meet their needs and wants. For example, the shopping center may include the Good Food supermarket, a pharmacy, a dry cleaner, and a children's furniture boutique. Rick Salazar, who has two children, might choose to buy furniture at the boutique if he likes the merchandise and thinks the prices are affordable. Similarly, Kerri Quinn, who has no children, might choose *not* to shop at the boutique.

ECONOMIC SYSTEMS *Competition is the economic rivalry that exists among businesses selling the same or similar products. **Why is competition important in a free-enterprise system?***

Competition Free enterprise gives businesspeople the right to choose what, how, and for whom to produce. Sometimes two or more businesspeople make the same production choices. These choices lead the businesspeople and their companies into competition. **Competition** is the economic rivalry that exists among businesses selling the same or similar products. Competition is important because it encourages producers to improve existing products and develop new ones in order to attract customers.

For example, suppose that Gillian Petrakis wants to buy a portable tape player. The Genco Electronics Company wants consumers like Gillian to buy one of their tape players instead of one produced by the Sanford Corporation or any of the many other electronics firms. Therefore, Genco will try to produce portable tape players that have better sound, are less likely to damage audiotapes, and need fewer batteries than tape players produced by their competitors. Similarly, the A-1 Appliance Store will try to sell tape players at a lower price than the Acme Appliance Store so that Gillian will choose to buy her tape player at A-1 Appliance. This high level of competition thus allows Gillian to find a portable tape player with the features she wants—at a price she is willing to pay.

Self-Interested Decisions As Adam Smith indicated, self-interest is the force that directs the actions of individuals and firms in a market system. In the United States, free enterprise allows producers and consumers to make choices for their own benefit.

Consider Toussaint Waller's decision to sell his land. He decided to sell the land to the BuildQuik development company because he felt that he would benefit from the exchange. Although the sale of the land also resulted in increased benefits to many other people in the form of more employment and more goods and services, Toussaint's decision was made on the basis of self-interest.

Limited Government Involvement Because the United States has a market economy, most

ECONOMIC INSTITUTIONS & INCENTIVES *The federal government provides national parks for public use.* **What reasons might the government have for preserving wilderness areas?**

production decisions are made by individuals or businesses—not by the government. The government does play an important role, however, by regulating the economy. For example, the government establishes health and safety laws, monitors banking practices, and prohibits discrimination in the workplace.

The government also provides public services. Funds are raised through taxation and spent on goods and services for members of society. For example, federal taxes are used to pay for national defense. Similarly, public education relies on funds from state and local taxes. The government also redistributes wealth—in other words, some funds from citizens' taxes are used to help needy individuals and struggling businesses. Finally, the government attempts to keep the economy stable by holding down prices and unemployment and by encouraging economic growth.

Economic Actors in Free Enterprise

As you know, free enterprise is driven by the decisions of producers and consumers, with a limited amount of government involvement. How do these three economic actors—producers, consumers, and the government—interact in the U.S. economy?

Producers As noted in Chapter 1, producers provide goods and services in the market. Through a combination of human resources, natural resources, and capital resources, producers work to satisfy the needs and wants of consumers. In doing so, producers rely on entrepreneurship to develop new products and production methods.

In a free-enterprise system, a successful producer also can benefit other economic actors. Suppose that Ross Anderson owns a company that produces digital pagers. If his business is successful—in other words, if the company makes more money than it spends—he may be able to expand his operations and hire more workers. Ross may choose to spend money on product development, creating new models of pagers with more features, thus providing consumers with new products.

Consumers Consumers influence production by purchasing goods and services. If Hannah Carroll feels that Ross's company provides quality digital pagers, she may choose to buy one. On the other hand, Hannah may not want to buy a pager, or she may prefer the features or price of a pager produced by a different company. Consumers such as Hannah communicate with producers by making these decisions. The level of product sales tells Ross if his company has accurately answered the basic economic questions of what, how, and for whom to produce.

Government As you know, government plays a limited but important role in the free-enterprise system of the United States. Although producers and consumers provide answers to the three basic economic questions of what, how, and for whom to produce, the government oversees and regulates the effects of these decisions on the economy as a whole. For example, Ross's company must produce its pagers in a factory that meets federal safety standards.

CIRCULAR FLOW OF GOODS AND SERVICES

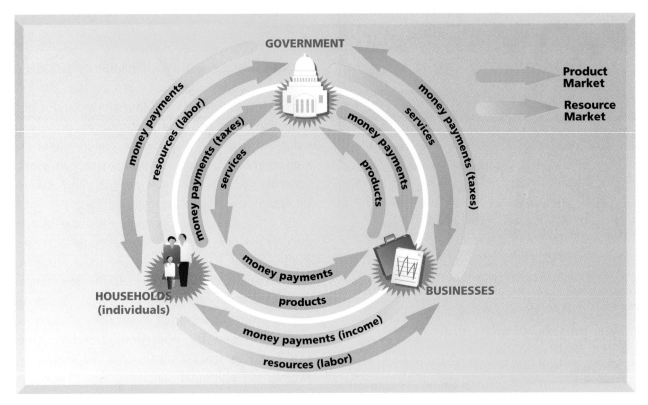

FIGURE 2.2 This circular flow model illustrates the exchange of resources, products, and money payments through the U.S. economy. **What is the government's role according to the circular flow model?**

Government, producers, and consumers play different—but connected—roles in a market system. To answer the economic questions of what, how, and for whom to produce, these economic actors also rely on a system of exchange.

Circular Flow Model

In a free-enterprise system, resources, products, and money payments are exchanged among the different actors in the economy. This exchange can be traced in a circular flow model. The model, shown in Figure 2.2, is a simplified view of how the U.S. economy functions.

Markets The circular flow model has two parts. The green arrows are the **product market**, which represents all of the exchanges of goods and services in the economy. Businesses develop products for sale to both households and the

government. Households and the government then pay the businesses for the products.

The gold arrows are the resource market. The **resource market** represents the exchange of resources between households—individuals like you who own the factors of production (natural, human, and capital resources)—and business firms and the government, who are the users of the resources.

The money paid to households by business firms and the government in exchange for the households' resources are called **income**. Households receive income such as rents (in exchange for natural resources), wages (in exchange for labor), and interest (in exchange for capital).

Flows Exchanges in the product and resource markets involve two different types of flows—the flow of resources and products and the flow of payments. Households supply the resources to businesses and the government in the resource market. Businesses then make products, which are sold to households and the government in the product market. For example, if you work in a restaurant, you (as a member of a household) provide a human resource (your labor) to the business. The business in turn provides food and service to customers, who, like you, are members of households.

Likewise, the government produces goods and services for the benefit of businesses and households. The government produces goods and services by using the resources that it purchases from households in the resource market.

In the resource market, businesses and the government make payments to households in exchange for the households' resources. Once households receive this payment, they continue circulating the money by purchasing goods and services in the product market. By doing this, households return money to businesses. Consider your job at the restaurant. The restaurant pays you for your work. In turn, customers such as yourself pay the restaurant for the food provided.

Businesses use the payments from households

ECONOMIC SYSTEMS *In a free-enterprise system resources, products and money payments can be exchanged among different parts of the economy.* **Is the sale of cookies at a bake sale part of the product market or the resource market?**

and the government to purchase additional resources from households. The money flow continues as businesses and households make payments to the government. These payments take the form of taxes. The government uses the payments to provide goods and services to businesses and households.

SECTION 2 — REVIEW

1. Define the following terms: free enterprise, private property, contract, competition, product market, resource market, income.

2. What separates the U.S. economy from the pure market model? What features does the U.S. economy share with the pure market model?

3. How does the product market differ from the resource market in the circular flow model? Describe an exchange you have made recently, and identify its place in the circular flow model.

4. What types of exchanges are shown in the circular flow model?

5. Thinking and Writing Critically
List the five main features of the U.S. economy. Describe personal experiences you have had with each of the five features.

6. Applying ECONOMIC SYSTEMS In your own words, explain how the Internet can be considered both a product and a promoter of free enterprise as practiced in the United States. Provide examples from an Internet search.

SECTION 3

THE U.S. ECONOMY AT WORK

Economics Dictionary
full employment
price stability
standard of living

Objectives

▶ How do nations decide how to use scarce resources?

▶ What are the major goals of the U.S. economy?

▶ Why do economic goals sometimes conflict?

What are your goals? You may hope to go to college or find a high-paying job. To reach your goals, you will need to take particular actions. For example, if you want to be an electrician, you will need to acquire skills and knowledge.

Nations—or economic systems—also set goals. As you have learned, economic systems are made up of economic actors. Households, businesses, and government officials together determine the general objectives—or goals—of their economic system. The government works toward the nation's economic objectives as the elected representatives of these actors. By setting goals, a nation's policymakers can choose how to use scarce resources.

U.S. Economic Goals

The United States has six major goals for its economy, many of which are also held by other nations around the world. These goals are economic

▶ freedom,
▶ efficiency,
▶ equity,
▶ security,
▶ stability, and
▶ growth.

Economic Freedom Maintaining freedom of choice in the marketplace is at the heart of economic freedom. In a free-enterprise system, consumers are free to decide how to spend their incomes on goods and services. Workers are free to choose an occupation, change jobs, or join a union. Savers and investors are free to decide when, where, and how to save or invest their money. Businesspeople are free to open new

THE WIZARD OF ID   **by Brant parker and Johnny hart**

ECONOMIC INSTITUTIONS & INCENTIVES *Security is one of the goals of the U.S. economy.* **What are the other five goals? Which goals are implied in this cartoon?**

ECONOMICS
in Action

"Extra, Extra!"

What would teens write about if they had the opportunity to publish their own work? The latest fashion trends? Celebrity profiles? Fad diets? The answer may surprise you. Although these topics are standard fare in many publications targeted at teen audiences, young writers are actually concerned about a wide variety of issues. Teenagers' writing can be found in newspapers and magazines focusing on the environment, sports, fiction, and even economics.

In fact, some publications contain only stories by teen authors. For example, the *21st Century*, run by John and Stephanie Meyer, is a newspaper written entirely by teenagers. The Meyers determined that "teens didn't need another publication with adults trying to figure out what they wanted to hear." So in 1989 they decided to create a newspaper that would provide teenagers with the opportunity to write articles that expressed their own thoughts and opinions.

Writing poetry, essays, and reviews offers students a way to present their ideas creatively and develop confidence in their writing skills. The Meyers believe that these rewards are improving teens' sense of self-worth and see the *21st Century* as an investment in the future. David Anable, chair of the Boston University journalism school and a member of the newspaper's board, believes that the *21st Century* gives student journalists a chance "to learn the craft and write with enthusiasm, not reluctance."

Contributors to the paper write about a number of controversial topics as well as dating, music, and humor. "American art is at a standstill," one teen writes. "Sapped by commercial capitalism and passive entertainment, our present culture seems inspirationless." Another argues about the impact of television: "I'm tired of society blaming its problems on television. The problem occurs when television sets start raising children. . . . Parents need to take responsibility for their children and their home."

Teen writers take their task very seriously. "We're just like any other journalists—we check and double-check sources for accuracy," says Jennifer Hill, who reports for *VOX*, another student newspaper written for and by high school students. During the 1996 Summer Olympic Games, 12 teenagers from Atlanta were chosen to cover the event for *VOX*.

These teen journalists wrote stories for several nationally-distributed publications, including *CNN On-line* and *USA Today*. Jimmy Kim, for example, sold a story to *CNN On-line* about how nearly 1,500 volunteers for the Atlanta Games provided translating services for athletes who did not speak English. Roya Rastegar, a high school senior, sold her story on the closing-ceremony performance by members of Atlanta's Symphony Youth. Although the reporters were paid a modest fee for their work, Roya argued, "The money is not a big deal— the big deal is that we're the first teens to cover the Olympics in history."

What Do You Think?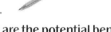

1. In your opinion, what are the potential benefits of teen writing and publishing?
2. If you were hired to write for a teen publication, what issues would you want to cover?

Publications such as the 21st Century *provide teen writers with a forum for their work.*

A key concern of economic stability is full employment. **How does low unemployment benefit the U.S. economy?**

businesses, change from one business to another, and expand or close existing enterprises.

Economic Efficiency

The goal of economic efficiency has to do with efforts to make the best use of scarce resources. Economic efficiency can be measured by how many goods and services a nation's workers produce. The more products each worker produces, the more efficient the economy will be.

Economic Equity

Economic equity, which is sometimes called economic justice, is hard to identify because it deals with questions of fairness and of right and wrong. Policymakers often face problems when trying to arrive at a fair decision. By studying the costs and benefits of a proposed course of action, policymakers try to judge whether a particular choice is fair. For example, policymakers in the United States attempt to ensure that members of society share in the costs and benefits of the free-enterprise system as equally as possible.

Economic Security

The goal of economic security refers to a nation's efforts to protect its members from poverty, business and bank failures, medical emergencies, and other situations that would harm the economic well-being of individual citizens and the nation as a whole. Economic security can result from individual and government actions. For example, you—and other consumers—can guard against the unexpected by purchasing different kinds of insurance or by saving some of your money. On the government level, federal, state, and local governments can promote economic security through such actions as providing unemployment compensation, insuring bank deposits, and giving economic assistance to troubled businesses.

Economic Stability

The goal of economic stability involves two concerns—achieving full employment and achieving stable prices. **Full employment** is the lowest possible level of unemployment in the economy. Although there will always be some amount of unemployment as workers move and change jobs and as new businesses open and others close, economic stability focuses on keeping the level of unemployment as low as possible.

The other element of economic stability is price stability. **Price stability** is achieved when the overall price level of the goods and services available in the economy is relatively constant. Price stability refers to the prices of all products taken together—not to changes in the price of an individual product.

A nation's standard of living is measured by per capita consumption during a specific period of time. **How is standard of living related to economic growth?**

Economic Growth Economic growth has to do with efforts to increase the amount of goods and services produced by each worker in the economy. The difference between simply increasing the economy's production and increasing the production from each worker is important. If the total number of workers increases more quickly than total production, on average each worker produces less. Lower production from each worker means that fewer goods and services are available for each person to consume.

A decrease in the number of available goods and services results in a decline in a nation's standard of living. **Standard of living** refers to people's economic well-being. Economists measure a nation's standard of living by how much the average person in that country is able to consume in a given period of time—usually one year. The standard of living improves when production from each worker increases faster than the total population, thus providing more goods and services for each person.

Economic Goals and Trade-Offs

Are you able to pursue all of your personal goals at the same time? Probably not. Sometimes you may have to decide that one goal is more important than another. For example, you may want to go to college and buy a car. If you cannot afford to do both at the same time, you may have to postpone one of your goals. Although you can work toward more than one goal over a period of time, you may have to make trade-offs at one particular point in time.

The goals of an economic system also can be affected by trade-offs. At various times, people's needs and wants may conflict. As a result, although different nations may share a number of economic goals, those nations will prioritize those goals differently.

Priorities Must be Assigned Scarcity forces individuals, businesses, and governments to make choices among various needs and wants. Nations also must decide which goals are most important and assign resources to them first. In

Immigration

Nearly 750,000 people legally immigrated to the United States in 1995 alone. Why do people want to move to this country? And how do they obtain legal status to live and work here?

Many immigrants come to the United States seeking employment. Relatively high wages and a high standard of living attract people from countries around the world. Additionally, television and movies often present an idealized image of life in the United States.

To obtain permission to live in the United States, an immigrant must apply for and meet the requirements of a visa. Most visas are sought by—and granted to—people who already have relatives living in the United States. Those without relatives may be considered for legal admission—known as "permanent resident status" and represented by a green card—based on their occupational skill level.

Skilled workers, such as doctors, teachers, and computer programmers, can obtain green cards relatively easily. The government allows 140,000 skilled workers to immigrate annually because skilled workers are needed in the U.S. economy.

A backlog of unskilled workers seeking green cards exists, however, because their work is not in as high demand. Only 10,000 unskilled workers are admitted into the United States each year. To admit these workers fairly, the U.S. Department of State conducts a visa lottery, randomly selecting and awarding green card visa numbers to eligible persons.

ECONOMIC INSTITUTIONS & INCENTIVES *Conflicts among goals force nations to prioritize their needs and wants.* **What are the trade-offs when resources are used to clean up pollution?**

World War II, for example, national defense and security became high priorities. The factors of production were shifted from business and industry to the war effort.

Priorities Can Change
Policymakers at all levels must decide which goals are most important according to the particular needs and wants of the time. For example, during the 1970s dramatic price increases encouraged many people in the United States to focus on economic stability. During the 1980s, however, concerns about unemployment and low productivity encouraged U.S. policymakers to focus on economic security and economic growth.

Priorities Can Conflict
Even at a single point in history, conflicts among goals arise because different groups in the nation have different needs. Low-income workers or the elderly, for example, generally are more concerned with economic security and equity than with other economic goals. Many businesspeople, on the other hand, want to emphasize economic growth and efficiency.

Solutions Can Conflict
Even if groups in a society agree on priorities, they may have conflicting ideas about the best means to achieve the selected goals. These differences are not always easy to resolve. For example, two groups of policymakers may agree that the most important goal is economic growth, but may propose strikingly different methods of achieving that growth. Suppose that one group believes that the government should raise taxes and use the money to help new businesses grow. The other group, however, wants to lower taxes to let businesses and individuals make and buy more goods to stimulate growth.

SECTION 3 — **REVIEW**

1. Define the following terms: full employment, price stability, standard of living.

2. Why do nations set economic goals?

3. List and explain the economic goals of the U.S. economy.

4. Why do economic goals sometimes require trade-offs?

5. **Thinking and Writing Critically** Consider your long-term and short-term personal goals. Which of these goals is most important to you? How do you establish priorities for your goals?

6. **Applying** SCARCITY & CHOICE Based on current events, which of the six goals that the United States has for its economy are priorities at this time? Explain your answer.

SECTION 1 Nations—as well as individuals respond to scarcity and answer the three basic economic questions of what to produce, how to produce, and for whom to produce. A nation's answers to these questions are determined by its economic system. An economic system is the way that a nation or society is organized to produce and distribute goods and services. Economists have identified four types of economic systems: traditional, command, market, and mixed. In the modern world all economies are mixed; pure traditional, command, and market economies are models that no longer exist.

Traditional economies depend on long-established patterns of behavior and belief. Command economies rely on government decision making and control of resources. Market economies allow individuals to control and allocate resources. Market economies also rely on self-interest and incentives.

Mixed economies have elements of traditional, command, and market models. Because mixed economies vary in their characteristics, economists classify them by their degree of government control. Nations whose economies are closest to the pure command model are said to practice authoritarian socialism, or communism. Nations whose economies are closest to the pure market model are said to practice capitalism. Nations with systems between these two extremes are said to practice democratic socialism.

SECTION 2 The economic system of the United States leans toward the market model. The fact that there is some government involvement and regulation, however, means that the U.S. economy is not a pure market model. Because the economic system of the United States is based on the freedom to make choices, it is often referred to as a free-enterprise system.

In the United States, individuals have the right to own private property and enter into contracts, make individual choices; engage in competition, and make decisions based on self-interest. Only a limited amount of government regulation and intervention exists in the U.S. economy.

Economists use the circular flow model to show how resources, products, and payments are exchanged in the U.S. free-enterprise system. The product market represents all of the exchanges of goods and services in the economy. The resource market represents the exchange of natural, human, and capital resources in the economy.

SECTION 3 The above features of the free-enterprise system assist the economy in reaching its six main goals. These goals are economic freedom, efficiency, equity, security, stability, and growth. Economic systems must assign priorities to these goals by determining where to use scarce resources. Changes in circumstances can cause these goals to take different priorities at different times. Different groups within a nation also can disagree over how to achieve economic goals.

Economics Notebook

Review what you wrote in your Economics Notebook at the beginning of this chapter about your personal economic goals. How do your short-term and long-term goals fit in with the economic goals of the United States? Record your answer in your Notebook.

REVIEW

REVIEWING CONCEPTS

1. Explain the differences between traditional, command, and market economies. Provide one example of each system.

2. According to Adam Smith, what is the economic role of self-interest? In which type of economic system does self-interest play a significant role?

3. Describe the three main types of mixed economies. Provide a current example of each economic system.

4. List the five main features of free enterprise in the U.S. economy. How does the level of government involvement in the U.S. system differ from the pure market model?

5. What does the circular flow model illustrate? Name the two markets represented in the model and list an example of each.

6. List the six major goals of the U.S. free-enterprise economy.

ECONOMIC SYSTEMS *Businesses in your community exemplify characteristics of the free-enterprise system.*

THINKING AND WRITING CRITICALLY

1. **ECONOMIC SYSTEMS** How do laws against false advertising promote economic equity? Which of the other goals of the U.S. economy might these laws promote? Explain your answer.

2. **ECONOMIC SYSTEMS** A city imposes restrictions on water use during a drought. Which economic goals are city leaders emphasizing? Explain your answer.

3. **ECONOMIC INSTITUTIONS & INCENTIVES** Why is completing a homework assignment in your self-interest?

4. **COMPETITION & MARKET STRUCTURE** What types of economic competition do you experience

during the course of one week? In what ways do you perform as an economic actor?

YOUR LOCAL ECONOMY

Choose a business in your community and explain how it exercises each of the five main features of the free-enterprise system. Provide a specific example of each feature in action.

INDIVIDUAL PORTFOLIO PROJECT

For each of the three types of mixed economies, select a country not mentioned in this chapter and research its economy. How do people in that country decide what, how, and for whom to produce? Identify each economy as a traditional, command, or market economy. Create a chart or table that illustrates how the three production questions are answered in each of the countries you have selected.

PRACTICING SKILLS: UNDERSTANDING CHARTS AND GRAPHS

Draw a poster of a circular flow model that illustrates your school's markets and flows. What is your school's resource market? What is your school's product market? Consider the direction of exchanges among students, teachers, and administrators; the physical structure of the school; and materials such as books, desks, and other equipment.

THE INTERNET: LEARNING ONLINE

Conduct an Internet search for information about different kinds of mixed economies. You might start with search words such as *authoritarian socialism*, *communism*, *capitalism*, and *democratic socialism*. Sketch a World Wide Web page entitled "Learning About Mixed Economies." Describe the information that you will include on the page as well as hyperlinks that will connect your page with the other Web sites found in your search.

ANALYZING PRIMARY SOURCES

"Adam Smith, Social Investor"

Janet Prindle and Farha-Joyce Haboucha are financial planners who manage more than $300 million of socially-responsive investments. Their opinion article below is a modern primary source that discusses the relevance of Adam Smith's economic theory to today's society. As you read the excerpt, try to identify the main points of the authors' argument. Then answer the questions that follow.

"In spite of capitalism's world-wide triumph over all competitors, it has become fashionable to think of capitalism as heartless and soulless. . . . This, then, seems a good time to go back to the roots of capitalist theory. The father of capitalism, Adam Smith (1723–1790), was perhaps history's most misunderstood philosopher. He was a progressive, even radical thinker, a far cry from his image in economic and political debates today. . . .

"If Adam Smith were alive, he would be a socially responsive investor. He clearly thought the financial success of an enterprise depended in large measure on the degree to which it contributed to the social good. . . . The way to improve society is to grow the economy. Increasing production increases wealth, which increases wages and purchasing power. The question for policymakers is how to facilitate this chain of cause and effect.

"And it is this question that leads Smith to develop his famous theory of the 'invisible hand.' We do not gain our supper through the benevolence [kindness] of the butcher. The butcher labors to promote his own interest, which includes a need to be seen as benevolent [kind]. This need and the pressures of a competitive environment produce the positive social effects: the growth of production, wealth, wages, and purchasing power.

"Society must promote competition. But unbridled [uncontrolled] competition is virtually the opposite of what Smith had in mind. He felt it was naturally checked by the individual's tendency toward benevolence and need for approval. He also believed that the role of government was to make certain that no one gained undue [unfair] advantages that would promote monopoly. . . . Smith saw commercial society as the force that would shape a better society, the ultimate purpose of his market system."

1. How do the authors interpret Smith's theory of the "invisible hand"?

2. According to the authors, how does economic growth improve society?

3. Why do the authors believe Smith would be a socially responsive investor? Do you agree with their assessment of Smith's ideas? Why or why not?

Economist for a Day

Imagine that a new international settlement has been planned for the moon. You and your classmates have been chosen by the Earth Federation to be part of the Federation's Moon Settlement Economics Committee. As members of this committee, your group is responsible for designing the economic system to be used in the settlement.

Because this is an international endeavor, you need to consider the pros and cons of all three modern economic systems on Earth: capitalism, democratic socialism, and authoritarian socialism (or communism). The Federation has supplied you with some basic information to begin your comparison. It also has included three documents for you to review: a letter from a citizen in the country of Richtany, a newspaper editorial from the country of Ziber, and a speech about the benefits of capitalism in Carnegia. These documents are located on the following pages.

In your Economics Notebook, write your notes and answers to the questions that accompany the documents. Then meet with your group and create an outline that summarizes the most important points about each system. Discuss your findings and formulate an argument for the economic system the group thinks will work best on the moon. Your group's completed recommendation should be in a speech format. Make sure to support your opinions with facts from the documents provided by the Federation.

EARTH FEDERATION

To: Moon Settlement Economics Committee
From: Earth Federation Executive Council

The General Assembly is looking forward to hearing your recommendation and plans for an economic system on the moon. Please use the attached information about the world's current economic systems to aid your research. We also have included a letter, a newspaper editorial, and a speech, each of which argues for one of the three systems.

Once you have made your determination, be sure to address these issues in your speech:
- How will the settlement answer the three basic economic questions?
- Who will own the factors of production?
- What will be the trade-offs in your system?

We realize that your task is a difficult one. However, it is vitally important to the success of the planned moon settlement, as well as to all space colonization efforts in the future, that you make a well-researched recommendation to the Earth Federation. Thank you for your time and effort.

EARTH FEDERATION	CAPITALISM	DEMOCRATIC SOCIALISM	AUTHORITARIAN SOCIALISM/COMMUNISM
TYPE OF POLITICAL SYSTEM	Nations are mainly democratic.	Some nations tend to be democracies, while other nations lean toward totalitarianism.	Most nations have a one-party totalitarian government.
CENTRAL PLANNING IN THE ECONOMY	Governments influence economic activity through tax credits, subsidies, low-interest loans, other financial incentives, and regulations.	Governments directly control production in large, state-owned facilities and are involved in planning the use of resources.	Almost all economic decisions are made by a single political party. Specific economic plans are devised by agencies in charge of planning for a particular industry.
ECONOMIC FREEDOM OF WORKERS	Workers choose jobs that fit their qualifications. Some join unions for collective bargaining power.	Workers choose jobs that fit their qualifications. Many join unions that bargain with private firms and governments.	The government controls employment and holds the power to reject job transfers. Unions are strictly controlled, and strikes are prohibited.
EXAMPLES	Carnegia	Richtany	Ziber

Economics Lab

From the Desk of Judit Steger

Dear Earth Federation Members,

As plans for the new moon settlement get under way, I am troubled by the widespread interest in establishing an economic system with little or no government intervention. In their unquenchable thirst for profits, some manufacturers have forgotten the ruin that an unregulated economy can bring on people who are prevented from working by age, illness, or disability. Without governmental protections for unemployment and market failures, even those who are able to work will be left vulnerable to economic depressions.

The citizens of Richtany believe that our system of democratic socialism will work best on the moon. Although most factors of production should be left in private hands, the moon settlement should own some of its major industries and use taxes to fund social programs that protect all of its citizens. We have both a moral and an economic obligation to provide social programs such as health care, education, and retirement pensions to the citizens of this new international settlement. I hope that when making your decision you will not ignore the value of moderate government control of the economy.

Sincerely,

Judit Steger

WHAT DO YOU THINK?

1. Who owns the factors of production in this system?

2. What are the trade-offs in this system?

3. How would this system affect an individual's budget, economic choices, and economic goals?

4. What are the incentives to produce in this system?

The Promise of Communism

The people of Ziber believe that authoritarian socialism, or communism, is a strong and fair economic system. We hope that the new moon settlement will model its economic system on that of this country and the economic theories of Karl Marx. Economic factors determine social and political change throughout the world. In many countries, the proletariat, or working class, is oppressed and exploited by those who own the factors of production. By owning the factors of production in Ziber, workers have created a classless society.

We believe that the government should own nearly all the industries in the settlement and should closely regulate any small private businesses. The government can then use these revenues to finance social programs such as low-cost public housing, free health care, and education and retirement pensions.

WHAT DO YOU THINK?

1. Who owns the factors of production in this system?

2. What are the trade-offs in this system?

3. How would this system affect an individual's budget, economic choices, and economic goals?

4. What are the incentives to produce in this system?

Three Cheers for Capitalism

Way back in 1993, Malcolm S. Forbes, Jr., encouraged all of us to give "Three Cheers" for the benefits of a capitalist economy. He said, "Capitalism works better than any of us can conceive. It is also the only moral system of exchange. It encourages individuals to freely devote their energies and impulses to peaceful pursuits, to the satisfaction of others' wants and needs, and to constructive action for the welfare of all.

"Capitalism is not a top-down system; it cannot be mandated [decreed] or centrally planned. It operates from the bottom up, through individuals—individuals who take risks, who often 'don't know any better,' who venture into areas where, according to conventional [customary] wisdom, they have no business going, who see vast potential where others see nothing. . . .

"There is another important thing to remember about capitalism: failure is not a stigma [sign of disgrace] or a permanent obstacle. It is a spur to learn and try again. Edison invented the lightbulb on, roughly, his ten-thousandth attempt. If we had depended on central planners to direct his experiments, we would all be sitting around in the dark today. . . .

"[Capitalism] stands not for accumulated wealth or greed but for human innovation, imagination, and risk-taking. It cannot be measured in mathematical models or quantified in statistical terms, which is why central planners and politicians always underestimate it."

Forbes's comments still are true today. That is why the people of Carnegia strongly urge the Earth Federation to use capitalism as the economic system for the moon settlement. Thank you.

WHAT DO YOU THINK?

1. Who owns the factors of production in this system?

2. What are the trade-offs in this system?

3. How would this system affect an individual's budget, economic choices, and economic goals?

4. What are the incentives to produce in this system?

THINGS TO DO

1. Discuss group members' notes about each system and opinions about which system should be established.

2. Create an outline summarizing the results of your study. You may want to start with a list of the benefits and limitations of each system. Then compare your answers to the questions about each system.

3. Determine which system you think will work best in the moon settlement.

4. Prepare a speech to be delivered to the class explaining why the economic system you selected is the best one for the settlement. Support your argument with information from this assignment.

UNIT 2

Economics Lab

How much money can you raise by decorating T-shirts? Find out by reading this unit and taking the Economics Lab challenge on pages 138–41.

ELEMENTS OF MICROECONOMICS

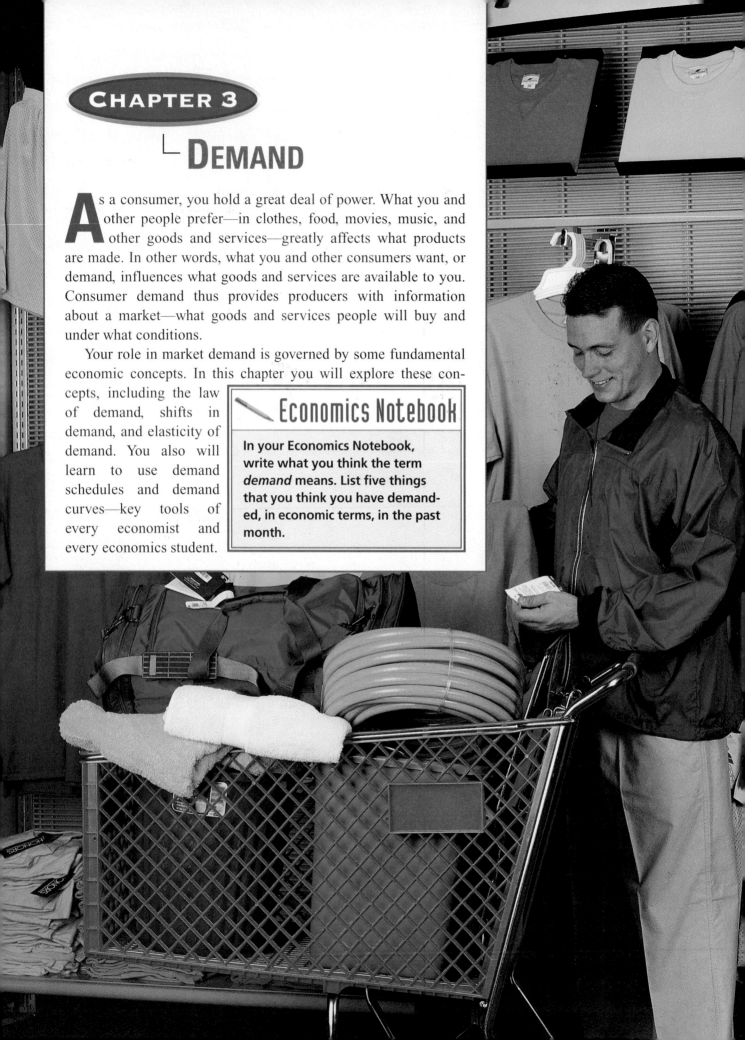

CHAPTER 3

DEMAND

As a consumer, you hold a great deal of power. What you and other people prefer—in clothes, food, movies, music, and other goods and services—greatly affects what products are made. In other words, what you and other consumers want, or demand, influences what goods and services are available to you. Consumer demand thus provides producers with information about a market—what goods and services people will buy and under what conditions.

Your role in market demand is governed by some fundamental economic concepts. In this chapter you will explore these concepts, including the law of demand, shifts in demand, and elasticity of demand. You also will learn to use demand schedules and demand curves—key tools of every economist and every economics student.

Economics Notebook

In your Economics Notebook, write what you think the term *demand* means. List five things that you think you have demanded, in economic terms, in the past month.

NATURE OF DEMAND

Economics Dictionary

demand
quantity demanded
law of demand
purchasing power
income effect
substitution effect
diminishing marginal utility
demand schedule
demand curve

Objectives

▶ How does demand differ from the quantity demanded?

▶ What does the law of demand state?

▶ What do demand schedules and demand curves illustrate?

You have wanted, or demanded, many things in your life. Everyone has. In economic terms, however, the concept of demand means more than simply wanting something.

Consider Linda Armstrong's situation. Suppose that she has been saving to buy a new car ever since she graduated and started her job a year ago. Linda wants a sports car that has a good safety record and a reputation for needing few repairs. After shopping around, Linda realizes that the cost of a new sports car is beyond her budget. At this point, she cannot afford the car she wants. Instead, she will have to look for a used sports car, buy a less expensive car, or wait until she can afford her first choice in cars.

At this particular time, Linda cannot add to the demand for new sports cars. This does not mean that she might not be part of that demand at some time in the future—if and when she can afford such a car.

As you can see from Linda's example, **demand** in economic terms is the amount of a good or service that a consumer is willing and able to buy at various possible prices during a given time period. **Quantity demanded** is a slightly different concept that describes the amount of a good or service that a consumer is willing and able to buy at each particular price during a given time period.

This definition of demand contains two important conditions. First, the consumer must be willing *and* able to buy the good or service. In other words, the person must not only want the product but also have the means to pay for it. Linda did not meet this condition because she could not afford the car she wanted. Second, demand for the product must be examined for a *specific time period*—a day, a week, a month, a year, or some other definite period. The time period under study must be specific because various factors that change over time can affect the demand for a product.

SUPPLY & DEMAND *Demand is more than just the desire to purchase a product.* **What conditions must a consumer meet in order to add to the demand for sports cars?**

Law of Demand

Linda's situation illustrates a basic economic principle: in a free-enterprise system, price is the main variable affecting demand. Specifically, there is an inverse, or opposite, relationship between price and the quantity demanded. This relationship is described by the **law of demand**, which states that an increase in a good's price causes a decrease in the quantity demanded and that a decrease in price causes an increase in the quantity demanded.

Suppose that you want to buy a compact disc (CD) player. You expect to buy a CD player for about $200, and you have saved that amount. One Saturday you go to the Avalon Electronics Store. When you arrive at the store, you discover that the price of CD players has increased from $200 to $300. You are not able to pay $300 for a CD player because you have not saved that much money. Even if you were able to pay the higher price, you might not be willing to do so. Similarly, some other consumers also will be unwilling or unable to buy CD players at the higher price. In other words, the price increase will lead to a decrease in the quantity demanded. In contrast, if the price for CD players falls to $100, the quantity demanded will increase as consumers are willing and able to buy more CD players.

Three economic concepts help explain the law of demand: the income effect, the substitution effect, and diminishing marginal utility. Together these concepts account for the inverse effect that changes in price have on the quantity demanded.

Income Effect

The amount of money, or income, that people have available to spend on goods and services is called their **purchasing power**. As a consumer's purchasing power increases, his or her demand for goods and services also tends to increase. On the other hand, a decrease in a consumer's purchasing power tends to decrease his or her demand. Any increase or decrease in consumers' purchasing power caused by a change in price is called the **income effect**.

For example, if a store lowers the price of its CDs from $15 to $10, a consumer can buy more CDs with the same amount of income. A person spending $30 can buy three CDs at the new price of $10, but could have purchased only two CDs at the previous price of $15. The lower price thus increases the consumer's purchasing power and increases the quantity of CDs demanded from two to three.

The income effect also exists when the price of a product rises and an individual can buy less of the product with the same amount of income. If the price of CDs jumps to $18, a consumer with $30 to spend does not have enough money to buy more than one CD. The consumer's purchasing power has decreased, resulting in a decrease in the quantity of CDs demanded from two to one.

In general, the income effect has a strong and predictable influence on the quantity demanded. Keep in mind, however, that the income effect does not always come into play. Although the price of CDs falls from $15 to $10, some people still may want only the two CDs they originally intended to buy at the higher price. Even though consumers' increased purchasing power has made them *able* to buy three CDs at the new price, they might not be *willing* to do so.

Likewise, people who really want these two CDs may be willing and able to buy them even if the price rises to $18. Although consumers' purchasing power has decreased, the quantity demanded would remain at two CDs instead of falling to one or none.

Substitution Effect

The **substitution effect** describes the tendency of consumers to substitute a similar, lower-priced product for another product that is relatively more expensive. This effect helps explain the relationship between price and the quantity demanded. For example, when the price of steak increases, many consumers reduce the quantity of beef demanded and buy more chicken, a lower-priced substitute. The substitution effect helps explain why a higher price for beef causes a decrease in the quantity of beef demanded.

Like the income effect, the substitution effect sometimes does not apply. If an essential good or service has no readily available substitute, a rise

SUPPLY & DEMAND *Generic products and store brands allow consumers to substitute similar, lower-priced goods for more expensive products.* **When does the substitution effect not apply to demand?**

in price may not lower the quantity demanded. Milk, for example, does not have a lower-priced, readily available substitute. Thus, a rise in the price of milk likely will not cause consumers to switch to a substitute. Most people will consume about the same amount of milk in spite of the higher price.

CASE STUDY

Generic Products

SUPPLY & DEMAND Consumer demand for generic products is an example of the substitution effect at work. Generic products are non-brand-name products. You may have purchased or seen such products on store shelves. When generic products were first introduced, they typically featured plain, white or yellow packaging with black lettering.

Long popular in Europe, generic products were first introduced to the U.S. market in 1977. They sell for up to 40 percent less than brand names even though the quality is roughly the same. How can generic products sell for so much less? They do not have costly packaging and are not the focus of expensive advertising campaigns like brand-name products.

Generic products had their highest U.S. sales to date in 1982, during a period of poor economic performance. Consumer purchasing power at that time had fallen, and many people chose to substitute lower-priced generic products for higher-priced brand names.

When the U.S. economy improved in the mid- and late 1980s, the demand for generic products decreased. Consumers' purchasing power had been restored to the point where many consumers who preferred brand-name products could afford to switch back to buying them.

Generic products still can be found on store shelves, however. In the 1990s many stores substituted "store" brands for their generic products. Instead of traditional generic packaging, these store brands feature more sophisticated packages and labels. The cost of redesigning and repackaging raises the price of generic and store-brand products somewhat, but they continue to cost less than brand-name products because of lower advertising costs.

Diminishing Marginal Utility The third concept involved in explaining the law of demand is based on utility. As noted in Chapter 1, utility describes the usefulness of a product, or the amount of satisfaction that an individual receives from consuming a product. A product's overall utility typically increases as more of the product is consumed. However, as more units of a product are consumed, the satisfaction received from consuming each additional unit declines. Economists call this **diminishing marginal utility** because the marginal, or additional, utility of each unit consumed diminishes, or lessens, with each unit.

Suppose that you and your friends play basketball on a Saturday morning. After the game, you all have lunch at the restaurant with the best tacos in town. The first taco is well worth the $1 it costs. In fact, you are so hungry you would have paid $1.50 for it. The second taco also is worth at least $1 to you.

As you consider eating a third taco, however, you realize that you are starting to get full. You are still a little hungry but not as hungry as you were before eating the first and second tacos. The third taco is not worth $1 to you. The restaurant is running a special, however. If you order two tacos, a third one is half price. At the lower price of 50 cents, the third taco is worth the cost to you. You eat the third taco and are full.

Although the total utility of eating the tacos has increased, the marginal utility has decreased with each taco consumed. What about a fourth taco? You cannot eat anything more, so you certainly would not be willing to pay $1—or even 50 cents—for a fourth taco. Even if this taco were free, you might not order it.

Diminishing marginal utility helps explain why the demand for a product is not limitless. At some point, consumers cannot use any more of a product. There is a limit to a product's utility to consumers and thus a limit to consumers' demand.

Demand Schedules

One useful way to show the relationship between the price of a good or service and the quantity that consumers demand is a **demand schedule**. This schedule lists the quantity of goods that consumers are willing and able to buy at a series of possible prices.

A demand schedule allows you to see the interaction of price and demand in a simple table format. Suppose that Ellen Lisiewicz, a jewelry store owner, wants to know how many Right On Time watches she can sell at various prices during a one-month period. Ellen may develop a demand schedule that indicates the quantity of watches demanded at several prices so that she can determine—and charge her customers—the most profitable price for the watch.

An example of a demand schedule appears in Figure 3.1. The schedule lists the quantity of watches demanded during the month at several possible prices. You can see that as prices increase from $100 to $600, the quantity demanded decreases. When the price is $100, the quantity of watches demanded is 5,000. When the price is $600 or higher, consumers do not buy any watches.

Demand Curves

Demand curves are another way to show the relationship between the price of a product and the quantity demanded. A **demand curve** plots this information on a graph.

In Figure 3.2, for example, demand curve D_1 plots all of the possible combinations of prices and quantities demanded during a one-month period for car stereos listed in the demand schedule on the left. The quantities that consumers might purchase appear along the horizontal axis at the bottom of the graph, increasing from left to right. The possible prices of the stereos appear along the vertical axis at the left side of the graph, increasing from bottom to top.

Each point plotted on the graph represents a specific combination of price and quantity demanded. The curve slopes downward, reflecting the greater quantity that consumers will buy at lower prices.

Why might a business owner plot a demand curve rather than simply referring to a demand

DEMAND SCHEDULE

Price per Watch	Quantity Demanded
$600	0
$500	1,500
$400	2,750
$300	3,750
$200	4,500
$100	5,000

FIGURE 3.1 A demand schedule shows the interaction between price and demand during a specific period. **During a one-month period, how many watches are demanded at a price of $300?**

DEMAND FOR CAR STEREOS

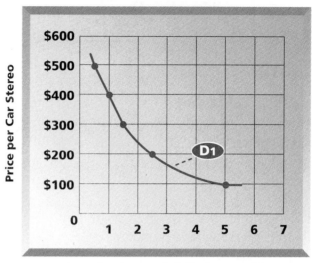

DEMAND SCHEDULE

Price per Car Stereo	Quantity Demanded
$500	500
$400	1,000
$300	1,500
$200	2,500
$100	5,000

DEMAND CURVE

FIGURE 3.2 A demand curve plots all of the information listed in a demand schedule. **If the price increases from $300 to $400, how will the demand for car stereos change in a given month?**

schedule? A demand curve can show at a glance the rate of change at each price. In some cases the demand curve will appear to be straight, as each change in price results in the same change in the quantity of the product demanded. Other demand curves, such as the one shown above in Figure 3.2, may reflect greater changes in the quantity of a product demanded at some prices than at others and therefore will have a more "curved" appearance.

SECTION 1 — REVIEW

1. Define the following terms: demand, quantity demanded, law of demand, purchasing power, income effect, substitution effect, diminishing marginal utility, demand schedule, demand curve.

2. Explain the difference between demand and quantity demanded.

3. How do the income effect, the substitution effect, and diminishing marginal utility help explain the law of demand?

4. What is the difference between a demand schedule and a demand curve?

5. **Thinking and Writing Critically** Give one personal example of each of the following concepts: income effect, substitution effect, diminishing marginal utility.

6. **Applying** SUPPLY & DEMAND Conduct an Internet search to find prices charged by Internet service providers (ISPs). How do the selected ISPs reflect the substitution effect?

CHANGES IN DEMAND

Economics Dictionary

determinant of demand
substitute good
complementary good

Objectives
▶ What does it mean for a product's demand to shift?
▶ What factors can shift demand for a product?
▶ How do substitute goods differ from complementary goods?

As noted in the previous section, a demand curve like the one in Figure 3.2 on page 55 illustrates a product's market during a specific period of time. In effect, the demand curve in Figure 3.2 is a snapshot of the car stereo market. And because the picture is taken at a single point in time, the only factor affecting the demand for car stereos is the one shown in the picture (graph): price. In other words, at the time this picture of the car stereo market was taken, nothing but a change in price could have caused a change in the quantity demanded.

By examining the demand curve, you can see that price is the only factor affecting the quantity demanded. Look again at the D_1 curve in Figure 3.2. What would have to happen for the number of car stereos demanded to increase

from 2,500 to 5,000? The graph shows that only a drop in the price from $200 to $100 will cause this change in the quantity demanded. Such a decrease in price will cause the intersection of price and demand to move to a new point along the demand curve.

Demand Shifts

Markets do not stand still, however, so new snapshots of demand for a product must be taken periodically. Indeed, the passage of time allows factors other than price to influence demand significantly. In economic terms, these factors can shift the entire demand curve of a product to the right or left, instead of simply causing movement along the old demand curve.

Figure 3.3 shows the old D_1 demand curve for car stereos from Figure 3.2, as well as two new demand curves. If, after the passage of time, a factor other than price causes an increase in demand for car stereos, the entire curve shifts to the right (D_2). Conversely, if this factor causes a decrease in demand, the entire curve shifts to the left (D_3). A shift in either the D_2 or D_3 curve means that a different quantity of car stereos is demanded at *each* and *every* price. This group of factors is called the **determinants of demand**.

SUPPLY & DEMAND *Concert ticket sales reflect a music group's popularity.* **How can consumer tastes and preferences influence demand?**

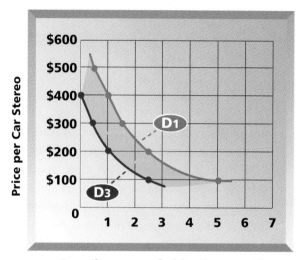

FIGURE 3.3 Many nonprice factors can shift the entire demand curve. **How do demand curves D₂ and D₃ reflect shifts in demand?**

What can cause these shifts in demand? The determinants of demand include

▶ consumer tastes and preferences,
▶ market size,
▶ income,
▶ prices of related goods, and
▶ consumer expectations.

Change in any one of these determinants can cause a change in the overall demand for a good or a service.

Consumer Tastes and Preferences

Changes in consumer tastes and preferences can have a major impact on demand for products. For example, think about the bands and singers you like. Are they the same ones your parents listen to? Are they even the same ones you liked just two or three years ago? Chances are they are not the same. The popularity of recording artists rises and falls frequently.

What happens to the demand curve when consumer preference for a recording artist grows?

For example, if the popularity of a new group called the Mock Turtles rises, the demand for the group's music also increases. The demand curve shifts to the right as consumers become willing to buy more Mock Turtles CDs at each and every price.

What happens when the Mock Turtles' next release receives terrible reviews from music critics? Some consumers no longer like the group, decreasing the quantity of Mock Turtles CDs demanded. As the group's popularity falls, the demand curve shifts to the left. Consumers will now buy fewer of the group's CDs at each and every price.

Market Size

Changes in the size of a market tend to affect demand. As a market expands, it has more consumers than before. A larger number of consumers in turn means a greater potential demand. Likewise, if a market contracts, it loses consumers, creating a smaller potential demand.

Markets expand and contract for several reasons. Decisions by private businesses are one

Market Researcher

Imagine that one Saturday you and your friends decide to go to the mall. As you enter the building, a woman at a demonstration table asks you to sample a new product and to answer some questions. You agree and spend the next few minutes tasting different types of peanut butter and comparing package labels.

Why is this woman asking questions about peanut butter? She is a market researcher. In order to know what products to make and how to present these products, companies need to find out what consumers like and dislike. Do consumers want organic peanut butter? Does a yellow label catch their eye more than a white one? Market researchers help companies answer these types of questions.

Sometimes market researchers conduct surveys, as in the "taste test" example above. Market researchers also rely on information collected by governments and businesses. For example, a toy company may use U.S. census data to pinpoint communities with large numbers of children in the population.

Market researchers need specific skills to do their job well. Because they deal with the public, researchers must have good communications skills. They also must be able to analyze statistics

and other data they collect. Most market research companies use computers to collect, organize, and analyze the massive amounts of data they handle, so good computer skills are necessary as well.

Market researchers provide companies with valuable insight into consumer habits and demand. Without this type of information, a company might develop the world's most delicious peanut butter—but not sell a jar of it because it is hidden behind an unattractive label.

Market researchers analyze consumer tastes and preferences.

cause of changes in market size. For example, suppose that Recreational Equipment Inc. (REI) launches a national advertising campaign for its boots and other hiking gear. People across the United States see the advertisements and learn about REI's products. More people take up hiking, thereby expanding the market and increasing demand for hiking products made by producers throughout the market. Because the quantity of hiking products demanded changes at each and every price, the entire demand curve shifts to the right. In contrast, decreased demand would cause the market to shrink and the demand curve to shift to the left.

Governments also make policy decisions that affect the size of markets. For example, North

Vietnam's victory in the Vietnam War led the United States to break off trade and diplomatic relations with Vietnam. In 1995, however, relations were restored. Suddenly, many U.S. companies found a whole new group of consumers for their goods in Vietnam. The demand curve for their products shifted to the right.

A third force affecting market size is new technology. Technology can create new products and markets, sometimes at the expense of older ones. The invention of small video cameras, or camcorders, for example, created a new market. The popularity of camcorders also caused the market for 16-millimeter movie cameras—and projectors—to contract until it virtually disappeared. Over time, the demand curve for camcorders shifted to the right, while the demand curve for 16-millimeter movie cameras shifted farther and farther to the left.

Income

Generally, when income increases, people have more money to spend. This increased spending results in a greater demand for goods and services, and thus in a shift to the right in the demand curve for the products people buy. Because of their higher incomes, consumers are willing and able to buy more products at every price. Similarly, a decrease in income leads to a

SUPPLY & DEMAND *Advertising can affect the size of markets, thereby increasing or decreasing demand.* **At what market is this targeted?**

decrease in demand because consumers are less willing and able to spend money and contribute to the demand for products.

Although the demand for most goods increases as income rises, a few exceptions exist. Suppose that a family eats beef for dinner once a week. As the household's income increases, the family switches from ground beef to the higher-priced—but now affordable—steak. This increase

cathy
by Cathy Guisewite

SUPPLY & DEMAND *A decrease in income decreases demand because consumers have less money to spend, regardless of price.* **How is a change in income different from the income effect?**

SUPPLY & DEMAND *Goods that can be used to replace the purchase of similar goods when prices rise are called substitute goods.* **How might an increase in the price of ice cream affect the demand for frozen yogurt?**

in the demand for steak, causes the demand for ground beef to decrease. In this situation the income effect is working in reverse. The higher-priced steak is being purchased rather than the lower-priced hamburger.

It is important to note that a change in people's income is similar to, as well as different from, the income effect. As noted in Section 1, the income effect deals with changes in consumers' purchasing power caused by a change in a product's price. For example, if Paul Sakamoto earns $18,000 a year and the price of various goods falls, his purchasing power increases as the $18,000 buys more of the same goods than it bought at higher prices. This results in a change in the quantity demanded, or movement along the demand curve.

In contrast, a change in a person's income brings a different amount of money into that person's household. For example, suppose that Paul receives a raise from $18,000 a year to $19,000. Paul has more money to spend, and his demand probably will increase. This results in completely new demand curves for the goods Paul buys. In this case, the actual change in income, rather than a change in price, causes the shift in demand as more product is bought at the same price.

Prices of Related Goods

The demand for a good is often connected to the demand for related goods. This means that changes in a product's price can affect demand for the product's related goods. There are two types of related goods: substitute goods and complementary goods.

Substitute Goods Goods that can be used to replace the purchase of similar goods when prices rise are called **substitute goods**. As noted in Section 1, consumers' tendency to switch to lower-priced substitutes is called the substitution effect.

How do price changes for one good affect demand for its substitutes? Consider two similar products—butter and margarine. Price changes for butter can affect the demand for margarine. When the price of butter increases, many people consume less butter and use margarine instead. Thus, the demand for margarine—a substitute good—increases. Likewise, when the price of butter decreases, many people who use margarine switch to butter, and the overall demand for margarine decreases.

SUPPLY & DEMAND *Paint brushes and paint are complementary goods.* **What other complementary goods come to mind?**

Linking Economics and → Psychology

Commercial Break

Could you become a better athlete simply by drinking a particular brand of soda? Of course not—and soft drink companies know this, too. One commercial shows a Sprite™-drinking teenager losing a basketball game to a National Basketball Association (NBA) star. Although the Sprite commercial pokes fun at the idea that the correct purchase can change your life, many other commercials encourage this attitude. Why?

Advertisers know that tapping into fantasies and emotions is a powerful way to reach consumers and increase demand for products. In fact, advertisers spend a great deal of money studying the psychological makeup of consumers—their attitudes, emotions, and behaviors. They use these findings to try to influence consumers' buying decisions and raise demand.

Some advertisements, for example, try to appeal to consumers' fantasies of who they want to be. Consider the commercial that suggests that consumers buy Gatorade™ if they want to "be like

Mike." This ad appeals to the many people who would like to be a famous basketball star like Michael Jordan. Of course, a sports drink can hardly improve someone's dunk shots—much less make that person taller.

Other ads focus on consumers' guilt, emphasizing who they feel they *should* be. A series of Quaker Oats™ commercials, for example, feature Wilford Brimley, an actor noted for authoritative and trustworthy roles. Sitting at a breakfast table, Brimley tells viewers to serve Quaker Oats because "It's the right thing to do." In the ad, breakfast is no longer simply a meal, but is treated as a moral issue.

Advertisers have several methods of determining the best way to appeal to consumers' emotions. One method is through focus groups. People in a focus group participate in activities designed to reveal opinions about and emotional responses to a product. Members of focus groups draw pictures to illustrate their reactions to a product, role-play scenarios that represent their need for or feelings about a product, and tell stories about how they might use a product. Based on the focus group results, advertisers develop campaigns to reinforce consumers' positive feelings about the product and relieve any anxieties they may have.

What does the link between psychology and advertising mean to you? As an alert consumer, you should always view advertising with a critical eye. Be aware of how ads try to tap into your fantasies and fears. Ask yourself if the product is what you need and can afford—not just if it will make you feel like an NBA star.

Advertising focus groups are designed to reveal consumers' opinions about and emotional responses to a product.

What Do You Think?

1. What are some of the positive and negative aspects of using psychological research in developing advertising campaigns?

2. In what ways can an understanding of psychology help consumers evaluate an advertisement?

By definition then, an increase in a product's price leads to increased demand for the product's substitute goods. Meanwhile, a decrease in the product's price leads to a decrease in the demand for the product's substitute goods.

Complementary Goods Goods that are commonly used with other goods are known as **complementary goods**. Paintbrushes and paint, for example, are complementary goods. As the price of a gallon of paint increases, the quantity of paint demanded *and* the quantity of paintbrushes demanded decreases. Along the same lines, if paint goes on sale, the quantity of both paint and paintbrushes demanded rises, even though the price of the paintbrushes has not changed.

Thus, an increase in a product's price causes decreased demand for that product's complementary goods. Similarly, a decrease in the product's price results in an increased demand for that product's complementary goods. Note that the effect of a price change on a product's complementary goods is the opposite of the effect of such a change on that product's substitute goods.

Consumer Expectations

Have you ever bought something in anticipation of having more money from a new job or from a raise in your allowance? If so, you probably shifted demand by way of expectations of your future income. Consumer expectations can dramatically influence shifts in the demand curve.

Suppose that you work at a restaurant on the weekends. The owner announces that all employees will receive a raise of 50 cents per hour. You have been hoping to buy a particular book, and you know that soon you will be able to afford the purchase. After some thought, you decide to buy the book today—even though you will not receive your raise for two weeks. By taking this approach, you have increased the demand for the book even though your income has not yet increased.

If, on the other hand, you anticipate a lower income because of a series of layoffs at the restaurant, you probably will choose to delay many of your purchases. Generally, when consumers are pessimistic about their future incomes, the overall level of demand for goods and services in the economy decreases.

SECTION 2 — REVIEW

1. Define the following terms: determinant of demand, substitute good, complementary good.

2. How is a shift in demand different from a change in the quantity demanded?

3. Name the five main determinants that can cause shifts in demand. Give at least two examples of how each of these determinants have affected your demand for a product.

4. Explain how the change in the price of a product affects demand for its substitute goods and its complementary goods.

5. **Thinking and Writing Critically** Suppose that consumer expectations about the overall economy are high. As a result, people make large purchases in anticipation of better wages. Unfortunately, over the next few months the economy does not perform as well as they had hoped. What happens to the general level of demand? How will this experience affect consumer expectations in the future?

6. **Applying** SUPPLY & DEMAND Describe three ways in which your personal economic decisions can affect the demand curve. Which determinants of demand do your decisions reflect?

ELASTICITY OF DEMAND

Economics Dictionary

elasticity of demand
elastic demand
inelastic demand
total revenue

Objectives

▶ What is demand elasticity?
▶ What is the difference between elastic and inelastic demand?
▶ How is demand elasticity measured?

As you have learned, the law of demand describes the inverse relationship between price and the quantity demanded. For example, if a movie theater increases the price of its matinees from $4 to $5, fewer people are likely to attend these showings. The quantity of movie tickets demanded decreases because of the ticket-price increase. But how much does the quantity demanded decrease when a product's price increases? How many fewer people will go to the matinees at the higher price?

Manufacturers, sellers, and other business-people need to know this type of information in order to make good business decisions. Will lowering their products' prices by 10 or 20 percent increase the quantity demanded and the theaters' income? Can they afford to lower their prices at all? If they increase prices, will their income still be high enough to stay in business?

Businesspeople can answer questions such as those described above by determining the elasticity of demand for their products. **Elasticity of demand** is the degree to which changes in a good's price affect the quantity demanded by consumers. The demand for a product can be elastic or inelastic.

Elastic Demand

Elastic demand exists when a small change in a good's price causes a major, opposite change in the quantity demanded. Thus, demand is elastic when a small decrease in a good's price causes a significant increase in the quantity demanded. Demand is also elastic when a small increase in a good's price results in a significant decrease in the quantity demanded.

Certain kinds of goods tend to have elastic demand. A good's elasticity can change if

▶ the product is not a necessity,
▶ there are readily available substitutes, or
▶ the product's cost represents a large portion of consumers' income.

SUPPLY & DEMAND *Portable tape players often are expensive and are not a necessity.* **Is the demand for portable tape players elastic or inelastic?**

ELASTIC DEMAND FOR PIZZA

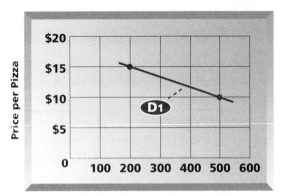

Price per Pizza

$20
$15
$10
$5
0

D1

100 200 300 400 500 600

Number Purchased per Week

FIGURE 3.4 A product has elastic demand when small changes in price result in major changes in demand. **How does the slope of the demand curve above indicate elastic demand for pizza?**

You can apply these three factors to determine if a product has elastic demand. Consider pizza, for example. Though some people are very fond of pizza, it is not a necessity. In addition, pizza has readily available substitutes. In fact, pizza has many substitutes, such as sandwiches and tacos. Competing restaurants often are located next to each other, so substitutes generally are only a few steps away.

Consider the third factor—the cost of a product compared to consumers' income. Here, the effect is not so clear-cut. If the price of the pizza represents a relatively large portion of your weekly income as a student, a rise in the price of pizza can have a large impact on your weekly budget. So if the price of a small pizza rose from $4.50 to $5.50, you probably would eat less pizza and switch to a less expensive meal.

The price of pizza represents a much smaller portion of the incomes earned by people with full-time jobs, however. A rise in the price of pizza might not affect their quantity demanded as much as it affects yours. Overall, however, the fact that pizza is not a necessity and that so many substitutes are readily available results in an elastic demand.

You can see the elastic demand for pizza in Figure 3.4. The curve indicating elasticity (D_1) is

almost horizontal, showing that a small increase in the price of pizza causes a large decrease in the quantity demanded as consumers switch to lower-priced substitutes. Likewise, a relatively small decrease in price causes a large increase in quantity demanded as sandwich-purchasers switch to pizza.

Inelastic Demand

Inelastic demand exists when a change in a good's price has little impact on the quantity demanded. Certain kinds of goods tend to have inelastic demand. A good usually has inelastic demand if

▶ the product is a necessity,
▶ there are few or no readily available substitutes for the product, or
▶ the product's cost represents a small portion of consumers' income.

Salt is an example of a good with inelastic demand. It is a necessity, it has few substitutes, and at a price of about 40 cents a box, salt represents a small portion of people's incomes. Even if the price of salt doubled, most people would

SUPPLY & DEMAND *Soap is a good that has inelastic demand. **What kinds of goods tend to have inelastic demand?***

Flour is a necessary good with inelastic demand in a general market. **Under what circumstances might the demand for flour be elastic?**

Elasticity in Specific and General Markets

In determining a product's elasticity, remember that consumers' responses to price changes can vary, depending on whether you are looking at a specific or general market for that product. Think again of the photograph metaphor—that is, think of looking at a product's demand as taking a snapshot at a particular point in time. When you take this picture, you can take a close-up shot or you can step back and take a wide-angle shot. The close-up shot reveals the specific market, capturing only a small part of the product's overall "scene." In contrast, the wide-angle shot shows the larger, general market for the product. This picture includes all the background of the product's market.

But how does the scope of the picture—whether it is a close-up shot or a wide-angle shot—affect how you will view the elasticity of demand for a product? Consider the market for a basic necessity: flour. If you take a wide-angle picture of this market, demand is inelastic. If the

consume the same amount because they must use salt, there is no alternative, and the higher price of 80 cents still represents only a tiny portion of their income.

Consider another example—soap. Is demand for this product elastic or inelastic? Determine how the three factors affect this product. It is essential—soap is necessary for washing.

This product does not have readily available substitutes. There are not many alternatives to soap. Other cleaning substances generally are too harsh for use on skin, making these substances poor substitutes.

Look at what portion of people's incomes the cost of soap represents. Soap is inexpensive and represents a small portion of people's incomes. Even if the price of soap doubled, it still would be very affordable.

The graph in Figure 3.5 illustrates the inelastic demand curve for soap. The demand curve D_1 on the graph is almost vertical, showing that even after a large increase in the price of soap there is a relatively small change in the quantity of soap demanded by consumers.

INELASTIC DEMAND FOR SOAP

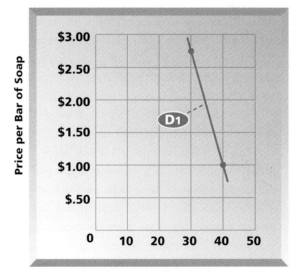

Quantity Demanded (in thousands)

FIGURE 3.5 The quantity of soap demanded during a one-month period indicates demand elasticity. **What is the relationship between price and demand for products with inelastic demand?**

Global Exchange

Movie Madness

What movies are hot at the box office in other countries? Probably the same movies you are going to see. The demand for movies made in the United States is high around the world. In fact, many movies—no matter how successful they may be in the United States—earn a large percentage of their profits in other countries.

Many movies became popular in other countries after earning recognition—and money—in the United States. In 1994 *The Fugitive* was released in Shanghai, China, earning about $120,000 in its first 2 days and $600,000 after 10 days. That same year, some 30 million people in India bought tickets to see *Jurassic Park*, which played in India for nearly 6 months.

Despite the enormous popularity of U.S. movies overseas, their success is not always greeted with enthusiasm by foreign trade officials. In a recent international trade agreement, members of the European Union (EU) decided that 60 percent of all movies shown on television in the EU must be European. French law is even more strict. It requires that 40 percent of televised movies in France be French, not just European.

The French government's policy did not lower demand for U.S. movies and raise demand for French films. Between the mid-1980s and mid-1990s, attendance at French movies fell from 94 million people per year to 35 million. Attendance at U.S. movies in France, on the other hand, rose from 70 million to 75 million. Governments do not have much luck in legislating consumer demand.

price of flour rises, the quantity demanded does not decrease proportionately. People still will consume about the same amount of flour because it is a basic staple that has no substitutes and it does not require a large portion of people's income.

If, however, you take a close-up shot of a specific, local market for flour, demand is elastic. Suppose that one of four grocery stores in town raises the price of flour by 75 cents per sack. The quantity of flour demanded at that store likely will fall off—not because people switch to lower-priced substitutes or consume less flour, but because they will buy the lower-priced flour at the other three grocery stores in town.

For these grocery store owners, demand for flour on the local level is elastic because of competition, even though the overall, general market for flour is inelastic. Looking only at the general, inelastic market for flour instead of at the specific, elastic market would lead these business owners to make incorrect pricing decisions based on incomplete and inaccurate information.

Measuring Elasticity

As noted at the beginning of this section, movie theater owners and other businesspeople try to determine demand elasticity so that they can set prices for their products. Businesspeople also can measure demand elasticity for their goods and services.

One of the simplest ways to measure demand elasticity is through the total-revenue test. **Total revenue**—sometimes called total receipts—refers to the total income that a business receives from selling its products. By monitoring any changes in a business's (or market's) total revenue before and after changes in the price of a product, you can determine the elasticity of demand for that product.

Keep in mind that the degree of elasticity of a product can vary for different price ranges. In fact, demand for a product can be elastic over one range of prices and inelastic over another. The total-revenue test indicates these changes in demand elasticity.

MOVIE TICKET REVENUE AND DEMAND ELASTICITY

DEMAND ELASTICITY AND TOTAL REVENUE

Price per Ticket	Quantity Demanded	Total Revenue
$5.00	10,000	$50,000
$4.50	22,500	$101,250
$4.00	30,000	$120,000
$3.50	31,250	$109,375
$3.00	32,500	$97,500
$2.50	33,750	$84,375

EFFECT OF DEMAND ELASTICITY AND TOTAL REVENUE

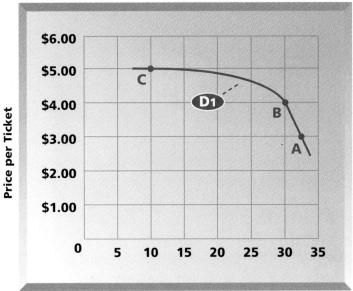

FIGURE 3.6 Demand for some products may be elastic in some price ranges and inelastic in other ranges. **During a one-month period, what price range shows inelastic demand for movie tickets?**

Total Revenue and Elastic Demand A drop in a business's total revenue from a price increase indicates elastic demand for the product. If, for example, movie theater owners raise the price of a matinee ticket from $4 to $5, many people likely will rent movies on videotape instead of going to movie theaters. Thus, even though the price per ticket is higher, the theater owners' total revenue decreases because so many more people will stay away from the theaters at the higher $5 price.

You can see this decrease in total revenue in the table in Figure 3.6. The table shows that when the price is $4 per ticket, the number of tickets sold during a one-month period is 30,000. The total revenue earned by the movie theaters in this town for this period of time is $120,000 ($4 × 30,000). When the price is raised to $5 per ticket, however, the number of tickets sold decreases to 10,000. Total revenue in turn decreases to $50,000 ($5 × 10,000). The drop in total revenue

indicates that the demand for movie tickets in this price range is elastic.

You can confirm this elasticity of demand by looking at the demand curve in Figure 3.6. The portion of the graph from point B to point C ($4 to $5) is not very steep. It shows that this change in price results in a drop in total revenue. In contrast, if the price was $5, then lowering the price to $4 would raise total revenue from $50,000 to $120,000. If lowering the price of a product raises total revenue, then demand is elastic.

Total Revenue and Inelastic Demand In contrast, a rise in a business's total revenue because of a price increase indicates inelastic demand for the business's good or service. Look again at the table in Figure 3.6. If the price of a movie ticket is only $2.50, some 33,750 people go to matinees. Total revenue is $84,375 ($2.50 × 33,750). If the price is raised to $3.50, the number of people attending the matinees

SUPPLY & DEMAND *Businesspeople—such as movie theater owners—need to measure demand elasticity in order to set prices.* **How can demand elasticity be measured?**

thus causes an increase in total revenue to $109,375 ($3.50 × 31,250). The rise in total revenue indicates that the demand for movie tickets in this price range is inelastic. Changes in total revenue and changes in price move the same direction on an inelastic demand curve.

The curve in Figure 3.6 illustrates this inelastic demand. From point A to point B ($3 to $4), the curve is very steep. It shows that a change in price in this part of the graph results in an increase in total revenue.

Maximizing Total Revenue Look again at the table in Figure 3.6. At what point is total revenue maximized for the movie theater owners? In other words, at this point in time and for this particular market, what is the price that theaters should charge to achieve the highest revenue? You can see that at $4 per ticket, 30,000 people flock to the matinees, for a total revenue of $120,000 ($4 × 30,000). If movie theaters charge either more or less than $4, total revenue drops. At the price of $4, therefore, the movie theaters' total revenue is highest. Measuring the varying elasticity of demand for their product directs the owners toward the pricing decision that will earn the most revenue.

remains high—31,250. Even after the price increase, many consumers consider matinees to be worthwhile, lower-priced entertainment than other recreational activities. The price change

---

SECTION 3 — REVIEW

1. Define the following terms: elasticity of demand, elastic demand, inelastic demand, total revenue.

2. What type of products tend to have elastic demand? Inelastic demand?

3. Why is determining demand elasticity important in economics?

4. How can a product have both elastic and inelastic demand? Think of an example that is not used in the book to illustrate this situation.

5. How does the total-revenue test indicate demand elasticity?

6. Thinking and Writing Critically Look up the word *elasticity* in a dictionary. Explain why this term is appropriate for describing the two different types of demand.

7. Applying SUPPLY & DEMAND Select three products and conduct an Internet search to determine their prices. Which products have elastic demand, and which have inelastic demand? Explain your answers.

SECTION 1 Demand is the quantity of a good or service that a consumer is willing and able to buy at various prices during a given time period. Price is one of the most important factors affecting demand. The law of demand states that an increase in price decreases the quantity demanded and that a decrease in price increases the quantity demanded, other things remaining the same.

The law of demand is explained by the income effect, the substitution effect, and diminishing marginal utility. The income effect appears when a change in price affects a person's purchasing ability. The substitution effect refers to consumers' tendency to substitute a similar, lower-priced product for a more expensive one. Diminishing marginal utility reflects the decreasing satisfaction experienced as increasing amounts of a product are consumed.

Demand schedules and demand curves can chart how changes in price affect quantity demanded for a specific period of time. A demand curve slopes downward, reflecting the greater quantity that consumers will buy at lower prices. A change in price results in movement along the product's demand curve.

SECTION 2 Factors other than price can affect demand for a product over time, causing a shift in its demand curve. These shifts illustrate a change in demand at each and every price.

The determinants of demand are consumer tastes and preferences, market size, income, prices of related goods (substitute goods and complementary goods), and consumer expectations. Changes in market size can be caused by private business decisions such as new advertisements, government policy decisions, and new technology. Changes in any of the determinants of demand can produce an entirely new demand curve for a product.

SECTION 3 To determine whether a price change is in their best interest, business owners need to determine elasticity of demand. The demand for a product can be either elastic or inelastic. When a small change in a good's price causes a major change in the quantity demanded, demand is elastic. In contrast, inelastic demand occurs when a change in a good's price has little impact on the quantity demanded.

Goods that have elastic demand usually are not necessities, have readily available substitutes, and represent a large portion of consumers' income. The opposite is true for goods with inelastic demand. Elasticity of a product can differ in specific and general markets.

The total-revenue test measures a product's elasticity of demand. A drop in total revenue following a price increase indicates elastic demand, while a rise in total revenue following a price increase indicates inelastic demand. Business owners try to find the price at which total revenue is maximized. This enables them to make pricing decisions that will earn the most revenue.

Economics Notebook

Review what you wrote in your Economics Notebook at the beginning of this chapter about the economic definition of *demand* and the things you have demanded in the past month. Now that you have studied this chapter, would you change your definition and examples? Why or why not? Record your answer in your Notebook.

CHAPTER 3

REVIEW

REVIEWING CONCEPTS

1. State the law of demand in your own words. Be sure to include how the income effect, the substitution effect, and diminishing marginal utility relate to the law of demand.

2. Choose three goods and services. Use the economic definition of demand to explain why you are or are not part of the demand for each of these products.

3. Why is determining demand elasticity important to business owners? How can business owners measure demand elasticity?

4. What factors can cause a shift in demand? Give one example of each of these factors at work for goods and services you have consumed.

5. What is the difference between a complementary good and a substitute good? Give an example of each kind of good for each of these products: ice cream, baseball game tickets, pencils.

6. What causes movement along a demand curve—in other words, a change in the quantity demanded? How does this movement differ from a shift in demand?

THINKING AND WRITING CRITICALLY

1. **SUPPLY & DEMAND** Determine whether demand for each of the following products is elastic or inelastic: Granny Smith apples, heart medicine, gasoline. Explain your reasoning.

2. **SUPPLY & DEMAND** Describe what happens to the demand curve for turkey in the United States in November. What happens to the curve after the holidays? Why do these changes occur?

3. **SUPPLY & DEMAND** Suppose that some children are planning to run a lemonade stand in your neighborhood this weekend. Given your newfound knowledge of demand, what advice would you give them in setting prices?

4. **SUPPLY & DEMAND** Fads are short-lived crazes for a particular item or style, such as baggy pants and miniskirts. Describe a current fad in economic terms. Be sure to note what is happening to demand and why.

YOUR LOCAL ECONOMY

Investigate the demand in your community for one category of products. For example, to study demand for grocery products, collect weekly advertisements for grocery stores from as many newspapers and in-store circulars as possible. Note which products are offered by all stores, which specialty products are offered by individual stores, and which products are on sale. Create a chart or collage that illustrates demand for these products. Write an extended caption that explains the economic reasoning behind your choice of images and information.

COOPERATIVE PORTFOLIO PROJECT

With your group, create a movie poster that "advertises" or illustrates one basic economic concept from the chapter. For example, you might create a poster of the movie *Cereal and Milk: A Love Story of Two Complementary Goods*. The poster should explain in words and images the economic concept your group has chosen. Assign members of the group to design the poster's layout, draw or find images, and write copy. Display your poster in class on a "movie marquee" of coming economic attractions.

The table below is a demand schedule for hair dryers. On a separate sheet of paper, use the schedule to draw a graph showing the demand curve. Then answer the questions that follow.

DEMAND SCHEDULE

Price per Hair Dryer	Quantity Demanded
$40	0
$30	10,000
$20	30,000
$10	40,000

1. How many hair dryers will consumers demand at a price of $20?

2. If the price of hair dryers were to drop from $20 to $10, how much would the quantity demanded change?

3. Perform the total-revenue test on all the possible price and quantity combinations listed in the demand schedule. At what price is total revenue maximized? Indicate this area graphically on your demand curve.

4. Does the demand elasticity of hair dryers change? How does your demand curve support you answer?

THE INTERNET: LEARNING ONLINE

Conduct an Internet search to find information about shopping on the Internet. Specifically, look for sites on the World Wide Web that are designed to meet teenagers' demand for goods. You might start with search words such as *shopping, compact discs, stereos,* and *bicycles.* Do you think the Internet is a good way to meet the demand of this market segment? Explain your answer.

ANALYZING PRIMARY SOURCES

"Summertime Blues"

You can find economic evidence of the law of demand and other economic concepts all around you, including in newspapers. The excerpt below is from *Community College Times*. As you read the excerpt, look for examples of the economic concepts you have read about in this chapter. Then answer the questions that follow.

"California's summer budget battles are becoming commonplace, but they are placing community colleges and their students in uncommon positions.

"In a compromise hammered out behind closed doors last week [June 1993], legislators agreed to a budget that assumes a 50 percent increase in community colleges' fees—from the current $10 per unit to $15 per unit. The total price tag for a semester would not exceed $150. . . .

"Exactly what effect the new fees will have on community college student enrollment is unknown, but last year's big fee hike—coupled with other budgetary changes such as further increased fees for students already holding baccalaureate [bachelor] degrees—was blamed for a 112,000 drop in attendance [last year].

"'We fully expect that we are going to lose a number of students,' [said a vice chancellor]. 'We could lose in the area of another 50,000 students.'"

1. What is the product in demand?

2. Is last year's drop in enrollment the result of a change in the quantity demanded or a shift in demand?

3. The article states that the effect of the new fees on community-college enrollment is "unknown." What effect do you predict it will have? Explain your answer.

4. Can you determine the elasticity of demand for this product from the information presented in the article? Why or why not?

CHAPTER 4

SUPPLY

ike most people, you probably think of yourself only as part of demand—as a consumer of goods and services. But you also are a producer, or supplier of goods and services. For example, you may have supplied your labor in a paid job, such as delivering newspapers. Or you may have supplied your labor in an unpaid job, such as working on community projects like planting trees and cleaning up graffiti. In this case the payment you received for your labor took a form other than money.

Like your role in market demand, your role in market supply is governed by some fundamental economic principles. This chapter explores these principles, including the law of supply, elasticity of supply, and shifts in supply. You also will learn to use supply schedules and supply curves, another set of basic economic tools. Additionally, you will learn how production decisions affect supply.

Economics Notebook

In your Economics Notebook, write what you think the term *supply* means. List five things you think you have supplied, in economic terms, in the past month.

NATURE OF SUPPLY

Economics Dictionary

supply
quantity supplied
law of supply
profit
cost of production
supply schedule
supply curve
elasticity of supply
elastic supply
inelastic supply

Objectives

▶ What is the difference between supply and quantity supplied?

▶ What does the law of supply state?

▶ What do supply schedules and supply curves illustrate?

▶ What is supply elasticity?

To meet consumers' demand, producers deliver goods and services to the marketplace. Consider, for example, the market for jackets. When are you most likely to buy, or demand, a warm jacket? Your demand for a jacket is highest in the fall and winter months, when cold weather arrives. When might you find the largest selection, or supply, of jackets in the stores? Again, the supply of jackets is highest in the fall and winter months, when demand is greatest.

In economic terms, however, supply is more than just the available selection of a good or service. **Supply** is the quantity of goods and services that producers are willing to offer at various possible prices during a given time period. During the winter months, for example,

jacket manufacturers offer a certain quantity of jackets at each price. The **quantity supplied** is the amount of a good or service that a producer is willing to sell at each particular price.

Law of Supply

In a free-enterprise system, price is the key factor affecting not only the quantity demanded but also the quantity supplied. That is, the quantity supplied is directly related to the prices that producers can charge for their goods and services. This relationship is described by the law of supply. The **law of supply** states that producers supply more goods and services when they can sell them at higher prices and fewer goods and services when they must sell them at lower prices.

For example, if producers of compact disc (CD) players can charge $300 for their products, they will make more CD players than if they could charge only $200. In other words, the higher price will lead to a larger quantity of CD

SUPPLY & DEMAND *These teenagers are supplying volunteer labor to build a house for a non-profit organization.* **What might they, as producers, consider to be a "price" for this volunteer work?**

players supplied. At the lower price, producers will supply a smaller quantity.

What causes producers to vary their supply of goods and services in this way? Their actions are based on the pursuit of profits. This critical motivation helps explain the law of supply.

Profit Motive

The amount of money remaining after producers have paid all of their costs is called **profit**. A business makes a profit when revenues are greater than **costs of production**. These costs include wages and salaries, rent, interest on loans, bills for electricity, raw materials, and any other goods and services used to manufacture a product.

To make a profit, producers must provide the goods and services that consumers want—at prices that consumers are willing and able to pay. For example, suppose that the Twin Wheels Bicycle Company is designing a new children's bike, aimed at 6- and 7-year-olds. The company is considering adding a tiny onboard computer system to the bike, much like those used in automobiles. The system will give young riders information such as their speed, direction, and tire pressure.

The system is so costly that the company would have to charge $1,000 for each bike. At this point the company owners tell the designers that the onboard computer system is not worth making. The owners know that the vast majority of consumers are not willing and able to pay $1,000 for a children's bike. If the company supplies this bike in the marketplace, it will not make a profit.

Profit and Markets

The profit motive has a far-reaching effect in free-enterprise markets. It not only governs how individual companies like Twin Wheels make decisions, it also helps direct the use of resources in the entire market.

For example, imagine that Twin Wheels introduces a line of children's bikes that sell for $150. The new model is extremely popular, and the company sells thousands of bikes and makes

---

SUPPLY OF CAR STEREOS

SUPPLY SCHEDULE

Price per Car Stereo	Car Stereos Supplied
$500	4,000
$400	3,750
$300	3,500
$200	2,500
$100	0

SUPPLY CURVE

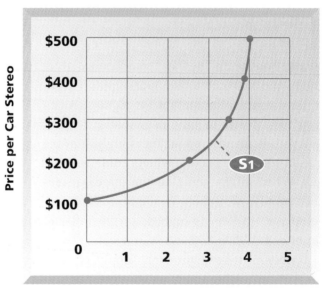

Quantity Supplied (in thousands)

FIGURE 4.1 A supply curve plots information from a supply schedule. **If the price of a car stereo changes from $200 to $300, how will the quantity supplied change during a given month?**

SUPPLY & DEMAND *The profit motive plays a key role in the law of supply.* **How does the profit motive help direct producers' use of resources?**

good profits. The company increases its production of the bike in pursuit of more profits.

Twin Wheels is not the only company to take notice of the market's high demand, however. On a broader scale, the company's sales and profits encourage other bicycle manufacturers to make more children's bikes. New bicycle manufacturers also may enter the market. All of these companies are pursuing profits.

What happens if Twin Wheels finds demand low for its new line of children's bikes? Even after lowering the price of the bikes, it barely makes back its investment. The company decides to decrease production of the bikes.

Likewise, the company's low sales and profits signal other suppliers that consumer demand in this market is low. Other bicycle manufacturers decrease their production of children's bikes and use their resources to make products that earn higher profits. The low demand also discourages new manufacturers from entering the market because they cannot expect to make good profits. In this way, profits help direct the use of resources.

Supply Schedules

One useful tool that shows the relationship between the price of a good or service and the quantity that producers will supply is a **supply schedule**. This schedule lists each quantity of a product that producers are willing to supply at various market prices.

An example of a supply schedule appears in Figure 4.1. The schedule lists the number of car stereos that the Audio Blast Company is willing to supply at several possible prices. You can see that as prices increase from $100 to $500, the quantity supplied increases. When the price is $100, the quantity of stereos supplied is zero. When the price is $500, Audio Blast supplies 4,000 stereos.

Supply Curves

Supply curves are another way to show the relationship between the price of a good or service and the quantity supplied. A **supply curve** plots on a graph the information from a supply schedule.

The supply curve S_1 in Figure 4.1, for example, shows all of the possible combinations of prices and quantities for Audio Blast's stereos, as listed in the supply schedule. The quantities of stereos that Audio Blast will supply appear along the horizontal axis, increasing from left to right. The possible prices of those stereos appear along the vertical axis, increasing from bottom to top.

Each point plotted on the graph represents a specific combination of price and quantity supplied. The curve slopes upward, reflecting the greater quantity that producers will supply at higher prices. Note that this is the opposite of what happens to demand curves, such as the one in Figure 3.2 on page 55.

Elasticity of Supply

The law of supply, supply schedules, and supply curves all point out the relationship between price and quantity supplied. They show that high prices for products lead to a large quantity of those products supplied, and low prices lead to a small quantity supplied. But how much of a change in price causes how much of a change in quantity supplied? As with demand, the answer lies in how elastic the supply of a product is.

Elasticity of supply is the degree to which price changes affect the quantity supplied. A

Careers in Economics

RESEARCHER CD-ROM

Buyer

Do you like to shop? Imagine being paid to buy the latest fashions, the hottest music, or the fastest computers. As a buyer, you would be required to make these kinds of purchases every day—but not for your own consumption.

Buyers are hired by stores to purchase merchandise from manufacturers. The stores then resell this merchandise to customers. All sizes of retail businesses—from small shops to large department store chains—employ buyers to determine what to buy, how much to buy, and from whom to buy consumer goods.

In effect, buyers must predict the future. Their job is to estimate what demand for particular products will be, and to choose the mix of prices, sizes, types, and colors. For example, when a buyer orders hot-pink sweaters for the fall line of clothes, he or she is estimating that the fashion tastes of shoppers and cooler weather will increase demand for this particular item.

Buyers have to replenish supplies quickly and economically as merchandise is sold. In addition, buyers price merchandise, create product displays, and manage sales personnel. They also must be good with numbers and able to use computers to track merchandise and inventory.

Buyers need to be skillful communicators. Those who are able to express their ideas to vendors, salespeople, managers, and customers generally obtain the best deals.

Most employers require a college education for this position. Courses in business management, merchandising, marketing, and math are helpful. A career as a professional buyer demands a lot of time and energy. Many buyers, however, find their role as the critical link between the consumer and producer to be exciting and rewarding.

Buyers use their knowledge of the market to predict demand and provide an adequate supply of goods and services.

product's supply, like demand, can be either elastic or inelastic.

Elastic Supply What goods tend to have elastic supply? **Elastic supply** exists when a small change in price causes a major change in the quantity supplied. Products with elastic supply usually can be made

▶ quickly,
▶ inexpensively, and
▶ using a few, readily available resources.

Suppliers can change the production rates of such goods easily in order to meet changing consumer demand.

Sports teams' souvenirs, such as T-shirts, posters, and hats, are an example of products with elastic supply. Consider what happens when a football team wins the Super Bowl. Demand for the team's souvenirs soars. They become more valuable to consumers, and prices rise.

What happens to the supply of these goods? Because these souvenirs can be produced quickly and inexpensively, the supply expands rapidly. In fact, within a few days of the team's victory, stores are literally flooded with the souvenirs.

The relatively small change in price results in an enormous change in supply.

You can see the elastic supply for posters of Super Bowl champions in Figure 4.2. The supply curve S_1 is more horizontal than vertical, showing that a small change in the price of posters causes a large change in the quantity of posters supplied. For example, at the price of $4.50, producers supply 100,000 posters. If the price increases to $9, producers supply 700,000 posters. A 100 percent increase in price leads to a 600 percent increase in the quantity supplied.

Inelastic Supply Some goods tend to have an inelastic supply. **Inelastic supply** exists when a change in a good's price has little impact on the quantity supplied. A product usually has an inelastic supply if production requires a great deal of

▶ time,
▶ money, and
▶ resources that are not readily available.

Suppliers cannot easily change the production rates of such goods in order to meet changing consumer demand.

ELASTIC SUPPLY FOR POSTERS

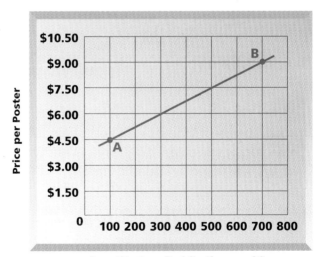

Quantity Supplied (in thousands)

FIGURE 4.2 A relatively horizontal line indicates elastic supply for posters during this one-week period. **What conditions are necessary for supply to be elastic?**

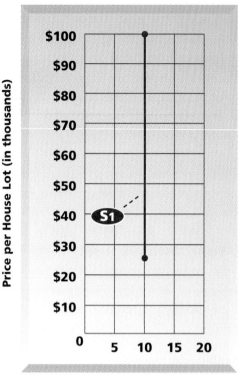

PERFECTLY INELASTIC SUPPLY

Price per House Lot (in thousands)

$100
$90
$80
$70
$60
$50
$40 S1
$30
$20
$10
0

5   10   15   20

Quantity Supplied

FIGURE 4.3 If a producer cannot increase supply regardless of price, supply is perfectly inelastic as it is for these house lots during a one-year period. **What characteristics indicate that a product has inelastic supply?**

Gold is one example of a product with a traditionally inelastic supply. If the price of gold rises, the quantity of gold supplied does not change much. Gold is a rare metal that is expensive to mine and requires time to refine, or purify. For these reasons, gold has an inelastic supply. Other rare, labor-intensive, and expensive items such as fine art and space shuttles have inelastic supply as well.

A perfectly inelastic supply exists when producers, regardless of price, cannot increase the quantity supplied. You can see a perfectly inelastic supply curve in Figure 4.3. Suppose that a building contractor wants to develop beachfront property and build Sandy Shores Homes. The contractor divides a piece of shoreline property into 10 lots. The lots are sized as small as local laws will allow. No matter what price the developer sets for each of the lots, the supply of shoreline properties at Sandy Shores is fixed. If demand is high, the developer might price the lots at $100,000 each. If demand is low, the developer might only be able to charge $25,000. At either price, however, the quantity supplied is 10 lots. Because price changes do not cause any change to the quantity of lots supplied, the supply of lots is perfectly inelastic.

SECTION 1 —REVIEW

1. Define the following terms: supply, quantity supplied, law of supply, profit, cost of production, supply schedule, supply curve, elasticity of supply, elastic supply, inelastic supply.

2. How does the concept of supply differ from the quantity supplied?

3. What is the law of supply? How does the profit motive help explain the law of supply?

4. What is the difference between a supply schedule and a supply curve?

5. What type of products tend to have an elastic supply? What are the usual characteristics of products with an inelastic supply?

6. Thinking and Writing Critically
Name at least two instances in which you supplied a good or service. Why were you willing to supply these products? What "price" did you receive for these products?

7. Applying SUPPLY & DEMAND Identify three products with elastic supply and three products with inelastic supply. Explain your choices.

CHANGES IN SUPPLY

Economics Dictionary

determinant of supply

tax

subsidy

regulation

Objectives

▶ What does it mean for a product's supply to shift?

▶ What factors might cause a product's supply curve to shift?

▶ How does a tax differ from a subsidy?

Like demand curves, supply curves illustrate a product's market at a specific period of time. The supply curve in Figure 4.1 on page 74, for example, is a snapshot of Audio Blast's stereo supply. Again, because the picture is taken at a set point in time, the only factor affecting the quantity of stereos supplied is the one factor shown in the picture (graph): price. Nothing but a price change is affecting the quantity of stereos

supplied by Audio Blast at the time this picture was taken.

By examining the supply curve, you can see that price is the only factor affecting the quantity supplied. Look again at the S_1 curve in Figure 4.1. What would have to happen for the number of car stereos supplied to increase from 2,500 to 4,000? The graph shows that only an increase in price from $200 to $500 will cause this change in the quantity supplied. Such an increase in price will result in the intersection of price and quantity supplied moving from point to point along the supply curve.

Supply Shifts

You already know, however, that markets do not stand still. New snapshots of a product's supply must be taken periodically because supply, like demand, is affected by factors other than price. In economic terms, these **determinants of supply**—or nonprice factors—can shift the entire supply curve of a product, instead of simply changing the quantity supplied along the original supply curve.

Figure 4.4 on page 80 shows movement of the entire S_1 supply curve from Figure 4.1. If the determinants of supply cause an increase in the supply of car stereos, the entire curve shifts to the right (S_2). Similarly, if the supply determinants cause a decrease in supply, the entire curve shifts to the left (S_3). A shift to either the S_2 or S_3

BLONDIE

SUPPLY & DEMAND *Businesses earn profits when revenues exceed resource costs.* ***How can a change in the price of resources affect the supply curve?***

curve means that a different quantity of car stereos is supplied at *each and every* price.

What causes these shifts in supply? The determinants of supply include

▶ prices of resources,
▶ government tools,
▶ technology,
▶ competition,
▶ prices of related goods, and
▶ producer expectations.

A change in one of these determinants can cause a change in the overall supply of a product.

Prices of Resources

One of the most common determinants that can shift the supply curve is a change in the price of resources, or factors of production. A resource is anything that is used in the production of a good or service. Resources include raw materials, electricity, and workers' wages. These resources contribute to a business's costs of production. Thus, any price change for a resource increases or decreases a business's production costs.

When the price of a resource falls, production costs fall accordingly. In turn, lower production costs mean that a business can supply more of the product for the same cost as before. Lower costs also generally go hand-in-hand with higher profits, which encourage the business to expand supply even more. For these reasons, a decrease in the price of a resource often causes producers to supply more product to the market at each and every price.

Suppose that the Fruit Bonanza Company makes fruit juices. The base ingredient of all of their juices is apple juice. An unexpectedly large crop of apples this year has been produced, reducing the price of apples by 10 cents a pound.

Given the large amount of apples that Fruit Bonanza buys, this price change significantly reduces the company's production costs. Lower costs allow the company to make more profit on the sale of each bottle of juice at each and every price. The higher profits encourage the owners of Fruit Bonanza to increase production even further. Thus, the supply curve shifts to the right as the company offers more bottles of juice at each and every price.

SUPPLY CURVE SHIFTS

INCREASE IN SUPPLY

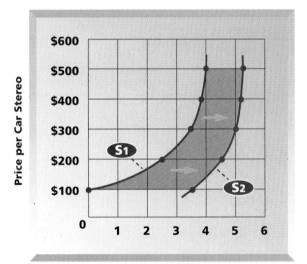

DECREASE IN SUPPLY

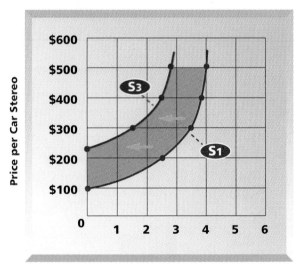

FIGURE 4.4 A shift in the supply curve results in new quantities of car stereos supplied at all possible prices. **What determinants cause a shift in the supply curve?**

An unexpectedly large crop of apples lowers the cost of products made with apples. **What would happen to the supply curve for applesauce in this instance?**

The opposite happens if the cost of a resource increases. If the price of apples rises by 10 cents a pound, for example, Fruit Bonanza's production costs also rise. Higher production costs mean that the company cannot supply as much of the product for the same cost as before. Higher costs also mean lower profits. The prospect of lower profits causes Fruit Bonanza to produce even less juice. Thus, the supply curve shifts to the left as the company offers less juice to the market at each and every price.

Government Tools

Various government tools can cause the supply curve for goods and services to shift either to the right or the left. The three main tools are taxes, subsidies, and regulation.

Taxes Like individual citizens, producers must pay taxes. A **tax** is a required payment of money to the government to help fund government services. Businesses may have to pay taxes on the materials they use, the property they own, and the profits they make. Taxes add to a business's

Acid Rain

Every government creates regulations that are designed to protect its citizens. Although such government regulations recognize international borders, sometimes the problems they address do not. Along the U.S.-Canadian border, for example, the problem of acid rain has introduced a sour note in the two countries' relations.

Acid rain is caused by sulfur dioxide and nitrogen oxide. Factories, cars, and refineries release these gases into the air, where they mix with water vapor. This falls to the earth as acid rain.

Why is acid rain a concern? Acid rain changes the soil's mineral content, altering the growth of plants. Some plants die; others grow but are not healthy. Acid rain also contaminates lakes and streams, killing fish and other aquatic animals.

For many years the problem of acid rain strained relations between the United States and Canada as pollutants crossed the border between the two countries. Canada has air quality objectives and strict emission standards for its cars and factories. The United States does not have nationwide policies aimed at reducing acid rain.

During the early 1990s a number of U.S. companies began participating in a new, market-based program. Each company received a pollution "allowance." When a company emitted more pollution than it was "allowed," it had to buy allowances from lower-polluting companies. This program is expected to lower pollution rates as companies buy newer equipment in the hope of selling unused allowances.

PRODUCTIVITY *The Ford assembly line revolutionized automobile production.* **How can technology cause the supply curve to shift?**

production costs, just like the cost of rent or raw materials does.

How do taxes affect supply? Higher taxes mean that businesses are faced with higher costs and the prospect of making less profit and will supply less of their product to the market. Thus, the supply curve shifts to the left.

Subsidies Payments to private businesses by the government are called **subsidies**. For example, to ensure consumers an affordable supply of flour, cereal, and other essential wheat products, the government might grant a subsidy to wheat farmers. By lowering the costs of planting wheat—compared to the costs of planting a non-subsidized crop—the subsidy encourages Gary Bryant, a wheat farmer, to plant more wheat. The lower costs of planting wheat also promise Gary greater profits on the sale of his wheat. The supply curve for wheat shifts to the right.

Subsidies and taxes thus have opposite effects on supply. As you can see from the above example, subsidies can reduce a business's production costs. These lower costs mean higher profits, which encourage producers to supply more of their product at each and every price.

Keep in mind, however, that subsidies have a cost. Taxpayers fund subsidies given to farmers and other private businesses.

Regulation To protect the public, the government passes many kinds of **regulations**, or rules, about how companies conduct business. Regulations are designed to prevent pollution, discrimination, and other problems that affect citizens. Loose government regulations tend to increase supply. Strict regulations, on the other hand, tend to decrease supply.

For example, strict pollution controls force companies to spend more money on finding safe ways to dispose of waste and toxic materials. Complying with the regulations thus increases the companies' production costs. As you have learned, higher production costs prevent producers from supplying as many goods and services, and the supply curve for their products shifts to the left.

Technology

New technology, such as a new tool or chemical process, can have a powerful impact on supply by changing the way in which products are made. Usually, new technology makes production more efficient and less expensive. This causes the costs of production to decrease. In turn, producers are able to supply more goods and services at each and every price because their costs are lower and their profits are higher.

Consider the case of automobiles. The first cars were produced individually by several workers. Because each car was made up of thousands of parts, production was time-consuming and expensive. In the early 1900s, however, technology revolutionized automobile production. Around 1913 Henry Ford used a new production technique—the assembly line—to make cars in his Detroit-area factory. Car frames moved along a conveyor belt past workers who performed their specified tasks in the assembly process. New machines produced the individual automobile parts, which were carried to workers on the assembly line.

This new technology had dramatic results. Assembly time was reduced significantly for Ford's Model T automobile. For the same amount of time and money as before, Ford's company could now produce many more Model T automobiles. Therefore, the supply curve for automobiles shifted to the right as it became profitable for producers to offer more cars at each and every price.

Keep in mind that technology also has a cost. A company may have to pay researchers or other companies for the desired technology. It is not uncommon for new technology to *add* to the costs of production at first. Henry Ford had to pay a great deal of money to install the new machines and the assembly line in his factory. However, Ford calculated that the increased efficiency and increased profitability of the new technology would outweigh the initial cost of installation.

Competition

Competition tends to increase supply, while a lack of competition tends to decrease supply. Why is this so?

Consider the market for home video games. When the first company offered these games, the selection was extremely limited. Demand for these games rose quickly, however, generating high sales and good profits for the company. These profits encouraged dozens of new video firms to enter the market. The supply and selection of games soon skyrocketed.

As this example shows, a larger number of suppliers in a market tends to increase supply. Each producer competes for a share of the market demand by supplying more of the product. This shifts the supply curve to the right as producers offer more goods at each and every price for the product.

Remember that suppliers can leave as well as enter a market. If the demand for video games were to fall, there would be more games (more supply) on the market than consumers wanted to purchase. Supply would be higher than demand. Some companies would not sell all of their games and might not make enough profit. These companies might then leave the market. Supply would shrink as fewer producers competed to deliver games to the market.

SUPPLY & DEMAND *Strong competition tends to increase supply, while weak competition tends to decrease supply.* **How might the entry of new carriers into the airline industry affect airfares?**

Internet Service Providers

SUPPLY & DEMAND Increased competition on the Internet has given consumers greater access to the global computer network. High profits for large online service providers such as America Online have encouraged others to enter the market.

Many of these new Internet service providers (ISPs) offer similar services—such as e-mail, bulletin boards, chat groups—at much lower prices than the larger companies. These lower prices attract customers and increase profits, which encourage still more entrepreneurs to offer online services.

In 1994, 14-year-old Michael Krause and his older brother Daniel started their own online service company from their parents' house, with one modem that could serve 10 callers. By 1996 the company, called Exchange Network Services Inc., provided online service to almost 5,000 customers and was adding about 20 new customers each day.

ISPs like the one established by Michael and Daniel compete for customers by offering faster service and less expensive rates than many large online services. This competition provides consumers with a greater number of choices—and therefore increases the supply of online connections.

At the same time, the spread of small ISPs increases public awareness of the Internet, and many new users subscribe to larger, more familiar services. Competition therefore has led to an increase of online services at many price levels and has caused the supply curve to shift to the right.

Prices of Related Goods

The supply for one good often is connected to the supply for its related goods. This means that changes in a product's price can affect the supply for the product's related goods.

For example, think again of Gary Bryant, the wheat farmer. In addition to wheat, Gary has several other choices of crops—corn, soybeans, and hay, for example. These goods are related as far as Gary is concerned because they share a common feature: they are potential crops that he may choose to plant.

Gary had planned to plant wheat, until the price of wheat dropped suddenly. The price of corn is now higher relative to the price of wheat. Because Gary can earn more profit on corn, he decides to plant corn instead of wheat. Thus, the drop in wheat prices results in an increase in the supply of its related good—corn—even though the price of corn did not change. The supply curve for corn shifts to the right.

Likewise, if the price of wheat were to rise relative to corn, more farmers would choose to plant wheat instead of corn in order to earn more profit. The rise in the price of wheat would result in a decrease in the supply of corn. The corn supply curve would shift to the left.

Producer Expectations

Just as consumers sometimes make current buying decisions based on their expectations of future income, suppliers make current production decisions based on their expected future income. Producers' income, of course, depends

COMPETITION & MARKET STRUCTURE *The popularity of the Internet has encouraged the development of many ISPs.* **How can competition contribute to an increase in quantity supplied?**

on the prices they can charge for their products. The expectations they have of future changes in the price of their products can affect how much of their product they supply to the market now.

For example, suppose that Sports Madness, a sports equipment manufacturer, expects the price of its basketballs to increase in the next few months. The company believes that the start of the school year—and later, the basketball season—will increase demand and prices. It decides to increase production of its basketballs now in order to meet the expected increase in demand. Thus, the supply curve for basketballs shifts to the right.

The effect of expectations on supply are difficult to predict, however. In the same situation, another sports manufacturer might decide to withhold a large portion of its basketballs by storing them in a warehouse. The company plans to deliver these basketballs to the market in a couple of months when prices will be higher. This decision leads to a decrease in the current supply of basketballs and shifts the supply curve in the opposite direction—to the left.

Manufacturers face similar options when they expect the price of their products to fall in the future. For example, if the above companies expect the price of basketballs to fall when the season ends, they may increase their production

SUPPLY & DEMAND *Suppliers make production decisions based on their expected future income.* **What happens to the supply curve for Valentine candy on February 15th?**

now in order to sell as many basketballs as possible before the price falls. Their expectations of future prices cause the supply curve to shift to the right. On the other hand, they may decrease their immediate production, anticipating that demand and prices will be lower. This decrease would shift the supply curve to the left.

SECTION 2 —REVIEW

1. Define the following terms: determinant of supply, tax, subsidy, regulation.

2. How is a shift in the supply curve different from a change in the quantity supplied?

3. List the determinants of supply and provide an example of each.

4. How can taxes and subsidies affect supply?

5. **Thinking and Writing Critically** Imagine that you own a cookie shop in a mall. What resources should you monitor for price changes? What related goods might you want to track?

6. **Applying** SUPPLY & DEMAND Describe an example of a recent technological change that affected a product's supply. How did this change affect the quantity of the product supplied?

MAKING PRODUCTION DECISIONS

Economics Dictionary

total product

marginal product

law of diminishing returns

fixed cost

depreciation

overhead

variable cost

total cost

marginal cost

Objectives

▶ Why do producers look at productivity when making supply decisions?

▶ How do varying levels of input affect the levels of output?

▶ How do changes in production costs affect producers' supply decisions?

You make production decisions every day. For example, you decide how to complete (produce) your homework assignments. You decide how to make your lunch. You decide how to make decorations for a school dance. Although you probably are unaware of it, when you make these types of daily choices, you go through a decision-making process much like the one that manufacturers use every day.

How do you and other suppliers make production decisions? You already know part of the answer. As noted in this chapter and in Chapter 3, the amount of goods produced is influenced by the laws of demand and supply, elasticity of demand and supply, and shifts in the demand and supply curves.

There are two pieces of the puzzle left to examine, however. Production levels also are influenced by productivity and the costs of production. Manufacturers must consider these two factors before deciding how much to produce for the market.

Productivity

As noted in Chapter 1, productivity is the amount of goods and services produced per unit of input. In other words, productivity tells business owners how efficiently their resources are being used in production.

Think about your own productivity regarding homework. Imagine that you have a test tomorrow in one of your classes. You estimate that it will take you about three hours to study for it. That is, for every three hours of input (study time) you produce one unit of output (a good grade on a test). Can you be more productive? Perhaps by studying with a friend—discussing the material and quizzing each other—you can increase the effectiveness of your study time. This type of studying allows you to produce a good grade on the test with only two hours of input instead of three.

Of course, productivity in businesses is much more complex—and involves more inputs—than the above example. But like you, business owners must examine their productivity in order to maximize efficiency and profits. And like you, they consider varying the amount of their inputs in order to increase productivity. To do this, business owners look at their total product, marginal product, and how the two figures change as inputs change.

Total Product To understand how output is affected by changes in input, a company first must calculate its output. All of the product a company makes in a given period of time—with a given amount of input—is called its **total product**, or total output. The table in Figure 4.5 contains a production schedule for the Golden Duck Company. The second column of the table lists the possible total product levels for the company. Golden can make anywhere between zero and 1,000 rubber ducks a day as it uses zero to 13 units of labor.

Marginal Product

Marginal Product To maximize productivity, business owners also need to know their marginal product. **Marginal product** is the change in output generated by adding one more unit of input. How do businesses calculate marginal product?

Return to the production schedule in Figure 4.5. The third column lists the marginal product for each level of production. That is, it shows how many additional units (ducks) are produced at each level of input. For example, if labor input increases from zero to 1, the marginal product is 10 because 10 ducks are produced. If the level of input rises again to 2, the marginal product is 40 because 40 more ducks are produced than before the increase (50 − 10 = 40).

Law of Diminishing Returns

Once total and marginal product have been calculated, a company is ready to vary one of its inputs to see the effect on output. This effect is governed by a basic economic principle: the **law of diminishing returns**. This law describes the effect that varying the level of an input has on total and marginal product. It states that as more of one input is added to a fixed supply of other resources, productivity increases up to a point. At some point, however, the marginal product will diminish. Eventually, it will result in negative marginal product.

Keep in mind that this principle applies to situations in which only *one* input is varied. Of course, a company like Golden would want to vary several of its inputs to find the most efficient combination. It might increase the number of its workers *and* add more machines to its

PRODUCTIVITY OF GOLDEN DUCK COMPANY

PRODUCTION SCHEDULE

Labor Input	Total Product	Marginal Product
0	0	0
1	10	10
2	50	40
3	110	60
4	175	65
5	245	70
6	320	75
7	400	80
8	485	85
9	575	90
10	675	100
11	875	200
12	985	110
13	1,000	15
14	975	-25
15	925	-50
16	825	-100

PRODUCTION CURVE

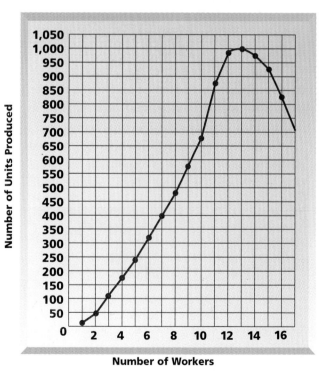

FIGURE 4.5 Production schedules and production curves illustrate productivity during a specific period of time. **How does this production curve reflect the law of diminishing returns during a one-week period at the Golden Duck factory?**

Dialing for Dollars

You may think of business leaders as men and women who have been part of the corporate world for many years. There are, however, some young people out there who already own and run their own businesses.

Bill Cunningham has been in business for himself since he was 17. While he was still in high school, Bill gained valuable experience working for a telemarketing company at night. Then with a telephone and about $700 in savings, he started his own business. He established Dial USA, a telemarketing firm based in Dallas.

Bill felt that telemarketing was an ideal business for a young entrepreneur. He said, "If I were to go to someone's office and try to sell him a copy machine in person at 17, it would be difficult. However, if I were able to communicate clearly and maturely over the telephone, I had a fighting chance."

Bill was responsible for every aspect of Dial USA's business. He had to find customers, pay the bills, and establish prices and policies. In the beginning, he also was Dial USA's only employee.

As the company grew, however, Bill needed people to help him. He was responsible for hiring new employees, training them, paying their salaries, and making sure that the company ran smoothly and earned a profit. Although Bill was happy to earn a profit, it was not the primary reason that he went into business. Bill said, "You don't go into business to make money. You go in because you are a creator. Money's a by-product, a way of keeping score." After only three years, Dial USA's "score" was an impressive $1.2 million in revenues, and Bill's client list continued to grow.

Why would a company hire a telemarketer like Dial USA? Telemarketers fill an important need by selling products, which allows a company's staff to concentrate on developing goods and services.

Making an organization known to the public is one of Dial USA's most important tasks. For example, Dial USA was hired by the Center for Success in Learning, an organization that develops techniques and programs for learning-challenged children. The center needed to raise funds, so Bill's company advertised a benefit rodeo. In a matter of weeks, Dial USA helped the Center for Success in Learning earn $35,000, which allowed the organization to stay in business.

Telemarketers usually are paid commissions, which means that instead of earning a fixed wage for every hour of work, their pay is based on the number of products sold. The more tickets Bill sold for the benefit rodeo, for example, the more money he made for himself as well as for the center. Bill said, "I believed that we could make a difference and make a profit at it."

Running a business takes hard work and determination. To any budding entrepreneurs, Bill suggests, "Examine all your options. But when you make up your mind, have laser-guided focus to work hard on your goals."

Bill Cunningham started his telemarketing company—Dial USA—at the age of 17.

What Do You Think?

1. What kinds of businesses offer a young entrepreneur the best chances for success? Explain your answer.

2. If you were starting your own business, what would you choose to do? Why?

factory. Varying several inputs at once, however, makes it difficult to determine clear cause-and-effect results. If production does increase at the Golden plant, was it a result of hiring more workers, adding new machines, or both? By looking at only one input at a time, the effect on total output is clearer.

The three stages of production that can be predicted by the law of diminishing returns are called increasing marginal returns, diminishing marginal returns, and negative marginal returns. The effect on output of varying levels of input can be seen by looking closely at these three stages.

Increasing Marginal Returns

Look again at the production schedule in Figure 4.5 on page 87. The first column shows one input in making rubber ducks: labor. As this input varies, so do the output levels of the company. Clearly, if there are no workers, no product is made. With one worker, the company makes 10 ducks a day. As the number of workers increases to 13, total product levels continue to increase. Extra workers allow each person to specialize, or concentrate, on a particular part of the process. This increases production.

Notice how the marginal product in column three also continues to increase with the addition of the first 11 workers. As each of these first 11 workers are added, output rises at a faster rate. The first worker boosts production by 10 units, the second by 40, the third by 60, and so on until the eleventh worker, who raises output by 200 units.

You can also see this rise in production in the production curve in Figure 4.5. The vertical axis of the graph shows Golden's total product, or output. The one varying input (labor) appears on the horizontal axis. As the number of workers increases from zero to 11, the total output rises at a steep rate.

Diminishing Marginal Returns

As the law of diminishing returns predicts, however, at some point output begins to increase at a diminished, or lower, rate. The twelfth worker only adds 110

PRODUCTIVITY *How many people does it take to change a lightbulb?* **Why do producers pay attention to marginal returns?**

units, whereas the eleventh worker added 200 units. Perhaps there is not enough machinery in the factory to keep the twelfth worker fully employed. Thus, even though total product continues to increase with the twelfth worker, marginal product begins to decrease. That is, total output increases at a slower rate than it did with workers 1 through 11.

The production curve in Figure 4.5 reflects this drop in the rate of increased production. As the number of workers increases from 11 to 12, the rise in total output begins to level off. Production with these workers is not rising as fast as in the first part of the graph.

Negative Marginal Returns

The fourteenth, fifteenth, and sixteenth workers make the situation even worse. At this point, workers are getting in each other's way, creating bottlenecks on the assembly line and actually lowering the level of output. In addition, the overcrowding results in frustrated workers and low morale, which further erodes productivity. The fourteenth worker, for example, lowers total production by 25 units.

You can see this drop in total product in the production curve. The graph curves downward after the addition of the fourteenth, fifteenth, and sixteenth workers. This reflects the negative marginal returns to labor.

Production schedules and curves like the ones in Figure 4.5 help businesspeople apply the law of diminishing returns to their production decisions. By discovering the point at which their inputs are most efficiently used, they can set production levels that will maximize profits.

Costs of Production

Manufacturers must also look at their costs of production when deciding how much to supply to the market. As noted in Section 1, a business's costs of production include any goods and services used to make a product. Manufacturers are particularly interested in their costs of production because these costs directly affect the amount of profit their business makes.

For example, imagine that you start your own lawnmowing service. Two of your customers want to have their lawns mowed by 10 a.m. Saturday. They are willing to pay you the same amount of money—$15. One lawn takes one hour to mow, and the other takes two.

You know you only have time to complete one of the assignments by the deadline. How do you choose? For a cost of two hours' work, you have the potential to earn $15. You can earn the same amount of money by working for one hour on a different lawn. But your cost in earning that money is lower—one hour of work instead of two. In search of the highest profit with the lowest cost, you decide that on Saturday morning you will mow the lawn that takes one hour to complete.

Manufacturers and other suppliers deal with complicated production costs and must consider many factors. To make analyzing costs easier, most producers divide them into several categories: fixed, variable, total, and marginal. Analyzing these various production costs helps

MARGINAL PRODUCT AND COSTS

Labor Input	Total Product	Marginal Product	Fixed Costs	Variable Costs	Total Costs	Marginal Costs
0	0	0	$3,400	$0	$3,400	–
1	10	10	3,400	215	3,615	$21.50
2	50	40	3,400	430	3,830	5.38
3	110	60	3,400	645	4,045	3.58
4	175	65	3,400	860	4,260	3.31
5	245	70	3,400	1,075	4,475	3.07
6	320	75	3,400	1,290	4,690	2.87
7	400	80	3,400	1,505	4,905	2.69
8	485	85	3,400	1,720	5,120	2.53
9	575	90	3,400	1,935	5,335	2.39
10	675	100	3,400	2,150	5,550	2.15
11	875	200	3,400	2,365	5,765	1.08
12	985	110	3,400	2,580	5,980	1.95
13	1,000	15	3,400	2,795	6,195	14.33
14	975	-25	3,400	3,010	6,410	–
15	925	-50	3,400	3,225	6,625	–
16	825	-100	3,400	3,440	6,840	–

FIGURE 4.6 Marginal costs indicate the cost of producing one more unit of output. **At what point are marginal costs lowest for the Golden Duck Company?**

producers determine production goals and potential profits.

Fixed Costs Some production costs do not change no matter how many goods are made. For example, whether the Golden Duck factory produces 10 ducks a day or 1,000—or even if it produces none—the rent that the factory pays stays the same. Production costs that do not change as the level of output changes are called **fixed costs**. Fixed costs include rent, interest on loans, property insurance premiums, local and state property taxes, and salaries.

Fixed costs also include routine wear and tear on machines and other capital goods. In the Golden Duck factory, for example, the machine that molds the toys was purchased five years ago. Each year, a portion of the value of that machine has been considered a fixed cost. Why?

Each year, the molding machine is older and less efficient. The older it becomes, the less value it has. This aging of the machine—and other capital goods—is thus seen as a cost.

Businesses do not determine the amount of **depreciation**, or lessening in value, on each and every capital good they own because these calculations would take too much time. Instead, tax laws and standard accounting practices allow them to divide the cost of a capital good over the life of the good.

You can see the total weekly fixed costs for the Golden Duck Company in Figure 4.6. The first three columns are the production schedule from Figure 4.5. Column 4 shows the fixed costs for each level of production. Notice that the fixed costs listed in this column do not change even though the production level changes. Whether the company produces zero ducks or 1,000 ducks a day, the company's total fixed costs, also called **overhead**, remain $3,400.

Variable Costs Unlike fixed costs, **variable costs** change as the level of output changes. Variable costs include raw materials and wages. In the case of the rubber duck factory, for example, as production rises from 10 to 1,000 ducks a day, the number of workers also rises. The wages

PRODUCTIVITY *Production costs are important to manufacturers because these costs directly affect their business's level of profits.* **What production costs can you identify in this photograph?**

of these workers are an added, or variable, cost. So are the added materials used to make the additional 990 ducks.

You can see Golden's variable costs in Figure 4.6. Column 5 shows the total variable costs of making ducks at each production level. As you would expect, the variable costs listed in column 5 change as production levels change. When no ducks are made, for example, variable costs are $0. At a production level of 1,000 ducks a day, variable costs are $2,795.

Total Costs The sum of the fixed and variable production costs is a company's **total costs**. At zero output a firm's total costs are equal to its fixed costs. If a company is not producing anything, it does not have any variable costs—no workers to be paid and no raw materials to be bought. Thus, its fixed costs are its total costs.

As soon as production begins, however, so do a company's variable costs. This in turn raises the company's total costs. Look again at Figure 4.6 on page 90. At a production level of 1,000 ducks a day, what are Golden's total costs per week? Adding the company's fixed costs ($3,400) and variable costs ($2,795) at this production level reveals weekly total costs of $6,195.

To make wise production decisions, this company must determine the additional costs of producing a tennis ball—one more unit of output. **How is marginal cost calculated?**

Marginal Costs To make production decisions, businesspeople need to know not only their company's total costs but also the marginal costs for the company. **Marginal costs** are the additional costs of producing one more unit of output. How do businesses determine marginal costs?

As you know, fixed costs do not change as production levels change. Therefore, to determine marginal costs as production levels change, a business must look at its variable costs alone. If Golden wants to increase production from 875 to 1,000 ducks a day, its variable costs increase by $430, from $2,365 to $2,795. The marginal cost of making each new duck is the additional cost ($430) divided by the number of additional ducks (125): $430 ÷ 125 = $3.44.

This figure means that each additional duck (numbers 876 to 1,000) costs $3.44 to make. If Golden wants to increase production from 875 to 999 ducks instead of to 1,000, it can calculate how much this will cost: 124 additional ducks at a marginal cost of $3.44 equals $426.56.

This allows businesspeople to calculate the exact cost of any change in production levels. Many businesspeople do indeed make marginal production decisions—decisions to produce a few more or a few less units of output. Marginal costs allow the business to determine the profitability of increasing or decreasing production by a few units.

SECTION 3 — REVIEW

1. Define the following terms: total product, marginal product, law of diminishing returns, fixed cost, depreciation, overhead, variable cost, total cost, marginal cost.

2. How does productivity influence supply decisions?

3. How do you determine what happens to productivity when a product's inputs change?

4. What happens in each of the three stages of production?

5. What is the difference between fixed costs and variable costs?

6. Thinking and Writing Critically Explain how the law of diminishing returns applies to a recipe for beef stew. Describe, in economic terms, what happens if you double, triple, or quadruple the amount of one of the ingredients (input). Are the results the same if you quadruple the amount of beef as when you quadruple the amount of salt? What happens to the quality of the stew (output) in each instance?

7. Applying SUPPLY & DEMAND Imagine that you own a photo-processing business. What production issues must you consider to make your business a success? Explain how each issue would relate to your business.

SECTION 1 Supply is the quantity of goods and services that producers offer at various possible prices during a given time period. Quantity supplied is the amount of a good or service that a producer is willing to offer at each particular price. The law of supply states that producers supply more goods and services when they can sell them at higher prices and fewer goods and services when they must sell them at lower prices.

Profit is the key motivation behind suppliers' behavior in providing goods to the marketplace. Supply schedules and supply curves are useful in charting the degree to which changes in prices affect quantities supplied.

The supply of goods can be either elastic or inelastic. When a small change in a product's price causes a major change in the quantity supplied, supply for the good is elastic. In contrast, inelastic supply occurs when a change in a product's price has little impact on the quantity supplied. A good usually has an elastic supply if it can be made quickly, inexpensively, and using a few, readily available resources. A good usually has inelastic supply, on the other hand, if producing it requires a great deal of time, money, and resources that are not readily available.

SECTION 2 Factors other than price can affect supply of a product over time, shifting the supply curve to the left or right. The determinants of supply are prices of resources, government tools, technology, competition, prices of related goods, and producer expectations.

Resources include raw materials and labor. A decrease in the price of resources causes an increase in supply. The opposite is true when an increase in the price of resources occurs. A tax hike causes a decrease in supply, while government subsidies increase supply. Loose government regulations tend to increase supply, while strict regulations tend to decrease supply. New technology and competition both usually increase supply. A change in the price of related goods can cause an increase or decrease in supply. Producer expectations also can cause an increase or decrease in supply.

SECTION 3 Production decisions are affected by the need to maximize productivity and by the costs of production. When setting production levels, business owners must consider total product (all of the product a company makes in a given period of time), marginal product (the change in output generated by adding one more unit of input), and the law of diminishing returns (the fact that marginal and total product will decrease after a certain production level).

Making these production decisions also requires business owners to determine their fixed costs (production costs that do not change as the level of output changes), variable costs (costs that change as output changes), total costs (the sum of fixed and variable costs), and marginal costs (the costs of producing one more unit of output).

✎ Economics Notebook

Review what you wrote in your Economics Notebook at the beginning of this chapter about the definition of _supply_ and the things you believe you have supplied in the past month. Now that you have studied this chapter, would you change your definition and examples? Why or why not? Record your answer in your Notebook.

CHAPTER 4

└REVIEW

REVIEWING CONCEPTS

1. Define the law of supply. Be sure to include how the profit motive relates to this law.

2. List three goods or services supplied by your school. Use the economic definition of supply to justify your choices.

3. Explain the difference between the following types of costs: fixed, variable, total, marginal.

4. What determinants can cause a shift in supply? Give examples of at least three of these factors at work for a company that manufactures televisions.

5. Explain what happens in the three stages of production described by the law of diminishing returns.

6. What causes movement along a supply curve—in other words, what prompts a change in the quantity supplied? How does this movement differ from a shift in supply?

THINKING AND WRITING CRITICALLY

1. **SUPPLY & DEMAND** Determine whether supply for the following products is elastic or inelastic: candy, diamonds, submarines, election campaign buttons. Explain your reasoning.

2. **SUPPLY & DEMAND** Explain what happens to the supply curve for swimsuits in the summer. What happens to the supply in the fall? Why do these changes in the supply of this product occur?

3. **SUPPLY & DEMAND** As a consumer, do you have more choice when the supply of a product is elastic or inelastic? Why?

4. **SUPPLY & DEMAND** Why might a government grant subsidies to certain individuals or businesses? Should U.S. taxpayers fund subsidies?

YOUR LOCAL ECONOMY

Create an economic supply map of your community. Contact a local chamber of commerce and newspaper to find out where and what products are grown and manufactured in your community or county. Create a set of symbols that represent the different economic products your community supplies. These symbols should appear in a legend on your map. You also might use colors to indicate large areas of production of a particular good. Be sure to title your map and include an extended caption that explains the supply of goods in your community or county.

INDIVIDUAL PORTFOLIO PROJECT

Create a cartoon or comic strip that illustrates one basic economic concept from the chapter. For example, you might create a cartoon of the law of diminishing returns in which an "increasing returns" character is climbing up the steep side of a "production" hill. Meanwhile, a "diminishing returns" character is about to reach the top of the mountain, and a "negative returns" character is tumbling down the other side of the hill.

PRACTICING SKILLS: UNDERSTANDING CHARTS AND GRAPHS

The table on page 95 is a production schedule for the Lightning Skateboard Company. On a separate piece of paper, use the production schedule to draw a graph showing how Lightning's output changes as its number of workers changes. Then answer the questions below.

1. How many skateboards can Lightning produce with eight workers?

PRODUCTION SCHEDULE

Labor Input	Total Product	Marginal Product
0	0	0
1	3	3
2	7	4
3	12	5
4	20	8
5	30	10
6	45	15
7	57	12
8	66	9
9	68	2
10	65	-3

2. If the number of workers increases from four to six, how much does marginal product increase?

3. For what levels of production does Lightning experience increasing returns? diminishing returns? negative returns? Indicate these three stages on your graph.

THE INTERNET: LEARNING ONLINE

Conduct an Internet search for information about government involvement in supply. You might start with search words such as *subsidy*. What kind of information about subsidies is available on the Internet? If possible, use e-mail to request additional materials about three or four subsidies. Create fact sheets on each subsidy you investigate and post these fact sheets in your classroom.

ANALYZING PRIMARY SOURCES

Only One Earth

For centuries, people believed that there was a limitless supply of the world's natural resources. Most people now recognize that the supply of petroleum, minerals, trees, fresh water, clean air, and other natural resources is indeed limited. Many people believe that these resources must be protected to guarantee their continued availability.

The excerpt below is from the book *Only One Earth*, written in 1972 by British economist Lady Barbara Ward. It discusses the economic consequences of depleting supplies of natural resources. Read the excerpt below and answer the questions that follow.

"When we turn to the materials used in industry, we begin to encounter the extreme difficulty of deciding just how large a reserve of this or that mineral is likely to be available over what span of time. Take a critical [necessary] substance like iron ore upon which man's industrial activities have been based for three or four thousand years. Annual consumption of iron ore has quadrupled since 1950, roughly 85 per cent of it in developed lands. If this rate of increase continues, estimates suggest that about 17 billion metric tons will have been used up by the year 2000—at which point there could be only another 88 billion metric tons left, a calculation which might suggest exhaustion of the ore bodies by the middle of the twenty-first century.

"But no such simple calculus can be made. These estimates were made on the basis of the 1968 price of $15 a ton. As reserves run down, four things will happen. Prices will rise, which will make it worthwhile using ore with a lower percentage of iron. This alone could triple and quadruple potential reserves. Next, a new wave of exploration will be unleashed which may . . . uncover unsuspected ore bodies with a high iron content or add to the scale of less valuable reserves. The third consequence will be much more careful use of scrap. . . . The fourth consequence will be a turn to other materials and to much greater research into reproducing in them the qualities that industrial processes require. . . . The plain truth is that iron ore at $20 a ton entails [involves] a completely different set of uses—and nonuses—than ore at $15."

1. What does Ward predict to be the consequences of depleting the earth's supply of iron ore?

2. Does iron ore have elastic or inelastic supply? Explain your answer.

3. According to Ward, how does demand affect the price of iron ore? Based on this information, do you predict that the demand for iron ore will increase or decrease in the future? Explain your answer.

CHAPTER 5

PRICES

Consumers and producers act in their own best interest. As a consumer, for example, you buy more pizza at low prices, when you can get the most pizza for your money. Producers, meanwhile, supply more pizza when they can receive a high price and make a good profit.

Self-interest thus leads producers and consumers—like you—to have different goals in the marketplace. How can consumers and producers compromise? How can consumers and producers determine a level of production that satisfies consumers' desire for affordable pizza and the producers' desire to make a profit?

Consumers and producers communicate through the price system. In this chapter you will learn how the price system works in a free-enterprise system, as well as how the market responds to surpluses and shortages.

Economics Notebook

In your Economics Notebook, list three items that you have purchased recently, and indicate how much you paid for them. Explain what you think these prices told you about the products.

THE PRICE SYSTEM

Economics Dictionary

market failure
externality
public good

Objectives

▶ What is the role of the price system?

▶ What are the benefits of the price system?

▶ What are the limitations of the price system?

How does the price system allow producers and consumers to communicate with each other? As you know, producers and consumers have different goals. To meet their goals, the two groups must work together. The price system guides producers and consumers to balance the forces of supply and demand by reaching compromises on production levels. That is, a free-enterprise economy primarily relies on the price system to answer the basic economic questions of what, how, and for whom to produce.

In this section you will learn not only how the price system works but also how well it works. The price system has both benefits and limitations in coordinating production decisions among producers and consumers.

The Language of Prices

Every time you buy a good or service, you are speaking the "language" of prices. It may sound strange to say that prices are a language, but prices do indeed serve as the main form of communication between producers and consumers in a free-enterprise market.

Prices are the way in which producers tell consumers how much it costs to produce and distribute a good or service. In essence, the price of a pizza translates to you, the consumer, as "If you want this amount of pizza, you have to pay this price." If you buy the pizza, your response to producers is "Yes, I want this amount of pizza at this price." Similarly, if you do not buy the pizza, your response is "No, I do not want this amount of pizza at this price."

If consumers buy a product at the established price, producers may be satisfied and maintain current production levels and prices. On the other hand, producers may decide to try to increase their profits. The owner of Palatial Pizza, for example, communicates this decision to consumers by increasing the price of a pizza. Consumers then have the chance to respond to Palatial Pizza's decision by accepting or rejecting the new price. If the price increase is acceptable, consumers will continue to buy about the same amount of pizza from Palatial, and revenue will increase. If the price increase is not acceptable, consumers will buy so many fewer pizzas from Palatial Pizza that revenue falls.

In contrast, if consumers do not buy a product at the established price, producers must determine whether they can charge a lower price for the product and still make a profit. If they can, producers communicate this to consumers by reducing prices.

Benefits of the Price System

Using the price system as a form of communication between producers and consumers has several benefits. It provides

▶ information,
▶ incentives,
▶ choice,
▶ efficiency, and
▶ flexibility.

Information Producers and consumers can gather information through the price system. For example, the prices of resources tell producers

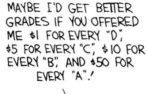

MARKETS & PRICES *Using the price system as a form of communication between producers and consumers provides several benefits, including incentives.* **What are the other benefits of the price system?**

how much they must pay to make their products. The market would be quite different if producers did not know this information. Businesses would make random decisions about what to produce because they would have no idea whether one product would be more profitable than another. A producer would have no way of knowing whether it would be more profitable to produce skateboards or microprocessors.

Like producers, consumers gather information through the price system. Consumers need to know the prices of goods and services to make informed buying decisions. Without prices, how could you shop effectively? You would have no way of knowing how the cost of a sweater compares with that of a jacket. Prices inform consumers of the relative worth of the goods and services they purchase.

Incentives The price system also provides producers and consumers with incentives to participate in the market. As noted in Chapter 2, an incentive is something that encourages you to behave in a particular way. High prices, when combined with low costs, generally encourage producers to supply more goods and services. This reflects the law of supply—that high prices encourage increases in the quantity supplied, while low prices encourage reductions in the quantity supplied. Low prices, meanwhile, give consumers an incentive to buy more goods and services. This, in turn, reflects the law of

demand, which states that high prices generally encourage reductions in the quantity demanded, while low prices tend to encourage increases in the quantity demanded. If there were no price incentives, producers and consumers would have a much more difficult time exchanging goods and services.

Choice By encouraging participation in markets, the price system also increases the choices available in those markets. The higher the incentive to supply products to the marketplace, the greater the choice of products supplied.

For example, consider the athletic clothing market. Demand for this type of clothing is high, which drives prices and profits higher in relation to many "basic" clothes like jeans and T-shirts. These higher prices and profits encourage competition among the various clothing manufacturers in this market.

In competing with one another the manufacturers create hundreds of different products, trying to match consumer preferences and generate the most profit. As a result, consumers can select from a wide range of styles and prices for athletic clothing and can choose to buy a $300 designer nylon jogging suit or a pair of $20 cotton sweatpants.

Efficiency Efficiency is a key benefit of the price system. The system brings about efficiency in two main ways. First, it provides for the wise

The Coming of the Computer Age

How would you describe a typical computer? You may think of monitors, hard drives, disk drives, and CD-ROM drives. Despite having all of these features, computers usually are small enough to sit on top of a desk. The computer has not always been so compact, however.

The first modern computer, called the Electronic Numerical Integrator and Computer (ENIAC), measured 50 by 30 feet. Development costs for the ENIAC, which was completed in 1945, totaled $400,000.

Over the next decade, computers were transformed from basic mathematical instruments into data-processing machines. The first successful business computer—the 1401®, created by International Business Machines (IBM)—rented for $2,500 per month in 1960 (equivalent to a purchase price of $150,000 at that time).

How did these large and costly computers, known as mainframes, develop into the desktop models we know today? During the 1950s and 1960s, a "revolution in miniature" swept the electronics industry. Large vacuum tubes were replaced by smaller transistors. Transistors then evolved into integrated circuits, or microchips, which measured only two tenths of an inch by one tenth of an inch. These tiny chips cost around $1,000 when they were first introduced in 1971, but within two years competition from other producers had driven the price down to $100.

Electronic innovations also meant that components could be produced more efficiently, lowering the price of the entire computer. By 1970 a "minicomputer" cost around $20,000.

The Altair 8800®—introduced in January 1975—is considered to be the first personal computer because it cost about $400 unassembled. The Altair consisted of only a single box with a panel of switches and neon bulbs. It had neither a display screen nor a keyboard and contained very little memory.

By 1977 the "microcomputer" was transformed from a hobbyist's machine into a consumer product. One of the many firms to join the market in the late 1970s was Apple Computer, selling a "home/personal computer" for $1,298 (excluding a monitor) in 1977.

Not to be outdone, in 1981 IBM launched a personal computer (PC) that sold for $2,880. Most software available at the time was easily converted to run on the PC, encouraging other companies to make clones, or copies of the IBM computer.

Competition and technological developments continue to decrease the price of PCs, thereby increasing demand. In fact, PC sales in the United States rose 14 percent during the first part of 1996, largely because of a 40 percent decrease in price over the previous year.

What Do You Think?

1. How do you think computers will change during the next 10 years?

2. Do you think that personal computers will become more or less affordable in the future? Explain your answer.

The first modern computer—the ENIAC—was extremely large and costly compared to today's machines.

MARKETS & PRICES *Prices immediately signal the value of a good in relation to another good.* **How does the price system encourage efficiency?**

use of resources. Prices tell producers which products consumers want to buy. High prices encourage producers to use resources to provide goods and services that consumers want. Low prices lead producers to stop using resources to provide goods and services that consumers do not want.

Without prices to indicate consumer demand, producers could unknowingly waste raw materials, their workers' labor, and other resources by making products that would sit unpurchased on store shelves. The pricing system tells producers how best to use their resources—natural, human, capital and entrepreneurial—to meet consumer demand.

The price system also encourages efficiency by quickly delivering information to producers and consumers. Prices immediately signal the value of a good or service in relation to other goods or services. Producers can easily compare the prices of resources, and consumers can do the same for goods and services. As a result, both groups can make decisions efficiently.

Think about how long it would take you to buy a pair of jeans at the mall if you could not compare prices. You might find four pairs you like equally, but be unable to determine which ones cost a lot of money and which ones are relatively inexpensive. The decision about which pair to buy would take you much longer—so long, in fact, that you might become frustrated and decide not to buy any jeans at all. By eliminating some choices, the price system allows consumers to make decisions efficiently.

Flexibility One of the price system's greatest strengths is its ability to deal with change. The supply and demand of goods changes almost constantly. A hit movie or music video can increase consumer demand for a particular hair or clothing style overnight. Sudden events such as floods, freezes, and work stoppages can reduce the supply of crops or manufactured goods. The price system can accommodate these changes quickly.

If, for example, a freeze destroys a large portion of the orange crop, the price of oranges increases. The higher prices determine how the low orange supply will be distributed: only those

MARKETS & PRICES *Limitations of the price system are known as market failures.* **What type of market failure is caused by a logging company that fails to plant new trees?**

people who are willing and able to pay the higher price can satisfy their demand for oranges.

If prices did not rise, the quantity of oranges demanded would be much higher than the quantity supplied. Consumers would have to compete for oranges—possibly by standing in long lines—only to have the supply run out before each person was able to make a purchase. In this case, many consumers who are willing and able to buy the lower-priced fruit would be unable to satisfy their demand.

Limitations of the Price System

On the whole, the price system is an effective way to coordinate the decisions of consumers and producers in a free-enterprise economy. The system does have limitations, however. These limitations are sometimes referred to as **market failures** because the market—or the price system—fails to account for some costs and therefore cannot distribute them appropriately.

Externalities One limitation of the price system is that it may not take into account all of the costs and benefits of production. The production of goods sometimes results in side effects for people not directly connected with the production or consumption of the goods. These side effects are called **externalities** and can be either negative or positive.

A negative externality exists when someone who does not make or consume a certain product nonetheless bears part of the cost of its production. Pollution is an example of a negative externality. Suppose that the air and water pollution emitted by the Paragon Paper factory affects a wide geographic area. If Paragon Paper is not held responsible for the costs of any negative health and environmental problems caused by this pollution, the price of the factory's goods is not an accurate measure of their entire cost. Instead, part of the cost—the externality cost of pollution—is "paid" by the people living near the Paragon Paper factory, rather than by the company and the consumers who buy Paragon's goods. In such situations the price system fails to

MARKETS & PRICES *The benefits of this home security system extend to nearby neighbors even though they did not pay for it.* **What positive externalities are you aware of in your community?**

assign the entire cost of production to the producers and consumers of the products.

A positive externality exists when someone who does not sell or buy a certain product nonetheless benefits from its production. For example, imagine that many workers eat lunch at The Hard Hat, a restaurant near the Paragon Paper factory. The Hard Hat's location allows it to benefit from the factory's production, even though it does not consume the factory's goods. The restaurant pays no part of the production cost, even though it benefits from that production. Instead, the Paragon Paper factory and consumers who buy the factory's goods bear the entire cost. In such situations the price system fails to assign the entire cost of production to all those who benefit from that production.

Public Goods The price system also fails to assign the cost of public goods to all consumers. A **public good** is any good or service that is

Law enforcement is one example of a public good. **How can public goods be market failures?**

consumed by all members of a group. Public goods include national defense, the judicial system, and law enforcement. If the government did not force people to pay for these goods and services through taxes, some of those who benefit from them would be unwilling to pay.

For example, if paying for U.S. national defense were voluntary, some citizens would choose not to pay. Yet as soon as the government supplied this service to the paying citizens, everyone in the United States would benefit from, or consume, the service. Suppose that a foreign nation attacked the United States, and U.S. armed forces stopped the invasion. All U.S. citizens—even those who had not contributed to the national defense budget—would benefit. In these situations the price system does not fairly distribute the cost of public goods.

Instability Although the price system's ability to adapt to change is generally considered a benefit, this flexibility can make the system somewhat unstable. As the system reacts to severe weather, natural disasters, worker protests, and other events, prices can swing quickly between extremes. A drastic drop in prices might cause some companies to go out of business. A tremendous price increase may make a certain necessity so expensive that most people cannot afford it. Even less dramatic price swings can prevent the market from functioning smoothly, because producers and consumers cannot rely on stable prices when making business or purchasing decisions.

SECTION 1 — REVIEW

1. Define the following terms: market failure, externality, public good.

2. How do prices coordinate the decisions of producers and consumers?

3. How is each of the five main benefits of the price system evident in a grocery store?

4. Give one example not mentioned in the text of each of the following: negative externality, positive externality, public good.

5. **Thinking and Writing Critically** Suppose that you go to the grocery store and none of the products have prices listed. How would you decide what—and how much—to buy? Explain your answer.

6. **Applying** MARKETS & PRICES Suppose that floods damage crops in the Mississippi River valley. How does the price system respond to the damaged harvest? Does this response reflect a benefit or a liability of the price system? Explain your answer.

SECTION 2

DETERMINING PRICES

Economics Dictionary
market equilibrium
surplus
shortage

Objectives
▶ What is market equilibrium?
▶ How does the price system handle product surpluses and shortages?
▶ How do shifts in demand and supply affect market equilibrium?

I f the price system is a type of unspoken language, how can you see—as well as feel—its influence on the decisions made by producers and consumers? You can see the price system at work most clearly in how it determines the amounts and prices of goods and services available in the marketplace.

Equilibrium

The price system helps producers and consumers reach **market equilibrium**, a situation that occurs when the quantity supplied and the quantity demanded for a product are equal at the same price. At this equilibrium point the needs of both producers and consumers are satisfied, and the forces of supply and demand are in balance. When a market reaches its equilibrium point, producers and consumers have communicated effectively.

You can see the equilibrium point for a product by plotting its demand and supply curves on the same graph. Examine Figure 5.1. The table on the left shows the demand and supply schedules for tennis shoes. The graph on the right plots this information in a demand curve (D_1) and a

DEMAND AND SUPPLY SCHEDULE FOR TENNIS SHOES

Price per Pair of Tennis Shoes	Quantity Demanded	Quantity Supplied
$15	180,000	0
$30	150,000	30,000
$45	120,000	60,000
$60	90,000	90,000
$75	60,000	120,000
$90	30,000	150,000
$105	0	180,000

EQUILIBRIUM PRICE FOR TENNIS SHOES

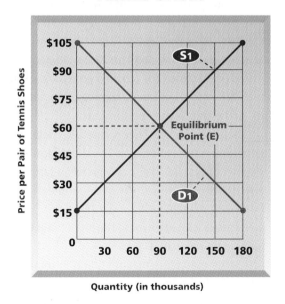

Quantity (in thousands)

FIGURE 5.1 Market equilibrium occurs when the quantity supplied and the quantity demanded for a product are equal at the same price. **How does the price system steer producers and consumers toward the equilibrium point?**

supply curve (S₁). The vertical axis lists the possible prices for a pair of tennis shoes. The horizontal axis lists the quantities that could be demanded and supplied.

The point at which these two curves intersect (point E) is the market equilibrium for tennis shoes. Equilibrium exists at a price of $60 and a quantity of 90,000 pairs of shoes.

How does the price system actually steer producers and consumers toward the equilibrium point? The process does not take place instantly. In fact, a certain amount of trial and error may be necessary, as producers change prices and quantities of the goods and services supplied. This adjustment process works to eliminate surpluses and shortages—situations in which the forces of

Careers

in Economics

RESEARCHER CD-ROM

Sales Manager

Suppose that your family is planning to go on vacation, and you need to earn spending money. You apply for a retail sales position at a department store in the mall. To prepare for your interview, you research the store and the role of the person who may be your supervisor.

What is a sales manager's job? A sales manager identifies applicants who seem likely to be effective salespeople and then teaches them about store and company policies. Additionally, the sales manager determines demand and establishes sales goals. How hot are in-line skates? How many pairs should salespeople sell every week? Once these sales goals are defined, the sales manager must supervise the salespeople and evaluate their performance.

Sales managers need specific skills. They generally have experience in sales. However, a manager must be able to assign tasks rather than attempting to "outsell" the salespeople. An effective sales manager also must be able to explain sales goals while providing the leadership needed to meet these goals.

Sales managers may be found in many businesses. For example, the sales manager for Sony or Panasonic may supervise sales of television sets and stereos to department stores. At the same time, the sales manager for a department store such as Sears or J.C. Penney oversees the retail sales clerks who sell the televisions and stereos to consumers.

Stores and companies need sales managers to analyze market demand, establish realistic objectives, and hire and train people to meet sales goals. Without these managers, a company might ignore potentially profitable consumers because of a lack of attention to the market and demand.

Sales managers are responsible for determining demand, teaching sales staff, and establishing sales goals.

SURPLUS AND SHORTAGE OF TENNIS SHOES

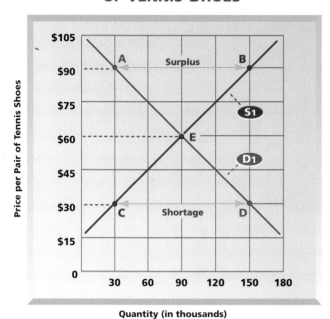

Price per Pair of Tennis Shoes

$105
$90
$75
$60
$45
$30
$15
0

A   Surplus   B
                S1
        E
                D1
C   Shortage   D

30   60   90   120   150   180

Quantity (in thousands)

FIGURE 5.2 The process of price determination may involve a period of trial and error. **What are the consequences of charging a price that is too high or too low for a product?**

supply and demand are not in balance and the market has not reached equilibrium.

Surpluses

A **surplus** exists when the quantity supplied exceeds the quantity demanded at the price offered. You can see an example of a surplus in Figure 5.2. Points A and B demonstrate what happens if producers decide to charge $90 for the shoes. At this price producers are willing to supply 150,000 pairs of tennis shoes (point B). The quantity demanded at this price, however, is lower than 150,000 pairs. At a price of $90, consumers are willing and able to buy only 30,000 pairs of shoes (point A). The result is a surplus of 120,000 pairs (150,000 – 30,000 = 120,000).

The surplus tells producers that they are charging too much for their shoes. After re-examining costs, producers decide they can lower their price and still make a profit. The lower price increases the quantity demanded and decreases the quantity supplied, eliminating the surplus and steering the market toward equilibrium (point E).

Shortages

A **shortage** exists when the quantity demanded exceeds the quantity supplied at the price offered. An example of a shortage appears in Figure 5.2. Points C and D show what happens if producers decide to charge only $30 for their shoes. At this price they are willing to produce 30,000 pairs of tennis shoes (point C). The quantity demanded at this price, however, is greater than 30,000 pairs. At a price of $30, consumers are willing and able to buy as many as 150,000 pairs of shoes (point D). The result is a shortage of 120,000 pairs (150,000 – 30,000 = 120,000).

How do producers react to this situation? The shortage tells them that they are charging too little for the shoes. They decide to raise the price. The higher price decreases the quantity demanded and increases the quantity supplied, eliminating the shortage and steering the market toward equilibrium (point E).

CASE STUDY

Mighty Morphin Power Rangers®

MARKETS & PRICES Every year as the holidays approach, toy manufacturers hope that they have developed the year's hot new product. Will their market research pay off? Will children around the world

MARKETS & PRICES *The price system steers producers and consumers toward market equilibrium.* **How might a bookstore react to a surplus of books?**

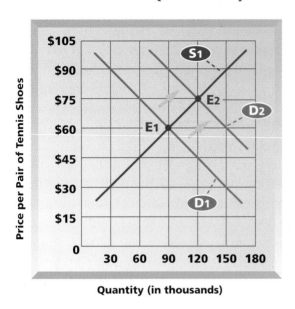
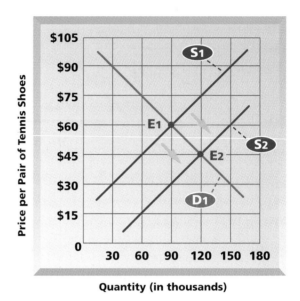

FIGURE 5.3 Many factors can shift a product's demand or supply curve. **What happens to the equilibrium point when either the demand or supply curve shifts?**

convince their parents to buy the company's new doll or game?

Sometimes this dream comes true far beyond the manufacturer's expectations. For example, the children's television show *Mighty Morphin Power Rangers* became so popular that consumers were frantic to purchase the merchandise inspired by the program. In fact, beginning in 1993, stores found themselves sold out of action figures, books, plastic swords, and other items sporting the Power Rangers logo. Consumers bought merchandise faster than the stores could stock it, leading to a dramatic shortage. Parents bought Power Rangers toys from other consumers at prices much higher than those set by stores. In some cases, a consumer who had purchased a Power Rangers item in a toy store for $10 would sell it to a desperate parent for $65. Sometimes people camped outside of stores, hoping to be the first customers when the doors opened.

The enthusiasm for Power Rangers merchandise was accompanied by controversy, however. Many people felt that *Mighty Morphin Power Rangers* contained too much violence for a television program aimed at children. In 1995, for example, officials in Germany announced that the program would no longer be aired on weekday mornings in that country, even though it was the nation's most popular children's show.

Despite this opposition, the popularity of the show and its related merchandise continued to grow. At one point, 57 percent of 6- to 11-year-olds in the United States watched *Mighty Morphin Power Rangers*. A 1995 Power Rangers movie led to even higher sales—and continuing shortages—of Power Rangers merchandise.

Shortages—and surpluses—occur throughout the marketplace. The price system steers all producers and consumers toward market equilibrium by responding to demand and supply imbalances.

Shifts in Equilibrium

As noted in Chapters 3 and 4, a variety of factors can shift a product's entire demand or supply curve to the right or left. Changes in consumer tastes and preferences, market size, income, prices of related goods, and consumer expectations can all shift the demand curve. Similarly, changes in government actions, technology, competition, producer expectations, and the prices of resources and related goods can all shift the supply curve. When either the demand or the supply curve shifts, the equilibrium point also shifts to the new intersection of the curves.

You can see an equilibrium shift in Figure 5.3. The graph on the left shows the results of a shift in demand for tennis shoes. Suppose that the tennis championship at Wimbledon is won by a new teenaged athlete. As a result of publicity for the sport, consumer preference for tennis shoes increases. Consumers now are willing to buy more tennis shoes at every possible price, so the demand curve shifts to the right from D_1 to D_2.

What happens to the equilibrium point? It moves from point E_1 on the old demand curve to point E_2 on the new demand curve. The new equilibrium price is $75, and the new equilibrium quantity is 120,000 pairs of shoes.

The graph on the right, however, shows the results of a shift in supply for tennis shoes. Suppose that many firms install new machinery in their factories. The new technology speeds up production and allows the companies to supply more shoes to the market at each and every price. As a result, the supply curve shifts from S_1 to S_2.

What happens to the equilibrium point? It moves from point E_1 on the old supply curve to

MARKETS & PRICES *During the 1996 holiday season, enormous demand for the Tickle Me Elmo™ doll caused widespread shortages.* **What were the likely results of this shortage?**

point E_2 on the new supply curve. The new equilibrium price is $45, and the new equilibrium quantity is 120,000 pairs of shoes. The quantity of tennis shoes demanded and the quantity supplied are once again equal at the same price.

SECTION 2 — REVIEW

1. Define the following terms: market equilibrium, surplus, shortage.

2. When is a market in equilibrium?

3. How does the price system respond to surpluses and shortages?

4. How do shifts in the supply and demand curves affect market equilibrium? Explain your answer.

5. **Thinking and Writing Critically** What would happen to both consumers and producers if a company did not change its product's price when faced with a surplus? when faced with a shortage?

6. **Applying** **MARKETS & PRICES** Explain what happens to the equilibrium point for pumpkins in September, October, and November. You may want to sketch a series of graphs to help determine the answer.

SECTION 3

MANAGING PRICES

Economics Dictionary

price ceiling
price floor
minimum wage
rationing
black market

Objectives

▶ Why do governments sometimes set prices?

▶ What do governments try to accomplish through price floors, price ceilings, and rationing?

▶ What happens when governments manage prices?

As noted in Section 1, the price system has a number of limitations. The price system does not accurately assign, or determine who should pay, the costs of externalities like pollution. Nor does it accurately distribute the costs and benefits of public goods like national defense. In addition, the system's occasional instability can complicate the attempts of producers and consumers to predict prices and plan for the future.

To address these limitations, governments sometimes become involved in the marketplace. Just as governments assign the costs of public goods, governments also can choose to assign the costs of externalities—for example, by making companies reduce the amount of pollution they emit and pay for any damage caused by that pollution. To keep the market functioning smoothly and to avoid instability caused by dramatic price swings, governments at times may choose to set prices and ration goods.

Setting Prices

Governments sometimes set prices to protect producers and consumers from dramatic price swings. They accomplish this through price ceilings and price floors.

Price Ceilings A **price ceiling** is a government regulation that establishes a maximum price for a particular good. Producers cannot charge prices above this set level.

Consider rent control, for example. Suppose that the city of New Populous is experiencing a population boom. So many people want to live in the city that prices for apartments and other rental properties have skyrocketed. As a result, many people who work in New Populous cannot afford to rent apartments or houses in town, near their jobs. Such a situation results from the forces of supply and demand. The high demand for the limited supply of New Populous rental properties drives up rents as consumers compete with one another by paying higher prices (rent).

Like many other communities, however, New Populous feels that affordable housing is an important priority. Therefore, to ensure that its citizens can afford to live in the city, the New Populous city council decides to intervene in the

MARKETS & PRICES *Rent control is one example of a price ceiling.* **Why do governments sometimes set prices?**

PRICE CEILING AND SHORTAGE

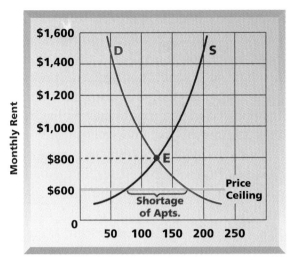

Quantity of Apartments (in thousands)

FIGURE 5.4 Price ceilings are governmental regulations that set the maximum legal price for a particular product. **How does this graph illustrate the consequences of setting price ceilings?**

market by setting a price ceiling on rents for apartments within city limits.

Price Floors Price floors are more common than price ceilings. A **price floor** is a government regulation that establishes a minimum level for prices.

In certain situations the government sets price floors for agricultural products. Suppose that good weather results in an unusually large corn crop. The huge supply drives the price of corn so low that farmers cannot make enough money to pay their bills, let alone make a profit. Many farmers face losing their land. To prevent this from happening, the government sets a base price for corn that will guarantee farmers a minimum level of income.

The **minimum wage** is another example of a price floor. Established by federal law, this wage is the lowest amount an employer legally can pay a worker for a job. In some types of work the number of workers exceeds the number of available jobs. As workers compete for jobs, they are willing to accept increasingly lower wages. Wages may fall so low that many people cannot

earn enough money on which to live. To help prevent this from happening, the government sets a minimum wage, ensuring workers a certain level of income.

Consequences of Setting Prices

Most economists advise against the use of price ceilings and price floors. Interfering in the normal interaction between supply and demand can cause unintended imbalances and can prevent markets from reaching equilibrium. Price ceilings tend to result in shortages, while price floors tend to result in surpluses. Think again about some of the examples already discussed.

The government of New Populous hopes that rent control—a price ceiling—will result in affordable housing. The government sets the price of a two-bedroom apartment at $600 per month, while the equilibrium price is $800 (see Figure 5.4). Unfortunately, by keeping rents artificially low, rent controls tend to shrink the supply of rental properties. Notice that a price ceiling of $600 creates a shortage of 100,000 (175,000 − 75,000 = 100,000) apartments. How does this happen?

MARKETS & PRICES *Minimum-wage jobs ensure workers a certain level of income.* ***What form of government price setting does this exemplify?***

PRICE FLOOR AND SURPLUS

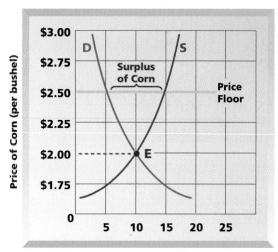

FIGURE 5.5 Price floors set the minimum legal price for a particular product. **What reasons might a government have for establishing price floors?**

Remember that the law of supply explains that higher prices encourage increases in the quantity supplied, while lower prices encourage reductions in the quantity supplied. By lowering prices, and therefore the potential profits that landlords can make on their properties, rent control programs discourage landlords from building new rental units. Likewise, landlords are less willing to invest money in repairing existing rent-controlled properties because they cannot increase rents to cover these expenses.

Thus, instead of increasing the quantity of affordable housing supplied, over time rent controls actually tend to decrease the quantity supplied. Because landlords cannot change prices according to their costs and in response to demand, the market does not reach equilibrium.

Now think again about the government's corn-pricing policy. As shown in Figure 5.5, a price floor of $2.50 per bushel encourages farmers to maintain a high level of corn production. Even when the market is flooded with surplus corn, farmers know that the price floor guarantees them a minimum income. By sending incorrect signals to farmers, the artificially high prices prevent the market from reaching equilibrium.

Rationing

Sometimes the supply of a good is so low that a government rations the good. **Rationing** is a system in which a government or other institution decides how to distribute a product. Under a rationing system, a product is distributed on the basis of policy decisions rather than on the basis of prices determined by supply and demand.

Rationing does not often occur in a free-enterprise system. In the United States, rationing has occurred mainly during wars and other crises. During World War II, for example, the U.S. government rationed many goods, such as tires, gasoline, meat, butter, and coffee. To coordinate its rationing efforts, the government distributed books of coupons that allowed citizens to buy specific amounts of rationed goods.

A national crisis is not the only time rationing occurs. Consider college sports tickets. Often the number of people who want to see a college team's games is greater than the number of tickets available. Under the price system, this shortage would be eliminated as the excess quantity demanded drove up prices. Fewer fans would be willing to pay the higher prices, and the quantity demanded would decrease.

Most colleges, however, believe that students and alumni should have priority over the general public when buying tickets for home games. To make sure that affordable tickets are available to

MARKETS & PRICES *During the 1970s, oil shortages in the United States forced gasoline rationing. **What current examples of rationing can you identify?***

these groups, colleges usually ration by setting aside tickets for alumni and for students.

Consequences of Rationing

Many people feel that rationing is an unwise economic policy. Critics charge that the system

▶ is unfair,
▶ is expensive, and
▶ creates black markets.

Unfairness One criticism of rationing is that it distributes goods and services unfairly. In the case of college sports tickets, for example, many people in the general public believe they have as much right to attend a team's games as do alumni and students. By rationing tickets, the college is giving both students and alumni special treatment over the general public.

Critics of rationing point out that the price system does not favor any one person or group over another. Prices are neutral because all consumers are treated equally. If the college tickets were distributed under the forces of supply and demand instead of under rationing, students, alumni, and the general public all would have an equal chance to buy tickets.

Cost Another criticism of rationing is that it is costly to put into effect. Colleges devote employees' work hours to carrying out and tracking the ticket rationing. Likewise, a government must not only determine who is to receive rationed goods and in what amounts but also must print and distribute ration coupons. In addition, a method of enforcing the rationing program must be developed to ensure that people do not receive more rationed goods than they should. These tasks can use significant amounts of human resources and financial capital.

Unlike rationing, the price system has no such administrative costs. When prices are determined by the normal interaction of supply and demand, governments and other institutions do not have to spend time and resources managing the distribution of goods and services.

Global Exchange

International Bargain Hunters

Many Japanese vacationers in the United States spend much of their time—and a third of their travel budget—on shopping. Prices in the United States often are dramatically lower than in Japan, allowing Japanese travelers to buy items that would be less affordable at home.

Many items that tourists buy—including electronic equipment, designer clothing, and jewelry—are purchased as gifts for family members. Some tourists, however, pay for their trip by selling the items that they have purchased overseas.

How dramatic are the price differences between the United States and Japan? In 1993 a pound of rice in Japan cost more than twice as much as in the United States. In Tokyo a tube of lipstick cost five times more than in New York.

Even though downturns in the Japanese economy during the mid-1990s lowered prices on goods, many of these prices would seem high to U.S. consumers. For example, in 1997 a movie ticket might cost $24 in Japan, and a bunch of grapes might cost as much as $30.

Some retailers have tried to lower prices in Japan. For example, Kou's—a discount warehouse—provides bulk products in the style of Price Club in the United States. U.S. producers such as the Gap and Eddie Bauer sell goods in Japan at prices lower than those offered by Japanese retailers.

Prices still remain high for many consumer goods in Japan. For many, overseas shopping may continue to offer bargains.

Ticket scalpers represent the black market that can be created by rationing. **What are other possible consequences of rationing?**

Black Markets The third problem with rationing is that it tends to encourage **black markets**, in which goods are exchanged illegally at prices that are higher than officially established prices. Rationing encourages black markets because it succeeds in distributing goods among consumers, but does not completely satisfy consumer demand.

After the college rations its tickets, for example, the quantity demanded remains high. Instead of allowing all consumers to compete for the tickets—which would drive up ticket prices and reduce the quantity demanded—the rationing program keeps prices artificially low. The high quantity demanded means that many people—including students and alumni—remain willing and able to buy tickets. Black markets have developed to meet this remaining demand.

At a sold-out football game, for example, the black market takes the form of people outside the gates offering to sell tickets—at prices higher than those set by the college. These black marketers, who buy rationed tickets from students and alumni who decide not to use them, sell them to the general public for a profit.

What is wrong with black markets? First, black markets are unfair. For example, if you buy a ticket from a black marketer, you may pay a great deal more than someone who bought a rationed ticket. Is it fair for you to pay so much more for the same good?

Black markets also pose other problems for consumers. If, for instance, the ticket you bought turns out to be fake, you probably cannot get your money back. Additionally, many governments outlaw black market activity because it defeats the very purpose of a rationing program—determining which consumers receive how much of a good.

SECTION 3 — REVIEW

1. Define the following terms: price ceiling, price floor, minimum wage, rationing, black market.

2. Why might the government place a $1 price ceiling on a gallon of milk? Why might it place a $5 price floor on a bushel of wheat?

3. What are the probable results of both the price ceiling and the price floor in question 2?

4. Under what circumstances do governments use rationing programs? What consequences do these programs have?

5. **Thinking and Writing Critically** Should the government try to manage prices in some situations? Why or why not? Give at least one example not used in the book to support your answer.

6. **Applying** MARKETS & PRICES Suppose that you have a part-time job, and the government announces a decision to eliminate the minimum wage. Describe how your income might be affected by the removal of this price floor. How would you respond to any changes in your income?

SECTION 1 In a free-enterprise market, prices are the main form of communication. They guide producers and consumers to reach efficient compromises on production levels of goods and services.

The price system has several benefits. It provides producers and consumers with information about, as well as incentives to participate in, the marketplace. The price system also increases the number of choices available in markets and promotes the efficient use of resources. In addition, the price system is flexible enough to deal with sudden changes in supply and demand.

The price system does have limitations, however. It does not accurately assign the costs of externalities like pollution. Nor does it accurately distribute the costs and benefits of public goods like national defense. In addition, the system's occasional instability can make it difficult for producers and consumers to predict prices and plan for the future.

SECTION 2 The price system coordinates production decisions by steering producers and consumers toward market equilibrium. Market equilibrium occurs when the quantity supplied and the quantity demanded for a product are equal at the same price, meeting the needs of both producers and consumers.

To reach market equilibrium, producers must avoid surpluses and shortages frequently through a process of trial and error. A surplus occurs when the quantity supplied is greater than the quantity demanded at a particular price. A shortage, on the other hand, occurs when the quantity demanded exceeds the quantity supplied at a given price.

A shift in either the demand or the supply curve can change a market's equilibrium point. These shifts may be the result of changes in consumer tastes and preferences, market size, income, prices of related goods, and consumer expectations. Changes in equilibrium may also stem from changes in government actions, technology, competition, producer expectations, and the prices of resources and related goods.

SECTION 3 The price system's limitations sometimes lead governments to intervene in the market. Governments may set prices by establishing price ceilings and price floors that are intended to protect producers and consumers from dramatic price swings. A price ceiling establishes a maximum price for a good or service, and a price floor establishes a minimum price.

Governments and other institutions also may ration goods that are in extremely short supply. Managing prices through price ceilings, price floors, and rationing interferes with the normal interaction between supply and demand, however, and can maintain or even worsen market imbalances. Additionally, many people feel that rationing is an unwise policy because it gives special treatment to some groups, is expensive, and encourages illegal sales through black markets.

Economics Notebook

Review what you wrote in your Economics Notebook at the beginning of this chapter about prices for items you have purchased recently and what those prices told you about the products. Now that you have studied this chapter, would you change your description of what you learned from the prices? Why or why not? Record your answer in your Notebook.

REVIEWING CONCEPTS

1. Explain the role of the price system. Be sure to include how the price system encourages market equilibrium.

2. Describe the limitations of the price system.

3. How can a shift in demand influence a market's equilibrium point?

4. Why might a government establish a price floor on one good or service and a price ceiling on another?

5. Why might a government begin rationing items in the market?

6. What are three common criticisms of rationing programs? Explain the reasoning for each criticism.

THINKING AND WRITING CRITICALLY

1. **MARKET FAILURES** Explain why you believe that each of the following is or is not a public good: fire protection, newspaper publication, road maintenance.

2. **MARKETS & PRICES** How can an advertising campaign cause a shift in a market's equilibrium?

3. **MARKETS & PRICES** You are in charge of selling tickets to your school play. Do you establish a rationing system to ensure that each performer's family is able to attend opening night? Why or why not?

4. **MARKETS & PRICES** A severe drought leads to a poor grain harvest. As a result, consumers face higher prices for chicken at the grocery store. Draw a flowchart that shows how and why the poor grain harvest has led to higher chicken prices.

YOUR LOCAL ECONOMY

Record the price of gasoline at several gas stations in your community. Read newspaper and magazine articles to find out the average price of gasoline nationwide. Is the price in your community the same as the national average? Consider factors that might influence gasoline prices in your community, such as the amount of competition, types of fuel used locally, and the location of your community and of local gasoline stations. Create a diagram that shows how these factors influence the price of gasoline in your community.

COOPERATIVE PORTFOLIO PROJECT

Conduct a panel discussion about introducing a price floor for soybeans. Choose one member of the group to act as mediator, and divide the remainder of the group into two teams. One team should argue in favor of the price floor, while the other should argue against it. Each team should research the subject carefully to disprove opposing arguments as well as to support its own point of view. After the discussion, prepare a table that lists the key arguments presented by each team. Have the rest of the class vote on the issue to determine which team presented its information most effectively.

PRACTICING SKILLS: UNDERSTANDING CHARTS AND GRAPHS

The table on page 115 lists the quantity of motor scooters demanded at various prices, as well as the quantity of motor scooters supplied before and after the factory introduces a new, more efficient assembly line. On a separate sheet of

DEMAND AND SUPPLY FOR MOTOR SCOOTERS

Price per Motor Scooter	Quantity Demanded	Quantity Supplied Before New Assembly Line (S₁)	Quantity Supplied After New Assembly Line (S₂)
$250	600,000	0	200,000
$500	500,000	100,000	300,000
$750	400,000	200,000	400,000
$1,000	300,000	300,000	500,000
$1,250	200,000	400,000	600,000
$1,500	100,000	500,000	700,000
$1,750	0	600,000	800,000

paper, draw a graph reflecting the demand and the supply curves for motor scooters. Then answer the questions that follow.

1. How is the supply curve affected by the introduction of the new assembly line?

2. What is the equilibrium point before the new assembly line is introduced?

3. What is the equilibrium point after the new assembly line is introduced?

THE INTERNET: LEARNING ONLINE

Conduct an Internet search to find information about price ceilings, using search words such as *price ceilings* and *rent control*. Organize the information by placing it in a chart or table. Be sure to identify the communities affected by rent control, the sources of the information—such as a bill or an editorial—and a description of the contents of this information. Use this information to create a brochure that explains both the benefits and the liabilities of rent control, and present your brochure to the class.

ANALYZING PRIMARY SOURCES

"Fighting a Formidable Force"

Information about the price system can be found in many sources. The following excerpt is from a 1996 New York Times Service article about electronic piracy—the illegal production, distribution, and sale of copyrighted goods such as videos, music, and software. Read the excerpt and answer the questions that follow.

"After losing an estimated $485 million annually to Mexican pirates in recent years, U.S. music, film, and software industries have set off alarm bells about the rapidly growing business of illegal entrepreneurs. . . .

"'Mexico has become one of the biggest pirate markets in the world,' the International Intellectual Property Alliance said in a recent report. . . .

"The Washington-based Alliance, which includes U.S. film, music, and business software companies, called Mexico's enforcement record 'abysmal' [extremely poor] . . . .

"The heart of the problem is in Tepito, a tough Mexico City neighborhood that is home to one of the world's biggest bazaars for pirated videos, music cassettes and software. . . .

"In the alleyways of Tepito there is no sign of a crackdown. In dozens of open-air stalls, commerce is thriving.

"Music cassettes are a favorite product of Tepito vendors because they are easy and cheap to copy. . . .

"Gabriel Abaroa, a Mexican executive who is president of the Recording Industry Federation of Latin America, said a recent census showed that pirates sold about 66 million cassettes, for a total of more than $85 million, in the Tepito market last year. By comparison, the entire legal music industry in all of Mexico sold only 30 million cassettes."

1. Why might people choose to make and sell pirated copies of cassettes?

2. How do you think the production and sale of pirated cassettes affects the music industry?

CHAPTER 6

MARKET STRUCTURES

When you shop, you probably have noticed that there are more choices available for some products than for others. There are dozens of brands of jeans in local stores, for example, but generally only one or two cable television services are available in your area. Why are there so many more choices in jeans than in cable television services?

The choices and prices available to you as a consumer depend in large part on how product markets are structured—specifically, on how competitive the markets are. In this chapter about market structures you will learn exactly how and why market competition affects you every time you shop.

Economics Notebook

In your Economics Notebook, list five brand-name products you buy consistently. For example, when you shop for tennis shoes, is there a particular brand you always look for? Is there a certain breakfast cereal you eat most mornings?

demand, supply, or prices. Instead, levels of production and prices are set by the market forces of supply and demand.

Note that in perfect competition, the many buyers and sellers must act independently. Otherwise, a group of sellers or buyers acting together could influence—or even set—prices. Of course, when there are many sellers and buyers in a market, they are less able to act together to control prices. Having a large number of independent buyers and sellers thus promotes competition.

Identical Products Under perfect competition, sellers offer identical products, so buyers make purchasing decisions by comparing "apples to apples" rather than "apples to oranges." This means that buyers choose one product over another primarily on price, not on unique characteristics. Buyers' decisions thus give sellers accurate information about whether they are charging the best price for their products.

What would happen if buyers chose among nonidentical products? In this case, buyers' purchases would not be based on price alone, as in perfect competition. Each product's unique features would lead to a separate market, with a single firm providing that product to the market. This type of single-firm market is the basis for the market structure known as **monopoly**, in which one seller controls all production of a good or service. Monopolies will be discussed in greater detail in Section 2.

Informed Buyers Under perfect competition, buyers must be knowledgeable about products. Without accurate and readily available product information, buyers cannot compare products effectively. Sellers can compete perfectly only when buyers can make informed decisions.

Easy Market Entry and Exit For sellers to compete perfectly, they must be able to enter a profitable market—or leave an unprofitable one—easily. The freedom to switch from market to market helps ensure that a single seller or small group of sellers cannot dominate a particular market.

The ease of entering or exiting a market depends on start-up costs, the level of technical knowledge needed, and the amount of control held by existing companies in the market. If any of these factors—known as barriers to entry—are high, sellers cannot compete easily and fully.

Perfect Competition As a Model

Of course, no market is perfectly competitive. As noted above, perfect competition is a model of an ideal competitive market structure. This model helps economists analyze markets and determine how competitive they are. (See Figure 6.1.)

Some markets do approach perfect competition, however. One example is the agricultural

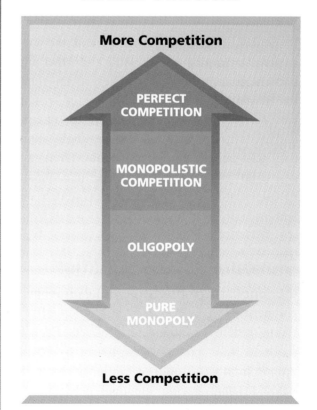

COMPETITION AND MARKET STRUCTURE

More Competition

PERFECT COMPETITION

MONOPOLISTIC COMPETITION

OLIGOPOLY

PURE MONOPOLY

Less Competition

FIGURE 6.1 Market structure is largely determined by the amount of competition among producers. **Which market structure involves the least competition?**

markets in the United States. Consider how well agricultural markets meet the four conditions of perfect competition.

First, many buyers and sellers act independently. Thousands of independent farmers and growers compete to sell their products to millions of buyers. No single buyer or seller controls enough of the market to affect the price of corn, peaches, or most other agricultural products.

Second, sellers offer identical products. Agricultural products are uniform: one apple is basically like another apple; one ear of corn is basically like another ear of corn. Buyers make their decisions based solely on the price of the apple or the corn, not on any distinguishing characteristics.

Third, buyers are well informed about the market's products. Labels on apples, for example, tell buyers the variety (McIntosh, Granny Smith, Golden Delicious), the price, the place of origin (Washington State, Michigan, Virginia), and often even how the apples were grown (organically, for example). Buyers can thus use this information to compare the price of identical products.

Fourth, sellers can enter or exit the market easily. The high price of land and other inputs prevent some potential suppliers from entering the market. But farmers who already own land can, for example, easily leave the carrot market and enter the tomato market if they believe tomatoes will become more profitable. Climate and soil conditions may restrict these decisions, but on the whole, U.S. farmers can switch easily among many agricultural markets.

Monopolistic Competition

Monopolistic competition differs from perfect competition in one key respect—sellers offer different, rather than identical, products. Each firm seeks to have monopolylike power by selling a unique product. Product variation is much more common than having identical products. As a result, monopolistic competition is much more common than perfect competition.

There are, however, similarities between the two systems. First, both buyers and sellers in

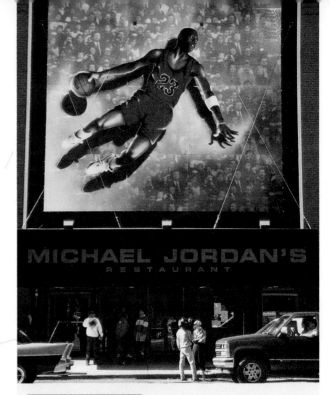

MARKETS & PRICES *This restaurant uses a famous celebrity to differentiate its product.* **What is the main goal of product differentiation?**

monopolistic competition compete under the laws of supply and demand, just as they do in perfect competition. In addition, both systems feature many buyers and sellers acting independently, buyers who are well informed about products, and ease of market entry or exit.

Product Differentiation Sellers in monopolistic competition try to **differentiate**, or point out differences, between their products and those of their competitors. By pointing out differences—which can be real or merely seem real to consumers—sellers use **product differentiation** to set their products apart.

Nonprice Competition Sellers differentiate their products through **nonprice competition**. That is, they compete on a basis other than price. Consider the jeans market, for example. Designer jeans that cost $75 and "no-name" jeans that cost $25 are basically the same product. If consumers decided which jeans to buy based solely on price, no one would buy the more expensive designer jeans. In this market, however, manufacturers have succeeded in competing on a nonprice basis. They compete through advertising and by emphasizing their brand names.

In fact, many manufacturers spend millions of dollars on advertising to persuade buyers to purchase a particular brand of jeans based on style or the brand name instead of price. Many consumers are persuaded by such advertising. They are willing to buy the more expensive jeans because they believe that the designer's brand name makes the jeans more stylish and thus more valuable.

Profits The main goal of product differentiation and nonprice competition is to increase profits. By setting its product apart from the competition and convincing buyers to base their decision on nonprice factors, a seller can raise the price of its product above the competitive level and make more profit. The seller does this by increasing demand for its product, thereby shifting the market price upward.

You can see this type of shift in demand and equilibrium price in Figure 6.2. The demand

Careers

in Economics

RESEARCHER CD-ROM

Advertising Account Manager

Who creates the attention-getting advertisements that you see on television or in your favorite magazine? One person responsible for bringing those advertisements from the drawing board to the television screen or magazine page is the advertising account manager.

Most ads are the result of a team effort by researchers, designers, and the account manager. While researchers analyze consumer needs and wants, designers develop an ad campaign that presents the product to the public. The account manager is the team captain, overseeing the campaign's development and ensuring that the client is happy with the ads.

Suppose that you are the account manager for Clinique cosmetics. You must determine what distinguishes Clinique products from other companies' cosmetics. Does the company offer makeup in a wider range of colors? Does a famous model or actress use Clinique products? As the account manager, you must persuade consumers to buy cosmetics from Clinique rather than from other companies such as Prescriptives and Max Factor.

Typically, account managers have college degrees in advertising. In addition to knowing how to produce an ad, communicate with the ad team and the client, and understand the market, an account manager must maintain a careful budget. By managing the team, market approach, and budget, an advertising account manager can create a winning campaign that ensures a successful product.

Advertising account managers organize the work of researchers and designers to meet the needs of the client.

SHIFT IN DEMAND AND EQUILIBRIUM PRICE

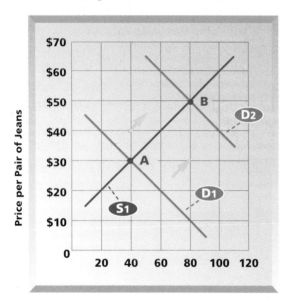

Price per Pair of Jeans

Quantity (in thousands)

FIGURE 6.2 A demand curve shift results in a new equilibrium price. **What does point B indicate about supply and demand?**

curve D_1 represents the initial demand for Jean Luc brand jeans. The equilibrium price is $30 (point A). After the company launches a successful national advertising campaign, demand for Jean Luc jeans soars. The demand curve shifts to the right (D_2) as consumers are willing and able to buy more jeans at each and every price.

The equilibrium price of Jean Luc jeans shifts upward to $50, from point A on the old demand curve (D_1) to point B on the new demand curve (D_2). Thus, although the product did not change and basically is the same as other jeans on the market, the equilibrium price is different for this brand of jeans.

Generally, by differentiating its product and creating brand-name loyalty, a seller can gain some monopolylike control over price. The seller can use nonprice competition to carve a niche, or small share, for itself in the market—a niche it can monopolize, or dominate, and from which it can profit.

Sellers realize, however, that they are still subject to the law of demand. If the maker of Jean Luc jeans increases its price too much, there will be a surplus of Jean Luc jeans. Many buyers will return to making their decisions based on price and switch to a lower-priced competitor's jeans.

SECTION 1 — REVIEW

1. Define the following terms: perfect competition, buyer, seller, monopoly, monopolistic competition, differentiate, product differentiation, nonprice competition.

2. What four conditions must exist for a market to be perfectly competitive?

3. How does monopolistic competition differ from perfect competition?

4. How do sellers in monopolistic competition compete with one another?

5. **Thinking and Writing Critically**
   Sellers try to differentiate their products in many ways. List three products that you buy. How do the manufacturers attempt to differentiate them? Is this market perfectly competitive? Explain your answer.

6. **Applying COMPETITION & MARKET STRUCTURE**
   Choose three products available for sale on the Internet. What type of competition exists for each one? Explain how each product fulfills the conditions necessary for either perfect or monopolistic competition.

SECTION 2

IMPERFECTLY COMPETITIVE MARKETS

Economics Dictionary

oligopoly

interdependent pricing

price leadership

price war

collusion

cartel

natural monopoly

economies of scale

geographic monopoly

technological monopoly

patent

copyright

government monopoly

Objectives

▶ How is an oligopoly structured?

▶ What is a monopoly?

▶ What types of monopolies exist?

▶ What factors affect price in oligopolies and monopolies?

You now know why you have such a large selection of jeans to choose from when you go shopping. The competitive structure of the jeans market encourages sellers to meet consumer demand but also encourages them to differentiate their jeans.

Not all markets, however, are structured as competitively as the jeans market. The cable television market, for example, typically has been imperfectly competitive, or even noncompetitive. In most areas of the United States, this market has been dominated by just one or two sellers.

Fewer sellers generally means fewer products and less choice for consumers like you. An imperfectly competitive structure also usually results in higher prices.

Oligopolies

The most common noncompetitive market in the United States is the **oligopoly**—a market structure in which a few large sellers control most of the production of a good or service. In general, an oligopoly exists when three conditions are present:

▶ There are only a few large sellers.
▶ Sellers offer identical or similar products.
▶ Other sellers cannot enter the market easily.

Few Large Sellers The existence of a few large sellers is the defining characteristic of an oligopoly. No other market structure has this feature. A market is considered an oligopoly when the largest three or four sellers produce most— perhaps 70 percent or more—of the market's total output.

Identical or Similar Products When there are a few large sellers, each one has a large share of the overall sales in the market. Because the sellers have so much at stake, they are less likely to take risks, such as offering new products. If a seller introduced a new product that failed, for example, that seller's share of the market—and its profits—likely would drop significantly. Thus, sellers in an oligopoly tend to offer identical or similar products.

Difficult Market Entry A few sellers can maintain their control only if other sellers cannot easily enter the market. The relative difficulty of entering an oligopolistic market depends on start-up costs, government regulation about entering the market, and consumer loyalty to the established sellers' products. If any of these factors is insignificant enough, other sellers can enter the market, compete with the original few sellers, and end those sellers' oligopoly.

COMPARING MARKET STRUCTURES

CHARACTERISTICS	PERFECT COMPETITION	MONOPOLISTIC COMPETITION	OLIGOPOLY	PURE MONOPOLY
NUMBER OF FIRMS IN EACH INDUSTRY	Many	Many	Few (Three or Four)	One
MARKET CONCENTRATION	Low	Low	High	Absolute
TYPE OF PRODUCT	Similar or Identical	Similar or Identical	Similar or Differentiated	Unique (No Substitutes)
AVAILABILITY OF INFORMATION	Much (Product Advertising)	Much (Product Advertising)	Much (Product Advertising)	Some (Product and Institutional Advertising)
ENTRY INTO INDUSTRY	Very Easy	Fairly Easy	Difficult	Prohibitive
CONTROL OVER PRICES	None	Little	Some	Complete
EXAMPLE INDUSTRIES	•Agriculture	•Telephone Companies •Airlines	•Automobiles •Breakfast Cereals	•Electric Power •Cable Television

FIGURE 6.3 Market structure involves several characteristics other than level of competition. **How do oligopolies and pure monopolies differ in terms of the availability of product information?**

Oligopolies at Work

The few sellers in an oligopolistic market have more control over prices than do the many sellers in a monopolistically competitive one. (See Figure 6.3.) This control stems mainly from legal methods of determining prices. Sometimes, however, oligopolies try to control prices through illegal means.

Nonprice Competition Like sellers in monopolistic competition, sellers in an oligopoly control prices somewhat through nonprice competition. That is, oligopolistic sellers attempt to differentiate their products through advertising and by encouraging consumers to develop loyalty to particular brand names.

Nonprice competition can become fierce among sellers in an oligopoly. Consider the market for breakfast cereals. Although a trip to the grocery store might make you think that dozens of cereal makers battle for the highest market share, three companies—Kellogg's, General Mills, and Post—account for about 80 percent of sales. The market is actually an oligopoly in which a few companies differentiate their products by creating numerous brand names.

Interdependent Pricing Sellers in an oligopoly also maintain a degree of control over price through **interdependent pricing**, or by being very responsive to—or dependent on—the pricing actions of their competitors. Interdependent pricing is particularly common in oligopolies because sellers are reluctant to risk their market share—causing them to not only offer similar products but also offer them at similar prices.

The most common form of interdependent pricing is **price leadership**, in which one of the largest sellers in the market takes the lead by setting a price for its product. If competitors also institute that price, the market leader has in effect controlled the price of all products.

What happens if the competing companies do not institute the same price as the market leader? In this case the leader has not successfully affected the price of its product. In fact, it may be forced to change its price again to be competitive with the other sellers' prices.

A failed pricing policy may spark a **price war**, in which sellers aggressively undercut each other's prices in an attempt to gain market share. Price wars can initially benefit consumers by lowering prices. Some sellers, however, can be severely hurt by price wars. If this level of competition lasts a long time, a seller may lose so much money that it is forced out of business— something that has happened to some airline carriers in the United States, for example.

When a price war ends, prices tend to rise again as oligopolistic sellers return to price leadership and nonprice competition. If one or more sellers have gone out of business, prices may rise even higher than before the price war because of reduced competition. Thus, in the long run, consumers may not benefit from severe price wars.

Collusion Nonprice competition and price leadership are legal methods of determining prices. On the other hand, **collusion**—when sellers secretly agree to set production levels or prices for their products—is illegal and carries heavy penalties such as fines and even prison sentences for those involved. Collusion tends to raise prices higher than they would be under the

International Jet Set

Have you ever dreamed of jetting off to an exotic place like Bora Bora or Sumatra? What prevents you from hopping on a plane and enjoying a relaxing getaway overseas? Chances are that such a trip is too expensive for you to take. It is for most people. That is why many wait for a price war between airline carriers before they purchase their dream vacation.

To encourage more people to take international flights, airlines sometimes reduce fares. For example, in 1995 Delta Airlines reduced fares for some of its more popular European routes. The price of a round-trip ticket from New York City to Paris dropped from $558 to $391. Similarly, the price of a trip from Atlanta to Madrid, Spain, went from $628 to $391, and a round-trip ticket from Cincinnati to Frankfurt, Germany, decreased from $658 to $447.

When one airline slashes its prices, others usually do the same to avoid losing customers. This creates a price war. To compete with Delta's reduced prices, the German airline Lufthansa dropped its fares from 10 U.S. cities to Milan, Italy; Stockholm, Sweden; Frankfurt and Düsseldorf, Germany; and Zurich, Switzerland. At the same time, Northwest Airlines and its European partner, the Dutch airline KLM, reduced fares on some of their routes.

Airlines hope that consumers will see the reduced fares as a bargain—and this is generally the case. Price wars often result in crowded travel offices and long waits on the phone as consumers try to take advantage of lower fares.

COMPETITION & MARKET STRUCTURE *South Africa's De Beers company produces a small portion of the world's diamonds, but through a cartel it controls the sale of rough gems by buying and stockpiling stones.* **Why are cartels illegal in the United States?**

competitive forces of supply and demand. This interference with competitive trade is viewed as undesirable, but the lure of higher profits may sometimes tempt companies in oligopolistic markets to set prices.

Cartels Collusion is sometimes based on an informal agreement to coordinate production decisions. In other cases, however, sellers form a **cartel**, in which companies openly organize a system of price setting and market sharing.

Cartels are illegal in the United States because they fix prices. Many other countries, however, allow the formation of cartels. Several cartels are international organizations that coordinate the production levels and prices of natural resources such as oil and diamonds. These types of goods lend themselves to being controlled by a cartel because they do not vary much—one country's oil is very much like another's. This means that sellers in the market cannot significantly

differentiate their product and thus encounter incentives to coordinate with other sellers.

Cartels often are unstable and short-lived. Members may be tempted to produce more than their agreed-upon market share in order to earn more profits. In response, the other sellers in the cartel may raise their output to protect their market share and profits. As production rises and supply increases, prices fall and competitive pressure increases among the cartel members. A price war can then break out, effectively dissolving the cartel.

Some cartels have maintained power over their markets for generations. For example, an international diamond cartel headed by South Africa's De Beers company has controlled the sale of rough diamonds around the world since the 1920s. Although De Beers directly produces only a fraction of the world's diamonds, it dominates the market, creating scarcity by buying and stockpiling stones from other producers.

Monopolies

Because a monopoly's market structure dictates that a single seller controls all production of a good or service, the conditions found in a monopoly are the opposite of those found in perfect competition. (See Figure 6.3 on page 124.) In general, a monopoly exists when three conditions are present:

▶ there is a single seller.
▶ no close substitute goods are available.
▶ other sellers cannot enter the market easily.

A Single Seller A monopoly is identifiable by the presence of only one seller. No other market structure has this feature. By establishing total control of the production of a good or service, the single seller can monopolize the market. In most regions of the United States, a single cable television company traditionally has controlled the market. Homes and businesses in a community must buy their cable television service from the single cable company because there are no other sellers in their area.

No Close Substitutes A lack of close substitute goods reinforces a single seller's monopoly over the market. As noted in Chapter 3, a substitute good is one that consumers will use to replace the purchase of a similar but higher-priced good.

In the case of a monopolistic cable television market, consumers cannot buy the service from another seller or easily substitute a similar good for it. Some households need cable to have basic television reception, including network broadcasts. Moreover, many viewers who receive network broadcasts without cable do not consider network programming to be a substitute for the hundreds of channels available on cable.

Difficult Market Entry For a single seller to maintain a monopoly, other sellers must not be able to easily enter the market. The difficulty of entering a monopolistic market depends on start-up costs and the level of technical knowledge needed. If either of these factors is low enough, other sellers can enter the market, compete with the original single seller, and end that seller's monopoly. The development of monopolies is made more difficult by government regulation.

The cable television market, for example, is hard to enter. Installing a cable system into homes—and then maintaining it—is an expensive task that requires technological expertise. In addition, government restrictions traditionally have prevented competitors from entering cable markets. Although the government is changing its regulations, most cable markets today remain monopolistic.

Types of Monopolies

How does a single seller establish a monopoly over a market? Certain conditions make it likely, and sometimes even advantageous for consumers, that a monopoly will form in a particular market. There are four main types of monopolies: natural, geographic, technological, and government. Each of these forms under different conditions.

COMPETITION & MARKET STRUCTURE *In a monopoly a single seller controls the total production of a good or service.* **What three conditions indicate the existence of a monopoly?**

Natural Monopolies In some markets, competition is inconvenient and impractical. These **natural monopolies**, feature a single large seller that produces a good or service most efficiently. Usually this seller can do so because of its **economies of scale**. That is, the seller's large scale, or size, allows it to use its human, capital, and other resources more efficiently and economically than if those resources were divided among several smaller producers.

Public and private utilities, like electric companies and cable television services, are natural monopolies. Because of the immense start-up, equipment, and maintenance costs of utilities, it would be

*In the United States, governments maintain monopolies over road construction and maintenance. **What purpose do government monopolies serve?***

inefficient for more than one seller to provide this type of service in an area. Imagine if several electric companies tried to compete in your community. Each company would have to build and maintain its own grid of electrical lines, and your street might have two or three times as many utility poles and electrical wires as it does now.

As a result, governments give utilities and other natural monopolies the exclusive right to provide certain goods or services in a specific area. The government closely regulates these monopolies, however, to ensure that they provide quality service at reasonable prices.

Geographic Monopolies

Sometimes a monopoly forms because a market's potential profit is so limited by its geographic location that only a single seller decides to enter the market. These markets are **geographic monopolies**. A general store in a remote community, for example, has a geographic monopoly on groceries and many common household items.

The number of geographic monopolies in the United States has declined in recent decades. One reason is that as people have become increasingly mobile, they can travel longer distances to shop. This means that even in rural areas more sellers can reach more buyers than

ever before. Sellers in remote areas also face competition from mail-order companies, which use telephones, fax machines, and delivery services to compete in markets that were once geographic monopolies.

Technological Monopolies

Some monopolies develop when a producer develops new technology that enables the creation of a new product or that changes the way an existing product is made. These types of markets are **technological monopolies**. General Dynamics, for example, developed the technology to build Trident submarines for the U.S. Navy. It is the only company with this technology, giving it a monopoly in the Trident submarine market.

What prevents other sellers from using General Dynamics's technology to produce Trident submarines and compete in the market? Sellers may protect the inventions or technology they develop by applying to the U.S. government for patents. A **patent** grants a company or an individual the exclusive right to produce, use, rent, and sell an invention or discovery for a limited time—17 years in the United States. In effect, a patent gives a seller a 17-year monopoly over its product.

Written works and works of art are protected in much the same way. By granting **copyrights**,

*Geographic monopolies have declined as mail-order shopping has become increasingly widespread. **How might the Internet affect geographic monopolies?***

the U.S. government gives authors, musicians, and artists exclusive rights to publish, duplicate, perform, display, and sell their creative works.

Government Monopolies
Governments often run monopolies, usually of basic necessities like public utilities. In the United States, cities and towns may monopolize water and sewer services. The federal and state governments have a monopoly over the building and maintenance of roads, bridges, and canals in the United States. Any market in which a government is the sole seller of a product is a **government monopoly**.

Government monopolies provide public goods that cannot always be supplied through the normal workings of the price system. Because these monopolies are providers of goods and services that enhance the general welfare, they usually have public support.

Monopolies at Work
The single seller in a monopolistic market has a great deal of control over prices. Think again about a cable television company. In theory, the company can dictate the price of its cable service. In practice, however, the seller in a monopoly cannot just charge any price it wants. Three forces limit the seller's control over prices: consumer demand, potential competition, and government regulation.

Consumer Demand
The first factor influencing the seller's ability to set prices is consumer demand for its product. At some point, the price of a product can become so high that the quantity demanded falls to zero. If the price of cable television, for example, were to reach $300 a month, most consumers would stop subscribing to the cable service.

Potential Competition
The second condition limiting the seller's control is potential competition. A monopolistic cable company may make enormous profits from an excessively high service price. At some point, however, these profits are high enough to attract other cable providers in the market, whereas high entry costs had kept competitors out at lower price levels.

Government Regulation
The third force affecting sellers in a monopoly is government regulation. To protect consumers from paying unnecessarily high prices, governments monitor and regulate monopolies. This regulation watches over quantity, quality, and prices of products.

SECTION 2 —REVIEW

1. Define the following terms: oligopoly, interdependent pricing, price leadership, price war, collusion, cartel, natural monopoly, economies of scale, geographic monopoly, technological monopoly, patent, copyright, government monopoly.

2. Compare the characteristics of oligopolies and monopolies.

3. What are the four main types of monopolies? Under what conditions do they tend to arise?

4. Identify the factors that affect prices in oligopolies and monopolies.

5. Thinking and Writing Critically
Why might a group of sellers feel that a cartel would offer more opportunity for profits than would a monopoly?

6. Applying COMPETITION & MARKET STRUCTURE
Identify two oligopolistic markets and describe how they exhibit the characteristics of an oligopoly.

MARKET REGULATION

Economics Dictionary

trust
laissez-faire
antitrust legislation
price discrimination

Objectives

▶ What was the relationship between the U.S. government and business before the 1880s?

▶ What was the purpose of early antitrust legislation?

▶ How has the government enforced antitrust legislation?

As noted in Section 2, in order to ensure competition and protect consumers, governments often monitor and regulate noncompetitive markets such as monopolies. In the United States, for example, the government has done so for more than 100 years.

Era of Big Business

In the decades after the Civil War ended in 1865, a wave of fierce competition swept through many U.S. markets. This competition affected the oil, steel, coal, sugar, tobacco, meatpacking, and railroad markets. Small companies were forced out of business or were taken over by larger companies. The result was an era of "big business" as huge monopolies called **trusts** dominated the marketplace.

At first the U.S. government did not interfere with the trusts. Most policy-makers at the time firmly believed in a **laissez-faire** economic philosophy. This philosophy states that economic systems prosper when the government does not interfere with the market in any way. (*Laissez-faire* is a French term meaning "let [the people] do [as they will].") Thus, the federal government initially favored leaving the market and the trusts alone.

By the 1880s, however, many people became concerned about the amount of control the trusts held over the marketplace. In response, the federal government passed a number of important laws that were intended to control unfair business practices in the United States.

Early Antitrust Legislation

The first antitrust laws passed were the Interstate Commerce Act (ICA) of 1887 and the Sherman Antitrust Act of 1890. These acts signaled a new era in the relationship between business and government. Called **antitrust legislation**, these acts were designed to monitor and regulate big business, prevent monopolies from forming, and dismantle existing monopolies. Two U.S. presidents who made "trust-busting" a priority of their administrations were Theodore Roosevelt and William Howard Taft.

Interstate Commerce Act The ICA created the Interstate Commerce Commission (ICC) in order to oversee the railroad freight business. Rates for transporting goods by train had soared under the control of trusts. Numerous complaints from farmers and merchants across the country prompted the government to act as it did. The ICC

President Theodore Roosevelt 1901–1909

President William Howard Taft 1909–1913

COMPETITION & MARKET STRUCTURE *The economic power of trusts became a concern during the late 1800s.* **How does this cartoon suggest that trusts—rather than voters—held the majority of political power as well?**

continued to regulate the railroads, along with trucks and other freight carriers, until the commission was abolished in 1995.

Sherman Antitrust Act

The Sherman Antitrust Act was more far-reaching. It banned any agreements and actions "in restraint of trade." This legislation was a milestone in the fight against trusts and set the tone of antitrust legislation for decades.

Unfortunately, the act did not clearly define what actions were or were not in restraint of trade. Because of its vague language, many trusts were able to avoid obeying the law. In fact, most of the lawsuits filed against trusts in the 1890s lost in court.

The Standard Oil Company was the best-known monopoly to be broken up as a result of the Sherman Antitrust Act. In 1870 John D. Rockefeller and his associates formed the Standard Oil Company of Ohio. By 1882 Rockefeller's group controlled almost all the U.S. oil industry through the Standard Oil Trust.

In 1911 the Supreme Court found that unlawful monopoly power existed and ordered the breakup of Standard Oil. Nevertheless, one branch of the company—Standard Oil of New Jersey—remained the largest single industrial corporation in the United States. In 1972 this company changed its name to Exxon, which is one of the largest industrial corporations in the United States and the world today.

Clayton Antitrust Act

To further define the principles in the Sherman Antitrust Act, the U.S. government passed additional antitrust legislation in the early 1900s. This period of time is sometimes called the Progressive Era because of the spirit of reform that swept through many areas of political, economic, and social life in the

United States. One such reform was the Clayton Antitrust Act, which the U.S. government passed in 1914.

This act prohibited a number of specific unfair business practices, including price setting and **price discrimination**—the practice of offering different prices to different customers under the same circumstances. Large manufacturers that buy great quantities of resources can pressure suppliers into charging them lower prices. Because this practice gives large sellers an advantage over smaller competitors, it can lead to the formation of monopolies.

Federal Trade Commission Act Another antitrust law passed in 1914 was the Federal Trade Commission Act. This act created the Federal Trade Commission (FTC) to investigate charges of unfair methods of competition and commerce. If the FTC discovers such practices, it can order a company to change its methods of doing business.

The Robinson-Patman Act With the 1936 Robinson-Patman Act, the federal government again strengthened antitrust legislation. This law reinforced the section of the Clayton Antitrust Act dealing with price discrimination.

More recent antitrust laws such as the Celler-Kefauver Act of 1950, the Antitrust and Procedures and Penalties Act of 1974, and the Parens Patriae Act of 1976 have strengthened the early antitrust legislation. For a summary of important antitrust legislation, see Figure 6.4.

Antitrust Policy in Recent Decades

The federal government must balance sellers' right to run their businesses with the need for market competition and consumer protection. To help accomplish this goal, the government has enforced the Sherman Antitrust Act and subsequent antitrust legislation.

COMPETITION & MARKET STRUCTURE *John D. Rockefeller was the founder of the Standard Oil Company of Ohio.* **Which piece of antitrust legislation was used to break up the Standard Oil Trust?**

C A S E   S T U D Y

Is Microsoft a Monopoly?

COMPETITION & MARKET STRUCTURE **In 1994 the U.S. Department of Justice filed a complaint in federal court against Microsoft Corporation, asserting that the computer software company used monopolistic practices to control its market.**

Microsoft develops and sells two kinds of software products—operating systems and applications. You probably are most familiar with applications, which come in the form of games, word-processing software, and other programs that can be purchased in retail stores. These applications, however, are useless without operating systems.

Operating systems form a sort of "central nervous system" for a computer. They tell the computers how to function and how to respond to commands from applications. Microsoft developed two very

U.S. ANTITRUST LEGISLATION

YEAR	LEGISLATION	PURPOSE
1887	Interstate Commerce Act	created the Interstate Commerce Commission (ICC) to oversee railroad rates; currently regulates railroads, motor vehicles, and other freight carriers
1890	Sherman Antitrust Act	prohibits any agreements, contracts, or conspiracies that would restrain interstate trade or cause monopolies to form
1914	Clayton Antitrust Act	clarified and strengthened the Sherman Antitrust Act by prohibiting price discrimination, local price cutting, mergers that reduce competition, and exclusive sales contracts
1914	Federal Trade Commission Act	created the Federal Trade Commission (FTC) to investigate charges of unfair methods of competition and commerce
1936	Robinson-Patman Act	(also called the Antiprice Discrimination Act) protects small retail businesses by prohibiting wholesalers from charging small retailers higher prices than they charged large retailers and by prohibiting large retailers from setting artificially low prices
1950	Celler-Kefauver Act	amended the Clayton Act to prohibit corporate acquisitions when they substantially decrease competition
1975	Antitrust Procedures and Penalties Act	increased penalties for violating antitrust laws
1976	Parens Patriae Act	gives states the right to sue companies on behalf of citizens harmed by the company's antitrust violations; requires large companies to notify the government of planned mergers; strengthened the federal government's power to investigate antitrust violations

FIGURE 6.4 The federal government has passed a number of laws designed to end or prevent monopolies. **How does the Robinson-Patman Act attempt to guarantee fair pricing policies?**

popular operating systems, called MS–DOS and Windows, and by the late 1980s had gained control of more than 70 percent of the operating-systems market.

How did Microsoft maintain control over such a large portion of the market? Generally, operating systems are sold only to manufacturers of personal computers (PCs). These hardware makers can choose to include any operating system on a PC. Microsoft, however, required hardware manufacturers that included Microsoft operating systems on *some* of their PCs to pay a fee to Microsoft for *all* of their PCs—even those that used operating systems developed by companies other than Microsoft. This type of agreement between software developers and computer manufacturers is called a "per processor" license.

Thus, a hardware maker wanting to use operating systems by both Microsoft and another company would have to pay two fees—one to the developer of the non-Microsoft system and another to Microsoft. This practice of requiring per processor licenses discouraged hardware manufacturers from using operating systems developed by companies other than Microsoft, contributing to the growth of a monopoly. Microsoft agreed to end the use of per processor licenses in 1995 after investigations by the FTC and the U.S. Department of Justice.

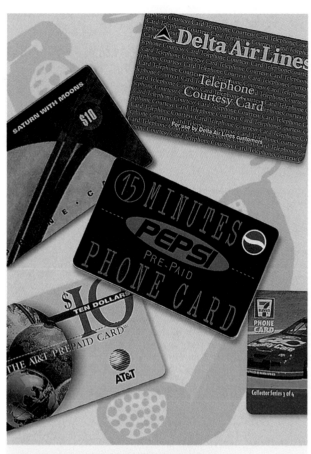

COMPETITION & MARKET STRUCTURE *In recent years, a number of companies have offered "pre-paid" phone cards to attract customers.* **How might the sale of these cards assist with product differentiation?**

Another recent example of the power of the Sherman Antitrust Act is the federal government's case against American Telephone and Telegraph (AT&T). In 1982 an antitrust decision broke up AT&T, which was the world's largest corporation and private utility. The government believed that this natural monopoly was no longer beneficial to the marketplace. New technology such as satellites and microwave-based communications had made it possible and more efficient for more than one company to provide telephone service. AT&T—sometimes called "Ma Bell"—was forced to create several independent companies, called "Baby Bells," from its local telephone service operation.

The federal government does not automatically oppose the existence or creation of large corporations, however. In fact, in 1996 the government permitted two of the Baby Bells—Pacific Telesis and SBC Communications—to combine into one company. The new company was by no means a re-creation of the AT&T monopoly, and the government did not believe the merger would pose a threat to competition in the marketplace. The creation of this new company encouraged a similar merger between Bell Atlantic and NYNEX, two other Baby Bells.

SECTION 3 — REVIEW

1. Define the following terms: trust, laissez-faire, antitrust legislation, price discrimination.

2. How did the relationship between government and business change in the late 1800s?

3. Why did the federal government pass the Sherman Antitrust Act and other antitrust legislation?

4. In what ways has the government attempted to ensure fair prices?

5. Why did the federal government end AT&T's monopoly on telephone service?

6. **Thinking and Writing Critically** What monopolies exist in your school? Consider how lunches, yearbooks, and other products are sold at your school.

7. **Applying** ECONOMIC INSTITUTIONS & INCENTIVES Identify three ways in which antitrust legislation might protect your or your family's economic interests.

SECTION 1 As a consumer, you tend to benefit most from highly competitive markets. These types of markets provide consumers with a range of products that are priced fairly and that reflect costs accurately. The forces of supply and demand promote competition by encouraging producers to supply consumers with a wide selection of goods and services.

Perfect competition is an ideal market structure in which buyers and sellers compete directly and fully under the laws of supply and demand. In general, perfect competition exists when four conditions are present: there are many buyers and sellers acting independently, sellers offer identical products, buyers are well informed about products, and sellers can enter or exit the market easily.

Monopolistic competition is much more common than perfect competition and differs from it in one important respect—sellers offer slightly different, rather than identical, products. In monopolistic competition, sellers exert some control over prices by differentiating their products through nonprice competition.

SECTION 2 In imperfectly competitive markets fewer sellers offer fewer products and usually at higher prices. The most common of these markets in the United States is the oligopoly. In oligopolies a few large sellers control most of the production of a good or service through nonprice competition and interdependent pricing. In general, an oligopoly exists when three conditions are present: there are only a few large sellers, sellers offer identical or similar goods and services, and other sellers cannot enter the market easily. Sellers in an oligopolistic market have more control over prices than do sellers in a monopolistically competitive market.

In monopolies a single seller controls the total production of a good or service. In general, a monopoly exists when three conditions are present: there is a single seller, no close substitute goods are available, and other sellers cannot enter the market easily. There are four main types of monopolies: natural, geographic, technological, and government. A single seller in a monopolistic market has a great deal of control over prices. However, this control over prices is limited somewhat by the forces of consumer demand, competition, and regulation.

SECTION 3 In the United States in the late 1800s, there existed an era of big business in which huge monopolies called trusts dominated the marketplace. In response to people's concerns about the control these trusts held, the U.S. government departed from its laissez-faire policy and passed several laws to protect consumers and ensure market competition. The Sherman Antitrust Act—later strengthened by the Clayton Antitrust Act—is the foundation of U.S. antitrust legislation. This act and subsequent legislation prohibit restraint of trade, the formation of monopolies, and unfair business practices such as price setting and price discrimination.

Economics Notebook

Review the products you listed in your Economics Notebook at the beginning of this chapter. Now that you have studied market structures, can you explain why you are "loyal" to these brand names? What nonprice factors persuade you to buy these products? Record your answers in your Notebook.

REVIEW

REVIEWING CONCEPTS

1. What is the purpose of product differentiation? How do sellers differentiate their products?

2. How are oligopolies different from monopolies?

3. How does a cartel operate? Why are cartels illegal in the United States?

4. How do oligopolies and monopolies affect product choice and price?

5. What factors encouraged the U.S. government to abandon its laissez-faire economic policies in the 1880s?

6. How did the government work to ensure competition and fair prices in the late 1800s and early 1900s?

THINKING AND WRITING CRITICALLY

1. **COMPETITION & MARKET STRUCTURE** Select a market in your community, such as movie theaters or shoe stores. How closely do these markets meet the conditions of perfect competition? Explain your answer.

2. **COMPETITION & MARKET STRUCTURE** Determine which of the following are examples of non-price competition: using a celebrity spokesperson, issuing discount coupons, holding a storewide sale, promoting product brand names.

3. **COMPETITION & MARKET STRUCTURE** Provide one example not listed in the chapter for each of the following: natural monopoly, geographic monopoly, technological monopoly, government monopoly. Explain how each example displays the characteristics of the corresponding monopoly.

4. **COMPETITION & MARKET STRUCTURE** Would you expect monopolies to develop as the result of competition or a lack of competition? Explain your answer, and then compare your response with the way in which monopolies developed after the Civil War.

YOUR LOCAL ECONOMY

Investigate product competition in a local grocery store by surveying the choices available for a specific type of product. Choose a product with many brands. Note the names of the brands, the companies that make them, the prices, the size or weight, the major ingredients, and the advertising claims on the packaging.

Present this information in a chart that includes an extended caption analyzing competition in this product's market. You should address the following questions: How many companies are really competing in this market—do the number of brands equal the number of companies? How are companies differentiating their products? Are these differences real or perceived?

INDIVIDUAL PORTFOLIO PROJECT

Create a puzzle of advertising slogans, such as a crossword or word search. Write down any advertising slogans—from magazines, newspapers, or television—that you think succeed in differentiating the product. (If the slogan makes you think of a particular brand name, it is probably successful in differentiating the product.) Use these slogans in your puzzle. For example, if the slogan is Nike's "Just do it. ™," a crossword clue might be "What product wants you to just do it?" Exchange puzzles with a classmate. Did the slogans you selected differentiate the products enough for your classmate to solve the puzzle?

Editorial cartoons have been used for hundreds of years to influence public opinion about a variety of topics. Using the guidelines that are described below the cartoon, write a brief paragraph explaining the significance and meaning of the cartoon.

How Much Higher Can the Poor Consumer Go?
CHORUS OF COAL MONOPOLISTS.—Hurry up and jump ↑ver, 'cos we want to put her up another peg!

1. Read the labels and captions and identify any symbols.

2. Determine what action is taking place. What is the significance of this action?

3. What overall message is the cartoonist trying to convey?

THE INTERNET: LEARNING ONLINE

Conduct an Internet search for a good or service provided by many producers. Start with search words such as the specific name of the product and the general type of good or service. Write a paragraph describing your findings, and explain how the Internet promotes monopolistic competition.

The Growth of the Standard Oil Company

Ida Tarbell was one of a small group of journalists that President Theodore Roosevelt called "muckrakers" because of their writing about the social evils and injustices of the time. The following excerpt is from a series of articles Tarbell wrote denouncing the business practices of John D. Rockefeller's Standard Oil Company at the turn of the century.

"The profits of the present Standard Oil Company are enormous. For five years the dividends have been averaging about $45 million a year. . . .

"Consider what must be done with the greater part of this $45 million. It must be invested. The oil business does not demand it. There is plenty of reserve for all of its ventures. It must go into other industries. Naturally, the interests sought will be allied to oil. They will be gas, and we have the Standard Oil crowd steadily acquiring the gas interests of the country. They will be railroads, for on transportation all industries depend, and, besides, railroads are one of the great consumers of oil products and must be kept in line as buyers. And we have the directors of the Standard Oil Company acting as directors on nearly all of the great railways of the country. . . .

"So long as it is possible for a company to own the exclusive carrier on which a great natural product depends for transportation, and to use this carrier to limit a competitor's supply or to cut off that supply entirely if the rival is offensive, and always to make him pay a higher rate than it costs the owner, it is ignorance and folly to talk about constitutional amendments limiting trusts."

1. What businesses does Tarbell suggest make up the trust known as the Standard Oil Company? Which one is the most important for sustaining the trust?

2. What kind of reaction do you think Tarbell's writing inspired in the American public?

Pricing to a "T"

Imagine that your school is planning a craft fair for next summer to raise funds to expand the school library. You and many other students have volunteered to help in the fund-raising. In fact, the fair's director has just assigned you and a group of your classmates to paint cotton T-shirts for sale at the fair. Before you decorate the shirts, however, the director needs your group to recommend a selling price that will bring in the most money for the school library project. She also wants your advice on what key points about the T-shirts to highlight in advertising flyers for the fair.

As you know, there are many factors to consider in determining the price of the shirts. To help you make your pricing and advertising decisions, the director has collected several newspaper articles and other sources of information for you to analyze. You will find these documents on the following pages.

After reviewing the documents, answer the accompanying questions in your Economics Notebook. Then work with other group members to develop a recommendation for the fund-raising director. Be sure to support your pricing and advertising decisions with clear arguments based on your document analysis. Discuss how the newspaper articles and other items influenced your decision. The recommendation should be neatly written or typed. In addition, you will need to create a sample of the advertising flyer.

John F. Kennedy High School

J
F
K

MEMO

To: T-Shirt Fund-Raising Volunteers

From: Ms. Albright, *Ms. Albright*
Fund-Raising Director

I am looking forward to hearing your pricing recommendation for the T-shirts. Please review the following price list of supplies you will need to make the T-shirts. I called several stores to find the best price on these materials, but of course, these prices could change by the time we are ready to make the shirts next summer.

I also have included two newspaper articles and an advertisement that might influence your pricing and advertising decisions. Look these materials over carefully.

Thanks for all your help. I know the fund-raising fair will be a success with you on the team. Good luck!

plain white cotton T-shirts
    $5 each if we buy fewer than 100
    $4 each if we buy 100 or more
paints (8 colors) $110
brushes $15
sequins, beads, ribbons $75
glue $10

Economics Lab

Discount Clothing Store Opens

Crazy Clothing announced that it will be opening two new stores this month within city limits. The new stores will employ 145 workers. The huge clothing discounter vows to compete fiercely for customers by slashing prices on its entire inventory. The store specializes in casual clothing, shoes, and accessories. Competition among clothing retailers is already tight, and local business owners believe a price war could break out when the new stores open.

Floods Cut Cotton Production

Some of the worst flooding of the decade has left thousands of acres of prime cotton farmland in several southern states under 10 inches of water. Heavy rain continued to batter the region over the weekend, and floodwaters are not expected to subside before Friday. Several states have asked that the flooded counties be declared federal disaster areas. As much as one fifth of the country's cotton crop may be lost. Economic analysts are already predicting that higher cotton prices will ripple throughout the clothing industry within the next month.

WHAT DO YOU THINK?

1. What impact might the floods have on the price and availability of cotton clothing? Might the prices you have to pay for your resources (plain white cotton T-shirts) change?

2. How might the clothing retailer's expansion and pricing policies affect the price you can charge for your T-shirts?

3. Will you be operating in a competitive market? If so, how can you differentiate your T-shirts from those of the competition?

Crazy Clothing... Is Coming to Town!

Attend our Grand Opening Sale!

All items in the store will be discounted 20, 40, even 60%!

- **Solid-Color Sweatshirts only $19.99!**
- **Solid-Color T-Shirts only $9.99!**
- **Sport and Other Printed T-Shirts only $15.99!**
- **Shoes, Sandals, and Boots $12.99–$39.99!**
- **Handbags only $14.99–$29.99!**

Shop from 8:00 AM to 10:00 PM Every Day!

T-Shirt Painters—

I almost forgot to give you these two tables. The one on the left is a supply schedule for the painted T-shirts. The one on the right is a demand schedule. These schedules are only preliminary, of course. I based them on the price information I collected and on a survey the school did for the fair. We asked parents and other community residents who are likely to attend the fair about what kinds of products they would like to be able to buy at the fund-raiser.

Mr. Albright

Supply Schedule

Price per T-Shirt	Quantity of T-Shirts Supplied
$24	400
$21	375
$18	325
$15	300
$12	275
$9	225
$6	175

Demand Schedule

Price per T-Shirt	Quantity of T-Shirts Demanded
$24	175
$21	225
$18	275
$15	300
$12	325
$9	375
$6	400

WHAT DO YOU THINK?

1. How many T-shirts will your group supply at $12 each? at $24?

2. How many shirts are consumers willing to buy at $6 each? at $21?

3. At what point does the market reach equilibrium?

4. Use the demand and supply schedules to graph demand and supply curves for your painted T-shirts. Label the market's equilibrium point on the graph.

5. How might the equilibrium point change between now and next summer because of nonprice factors such as resource costs?

THINGS TO DO

1. Compare group members' notes and ideas about each document you have been given to review.

2. Discuss the factors that can influence price, and determine which ones affect your particular pricing decision.

3. Discuss the competition you face from other T-shirt sellers and how you can differentiate your T-shirts.

4. Prepare a formal report with the group's recommendation on pricing and advertising. Be sure to explain the reasons for the group's decision and how the information in this Economics Lab influenced your recommendation.

5. Create a sample of the advertising flyer.

UNIT
└3

Economics Lab

How would you run your own business? Find out by reading this unit and taking the Economics Lab challenge on pages 222–25.

FREE ENTERPRISE
AT WORK

BUSINESS ORGANIZATIONS

Would you like to start your own business? For many people, owning a business provides the opportunity to make their own decisions and to earn a profit. A successful business, however, requires a great deal of work. In addition to deciding what products to provide, a businessperson must determine how that business will be organized.

Free enterprise allows business owners to select the type of organization that suits their needs. Most businesses are organized as sole proprietorships, partnerships, or corporations. This chapter describes the forms of business organization in the United States.

Economics Notebook

In your Economics Notebook, list the names of at least 10 businesses in your community. You might include restaurants, clothing alteration shops, bookstores, shoe repair shops, law firms, jewelers, department stores, and music stores.

SOLE PROPRIETORSHIPS

Economics Dictionary

sole proprietorship
zoning law
liability
collateral
longevity

Objectives

▶ What are the advantages of establishing a sole proprietorship?

▶ What are the disadvantages of establishing a sole proprietorship?

Suppose that you decide to start a weekend house-cleaning business. You must determine which type of organization will best suit your needs. If you alone will own and control the house-cleaning service, your business may be a **sole proprietorship**. A sole proprietorship is a business owned and operated by one person. The sole proprietorship is the oldest, simplest, and most common type of business organization.

What kinds of businesses are typically organized as sole proprietorships? The financial resources available to one person often are limited. As a result, sole proprietorships generally tend to be enterprises that require

small amounts of financial capital, or money, to start and operate. Many lawyers, plumbers, carpenters, hairstylists, florists, and farmers are sole proprietors. (See Figure 7.1.)

Advantages of Sole Proprietorships

Why might someone choose to organize his or her business as a sole proprietorship? There are a number of advantages to this type of business organization:

▶ ease of start-up,
▶ full control, and
▶ exclusive right to profits.

Easy Start-up The chief advantage of sole proprietorships is that they are easy to form. Sole proprietorships require fairly small amounts of financial capital and involve few legal considerations. For example, to start your house-cleaning business, you would not need to file complicated legal documents with your state or federal government.

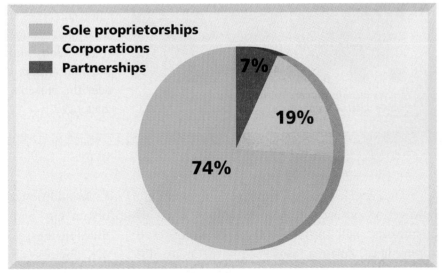

TYPES OF BUSINESS ORGANIZATIONS, 1993

- Sole proprietorships
- Corporations
- Partnerships

7%

19%

74%

Source: *Statistical Abstract of the United States: 1996*

FIGURE 7.1 Sole proprietorships are the most common type of business organization. **What percentage of businesses are established as sole proprietorships?**

Entrepreneur

If you like the idea of being your own boss, you might consider a career as an entrepreneur. Everyone from a pushcart vendor to a television station owner can be considered an entrepreneur. Some of these people have graduate degrees in business or finance, while others may never have attended college.

Successful business owners tend to be confident, creative, persistent, hardworking, and flexible. Adeena Smith and Ted Turner are two entrepreneurs who share these qualities—even though their businesses are very different.

Adeena Smith is one of a growing number of people who own specialty retail businesses. Smith's Hats Under Atlanta store in the popular

Entrepreneur Ted Turner created CNN and owns the Atlanta Braves baseball team.

Underground Atlanta Mall brought in close to $200,000 in its first year alone. However, it took considerable time, persistence, and flexibility for Smith to reach this point.

Smith sold Georgia nuts from a pushcart in the mall's thoroughfare, or main hallway. Six months later, she began selling customized caps from her pushcart. Eventually she was able to open Hats Under Atlanta.

Imagination and foresight have made Ted Turner a billionaire. Drawing on his experience running Superstation TBS, a satellite television station based in Atlanta, Turner developed a creative new format for broadcast news. In 1980 he established the Cable News Network (CNN) to broadcast news 24 hours a day. Despite a shaky start, CNN became a respected news organization as well as a profitable cable station.

Although becoming an entrepreneur can bring financial rewards, many people simply enjoy being their own boss. With this benefit, however, comes responsibility. Business owners often must endure long hours, oversee every area of operation, and risk failure. You—and other potential entrepreneurs—nevertheless may consider the possible rewards to be well worth the challenges.

Some legal and governmental restrictions, however, do affect sole proprietorships. Like all businesses, sole proprietorships must observe zoning laws. **Zoning laws** specify the areas of a city or county where various types of business activities can be pursued. For example, zoning laws in your neighborhood may not permit you to operate your business from your home.

In addition, sole proprietorships may have to obtain city and county licenses before opening their businesses. Some professionals—for example, doctors, child-care providers, and hair stylists—also must be licensed by the state.

Control A second advantage of sole proprietorships is control. While the operation of a larger firm often requires extensive paperwork or group decisions, a sole proprietor can act quickly to correct problems or take advantage of opportunities. If you want to hire more workers so that you can clean more houses, for example, you can expand your staff right away. Similarly, if few people in your neighborhood want to pay for house-cleaning services, you can reduce your staff without the complicated procedures experienced by larger firms.

This control gives sole proprietors a high degree of personal satisfaction. If your house-cleaning business succeeds, you will know that you earned that success through your own efforts—because you alone run the business. A sole proprietorship thus can be rewarding both personally and financially.

Profit Another advantage of the sole proprietorships is that the owner keeps all of the profits. In fact, for many people profit is the main reason

ECONOMIC INSTITUTIONS & INCENTIVES *Sole proprietors have the responsibility of running all aspects of their business.* **What are some other disadvantages of sole proprietorships?**

for starting a business. Will you make a fortune from your house-cleaning business? Perhaps not. In some cases, however, people who started out as small proprietors have made huge fortunes. This possibility of wealth is at the heart of the free-enterprise system.

Disadvantages of Sole Proprietorships

Although sole proprietorships have some appealing advantages, they also have several disadvantages. Sole proprietors face

▶ unlimited liability,
▶ sole responsibility,
▶ limited growth potential, and
▶ lack of longevity.

Unlimited Liability According to the law, sole proprietors personally are responsible for all business debts. This responsibility for debt is called **liability**. Suppose that you borrow money to publicize your house-cleaning business. If the publicity fails and your company cannot repay the loan, you as a sole proprietor must make the payments—even if that means selling personal

ECONOMIC INSTITUTIONS & INCENTIVES *Ninfa Laurenzo started her business as a sole proprietorship.* **What are the advantages of sole proprietorships?**

Encouraging Small Business Growth

Why would someone want to start a business? Although the amount of effort involved in forming a new business can be overwhelming, working for oneself gives people the opportunity to profit directly from their hard work. As a result, in the past few decades, an increasing number of people have opened their own small businesses.

Traditionally, the U.S. government has offered tax breaks and subsidies to small businesses because they create jobs and provide goods and services that stimulate the economy. However, some government regulations on businesses pose particular challenges for small companies.

One of these challenges involves interpreting complex federal rules and completing the accompanying paperwork. Unlike large corporations, small-business owners often do not have the funds to hire lawyers, accountants, and other personnel who can make sure their company meets federal regulations.

Without the skills of such professionals, small businesses can be less efficient than larger businesses. For example, small businesses that employ fewer than 20 people spend an average of $5,106 per employee every year to process the paperwork required by the federal government, while businesses with more than 500 employees spend an average of $3,404 per employee.

The newest companies generally suffer the most from federal regulations. For example, owners in the dry-cleaning industry have to complete up to 100 forms, obtain permits, pay high start-up fees, and follow strict reporting requirements—all before opening their doors for business.

In response to these problems, the Clinton administration designed several new programs to ease the burden of complying with federal regulations on small businesses. One program of President Clinton's first administration gave small companies a six-month grace period to correct any violations of federal environmental regulations. First-time offenders who fixed the problems within this period had their fines dismissed or reduced.

Another Clinton program implemented a "store for business" in Houston, Texas, in 1995. This pilot, or test, program sought to simplify small companies' interaction with the government. Small-business owners could go to the store—which is staffed by federal workers—for tax, regulation, and finance advice. If the pilot store in Houston succeeds, the federal government may open similar stores in other cities. The government's effort to balance economic growth with protective regulations will no doubt continue in the future.

What Do You Think?

1. What are the advantages and disadvantages of owning a small business?

2. Why does the federal government support small businesses?

3. How might the federal government slow small-business growth?

The U.S. government's store for business offers tax, regulation, and financial advice for small businesses.

property that belongs to you as an individual rather than to the business.

Sole Responsibility A second disadvantage of sole proprietorships is the owner is responsible for all aspects of running the business. What does this mean for your house cleaning business, for example? You will have to be a market analyst, advertiser, accountant, and cleaner—at least until you are able to hire others to fill some of these jobs. With so many job requirements, you will need to have skills in many different fields. Even if you hire people to fill these positions, you must check their work if the business is to be successful. These demands on your time and energy may create frustration and reduce your sense of satisfaction and accomplishment.

Limited Growth Potential A third disadvantage of sole proprietorships is the limited potential for growth. You probably will start your house cleaning business by using your savings or borrowing a small amount of money. To guarantee repayment, a bank or other lender often will require you to put up **collateral**—anything of value that a borrower agrees to give up if he or she is not able to repay a loan. Sole proprietors generally have limited collateral, which may include the business itself, supplies and unsold merchandise, and even their homes and other personal possessions.

Like other businesses, sole proprietorships need financial capital to make improvements and to expand their companies. Creditors, however, usually will not lend money that exceeds the value of the borrower's collateral. In other words, if your business and all your personal possessions are already serving as collateral for existing loans, you probably will have trouble finding more credit to expand your business. To increase your credit, you will have to increase your collateral—a difficult task if you cannot expand your business. Thus, because most owners have limited collateral, sole proprietorships often have a limited potential for growth.

Lack of Longevity A final disadvantage of sole proprietorships is lack of longevity. **Longevity** is the length of a firm's life, or the amount of time the business operates. Because sole proprietorships depend on the health, commitment, and competence of one person, they often have a shorter life span than other types of business organizations. For example, your house cleaning service may fail if you become sick or lose interest in the enterprise. Because a sole proprietorship depends on one person, the risk of failure is very great.

SECTION 1 — REVIEW

1. Define the following terms: sole proprietorship, zoning law, liability, collateral, longevity.

2. Why might a someone organize his or her business as a sole proprietorship?

3. What are the main government restrictions on sole proprietorships?

4. What challenges does a sole proprietor face?

5. **Thinking and Writing Critically**
   Think about your role as a student. How might you consider yourself a sole proprietor who is paid in grades? How are you affected by the advantages and disadvantages associated with sole proprietorships?

6. **Applying** ECONOMIC INSTITUTIONS & INCENTIVES
   If you could start your own sole proprietorship, what type of business would you choose? Explain your answer.

PARTNERSHIPS

Economics Dictionary

partnership
general partnership
limited partnership

Objectives

▶ How do general partnerships and limited partnerships differ?

▶ What are the advantages of organizing a partnership?

▶ What are the disadvantages of organizing a partnership?

You know that a sole proprietorship is a business that is owned and controlled by one person. A business that is owned and controlled by two or more people is called a **partnership**. Like sole proprietorships, partnerships are most often found in enterprises that require relatively little financial capital to start and operate.

What kinds of businesses are typically formed as partnerships? In many cases, partnerships are the same types of businesses that are formed as sole proprietorships. Doctors, lawyers, and accountants may form partnerships. Small retail stores, farms, and construction companies also may be organized as partnerships.

Forms of Partnerships

Partnerships take different forms. In a **general partnership**, partners enjoy equal decision-making authority. They also have unlimited liability. Unlimited liability means that general partners, like sole proprietors, are responsible for paying all of the business's debts and other financial losses. A general partner's personal property is therefore at risk if the business fails.

A second type of partnership is a **limited partnership**, in which partners join as investors who provide financial capital in exchange for a share of the profits, but rarely take an active role in business decisions. Additionally, their liability is limited, or confined to the amount of money they invest in the business. Unlike sole proprietors or general partners, limited partners cannot lose personal property to creditors if the business fails.

Advantages of Partnerships

Many partnerships begin as sole proprietorships. Business owners often decide to transform their sole proprietorships into partnerships because of the following advantages:

▶ ease of start-up,
▶ specialization,
▶ shared decision making, and
▶ shared business losses.

Easy Start-up Like sole proprietorships, partnerships are fairly easy to form. Few government

ECONOMIC INSTITUTIONS & INCENTIVES *Ben Cohen and Jerry Greenfield started their ice cream business as a partnership.* **Why might they have chosen this form of business organization?**

regulations apply to partnerships, and costs tend to be low.

A partnership begins when two or more people agree to operate a business together. To avoid later conflicts, the partners usually develop a written agreement called a partnership contract. This contract outlines the distribution of profits and losses among the partners. It also details each partner's responsibilities and includes conditions for adding or dropping partners and for dissolving the partnership.

Specialization Another advantage of partnerships is specialization. Specific business duties can be assigned to different partners depending on the partnership contract. Unlike sole proprietors, partners are better able to specialize in those areas of the business in which their skills and talents can best be used.

For example, suppose that Jason Fernandez, Tom Reiner, and Stacey Caserma are partners in a sporting-goods store. Jason is an excellent accountant and money manager, Tom is an experienced salesperson, and Stacey is skilled in sales promotion and maintaining inventory. The three partners are able to pool their skills so that one person does not need to meet all of these job requirements.

Shared Decision Making A third advantage of partnerships is shared decision making. Partners can minimize mistakes by consulting with each other on business matters. For example, to make wise purchasing decisions, Stacey needs to consult with Tom about which items are selling well and which are selling poorly. Without this information, she might order too many footballs and too few tennis rackets. Similarly, Tom and Jason need to work together to determine prices that customers will be willing to pay but that will bring the store as much profit as possible. This decision-making process allows the partners to compare points of view, rather than relying on one person for ideas.

Shared Business Losses Just as partners share the process of decision making, they also

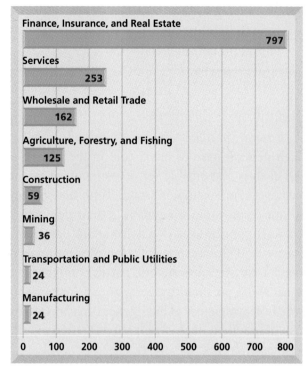

PARTNERSHIPS BY INDUSTRY 1992

Finance, Insurance, and Real Estate — 797
Services — 253
Wholesale and Retail Trade — 162
Agriculture, Forestry, and Fishing — 125
Construction — 59
Mining — 36
Transportation and Public Utilities — 24
Manufacturing — 24

Number (in thousands)

Source: *Statistical Abstract of the United States: 1996*

FIGURE 7.2 Partnerships offer many advantages, including shared risks. **Which industry contains the largest number of partnerships?**

share any business losses. The sharing of losses may enable a partnership to survive a situation that would cause a sole proprietorship to fail. Furthermore, partnerships usually are better able than sole proprietorships to obtain needed financial capital for business expansion and modernization. Creditors are more likely to extend larger loans to partnerships than to sole proprietorships because the risk is shared among several people. Groups of people typically are better able to repay a debt than is a single owner and are likely to have more collateral. Banks and other lenders thus feel more confident that loans to partnerships will be repaid.

Disadvantages of Partnerships

Some of the problems associated with sole proprietorships are less severe for partnerships.

However, partnerships do have three distinct disadvantages:

▶ unlimited liability,
▶ potential for conflict, and
▶ lack of longevity.

Unlimited Liability One major disadvantage of general partnerships is unlimited liability. Each general partner has a role in the business, and each is responsible for debts incurred by the business. For example, Jason, Tom, and Stacey all are responsible for repaying their company's loans. If Tom refuses to pay his share, Jason and Stacey still are responsible for the entire payment. Like sole proprietors, partners might have to sacrifice personal property to cover the debts of a failed business. Thus, general partners may lose more than they originally invested in the business.

Potential for Conflict A second disadvantage of partnerships is that disagreements or other conflicts may arise among partners. Partners may have personality conflicts and different management styles. A partner with poor communication skills might fail to relay important information either to the other partners or employees. Partners who have opposing views may have trouble compromising. These types of conflicts can lower employee morale, delay important business decisions, and decrease overall efficiency. Disagreements also can affect the personal satisfaction that the partners get from the business.

Suppose that Tom thinks that the sporting-goods store should introduce a new line of exercise gear with a celebrity endorsement. Jason, on the other hand, feels that a celebrity endorsement would cost the store more money than would be earned from the new product. If this conflict is not resolved, Tom and Jason could spend too much time arguing and not enough time on their main responsibilities.

Lack of Longevity A final disadvantage of partnerships is that the life of the business is dependent on the willingness and ability of the partners to continue working together. Illness, death, conflict among partners, and other problems can end the partnership.

Following the disagreement about celebrity endorsements, Jason may decide that he can no longer work effectively with Tom. If he withdraws from the partnership, Stacey and Tom will have to find a new partner to assume Jason's responsibilities, divide Jason's former responsibilities between them, or dissolve the partnership and close the business.

SECTION 2 —REVIEW

1. Define the following terms: partnership, general partnership, limited partnership.

2. Compare general and limited partnerships. Would you rather be a general partner or a limited partner? Explain your answer.

3. Why might two or more people agree to become partners in a business?

4. What challenges do partnerships face?

5. **Thinking and Writing Critically** Why might a sole proprietor such as a hot dog vendor decide to take on a partner? Why might that proprietor decide not to take on a partner?

6. **Applying** ECONOMIC INSTITUTIONS & INCENTIVES Describe a situation in which you have worked with one or more partners. What were the advantages and disadvantages compared with working alone?

SECTION 3

└ CORPORATIONS

Economics Dictionary

corporation
articles of incorporation
corporate charter
board of directors
stock
share
dividend
common stock
preferred stock
corporate bond
principal
interest

Objectives

▶ How is a corporation formed?

▶ How is a corporation organized?

▶ How do stocks and bonds differ?

▶ What are the advantages and disadvantages of organizing a corporation?

You have learned that sole proprietorships and partnerships are forms of business organization that are owned and controlled by one or a few people. Unlike sole proprietorships and partnerships, **corporations** are legally distinct from their owners and are treated as if they were individuals. This means corporations can own property, hire workers, make contracts, pay taxes, sue and be sued, and make and sell products.

What kinds of companies are organized as corporations? Companies in industries such as food, steel, and oil tend to be organized as corporations. Insurance companies, supermarket chains, and major companies that sell to businesses or consumers also tend to be organized as corporations. (See Figure 7.3.)

Forming a Corporation

As you have learned, forming a sole proprietorship or a partnership is fairly simple. Forming a corporation, however, is much more complex.

Suppose that Michael Abeyto, Lisa Arnaud, Ben Wallace, and Caroline Jee are partners in a company that develops and sells computer games for a small market in California. The four partners want to expand their business and market their games nationally. Adding a fifth partner would not increase their borrowing power enough to pay for the planned expansion. To put themselves in a better financial position, they decide to transform their partnership into a corporation. Caroline suggests that they consult a lawyer to handle the extensive paperwork and many legal issues.

The first step in forming the new corporation is to apply for a state license known as the

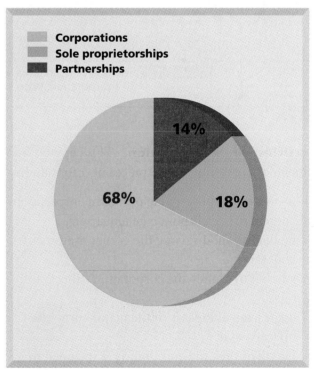

NET INCOME OF BUSINESSES, 1993

Corporations
Sole proprietorships
Partnerships

14%
68%
18%

Source: *Statistical Abstract of the United States: 1996*

FIGURE 7.3 A corporation is considered to be legally distinct from its owners. **What percentage of net profits is earned by corporations?**

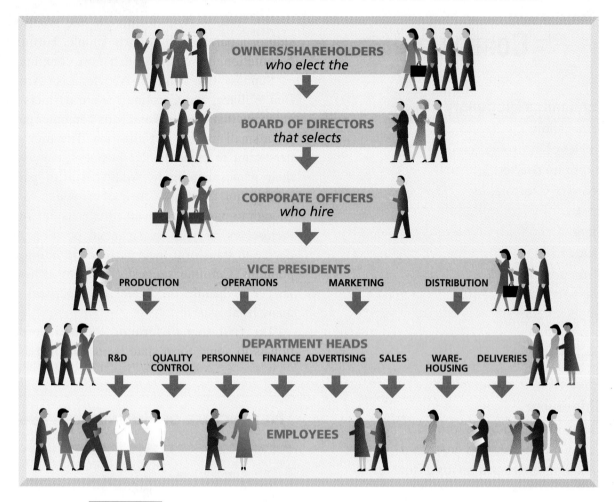

OWNERS/SHAREHOLDERS
who elect the

BOARD OF DIRECTORS
that selects

CORPORATE OFFICERS
who hire

VICE PRESIDENTS

PRODUCTION   OPERATIONS   MARKETING   DISTRIBUTION

DEPARTMENT HEADS

R&D   QUALITY CONTROL   PERSONNEL   FINANCE   ADVERTISING   SALES   WARE-HOUSING   DELIVERIES

EMPLOYEES

FIGURE 7.4 The board of directors is the most important decision-making body in a corporation. **Who selects the board of directors?**

---

articles of incorporation. This application includes the following six pieces of information:

▷ name and purpose of the proposed corporation,
▷ address of the corporate headquarters,
▷ method of fund-raising the corporation will undertake,
▷ amount of money the corporation expects to raise,
▷ names and addresses of the major corporate officers, and
▷ length of time the corporation is intended to exist—either indefinitely or for a specified period of time.

The articles of incorporation are reviewed by state officials, who—if everything is in order—

grant a license, or **corporate charter**, which permits the formation of the new corporation. Michael, Lisa, Ben, and Caroline submit their articles of incorporation and receive the corporate charter for their business, which they have named CompuFun.

Corporate Structure

The corporate charter identifies the corporation's officers—for example, Lisa as president and chief executive officer (CEO), Caroline as vice president of sales, Michael as vice president of product development, and Ben as treasurer. Corporations have other formal structures as well—and generally many more of these structures than do businesses organized as sole proprietorships or partnerships.

Figure 7.4 shows the structure of a typical corporation. The structures of specific corporations may vary somewhat from the diagram because corporations differ in size and in the goods and services they produce. In any corporation, however—including CompuFun—the **board of directors** is made up of people from inside or outside of the company. The board is the corporation's key decision-making body.

What kinds of decisions does the board of directors make? The board must determine how the corporation should develop and what policies it will follow. Michael recommends that CompuFun develop a series of educational games to help children study geography, math, and biology. This new product line would require hiring additional product development specialists and programmers. The board must determine if expansion into educational software is in the company's best interest.

In addition, the board selects new corporate officers as needed. Although the original corporate officers are identified in the articles of incorporation, these individuals may leave the company. The board of directors would then select new officers to ensure that business continues smoothly. Corporate officers typically are experienced, professional managers hired to make day-to-day decisions and to advise the board about production plans. These officers also see that the policies and plans approved by the board are carried out by the corporation's various department heads.

Corporate Finances

The board of directors also is responsible for deciding how the corporation will raise funds. The most common way in which corporations raise funds is by selling stock. **Stock** represents ownership of the firm. This ownership is issued in portions known as **shares**. If you buy 100 shares of stock in a company, you own 100 pieces of that company. If that company has issued 10,000 shares, you own 1 percent of the firm.

Why might you want to own stock? It is an investment—you hope that the company will do well, so that your shares will increase in value and you will receive part of the profits. The profits paid to you as a shareholder are called **dividends**. You receive dividends as a "return," or profit, on your investment.

What other benefits do you enjoy as a shareholder? The answer depends on the type of stock you own. Corporations issue two kinds of stock—common and preferred. **Common stock** provides shareholders with a voice in how the company is run and a share in any potential dividends. **Preferred stock** provides guaranteed dividends—paid before any received by holders of common stock—but does not grant shareholders a voice in running the corporation.

Corporations can have thousands of shareholders and, therefore, thousands of owners. As a result, corporations can raise enormous amounts of money through the sale of stock.

Corporations also raise money by issuing corporate bonds. A **corporate bond** is a certificate issued by a corporation in exchange for money borrowed from an investor. How do stocks and bonds differ? Stock, as you have learned, represents ownership in a corporation. A bond, on the other hand, indicates that the corporation is in debt to the person who holds the bond. The bondholder does not own any part of the company.

As a moneylender, the bondholder is repaid the principal of the loan, plus interest. The **principal** is the actual amount of money that was borrowed. **Interest** is the amount that the borrower—the corporation in this case —must pay for the use of those funds. For example, if you hold a one-year $1,000 bond that pays interest at a rate of 5 percent, you are in fact lending $1,000 for one year. In return, at the end of the year you will receive your $1,000 of principal plus $50 interest ($1,000 $\times$ 5% = $50), thereby earning $50 on the loan.

After analyzing the different methods of raising money, the CompuFun board of directors decides to sell common stock. After its first year of sales, CompuFun finds it has made enough profit to issue a dividend of 10 cents per share.

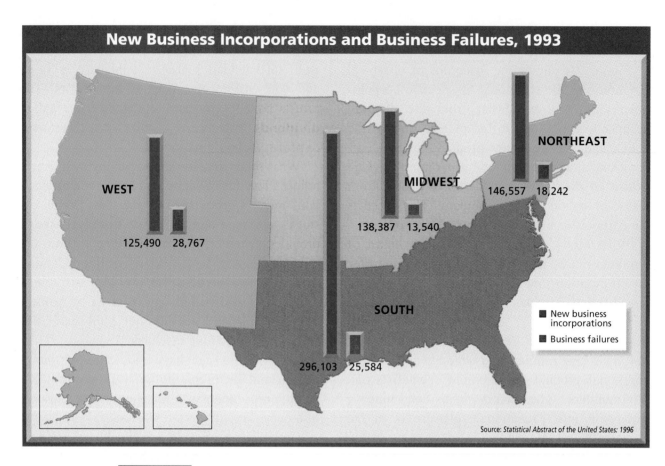

New Business Incorporations and Business Failures, 1993

NORTHEAST
146,557 18,242

MIDWEST
138,387 13,540

WEST
125,490 28,767

SOUTH
296,103 25,584

■ New business incorporations
■ Business failures

Source: *Statistical Abstract of the United States: 1996*

FIGURE 7.5 Many new businesses are opened each year. **Which region is home to the largest number of new businesses?**

This means that a person owning 1,000 shares of CompuFun stock receives $100 of the company's profits for the first year (1,000 × $0.10 = $100). Additionally, CompuFun shareholders are able to vote on company policies and elect the board of directors.

Advantages of Corporations

Corporations have two sets of advantages. One group of advantages is enjoyed by the stockholders, and the other is enjoyed by the corporation itself.

Benefits for Stockholders For stockholders, the major advantage is limited liability. If a corporation fails, the loss to its stockholders, for example, is limited to the amount they invested. A shareholder's assets, or private property, cannot be seized to pay corporate debts. If you buy

100 shares of CompuFun stock and the company goes out of business, you will not have to pay the company's remaining debts. You will lose only what you paid for the stock.

The corporate structure also gives stockholders flexibility, allowing them to take back all or part of their investment by selling shares. You can sell your CompuFun shares at any time, provided that you can find someone who is willing to buy the shares of stock at a price you are willing to accept.

Benefits for Corporations Limited liability also benefits a corporation's founders. The owner of a sole proprietorship who intends to borrow in order to expand the business may decide to incorporate to avoid losing his or her personal possessions. Similarly, partners who incorporate are no longer liable for the loss of anything beyond their own investments.

A second advantage for a corporation is the separation of ownership from management. Because the owners are not involved in daily operations, the corporation can assign specialists to complex management tasks. For example, the CompuFun shareholders do not make day-to-day decisions about company activities. Instead, professional managers, who are skilled at operating a business, make the decisions concerning the production and marketing of the corporation's products. A corporation also can hire additional specialists, such as lawyers and accountants, to advise the professional managers.

A third advantage for a corporation is the relative ease with which capital can be raised. Unlike sole proprietorships and partnerships, which generally rely on collateral to gain credit, corporations can raise money by expanding ownership through the sale of stock. Bonds allow corporations to borrow from individuals as well as from institutions such as banks. A corporation, therefore, has many more potential sources of capital than does a sole proprietorship or a partnership.

The final advantage for a corporation is longevity. A corporation often continues to exist after the deaths of its founders and original management. This long life span is possible because the corporation's structure is not dependent on one or a few individuals, as in a sole proprietorship or partnership. A corporation's pool of ownership changes constantly as stock is bought and sold, and as corporate directors, officers, and employees quit, retire, and are hired and fired. Although these changes could force a proprietorship or partnership to close, a corporation would most likely continue to exist. CompuFun, for example, can continue to do business even if Ben is fired, Caroline quits her job to go back to school, or you sell your stock.

Disadvantages of Corporations

Although there are several disadvantages to this form of business organization, most affect the corporation itself rather than individual stockholders. What are these disadvantages?

Corporate Issues First, a corporate charter can be expensive and difficult to obtain. Costs vary from state to state, but attorney fees and filing expenses may total several thousand dollars.

Second, the federal and state governments regulate corporations much more closely than they do sole proprietorships and partnerships. In addition to obtaining a license, a corporation must follow specific government guidelines when selling stock. A corporation also may face stiffer legal regulations, such as having to publicize financial information about its sales and profits.

A third disadvantage for a corporation is the slow process of decision making. In a corporation—particularly a large one—decisions are made only after extensive study of the issues by specialists and discussion and debate among managers. The process can be further slowed if

ECONOMIC INSTITUTIONS & INCENTIVES *Annual stockholder meetings offer stockholders the opportunity to vote on company policies.* ***What are some of the advantages of forming a corporation?***

disagreements take place between top-level managers and the board of directors over such matters as establishing hiring practices and setting production goals.

Stockholder Issues The main disadvantage for stockholders seems, at first glance, like an advantage. Stockholders can earn a profit without actually working for the company. This may seem very appealing as a way of earning an income without having to work for it. In reality, however, this situation means that stockholders are far removed from the actual running of the business. Although you earn money in the form of dividends from your CompuFun stock, you have no direct participation in developing and selling new products. As a result, you—and other stockholders—are not likely to have the sense of pride, accomplishment, and personal satisfaction often felt by sole proprietors or partners, even though you are an owner of the corporation.

A second related disadvantage for stockholders is lack of control. Although stockholders technically are able to influence the company, their power generally is limited. Annual shareholder meetings offer owners a chance to vote on company policies. Most stockholders, however, own only a small percentage of a company's shares, making it difficult to influence policy and corporate objectives unless a majority of shares are held by people with similar views. In addition, stockholders cannot affect a corporation's day-to-day activities. For example, if you as a shareholder think that CompuFun should sell a computerized time-management program, you must count on the corporation's officers to decide whether to develop such a product.

Shared Issues For some people, there is an additional disadvantage that applies both to the corporation and to its stockholders. These people point out that corporate profits are taxed twice—once as corporate profits and again as dividends. The income, or profit, of a corporation is taxed because legally—as you learned earlier in this section—the corporation is treated as if it were an individual. Next, these after-tax profits are distributed to shareholders as dividends. The government views dividends as income for the stockholder, so he or she must pay income tax on this money in addition to the taxes paid by the corporation.

SECTION 3 —REVIEW

1. Define the following terms: corporation, articles of incorporation, corporate charter, board of directors, stock, share, dividend, common stock, preferred stock, corporate bond, principal, interest.

2. Legally, how is a corporation treated as an individual?

3. How are corporate bonds different from shares of stock?

4. What advantages does incorporation give to shareholders and to the company?

5. What disadvantages does incorporation give to shareholders and to the company?

6. **Thinking and Writing Critically** How might you consider your school to be a corporation? Who makes up the board of directors? Who are the officers? Who are the shareholders, and what dividends are paid?

7. **Applying** ECONOMIC INSTITUTIONS & INCENTIVES Conduct an Internet search using the search words *stocks* and *bonds*. What possibilities exist for buying or selling stocks and bonds on the Internet?

SECTION 4

OTHER FORMS OF ORGANIZATION

Economics Dictionary

merger
horizontal combination
vertical combination
conglomerate combination
subsidiary
franchise
cooperative
nonprofit organization

Objectives

▶ How do vertical combinations differ from horizontal and conglomerate combinations?
▶ Why might a business owner decide to open a franchise?
▶ What is the customer's role in a cooperative?
▶ How does a nonprofit organization differ from other types of business organizations?

Sole proprietorships, partnerships, and corporations are the three most common forms of business organization in the United States. There are, however, other forms business owners may choose, including

▶ corporate combinations,
▶ franchises,
▶ cooperatives, and
▶ nonprofit organizations.

Like sole proprietorships, partnerships, and corporations, these business organizations meet the needs of particular enterprises. As you read this section, consider how each form can benefit a business.

Corporate Combinations

Many of the advantages associated with forming a corporation—longevity, separation of ownership from management, and ease of raising financial capital—are associated with one characteristic: size. As noted in Chapter 6, large size often brings economies of scale. In order to make the most of these advantages, many corporations try to expand. To expand, a corporation either grows from within by building new facilities or legally combines with another enterprise.

The most common method of joining businesses is through mergers. A **merger** occurs when one company joins with or absorbs another. In a merger the absorbed company often loses its identity. Suppose that the computer games company known as CompuFun Corporation is purchased by a company known as CyberAce Corporation. If CompuFun's games are popular, CyberAce will probably continue to produce them, but under the CyberAce name.

Companies may form different types of corporate combinations. The three most common types of combinations are

▶ horizontal,
▶ vertical, and
▶ conglomerate.

Horizontal Combinations A merger between two or more companies producing the same good or service is called a **horizontal combination**. A horizontal combination also may involve companies that dominate one phase of production.

As noted in Chapter 6, John D. Rockefeller and his associates organized the Standard Oil Trust—which was later broken up by the federal government—to control the U.S. oil industry. This trust was a horizontal combination in that it included many companies involved in the same industry—oil refining.

Vertical Combinations A merger between two or more companies involved in different production phases of the same good or service is a **vertical combination**. For example, the United

States Steel Corporation, founded in 1901, combined companies that owned ore deposits, iron mines, steel mills, railroads, and shipping lines. All of these companies were involved in different phases of the production and distribution of steel. Today the company, which is now a part of USX Corporation, produces 10 percent of all the steel manufactured in the United States.

Conglomerate Combinations A merger of companies producing unrelated products is known as a **conglomerate combination**. (See

Figure 7.6.) Whereas horizontal and vertical combinations have existed since the late 1800s, conglomerate combinations did not become common until the 1960s and 1970s.

One example of a conglomerate is the International Telephone and Telegraph Corporation (ITT). Until the 1950s, ITT manufactured only telecommunications equipment. During the 1960s and 1970s, however, ITT acquired hundreds of companies that became **subsidiaries**, or distinct divisions, of ITT. Although owned by ITT, these subsidiaries continued to manufacture

CONGLOMERATE COMBINATION

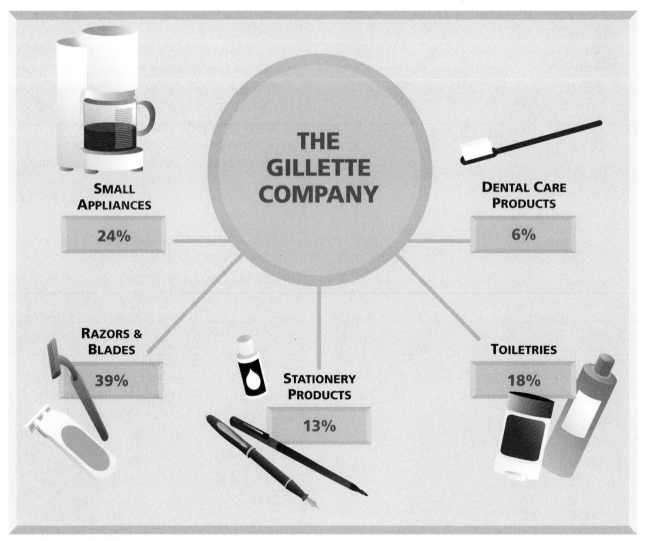

Source: *Hoover's 500: 1996*

FIGURE 7.6 A conglomerate combination produces two or more unrelated products.
What is the Gillette Company's largest product line?

products under their own names—often noting that the companies were subsidiaries of ITT. Today ITT has subsidiaries in such varied enterprises as insurance, financial services, defense technology, and automotive products.

To ensure competent and knowledgeable decision making, combinations often allow subsidiaries to keep their own top management. For example, when General Motors (GM) acquired Hughes Aircraft Company in the mid-1980s, GM permitted Hughes to conduct its own affairs largely without interference.

Advantages of Combinations
One major advantage of corporate mergers is efficiency. By centralizing decision making within an industry, a combination usually can increase efficiency through the elimination of overlapping jobs and departments. For example, when CyberAce purchases CompuFun, the new combination will not need two vice presidents of product development and may eliminate Michael's job.

A second advantage is the potential for lower costs. Buying an existing business is often less expensive than building new plants and offices, hiring new employees, and acquiring additional financial capital to expand. CyberAce will not need to pay to recruit and relocate new employees because the merger has brought CompuFun's employees into the corporation.

A third advantage is that the increased size of a combination often makes it easier to acquire financial capital. Just as partnerships typically have more collateral than sole proprietorships, combinations typically have a greater ability to raise financial capital than separate corporations. Additionally, larger companies often are believed to be more successful, which encourages shareholder investment. The new financial capital that CyberAce raises can be used to increase the sales force or to modernize production facilities, enabling the combination to compete more effectively in the marketplace.

Disadvantages of Combinations
Although combinations can lead to increased efficiency, their practices also can lead to higher rates of

Shared Risks and Rewards

A joint venture is created when two or more companies formally come together to work toward common goals. In an international joint venture, ownership and control of a business are shared by companies in two or more countries.

Unfortunately, many joint ventures quickly fail. These failures generally result from disagreements between partners about control issues and about the new company's strategy and goals.

A success story in the risky world of joint ventures is Fuji Xerox, a partnership founded in 1962 between Xerox Corporation of the United States and Fuji Photo Film of Japan. The long life of this Tokyo-based business stems from its combination of the best aspects of the original companies, as well as its ability to adapting to market changes.

For example, in its early years Fuji Xerox adopted some of Xerox's business techniques, such as renting copiers. Few Japanese companies were renting out equipment at the time, so Xerox's strategy opened up a vast new market.

Meanwhile, Fuji Xerox's product development methods benefited Xerox's business in the United States. Facing stiff competition during the 1980s, Xerox was able to protect their market share by introducing new copiers developed by Fuji Xerox.

Doing business in a foreign country is not easy. Businesspeople must be familiar with that country's language, government, customs, and even cultural taboos. With flexibility and teamwork, however, an international joint venture can succeed.

ECONOMIC INSTITUTIONS & INCENTIVES *Franchises share the original company's name but are individually owned.* **What franchises are you familiar with?**

unemployment. Employees may be reassigned or may lose their jobs. If Michael no longer works as vice president of product development, he may become unemployed or be assigned to new duties—perhaps as vice president of production. Even employees who keep their jobs, however, sometimes suffer low morale from altered job descriptions or other changes in working conditions. Michael may not enjoy his new job, or employees in product development may not like working for the CyberAce vice president.

Additionally, because mergers may result in reduced competition in the marketplace, they can lead to higher prices for consumers. Since CyberAce games no longer need to compete with CompuFun games—because they all are now produced by CyberAce—prices may increase.

Franchises

Some businesses share a name even though they are separately owned. In this case, one company agrees—for a fee—to let another person or group set up a **franchise**, an enterprise that uses the

original company's name to sell goods and services. The parent company—the company owning the name—is called the franchisor. The person or group opening the franchise is called the franchisee.

What kinds of businesses are operated as franchises? Hotel and motel chains such as Holiday Inn, restaurants such as Burger King, and real estate agencies such as Century 21 are organized as franchises.

Franchise agreements generally include requirements designed to uphold the reputation of the parent company. For example, the franchisee has to maintain quality standards and must provide a particular good or service.

To ensure consistent quality and service, the franchisor often provides training for employees. It also may pay for national advertising. Because of these advantages, as well as use of the parent company's name, the franchisee can lower the costs associated with starting a business.

For example, suppose that Nalani Ling wants to open a shoe repair store. She can establish a sole proprietorship, but she also has the opportunity to open a franchise of the widely known Zippy Fix Shoe Repair company. Nalani may

ECONOMIC INSTITUTIONS & INCENTIVES *Cooperatives are owned collectively by their members.* **Why might a consumer join a co-op such as the one pictured here?**

decide to become a franchisee because even though she will have to pay for the use of the Zippy Fix name, she knows that she can count on the franchisor to provide standards of quality, access to tools and materials, and advertising. Additionally, she knows that customers will recognize the Zippy Fix name from the moment she opens the doors of her business, increasing her share of the shoe repair market. The name Ling Shoe Repair, on the other hand, would be less familiar to the public and would take longer to attract customers. Nalani may determine that a franchise suits her business needs better than a sole proprietorship.

Cooperatives

Some businesses are organized as **cooperatives**, or co-ops—businesses that are owned collectively by their members. For example, residents of an apartment building may join together to buy their building as a housing cooperative, rather than allow it to be purchased by a shopping-mall developer. Suppose that residents of Blue Moon Apartments decide to form a cooperative and buy the building. Some of the residents decide to move, but Janelle Franklin is one of many who agrees to invest money and join the cooperative. Janelle now owns shares in the Blue Moon Apartment Cooperative and has the right to occupy one of the apartments. As an individual, however, she does not own part of the physical structure of the building. Additionally, she and the other co-op members share the building's maintenance costs.

There are many types of cooperatives. Purchasing cooperatives like Price Club and Sam's Club are retail stores that buy large quantities of merchandise at reduced prices and pass these savings on to their members. Marketing cooperatives are commonly established by groups of farmers who hope to secure higher prices for their farm products. Service cooperatives provide members with services such as electrical power, health care, or legal assistance. Credit unions are financial cooperatives that allow members to borrow money at reduced interest rates.

ECONOMIC INSTITUTIONS & INCENTIVES *Nonprofit organizations provide goods and services without financial gain.* **How do nonprofit organizations raise money?**

Nonprofit Organizations

One form of business organization does not focus on financial gain for its members. Instead, a **nonprofit organization** works in a businesslike way to provide goods and services while pursuing other goals, such as improving educational standards, providing health care, or maintaining museums and other cultural institutions. Nonprofit organizations include the American Red Cross, the Boy Scouts of America, the Girl Scouts of the U.S.A., and the American Heart Association, as well as churches, labor unions, and some hospitals.

Nonprofit organizations often are structured like corporations, in part so that they can benefit from unlimited longevity. Revenues for nonprofit organizations generally come from the sale of products, fees for services, and charitable contributions. The income of nonprofit organizations is not taxed by the government.

C A S E   S T U D Y

The Green Bay Packers

ECONOMIC INSTITUTIONS & INCENTIVES Owners of pro sports teams look for many things in a hometown—a large population, a modern stadium, and widespread local television coverage. Because of this, many teams have left familiar cities and fans for greener, richer hometowns. Why, then, have the Packers stayed in Green Bay, Wisconsin since 1919, when in 1995 the city was only the 199th-largest in the United States and the 71st-largest television market?

Most sports teams are organized as sole proprietorships, partnerships, or parts of corporations. The Green Bay Packers, however, are a nonprofit corporation. The 4,634 shares of Packer stock originally were purchased by Green Bay residents. A shareholder can pass his or her shares on to a relative, but cannot sell the shares to a nonresident unless the corporation approves. The corporation also limits stock ownership to 200 shares per person and has set the price of the shares at $25 each. These rules ensure that residents of all income levels can afford a "stake" in their team. The low price offers an investment in civic pride, not a chance to earn a profit. Any profits earned by the Packer organization are spent on improvements to the stadium and facilities.

Is the choice to make the team a nonprofit organization working? Fans think so. Packer games consistently are sold out, and the waiting list for season tickets contains about 23,000 names.

SECTION 4 — REVIEW

1. Define the following terms: merger, horizontal combination, vertical combination, conglomerate combination, subsidiary, franchise, cooperative, nonprofit organization.

2. Compare horizontal, vertical, and conglomerate combinations.

3. What are the advantages of opening a franchise?

4. What are the advantages of membership in a cooperative?

5. What is the purpose of a nonprofit organization? List three nonprofit organizations not mentioned in the text.

6. **Thinking and Writing Critically**
Is your school more like a franchise, a cooperative, or a nonprofit organization? Explain your answer.

7. **Applying** ECONOMIC INSTITUTIONS & INCENTIVES
Select three companies and conduct an Internet search to determine the business organization of each.

SECTION 1 The most common form of business organization is the sole proprietorship. A sole proprietorship relies on the work and organizational abilities of one person. Sole proprietorships are easy to start up, provide the single owner with full control of the business, and allow the owner to keep all the profits. There are several problems related to sole proprietorships. First, the proprietor has unlimited liability for business debt. Second, the proprietor is completely responsible for all aspects of the business. Third, sole proprietors often have difficulty raising capital. Fourth, a sole proprietorship lasts only as long as the proprietor is willing and able to maintain the business.

SECTION 2 Partnerships spread the risk and workload of a company among partners. A partnership may be organized either as a general partnership or as a limited partnership.

Like sole proprietorships, partnerships are easy to set up. Unlike proprietorships, however, partnerships allow specialization and shared responsibility, shared decision-making, and shared business losses. Disadvantages for partnerships include unlimited liability, the potential for conflict, and a lack of longevity.

SECTION 3 A more complex type of business organization is the corporation. It is supervised by a board of directors. Legally, a corporation is treated as if it were an individual.

The corporation offers several advantages. First, stockholders and corporations have limited liability. Second, corporations permit the separation of ownership from management. Corporations also have relatively little trouble raising capital, and they offer longevity.

The disadvantages of corporations include expenses of establishing the business, strict government regulation, and a slow decision-making process. Additionally, shareholders are removed from daily company activities. Some people also think that it is unfair to tax dividends twice—first as corporate profits and again as shareholder income.

SECTION 4 Corporations are able to expand their operations by combining, or merging, with other firms. Horizontal combinations occur between companies that produce the same goods or services. Vertical combinations are mergers between companies involved in different phases of production of the same good or service. A conglomerate combination occurs between companies producing or marketing significantly different products.

Franchises, cooperatives, and nonprofit organizations are three additional types of business organization. In a franchise, one business agrees to let its name be used by another business—for a fee—to sell goods or services. A cooperative is a voluntary association of consumers or producers in some kind of business activity. Nonprofit organizations provide goods or services but do not seek profits for individual members.

Economics Notebook

Refer to the businesses you listed in your Economics Notebook at the beginning of this chapter. Classify each of these businesses as a sole proprietorship, partnership, corporation, franchise, cooperative, or nonprofit organization.

CHAPTER 7

⌐REVIEW

REVIEWING CONCEPTS

1. Why is a sole proprietorship the easiest type of business to establish?

2. How does forming a partnership solve many of the problems that are associated with sole proprietorships?

3. Compare stocks and corporate bonds. How do corporations raise money through stocks and bonds?

4. Explain how vertical combinations differ from horizontal combinations.

5. What are the benefits of opening a franchise? Why do you think a parent company might want to encourage the development of franchises?

6. How do nonprofit organizations differ from other forms of business organizations?

THINKING AND WRITING CRITICALLY

1. **ECONOMIC INSTITUTIONS & INCENTIVES** Collect newspaper advertisements for each of the following types of businesses: sole proprietorship, partnership, corporation, franchise.

2. **ECONOMIC INSTITUTIONS & INCENTIVES** Suppose that you want to start a business selling pizza. Which type of organization do you feel would best suit your business needs? Explain your answer.

3. **ECONOMIC INSTITUTIONS & INCENTIVES** If you purchase stock in a corporation, what is your role as an owner?

4. **ECONOMIC INSTITUTIONS & INCENTIVES** Have you ever participated in—or benefited from—the activities of a nonprofit organization? Explain your answer.

YOUR LOCAL ECONOMY

Draw a map of the main commercial street of your community. Label businesses along the street as sole proprietorships, partnerships, corporations, franchises, cooperatives, and nonprofit organizations. Which type of business organization is most common in your community? Why do you think this is so? Explain the map's content and your conclusions in an extended map caption, and present your map to the class.

COOPERATIVE PORTFOLIO PROJECT

As a group, select a good or service that you wish to provide and organize a corporation in order to limit your liability. Assign the roles of president, vice president of product development, vice president of marketing, and treasurer. Prepare a pamphlet that explains your corporate structure, describes the good or service provided by your corporation, and identifies whether your corporation will sell common stock, preferred stock, or corporate bonds. You may wish to include charts or diagrams in your pamphlet. Display your pamphlet in the classroom.

PRACTICING SKILLS: UNDERSTANDING CHARTS AND GRAPHS

The circle graph, or pie chart, on page 167 illustrates business receipts for sole proprietors. The graph has five "pie slices" that together represent the whole number (15,442,000 or 100%) of tax returns submitted by sole proprietorships in

SOLE PROPRIETORSHIPS, 1993 BY SIZE OF RECEIPTS

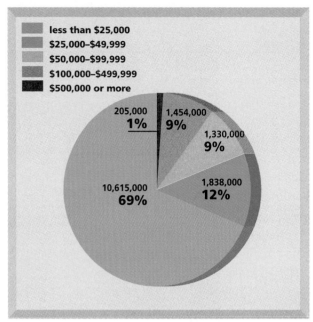

- less than $25,000
- $25,000–$49,999
- $50,000–$99,999
- $100,000–$499,999
- $500,000 or more

205,000
1%

1,454,000
9%

1,330,000
9%

10,615,000
69%

1,838,000
12%

Source: *Statistical Abstract of the United States: 1996*

the United States in 1993. Read the labels on the graph, and study the relative size of the "slices" to answer the questions that follow.

1. In what income range did most sole proprietors fall in 1993?

2. How many sole proprietors made more than $500,000?

3. What percentage of sole proprietors made less than $100,000?

4. Approximately what percent of sole proprietors earned more than $25,000?

THE INTERNET: LEARNING ONLINE

Conduct an Internet search to find information about conglomerates. You might start with search words such as *conglomerate* or the name of a business you think is a conglomerate. Find a conglomerate with at least 10 subsidiaries, and research the history of the company. What goods and services did the company provide when it was founded? How did the company expand, and what goods and services does it provide today? Create an illustrated time line of the mergers and acquisitions that developed the conglomerate you have chosen to study.

ANALYZING PRIMARY SOURCES

Iacocca: An Autobiography

Lee Iacocca—a famous businessman who successfully brought Chrysler Corporation back from the brink of bankruptcy—published a well-known autobiography in 1984. In the passage below, he describes the situation he inherited when he became president of Chrysler, just weeks after having been fired as president of Ford Motor Company.

"It turned out that my worries were justified. I soon stumbled upon my first major revelation: Chrysler didn't really function like a company at all. Chrysler in 1978 was like Italy in the 1860s— the company consisted of a cluster of little duchies [independent territories], each one run by a prima donna [temperamental person]. It was a bunch of mini-empires, with nobody [caring] about what anyone else was doing.

"What I found at Chrysler were thirty-five vice-presidents, each with his own turf. There was no real committee setup, no cement in the organizational chart, no system of meetings to get people talking to each other. I couldn't believe, for example, that the guy running the engineering department wasn't in constant touch with his counterpart [peer] in manufacturing. . . . Everybody worked independently. I took one look at that system and I almost threw up. That's when I knew I was in really deep trouble. . . .

"The contrast between Chrysler's structure and Ford's was simply amazing. Nobody at Chrysler seemed to realize that you just can't run a big corporation without calling some pregame sessions to do blackboard work. Every member of the team has to understand what his job is and exactly how it fits in with every other job."

1. What was Iacocca's main complaint about the Chrysler company?

2. Identify three values that Iacocca would consider to be important for running a successful company.

CHAPTER 8

⌐ LABOR AND UNIONS

What kind of job would you like to have? Perhaps you would like to be an accountant or a television reporter. You might opt to become an artist or a zoologist. When you choose a career, you decide how you will use one of the factors of production—human resources.

Referring to people as resources may seem odd, because the term is generally used to describe tools, raw materials, or money. In an economic sense, however, labor is a valuable resource—one that cannot be separated from the people who provide it. In this chapter you will learn about the labor force in the United States, and the choices you will face when you enter it. Additionally, you will learn how the people who make up the labor force can organize to achieve their shared goals.

✎ Economics Notebook

In your Economics Notebook, list the kinds of labor you perform during the course of one week. Consider the work you do as a student, as a member of a household, and—if you have an after-school job—as an employee.

SECTION 1

THE U.S. LABOR FORCE

Economics Dictionary

labor force
wage
intrinsic reward
derived demand
industrialization
capital-intensive
labor-intensive
affirmative action
quota

Objectives

▶ What factors affect workers entering the labor force?

▶ How has the U.S. labor force changed over time?

▶ How does the U.S. government affect labor?

A re you part of the U.S. labor force? The **labor force** includes all people who are at least 16 years old and are working or actively looking for work. In the United States more than 130 million people—two thirds of all people 16 years of age or older—are members of the civilian labor force. The civilian labor force makes up about 98 percent of all people in the United States who are working or looking for work. The remainder are members of the armed forces or are employed by the military (see Figure 8.1).

How do people decide what kinds of jobs they want in the labor force? For many people, the most important factor in choosing an occupation is the salary or **wage**—the hourly, weekly, monthly, or yearly pay that a worker receives in exchange for his or her labor.

Entering the Labor Force

Suppose that Sally Cromwell is looking for a job. In her search she considers

▶ wages,
▶ skills,
▶ working conditions,
▶ location,
▶ intrinsic rewards, and
▶ market trends.

Wages First, Sally should consider what kinds of jobs are in demand and the supply of different kinds of workers. Why is this information important? Just as supply and demand affect the prices of other resources, they also affect the price of labor, or workers' wages.

LABOR FORCE, 1995

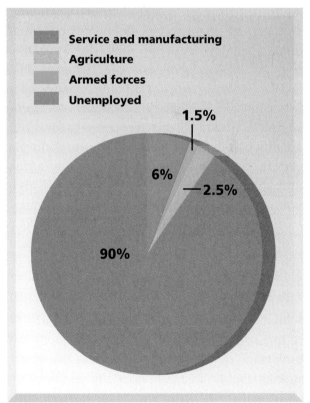

Source: *Statistical Abstract of the United States: 1996*

FIGURE 8.1 The labor force is made up of U.S. residents who are working or looking for work. **Which employment category provides jobs for the largest percentage of workers?**

EQUILIBRIUM WAGE

WAITERS

BRAIN SURGEONS

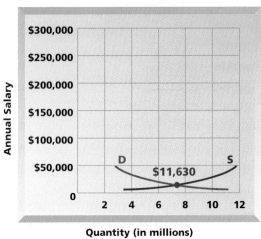

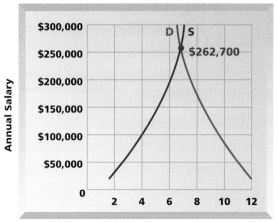

Source: *Statistical Abstract of the United States: 1996*

FIGURE 8.2 The equilibrium wage is established when the quantity of workers supplied and the quantity of workers demanded is the same at a particular salary. **Why is the equilibrium wage for brain surgeons so much higher than that for waiters?**

When an occupation has many potential workers but few available jobs, the wage rate tends to be low. For example, imagine that Charles Bernini wants to find a job as an admissions counselor for a university. Many other people are interested in this type of job, however, and although there are many colleges and universities in the United States, each has only a few admissions jobs. Because so many people (a high quantity supplied) are interested in a small number of jobs (a low quantity demanded), there is a surplus of workers and the wages are lower than Charles—and other applicants—might hope to receive.

High wages, on the other hand, occur when the number of workers who are interested in—or are qualified for—an occupation is limited, and the demand for them is high. Suppose that housing construction increases in a city and the current number of workers is insufficient to complete the construction projects. Additional workers cannot appear instantly, so a shortage of workers results. If Joe Wilson, a general contractor for house-building projects, wants to ensure that he will have enough workers to complete his

projects on time, he must offer a higher wage than that offered by other contractors.

So how do supply and demand affect what occupation Sally should choose? She is more likely to find a good-paying job in an occupation with a high demand for—and a low supply of—workers. This does not mean, however, that she should base her decision solely on this consideration. Sally should also consider her skills.

Skills Think about your skills as a worker. Education, experience, and abilities all affect your skills and help determine what jobs you are—and are not—eligible to hold. Do you have the skills needed to be a brain surgeon, an airline pilot, or a chef? Probably you have yet to develop all the skills needed for these jobs, and employers likely would not hire you for these positions.

Because businesses want to hire only qualified people, skill level can limit the supply of workers (see Figure 8.2). For example, relatively few people attain the skills required to be a professional baseball player or an intensive care nurse. The more skills a particular job requires, the fewer qualified people there are who can perform the job. As you know, this limited supply of labor means that jobs requiring high skill levels usually offer higher wages. Conversely, the fewer skills a job requires, the greater number of qualified people there are for the position. Because of this large supply of labor, low-skilled occupations usually offer lower wages.

You, Sally, and other workers thus face the same skill-related questions. Do you want to invest a great deal of time, money, and effort in acquiring the skills needed for a high-paying job? Or are there other considerations you might take into account when entering the labor force?

Working Conditions

As Sally continues her job search, what might she want to know about conditions in the workplace? In most U.S. workplaces, federal and state laws carefully regulate health and safety concerns such as noise levels and cleanliness. Some high-risk occupations, however, are simply more dangerous to workers. Skyscraper construction, fire fighting, and coal mining are examples of hazardous occupations. To compensate for these dangers and to encourage qualified workers to apply, hazardous occupations sometimes pay higher wages than those jobs with low risks to life and limb.

Location

In addition to workplace conditions, Sally should consider the locations of the jobs that interest her. Does she want to move to a new area, or would she rather continue to live where she does now? Sometimes employers offer higher wages to encourage workers to move to a different area. In some cases, jobs in distant or remote locations pay higher wages to help make up for the isolation. For example, engineers and other specialists who are recruited to work in other nations may receive high salaries. Workers performing the same jobs in more desirable locations generally receive lower wages.

Intrinsic Rewards

Although Sally certainly wants to earn a good salary, she might seek other types of job satisfaction. **Intrinsic rewards** are nonmonetary reasons for working at a particular job. They include a worker's pride and satisfaction in the quality of work done and the status, prestige, or respect that accompanies a job.

People who value a particular intrinsic reward often are willing to accept lower salaries than they might receive in another job that calls for comparable levels of skill and training. Consider the case of Patrick Sloan, who is graduating from college with a degree in English. He has the skills to go to law school or to earn a teaching certificate. He knows that he may be able to earn a higher salary as a lawyer than as a teacher. Patrick, however, wants to increase people's appreciation for literature. He decides to pursue a teaching career because he believes that the intrinsic rewards of teaching are greater than the possible financial rewards of a legal career.

Market Trends

Sally also should investigate trends in the careers that interest her. What industries are expanding or contracting? Industries expand to meet increasing needs and wants of consumers, leading to an increase in the need for workers. In other words, consumers' demand for a particular good creates a demand for the labor—and other resources—needed to produce that good. This process is called **derived demand**, because the demand for workers and other resources is derived, or follows, from the consumers' demand for the good.

Derived demand can cause great changes in employment patterns as producers try to meet the

INCOME DISTRIBUTION *Jobs in remote locations such as Alaska may pay relatively high wages to make up for the isolation.*

new needs and wants of consumers. For example, in the early 1900s consumer demand shifted from the horse and carriage to the automobile. As a result, the demand for industrial workers in automobile plants increased, while the demand for skilled carriage makers declined.

Changes in the Labor Force

Now you know what people consider before entering the labor force, but who exactly is looking for jobs? The people who make up the labor force—and the jobs that they hold—are very different today from laborers and jobs in the past. Why is this so?

Capital-Intensive Economy For much of American history, most people in the United States earned their living from agriculture. The introduction of new technologies during the late 1700s and early 1800s, however, encouraged **industrialization**—the process of mechanizing all major forms of production.

Widespread industrialization first occurred in Great Britain in the mid-1700s, during a period that became known as the Industrial Revolution. Soon other nations—including the United States—followed Britain's lead.

Industrialization created new, factory-based jobs, which contributed to an economic shift away from agriculture. This shift led not only to a vast increase in the number and kinds of goods and services available but also to a greater reliance on the capital goods needed in factory production. Industrialization thus caused the U.S. economy to become **capital-intensive**, or dependent on machines to produce goods. In contrast, agricultural economies are **labor-intensive**, producing goods primarily through animal and human power.

How did the shift to an industrialized, capital-intensive economy change the makeup of the U.S. labor force? In the late 1700s about 80 percent of the labor force was employed in farm labor. By 1850, farm workers made up only 63 percent of the labor force, and by 1900 they made up only 37 percent. Today less than 3 percent of the U.S. labor force works in agriculture. In contrast, about 90 percent of workers hold service and manufacturing jobs.

Women in the Labor Force Industrialization also increased the number of females who received wages for their labor. Women often worked on family farms without being paid a separate income. In the early 1800s, however, textile factories in New England began to employ women. By 1900, women working for wages outside the home made up about 18 percent of the labor force.

The number of females in the labor force increased again during World War I, when many women took jobs in defense plants to replace men who had entered the military. In fact, during the war some 1.5 million American women worked as automobile mechanics, truck drivers, bricklayers, metalworkers, railroad engineers, and other industrial laborers.

Although many of these women stopped working outside their homes when the war ended, women again entered the labor force in large numbers during World War II. From 1940 to 1944 more than 4 million women held jobs in workplaces such as airplane factories, newspaper offices, and shipyards. The millions of women who joined the labor force in these times of national emergency helped establish a pattern for working outside the home and contributed to a change in public attitudes toward women in the workplace.

The number of women in the labor force continues to increase. In 1995, 58.9 percent of women in the United States were members of the labor force, compared to 75 percent of men. Smaller family size and an increase in affordable day care have enabled many women to pursue careers outside the home. In addition, improved access to educational facilities allows women to gain the same level of training as men, and therefore to compete for jobs traditionally held by men. Legislation protecting equal access to jobs also has opened up employment opportunities for women.

Higher Education Levels

As you know, increased education has helped improve employment opportunities for women. These improvements have not been limited to women, however. The U.S. labor force in general has become better educated over the years.

Many states did not have public school systems until the early 1900s, so education in some areas was largely limited to the wealthy. The development of free public schools and the passage of mandatory-attendance laws, however, caused education levels to rise dramatically throughout the 1900s.

For example, in 1960 about 41.1 percent of people over the age of 25 had completed high school. By 1995 this number had nearly doubled, with almost 82 percent completing high school. Similarly, the number of U.S. residents completing at least four years of college increased, from 7.7 percent in 1960 to 23 percent in 1995.

How do workers benefit from greater access to education? A direct relationship exists between a worker's level of education and his or her income. If you stay in school for at least 16 years—earning a college degree—you probably will be able to get a better job and earn a higher salary than workers with less education. How much more could you earn? In 1993 the average salary for a college graduate in the workforce

was $31,500 per year, while the average salary for a person with a master's degree was $40,932. In contrast, the average salary for a high school graduate without any further education was $16,560 per year, and the average high school dropout earned only $10,872. (See Figure 8.3.)

Government and Workers

You read earlier that governments passed attendance laws so that more workers would get an education. This is one example of how the government can affect the labor force. In fact, over time the U.S. government has become more

EDUCATION AND SALARY, 1993

HIGHEST EDUCATION LEVEL ATTAINED	AVERAGE YEARLY INCOME
Professional degree	
Doctoral degree	
Master's degree	
Bachelor's degree	
Associate's degree	
Vocational degree	
Some college, no degree	
High school graduate	
Not a high school graduate	

= $10,000

Source: *Statistical Abstract of the United States: 1996*

FIGURE 8.3 Higher levels of education generally increase the potential for higher wages. **How does the average yearly income of a person with a professional degree compare to that of a person who did not complete high school?**

Global Exchange

Maquiladoras

Business owners often find that labor is one of their highest costs. To remain competitive in the global market, businesses always are searching for ways to pay less for labor.

For this reason, many U.S. companies have built factories called *maquiladoras* (mah-kee-lah-DOHR-ahs) on the Mexican side of the 2,000-mile border between the United States and Mexico. These factories save money by employing Mexicans, who typically are paid less than workers in the United States. *Maquiladoras* began as a result of a 1965 agreement between the United States and Mexico that was designed to generate jobs for Mexicans while allowing U.S. companies access to low-cost labor.

The passage of the North American Free Trade Agreement (NAFTA) among the United States, Mexico, and Canada in 1993 created a surge in the number of *maquiladoras*. For a product to qualify for NAFTA's lower tariff rates, a certain percentage of its parts must come from a NAFTA country. Of the three countries involved, Mexico usually has the lowest labor costs, making it a prime location for factories.

Although *maquiladoras* added close to 200,000 jobs in the border region in 1995 and 1996, not all the effects have been positive. In 1996, for example, the population of the border town Tijuana grew at twice the pace of population growth for Mexico as a whole. A lack of adequate housing has forced many people in Tijuana and other border towns to live in unsafe shelters. In addition, roads and bridges are overburdened, and water and energy supplies are running low.

involved in the economy and other issues affecting the labor force. Specifically, since the 1960s the federal government has passed several antidiscrimination and minimum-wage laws to protect the rights of individual workers. During the 1900s the government also has passed legislation concerning labor unions, which you will learn about in Section 2.

Antidiscrimination Laws During the 1960s Congress passed a series of laws aimed at protecting workers from discrimination in hiring, promotion, and firing. For example, the Equal Pay Act of 1963 requires that employers pay the same wages to male and female workers who perform the same job. The Civil Rights Act of 1964 protects workers from employer discrimination based on race, sex, religion, or national origin. The act also established the Equal Employment Opportunity Commission (EEOC). The main task of the EEOC is to monitor and enforce the act's provisions.

In addition, in 1965 President Lyndon Johnson began pursuing a policy of **affirmative action**, or making up for patterns of discrimination against women, members of minority groups, and others who were traditionally disadvantaged in the workplace. Programs were aimed at eliminating racial and gender bias in the employment practices of firms doing business with the federal government. The Department of Labor soon established a practice of relying on what amounted to **quotas**, or numerical goals, for hiring and promoting women and minorities.

Affirmative action has stirred up controversy between employees and employers. Supporters have argued that affirmative action is the only effective method of ending workplace discrimination. Opponents counter that affirmative action is itself a form of discrimination because it offers special treatment to one group of citizens at the expense of another.

The Supreme Court has acted to make sure that affirmative action does not discriminate against people who are not members of minority groups. In the case *Regents of the University of California* v. *Bakke* (1978), the Court ruled that a

ECONOMIC INSTITUTIONS & INCENTIVES *President Lyndon Johnson signs civil rights legislation.* **What was the name given to Johnson's antidiscrimination policy?**

California medical school could not reserve a certain number of seats for minority students in an incoming class. According to the Court's ruling, that quota violated the Civil Rights Act of 1964 because it made race the sole factor in admissions. The Supreme Court did maintain, however, that race could be one of several factors used to determine admissions.

A shift away from quotas has continued. In *Hopwood* v. *University of Texas* (1996), a federal appeals court ruled that the University of Texas law school could not use race alone as a factor in admissions. Later that year, California voters approved a state constitutional amendment forbidding state agencies—including universities—to consider race or gender in admissions, hiring, promotions, and firing. A federal judge, however, prevented the amendment from going into effect until a federal court could determine whether it violated the U.S. Constitution. In 1997 a federal appeals court ruled that the amendment was constitutional.

CASE STUDY

Equal Pay for Equal Work

INCOME DISTRIBUTION Legally, men and women who perform the same or similar jobs must be paid the

same amount of money. But in 1996, women made only 71 cents for each dollar earned by a man. Why?

Historically, men and women have held different jobs. Some occupations—including nursing, secretarial work, and child care—traditionally have been dominated by women. Similarly, men have dominated the fields of law, construction, and engineering. Different jobs pay different wages, and in the past "women's jobs" generally paid less than "men's jobs."

To guarantee women fair wages, some people support the concept of comparable worth, which calls for analyzing the requirements for various jobs in order to set similar wages for jobs requiring similar skill levels. Supporters of comparable worth argue that assigning wages based on job knowledge, problem solving, accountability, and working conditions would remove the traditional wage bias.

Opponents of comparable worth, on the other hand, argue that the laws of supply and demand already are impartial. If women earn less money than men, they say, it is because wages in so-called women's jobs have been driven down by a surplus of available workers. Rating jobs, they argue, thus would interfere with supply and demand and discourage free enterprise.

Minimum-Wage Laws In addition to antidiscrimination laws, the government has passed legislation to ensure that workers are paid a basic level of income. One of the most important pieces of legislation to do this established a national minimum wage, or the lowest hourly wage an employer legally can pay a worker for a job.

The first minimum wage was set at 40 cents per hour by the 1938 Fair Labor Standards Act. This wage applied only to businesses engaged in interstate commerce—trade that crosses state boundaries. Furthermore, the law did not apply to farm laborers, domestic servants, and some other groups.

Over time the Fair Labor Standards Act was extended to a wider range of jobs. For example, the Supreme Court ruled in *Garcia* v. *San Antonio Metropolitan Transit Authority* (1985) that

MINIMUM WAGE, 1950–1997

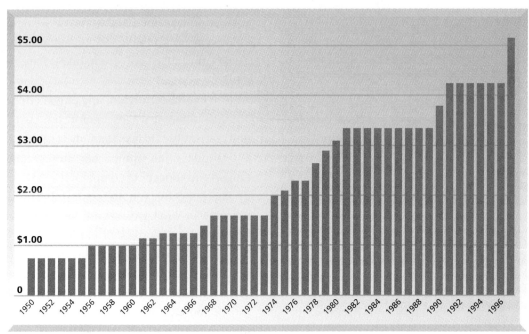

Source: *Statistical Abstract of the United States 1996; Facts On File: 1996*

FIGURE 8.4 The minimum wage is designed to provide workers with a base level of income. **In which year did the minimum wage increase by the greatest amount?**

the federal minimum-wage and overtime regulations should be applied to the millions of people who work for state and local governments. Today more than 80 percent of all employees are covered by the minimum-wage law. (For minimum-wage rate changes since 1950, see Figure 8.5.)

SECTION 1 —REVIEW

1. Define the following terms: labor force, wage, intrinsic reward, derived demand, industrialization, capital-intensive, labor-intensive, affirmative action, quota.

2. What are the six factors that affect a worker's job choice? Which factor is most important to you when you search for employment? Explain your answer.

3. List three ways in which the composition of the labor force in the United States has changed since the 1700s.

4. How does the government ensure fair treatment of workers?

5. **Thinking and Writing Critically**
How would you define the labor force at your school? How does the labor force at your school differ from the national labor force?

6. **Applying** ECONOMIC INSTITUTIONS & INCENTIVES
Conduct an Internet search for information on antidiscrimination laws. Discuss whether your findings support or oppose these laws.

THE GROWTH OF LABOR UNIONS

Economics Dictionary

labor union
open shop
closed shop

Objectives

▶ Why did labor unions develop?

▶ How are labor unions organized?

▶ What is the main challenge facing unions today?

▶ How have government attitudes toward labor unions changed?

As you know, in the last several decades the government has acted to protect the rights of workers. For more than two centuries, however, workers in the United States have taken their own steps to secure their rights. For example, as early as 1778, printers in New York joined forces to demand higher pay.

Workers also have organized into labor unions. A **labor union** is an organization of workers that negotiates with employers for better wages, improved working conditions, and job security. Labor unions—and the government's attitude toward them and their activities—have a long and varied history in the United States. Today, unions face some of their greatest challenges.

Development of Unions

You have learned how industrialization affected the kinds of jobs available to workers. Industrialization also changed the relationship between employers and their workers. The switch from labor-intensive agriculture to capital-intensive industries meant that employers, or the owners of capital, had increasingly more power than workers, or the owners of labor. This shift in power allowed some industrial business owners to make enormous profits while paying their workers only pennies a day. Owners grew increasingly rich, while workers remained poor and ever more dependent on the low wages they were forced to accept.

Thus, in the mid- and late 1800s, owners had almost complete control over both pay scales and the length of the workday. In 1860, for example, the average workweek for a factory laborer was 60 hours, for which he or she received just over 10 cents an hour. To make ends meet, families often sent their children to work in jobs outside the home. By 1890 nearly 20 percent of children aged 10 to 15 worked for wages.

At that time workplaces frequently were unsafe, noisy, and unsanitary. In 1911 more than 140 people died in a fire at the Triangle Shirtwaist Company in New York City because most of the exits were locked. In his novel *The Jungle*, Upton Sinclair described conditions in meatpacking plants, where people's hands were eaten away by the acid used to help remove the wool from sheep carcasses and where infectious diseases like tuberculosis thrived and spread in the rooms where meat was cooked.

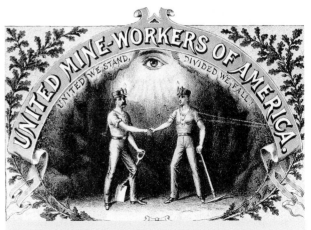

ECONOMIC INSTITUTIONS & INCENTIVES *During the late 1800s workers began to join together in labor unions to protect their rights.* **What are the two major types of unions?**

Recognizing that they could bring about change only by acting together, workers formed a number of labor unions. The two major types that developed were craft unions and industrial unions. A craft union is composed of one trade's skilled workers—for example, plumbers, electricians, or carpenters. The International Union of Bricklayers and Allied Craftsmen is a craft union. An industrial union, on the other hand, includes all workers in an industry, whether they are skilled, semiskilled, or unskilled. The United Auto Workers is an industrial union.

Knights of Labor

The most successful of the early unions was the Knights of Labor, an industrial union that was open to workers from nearly all trades. A loosely structured organization, the Knights brought together skilled and unskilled workers from a wide variety of crafts and industries. Additionally, the union offered membership to women and African Americans. At the height of its power in 1886, the Knights had nearly 700,000 members.

The Knights of Labor supported setting an eight-hour workday, ending child labor, and replacing capitalism with a system of consumers'

and producers' cooperatives. The Knights worked to achieve social and political reform through a combination of marches, demonstrations, and violent protests.

The loose structure of the Knights of Labor and its support of radical political change eventually led to its downfall. In addition, when the Knights attempted to improve the working conditions of unskilled laborers, skilled members refused to support the union's actions. Without the support of skilled workers, the union began to lose power. By 1900 it was no longer a significant force.

American Federation of Labor

The modern period of the U.S. labor movement began in 1886, when a loose association of craft unions organized as the American Federation of Labor (AFL). Samuel Gompers, the first AFL president, felt that unions should focus their efforts on gaining higher wages and better working conditions rather than striving for social changes such as the cooperatives supported by the Knights. The AFL mainly included unions of skilled workers, excluding unions of unskilled workers. In 1914 the AFL had more than 2 million members. By 1920 its membership had doubled.

The 1920s, however, were difficult for labor unions. Internal struggles plagued the AFL, and opponents challenged Gompers' leadership. When he died in 1924, the presidency of the union changed hands, but the internal struggles did not disappear. At the same time, a strong antiunion sentiment arose as many unions supported radical platforms and actions. Businesses, with the aid of the government, attacked organized labor. Many business owners set up **open shops**, in which workers did not have to join a union. Unions, of course, preferred **closed shops**, in which workers could be hired only if they first joined a union. (See Figure 8.5.)

Massive unemployment during the Great Depression of the 1930s decreased the AFL's membership. The continuing internal disputes, particularly over the inclusion of unskilled workers, eventually pushed several AFL unions to form a new, separate labor organization.

Congress of Industrial Organizations

Although the AFL was made up primarily of craft unions, a few industrial unions did join. To further widen the AFL's membership, John L. Lewis, president of the United Mine Workers (UMW), formed the Committee for Industrial Organizations within the AFL in 1935. One of the committee's main goals was to organize both unskilled and semiskilled workers in several industries and bring them into the American Federation of Labor.

By 1937, AFL leaders—determined to keep the organization focused on craft unions—had expelled Lewis and all of the industrial unions that he had helped organize. A year later, Lewis became president of the newly named Congress of Industrial Organizations (CIO). Under his leadership, millions of unskilled industrial workers—including women as well as African Americans and other minorities—were organized. Large industrial unions that joined the CIO included the United Steel Workers (USW), the United Automobile Workers (UAW), and Lewis's own UMW.

Union Organization

As workers in many industries and regions joined together to claim their rights, labor unions began to structure themselves in certain ways. What are these forms of organization?

Local Unions Local unions are made up of people who work for a particular company or in a particular area. One local union might be made up of all the workers at the Fantastic Furniture Company. Another might include only saw operators from several lumber companies in the same city.

National Unions At the next level of organization, local unions from different parts of the country are organized into national unions. Suppose, for example, that the Saw Operators Union of Toledo is one chapter of the Saw Operators Union of America. Although union members are more likely to be active in their local unions, national unions often are better known to the public and hold greater political and economic

States with Right-to-Work Laws

- ■ States with right-to-work laws
- □ States without right-to-work laws

Source: *Statistical Abstract of the United States: 1996*

FIGURE 8.5 States establish right-to-work laws, which prohibit shops that are closed to nonunion workers. **Which states have right-to-work laws?**

CHANGES IN UNION MEMBERSHIP

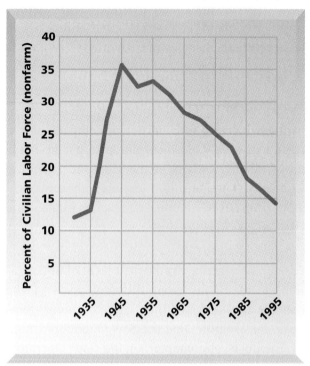

Source: *U.S. Bureau of Labor Statistics: 1986; Statistical Abstract of the United States: 1996*

FIGURE 8.6 Union membership declined in the decades after World War II. **What factors contributed to this decline?**

power because of their size. National unions provide their local chapters with leadership on national issues, as well as lawyers and other specialized staff to support local causes.

One of the best-known national organizations is the AFL–CIO. By the mid-1950s, union leaders in the AFL and the CIO acknowledged that all laborers—skilled and unskilled alike—had similar economic concerns. In 1955 the two organizations merged, forming the AFL–CIO. Today this organization includes dozens of smaller unions and more than 13 million members across the nation.

Independent Unions Many labor unions are not affiliated with the AFL–CIO. For example, the National Education Association is an independent union with more than 2 million members. Local unions also may be independent of national organizations.

Challenges to Labor Unions

In recent decades the labor movement in the United States has experienced a period of crisis. Union membership has dropped dramatically, as shown in Figure 8.6. The three main reasons for the decline are

▶ employer opposition,
▶ changes in employment patterns, and
▶ negative public opinion.

Employer Opposition The managements of many companies have opposed the development of unions because increased wages for workers mean lower profits for owners. Rather than attacking the unions directly, however, in recent years some employers have tried to make unions seem unnecessary by changing company labor policies to recognize the invaluable role of workers. For example, some employers have made workers part of management teams. Others have allowed employee representatives to sit on their boards of directors, thus giving workers a voice in company decision making.

Other companies simply try to avoid dealing with unions. For example, some companies in the Northeast and the Midwest, where unionism traditionally has been strong, have moved their headquarters or production facilities to cities in the South and the Southwest, where unions tend to hold less power. Similarly, some companies have moved production to other countries, where wages are low and a lack of unionization enables employers to cut costs significantly.

Changes in Employment Patterns A second factor contributing to the decline of unions in the United States is the shift from a manufacturing-based economy to a service-based economy. Labor union membership traditionally has been strong in the manufacturing sector, such as the automobile and appliance industries. However, employment in this sector has dropped in recent years, while employment of office and service workers—who generally have low union participation rates—has increased.

Union Summer

Meet the face of modern organized labor: University of Texas student Gladiola Campos. Although most labor activities in the past were carried out by older white males, many labor activists today are—like Gladiola—female, members of minority groups, and in their twenties and thirties.

The American Federation of Labor–Congress of Industrial Organizations (AFL–CIO) is working to energize the labor movement by recruiting young people like Gladiola, who was one of more than 1,000 student volunteers chosen to participate in the AFL–CIO's 1996 "Union Summer." The campaign was modeled after the historic Freedom Summer of 1964, which promoted civil rights and voter registration for African Americans.

Union Summer volunteers worked in more than 20 cities across the United States. For $210 a week and free housing, the students demonstrated against unfair labor practices on riverboat casinos in St. Louis, registered voters door to door and encouraged local union activism in San Diego, and urged farmworkers in California to become union members.

As an immigrant and the daughter of an El Paso janitor, Gladiola Campos felt it her duty to fight for immigrants who were not able to attend college, as she was. "Around campus, I see so many Mexicans cleaning dorms. We are all immigrants, but I got lucky." She also knows firsthand the power of unions: before her mother's workplace was unionized in 1989, "she had to work two jobs and we couldn't afford health insurance."

Rafael Garcia, Jr., a volunteer from Santa Monica College, was eager to work with the United Farm Workers (UFW). Inspired to join Union Summer by his idol, the late UFW leader and founder César Chávez, Rafael explained his reasons for union activism: "People aren't active. They don't want to get involved in things. . . . A lot of workers don't want to unionize because they're afraid of being fired. . . . I'm hoping to get workers to join unions and not to be afraid to stand up for themselves."

Employers' reactions to the enthusiasm of young union activists have been lukewarm. Jeffrey McGuiness—president of the Labor Policy Association in Washington, D.C., which represents the interests of large corporations—says, "College students breezing in and telling people they are better off joining a union—and then breezing back to school again—that's not likely to be very effective." In addition to their academic experience, however, many of Union Summer's handpicked volunteers have worked in blue-collar jobs and have parents or other relatives who have benefited from union membership.

The AFL–CIO is counting on long-term results from their efforts in the summer of 1996. Organizers hope not only that union membership and awareness will increase in the short run, but that young people who participated in Union Summer will consider careers in the labor movement.

What Do You Think?

1. Why would the AFL–CIO want to recruit union members and organizers with a variety of backgrounds?

2. Why might college students be attracted to a project like Union Summer?

More than 1,000 student volunteers participated in the AFL–CIO's 1996 Union Summer.

MAJOR LABOR LEGISLATION

YEAR	LEGISLATION	PURPOSE
1914	Clayton Antitrust Act	exempts unions from antitrust suits and gives labor the right to strike, picket, and organize a boycott of a firm's products in an effort to settle contract disputes; made it more difficult for businesses to obtain injunctions against unions; not always effective because courts often sided with businesses
1932	Norris–La Guardia Act	guarantees the right of a worker to join a union and engage in normal union activities; outlaws contracts prohibiting employees from joining unions; restricts the issuing of court injunctions during labor disputes
1935	Wagner Act	(also called the National Labor Relations Act) guarantees workers the right to form unions and to bargain collectively; requires management to bargain in good faith and refrain from unfair labor practices; established the National Labor Relations Board
1938	Fair Labor Standards Act	(also called the Wages and Hours Law) established a minimum wage and set a maximum workweek of 44 hours (which was later reduced to 40 hours); guarantees time-and-a-half pay for overtime, and restricts child labor
1947	Taft-Hartley Act	(also called the Labor-Management Relations Act) reversed some earlier union gains by prohibiting closed shops; allows states to enact right-to-work laws, which prohibit closed shops; requires a "cooling-of" period of 60 days prior to strike or termination of a contract and allows federal injunctions to block certain strikes for up to 80 days; outlaws union campaign contributions to national political candidates
1959	Landrum-Griffin Act	(also called the Labor-Management Act) passed in an effort to prevent corrupt union practices; requires union officials to be elected democratically; requires that union funds be recorded with the Department of Labor; set up strict guidelines to be followed in establishing unions and in conducting union activities
1964	Civil Rights Act	title VII established the first federal fair employment practices law, prohibiting employers to discriminate on the basis of race, color, religion, national origin, or sex; established an Equal Opportunity Commission to investigate and rule on complaints

FIGURE 8.7 The federal government has passed a number of laws designed to regulate the workplace. **How do the laws listed here reflect changes in government attitudes toward unions?**

Additionally, growing numbers of women and teenagers have entered the labor force. Although unions do not exclude them, such workers have not been at the center of union organizing efforts and often have not been attracted to union membership. Thus, as employment of women and teenagers has increased, the percentage of employees involved in unions has declined.

Negative Public Opinion
The third factor in the decline of unions is the public's generally negative view of them. Many people—including economists—feel that union demands for higher wages and increased benefits have encouraged companies to move their factories outside of the country, thereby decreasing the number of jobs available to workers in the United States. Some also believe that union members' wages are too high considering the skill level needed to perform their jobs.

In addition, the public has at times opposed the actions of union leaders, some of whom have been accused of accepting political favors in exchange for lowering union demands. Others are thought to have used violence and other offensive tactics to maintain their power. These incidents have contributed to a negative public attitude toward unions.

Union Responses

One union response to the drop in membership has been to adopt a more cooperative spirit in their dealings with management. For example, during the 1980s labor and management in some industries agreed to wage and benefit reductions to help their companies remain competitive in the marketplace.

Additionally, labor and management have come together on other national issues. For example, both groups have opposed rapidly rising insurance costs for businesses.

To increase membership, organized labor has addressed new issues that are of concern to workers, such as skill training, career development programs, quality of life in the workplace, and worker involvement in decision making on the job. Other issues, such as the availability of day care facilities, are designed to appeal to parents and other specific groups of workers.

Unions also have attempted to gain members by improving the training they provide to union organizers. Unions also are hiring professional union organizers to explain the benefits of membership to nonunion workers.

Finally, unions have experimented with a number of incentives to make membership more attractive. For example, unions have offered incentives such as life and health insurance plans, retirement accounts, low-interest credit cards, and legal services.

Government and Unions

The government's responses to unions have changed over time. During the 1800s the government generally favored business interests over those of labor unions. For example, in 1894, workers at Chicago's Pullman Palace Car Company factory, which produced sleeping cars for trains, protested wage cuts by refusing to work. Eugene V. Debs, leader of the American Railway Union, then urged union members to refuse to work on any train with a Pullman car. When railroad traffic across the country was disrupted, the railroad companies attached mail cars to Pullman cars. This action caused the government to oppose the protests on the grounds that they were preventing mail delivery. Federal troops were sent to enforce order, and protesters were jailed.

The government's attitude toward unions changed during the first decades of the 1900s, however, when the country entered a period of social and political reform. The U.S. Congress and state legislatures passed laws protecting the rights of workers. Since 1940, though, legislation once again has tended to place limits on the power of unions. (For a description of major labor legislation, see Figure 8.7.)

SECTION 2 — REVIEW

1. Define the following terms: labor union, open shop, closed shop.

2. What conditions led to the development of labor unions?

3. How do national unions support local unions?

4. What are the main reasons for declining union membership? How have unions responded?

5. **Thinking and Writing Critically** Research a local union in your area. You might start by contacting one listed in the local newspaper or telephone directory. Be sure to find out its size, goals, and organization.

6. **Applying** ECONOMIC INSTITUTIONS & INCENTIVES In your opinion, how should the government interact with unions? Should it be supportive? regulatory? confrontational? Explain.

UNIONS AND MANAGEMENT

Economics Dictionary

fringe benefit
seniority
collective bargaining
mediation
arbitration
strike
primary boycott
secondary boycott
coordinated campaigning
lockout
injunction

Objectives

▶ What major issues are discussed in labor contract negotiations?

▶ How do unions and management reach a contract agreement?

▶ What negotiation tactics do unions and management use?

As noted in Section 2, unions are organizations of workers who pool their resources and efforts to secure fair pay, better benefits, safe working conditions, and job security. How can labor unions work to achieve these goals? What tactics do dissatisfied workers sometimes employ? How does management respond to these tactics?

Labor Contract Issues

The labor movement in the United States traditionally has focused on practical issues that affect workers on a daily basis. In negotiations between labor and management, five major issues usually are discussed:

▶ wages and fringe benefits,
▶ working conditions,
▶ job security,
▶ union security, and
▶ grievance procedures.

Suppose that Kara Langley is a leader of the Tour Workers Union in San Francisco. The union includes local tour guides, bus and van drivers, and office workers. For several years Kara worked as a tour guide, so she understands many of the challenges faced by tour workers. The union is currently negotiating a labor contract with a new tour company, and the five issues listed above are under discussion.

Wages and Fringe Benefits The union's first major concern is about wages paid to tour guides, drivers, and office workers. Wages are set by labor contracts and vary according to the type of position held and the number of years a worker has been on the job. Tour guides and drivers probably will be paid different amounts, just as a guide with 10 years of experience will most likely earn more money than a newly hired guide.

ECONOMIC INSTITUTIONS & INCENTIVES *Workers' concerns usually are focused on issues that they confront on a daily basis.* ***What are the five major issues that generally are discussed in labor negotiations?***

The labor contract also outlines the policy for paying overtime to tour employees working more than the standard 40-hour work week. In addition, the contract includes a cost-of-living adjustment (COLA). A COLA automatically raises employee wages to match widespread price increases, allowing workers to maintain their purchasing power.

In addition to negotiating for higher wages, Kara—as a union representative—tries to ensure that the tour workers will receive fringe benefits in the labor contracts. **Fringe benefits** are nonwage payments, commonly including paid sick days, holidays, and vacation days; health and life insurance; and savings and retirement plans. Many companies also provide profit sharing as well as employee stock ownership plans (ESOPs). Under profit sharing, a firm distributes a portion of its profits to workers. An ESOP provides workers with stock in the company. By providing higher benefits only if the company does well, profit sharing and ESOPs provide an incentive for employees to work hard.

Working Conditions

Kara also tries to secure good working conditions for union employees. In addition to conditions at the tour office, Kara works to improve conditions at the tour locations that workers will visit, such as Fisherman's Wharf, Golden Gate Park, and Lombard Street. Desirable working conditions include a clean and safe workplace, clearly defined work responsibilities, and reasonable working hours. Kara tries to make sure that the labor contract specifies the number of tours a guide is expected to lead each week, the types of vehicles drivers will operate, the ease of contacting and gaining assistance from the tour office, and the maximum number of visitors on each tour.

ECONOMIC INSTITUTIONS & INCENTIVES *American Airlines pilots fought to gain better job security and wages in their 1997 contract negotiations.* **What other labor issues might be important to pilots?**

Job Security

As she negotiates the contract, Kara focuses on the need for the new company to provide job security. The legal system provides some job security for workers. For example, the law prohibits an employer from firing an employee because of race, sex, religion, age, or union activity.

Union negotiators typically seek contracts that give greater job security through the seniority system. **Seniority** is the holding of privileges based on the number of years a worker has been employed by a firm. Labor contracts usually protect seniority by requiring that workers with the least seniority be the first to lose their jobs in the event that the company must reduce its workforce. In other words, if the tour company is forced to lay off workers, a tour bus driver who has been working for six months will lose his job before a driver who has held her job for three years.

Union Security

As she negotiates the terms of the labor contract, Kara also ensures that workers are free to join the union. In other words, employees of the new tour company will be able to participate in the union without worrying

ECONOMIC INSTITUTIONS & INCENTIVES *Union organizers negotiate for union security.* **What organization enforces workers right to organize and join a union?**

about whether company owners approve of union activities.

In its broadest sense, union security provides workers with the right to organize and join a union. This right is enforced by the National Labor Relations Board (NLRB).

How does a union become the negotiating body for workers in a company? First, at least 30 percent of a firm's employees must sign a petition informing the NLRB that they want to hold an election to determine whether a majority of employees want to unionize. Second, the NLRB conducts the election using a secret ballot, which allows workers to vote without fear of harassment or intimidation. If the majority of workers favor unionization, the NLRB recognizes the union as the only bargaining representative for the company's employees.

Grievance Procedures When a work-related dispute arises, either labor or management may seek resolution by following a particular set of steps. For example, suppose that one of the tour guides feels that she is not receiving as many tour assignments as she should. If union representatives agree and feel that management has violated provisions outlined in the labor contract, the union may begin grievance procedures.

Grievances, or formal complaints, usually are resolved by committees made up of representatives of the union and the management. If this procedure does not resolve the problem, a negotiator is brought in by the NLRB. Both sides—union and management—must agree to give the negotiator all applicable information and to abide by the negotiator's decision.

Contract Negotiations

You have learned about the major issues in contract negotiations. How do union representatives and management arrive at an agreement on these issues?

Collective Bargaining When negotiating a new contract with management, union leaders speak for all the members they represent. During this process, known as **collective bargaining**, union and management representatives meet to discuss their goals and offer solutions and compromises. In most cases, collective bargaining results in a contract settlement. At times, however, other negotiation methods must be used.

Mediation Sometimes the bargaining process breaks down, and labor and management are unable to make any progress. In this case, they may resort to mediation. In **mediation**, negotiators call in a neutral third party, or mediator, to listen to the arguments of both sides and to suggest ways in which an agreement may be reached.

Who serves as a mediator? Mediation services are offered by private citizens and government agencies alike. In addition, the Taft-Hartley Act of 1947—which gives the government the power to regulate relations between labor and management—established the Federal Mediation and Conciliation Service (FMCS). The FMCS mediates thousands of disputes every year.

Arbitration In some cases, neither collective bargaining nor mediation results in a contract settlement. A third method of reaching an agreement is **arbitration**. Like mediation, arbitration calls for the assistance of a negotiator to arrive at a contract. An arbitrator, like a mediator, is a neutral third party. Unlike in mediation, however, an arbitrator's decision is legally binding.

Union Tactics

What happens when unions and management are unable to reach an agreement through collective

Careers in Economics

Labor Relations Consultant

As business decisions become increasingly complex, many companies are turning to outside experts for information and ideas. These experts—called consultants—bring their experience and knowledge to many kinds of companies.

Consultants generally have undergraduate and professional degrees in business or law, as well as several years of work experience in a particular field or industry. In addition, many consultants take courses to improve their skills and expand their understanding of business practices and policies.

Consultants are often called in during contract negotiations between labor and management. Suppose, for example, that union representatives want to know if their fringe benefits are comparable to those received by workers in other companies. They may hire a labor relations consultant who can bring knowledge of employment conditions in many regions and industries. Similarly, management may hire a labor relations consultant who can analyze union demands and support management's position during negotiations.

Labor relations consultants have to be intelligent, well informed, persistent, and able to think quickly under pressure. Experience in public speaking and debate, as well as strong research abilities and writing skills, can help a consultant be both persuasive and knowledgeable.

One of the most important skills for a labor relations consultant is the willingness and ability to compromise. Although a consultant may support union positions and have strong views about what actions should be taken, he or she must recognize when to agree to management's terms in order to gain other advantages. You might think of labor relations as a game of checkers. Although your goal is to capture as many pieces—or win as many concessions—as possible, sometimes you may have to lose some of your own pieces—or give up on some issues—to keep moving forward.

Labor relations consultants must be highly skilled in the art of compromise.

bargaining, mediation, or arbitration? In some cases unions may resort to a **strike**, in which they call for union members to stop working until contract demands are met.

Most strikes are called over wage disputes. For example, a salary dispute between professional baseball players and major-league team owners led to a shortened 1994 season and the cancellation of that year's World Series, as well as a delayed start for the 1995 season.

Other strikes have been called because of poor working conditions, lack of benefits, and unfair management practices. In August 1997, for example, the Teamsters Union organized a strike against United Parcel Service (UPS). Demanding more full-time jobs and improved benefits such as pensions, some 185,000 employees participated in the strike. The company's delivery rate dropped from an average of 12 million packages a day to about 120,000. Mediation by the federal government helped to end the

15-day strike, as UPS management agreed to a number of union demands.

Strikes often involve more than the stoppage of work. Three tactics commonly are used in carrying out strikes:

▶ picketing,
▶ boycotting, and
▶ coordinated campaigning.

Picketing Imagine that the assembly line workers at the Merry Marker Crayon Company go on strike. They decide to picket the company, parading in front of the plant while carrying signs that explain their grievances. Why might they decide to adopt this tactic?

The tactic of picketing has three purposes. First, it informs the public that a strike is in progress. Passersby will see the striking workers and read the grievances listed on their signs. Second, picketing may arouse public support. Some

ECONOMIC INSTITUTIONS & INCENTIVES *More than 185,000 Teamsters went on strike against United Parcel Service in August 1997.* ***What are three common strike tactics?***

members of the public will identify with the problems of the striking workers. Third, picketing discourages nonstrikers from entering the plant. Some workers who did not join the strike may be too intimidated to return to work if they must walk through the group of striking workers. Workers who cross the picket line, called scabs, are often insulted by strikers.

Boycotts If picketing does not help resolve a contract dispute, a union might decide to organize a boycott. A **primary boycott** is an organized effort to stop purchases of a firm's products.

Most primary boycotts are organized on a local level, but some have been successful on a national scale. During the 1960s César Chávez led the National Farm Workers Association in an attempt to improve the wages and working conditions of migrant agricultural laborers. The union expanded and became known as the United Farm Workers (UFW). In 1965 the union organized a primary boycott of grapes. Millions of consumers across the United States supported the union by refusing to buy grapes. This primary boycott lasted for five years, until grape growers in California agreed to a contract with the union.

A **secondary boycott** is a refusal to buy the goods or services of any firm that does business with a company whose employees are on strike. For example, you would be participating in a secondary boycott if you refused to buy lunch or any other goods at the Griffin's Nook Comic and Sandwich Shop because the store carried comic books by White Tiger Press, whose employees are on strike. The Taft-Hartley Act, however, made secondary boycotts illegal if workers are striking in an attempt to make that employer join a boycott of another firm.

Coordinated Campaigning The third tactic that unions may use is called **coordinated campaigning**, which involves the use of picketing as well as boycotts. For example, in 1985–86 a local union of the United Food and Commercial Workers (UFCW) organized a coordinated campaign against George A. Hormel & Company, which makes hot dogs, chili, and many other

ECONOMIC INSTITUTIONS & INCENTIVES *César Chávez led the United Farm Workers in an attempt to improve working conditions for migrant laborers.* **What is a boycott?**

food products. The UFCW local picketed and boycotted the Hormel company as well as corporations and banks that did business with Hormel. Union members also distributed leaflets to community members and to other unions to try to gain support for the UFCW local's demands.

Management Responses

Suppose that the dispatchers at the local police department go on strike. How will the city government respond to the strike? Officials might agree to the demands of the dispatchers' union. On the other hand, they might oppose the strike. Three common management actions are

▶ hiring replacement workers,
▶ introducing a lockout, and
▶ asking for an injunction.

Replacement Workers The police department may decide to hire replacement dispatchers so that police officers will be able to respond to reports of crime. Finding qualified workers can be difficult, however, and picketing workers often try to intimidate strikebreakers as they attempt to go to work.

ECONOMIC INSTITUTIONS & INCENTIVES *These workers have been locked out of their jobs.* **What are three common management responses to a strike?**

Lockouts A **lockout** occurs when an employer closes a company's doors to striking workers until negotiators reach a contract agreement that is satisfactory to management. Striking dispatchers who have been locked out by the police department will not be allowed to return to work—even if the strike ends before an agreement is reached. Lockouts can cause problems for employers, however. Employers may lose money if they are unable to hire other workers and production stops.

Injunctions The police department also might ask the government to issue an **injunction**, or court order, to prohibit the dispatchers from striking. There are restrictions on injunctions, but the Taft-Hartley Act permits the issuing of an injunction when a strike threatens the health or safety of the public. A police dispatcher strike might pose just such a threat, as police officers would not be informed of which crimes or disturbances required their attention.

SECTION 3 — REVIEW

1. Define the following terms: fringe benefit, seniority, collective bargaining, mediation, arbitration, strike, primary boycott, secondary boycott, coordinated campaigning, lockout, injunction.

2. What major issues generally are discussed in contract negotiations? Describe how each of these issues affects workers.

3. Compare mediation and arbitration.

4. What options are available to unions and to management when contract negotiations fail to reach a labor agreement? Which of these methods do you think would be easiest to organize? Explain your answer.

5. **Thinking and Writing Critically** Describe a dispute you have had with a friend or classmate. What methods did you use to resolve the dispute? How were your methods similar to—or different from—those used in union negotiations?

6. **Applying** ECONOMIC INSTITUTIONS & INCENTIVES Think about why workers use picketing, boycotts, or coordinated campaigning as strike tactics. Which do you think would be most effective? Explain your answer.

SECTION 1 The U.S. labor force, which includes more than 130 million people, is made up of all people who are at least 16 years old and who are working or looking for work. These people are part of the civilian labor force.

Workers usually consider six main factors when they enter the labor force. These factors are wages, skill levels, working conditions, location, intrinsic rewards, and market trends.

The labor force has undergone numerous changes throughout the nation's history. Among these changes are a shift from a labor-intensive economy to a capital-intensive economy, increased numbers of women in the labor force, and higher levels of education among workers. Additionally, the government has passed a series of laws aimed at protecting workers from discrimination in hiring, promotion, and firing. These laws include the Equal Pay Act of 1963 and the Civil Rights Act of 1964. In addition, the 1938 Fair Labor Standards Act established the first minimum wage and protections for the rights of individual workers.

SECTION 2 To secure their rights, many U.S. workers organized labor unions. These unions struggled for higher wages, improved working conditions, and job security for workers. Well-known unions have included the Knights of Labor, American Federation of Labor, and Congress of Industrial Organization. In 1955 the American Federation of Labor and the Congress of Industrial Organization merged to form the AFL–CIO. Today the AFL–CIO, with its more than 13 million members, is the largest and most powerful labor organization in the United States.

Labor union membership, however, has declined in recent years. This trend has resulted from several factors, including employer opposition, changes in employment patterns, and negative public opinion of unions. Unions have tried to face these challenges by cooperating more with employers and by addressing new issues of concern to workers.

The government's attitude toward unions has changed during the last century. In the late 1800s the government regularly supported business owners. However, in the early 1900s—during times of social and political reform—activists were able to persuade the government to support unions by passing laws to protect the rights of workers. After 1940 the government again changed its attitude, and passed new laws limiting the power of unions.

SECTION 3 Common labor contract issues between workers and management include wages and fringe benefits, working conditions and hours, job security, union security, and grievance procedures. Labor unions rely on collective bargaining, mediation, and arbitration to improve working conditions and wages for their members. If an agreement is not reached, unions resort to such tactics as strikes, picketing, boycotts, and coordinated campaigning. Management can counter these tactics by hiring replacement workers, introducing lockouts, and requesting injunctions.

Economics Notebook

Review the list you wrote in your Economics Notebook of the kinds of labor you perform. How do you decide how to use your own labor? What influences your decisions about where and how to work? Explain your answer in your Notebook.

└REVIEW

REVIEWING CONCEPTS

1. Explain how supply and demand affect the labor force.

2. How has the composition of the U.S. labor force changed since the 1800s?

3. Why did workers in the 1800s and early 1900s begin to organize unions?

4. Describe how government attitudes toward labor unions have changed over time.

5. What major issues generally are addressed during labor contract negotiations?

6. What tactics might a labor union use during contract negotiations? What tactics might management use?

THINKING AND WRITING CRITICALLY

1. **SUPPLY & DEMAND** Investigate three occupations that you are interested in pursuing. What is the average wage? What working conditions might you expect to encounter? Where are most of these jobs located? What intrinsic rewards are offered? Create a chart that answers these questions for each job.

2. **ECONOMIC INSTITUTIONS & INCENTIVES** Research the activities of a national union such as the United Steel Workers (USW) or the International Ladies' Garment Workers' Union (ILGWU). Create a poster or chart that reflects the union's major activities.

3. **EXCHANGE, MONEY, & INTERDEPENDENCE** Consider your school as a workplace for both teachers and students. Create a table that describes wages and fringe benefits, working conditions and hours, job security, union security, and grievance procedures for each of these groups.

4. **ECONOMIC INSTITUTIONS & INCENTIVES** Describe an example from your own experience of each of the following: collective bargaining, mediation, arbitration.

YOUR LOCAL ECONOMY

Visit your local library or chamber of commerce, and research the labor force in your community. What percentage of workers are employed in manufacturing jobs? How many workers in your community have high school diplomas? How many have college degrees? What is the average salary for a worker in your community? Use your findings to create a labor force profile of your community. Be sure to compare your local labor force with the national labor force.

INDIVIDUAL PORTFOLIO PROJECT

Research the symbols, emblems, and logos used by unions to identify products made by union members. Create a board game that challenges players to identify which logo matches which union, and then share the game with your classmates.

PRACTICING SKILLS: UNDERSTANDING CHARTS AND GRAPHS

Using the information in the table on page 193, create a bar graph that illustrates the change in women's participation in the labor force over time. Your bar graph may be either horizontal or vertical. You may wish to use Figure 8.4 on page 176 as a model. After you have created your graph, answer the questions below.

1. Does the graph indicate that women's labor force growth between 1900 and 1995 has been consistent or uneven?

Year	Women in the labor force (in thousands)	Percent of women in the labor force	Women as percent of total labor force
1900	5,319	18.8	18.3
1910	8,076	23.4	21.2
1920	8,550	21.0	20.5
1930	10,752	22.0	22.0
1940	12,887	25.4	24.5
1950	18,389	33.9	29.6
1960	23,240	37.7	33.4
1970	31,543	43.3	38.1
1980	45,487	51.5	42.5
1990	56,829	57.5	45.2
1995	60,944	58.9	46.1

Sources: *Historical Statistics of the United States: Colonial Times to 1970, Part 1:* U.S. Bureau of Statistics

2. What differences do you notice between the percentage of women in the labor force and the percentage of the labor force made up by women? What conclusions might you draw from your findings?

THE INTERNET: LEARNING ONLINE

Conduct an Internet search for union home pages. You might start by using search words such as *union* or the name of a particular union. Create a fact sheet on one of the unions you have researched, describing what information is included on its home page.

ANALYZING PRIMARY SOURCES

César Chávez and the Council of California Growers

On January 15, 1974, nineteen farm workers on their way to work died in a bus accident in southern California. The following passage is from a speech that César Chávez delivered at a memorial mass for the workers. As you read the excerpt, consider the author's point of view.

"There have been too many accidents in the fields, on trucks, under machines, in buses; so many accidents involving farm workers. People ask if they are deliberate. They are deliberate in the sense that they are the direct result of a farm labor system that treats workers like agricultural implements [tools] and not human beings.

"These accidents happen because employers and labor contractors treat us as if we were not important human beings. . . . The workers learned long ago that growers and labor contractors have too little regard for the value of any individual worker's life. The trucks and buses are old, and unsafe. The fields are sprayed with poisons. The laws that do exist are not enforced. How long will it be before we take serious the importance of the workers who harvest the food we eat?

"We are united in our sorrow, but also in our anger. This tragedy happened because of the greed of the big growers who do not care about the safety of the workers and who expose them to grave dangers when they transport them in wheeled coffins to the field."

A few days later Don Curlee—a grower representative and former executive assistant to the Council of California Growers—responded by writing a letter to the *Los Angeles Times*. Consider point of view as you read the following excerpt from Curlee's letter.

"This [Chávez's writing] is inflammatory [anger-inciting], irresponsible, and unnecessarily harsh rhetoric [inflated speech] that has no basis in fact . . . the bus was not owned, maintained, or operated by a grower, big or small. Only the shallowest, most reactionary [backward] thinking can associate this accident with greediness on the part of anybody.

"Sympathy certainly is extended to the families of the victims, especially since they have been exploited [used] in the publicity-seeking stunts of Chávez consoling them publicly. The greater tragedy here is an intellectual and moral one, in which the demagog [agitator] Chávez capitalizes on the deaths of people he purports [claims] to represent and seeks to use the occasion as a platform from which to spew his unfounded vilification of [wrongly giving a bad name to] growers."

1. Why do you think Chávez thought as he did? Why did Curlee think as he did?

2. How might Chávez's cause have gained from publicity surrounding the workers' deaths?

3. Do you agree with Chávez's argument that the accident occurred "because of the greed of the big growers?" Explain your answer.

CHAPTER 9

SOURCES OF CAPITAL

Because you are part of a free-enterprise economy, you can choose how to use your money. You may decide to buy products such as a stereo or in-line skates. You may decide to save your money, or to invest it.

At some point you also may decide to borrow money. Major expenses often require consumers to take out loans. Although borrowing can present hazards to people who are unable to pay their debts, it can also encourage economic growth and economic stability.

In this chapter you will learn how consumers can save, invest, and borrow money. Additionally, you will learn how the government regulates these activities.

✎ Economics Notebook

Imagine that you have just won $500 in a trivia contest on the radio. Write a brief paragraph in your Economics Notebook explaining what you will do with the money and how you made your choices.

SECTION 1
SAVING

Economics Dictionary
disposable income
balance
liquidity
time deposit
maturity
savings rate

Objectives
▶ What benefits do people gain by saving money?
▶ How do savings accounts differ from time deposits?
▶ How do economists measure savings?

In a free-enterprise economy business owners can choose how to organize their companies and workers can make choices about how to use their labor. Similarly, consumers have an important choice to make—how to use the income at their disposal. They may spend this income or save it, consume it or not consume it. Spending is the consumption of **disposable income**—money available after taxes have been paid. Saving is the nonconsumption of disposable income.

Spending and saving are equally important to a strong economy. Spending reflects demand—how much of a product consumers will buy at a particular price. As spending increases, producers expand supply, and as spending decreases, producers reduce supply. But how is saving important?

Why Save Money?

Think about what people can do with money they have saved. In general, people save for five main reasons: for major purchases such as a car, house,

or refrigerator; to pay large annual or semiannual bills such as property taxes or automobile insurance; for unexpected expenses such as medical treatment or home repairs; for major long-term expenses such as college tuition or retirement needs; and to amass wealth or leave an inheritance to their children.

No matter what reasons people have for saving money, they experience two benefits: security and interest.

Security Saving money in a bank or other lending institution provides two types of security. First, money in a bank account cannot be lost because of misfortunes in the home, such as fire or theft. Second, most financial institutions are protected by state and federal deposit insurance. These insurance plans protect savers from losing their money if the institution closes.

Interest When you deposit money in a financial institution, you may receive a payment called interest. The financial institution pays interest in exchange for the use of your money while it is deposited. (See Figure 9.1 on page 196.)

Interest rates on savings vary according to the type of account chosen and the financial

ECONOMIC INSTITUTIONS & INCENTIVES *One major expense that many people save for is college. **What are two benefits of saving?***

COMPOUND INTEREST

Compounded Interest on a Single Investment of $1,000

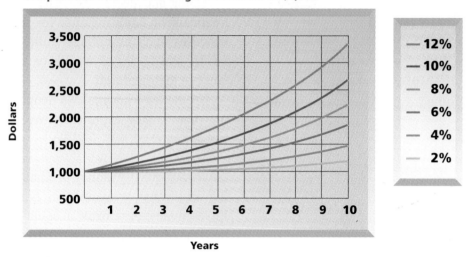

Financial institutions pay interest in exchange for the use of customers' money. **What causes interest rates to change?**

institution in which the money is deposited. Interest rates also fluctuate, or change, to reflect the general availability of money in the economy. When the supply of money in the economy is reduced, interest rates generally increase. When more money is available, on the other hand, interest rates are lower.

Financial institutions such as banks also *charge* interest on the loans they make to individuals and businesses. Again, this interest is a payment for the use of the loaned money. Basically, a bank or other financial institution makes a profit in part by charging more interest on loans than it pays on savings deposits.

Savings Accounts

Suppose that Monique Foster decides to open a savings account. She already knows that savings accounts offer very little risk. While her money is deposited in a financial institution such as a bank, her funds—up to $100,000—are insured by the federal government. When Monique arrives at her local bank, she discovers that she can choose from among different types of accounts, including regular savings accounts and money market deposit accounts.

Regular Savings Accounts Regular savings accounts, which are among the most common types of accounts, usually require only a small deposit. Many financial institutions, however, charge a fee if the **balance**—the amount of money in the account—drops below a specified level.

Some depositors open regular savings accounts because they offer liquidity. **Liquidity** means that assets such as an account can be converted into cash with little or no loss in interest payments. Monique could withdraw her savings from this type of account at any time. In exchange for high liquidity, the interest rate on a regular savings account is relatively low compared to the interest paid on other types of savings accounts.

Money Market Deposit Accounts Monique may decide to open a money market deposit account. Like regular savings accounts, money market deposit accounts pay interest and allow relatively easy access to savings. These accounts offer variable interest rates that generally are higher than those of regular savings accounts.

To determine interest rates for money market deposit accounts, financial institutions invest funds from these accounts in interest-bearing securities such as Treasury bills. The financial institution passes on part of the interest to account holders and keeps the rest as profit. Because these interest rates fluctuate, however, account holders may not always receive higher interest rates.

Money market deposit accounts have a fair amount of liquidity. Account holders can make withdrawals without penalty, but they are usually restricted to making a certain number of withdrawals each month. Some financial institutions place other restrictions on these money market accounts as well, such as requiring advance notice of withdrawals.

Time Deposits

Suppose that Monique decides that savings accounts do not offer enough interest. She may open an account known as a time deposit. **Time deposits** require the saver to leave money in the account for a specific amount of time. Savers who want to open time deposits probably will buy certificates of deposit or savings bonds.

Certificates of Deposit
Monique may decide to deposit her money for a particular length of time. If she does, she will receive a certificate of deposit (CD) that represents her funds. The length of time that money must be deposited is called the **maturity**. The maturities of CDs range from less than a month to several years.

CDs with longer maturities generally offer higher interest because the higher rates compensate for reduced liquidity. Because people who invest in CDs lose the use of their money for a longer period of time, they receive a higher interest rate. In return, someone who withdraws funds before the maturity date must pay a penalty. CDs usually require a minimum deposit, which may range from $250 to $100,000.

Both the maturity and the interest rate are established when the account is opened, and the interest rate stays constant until the maturity date. Fixed interest rates offer both benefits and

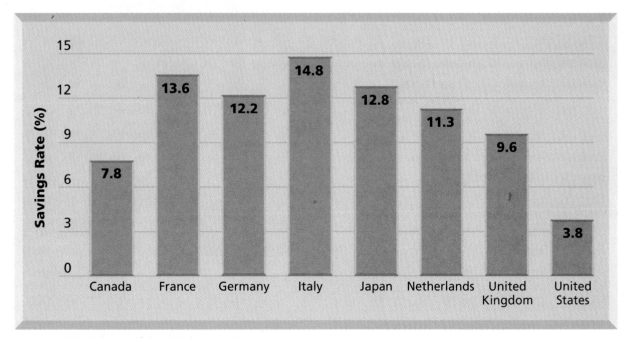

NATIONAL SAVINGS RATES

Savings Rate (%)

Canada 7.8
France 13.6
Germany 12.2
Italy 14.8
Japan 12.8
Netherlands 11.3
United Kingdom 9.6
United States 3.8

Source: *Statistical Abstract of the United States: 1996*

FIGURE 9.2 Savings rates vary considerably from country to country. **What are some of the reasons for this variation?**

Savings Around the World

Because many factors influence savings rates, it is not surprising that such rates vary dramatically from country to country. In some countries—Singapore, for example—workers must contribute a portion of their pay to a government-sponsored savings plan, making savings rates relatively high.

The availability of goods for consumers to purchase is another factor that influences savings rates. For example, before the fall of communism, Eastern European countries often suffered from chronic shortages of consumer goods. Without products to purchase, many Eastern Europeans simply saved their money.

Savings rates are naturally lower in countries where incomes are low. In the poorest countries, food purchases might account for as much as 60 to 70 percent of a household's budget. In addition, many workers in poor countries do not have easy access to financial institutions in which they can deposit money they do not spend.

On the other hand, workers in wealthy countries do not necessarily have high savings rates. The personal savings rate in the United States dropped from more than 8 percent of income to less than 5 percent between 1970 and the mid-1990s. Economists suggest different reasons for this decline, such as high levels of debt carried by many consumers. Some economists believe, however, that the U.S. savings rate will rise as members of the baby boom generation—people born between 1946 and 1964—get older and put more money away for retirement.

drawbacks. If interest rates in general go down after Monique buys a CD, she will still receive the higher, agreed-upon rate. On the other hand, interest rates may go up—but Monique will receive only the CD's relatively lower, established interest rate.

Savings Bonds Monique may decide to limit her risk by purchasing savings bonds, which are issued by the federal government to pay for federal programs. The purchasers assume little risk because the savings bonds are guaranteed by U.S. government funds.

Savers like Monique purchase the bonds for less than face value and redeem them at their face value upon maturity. Savers can purchase a $50 Series EE government savings bond for $25 and redeem it later for $50. If a bondholder chooses to keep the savings bond beyond its

SIGN UP FOR PAYROLL SAVINGS TODAY.

ECONOMIC INSTITUTIONS & INCENTIVES *Savings bonds are issued by the U.S. government.* **How does a bond acquire value?**

maturity date, the bond continues to earn interest until redeemed.

Like corporate bonds, government bonds are a kind of loan. By selling bonds, the government gains money for programs. Similarly, consumers know that they will receive interest while they hold the bond. The increased value of a bond reflects the money borrowed from, plus the interest paid to, the bond buyer. Someone redeeming a $50 bond, for example, gets back the initial $25 plus $25 in interest.

ECONOMIC INSTITUTIONS & INCENTIVES *Economists use the savings rate to measure the strength of an economy.* **How is the savings rate determined?**

Measuring Savings

Economists measure savings to help determine the health of the economy. The main factor they consider for this process is the savings rate. The **savings rate** is the percentage of people's disposable income—money available after taxes are paid—that is not spent.

One of the most important determinants of the personal savings rate in the United States is income. High-income households tend to save more money than low-income households. As a result, the average rate of personal savings for the nation is likely to be high when wages are high. In contrast, the average rate of personal savings is usually lower when wages are lower—for example, during economic slowdowns and periods of high unemployment. (See Figure 9.2 on page 197.)

SECTION 1 —REVIEW

1. Define the following terms: disposable income, balance, liquidity, time deposit, maturity, savings rate.

2. How do people gain security and profits through savings?

3. How do liquidity and interest rates influence people's choice between savings accounts and time deposits?

4. Describe how economists measure savings.

5. Thinking and Writing Critically
Explain how your personal savings rate is affected if you purchase a new stereo.

6. Applying OPPORTUNITY COSTS & TRADE-OFFS
Suppose that you have an after-school job in a music store, and you decide to save $10 from each paycheck. What are the trade-offs?

INVESTING

Economics Dictionary

investment
budget
fixed expense
flexible expense
diversification
real investment
capital accumulation
infrastructure
venture capital

Objectives

▶ What are the goals and elements of a personal financial plan?

▶ How do financial investment and real investment differ?

▶ How does real investment affect economic growth?

As you decide what to do with your money, saving and spending are not your only options. In the United States, freedom of choice also extends to investment. **Investment** occurs when people exchange their money for something of value with the expectation of earning a profit on it in the future.

Some people who make investments must decrease their current consumption of goods and services because invested money cannot be spent on other goods. These investors make a trade-off, choosing to sacrifice some purchasing power in the present in exchange for the chance of maintaining or increasing their purchasing power in the future.

As you know, keeping your savings in a bank or buying a savings bond involves relatively little risk. On the other hand, most investments—such as stock and corporate bonds—involve greater

risk because of the possibility that the firm you invested in will go out of business. Governments do not guarantee such investments.

Suppose that Janis Johansen decides to invest some of her money. She knows that as her potential profit increases, her risk is likely to be greater. Why might Janis decide to take the increased risk? She might do so because she feels that the potentially higher returns offered by investments outweigh the greater level of risk.

Financial Planning

As Janis decides how to invest her money, she develops a personal financial plan. A financial plan provides Janis with an organized system of balancing her wants and needs with her ability to pay for them. Such a plan includes a spending and saving plan, an investment plan, a retirement plan, and an estate plan. Janis practices financial planning to ensure that she uses her money wisely and meets her investment goals.

Spending and Saving Plan All financial planning begins with a spending and saving plan, or **budget**. The budget lists fixed expenses and

ECONOMIC INSTITUTIONS & INCENTIVES *Financial planning begins with a spending and savings budget. **Is eating out a fixed or a flexible expense?***

flexible expenses. **Fixed expenses** are those payments that remain constant from month to month, such as payments for a mortgage and insurance premiums. Your own fixed expenses might include monthly car payments or, in the future, rent. **Flexible expenses** can vary from month to month. Examples include expenditures for pizza and movies. The budget should also include the amounts that a person is willing and able to set aside for saving and investing.

Investment Plan An investment plan is the way Janis puts her money to work. To devise an investment plan, Janis first must determine her reasons for investing. For example, does she want her investments to provide current income, or does she want them to increase in value over time? Once she answers this question, Janis can decide what kinds of investments to make.

An investment plan often reflects a program of diversification. **Diversification** means that a person chooses a variety of investments—CDs, stocks, bonds, and so on. By diversifying her investments, Janis can balance risk, income, and liquidity. Investment choices will be discussed more fully later in this section.

Retirement Plan Janis knows that it is time to begin saving for retirement. She must decide how much money to set aside, choosing investments that will grow while she is working.

Janis's retirement plan probably will be influenced by her employer. If she works for a company, it may offer her a pension or other plan such as a 401(k). If she is self-employed, however, she may establish her own program such as an individual retirement account (IRA).

Estate Plan An estate plan provides for a smooth transfer of a person's property after death. Janis does not yet own a home or have large amounts of savings and investments, but she has designated a beneficiary—or person who will receive payments—for her life insurance. Additionally, her new investments will become part of her estate. Financial experts recommend that people develop estate plans to avoid paying

ECONOMIC INSTITUTIONS & INCENTIVES *Saving for retirement is an important part of an individual's financial plan.* **What are three other common components of financial planning?**

large estate taxes and to guarantee that their inheritance is distributed according to their wishes.

Types of Investment

Now you know how to go about creating an overall financial plan. Several investment decisions remain, however, to make the plan complete. For example, what goals do you (the investor) have for your money? Perhaps you hope only that an investment will grow in value during the time you own it. On the other hand, you may hope that your investment increases in value by helping to create new goods. These two types of investment are financial investment and real investment.

Financial Investment The exchange of property ownership and payment between two individuals or groups is known as a financial investment. Although ownership of the property changes hands, financial investment produces no new goods. People make financial investments when they buy existing stocks, bonds, real estate, or other property. Both individuals and firms make financial investments, in the hope of profiting from them in the future. For example, suppose that two brothers—Johnny and Charlie

*Building construction represents real investment. **What is the difference between real and financial investment?***

Abela—buy a sizable plot of land as a financial investment. The Abelas have created no new capital goods. They have purchased the property only in the hope that it will increase in value so they can resell it at a profit in the future.

Real Investment When investors use money to create a new capital good, they practice **real investment**. Suppose that Johnny and Charlie decide to form a development company. The new company clears the land and constructs an apartment complex. Johnny and Charlie have now created a new capital good—the apartment complex. The money spent on the complex now represents a real investment. Such investments are not only made by individuals, but also by firms and by the government.

Investment and Economic Growth

How does real investment in the public and private sectors promote economic growth? Real investment increases the number of capital goods used by producers. The expansion of the capital goods existing in an economy is called **capital accumulation**. Money spent to *replace* existing capital merely keeps the capital stock at its present level. Capital accumulation, on the other hand, promotes economic growth.

For example, suppose that Brian Flanagan is the owner of a shipping company. If one of his barges sinks in a hurricane and he purchases a replacement barge, he is maintaining his capital stock. If, on the other hand, Brian decides to expand his business and purchases three more barges, he is practicing capital accumulation. In expanding his own business, Brian has provided money to a shipbuilding company, which hires more workers to meet the increased demand for barges. These new jobs provide income to more people, enabling them to purchase consumer goods and further expanding a variety of businesses.

In the public sector, federal, state, and local governments make real investments when they improve the nation's economic **infrastructure**—transportation systems including roads, bridges, harbors, and airports, and public facilities such as schools and universities. The infrastructure is the network that enables producers and consumers to participate in the economy. In the private sector, real investment stimulates technological change and entrepreneurship.

Technological Change How can real investment stimulate technological change? Real investment enables companies to develop or purchase new technology, which increases productivity and economic growth. The development of these new technologies is the result of research and development by major firms or by individual entrepreneurs.

Suppose that Alex Kihara invests in a local business called Print 'n' Copy Store. As a result of this investment, the owners of the copy store are able to afford new software to computerize their billing system. Real investment has improved the technology used by Print 'n' Copy. Additionally, higher sales of the computerized billing program encourages the owners of the software company to develop a new upgraded version of the program.

Entrepreneurship Real investment also can encourage entrepreneurship, which in turn fosters economic growth and the development of new products. Money invested in entrepreneurial enterprises is called **venture capital**, and it encourages economic growth. Venture capital helps entrepreneurs develop an idea into a marketable product, improve production facilities, or finance product distribution.

For example, suppose that Ana Guajardo wants to start a new music magazine. She is able to write the articles, but she needs venture capital to hire a designer to create a "look" for the magazine, pay for photographs and printing, and cover the distribution costs.

Where will Ana acquire this venture capital? She may know friends and local business owners who are willing to invest their money, or she may take out a loan. She might acquire capital from a private venture capital firm that specializes in seeking out and financing promising businesses. In the United States these firms spend billions of dollars annually to support entrepreneurs and their projects.

ECONOMIC INSTITUTIONS & INCENTIVES *Entrepreneurship fosters economic growth and the development of new products.* **How would venture capital encourage economic growth and help a small business such as this one?**

The government also provides funding to entrepreneurs with promising businesses. The Small Business Administration, a federal agency, invests money in smaller-size firms by extending low-interest loans. Some state governments also provide venture capital to small businesses.

SECTION 2 — REVIEW

1. Define the following terms: investment, budget, fixed expense, flexible expense, diversification, real investment, capital accumulation, infrastructure, venture capital.

2. Describe the four elements of a personal financial plan.

3. How do the purposes of financial and real investment differ?

4. Explain how real investment promotes economic growth.

5. Thinking and Writing Critically
Suppose that you have a part-time job after school. After paying your monthly bills, you have $150 remaining. Describe the spending and saving plan, investment plan, retirement plan, and estate plan that make up your personal financial plan.

6. Applying ECONOMIC INSTITUTIONS & INCENTIVES
Conduct an Internet search using the search word *investment* to determine what investment services are available online. Write a paragraph describing your findings.

SECTION 3

STOCKS, BONDS, AND FUTURES

Economics Dictionary

capital gain
capital loss
stock split
broker
investment bank
bull market
bear market
yield
future
prospectus

Objectives

▶ Why and how do people invest in stocks?

▶ What factors influence stock prices?

▶ How do corporate and government bonds differ from stocks?

▶ What are the advantages and disadvantages of futures?

Saving and investing require you to make decisions about how to use your money. If you decide to invest your money, further choices arise. For example, do you want to own part of a corporation by becoming a shareholder, or simply lend money by becoming a bondholder? Are you most concerned about low risk or high return? As you read this section, think about the factors that contribute to financial decisions.

Why Buy Stocks?

"Stock Prices Rise." "Experts Predict Market Downturn." You may have seen newspaper headlines like these. Sometimes stocks can seem like an

uncertain investment with random price changes. Why, then, do people buy stocks?

There are three main reasons that people choose to invest in stocks. People often hope to

▶ gain a profit,
▶ limit the risk on their investment, and
▶ become a part owner of a corporation.

Profit Potential Stocks can provide a profit in two ways. First, many stockholders receive regular dividends on the money invested in stocks. As noted in Chapter 7, dividends are paid to a shareholder in return for an investment. Most corporations pay dividends quarterly, while others pay them annually or semiannually.

Stocks that pay consistent dividends are called income stocks. These stocks provide a steady amount of current income to investors. Stocks that pay few or no dividends but that increase in value are called growth stocks. Investors generally purchase growth stocks in order to increase the value of their assets.

A second way to earn profit on a stock is to sell it at a higher price than the original purchase

ECONOMIC INSTITUTIONS & INCENTIVES *Owning stock in a utility company is a popular form of investment.* ***What are the three main reasons that people choose to invest in stocks?***

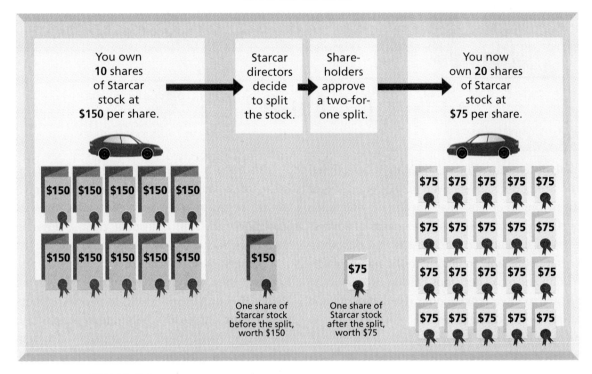

FIGURE 9.3 When the price of stock becomes so high that it discourages potential investors from buying it, the directors of a company may decide to split each share into two. **What usually happens to stock prices after a split?**

price. The difference between the higher selling price and the lower original purchase price is the investor's **capital gain**. An investor who sells a stock at a price lower than the purchase price, however, incurs a **capital loss**.

Limited Risk Stockholders are protected from some risks. Unlike sole proprietors and partners, stockholders in corporations enjoy limited liability. As noted in Chapter 7, the amount of money a stockholder can lose is limited to the amount he or she invested in the stock.

Ownership People also invest in stocks to become owners in a corporation and to vote on company matters. The number of votes a shareholder has is equal to the number of shares of stock he or she owns.

As owners, shareholders vote to elect the board of directors as well as to decide a variety of other business issues. One such issue involves

when to initiate a **stock split**. (See Figure 9.3.) Suppose that the directors of Gadsen Publications determine that the price of Gadsen's stock has become so high that it discourages potential investors from purchasing shares. The directors may decide to "split" each share into two. After the shareholders approve the two-for-one stock split, a shareholder will have two shares of Gadsen stock for every single share held before the split. The price is divided along with the stock, so that stock previously selling for $100 will sell for $50 after the split. Shareholders generally like stock splits because share prices tend to rise afterward.

How Stocks Are Traded

Suppose that Brad Halsey wants to buy stock. Does he call a corporation and place a purchase order? Probably not—very few corporations sell stock directly. Instead, Brad contacts a company

Stockbroker

Imagine a business in which timing is everything. The wrong decision—or even the right decision at the wrong moment—may mean the difference between collecting or losing thousands of dollars.

To a stockbroker, timeliness is vital. Stockbrokers must be able to find up-to-the-minute information and make decisions quickly. Brokers must be able to interpret economic developments and predict price changes on the stock market. To meet these goals, research skills and a college degree in business or finance are essential.

Stockbrokers must be able to find up-to-the-minute information and make wise financial decisions quickly.

Basically, a stockbroker is a salesperson. Instead of selling cars, shoes, or kitchen appliances, however, a broker sells stock. Brokers generally work with individual clients, advising these investors to buy or sell particular stocks.

Brokers often must find their own clients. Because they must be comfortable introducing themselves and their services to people, brokers typically are aggressive, determined people who like to take risks. These characteristics also help brokers make decisions about how their clients' money would best be invested.

Stockbrokers usually do not receive hourly wages or a yearly salary. Instead, brokers are paid commissions—percentages of each sale. These commissions pay stockbrokers for their services, including time, research, and professional advice. To maximize profits—and earn a high commission—brokers work to purchase stock at the lowest possible price and sell it at the highest possible price.

Earning money on commissions can be both risky and rewarding. On the one hand, stockbrokers may not receive steady paychecks. On the other hand, they have the potential to earn much more money from commissions than they might earn from a fixed salary.

that specializes in selling stocks. These companies belong to a network of brokerage firms, investment banks, and stock exchanges.

Brokers and Analysts Stockbrokers, often called **brokers**, link buyers and sellers of stock. Brokers work for brokerage firms, which are businesses that specialize in trading stocks and

other securities. Brokers and brokerage firms earn a profit by collecting a commission, or fee, on each transaction.

Investment Banks Corporations usually do not issue new stock or trade large blocks of other stocks without help. They usually contact an **investment bank**, which buys and sells large blocks of stock. Investment banks usually buy the stock when offered by a company and then offer that stock to the general public. Like brokers, investment banks collect commissions on transactions.

Stock Exchanges When people speak of the "stock market," they generally are referring to the New York Stock Exchange (NYSE). The NYSE, the largest stock exchange in the United States, began informal operations in 1792 on Wall Street in New York City, providing a place to buy and sell corporate stocks and government bonds.

Before the Civil War, other brokers founded the New York Curb Agency, a name that arose because the brokers actually met on the street. In 1953 the name was officially changed to the American Stock Exchange (AMEX). Besides the NYSE and the AMEX, five regional stock exchanges are located in other U.S. cities. Major world cities such as Tokyo, Hong Kong, London, Frankfurt, and Paris also have stock exchanges on which some U.S. firms are able to trade.

Changes in technology have improved the buying and selling of stocks on the NYSE. For example, the NYSE spent millions of dollars modernizing its equipment from 1980 to 1985. Powerful computers in the exchange and in other locations throughout New York City connect with similar equipment in the nation's major brokerage firms. The computer linkup makes it possible to handle as many as 1,000 stock transactions each second. On January 23, 1997, more than 683 million shares were traded on the NYSE, setting a record for daily trading volume.

The nearly 3,000 companies that now have their shares traded on the NYSE must meet rigorous standards concerning number of shareholders, number of shares, and minimum earnings. Companies on the NYSE also must follow standard accounting practices in calculating their earnings.

Before a brokerage firm's representatives can buy and sell shares on the NYSE, it must purchase a "seat" on the exchange. Prices for the 1,366 seats vary. In August 1996, for example,

the auction price of a seat was $1,162,500. The all-time high for a seat was $1,475,000 in July 1997; the low was $2,750 in 1871.

Over-the-Counter Market Stocks that are not listed on the NYSE or other stock exchanges are traded on the over-the-counter (OTC) market. Many smaller corporations that do not meet the standards set by the nation's stock exchanges can still trade their stocks OTC. These stocks are sometimes called OTC stocks.

Investors still need brokers to trade OTC stocks. First, buyers and sellers place buy or sell orders with their brokers. Second, the brokers arrange the purchase or sale by using a market service called the National Association of Securities Dealers Automated Quotations (NASDAQ), which lists thousands of stocks not listed on the stock exchanges. To arrange for the sale or purchase of stocks not listed on NASDAQ, the brokers telephone other brokers who might have clients interested in trading the stock directly.

Determinants of Stock Prices

Suppose that you decide to invest in a company's stock. How can you find out the price? If you look in the business section of the local newspaper, you will find a list of stock prices. They do

EXCHANGE, MONEY, & INTERDEPENDENCE *The NYSE began informal operations in 1792 on Wall Street in New York City.* **What other cities in the world have major stock exchanges?**

UNDERSTANDING STOCK MARKET REPORTS

The annual dividend is 46 cents per share.

Trading volume of the week, in 100-share lots— thus, 19,532,000 shares were traded.

PepsiCo closed at $31.75 per share.

PepsiCo stock price has risen 8.5% this year.

52 week		Name	Div	Yield	PE	Volume Wkly.	Wkly Hi	Lo	Last	Charge Fri	Wkly	YTD % Chg
Hi	Lo											
16	$7^{3}/_{8}$	Kmart			26	238,786	$13^{1}/_{2}$	$12^{1}/_{4}$	$12^{1}/_{2}$	$-^{1}/_{4}$		+20.5
$53^{3}/_{4}$	41	McDnlds	.30	0.7	21	165,646	$45^{1}/_{8}$	$42^{1}/_{2}$	$44^{1}/_{2}$	$-^{1}/_{4}$	$+1^{1}/_{4}$	-1.9
$35^{7}/_{8}$	28	PepsiCo	.46	1.4	34	195,320	$33^{5}/_{8}$	$31^{5}/_{8}$	$31^{3}/_{4}$	$-^{1}/_{8}$	$-1^{1}/_{4}$	+8.5
$52^{7}/_{8}$	26	Reebok	.30	0.6	25	13,269	$51^{3}/_{8}$	$45^{3}/_{4}$	$50^{1}/_{8}$	$+1^{1}/_{8}$	$+3^{3}/_{8}$	+19.3

$35.875 is the highest and $28.00 is the lowest price of PepsiCo stock in the past 52 weeks, adjusted for splits.

The yield tells what percentage of each share would be returned as dividends, given the current closing price.

The price-to-earnings (PE) ratio is calculated by dividing the stock's last closing price ($31.75) by the company's earnings per share. A higher PE indicates lower earnings, and a lower PE indicates higher earnings.

PepsiCo stock went as high as $33.625 and as low as $31.625 per share during the week.

PepsiCo stock dropped 12.5 cents per share on Friday but dropped $1.25 for the week as a whole.

FIGURE 9.4 Most newspapers print current stock prices in their business section. **What is the dollar value of the highest price for PepsiCo stock during the last 52 weeks?**

---

not appear to be listed in dollars and cents, however, but in fractions. Actually, these numbers represent dollars and cents. For example, a stock listed at 38 1/8 means that the price for one share of stock is $38.125 (1/8 = .125). Shares usually are traded in lots, or amounts, of 100. Smaller amounts are referred to as odd lots.

The stockbroker's task is to make a sale by reconciling a "bid" price with an "asked" price. For example, a buyer bids 37 3/8, or $37.375 a share, and the seller asks 38 1/8, or $38.125. If the stockbroker persuades the buyer to pay 50 cents more for a share and the seller to sell for 25 cents less, a sale is made at 37 7/8, or $37.875. (See Figure 9.4.)

When many buyers compete for a scarce supply of stock, demand pushes up the price. Similarly, when there is a large supply of stock and few buyers, low demand pushes down the price. In this way, demand affects stock prices. The main factors influencing demand for a stock are corporate finances, investor expectations, and external forces.

Corporate Finances
A corporation's financial strength usually is measured in terms of profits and losses. A company's quarterly and annual earnings reports are read carefully by investors, market analysts, and brokers. When confident that a corporation produces high-quality products and has good long-term prospects, investors will buy its stock. Such stocks are called "blue chip" stocks and are in high demand during both upswings and downswings of the stock market because of their long-term stability and value.

Investor Expectations
As noted in Chapter 3, consumer expectations can influence demand. Similarly, investors' expectations about the future price of a stock can affect the stock's current market price. Investors increase their demand for (buy) a stock when they expect it to increase in

value and tend to decrease their demand (sell) when they believe a stock's value will decrease. (See Figure 9.5.)

Investors, market analysts, and brokers form their expectations in part by watching fluctuations in stock indexes, such as the Dow Jones Industrial Average, or the Dow. The Dow records changes in the stock prices of a select group of 30 major industrial companies.

When the Dow steadily rises over a period of time, a **bull market** is said to exist. When the Dow average falls for a period of time, on the other hand, a **bear market** is said to exist. In a bull market, investors expect an increase in profits and thus buy stock. During a bear market, however, investors sell their stock in the expectation of reduced profits. (See Figure 9.5.)

External Forces Sometimes forces over which neither the stock market nor private firms have any control influence the price of stocks. For example, the price of Johnson & Johnson stock fell in 1982 after someone put poison in a few bottles of Tylenol® capsules in the Chicago area. Johnson & Johnson voluntarily withdrew all Tylenol capsules from store shelves.

Some investors feared that Johnson & Johnson's profits would fall. These investors rushed to sell their Johnson & Johnson shares, contributing to a drop in the stock's price. This drop was temporary, however. After Johnson & Johnson introduced new forms of Tylenol that were more difficult to tamper with, public confidence increased and the stock's price rose again.

Other external forces include government statistics on unemployment, inflation, interest rates, and the number of new houses being built. National and international events such as revolutions, assassinations of world leaders, and elections also can affect investor confidence. For example, when Mexican presidential candidate Luis Donaldo Colosio Murrieta was assassinated in 1994, prices on the Mexican stock exchange plunged as investors sold large amounts of stock. Prices recovered quickly, however, in part because the Mexican and U.S. governments worked together to avoid an economic slowdown that might have harmed both nations.

Why Buy Bonds?

Corporate bonds and government bonds are other forms of investment. Although bond **yields**—or interest on money owed to a bondholder—are frequently lower than stock dividends, they generally offer less risk. Additionally, if a company goes out of business, bondholders must be paid before stockholders.

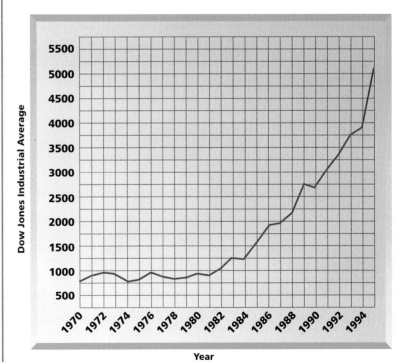

STOCK MARKET PERFORMANCE

Sources: *Statistical Abstract of the United States: 1975, 1980, 1996*

FIGURE 9.5 Investors buy stock when they expect it to increase in value and sell stock when they expect it to decrease in value. **In the above graph, identify a time period in which a bull market existed and a time period in which a bear market existed.**

Corporate Bonds As noted in Chapter 7, corporations sell bonds to raise large sums of money that might be difficult to obtain from a bank. Corporate bonds come in large units, such as $1,000, $5,000, or $10,000 each. The investor purchases a bond at face value—the value listed on the bond when issued—and receives an annual interest payment. On the maturity date, the investor collects the final interest payment and the principal, or the amount of the original bond. Brokerage firms sell the corporate bonds to the public over the counter or on the NYSE and AMEX bond markets.

Government Bonds Corporate bonds are similar to government bonds that, as noted in Section 1, represent debt that the government must repay the investor. The U.S. government—specifically the Treasury Department—issues not only Treasury bonds, but also Treasury bills and notes.

These three investments offer different lengths of maturity and require different minimum investments. They all carry fixed interest rates and are redeemable at stated maturity dates, which vary in length from 90 days to 30 years past the date of purchase. In contrast to corporate bonds, whose interest is taxed as normal income, bonds issued by the federal government pay interest that is exempt from state and local taxes but not from federal income taxes. Backed by the "full faith and credit" of the federal government, these Treasury bonds, bills, and notes are among the safest of all investments. For information about the differences among these three investments, see Figure 9.6.

State, county, and local governments and municipalities such as water districts also issue bonds. For the most part, these bonds have been safe investments since the Great Depression, but they do carry an element of risk. For example, for 18 months beginning in late 1994, people were uncertain whether they would be able to redeem municipal bonds they had purchased from Orange County, California. Orange County was in severe financial difficulty as a result of risky investments by Orange County officials.

TREASURY BONDS, BILLS, AND NOTES

TYPE OF FEDERAL SECURITY		
Treasury Bill	**Treasury Note**	**Treasury Bond**
• short-term U.S. government security • maturity ranging from three months to one year • liquid and safe • minimum order: $10,000 • denomination: $1,000 • yield rate usually lower than on long-term securities • price fluctuation usually lower than for other government securities	• long-term U.S. government security • maturity ranging from 1 to 10 years • safe • minimum order ranging from $1,000–$5,000, depending on maturity • denomination: $1,000 • pays at a stated interest rate semiannually • redeemed at face value at maturity	• long-term U.S. government security • maturity ranging from 10 to 30 years • safe • minimum order: $5,000 • denomination: $1,000 • pays at a stated interest rate semiannually • redeemed at face value at maturity

(left margin: CHARACTERISTICS)

FIGURE 9.6 Treasury bonds represent debt that the government must repay the investor. **How do the maturity periods differ between these three government investments?**

The Crashes of 1987 and 1929

History often holds important clues to understanding economic events in more modern times. Take, for example, the stock market crashes of 1987 and 1929. On October 19, 1987, the Dow Jones Industrial Average dropped 508 points—a record 22.6 percent. Coming on top of earlier, steep declines in the Dow, the "Black Monday" crash rocked stock markets around the world. Panic set in among some investors and stock traders, adding to fears that the stock slide would batter the U.S. economy and throw people out of work.

To many economists and historians, the crash seemed eerily similar to a stock market crash 58 years earlier. On October 29, 1929—"Black Tuesday"—the Dow fell 12.8 percent. This crash helped trigger a financial panic as stock values continued to plunge for weeks. Banks were forced to close as people rushed to withdraw savings. With access to capital sharply limited, businesses closed, and millions of people lost their jobs.

Prior to the 1929 crash, the U.S. economy appeared to many observers to be very healthy. Stock values were soaring, profits for many companies were high, and consumers were spending—and investing—like never before. Many investors in 1929 and 1987 simply did not see—or refused to see—signs of a coming crash. Reports in 1929, for example, warned that industrial production, certain stock values, and other economic indicators in the United States were falling. Prior to the 1987 crash, some observers warned that the U.S. government was borrowing too much money, thus making capital for private industry more expensive and difficult to obtain.

Certain factors made the effects of the 1929 crash much worse than those in 1987. For example, investors in 1929 often purchased their stocks with credit. An investor would pay cash for only a small portion of the price of the stock and agree to pay off the debt later with profits from the stock after it rose in value. Unfortunately, when brokers began to worry that values might not continue to rise, they began to require purchasers to come up with the money owed, or lose the stock. When prices began to fall, investors who had bought stock with credit could not cover their debts.

In 1987, however, various reforms instituted by the government in response to the 1929 crisis worked to keep a similar financial catastrophe from occurring. One reform restricts the purchase of stocks with credit. Also, the federal government now insures bank deposits. If a bank does not have enough money to cover its deposits during a crisis, a federal agency steps in to pay depositors. In 1987, then, while stock investors indeed lost a great deal of money—at least on paper—U.S. consumers did not have to worry that they would lose money they had deposited in banks.

What Do You Think?

1. Do conditions similar to those that preceded the 1929 and 1987 crashes exist in today's economy? Explain your answer.

2. In a free-enterprise system, people are free to risk their money in an attempt to make more. Should the government make stock investments as safe as bank deposits? Explain your answer.

SECURITY REGULATIONS

YEAR	LEGISLATION	PURPOSE
1890	Sherman Antitrust Act	prohibits business trusts; because its vague language left loopholes it was strengthened in 1914 by the Clayton Antitrust Act
1933	Federal Securities Act	(also called the Truth-in-Securities Act) requires anyone offering securities for public sale to disclose information about them; requires companies to disclose the securities holdings of their officers and directors
1934	Securities Exchange	sought to eliminate dishonest practices in the stock market; created the Securities and Exchange Commission (SEC) to enforce the regulations
1984	Insider Trading Sanctions Act	established triple penalties against violators in addition to requiring the return of any illegally acquired money or property; was extended in 1988 to include corporate supervisors

FIGURE 9.7 During the past 100 years, Congress passed several acts to regulate the securities industry and protect investors. **What is the role of the Securities Exchange Commission?**

Not until June 1996 did the municipal bonds become redeemable.

Why Buy Futures?

Futures are another type of investment. In futures markets such as the Chicago Board of Trade, instead of trading stock, investors trade various types of products called **futures**. Futures include agricultural products such as corn, wheat, soybeans, and oats. They also include industrial goods such as steel and coal, and precious metals and gemstones such as gold, silver, and diamonds. Because futures trading carries a high risk, investors must have specialized knowledge about the commodities being bought and sold.

How does futures trading work? When traders sell futures, they accept an investor's money today in exchange for a promise to deliver a commodity to the investor at a later date. The terms of a futures trade are stated in a contract.

For example, suppose that Joanne Kaehler decides to invest in hog futures. She signs a contract in which she agrees to pay a certain amount of money for a later delivery of hogs—perhaps six months after the purchase. Joanne probably does not want to own the hogs, however. She is hoping that the price of hogs will increase within the six-month period so that she can resell the contract and make a profit.

How can the futures market benefit Joanne? If the market price of hogs rises above the price listed on the contract, the hog owner still must honor the contract and deliver the hogs to Joanne at the lower-than-market price that it lists. Joanne then can resell the hog contract at the current market price and make a profit.

The hog owner, on the other hand, hopes that the price will drop within the contract's six-month period. Why? If the market price of hogs drops below the price that Joanne paid in the contract, the hog owner has made a greater profit than is available at the current market price. If the owner had not sold the hogs in advance, he or she would have received the later, lower market price for the hogs.

Both Joanne and the hog owner face tremendous risks. The buyer and the seller essentially are betting that the price of hogs will reach a certain level by a particular time. Depending on whether the price rises or falls, either the seller or the buyer could lose a great deal of money.

Regulation of the Securities Industry

Throughout the 1800s, trade in securities was not monitored by any organizations outside the stock exchanges. As a result, dishonest securities dealers often provided investors with misleading or false information.

During the early 1900s, Congress passed several acts to regulate trading in securities. As noted in Chapter 5, the Clayton Antitrust Act (1914) outlawed many monopolistic practices. The act discouraged the formation of monopolies by forbidding corporations from buying stock in competing companies when doing so could result in monopolistic control over an industry.

The next key piece of legislation came in 1933. The Federal Securities Act, also called the Truth-in-Securities Act, requires all companies to register their securities with the Federal Trade Commission (FTC). Just a year later the Securities Exchange Act established the Securities and Exchange Commission (SEC) to enforce the Federal Securities Act. For a summary of securities regulations, see Figure 9.7.

Companies must meet rigorous standards to sell their stock in a stock exchange. Additionally, companies register their securities by providing a detailed financial statement to the SEC and a prospectus to potential investors. A **prospectus** is a fact sheet containing data on the company's finances. Investors use the prospectus to evaluate securities that are offered for sale. The SEC is empowered to charge heavy fines for violations of these requirements.

The SEC also regulates the procedures for the trading of securities. The SEC licenses all stock exchanges in the United States and regulates the activities of brokers and brokerage houses to guard against fraud and other unethical actions.

SECTION 3 — REVIEW

1. Define the following terms: capital gain, capital loss, stock split, broker, investment bank, bull market, bear market, yield, future, prospectus.

2. List the main reasons people choose to purchase stock.

3. How does an investor purchase stock?

4. How do corporate finances, investor expectations, and external forces influence stock prices?

5. How does the futures market offer risks to sellers as well as to investors?

6. **Thinking and Writing Critically**
   Suppose you own stock in a corporation, and you hear that the stock is about to split. How can you benefit from ownership of this stock?

7. **Applying** ECONOMIC INSTITUTIONS & INCENTIVES
   Visit the NYSE and NASDAQ Web pages. From the information available, determine whether a bull or bear market currently exists.

SECTION 4

└ BORROWING AND CREDIT

Economics Dictionary

installment

credit rating

credit bureau

finance charge

annual percentage rate

usury

bankruptcy

Objectives

▶ How do lenders make money on loans?

▶ What factors influence a credit rating?

▶ How can credit help the economy?

S uppose that you want to buy a car. You know that your friend's parents are selling their car for $5,000. For the past two years you have been saving money from your after-school job and have saved $1,500. If you want to buy the car, you will need to borrow the remaining $3,500 or perhaps pay for the car on credit. Before you do so, however, there are several things you need to know about borrowing and credit.

Borrowing is the transfer of a specified amount of money from a lender to a borrower for a specified length of time. Business owners borrow money to begin or expand their businesses. Governments borrow money to finance their programs and operations.

People also may rely on credit when they do not have enough money for a purchase. Even wealthy consumers may use credit when purchasing expensive items such as houses and cars.

Why do consumers borrow money or rely on credit? Try considering the used-car purchase

mentioned earlier. A loan or credit will enable you to use the car now while paying off the loan or credit debt, and you can extend payments for the car over a period of time. Paying a smaller amount every month thus makes large purchases more affordable for many people.

Borrowing Money

As noted in Chapter 7, the amount borrowed in a loan is called the principal. The amount paid by the borrower for the privilege of using the money is called the interest. Both the principal and the interest are included in the loan's repayment.

Most loans require that borrowers put up collateral. Collateral is something of value offered by the borrower as a guarantee that the loan will be repaid. In a mortgage loan the house is the collateral, and in an automobile loan the car is the collateral. If the loan is not repaid according to the terms of the loan agreement, the lender may take possession of the borrower's collateral. That is, the lender can foreclose on the house or repossess the car.

How are loans repaid? In the repayment of most loans, the principal and interest are divided

EXCHANGE, MONEY, & INTERDEPENDENCE *Credit is the purchase of goods and services on the promise to pay later.* ***Why do consumers use credit?***

into equal amounts, or **installments**, according to the length of the loan period. The length of repayment is important in determining the monthly payment amount. The longer the loan period, the smaller the amount of money the consumer must pay each month. A longer loan period, however, means that the total interest payment is greater.

Buying on Credit

Unlike borrowing, buying on credit does not involve the direct exchange of money. Instead, businesses allow customers to charge their purchases and to pay for them later. This is done through the use of a charge, or credit, account. Think of a charge account as a type of loan offered by businesses to their clients. Businesses that offer credit include banks, department stores, gasoline companies, and financial service firms such as VISA®, MasterCard®, and American Express®.

Credit Ratings Consumers cannot use credit without first applying for it and being approved. The creditor evaluates information about the purchaser and assigns that person a credit rating. A **credit rating** is an estimation of the probability of repayment. Creditors are particularly concerned about three factors that can influence the likelihood that an applicant will repay credit:

▶ ability to pay,
▶ assets, and
▶ credit history.

Suppose that Julie Solomon is applying for credit. A creditor evaluates the three factors and assigns a credit rating. If Julie's financial status satisfies the creditor, she receives a high credit rating—meaning that she is a good credit risk. Perhaps Julie has no assets, however, or has failed to repay an earlier loan. In that case she may receive a low credit rating. The higher the credit rating a person has, the easier it is for him or her to receive credit.

How do creditors obtain financial information about applicants? Many creditors consult a credit

"Sorry, but I hope you'll try us again sometime when you don't need it quite so badly."

Drawing by Mirachi; © 1975 The New Yorker Magazine, Inc.

ECONOMIC INSTITUTIONS & INCENTIVES *If consumers want credit, they must apply for it.* **What factors do creditors consider?**

bureau. A **credit bureau**, or credit reporting service, is a business that specializes in collecting financial information about consumers. Consumer information comes from banks and other financial institutions as well as stores and credit card companies. Consumers also may request a copy of their own credit report to guarantee that the information is accurate.

Credit Terms Once a customer is approved for a charge account, he or she can make purchases with a credit card. The consumer is then billed—usually every 28 or 30 days—for the amount of their purchases. These accounts have specified credit limits that indicate the maximum amount the customer can purchase on credit.

A customer who does not pay his or her balance in full will have to pay an additional **finance charge**—the total cost of credit expressed in dollars and cents. This charge includes interest, service charges, and any other miscellaneous fees. Most states allow credit card issuers to set their interest rates as high as 1.5 percent per month, or 18 percent per year. This 18 percent figure is the **annual percentage rate** (APR), or the total cost of credit expressed as a yearly percentage. Some credit card companies also charge annual fees that must be paid whether or not the card is used.

Credit Card Incentives

EXCHANGE, MONEY, & INTERDEPENDENCE Have you ever received an offer from a credit card company? In 1995 some 2.7 *billion* credit card offers were mailed to people across the country. Some companies now even offer credit cards to high school seniors. Why are these companies trying so hard to lend you and other consumers money?

Because the credit card market is highly competitive, many credit cards offer a variety of incentives to gain consumers' business. Some target specific groups of consumers, such as college students or school alumni. For example, in 1996 the University of California, Los Angeles, (UCLA) offered alumni association members a selection of cards with no annual fee and an APR of only 6.9 percent for the first year of card use.

In addition to low APRs and no annual fees, some other cards offer a rebate. For example, General Motors (GM) issues credit cards that offer rebates on the price of a GM automobile.

Still other cards try to appeal to the consumer's interests. Some cards are printed with a picture of the cardholder's college, while others show artwork by celebrities such as basketball player Michael Jordan. In Virginia, Leader Federal Bank for Savings even offers a credit card with a picture of Elvis Presley .

Because credit card offers are so numerous and present such a wide range of incentives, consumers need to choose carefully. How much credit is necessary? Which is more important—a low APR or a low annual fee? To use credit wisely, you must examine more than the artwork on the card. Take a critical look at the incentives and costs to determine which card, if any, best meets your needs.

Credit Regulation Some critics claim that the interest rates on credit card balances are too high. Banks and credit card companies, however, point to the high number of defaults by credit card users, the lack of collateral for the extended credit, and the high costs of processing credit card loans compared with other types of loans.

To balance the interests of both consumers and creditors, the government limits the amount of interest that can be charged. Charging credit above that limit is illegal and is called **usury**.

The federal government also has passed a number of laws to protect consumers from other kinds of unfair credit practices. Additionally, during the 1960s and 1970s, Congress passed a series of laws to define more clearly the rights and responsibilities of borrowers and lenders. (See Figure 9.8.)

Credit Abuse Increasingly, credit abuse has become a problem for both consumers and businesses. Consumers sometimes take on more credit debt than they can handle. When repayment of loans and credit debts becomes a problem, consumers usually have two courses of action. First, they can seek credit counseling. Counselors advise consumers on ways to pay off present debts through a repayment program and how to avoid recurring credit problems.

Counselors sometimes advise people with severe credit problems to take out a debt consolidation loan to repay several smaller loans and credit balances. Debt consolidation loans carry high interest rates because of the high risk they pose to creditors.

Second, consumers with large debts may be advised to declare bankruptcy. **Bankruptcy** is a legal declaration of inability to pay debts. Those who have abused credit, particularly individuals, usually declare bankruptcy only as a last resort, for it has serious consequences. By law, bankruptcy information remains on a person's credit history for 14 years, making it nearly impossible for the person to borrow money or receive credit.

For businesses, bankruptcy may mean the end of the firm's existence, a reduction in size, or intense regulation by courts and government agencies. Declaring bankruptcy, however, often saves a business by giving it time to rebuild much of its strength.

Credit in the Economy

The use of credit helps people to satisfy many of their personal wants and needs. It also can have a major effect on the economy of the United States by stimulating economic growth and by promoting economic stability—two important goals for the nation.

Stimulating Growth Economic growth is a major goal of the United States. Economic growth occurs when the per capita, or per person, output of goods and services in a nation increases during a specified period of time.

Figure 9.9 on page 218 illustrates how credit—as well as saving and borrowing—helps

FEDERAL REGULATION OF CREDIT

NAME OF LEGISLATION	MAJOR PURPOSE	PROVISIONS
Civil Rights Act, 1968	to outlaw discrimination by lenders in providing home mortgages	•forbids lenders from rejecting a home loan application because of the applicant's race, national origin, religion, or sex
Truth-in-Lending Act, 1968	to ensure that borrowers are fully informed about the costs and conditions of credit	•requires lenders to disclose all costs and finance charges, as well as the annual percentage rate, so that consumers can comparison-shop for credit •sets a $50 maximum that credit card users can be required to pay for charges incurred on a card that is reported lost or stolen and eliminates all liability for purchases made after the loss is reported •establishes a 3-day "cooling off period" during which consumers can cancel most credit contracts except first-home mortgages •requires that credit advertisements include all credit conditions of the agreement
Fair Credit Reporting Act, 1971	to protect consumers against the use of any inaccurate or outdated information gathered by credit bureaus	•entitles consumers to see a summary of their credit reports •allows consumers to insist that disputed information be reinvestigated and corrected and permits consumers to insert in the reports their own versions of the disputed information •requires that most negative credit information be removed from the reports after 7 years, but permits bankruptcy information to remain for 14 years
Equal Credit Opportunity Act, 1974 and 1977	to expand the 1968 Civil Rights Act's protection against discrimination in credit matters	•prohibits discrimination in granting credit because of such personal factors as race, national origin, religion, sex, or marital status •requires that the same credit guidelines be applied to all applicants •requires that applicants be notified within 30 days of a decision on their credit application
Fair Credit Billing Act, 1975	to promote prompt correction of billing errors	•sets up a procedure that allows consumers to challenge billing errors •requires consumers to notify creditors of errors within 60 days of receiving a bill and requires creditors to respond to that notification within 30 days •permits unresolved disputes to be settled in court or through other legal means
Fair Debt Collection Practices Act, 1977	to protect consumers from harassment by professional collection agencies	•prohibits bill collectors from making harassing telephone calls to consumers and their families and friends and from using other methods of intimidation

FIGURE 9.8 The federal government has passed a number of laws to protect consumers from unfair credit practices. **Which law protects consumers against inaccurate credit reports?**

promote economic growth. Individuals use the borrowed money and credit to buy consumer goods and services, while businesses buy capital goods such as new equipment and raw materials. Governments provide schools, bridges, and fire and police protection.

As businesses, individuals, and governments spend the borrowed money and use credit, more goods and services are purchased, and demand increases. Businesses then increase their supply of goods to meet consumer demand.

Promoting Stability
Credit also affects a nation's economic stability, a companion goal to economic growth. Key indicators of a nation's economic stability are employment and price stability. Credit, when used in moderation, promotes high employment and stable prices.

How does the use of credit accomplish this stability? As consumers use credit to buy goods and services, demand increases. To meet this demand, business owners speed up production and hire more workers, increasing employment. With the supply now sufficient to meet demand, prices reach a level that is acceptable to both producers and consumers. Prices remain stable at this level until supply or demand decreases.

PROMOTING ECONOMIC GROWTH THROUGH SAVING AND CREDIT

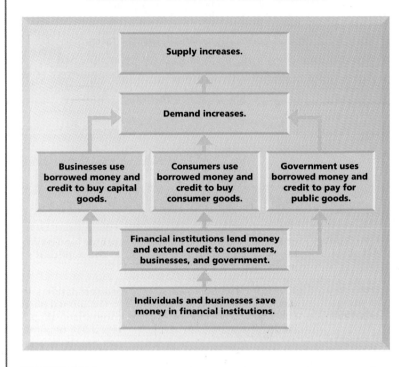

FIGURE 9.9 Economic growth occurs when per capita output of goods and services in a nation increases. **In this diagram, how does the use of credit affect economic growth?**

SECTION 4 — REVIEW

1. Define the following terms: installment, credit rating, credit bureau, finance charge, annual percentage rate, usury, bankruptcy.

2. Why do lenders charge interest on loans?

3. How is a credit rating determined?

4. Describe the impact of credit on the U.S. economy.

5. **Thinking and Writing Critically**
How can having too much credit be harmful to a consumer? For example, would it truly benefit you to have a credit card with a $50,000 credit limit? Explain your answer.

6. **Applying** EXCHANGE, MONEY, & INTERDEPENDENCE
Why is bankruptcy considered a last resort for a credit abuser? How can declaring bankruptcy affect a person's life?

SECTION 1 When people choose not to consume their disposable income, they are saving. In general, people save money for five major reasons: for major purchases, to pay large annual or semiannual bills, for unexpected expenses, for longterm expenses, and to amass wealth or leave an inheritance. By saving money, people gain financial security and interest, whether they rely on savings accounts or time deposits. Economists examine savings rates to determine the amount of money being saved throughout the economy.

SECTION 2 Investing allows consumers to exchange their money for something of value, with the expectation of future profits. To meet their goals, investors develop financial plans that include spending and savings plans, investment plans, retirement plans, and estate plans. Investors who hope only that the value of their investments will grow with time are practicing financial investment, while investors who hope to increase their investment while creating new capital goods are practicing real investment. Real investment contributes to economic growth by creating new products and, indirectly, new jobs.

SECTION 3 Investors buy stock to increase their profits, limit risk, and become owners of a corporation. Stocks are purchased from brokerage firms, which hold seats on stock markets such as the New York Stock Exchange (NYSE). Stocks not listed on stock exchanges can be purchased in the over-the-counter (OTC) market. Stock prices are determined by corporate finances, investor expectations, and external forces. Bonds offer lower returns than stocks, but because they are offered by federal, state, and local governments, they generally have less risk as well. Futures provide investors with the chance to collect future profits, although the high risks for businesses and investors discourage many people from participating. All of these securities are regulated by the federal government.

SECTION 4 Borrowing and credit serve as other sources of financial capital. Borrowing enables people to enjoy their purchases now while paying for them later, spreading payments out over a period of months or years. Credit allows purchases to be made without an actual exchange of money. To develop a credit rating, a credit bureau evaluates a consumer's financial background on the basis of ability to pay, assets, and credit history. Consumers who abuse their credit may have difficulty paying debts and in some cases may be forced to declare bankruptcy.

There are economic benefits to credit as well. Credit can stimulate economic growth by enabling people to buy goods and services, thus promoting investment and job growth. Economic stability also can stem from credit, as supply rises to match increased demand. Increased supply requires producers to hire more workers, providing more people with incomes.

Economics Notebook

Review the financial plan you outlined for your contest winnings in your Economics Notebook at the beginning of the chapter. Now that you have learned about saving, investing, borrowing, and credit, would you make any changes to your plan? Explain your answer in your Notebook.

CHAPTER 9

REVIEW

REVIEWING CONCEPTS

1. Identify which of the following savings plans would provide the greatest possible liquidity: regular savings account, certificate of deposit, savings bond. Explain your answer.

2. Why do economists study savings rates? Name one important determinant of savings rates in the United States.

3. Explain the difference between financial investment and real investment. Provide an example of each type of investment.

4. Describe the different ways you can earn profits from stock purchases. Compare a *capital gain* and a *capital loss*.

5. How does a broker's job differ from that of a market analyst?

6. What are the benefits and liabilities of credit? Describe three pieces of legislation that protect consumers from unfair credit practices.

THINKING AND WRITING CRITICALLY

1. **ECONOMIC INSTITUTIONS & INCENTIVES** Choose three goods and services that you need or want to purchase in the future. Explain why either a savings account or time deposit is the most appropriate method of saving for each purchase.

2. **PRODUCTIVITY** Does construction of a new school represent financial investment or real investment? Explain your answer.

3. **EXCHANGE, MONEY, & INTERDEPENDENCE** Suppose that you receive an inheritance of $1,000, with the limitation that it must be invested in stocks and bonds for five years before you can spend it. Tell whether you will purchase stocks, bonds, or a combination. Explain your answer.

4. **EXCHANGE, MONEY, & INTERDEPENDENCE** Suppose you want to buy a new stereo but have saved only $100 of the total cost of $200. Would it be in your best interest to purchase the stereo on credit or wait until you have saved another $100? Explain your answer.

YOUR LOCAL ECONOMY

Identify at least two companies in your community that have their shares traded on stock exchanges. Track the stocks for a month, and create a graph that reflects price changes. Then write a paragraph discussing the advantages and/or disadvantages of investing in these companies.

COOPERATIVE PORTFOLIO PROJECT

With your group, develop a prospectus describing the financial status of an imaginary company. Divide tasks for the project among the various "company officers" in your group. For example, the vice president of sales might develop a report on sales performance over the past year. You may want to model your prospectus after existing companies' reports that you can find in the library. As a group, design a portfolio that contains charts and graphs illustrating what you determine to be the most important company information and statistics.

PRACTICING SKILLS: UNDERSTANDING MEASUREMENT CONCEPTS AND METHODS

Study the information and the guidelines presented in Figure 9.4 on page 208 to learn how to read stock market reports. Then consider the stock market report on page 221.

This stock market report represents a daily newspaper listing rather than the weekly report shown in Figure 9.4 on page 208. The daily report is an abbreviated version of the weekly report. Use the stock market information below to answer the questions that follow.

	Div	Sales	Last	Change
IBM	1.60	3448	173$7/8$	+$1/4$
Disney	.53	9790	83$5/8$	
EsteeLdr	.34	1536	48$1/2$	-1

1. How many lots of Estee Lauder were traded? How many shares of Disney were traded?

2. By how much did Disney stock rise or fall on Friday?

3. At what price did IBM's stock close?

4. What was the value of 200 shares of Estee Lauder stock?

5. What was the annual dividend for IBM stock?

THE INTERNET: LEARNING ONLINE

Conduct an Internet search to compare credit card offers. Type in search words such as *credit* or names of credit card companies with which you are familiar. Collect information on at least three different companies and create a chart comparing the terms of their offers, such as the APR, fees, and rebates.

ANALYZING PRIMARY SOURCES

"The Gospel of Wealth"

Andrew Carnegie (1835–1919) was a leading American industrialist, author, and philanthropist, or charitable donor. In this, his most famous essay, Carnegie argued that the rich are the rightful "trustees" of society's wealth—a view widely accepted during the nineteenth and early twentieth centuries.

"This, then, is held to be the duty of the man of wealth: To set an example of modest . . . living, shunning display or extravagance; to provide moderately [reasonably] for the legitimate [proper] wants of those dependent upon him; and, after doing so, to consider all surplus revenues which come to him simply as trust funds, which he is called upon to administer . . . as a matter of duty . . . in the manner which, in his judgment, is best calculated to produce the most beneficial results for the community—the man of wealth thus becoming the mere trustee and agent for his poorer brethren, bringing to their service his superior wisdom, experience, and ability to administer, doing for them better than they would or could do for themselves. . . .

"In bestowing charity, the main consideration should be to help those who will help themselves; to provide part of the means by which those who desire to improve may do so; to give those who desire to rise the aids by which they may rise; to assist, but rarely or never to do all. . . .

"[The] best means of benefiting the community is to place within its reach the ladders upon which the aspiring [hopeful] can rise—free libraries, parks, and means of recreation, by which men are helped in body and mind; works of art, certain to give pleasure and improve the public taste; and public institutions of various kinds, which will improve the general condition of the people; in this manner returning their surplus wealth to the mass of their fellows in the forms best calculated to do them lasting good. . . .

"Such, in my opinion, is the true gospel concerning wealth, obedience to which is destined some day to solve the problems of the rich and the poor, and to bring 'Peace on earth, among men good will.'"

1. In Carnegie's view, who are the trustees of society's wealth? Why are they called trustees? What type of lifestyle should they live?

2. According to Carnegie, what types of causes are worthy of support? How was Carnegie's philanthropy a type of investment in American society and culture?

3. Do you agree or disagree with Carnegie's philosophy? Why?

YOUR ASSIGNMENT

Opening a Bagel Franchise

Imagine that you and the other members of your group want to open a Spaegel's Bagels franchise. You and your partners are convinced that you can offer a wide variety of bagels in a location that is easily accessible to many potential customers. Plus, you want your shop to be part of a well-known, national bagel shop chain like Spaegel's.

To open your shop, you will need to obtain a small-business loan from a bank. The bank will want to know how you plan to spend the money it loans you, so you should prepare a report outlining your projected costs and profits. The documents on the following pages have been provided by Spaegel's to give you the information necessary to write your report. First, the president of Spaegel's has sent you a promotional brochure explaining the benefits her company provides to franchise owners, as well as a summary of suggested wages and benefits for Spaegel's franchise employees. You can compare these suggestions with information taken from the *1996 Statistical Abstract of the United States* describing wages and compensation in other service industry businesses. Finally, Spaegel's has provided an outline of projected costs and sales.

In your Economics Notebook, answer the questions that accompany the documents. Then review and share your answers with other members of your group. Finally, prepare a sample help-wanted advertisement and a financial plan for your bagel shop. This report should be neatly written or typed, as it will be presented to other potential investors and to the bank you want to provide your business loan.

SPAEGEL'S bagels

Dear Prospective Franchisee:

Thank you for expressing interest in opening a Spaegel's Bagels franchise in your town. Spaegel's Bagels' first shop opened in 1978 in Brooklyn, New York. Today, more than 100 Spaegel's Bagels' shops employ more than 1,200 people in the United States. Our tasty, chewy bagels are loved by customers around the country, and we believe our bagels will be very popular with customers in your town, too.

Spaegel's Bagels offers its franchisees a variety of benefits, including the use of our special bagel recipe and cooking methods. Potential customers from other towns will see our name on your shop and know that they can stop in for a quality bagel.

In addition, opening a Spaegel's Bagels franchise will help keep your costs down. We will pay for national advertising, for example, leaving to your franchise the responsibility only for local advertising.

Spaegel's Bagels also will train your employees in the "Spaegel way" of service, thereby saving you money on training costs. Last, but not least, we will serve as a resource of information and materials you need to make your business a success. For example, all Spaegel's Bagels franchises can purchase supplies, such as flour and spices, at discount rates from one supplier.

If you are interested in opening a Spaegel's Bagels shop, please write us for more information about employee benefits and projected costs and sales for your franchise. Those estimates should help you in developing financial plans for your business and yourselves. I look forward to hearing from you.

Molly Spaegel
President, Spaegel's Bagels

WHAT DO YOU THINK?

1. What are the advantages of opening your bagel shop as a franchise rather than as a sole proprietorship, partnership, or corporation?

2. What might be the disadvantages of opening a national franchise? For example, could problems with a franchise in one town affect other franchises?

3. How could opening a Spaegel's Bagels franchise save on business costs?

Economics Lab

SUGGESTED WAGES AND BENEFITS FOR SPAEGEL'S BAGELS FRANCHISE EMPLOYEES

Starting wage for sales clerks: $5.15/hour

Starting wage for bagel makers: $7.00/hour

Starting wage for shift supervisors: $8.50/hour

Other benefits: job training, potential for advancement, health insurance, two weeks' paid vacation, five company holidays, company retirement plan

COMPANY PHILOSOPHY:

Spaegel's Bagels values its many hard-working employees. To show our support and appreciation for their hard work, Spaegel's Bagels offers a valuable package of benefits for franchise employees. These benefits include health insurance, vacation and other paid time off, and a company pension plan for longtime employees. These benefits are designed to help our employees support themselves and their families, enjoy their time off, and prepare for their retirement. In return, each Spaegel's Bagels franchise receives the support of a loyal, committed workforce.

FACTS TO CONSIDER:
- In the U.S. about one fourth of service industry labor costs involve benefits such as health insurance, vacation and sick days, Social Security, and unemployment and workers' compensation insurance.
- The average hourly wage for restaurant employees is $5.59, although the minimum wage for servers is $2.13 because these workers also receive tips.

Source: *Statistical Abstract of the United States: 1996*

WHAT DO YOU THINK?

1. From a business owner's point of view, what are the advantages and disadvantages of the required minimum wage? What would be the advantages and disadvantages of paying workers at a rate higher than the minimum wage?

2. From the fact sheet, you can see that paying for health insurance, vacation days, and other nonwage benefits can be a big part of an employer's costs. Nevertheless, Spaegel's Bagels' officials believe that paying for those benefits is important. Why do you think this is so?

3. What parts of the suggested employee wages and benefits would you emphasize in recruiting new employees for your store? Explain your reasoning.

SPAEGEL'S bagels

PROJECTED COSTS AND SUGGESTED FINANCING

START-UP COSTS:
Franchise fee to Spaegel's Bagels: $20,000
Other start-up costs (construction, supplies): $50,000

SUGGESTED FINANCING:
$20,000 from partners' savings and other resources
$50,000 business loan

Projected monthly sales: $17,000

PROJECTED MONTHLY COSTS

Item	Cost	Percent of Sales
Rent	$1,700	10
Labor	$5,100	30
Supplies	$1,700	10
Loan repayment ($50,000 at 9.5% for 5 years)	$1,000	06
Total	$9,500	56

Projected monthly profit: $7,500
(before payments to partners)

WHAT DO YOU THINK?

1. How high is the projected start-up cost for the Spaegel's Bagels franchise? According to the tables, what percent of sales will be left as profit (before partners are paid)?

2. What additional costs might your bagel shop face in the future?

3. How much of each month's profits do you think should be saved? How much should be used to pay the partners a monthly salary?

4. What elements would you include in a personal financial plan for managing the money you earn from the bagel shop? Use the information you learned in Chapter 9 to describe how you would save and invest your money.

THINGS TO DO

1. As a group, compare notes and ideas about the information presented by Spaegel's Bagels. Compile a list of the reasons why you should open a Spaegel's Bagels franchise.

2. Work as a group to prepare a help-wanted ad for the franchise. The ad should highlight the reasons why a potential employee would want to work at your franchise. This ad will be part of your business report.

3. Working with your group, prepare a financial plan for the bagel shop. A bank will be looking for information about projected costs, sales, and profits, so be sure to include the information provided by Spaegel's Bagels and information about how much of the profits will go to the business partners. In addition, explain how profits (after partners have been paid) will be saved, invested, and used for business development.

4. Compile all of your information into a formal business report to be presented to the bank.

UNIT
4

ECONOMIC
PERFORMANCE

ECONOMIC
CHALLENGES

Economics Lab

How would you predict
the future of the U.S. economy? Find out by reading
this unit and taking the
Economics Lab Challenge
on pages 272–275.

ELEMENTS OF
MACROECONOMICS

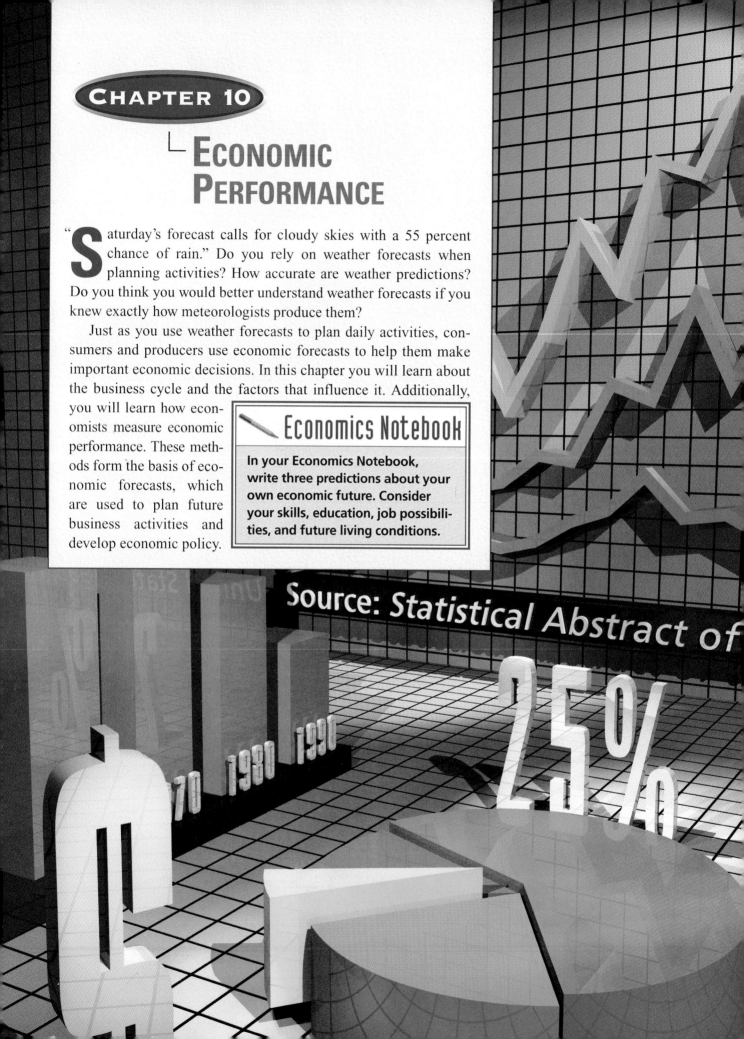

CHAPTER 10

ECONOMIC PERFORMANCE

"Saturday's forecast calls for cloudy skies with a 55 percent chance of rain." Do you rely on weather forecasts when planning activities? How accurate are weather predictions? Do you think you would better understand weather forecasts if you knew exactly how meteorologists produce them?

Just as you use weather forecasts to plan daily activities, consumers and producers use economic forecasts to help them make important economic decisions. In this chapter you will learn about the business cycle and the factors that influence it. Additionally, you will learn how economists measure economic performance. These methods form the basis of economic forecasts, which are used to plan future business activities and develop economic policy.

Economics Notebook

In your Economics Notebook, write three predictions about your own economic future. Consider your skills, education, job possibilities, and future living conditions.

Source: Statistical Abstract of

GROSS DOMESTIC PRODUCT

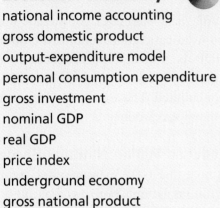

Economics Dictionary

national income accounting
gross domestic product
output-expenditure model
personal consumption expenditure
gross investment
nominal GDP
real GDP
price index
underground economy
gross national product

Objectives

▶ How do economists calculate gross domestic product?

▶ What are some of the limitations of gross domestic product?

▶ What other statistics do economists use to measure the economy?

How do economists predict economic performance? Although predicting the future might seem like something done by a fortune teller at a carnival, economists do not rely on crystal balls or tea leaves for their information. Instead, they study the past and current performance of the economy as a whole.

As noted in Chapter 1, the study of entire economies, as opposed to individual actors or markets within an economy, is called macroeconomics. Macroeconomists use measures called national income and product accounts (NIPAs) to track production, income, and consumption in a nation's economy. This tracking process is known as **national income accounting** and provides information about a nation's economic activities.

Measuring Economic Production

Total production, or output, is one measure of an economy's strength. The most widely used NIPA is **gross domestic product** (GDP)—the total dollar value of all final goods and services produced within a country during one calendar year. A closer look at three components of the definition of GDP will help you better understand what it says about a nation's economy.

Final Output To avoid counting products more than once, economists include only the value of final goods and services when calculating GDP. How is a good identified as "final"?

Suppose that a woodcutter cuts down a tree and sells it to a sawmill operator. The sawmill then processes the tree into lumber, which is sold to a furniture manufacturer. The furniture manufacturer in turn uses the lumber to build a dining table, which is purchased by a consumer.

"HOW DO YOU WANT IT — STATISTICAL PROBABILITY, OR THE ANCIENT ART OF CRYSTAL GAZING?"

© 1999 by Sidney Harris

GROSS DOMESTIC PRODUCT *Economists generally do not use crystal balls to predict the future of the economy.* **What measures do macroeconomists use to predict economic performance?**

All Work and No Play . . .

Many companies in the United States hope to increase profits by participating in global markets. One of these firms is Toys "R" Us, America's largest chain of toy stores. As the biggest toy store in the world, Toys "R" Us has opened stores all over the globe, including Japan, Hong Kong, Spain, Germany, and Singapore.

The chain often has had to adjust its way of doing business in order to respond to local conditions. For instance, in Japan Toys "R" Us officials had to undergo a difficult approval process and were required to follow regulations designed to keep smaller stores from going out of business.

The chain also has had to adapt toys for the foreign market. In Hong Kong, for instance, the board game Monopoly® replaces Boardwalk and Park Place with local suburbs Sheko and Repulse Bay.

Even the company name required modification in foreign countries. The backward *R* was unfamiliar to non-English speakers, so many overseas stores added the name by which the store was locally known. Hong Kong toy shoppers therefore can visit Big Toy City, while in Germany the chain is called *Spielwaren das sind wir.*

While Toys "R" Us has had to make adjustments in order to compete in global markets, the company's founder and chairman Charles Lazarus is confident about its success. "Kids are the same all over the world. They all know what Nintendo is; they all know what Ninja Turtles are," he says. Lazarus is hoping that kids the world over will soon add Toys "R" Us to that list.

Of these items, only the dining table is considered the final product. The tree and the lumber are considered intermediate products—goods and services used to make other products. The value of the tree and the lumber are figured into the value of the dining table. To avoid counting these intermediate products twice, GDP includes only the value of the dining table.

Current Year GDP also does not include products such as used cars and secondhand clothing. Because GDP is a gauge of production—not sales—for the current year, sales of secondhand items are not counted. These goods were counted in the year they were produced.

Output Produced Within National Borders

You should note that GDP measures only output produced within a nation's borders, regardless of who produces it. For example, the Coca-Cola Company owns several production plants in Russia. When economists calculate U.S. GDP, however, they do not include these plants' output because the production occurs outside U.S. borders. U.S. GDP does include, however, the output of foreign workers and firms within the United States—for example, the automobiles that are produced at the Japanese-owned Nissan factory in Tennessee.

Output-Expenditure Model

How is GDP determined? Four sectors of the product market combine to make up GDP:

▶ personal consumption expenditures (C);
▶ gross investment (I);
▶ government purchases of goods and services (G); and
▶ net exports of goods and services, or exports minus imports (X − M).

Figure 10.1 uses these categories to represent the 1995 U.S. GDP. To actually compute GDP, economists add the output produced by these four sectors by using the **output-expenditure model**. This process is represented by the formula C + I + G + (X − M) = GDP.

Personal Consumption Expenditures The first element of GDP is **personal consumption expenditures**, or consumer purchases. Personal consumption expenditures include durable goods, nondurable goods, and services. Durable goods are items that have a useful lifetime of more than a year, such as automobiles and computers. Nondurable goods are items that have a short useful lifetime, such as food and cosmetics. Services—such as medical care, entertainment, and public education—are the fastest-growing area of consumer expenditures.

Gross Investment As noted in Chapter 9, real investment is the use of money to produce new capital goods. The results of this real investment—the capital goods produced—are measured as gross investment, which is the second part of GDP. **Gross investment** is the total value of all capital goods produced in a given nation during one year as well as changes in the dollar value of business inventories. Economists divide gross investment into two subcategories: fixed investment and inventory investment.

Fixed investment includes spending on residential structures, nonresidential structures such as office space and factories, and capital goods such as new machinery and office equipment. Inventory investment refers to the increase or decrease in the total dollar amount of the stock of raw materials, intermediate goods, and final goods of domestic businesses during a given period. Note that gross investment does not include the purchase of financial assets—such as stocks, bonds, and land—because these purchases do not result in the production of any new goods or services.

Government Purchases The third component of GDP consists of the total dollar value that federal, state, and local governments spend on goods and services such as highways, public education, and national defense. Government transfer payments—expenditures for which the government receives no goods or services in exchange—are not included when calculating government purchases. Transfer payments include Social Security payments and various types of government aid.

Net Exports The final component of GDP is net exports—total U.S. exports minus total U.S. imports. As you have learned, GDP measures goods and services produced within a given nation's borders. Thus, GDP includes the value of goods and services produced domestically but sold in other countries (exports) and does not include goods and services produced in other countries but purchased locally (imports).

Some goods and services included in GDP, however, are actually produced in other countries. Likewise, some items produced in the

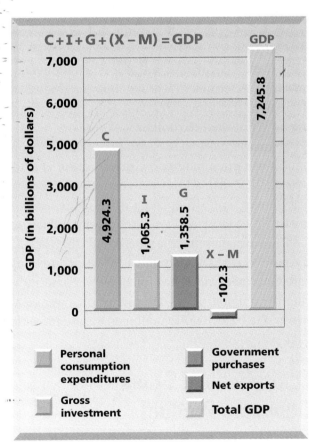

GROSS DOMESTIC PRODUCT, 1995

C + I + G + (X – M) = GDP

GDP (in billions of dollars)

C — 4,924.3
I — 1,065.3
G — 1,358.5
X – M — -102.3
GDP — 7,245.8

Legend:
- Personal consumption expenditures
- Gross investment
- Government purchases
- Net exports
- Total GDP

Source: *Statistical Abstract of the United States: 1996*

FIGURE 10.1 The most common measure of an economy's output, or strength, is gross domestic product. **What four sectors of the product market combine to make up GDP?**

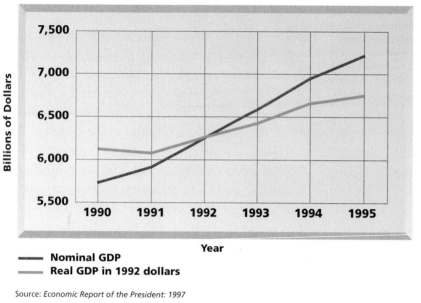

NOMINAL AND REAL GDP

Billions of Dollars

7,500

7,000

6,500

6,000

5,500

1990   1991   1992   1993   1994   1995

Year

—— Nominal GDP

—— Real GDP in 1992 dollars

Source: *Economic Report of the President: 1997*

FIGURE 10.2 Nominal GDP grew more than 21 percent from 1990 to 1994, while real GDP grew only about 9 percent. **What is the difference between nominal and real GDP?**

it was in 1980. As in Rosa's case, however, these increases do not necessarily derive from real increases in the output of goods and services. As prices increase, so does GDP. Consequently, economists calculate GDP in both nominal and real prices.

Nominal GDP, or current GDP, is GDP expressed in the current prices of the period being measured. **Real GDP** is GDP adjusted for price changes. Figure 10.2 shows the nominal and real U.S. GDP for 1990 through 1995. A close examination shows that while nominal GDP grew more than 26 percent during that period, real GDP increased by only about 10 percent. Calculating real prices allows economists to determine if production increased or decreased, regardless of changes in the purchasing power of the U.S. dollar.

To measure changes in prices over time, economists use price indexes. A **price index** is a set of statistics that allows economists to compare prices over time. To create a price index, economists first select a base year against which to measure changes in prices. Second, they assign the base year an index number of 100. Third, they calculate index numbers for other years to indicate the amount prices are higher or lower relative to the base year. Economists update the base year every few years.

United States are sold in other countries and fail to get included in the other components of GDP. To account for this movement of goods and services in and out of countries, economists subtract total imports from total exports and add the result to the other GDP components to obtain total domestic output.

Adjusting GDP for Price Increases

Suppose that Rosa Quintanilla serves as treasurer for the math club at her high school. In preparation for the club's annual candy sale, Rosa reviews the sales figures for the last two years. Although the club raised almost twice as much money last year as the year before, Rosa notices that the price collected by the club for each candy bar increased from $1.25 to $2.50 from the first year to the next. However, the number of candy bars sold each year was approximately equal. The rise in price had masked the lack of increase in candy-bar sales.

In 1995 U.S. GDP was nearly seven times greater than in 1970, and almost three times what

Limitations of Gross Domestic Product

Although GDP is the most common measure of the state of a nation's economy, it is not an entirely accurate measure of output and economic growth. To properly interpret GDP and other national accounts based on it, one must understand its limitations.

Accuracy and Timeliness of Data
When computing GDP, economists use estimates and sampling techniques to determine prices and quantities of goods and services. Gathering the necessary data is a slow and time-consuming process. As a result, initial GDP figures are often inaccurate, and the Commerce Department may have to issue revised figures. Government and business decision makers who use GDP and other NIPAs must either rely on initial figures that may change or they must wait several months for more accurate figures to be calculated. Even then, decision makers must keep in mind that GDP and other NIPAs are only approximations of total output and income.

Nonmarket Activities
Suppose that every Saturday, Tim Murphy mows his parents' lawn. Routinely, he also makes his bed, cleans his room, and washes the car—all at no charge. Although these activities are productive, no financial exchange takes place. As a result, Tim's household chores are not included in GDP.

For the most part, GDP measures only market transactions—exchanges of goods and services for money that are recorded in the marketplace. Transactions that do not involve money and are not recorded are nonmarket activities. Barter transactions, housework, and do-it-yourself home repairs are examples of nonmarket activities.

If Tim decides to start charging his parents for the household chores he performs, measured GDP will increase; however, the amount of real output will not have changed. Thus, GDP does not measure all output, and changes in GDP do not necessarily equate to changes in real output.

Underground Economy
Suppose that Fran LaSalle spends many of her afternoons working at her auto repair business. She works out of her garage, does not advertise, and accepts only cash for payment. In this way, Fran avoids reporting her income and paying taxes to the Internal Revenue Service.

Fran is taking part in the **underground economy**—illegal activities and unreported legal activities. Although Fran's business is a legally acceptable activity, her failure to report that activity—and any income from it—is illegal.

"Goods" and "Bads"
Just as GDP is an imperfect indicator of economic growth in a nation, it is also an imperfect indicator of a nation's overall well-being. The value of many "goods"—things that make for a better society—are not reported in GDP, while the value of many "bads"—things that make society worse—are.

Governments and economists must carefully analyze costs and trade-offs when considering policies designed to stimulate economic growth. Some policies that protect the environment or improve society result in decreased GDP. Nevertheless, the government sometimes decides the trade-off is worthwhile. Automotive emissions standards and regulations that prohibit development in ecologically sensitive areas reduce GDP but improve the nation's well-being.

Some economists have proposed using a new measure of the economy that accounts for the "goods" and "bads," and thus more accurately measures a nation's well-being. Positive dollar values would be assigned to "goods" such as

GROSS DOMESTIC PRODUCT *GDP does not measure all output in an economy—only money transactions that are recorded in the marketplace. **What other limitations must be considered in the interpretation of GDP?***

NATIONAL INCOME AND PRODUCT ACCOUNTS, 1995

	in billions
Gross Domestic Product (GDP)	**$7,245.8**
PLUS: The value of goods produced in foreign countries with U.S. capital	+ 206.7
LESS: The value of goods produced in the U.S. with foreign capital	- 215.0
Gross National Product (GNP)	**7,237.5**
LESS: Fixed capital depreciation	- 825.9
Net National Product	**6,411.6**
PLUS: Subsidies	+ 18.2
LESS: Indirect business taxes, nontax liabilities, and other items	- 595.5
National Income	**5,799.2**
PLUS: Personal interest and dividend income and transfer payments	+ 1,952.0
LESS: Corporate profits, net interest, and social insurance contributions	- 1,649.5
Personal Income	**6,101.7**
LESS: Personal taxes and nontax payments	- 794.3
Disposable Personal Income	**$5,307.4**

Source: *Statistical Abstract of the United States: 1996*

FIGURE 10.3 In addition to GDP, economists use a number of other measures of macroeconomic performance. **What are the five most common national income and product accounts?**

leisure time and urban renewal. Likewise, negative dollar values would be assigned to "bads" such as pollution and traffic congestion.

Other National Income and Product Accounts

Besides GDP, economists use a number of other national income and product accounts to track and measure a nation's economy. The five most common accounts are

▶ gross national product,
▶ net national product,
▶ national income,
▶ personal income, and
▶ disposable personal income.

Figure 10.3 shows the relationship between GDP and the other accounts. Although all five measures are important in macroeconomics, economists most often use the measure of GDP.

Gross National Product   Until December 1991 the Commerce Department used a NIPA

called **gross national product** (GNP) to measure the U.S. economy. GNP measures the total dollar value of all final output produced with factors of production owned by residents of a country during one year. Consider the Coca-Cola plants from the earlier example. The plants employ mostly local labor. The contribution that these Russian workers make to production would count as part of Russian GNP. If production involves any capital owned by U.S. residents, however, the value of that production would count as part of U.S. GNP.

Although GDP and GNP are similar, GDP more accurately reflects short-term resource use changes in the economy. In addition, the United Nations and most countries use GDP as the primary measure of economic production. For this reason, the Commerce Department switched to GDP—and stopped using GNP—in December 1991. The change has made it easier for U.S. economists and business firms to make international economic comparisons.

Net National Product   As you have learned, GDP includes money invested in capital goods.

This investment includes money spent on replacing defective or outdated equipment and machinery. When this depreciation is subtracted from GNP, the result is a nation's net national product. Because net national product does not include investment spent to maintain current equipment, it is a more representative measure than GNP of a nation's actual output of new goods and services during a given year. Nevertheless, even though net national product is a better measure of a nation's output, economists use it less frequently than they use GNP. Net national product usually accounts for about 90 percent of GNP.

National Income To determine the total income paid to the owners of a nation's factors of production, economists use the measure national income. National income refers to the sum of employees' and proprietors' income, real and estimated rental income, corporate profits, and net interest.

To calculate national income, economists subtract subsidies and indirect taxes from net national product. Indirect taxes—as opposed to direct taxes on income—are taxes included in the final price of goods and services.

Personal Income Sometimes economists are interested in the total amount of income earned by people in a given nation. To estimate this measure, economists subtract from national income all income that does not go to people, such as profits that firms retain and reinvest and money that firms spend on corporate income taxes and employees' Social Security. Economists then add to this amount the money that individuals receive from government transfer payments, such as Social Security checks. The result is personal income, the total amount of income paid to individuals living in a given nation.

Disposable Personal Income If you have ever received a paycheck, you are familiar with the difference between your gross pay and your net pay, or the amount of money that you actually take home. Your take-home pay shrinks noticeably once deductions are made for government programs such as Social Security and income tax. Thus, only a portion of personal income is available to consumers.

To estimate a given nation's disposable personal income—the total amount of income available to a nation's people to spend or save—economists subtract personal taxes and nontax payments from personal income. Personal taxes include income, estate, gift, property, and motor vehicle taxes. Nontax payments include fines and passport fees.

SECTION 1 — REVIEW

1. Define the following terms: national income accounting, gross domestic product, output-expenditure model, personal consumption expenditure, gross investment, nominal GDP, real GDP, price index, underground economy, gross national product.

2. What are the main components of GDP, and how are they determined?

3. What are the limitations of GDP?

4. How does GNP differ from GDP?

5. **Thinking and Writing Critically** Do you think that economists should include output that results in negative externalities when computing GDP? Explain your answer.

6. **Applying** GROSS DOMESTIC PRODUCT How might you calculate GDP for your school? What products would you include? Which ones would you exclude? Explain your answers.

SECTION 2

BUSINESS CYCLES

Economics Dictionary

business cycle
expansion
peak
contraction
recession
depression
trough
leading indicators
coincident indicators
lagging indicators

Objectives

▶ What are the four phases of the business cycle?

▶ What factors influence the business cycle?

▶ What are the three leading indicators used to determine the current phase of the business cycle and predict where the economy is headed?

Business cycles are fluctuations, or changes, in a market system's economic activity. These fluctuations are measured by increases or decreases in real GDP. While fluctuations are inevitable, the duration of upturns or downturns varies and can last from a few months to several years.

Phases of the Business Cycle

The business cycle is divided into four stages or phases:

▶ expansion, or recovery,

▶ peak,

▶ contraction, or recession, and

▶ trough.

Figure 10.4 on page 238 illustrates the business cycle and its four phases. The **expansion** phase is a period of economic expansion and growth. For example, between 1940 and 1944 current GNP in the United States increased from $99.7 billion to $210.1 billion, indicating a period of economic expansion. This tremendous growth was mainly because of high levels of military spending during World War II.

Periods of expansion eventually hit a **peak**, or a high point, at which the economy is at its strongest and most prosperous. At a peak, high consumer demand encourages producers to use plant capacity more fully and to hire workers.

When real GDP stops increasing, the business cycle enters a period of business slowdown known as a **contraction**, or a recession. Technically, a **recession** is a decline in real GDP for two or more consecutive quarters—that is, for six months or more. **Depressions** are prolonged and severe recessions, such as the Great Depression of the 1930s—the most severe contraction in U.S. economic history.

The final stage in the business cycle is the **trough**, which occurs when demand, production, and employment reach their lowest levels. Following the trough, the economy enters a period of recovery, and the expansion phase begins once again.

Influences on the Business Cycle

The factors that affect supply and demand also cause the fluctuations in the business cycle. Many economists agree that the level of business investment, availability of money and credit, expectations about future economic activity, and external factors affect the business cycle.

Business Investment Businesses invest in capital goods—such as new machinery—to increase their production. High levels of business investment promote expansion in the business cycle, while low levels of investment contribute to contractions.

How Does Your Garden Grow?

Many students hope to attend college after graduating from high school. However, with the costs of a college education rising, students and their families find paying for college to be increasingly difficult. A group of high school students in South Central Los Angeles have come up with a solution to the problem of financing their college education: they started their own business.

Shortly after the 1992 Los Angeles riots, 39 students at Crenshaw High School—with the help and encouragement of their biology teacher—converted an empty field next to their school into a vegetable garden. They then formed a company, Food From the 'Hood, to sell their produce at local farmers' markets. Soon the students were turning a profit while helping to clean up and beautify their neighborhood.

This business was so successful that the students began to think of ways to expand. With the help of several start-up grants and the donated expertise of local investment bankers, financial planners, and public relations consultants, the students decided to introduce their own brand of salad dressing—Straight Out 'the Garden. Within months 50,000 bottles of the dressing were sold in over 2,000 stores throughout southern California. Soon the students were promoting their product nationwide at food trade shows.

Business decisions are made by vote at weekly meetings held at Food From the 'Hood's company office. The headquarters, a converted storage building at the high school, is equipped with a large conference table and several computer workstations loaded with everything from accounting and financial software to Scholastic Aptitude Test (SAT) review programs.

Students receive a share of the profits in the form of college tuition grants. The grant amount is based on the number of hours each semester a student works, his or her performance in school, and other factors such as working as a tutor for fellow students. After three years of service in the company, a student can earn as much as $45,000 in scholarship money.

Running a company has influenced the future career choices of many of the owners. For instance, Ben Osborne's experience designing the label for the dressing encouraged him to study commercial art in college, with the goal of working as an art director at an advertising firm. Dennis Famond, who in 1994 earned a football scholarship to the University of California, thinks the experience of running a business could help provide an alternative career. "I know I can always garden. And my friends and I, we think of opening a restaurant someday."

High school students in South Central Los Angeles formed their owned company to finance their college educations.

What Do You Think?

1. What role did the idea of community play in the founding of Food From the 'Hood?

2. The salad dressing market is extremely competitive. If you were planning an advertising campaign for Straight Out 'the Garden, how might you differentiate the product from its competitors?

BUSINESS CYCLE

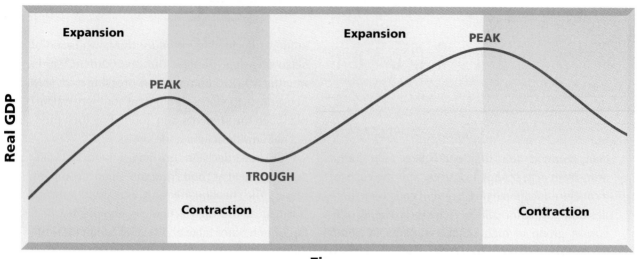

FIGURE 10.4 Increases and decreases in GDP represent fluctuations in the business cycle. **What factors influence the business cycle?**

Business investment is important to expansion for three reasons. First, by purchasing new capital goods, businesses create a demand for these goods. This demand encourages further increases in production. Second, businesses use the new capital to moderate production methods and promote efficiency. Third, increased business investment, particularly in the research and development (R&D) of new capital goods, tends to stimulate technological change and generally results in higher output at lower production costs.

Money and Credit The availability of money and credit also affects the business cycle. The amount of money in circulation depends mainly on government policies. Individuals and businesses generally borrow more money to make purchases when interest rates are low. When interest rates are high, borrowing tends to fall. Thus, total output changes as the availability and affordability of credit rise and fall.

Public Expectations Expectations about future economic conditions can shape current economic behavior as well. For example, if consumers believe that the economy is heading toward a recession, they may decide to limit their

spending in order to save money for the hard times ahead. When consumers believe that the economy is strong and the future looks prosperous, however, they tend to increase spending.

Expectations also contribute to fluctuations in the business cycle. The possibility of prosperity encourages business owners to invest in new capital or to hire more workers. Conversely, a negative view of future business prospects causes firms to decrease investment and hiring.

Copyright, 1974. Distributed by Los Angeles Times Syndicate. Reprinted with permission.

INFLATION & DEFLATION *External factors can affect the business cycle in the United States.* ***What effect did sharp increases in OPEC oil prices have during the 1970s?***

External Factors Changes in the world's economic or political climate also affect the business cycle in the United States. For example, the sharp increase in world oil prices in 1973–74 and again in 1979–80 contributed to recessions in 1974–75 and 1980–82. The Organization of Petroleum Exporting Countries (OPEC) quadrupled oil prices beginning in late 1973, causing severe price shocks throughout the U.S. economy. This external factor kept oil prices high and eventually led to an energy crisis in the United States. Conversely, the dramatic decline in oil prices in the mid-1980s strengthened the expansion phase of the business cycle.

War is another external factor that affects the business cycle. Large government expenditures

Careers

in Economics

RESEARCHER CD-ROM

Financial Analyst

Suppose you want to invest your hard-earned money in a business. How would you go about determining which one would provide the highest profit—without being too risky? You might start by looking at the stock market quotations in the business section of a newspaper. For more detailed advice you might consult a financial analyst. In many ways, a financial analyst is like a weather forecaster. Instead of predicting the week's weather, he or she predicts the long-range performance of a company or industry.

A financial analyst usually chooses one of three job specializations. First, he or she may analyze the performance of a particular company or industry, focusing on how well it will perform in the future. To do this, analysts review the company's or institution's history, products, markets, operations, and financial stability. Other financial analysts are responsible for evaluating the "health" of the overall economy by studying factors such as the timing of business cycles, interest rates, and the performance of the global economy.

Finally, analysts may manage a large number of investments at one time. This "portfolio" is a group of investments spread over various types of businesses and industries. By distributing investments in this way, financial analysts hope to create the most profit with the least amount of risk. In other words, they try to avoid poor returns by not putting all their clients' eggs (investments) in one basket (business or industry).

Financial analysts usually work for large businesses or investment funds with substantial portfolios. They also usually specialize in a particular type of business such as banking, airlines, or oil and gas. Financial analysis can be a high-paying career. A career in financial analysis requires extensive college training in business and finance, including a familiarity with statistics and the way governments manage the economy.

Financial analysts predict the long-range performance of businesses.

for national defense traditionally have strengthened business activity in the United States. For example, periods of expansion accompanied U.S. involvement in World War I, World War II, and both the Korean and the Vietnam Wars.

Predicting the Business Cycle

Economists try to predict fluctuations in the business cycle. Decision makers in business use these predictions of future economic activity to help plan for plant construction, expansion, or modernization, production goals, and hiring. Similarly, government decision makers rely on economic forecasts when they develop taxation and spending policies.

Economists often rely on three types of economic indicators to determine what phase of the business cycle the economy is currently in and in which direction it is heading. The three types of economic indicators are

▶ leading indicators,
▶ coincident indicators, and
▶ lagging indicators.

All three types are sets of statistics collected by the U.S. Department of Commerce.

Leading Indicators When attempting to predict changes economists often examine **leading indicators**, which anticipate the direction in which the economy is headed. Among the most important leading indicators are changes in the number of building permits issued, the number of orders for new capital and consumer goods, the price of raw materials and stock prices.

Coincident Indicators Some indicators provide information about the current status of the economy. These **coincident indicators** change as the economy moves from one phase of the business cycle to another and tell economists that an upturn or a downturn in the economy has arrived. The most important coincident indicators include personal income, sales volume, and industrial production levels.

Lagging Indicators Not all changes take place instantly. **Lagging indicators** change months after an upturn or a downturn in the economy has begun and help economists predict the duration of economic upturns or downturns. Important lagging indicators include the use of consumer installment credit and the number and size of business incomes.

SECTION 2 —REVIEW

1. Define the following terms: business cycle, expansion, peak, contraction, recession, depression, trough, leading indicators, coincident indicators, lagging indicators.

2. What are three signs that the business cycle is entering a period of expansion?

3. What are three signs that the business cycle is entering a period of recession?

4. List the four factors that influence the business cycle.

5. List and describe the three types of economic indicators that economists use to determine the current phase of the business cycle and where the economy is headed.

6. **Thinking and Writing Critically** How might a prediction by a well-known economist shape future economic activity?

7. **Applying** ROLE OF GOVERNMENT What are some actions that the government might take to help the economy when the nation is experiencing a recession?

ECONOMIC GROWTH

Economics Dictionary

real GDP per capita
labor productivity
productivity growth
capital-to-labor ratio
capital deepening

Objectives

▶ Why is economic growth important?

▶ What are the requirements of economic growth?

▶ What is the relationship between economic growth and productivity?

As noted in the previous section, economic activity fluctuates in business cycles. These expansions and contractions usually represent short-term changes in the economy. Economic growth, however, refers to long-term overall improvements in the economy.

For example, consider the Keynes High School basketball team, the Wizards. Throughout the season, they experience both winning and losing streaks. By the end of the season, however, they have won far more games than they have lost, and consider it a winning season. Similarly, even though the economy may fluctuate in short-term ups and downs, as long as the ups are more frequent, the economy will experience growth.

Importance of Economic Growth

As a nation's economy grows, its capacity to produce goods and services increases. Thus, this economic growth is defined as the increase in the output of final goods and services produced within a nation's borders over a specified period of time—that is, an increase in a nation's real GDP over time. To account for population increase, economists usually measure economic growth in terms of *per capita* increase in real GDP. **Real GDP per capita** is an increase in the real dollar value of all final goods and services that are produced *per person* for a specified period of time. (See Figure 10.5 on page 242.)

As noted in Chapter 2, economic growth is one of the six major goals of the U.S. economy. Continued economic growth is important to the welfare of the United States for a number of reasons—to maintain a high standard of living, to compete effectively in global markets, and to provide the resources to deal with domestic problems.

Increasing the Standard of Living Without long-term economic growth, a nation's standard of living declines. The standard of living—the economic well-being of a nation's people—improves when production per person increases

PRODUCTIVITY *The late trade secretary Ronald Brown was in charge of the opening of a U.S. technology office in Beijing, China.* **Why is continuous economic growth important for the United States to remain competitive in the global market?**

REAL GDP PER CAPITA, 1960–1995

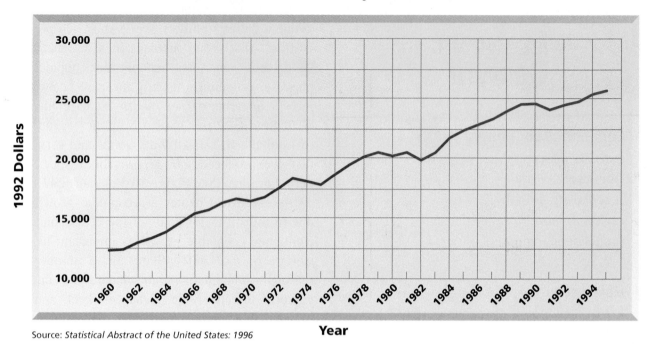

Source: *Statistical Abstract of the United States: 1996*

Year

FIGURE 10.5 Real GDP per capita provides a good estimate of a nation's standard of living. **Despite this fact, how might this measure be an inaccurate indication of a people's well-being?**

---

faster than the total population. Thus, people have more money to spend, an increased supply of goods and services to choose from, and the means to enjoy more leisure time. On the other hand, a decrease in the number of available goods and services results in a decline in the standard of living.

A higher standard of living can benefit society in many ways. People do not have to devote so many hours to work and have more time to spend on family, travel, and entertainment. In addition, people have more time to spend helping their community and can better afford to volunteer their time. More money in the economy also may help lessen domestic problems such as poverty, crime, and lack of health care—all of which are associated with low incomes.

Keep in mind, however, that an increase in a nation's real GDP per capita is not a true measure of that nation's standard of living. As noted in Section 1, real GDP does not measure quality of life or differentiate between "goods" and "bads," and it says nothing about the distribution of

income across the population. Obviously, if most material possessions are in the hands of only a few people, then many people are not experiencing a high standard of living. Nevertheless, real GDP per capita does provide a good approximation of a nation's standard of living.

Competing in the Global Market During the twentieth century the United States was the leading economic world power among industrialized nations in terms of GDP. To maintain this position, however, it must continue to experience economic growth. Although the U.S. economy leads the world in overall production levels, the economies of some other nations are growing at a faster rate.

Increasing Domestic Resources Another benefit of economic growth is an expanded tax base. As people's incomes increase, they generally pay more in taxes. Thus, the government can spend more money on national defense, education, fire protection and police services, and other important services such as welfare and job training programs. In addition, the government can devote more money to reducing the federal deficit. Alternatively, the government might lower taxes.

Requirements for Economic Growth

As you can see, economic growth is essential to the strength and prosperity of a nation and its people. Thus, macroeconomists devote a great deal of time to examining ways to stimulate the economy. In order to devise policies that promote growth, economists first examine the factors that contribute to growth.

For a nation to increase its long-term output and income, it must either increase its inputs—its factors of production—or increase the productivity of these inputs. Policies designed to promote economic growth usually seek to increase both available resources and productivity levels, in combination.

Natural Resources The United States possesses a wealth of natural resources. Businesses

PRODUCTIVITY *Natural resources—such as the diamonds used in this industrial saw—are important for economic growth.* ***What other factors affect economic growth?***

in the United States, for example, have access to plentiful amounts of timber, coal, natural gas, and minerals. Despite this wealth of natural resources, however, the United States still must import many resources, such as oil and diamonds. As a result, economic growth in the United States is, to a certain extent, dependent on the state of international markets and politics—conditions that can change with little warning. Therefore, it is important that the existing resources be protected, particularly those that cannot be replenished or restocked.

Human Resources When estimating a nation's capacity to produce goods and services, economists examine the amount of labor input that is available. Labor input is the size of the employed labor force multiplied by the length of the average workweek. Although the average workweek has decreased in length significantly since the early 1900s, the size of the labor force has increased. As noted in Chapter 8, this increase has been a result of dramatic population growth and more women and minorities joining the labor force.

Capital Resources Increasing the total stock of capital goods increases total production. The more farmland, machines, factories, and production plants in a nation, the more it is likely to produce and the more its economy will grow. A workforce that has access to plentiful supplies of modern, quality equipment and facilities is generally more productive and more efficient. Just as a high level of investment in capital goods promotes expansion in the business cycle, it also leads to long-term economic growth. The relationship between capital stock and economic growth is examined in further detail later in this section.

Entrepreneurship The willingness of entrepreneurs to take the risks involved in starting new businesses and creating and selling new products is vital to economic growth. These entrepreneurs create new products, new markets, and new jobs, all of which contribute to

RESEARCH & DEVELOPMENT EXPENDITURES, 1992

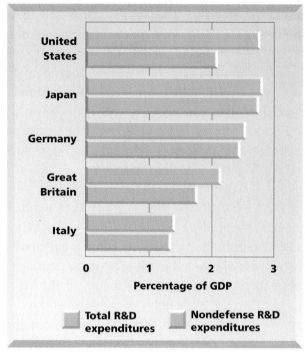

Percentage of GDP

- Total R&D expenditures
- Nondefense R&D expenditures

Source: *Statistical Abstract of the United States: 1996*

FIGURE 10.6 R&D expenditures indicate the percentage of total GDP that a nation uses to improve technology. **Which of these nations devotes the smallest percentage of GDP to R&D?**

factors that have a significant impact on productivity growth are

▶ level of available technology,
▶ quantity of capital goods available per worker, and
▶ education and skill level of the labor force.

Technological Advances Invention and innovation—new knowledge and new ways of applying this knowledge—are the leading sources of productivity growth. New ideas, methods, and tools increase efficiency and output and often lower costs.

Research and development (R&D) expenditures indicate the percentage of total GDP that a nation devotes to improving its technology. Figure 10.6 shows the R&D expenditures for a sample of industrialized nations.

Capital Deepening Another measure of productivity is the **capital-to-labor ratio**, or the amount of capital stock available per worker. This ratio is calculated by dividing the total amount of capital stock by the size of the workforce. When the amount of a nation's capital goods increases faster than the size of that nation's workforce, **capital deepening**—an

increased output and demand. Policies that make it easier for entrepreneurs to start new businesses and to compete successfully in the marketplace help a nation's economy grow. At the same time, the new goods and services that entrepreneurs provide give consumers more choices and improve the overall standard of living.

Increasing Productivity

When estimating and determining ways to increase a nation's capacity to produce goods and services, economists often focus on labor productivity. **Labor productivity** is a measure of how much each worker produces in a given period of time, usually one hour. Economists define **productivity growth** as an increase in the output of each worker per hour of work. The

Reprinted by permission of Josh Beutel from the "New Brunswick Telegraph Journal"

PRODUCTIVITY *An educated and skilled labor force is critical to a nation's productivity.* **What are two other sources of productivity growth?**

LABOR PRODUCTIVITY, 1960–1995

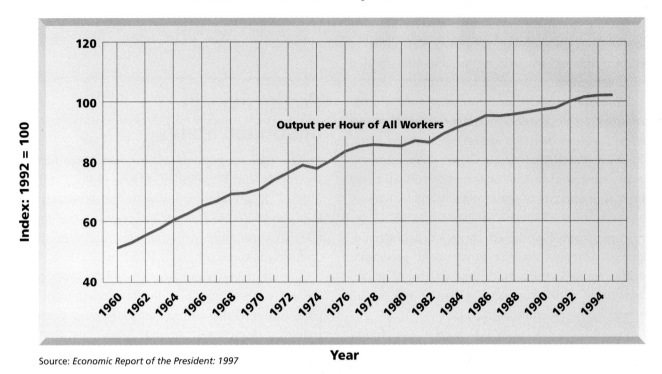

Source: *Economic Report of the President: 1997*

Year

FIGURE 10.7 Economists use labor productivity to estimate a nation's capacity to produce goods and services. **Did U.S. productivity increase or decrease between 1960 and 1995?**

increase in the amount of capital goods available per worker—results.

Workers who have access to more and better capital goods—machines, tools, equipment, and work facilities—usually will produce more in less time. Thus, capital deepening results in increased labor productivity.

Educated and Skilled Labor Force The third influence on productivity is the education and skill level of the labor force. As trade becomes more global and people become more mobile, workers entering the labor force face greater and stiffer competition for jobs. In addition, as the level of skill required to perform certain jobs increases, employees must continue to learn and to improve their skills to keep their jobs. For U.S. citizens to compete in the workplace, it is vital that the nation and its businesses invest in human resources through better education, improved access to college and vocational programs, and increased numbers of job training programs.

CASE STUDY

Retraining

ECONOMIC INSTITUTIONS & INCENTIVES One business that recognizes the importance of education in the global marketplace is the Will-Burt Company in Orrville, Ohio. During the mid-1980s the machine parts producer found itself losing business to both domestic and foreign manufacturers.

Will-Burt's chairman, Harry Featherstone, realized that his company's main problem was its percentage of machine parts with problems. This high defect rate forced customers to look to competitors for better-quality parts. The defect rate was blamed mostly on undereducated workers. Will-Burt's workers, on average, had a 10th-grade educational level, and most did not have the skills to perform technically complex tasks such as reading blueprints.

Featherstone decided it was time for the company to invest in retraining its workers. The company hired a high school teacher, a university instructor, and a specialist in industrial training to teach classes in everything from basic math and blueprint reading to algebra, geometry, and statistics. Over the next several years the company spent over $200,000 of its own money, as well as several state-funded retraining grants.

The program was an astounding success. The company's defect rate fell dramatically, from 10 percent to less than 3.7 defects per million parts. Moreover, the program led to higher worker morale. For instance, workers took far fewer days off work, and the cost of workers' compensation claims for injuries dropped from $500 per person per year to $3.

Investment in worker retraining can pay off handsomely. Whether through government programs, local community colleges, or the initiative of private companies, retraining plays a crucial role in an increasingly competitive marketplace.

Additional Factors Many factors other than education can affect productivity levels. The attitudes and motivation levels of workers, their dedication to their jobs, and the amount of loyalty they have to their companies directly affect productivity. Highly dedicated workers produce more, as do workers who enjoy their jobs.

A larger percentage of the labor force working in highly productive fields also results in increased productivity. As noted in Chapter 8, industrialization provided many new jobs for U.S. workers. As more people went to work in industry, productivity increased.

Productivity in the United States

Figure 10.7 on page 245 shows labor productivity levels for the United States from 1960 to 1995. U.S. productivity growth has slowed since the mid-1960s. Moreover, in several of the countries that compete with the United States, productivity is increasing at a faster rate.

Economists disagree as to why U.S. labor productivity is increasing at slower rates than in the past. Some of the more commonly cited reasons include decreased saving and investment, decreased investment in research and development, increased government regulation, and the shift to a more service-oriented economy.

Economists also disagree as to the best ways to stimulate economic growth in the United States. As mentioned before, policies designed to promote economic growth usually seek to increase both input and productivity. Different approaches and specific government policies for doing this are discussed in later chapters.

SECTION 3 — REVIEW

1. Define the following terms: real GDP per capita, labor productivity, productivity growth, capital-to-labor ratio, capital deepening.

2. Describe the relationship between economic growth and a nation's standard of living.

3. What changes result in economic growth?

4. List and describe the three factors that lead to increased productivity.

5. **Thinking and Writing Critically** Explain why it is important for the United States to be able to compete in the global economy.

6. **Applying** PRODUCTIVITY Consider the ways productivity applies to your own life. List five ways that you can improve your productivity at school. Are any of the actions you listed similar to ways in which nations can increase their productivity? Explain your answer.

SECTION 1 Macroeconomists use national income and product accounts (NIPAs) to measure the output and income of national economies. This process is known as national income accounting. The primary account used to measure a nation's output is gross domestic product (GDP), the total dollar value of all final goods and services produced within a given country's borders during one year. Other commonly used measures of a nation's economy are net domestic product, national income, personal income, and disposable personal income.

In computing GDP, economists use the output-expenditure model, which is the sum of a nation's personal consumption expenditures (C), gross private domestic investment (I), government purchases of goods and services (G), and net exports (X – M). Nominal GDP is GDP expressed in the current prices of the period being measured. Real GDP is GDP adjusted for the change in prices.

Because GDP is limited to market transactions and excludes nonmarket activities and the underground economy, it is only an approximate measure of a nation's total output. In addition, GDP does not differentiate between "good" and "bad" output and, as a result, is only an approximate measure of a nation's well-being.

SECTION 2 Business cycles are fluctuations in economic activity that occur in a market system as measured by increases or decreases in real GDP. The business cycle is divided into four stages or phases: expansion, or recovery; peak; contraction, or recession; and trough. Most economists agree that the level of business investment, the availability of money and credit, expectations about future economic activity, and other external factors have an impact on the business cycle. Economists analyze leading, coincident, and lagging indicators to determine the occurrence or duration of a particular phase in the business cycle and to predict where the economy is headed.

SECTION 3 Economic growth refers to long-term overall improvements in a nation's economy and standard of living. Economic growth is defined as the increase in a nation's real GDP over time. To account for population growth, economists usually measure economic growth in terms of an increase in real GDP per capita. Strong economic growth enables the United States to maintain a high standard of living and compete effectively in global markets.

Achieving economic growth requires an increase either in a nation's inputs—its factors of production—or in the productivity of these inputs. To measure productivity, economists look at labor productivity, or the amount that each worker produces in a given period of time, usually one hour. Productivity growth is defined as an increase in output per worker per hour. The level of available technology, the capital-to-labor ratio, and the education and skill level of the labor force have an impact on productivity growth.

Economics Notebook

Review the predictions you wrote in your Economics Notebook at the beginning of this chapter about your economic future. Are your predictions similar to economic predictions made on the national level? Record your answer in your Notebook.

REVIEWING CONCEPTS

1. Which of the following goods and services does GDP include: leather used to make saddles, clothing sold in a retail store, lawn services provided free-of-charge, used cars, athletic shoes sold at a mall?

2. Explain the difference between nominal GDP and real GDP. Why is real GDP a better measure to use when examining changes in GDP over time?

3. Describe the relationship between a nation's total output and its total income.

4. Explain the difference between personal income and disposable personal income.

5. Explain the difference between expansion in the business cycle and economic growth.

6. How are economic growth and productivity related?

THINKING AND WRITING CRITICALLY

1. INFLATION & DEFLATION How does warfare affect the business cycle? Explain your answer.

2. GROSS DOMESTIC PRODUCT What might happen to GDP if all nonmarket and underground products and services were included? Would this GDP then reflect a higher quality of life? Why or why not?

3. GROSS DOMESTIC PRODUCT What would happen to the economy in terms of GDP if the interest rate were lowered to 5 percent?

4. PRODUCTIVITY Imagine that the DoRite Company has started an in-house day care and a job skills training program for its employees. What impact might this have on the company's productivity? Explain your answer.

YOUR LOCAL ECONOMY

Make a list of 10 goods and services that you see in your classroom and the intermediate products used to make them. Estimate the value of these final products and calculate the total value of the final goods and services you use everyday.

INDIVIDUAL PORTFOLIO PROJECT

Imagine that you are an economist who foresees a recession in the near future. Write an editorial about the recession's impact.

PRACTICING SKILLS: UNDERSTANDING MEASUREMENT CONCEPTS AND METHODS

The graph below shows the 11 leading indicators that economists use to predict the future of the

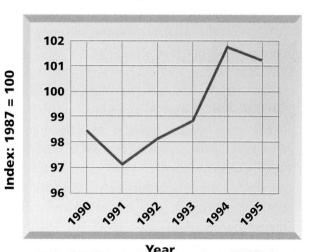

LEADING ECONOMIC INDICATORS, 1990–1995

Source: *Statistical Abstract of the United States: 1996*

economy. Use the information presented on the graph on page 248 to answer the questions that follow.

1. In what year were the indicators at the highest point?

2. In what year did the indicators rise above the index number? What does this point signify?

3. What does the graph indicate about the economy in general from 1990 to 1995? Explain your answer.

THE INTERNET: LEARNING ONLINE

Conduct an Internet search to learn about the Great Depression using key words such as *Great Depression*, *New Deal*, and *Franklin Roosevelt*. What can you learn about the economic factors that led to the depression? What programs were developed to help relieve the depression? Make a poster that illustrates some of the main causes of the depression, the programs put into place to relieve the depression, and information about the effectiveness of these programs.

ANALYZING PRIMARY SOURCES

"The Sky Is Always Falling"

The following is an excerpt from Gregg Easterbrook's article "The Sky Is Always Falling" which appeared in *The New Republic* magazine on August 21, 1989. The article takes a humorous look at the practice of interpreting economic performance. Read the excerpt and answer the questions that follow.

"Better sit down and brace yourself: there's an economic trend in progress. It's bad, real bad. What trend? Makes no difference.

"Let's take employment. U.S. ECONOMY ADDS 400,000 JOBS IN MONTH: REPORT SPURS FEARS, declaimed the *Washington Post* last February. Some economic naïf [uninformed person] might consider job growth to be good news. To the cognoscenti [especially knowledgable people], though, it was a frightening omen: high employment might inspire the Federal Reserve to raise interest rates, the *Post* worried. . . . Of course, later when employment expansion slowed somewhat, that was bad too: APRIL JOB GROWTH EASED DECISIVELY, STIRRING CONCERN, the *New York Times* warned . . . .

"You may recall that during the 1970s high oil prices were considered less than optimal [ideal]. Now that prices are down, that's a crisis too. . . . Though when oil prices poked up after the Exxon *Valdez* [oil spill], that was bad too. COFFEE PRICES AT 8-YEAR LOW AFTER BRAZIL IS SPARED FROST, the *Times* recently noted. Should we raise our mugs in a toast? Not at all. The *Times* sympathized with 'a battered market' upset because 'an expected freeze in the Brazilian coffee fields had not materialized.' . . .

". . . The sentiment that disaster is a great story while normalcy is boring animates not just the media but Congress, where congressional hearings and members' statements enthusiastically embrace that day's sky-is-falling economic line.

"The fact that such a line is always available reflects a central truth about economics: almost any economic development is both good *and* bad—good in some ways, bad in others. An expanding economy reduces unemployment, but at some point risks inflation. . . .

"If you're determined to concentrate on the cons, there is always a full panoply [array] to choose from. On the other hand, relentless emphasis on the good news in any set of economic statistics . . . can be just as fatuous [empty] as relentless emphasis on the bad news, and somewhat more dangerous. . . . But sometimes it makes sense to risk today's good news to avoid tomorrow's bad news."

1. According to the article, what are the pros and cons of job growth?

2. How did producer expectations affect the price of Brazilian coffee in 1989? How was this good for consumers yet bad for the market?

3. What point is Easterbrook trying to make about the media and about economics?

4. Does Easterbrook think it is better to always look at the pros, or the cons, of economic developments?

CHAPTER 11

ECONOMIC CHALLENGES

How much money will you need to save for college? What will the job market be like when you graduate? Will you be able to earn enough to meet your expenses? How much will a house cost? How much money will you need to set aside for retirement?

To plan for the future, people must anticipate many unknown factors, such as changes in prices, the job market, and technology. The government also encounters these challenges as policy makers try to meet the nation's economic goals. In this chapter you will learn about three challenges faced by individuals and the U.S. economy as a whole: unemployment, inflation, and poverty and income distribution.

Economics Notebook

In your Economics Notebook, list five economic challenges you have faced in the last month, such as a job search or an increase in movie ticket prices. Describe how you responded to each challenge.

UNEMPLOYMENT

Economics Dictionary

unemployment rate
marginally attached worker
discouraged worker
underemployed
frictional unemployment
structural unemployment
seasonal unemployment
cyclical unemployment

Objectives

▶ What is the unemployment rate?
▶ What are the four major types of unemployment?
▶ What are the main economic costs of high unemployment?

Why is unemployment part of macroeconomics? You may think that unemployment is an issue for microeconomics, since it affects individuals. After all, unemployment threatens the security and well-being of Americans and their families every day. People who want to work but are unable to find jobs face many hardships. They may experience low self-esteem and other personal problems. They may be unable to afford many of the goods and services they need and may even lose their homes and belongings.

True, individuals can be greatly affected by unemployment. At the same time, however, high rates of unemployment also hurt the economy as a whole. The nation loses the goods and services that the unemployed would produce if they were working. Businesses lose sales because the unemployed cannot buy as many products. Moreover, the government must decide how and to what extent to support the unemployed and their dependents.

Measuring Unemployment

Policy makers and economic analysts gauge the health of the U.S. economy by examining the labor force and unemployment: How many workers are unemployed? How long have they been jobless? How does unemployment differ for specific industries and geographic regions?

To answer such questions, the U.S. Bureau of the Census, also known as the Census Bureau, conducts a monthly study called the Current Population Survey. Census Bureau employees interview a sample of about 60,000 households across the country. These data are then analyzed and published by the Bureau of Labor Statistics (BLS) in the U.S. Department of Labor.

Identifying the Employed and Unemployed

The Census Bureau uses specific definitions for the terms *employed* and *unemployed*. Individuals ages 16 and older are classified as employed if during the survey week they

▶ worked for pay or profit one or more hours,
▶ worked without pay in a family business 15 or more hours, or
▶ have jobs but did not work as a result of illness, weather, vacations, or labor disputes.

UNEMPLOYMENT *Economists measure the health of the U.S. economy by examining unemployment.* **Which government bureaus study unemployment?**

The bureau classifies individuals as unemployed if during the survey week they do not meet any of the criteria for employed status. In addition, these people must have been actively looking for work during the past four weeks.

These definitions do not account for every person in the United States. Anyone who is not classified as either employed or unemployed is considered to be "not in the labor force."

Unemployment Rate

The most closely watched and highly publicized labor force statistic is the **unemployment rate**, the percentage of people in the civilian labor force who are unemployed. Unemployment tends to increase during times of recession and decrease during times of expansion.

Problems with the Unemployment Rate

The unemployment rate does not measure all aspects of unemployment. First, it does not indicate the differences in intensity with which people look for jobs. Second, the conditions for being included among the unemployed exclude some individuals who most people would think of as unemployed. Among this group are **marginally attached workers**—people who once held productive jobs but have given up looking for work. In 1995 some 5.7 million people were marginally attached workers. **Discouraged workers**—a subset of marginally attached workers—are people who want a job but have stopped looking for work for job-related reasons.

Suppose, for example, that Ben Greene is a discouraged worker. Ben is 57 years old and worked as a senior programmer for a computer company for 15 years. Two years ago a company merger eliminated his department. He actively searched for employment for over a year, but without success. Now, faced with stiff job competition, Ben has stopped looking. He still wants a job, but sees no point in continuing to look.

A third shortcoming of the unemployment rate is that it does not indicate the number of underemployed workers. Workers who have jobs beneath their skill level or who want full-time work but are only able to find part-time jobs are considered to be **underemployed**. Like unemployment, underemployment represents wasted resources and lost output. For example, a recent college graduate who is unable to find a job in his or her field and takes a job waiting tables is underemployed.

Labor Force Statistics Figure 11.1 shows the main labor force statistics for the civilian population for 1995. Because unemployment can vary widely among different groups, the BLS provides employment and unemployment information for the total population as well as figures that have been broken down by age, sex, race, marital status, industry, and occupation. In addition, the BLS provides unemployment information based on job-seeking methods and reasons for—and duration of—unemployment.

Determining Full Employment As noted in Chapter 2, full employment is an important part of economic stability. Full employment does not, however, mean that everyone has a job and the employment rate is zero. Some unemployment is unavoidable and a natural part of even a healthy economy. As a result, economists generally consider an unemployment rate of about 5 percent—that is, employment of about 95 percent of the labor force—to represent full employment.

In addition, some economists assert that extremely high levels of employment can cause dramatic increases in the average prices of goods and services. These economists state that a "natural rate of unemployment" exists when prices are relatively stable.

Types of Unemployment

To better analyze the factors that contribute to joblessness, economists break unemployment into four categories:

▶ frictional,
▶ structural,
▶ seasonal, and
▶ cyclical.

Some types of unemployment do not hurt the economy as much as others. In addition, different approaches and policies are needed to deal with the different types of unemployment.

Frictional Unemployment

When workers are moving from one job to another, they experience what is known as **frictional unemployment**. This category includes people who have decided to leave one job to look for another, as well as new entrants and re-entrants into the labor force. For example, suppose that Heather Gibson leaves her job as a receptionist to find a job as a data processor. During her job search, Heather is considered frictionally unemployed.

Economists consider frictional unemployment a normal part of a healthy and changing economy. This type of unemployment reflects workers' freedom of choice in the labor market, as they select the jobs that are most satisfying to them. Frictional unemployment often is a signal that new jobs in new industries are becoming available.

Structural Unemployment

Unemployment that occurs as a result of changes in technology or in the way the economy is structured is known as **structural unemployment**. Technological advances and shifts in consumers' tastes can result in the change or decline of entire industries. For example, when the television industry began to build TVs that relied on transistors rather than tubes, this technological change reduced the need for television repair specialists. (See Figure 11.2 on page 255 for information on unemployment and current occupations.)

Some industries decline and even disappear as natural resources in a region are used up. Industries in Appalachia, for example, enjoyed high employment and prosperity during the late 1800s and early 1900s because many natural resources such as timber and coal were available there. As

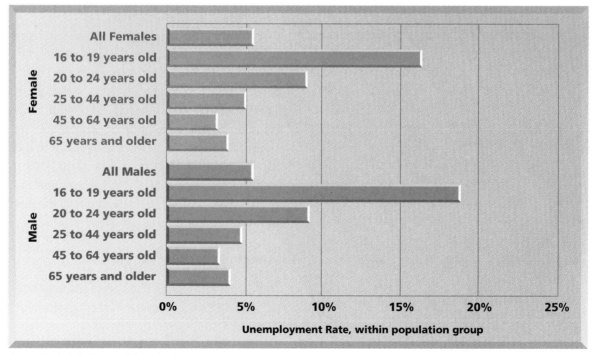

UNEMPLOYMENT BY SEX AND AGE, 1995

Source: *Statistical Abstract of the United States: 1996*

FIGURE 11.1 The unemployment rate is the percentage of unemployed people in the civilian labor force. **Which population group has the highest unemployment rate?**

Civilian Conservation Corps

The Great Depression of the 1930s was the most serious economic crisis the United States has ever faced. At its worst point in 1933, about one in every four working Americans was unemployed. The unemployment rate among young men was even higher. As many as 250,000 jobless youth had taken to wandering the country in search of employment.

In the first few years of the depression, the federal government did little to lessen the hardships created by severe unemployment. However, with Franklin D. Roosevelt's election to the presidency in 1932, the government began to take action. Within days of taking office in 1933, President Roosevelt set out a recovery plan that became known as the New Deal. One of the plan's first steps was to employ the nation's youth.

To this end, Roosevelt called for the immediate creation of the Civilian Conservation Corps (CCC), a program designed to put young men back to work while helping to maintain the nation's natural resources. Roosevelt believed that forests and farmland were valuable resources that should be managed and protected to ensure their survival for future generations of Americans. The CCC hired young men between the ages of 18 and 25 to work on a variety of conservation-related projects such as combating soil erosion on farmland, replanting overlogged forests, and building dams and other flood control barriers.

The CCC was one of the most successful New Deal programs. From its founding in 1933 until 1942, when it was discontinued because of America's entrance into World War II, the program employed almost 3 million young men, paying them $1 a day, plus room and board.

The program had other economic benefits as well. Farmers benefited from reduced soil erosion, businesspeople received profits from trade with local work camps, and CCC workers sent paychecks to their families. Workers also planted millions of acres of trees, built hundreds of miles of flood control levees, and constructed improvements in the National Park system that are still being enjoyed across the country today.

In recent years there have been calls to recreate the Civilian Conservation Corps. Supporters claim it could provide useful work for many unemployed young people and expose urban youth to the healthful effects of the great outdoors. They also argue that it could bring together urban and rural youth. Finally, a new CCC could work to protect the country's natural environment. Others object to any such program on the grounds that private businesses are better suited than the government to employ the nation's youth efficiently.

The Civilian Conservation Corps, which employed depression-era youth, encouraged hard work, discipline, and cooperation.

What Do You Think?

1. Should the government provide work programs like the CCC for young Americans? Explain your answer.

2. If you were going to establish a program like the CCC today, what would be its focus? Explain your answer.

FASTEST-GROWING AND FASTEST-DECLINING OCCUPATIONS, 1994–2005

Personal and home care aides	Letterpress operators
Home health aides	Typesetting and composing machine operators
Systems analysts	Directory assistance operators
Computer engineers	Telephone station installers and repairers
Physical and corrective therapy assistants	Central office operators
Electronic pagination systems workers	Billing, posting, and calculating machine operators
Occupational therapy assistants	Data entry keyers
Physical therapists	Shoe-sewing machine operators
Residential counselors	Roustabouts—deckhands, dock workers, oil rig workers
Human services workers	Electronic data–processing equipment operators

Source: *Statistical Abstract of the United States: 1996*

FIGURE 11.2 Structural unemployment can cause entire industries and occupations to disappear. **What industries appear to be most affected by structural unemployment?**

these resources were used up, however, the region developed high structural unemployment.

Seasonal Unemployment
The unemployment rate may also fluctuate in a predictable way from season to season as a result of regular occurrences such as holidays, the school year, harvest schedules, and industry production schedules. Economists call these regular fluctuations in jobs **seasonal unemployment**. Agricultural workers are particularly affected by seasonal unemployment. Spring, summer, and fall are busy seasons for many farmers because most crops can be planted, cultivated, and harvested only during warm weather. During the winter months, however, many farmworkers temporarily lose their jobs.

CASE STUDY

Migrant Workers in California

UNEMPLOYMENT For years, California has been an important source of agricultural products. Farming is the state's largest business. In fact, Californians grow over half the nation's fruit and vegetables.

Although this level of productivity might suggest high levels of employment, the nature of the work instead results in significant seasonal unemployment. The instability, low pay, and grueling labor involved in agricultural work, along with the fact that workers frequently have to live in over-crowded labor camps, discourages many U.S. citizens from becoming migrant farm laborers. For more than 100 years, therefore, California growers have relied on the labor of migrant workers—many of whom come from other countries—to harvest their crops.

The state's strawberry industry provides a glimpse of the lives of migrant laborers, as the vast majority of the labor force consists of migrant workers. While strawberries can be highly profitable, they require intensive labor. The berries are planted, tended, and picked by hand, and they have a short harvest period.

When the harvest is at its peak, workers can make as much as $100 a day. These wages—and the prospect of employment—attract many workers. Soon, however, this intense competition causes wages to drop. Additionally, workers often have to live in overcrowded labor camps. Because employment is so short-term, most migrants spend as much as three months each year seasonally unemployed.

UNEMPLOYMENT *The strawberry industry depends on migrant workers to harvest its crops.* **What type of unemployment affects agricultural laborers?**

Cyclical Unemployment Unemployment resulting from recessions and economic downturns is called **cyclical unemployment**. This type of unemployment harms the economy more than any other type of unemployment. When sales decline, producers tend to reduce output and lay off workers. Increased unemployment further reduces total demand and leads to more layoffs and even higher unemployment. When the economy begins to expand again, total demand for goods and services rises, producers hire more workers to increase output, and the level of unemployment begins to decrease.

Cyclical unemployment has challenged the U.S. economy during the 1900s. In 1933, during the Great Depression, unemployment reached an all-time high of about 25 percent of the labor force, or some 12.8 million workers. Serious recessions in 1974–75, 1980–82, and 1990–91 also were characterized by high levels of cyclical unemployment. Increased unemployment rates may lag slightly behind the development—or even the end—of a recession. For example, in the case of the 1990–91 recession, the unemployment rate did not reach its peak of 7.5 percent until 1992. The complete elimination of cyclical unemployment, on the other hand, indicates that the economy has reached full employment.

Although seasonal fluctuations in unemployment are fairly easy for economists to predict, these changes make it difficult to determine whether unemployment shifts between two periods are the result of changing conditions or normal seasonal changes.

SECTION 1 — REVIEW

1. Define the following terms: unemployment rate, marginally attached worker, discouraged worker, underemployed, frictional unemployment, structural unemployment, seasonal unemployment, cyclical unemployment.

2. Does the unemployment rate accurately estimate the number of people who are unemployed? Explain your answer.

3. Explain the concept of full employment.

4. Give an example not mentioned in the text of each of the major types of unemployment.

5. **Thinking and Writing Critically** What are some possible disadvantages of a zero unemployment rate?

6. **Applying** UNEMPLOYMENT Explain the relationship between recessions in the business cycle and high rates of unemployment. Provide an example to illustrate your explanation.

INFLATION

Economics Dictionary

aggregate supply

aggregate demand

inflation

deflation

demand-pull inflation

cost-push inflation

supply shock

wage-price spiral

consumer price index

market basket

producer price index

inflation rate

hyperinflation

Objectives

▶ What do economists look at when evaluating price changes over time?

▶ What causes inflation?

▶ What are the two main price indexes that economists use to measure inflation?

▶ How does inflation affect the U.S. economy?

As noted in Chapter 5, when quantity demanded exceeds quantity supplied, prices go up and the purchasing power of a dollar goes down. When quantity supplied is greater than quantity demanded, prices go down and the purchasing power of a dollar goes up. These changes in prices and in the purchasing power of money have many immediate and far-reaching effects for society and can threaten the stability of a nation's economy. To understand the effects of these forces, economists study price changes throughout the economy.

Examining Price Fluctuations

When discussing prices, economists talk about the price level, inflation, and deflation. The price level reflects prices throughout the economy at a particular time. Inflation and deflation refer to changes in the price level over time.

Price Level The price level influences aggregate supply and aggregate demand. **Aggregate supply** is the total amount of goods and services produced throughout the economy. As noted in Chapter 4, the law of supply states that quantity supplied increases as prices rise. Similarly, the aggregate quantity of goods supplied is likely to be higher when the price level is higher.

Aggregate demand is the total amount of spending by individuals and businesses throughout the economy. The law of demand applies to aggregate demand, which means that there is a greater aggregate quantity of products demanded when the price level is lower.

Although the price level reflects a particular point in time, it is used for comparative purposes. For example, economists may compare today's

MARKETS & PRICES *Changes in prices have many effects on society and can threaten the stability of a nation's economy.* **What terms describe changes in price level over time?**

INFLATION & DEFLATION *Inflation reduces the real purchasing power of the dollar.* **What are the two types of inflation?**

Causes of Inflation

Economists classify inflation into two general categories based on cause—demand-pull inflation and cost-push inflation. Prices can either be *pulled* up by high demand or *pushed* up by high production costs. In addition, expectations about future prices strongly affect inflation.

Demand-Pull Inflation When aggregate demand increases faster than the economy's productive capacity, **demand-pull inflation** results. Following the laws of supply and demand, prices increase when quantity demanded exceeds quantity supplied. As demand continues to increase, the prices of goods are *pulled* even higher. Demand-pull inflation can result from an increase in the money supply or an increase in the use of credit.

The Federal Reserve system, commonly known as the "Fed," controls the money supply in the United States. (The Federal Reserve system is discussed in greater detail in Chapters 13 and 14.) When the Fed increases the supply of money and credit, aggregate demand increases as consumers, businesses, and governments purchase more goods. Spending thus outpaces the available supply of goods, and demand-pull inflation results. Economists refer to this situation as "too much money chasing too few goods."

price level with price levels in 1990 or 1995 to see how the economy has changed.

Inflation An increase in the average price level of all products in an economy is called **inflation**. Usually, inflation occurs when aggregate demand increases faster than aggregate supply. When quantity demanded exceeds quantity supplied, consumers must compete for limited products, and prices go up. As prices increase, the amount that a dollar buys decreases. Thus, inflation reduces the real purchasing power of the dollar.

Deflation A decrease in the average price level of all goods and services in an economy is known as **deflation**. Deflation may occur when aggregate demand decreases more rapidly than aggregate supply. In such situations, sellers are forced to lower prices to attract buyers. As prices decrease, the amount a dollar buys increases. Thus, deflation boosts the real purchasing power of the dollar. The most prolonged—and most recent—deflationary period in U.S. history occurred during the Great Depression, when high unemployment coupled with reductions in wages caused aggregate demand and prices to fall.

Cost-Push Inflation When producers raise prices to cover higher resource costs, **cost-push inflation** results. As noted in Chapter 4, resource costs are one of the determinants of supply. Producers must set prices high enough to cover their costs and to earn a profit. Thus, increased production costs *push* producers to raise prices even if demand has not increased.

Supply shocks are one of many sources of cost-push inflation. A **supply shock** is an event that increases the cost of production for all or many firms, resulting in overall higher prices. Crop failures, natural disasters, and political upheavals can cause supply shocks. As noted in Chapter 10, for example, in 1973–74 members of the Organization of Petroleum Exporting Countries (OPEC) quadrupled the price of oil after a war with Israel. Producers in the United States had to raise prices to cover increased energy costs. The result was a ripple of price increases for everything from gasoline and home heating oil to plastics and cosmetics. By 1974 inflation had spiked to 11 percent, up from 6 percent in 1973.

The relationship between wages and prices can also lead to cost-push inflation. Suppose that a worker bargains for a wage increase. These higher wages—when paid to workers throughout

Careers in Economics

Loan Officer

The use of credit often spurs economic growth. At some point, nearly all companies must borrow money to buy new equipment and finance other improvements that will help their business grow. Families and individuals also borrow money to purchase a new house or car or finance a college education. The high demand for credit means that loans are an important source of income for financial institutions.

To borrow money from a bank, you would need to meet with a loan officer, the person responsible for loan applications. Loan officers determine whether a potential borrower is likely to repay the loan. Once money is lent, the loan officer keeps track of whether the borrower is keeping up with his or her loan payments.

In the 1980s some U.S. banks and savings institutions made unwise lending decisions. When some borrowers stopped making loan payments, the lost revenue threatened the entire banking system. In part to avoid repeating this crisis, the banking industry has since made a concerted effort to raise the training standards for loan officers.

Most banks look for loan officers with training beyond an undergraduate college degree. A loan officer is expected to have business school training in finance and a familiarity with the many federal laws that apply to lending money. He or she is also expected to have excellent writing skills and to possess the ability to communicate clearly.

While becoming a loan officer requires extensive training and preparation, the rewards can be generous. The loan officer is a highly paid employee and has an opportunity to participate in the economic growth of his or her community.

Loan officers evaluate borrowers' needs and their ability to repay loans.

the economy—encourage producers to raise prices, continuing the cycle. Some economists refer to this cycle as the **wage-price spiral**.

Price Expectations Expectations about future prices can affect inflation. When consumers expect prices to increase, they tend to buy immediately to take advantage of lower prices. As a result, aggregate demand increases and inflation rises. When consumers expect future prices to be lower, they are likely to postpone buying, which decreases aggregate demand and slows inflation.

Similarly, producers adjust prices to match their expectations of future inflation. When producers expect inflation to increase, they raise prices. As prices continue to rise, consumers' and producers' expectations of future inflation grow even more, and prices spiral upward.

Measuring Inflation

When measuring price level fluctuations, economists look at changes in the average price level of goods and services in a nation. They look at the average price level as opposed to specific prices, because in any given period the prices of some goods are rising while the prices of others are falling. Even though specific items might be cheaper than they used to be, if most items are more expensive, then the purchasing power of the dollar in general has decreased.

To measure the price level, economists construct a price index. The two most common price indexes are the consumer price index and the producer price index.

Consumer Price Index

When news reports declare that inflation is up or down, they are usually referring to a change in the consumer price index. The **consumer price index** (CPI) is a measure of the average change over time in the price of a fixed group of products.

The Bureau of Labor Statistics (BLS) calculates and reports the CPI each month. First, the bureau selects a base year against which to measure price changes. Currently the CPI is based on the period 1982–84 instead of a single base year.

Second, the bureau selects a representative sample of commonly purchased consumer items, called the **market basket**. This sample includes items that the typical urban consumer might buy, such as food, clothing, shelter, utilities, transportation, entertainment, and health care. Each item in the market basket is weighted based on its importance in consumers' budgets. The bureau then samples the prices of these goods and services in selected areas across the nation. Some prices are reviewed every month; others every other month. Every 8 to 10 years the BLS conducts a survey to identify items that should be included in the market basket.

Economists set the index price for the base year at 100. To calculate the CPI for another year, the BLS determines the price of the market basket for that year, divides the amount by the cost of the market basket in the base year, and multiplies the result by 100. For example, if the market basket cost $4,000 in 1982–84 and $7,000 in a later year, the CPI for the later year would be 175: ($7,000 ÷ $4,000) × 100 = 175. The average price level in the later year is 75 percent higher than it was in 1982–84. In other words, purchasing power has declined, and consumers must spend 175 percent of the cost in 1982–84.

Producer Price Index

The **producer price index** (PPI) is a measure of the average change over time in the prices of goods and services bought by producers. PPIs are compiled for selected types of products as well as for production stages or particular industries. Price data are based on some 3,200 products. The current base year for the PPI is 1982 and, like the CPI base year, has a value of 100.

Inflation Rate

Economists use price indexes like the CPI to calculate the **inflation rate**, the monthly or annual percentage change in prices. To use the CPI to calculate the inflation rate from one year to another, economists use the formula: inflation rate = [(CPI Year B − CPI Year A) ÷ CPI Year A] × 100. For example, if the price level, or CPI,

CONSUMER PRICE INDEX, 1940–1996

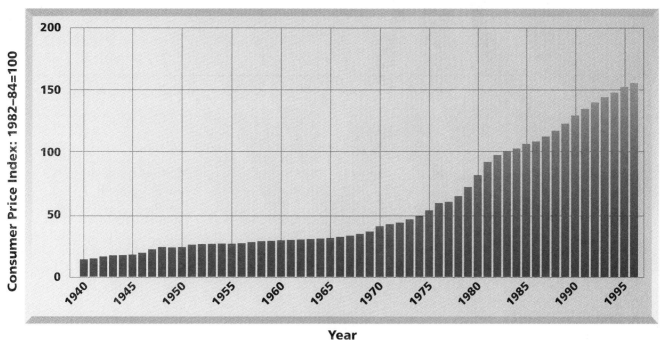

Sources: *Statistical Abstract of the United States: 1996;*
Economic Report of the President: 1997

FIGURE 11.3 The consumer price index measures prices for a specific group of products. **What was the consumer price index for 1995?**

is 140 in Year A and 145 in Year B, the inflation rate is 3.57 percent for that period: [(145 − 140) ÷ 140] × 100 = 3.57 percent. Figure 11.3 shows the CPI for the United States from 1940 to 1996, and Figure 11.4 on page 262 graphs the inflation rate, based on the annual percent change in CPI, for the same period.

Most economists consider inflation rates from 1 to 3 percent to be low to moderate, with inflation rates of less than 1 percent to be negligible. Depending on the severity of the inflation rate, economists may describe it as *creeping* or *galloping*. **Hyperinflation**, the worst degree of inflation, is a situation in which inflation is increasing at a rate of several hundred percent a year. Hyperinflation can result in complete economic collapse. After Germany lost World War I, for example, it was forced to pay heavy reparations to the victorious countries. Germany tried to pay this debt simply by printing more money. By November 15, 1923, it took 4.2 trillion marks (German currency) to equal the value of one U.S.

dollar—meaning that the mark was worth so little that even the paper on which it was printed had greater value.

Effects of Inflation

Although inflation benefits some people, it affects most people negatively. Inflation causes changes in

▶ the purchasing power of the dollar,
▶ the value of real wages,
▶ interest rates,
▶ saving and investing, and
▶ production costs.

Decreased Purchasing Power You may have heard an older family member or friend talk about how inexpensive things were when they were young. They are discussing one of the effects of inflation—decreased purchasing power. (See Figure 11.5 on page 263.)

INFLATION RATE, 1940–1996

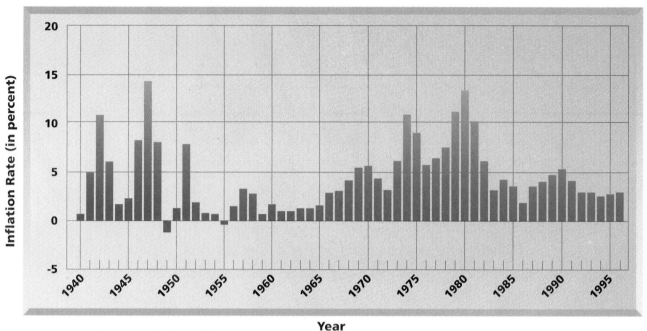

Source: *Economic Report of the President: 1997*

FIGURE 11.4 The inflation rate is the percentage change in prices during a specific period such as a month or a year. **In which years did the U.S. economy experience a negative inflation rate?**

The decreasing value of the dollar particularly hurts people on fixed incomes. As the value of the dollar falls, the purchasing power of people who rely on set pension checks or other fixed income decreases as well. To combat this problem, many labor contracts, government benefits, and retirement plans include cost-of-living adjustments (COLAs). As noted in Chapter 8, COLAs automatically raise wages or payments to account for inflation.

Decreased Value of Real Wages Inflation also reduces the value of workers' real wages when pay increases fail to keep pace with rising prices. For example, suppose that Donald Ming earned $20,000 in 1979 and $40,000 in 1995. In current dollars, Donald's $40,000 salary is double what he made in 1979. Once Donald's 1995 income has been adjusted for inflation, however, it becomes clear that his purchasing power has remained about the same. Therefore, his salary increase has just enabled him to keep pace with

the cost of living. Overall, wages tend to stay ahead of or at the pace of inflation.

Increased Interest Rates As prices increase, interest rates—the price of borrowing money—tend to increase as well. High interest rates can decrease consumer spending, particularly on goods that are usually purchased on credit or through loans, such as computers, automobiles, and houses. High interest rates can double or even triple consumers' monthly credit card or loan payments.

Decreased Saving and Investing The inflation rate also affects the return that people receive from their savings and investments. For example, suppose that Jody Bailey deposited $2,000 in a savings account yielding 5 percent interest. After a period of five years, during which time the inflation rate averaged 7 percent, she withdrew her savings—which had grown to $2,550. Although Jody has more money than when she started, she has "lost" money overall because inflation was running at a higher rate than the interest she earned on her savings. As a result, the purchasing power of Jody's savings has declined. High inflation thus tends to discourage saving.

Increased Production Costs

Businesses that issue long-term bonds with interest rates lower than the inflation rate benefit from inflation. For the most part, however, high inflation rates hurt businesses because inflation increases their costs of production. Businesses that can pass these additional costs on to buyers survive. Consumers, however, may refuse to pay the higher prices.

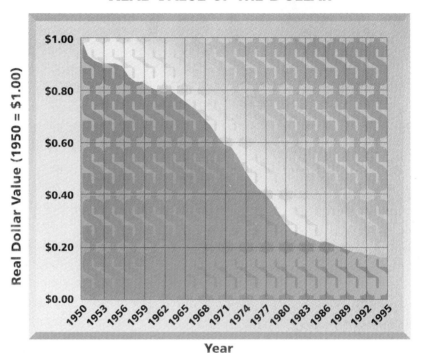

REAL VALUE OF THE DOLLAR

Source: *Statistical Abstract of the United States: 1996*

FIGURE 11.5 Inflation reduces the purchasing power of a dollar. **How much was a 1950 dollar worth in 1995?**

SECTION 2 —REVIEW

1. Define the following terms: aggregate supply, aggregate demand, inflation, deflation, demand-pull inflation, cost-push inflation, supply shock, wage-price spiral, consumer price index, market basket, producer price index, inflation rate, hyperinflation.

2. How is price level different from inflation and deflation?

3. What are the two major types of inflation?

4. What are the two most common price indexes? What do economists measure with these two price indexes?

5. Which of the following would be hurt by a high rate of inflation and why?

(a) a person hoping to buy a home
(b) a retired auto worker
(c) a retail salesperson who has not received a raise in three years

6. **Thinking and Writing Critically**
Suppose that you are going to calculate a price index for your classroom. What products would you put in your market basket? Explain your choices.

7. **Applying** INFLATION & DEFLATION
Imagine that a political revolution in a country containing most of the world's gold mines results in a 15 percent increase in the price of gold in the United States. How might this event affect the rate of inflation? Explain your answer.

POVERTY AND INCOME DISTRIBUTION

Economics Dictionary

poverty threshold
poverty rate
Lorenz Curve
Gini Index

Objectives

▶ How do economists determine the number of poor people in the United States?

▶ How do economists measure the distribution of income?

▶ What policies does the U.S. government use to reduce the income gap and decrease poverty?

The income gap between the richest and the poorest Americans was wider in the 1990s than at any other time since World War II. Moreover, income inequality in the United States had become greater than in any other large industrialized country. How does a growing income gap affect a nation's economy and society? Should the U.S. government take action to reduce this gap? These are the sorts of questions that U.S. policy makers must address as they try to balance economic equity with other goals in an increasingly competitive and global economy.

Poverty in the United States

Another way to examine the economic well-being of a nation is to measure the number of people who are living in poverty. In 1995, for example, 36.4 million people in the United States—13.8 percent of the total population—were living in poverty.

How is poverty defined? According to the Census Bureau, individuals, families, or households are living in poverty if their total incomes fall below designated income levels. The **poverty threshold**, or poverty level, is the lowest income—as determined by the government—that a family or household of a certain size or composition needs to maintain a basic standard of living. In 1995 the poverty threshold for a family of four was $15,569.

The official method of determining the poverty threshold was established in 1963–64 by the Social Security Administration (SSA). The thresholds are based on economical food plans. A 1955 study of food consumption found that the average family of three or more spent approximately one third of its after-tax income on food. Based on this information, the Department of Agriculture designed economical, nutritionally balanced food plans for different family sizes. The SSA then multiplied each plan by three to determine the poverty thresholds. Today poverty thresholds are adjusted annually based on changes in the consumer price index (CPI).

The **poverty rate** is the percentage of individuals or families in the total population, or a

INCOME DISTRIBUTION *Many people in the United States with incomes below the poverty threshold are white and live in rural areas.* **How is the poverty threshold determined?**

subset of the population, that are living in poverty. Figure 11.6 shows the number and percentage of individuals and families living in poverty from 1977 to 1995. Both the number and rate of Americans living in poverty have dropped in the last several years. In 1995 the poverty rate was 13.8 percent.

Distribution of Income

In his 1890 book *How the Other Half Lives*, journalist Jacob Riis wrote about the widening gap between the rich and the poor. The situation that Riis described was not limited to the late 1800s, an era often called the Gilded Age. Economists refer to this inequality in income among individuals and households as the distribution of income.

Several factors contribute to differences in income. People come from different economic and social backgrounds. They have different skills and talents, grow up in different neighborhoods, attend different schools, and face different economic and social difficulties. Moreover, in a market economy, an individual's income is determined in large part by the market value of the goods and services that person has to offer. People with resources or talents that are in high demand will earn more money than people whose resources and talents are not in such high demand. For example, in the United States a professional basketball player's income will likely dwarf a pro soccer player's income because basketball games draw larger crowds and generate more money than soccer games do.

Measuring Income Inequality When news reports describe the "income gap," they are referring to the amount of income inequality in the nation. If the richest 20 percent of families earn 49 percent of the total income and the poorest 20 percent of families earn only 5 percent of the total income, as in 1995, there is a high level of income inequality.

To measure the amount of inequality in the distribution of income, economists plot a **Lorenz Curve**, which illustrates the amount that a

POVERTY RATE, 1977–1995

Year	Individuals		Families	
	Number in Poverty (in millions)	Percent in Poverty	Number in Poverty (in millions)	Percent in Poverty
1977	24.7	11.6	5.3	9.3
1978	24.5	11.4	5.3	9.1
1979	26.1	11.7	5.5	9.2
1980	29.3	13.0	6.2	10.3
1981	31.8	14.0	6.9	11.2
1982	34.4	15.0	7.5	12.2
1983	35.3	15.2	7.6	12.3
1984	33.7	14.4	7.3	11.6
1985	33.1	14.0	7.2	11.4
1986	32.4	13.6	7.0	10.9
1987	32.2	13.4	7.0	10.7
1988	31.7	13.0	6.9	10.4
1989	31.5	12.8	6.8	10.3
1990	33.6	13.5	7.1	10.7
1991	35.7	14.2	7.7	11.5
1992	38.0	14.8	8.1	11.9
1993	39.3	15.1	8.4	12.3
1994	38.1	14.5	8.1	11.6
1995	36.4	13.8	7.5	10.8

Source: *Economic Report of the President: 1997*

FIGURE 11.6 The poverty rate is the percentage of individuals or families in the population that are living in poverty. **In what year was the poverty rate highest for individuals? for families?**

nation's distribution of income varies from a perfectly proportional distribution of income. To create a Lorenz Curve, economists plot the proportion of the total income that various percentages of the population received.

Figure 11.7 on page 266 shows the Lorenz Curve for U.S. household incomes in 1994. Point A equals the percentage of the total income that the lowest population quintile, or the poorest 20 percent of the population, earned. Point B equals the percentage of the total income that the bottom two population quintiles, or the poorest 40 percent of the population, earned. Point C equals the percentage of the total income that the bottom three population quintiles earned, and so on. A perfectly proportional distribution of income—one in which each population quintile earns exactly 20 percent of the nation's total income—results in a 45-degree diagonal line

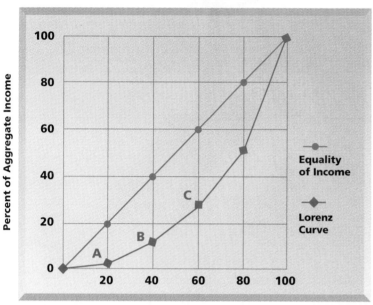

LORENZ CURVE, 1994

Percent of Aggregate Income (y-axis: 0, 20, 40, 60, 80, 100)

Points labeled A, B, C along the Lorenz Curve

Equality of Income

Lorenz Curve

Percent of Total Households (quintiles) (x-axis: 20, 40, 60, 80, 100)

Source: U.S Census Bureau

FIGURE 11.7 The Lorenz Curve illustrates income distribution. **What percentage of income did the lowest 60 percent of households earn in 1994?**

The data used to plot a Lorenz Curve enable economists to compute the **Gini Index**, another statistical measure of income inequality. The Gini Index ranges from 0.0, where each family or household receives an equal share of the total income, to 1.0, where one family or household receives all of the income. To compute the Gini Index, economists take the area between the 45-degree equality line and the actual Lorenz curve and divide it by the area below the 45-degree line. Figure 11.8 shows the Gini Index from 1967 to 1995.

Limitations of Income Distribution

Measures of income distribution tend to overemphasize income inequality for two main reasons. First, the definition of income for this purpose is very limited. The data that are used to determine the distribution of income are based on families' or households' gross incomes before deductions for such expenses as personal income taxes, Social Security, Medicare, health insurance, and union dues. Income does not include capital gains or the value of noncash benefits that families or households may receive,

extending from the bottom left corner of the graph to the upper right corner. The more an actual Lorenz Curve dips below this 45-degree line of absolute equality, the greater the amount of income inequality.

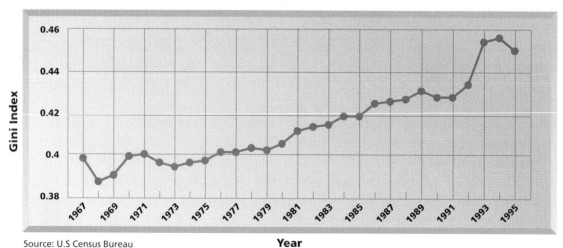

GINI INDEX, 1967–1995

Gini Index (y-axis: 0.38, 0.4, 0.42, 0.44, 0.46)

Year (x-axis: 1967, 1969, 1971, 1973, 1975, 1977, 1979, 1981, 1983, 1985, 1987, 1989, 1991, 1993, 1995)

Source: U.S Census Bureau

FIGURE 11.8 The Gini Index indicates whether the income gap is increasing or decreasing. **Based on this graph, in what year did the Gini Index reflect the greatest income gap?**

such as food stamps, health benefits, or low-cost housing.

Second, most measures of income distribution do not differentiate among families or households of different sizes or ages or with different numbers of wage earners. People tend to earn different amounts of income at different stages in their lives, and families of different sizes and ages need different amounts of income. As a result, families or households in the same income bracket can have very different standards of living.

Growing Income Gap

Are the rich getting richer and the poor getting poorer? This question has become a heated political issue in the United States in recent decades. Some politicians and economists assert that the income gap is not really increasing as much as it may seem, since income estimates are based on pretax figures and do not include noncash benefits. Others argue that even if the gap is increasing, the increase may simply be occurring at a faster rate for rich families than for poor, rather than only at the upper end of the scale.

The growing income gap in the United States stems from a variety of economic and social changes. Economists usually cite the following factors as the main causes of the widening disparity in income:

▶ changes in households,
▶ changes in the labor market,
▶ rapid changes in technology, and
▶ the growth of a global economy.

Changes in Households Historically, married couples living with their children have made up a large percentage of the wealthier households in the United States. Well-paid men and women tend to marry each other, thus concentrating wealth in one household and boosting income at the top of the income distribution. Single-parent and single-person households, on the other hand, have tended to have lower incomes. Higher divorce rates, more out-of-wedlock births, and

New Horizons

Some Americans respond to economic challenges in the United States by seeking better prospects in other countries. Each year some 250,000 to 300,000 U.S. citizens—about one third the number of people immigrating to the United States—move overseas. Although many are returning to their nation of origin, as many as 100,000 were born in the United States.

Why are these people moving to other countries? Some seek better job opportunities, while others want a more relaxed lifestyle. Still others are in search of a safer place to live, with less social tension.

The growth of a global economy, improved communications networks, and convenient travel opportunities have made living overseas seem very appealing to some people. Dennis Raphael, for example, left Brooklyn, New York, for Toronto, Canada, to attend graduate school in the 1970s. In 1995 he became a Canadian citizen. "Americans are concerned with individualism and the pursuit of happiness. Canadians are concerned with peace, order, and good government," he said.

Others have moved elsewhere for the opportunity to test themselves in a society undergoing dramatic change. For example, Barbara Duvoisin found that her studies of Russian history, economics, and international finance provided her with the ideal qualifications for running the Moscow office of a corporation. "There is no doubt . . . that in Russia you are given more responsibility and more exposure within your organization than anyplace else in the world," she said.

increasing numbers of people who live alone have resulted in more of these households.

Changes in the Labor Market Analysts cite changes in the labor market—such as have resulted from corporate downsizing—as one cause of the income gap. The heavy corporate downsizing and restructuring of the late 1980s and early 1990s increased unemployment and resulted in many workers settling for lower-paying jobs. The decline in the real value of the minimum wage due to inflation and the increased use of temporary workers, who generally are paid less and receive fewer fringe benefits, have also contributed to lower income levels.

In addition—as noted in Chapter 8—labor union membership has decreased since the 1970s. As the power of labor unions declines, workers lose an important means of negotiating salaries with employers. In countries where labor unions are not as powerful, a greater income gap exists between workers with similar jobs.

Changes in Technology Rapid changes in technology have led to a drop in demand for lower-skilled workers. Additionally, increased automation has lowered income levels for the bottom 20 percent.

The increase in jobs for highly skilled, trained, and educated workers has helped boost incomes for the top 20 percent. Income levels tend to reflect education levels because technological changes make advanced education and computer skills a necessity. The need for education is more important than ever.

Growth of a Global Economy As the economy becomes more global, more U.S. companies are relocating production to other countries where laborers will work for less pay. As a result, the demand for unskilled workers in the United States has decreased, and low-skilled workers in the United States find it harder to find employment. This means that these U.S. workers end up at the bottom of the income distribution.

Narrowing the Income Gap

A variety of policies can narrow the income gap. Programs that increase access to educational resources and provide training for low-skilled workers may help narrow the income gap. The government also can redistribute income by increasing taxes for the wealthy or spending more on programs that provide assistance to low-income groups. Other suggestions for improving income equality include raising the minimum wage, setting wage levels, and prohibiting companies from building plants in foreign countries where labor is cheaper.

SECTION 3 —REVIEW

1. Define the following terms: poverty threshold, poverty rate, Lorenz Curve, Gini Index.

2. How is the poverty threshold determined?

3. What factors have contributed to the income gap in the United States?

4. Describe three programs that experts think would decrease the U.S. income gap?

5. **Thinking and Writing Critically** In your opinion, should the U.S. government respond to the factors that contribute to the income gap? Explain your answer.

6. **Applying** INCOME DISTRIBUTION Many economists maintain that a certain level of income inequality is a natural side-effect of a free-enterprise system. Do you agree or disagree? Explain your answer.

SECTION 1 Unemployment is an important macroeconomic issue because it hurts the economy as a whole. Economists measure unemployment by identifying the number of employed and the number of unemployed and by determining the unemployment rate. The unemployment rate is the percentage of people in the civilian labor force who do not have jobs but are actively seeking employment. It is not entirely accurate, however, because it does not include the number of people who either lack jobs but have stopped looking for work or who are underemployed.

Four major types of unemployment exist: frictional unemployment, structural unemployment, seasonal unemployment, and cyclical unemployment. Although some frictional and structural unemployment occurs even in a healthy economy, unemployment in general has great economic and social costs.

SECTION 2 Economists analyze price fluctuations by examining the price level, inflation, and deflation. The price level influences aggregate supply, or total production throughout the economy, and aggregate demand, or total spending and investment throughout the economy. Inflation is an increase in the average price level of all goods and services in the economy, and deflation is a decrease in the average price level of products. Inflation caused by demand growing faster than supply is known as demand-pull inflation. Inflation caused by rising production costs is known as cost-push inflation.

Economists use both the consumer price index (CPI) and the producer price index (PPI) to measure the amount of price fluctuations. These price indexes estimate the inflation rate, or the pace at which the price level increases. Inflation affects the purchasing power of the dollar, the value of real wages, interest rates, saving and investing, and production costs.

SECTION 3 Growing income inequality in the United States can be seen in a large gap between the incomes of the rich and the poor. In 1995 some 36.4 million people in the United States lived in poverty.

The Census Bureau classifies people as living in poverty if their total income falls below designated income levels known as the poverty threshold. This threshold is determined largely by the cost of food. The poverty rate is the percentage of people in the total population who are living in poverty.

The Lorenz Curve illustrates how a nation's distribution of income differs from a perfectly proportional distribution of income. The Gini Index provides a statistical measure of income inequality.

Economists believe that the income gap has grown for a variety of reasons. First, the composition of households in the United States has changed. Second, the labor market has changed. Third, technology has caused dramatic shifts in employment and income. Fourth, the growth of a global economy has encouraged many U.S. companies to relocate production to other countries.

Economics Notebook

Refer to the list you made in your Economics Notebook at the beginning of this chapter. Does your list include items that might correspond to inflation, unemployment, or poverty? Of these three economic challenges, which do you think harms the U.S. economy the most? In your Notebook, provide reasons to support your answer.

REVIEWING CONCEPTS

1. Classify each of the following individuals as employed, unemployed, or outside of the labor force: (a) Charles Renaud—owner of the Cityscape Bar and Grill; (b) May Lau—a high school student hired to work at Bud's Burger Barn for the summer, who starts in three weeks; (c) Jared Turner—a full-time college student who often works about 20 hours for his parents at their business; (d) Jill Scott—an on-call substitute teacher who did not receive any calls to work this week.

2. Which type of unemployment is most damaging to the U.S. economy? Explain your answer.

3. Identify the following as examples of demand-pull inflation or cost-push inflation: (a) an increase in price of a popular toy at Christmas when the stores sold out of the product, (b) an increase in the price of orange juice because of a drought in Florida, (c) an increase in the price of Chunky Chicken products because of a union-negotiated wage increase for production workers.

4. Calculate the consumer price index using the following hypothetical information, and determine the percentage of change in the price level from 1995 to 1997: 1995 market basket ($7,000), 1997 market basket ($10,000).

5. What are some of the limitations of income distribution measurements?

6. What is the relationship between the Lorenz Curve and the Gini Index?

THINKING AND WRITING CRITICALLY

1. AGGREGATE SUPPLY & AGGREGATE DEMAND Explain the relationship between price level, aggregate supply, and aggregate demand.

2. UNEMPLOYMENT Why does unemployment increase during a recession and decrease during expansion?

3. UNEMPLOYMENT Give an example of someone who is underemployed and explain why the person is underemployed.

4. INCOME DISTRIBUTION Explain how changes in technology have influenced the growth in the income gap.

YOUR LOCAL ECONOMY

How would a 50 percent increase in the inflation rate affect your local economy? Write a newspaper article detailing the changes in the local economy due to the inflation.

COOPERATIVE PORTFOLIO PROJECT

Imagine that you are economists who have just received information about the personal distribution of income for the current year. You learn that the richest fifth of the population earns 68 percent of the total income, while the poorest fifth earns only 7 percent of the total income. With your group, write a proposal to the government suggesting specific ways to narrow the income gap. Some members of the group might outline your suggestions while others create visual aids such as tables and graphs to illustrate your proposal.

PRACTICING SKILLS: UNDERSTANDING MEASUREMENT CONCEPTS AND METHODS

Suppose that you have earned $2,000 every summer for the past four years. To determine your real wage, however, you must adjust your nominal wage of $2,000 by taking inflation into account. Real wages depend on the general price level, because purchasing power increases with lower prices and decreases with higher prices.

Changes in the price level are measured by means of a price index—the ratio of one price to the price of the same item at a different time. A real wage is calculated by dividing the nominal wage by an index number of general prices, as illustrated below:

N [nominal wage] $\div$ P [price index] $\times$ 100 = R [real wage]

Based on this method of measuring wages, compute your annual real wage for the past four years, using these price index features—Year 1: 100, Year 2: 125, Year 3: 105, Year 4: 138.

If the price index rises next year, will you adjust your saving and spending according to your real and nominal wages? Explain your answer.

THE INTERNET: LEARNING ONLINE

Use the Internet to find information on employment, unemployment, and poverty for different regions of the United States. You might visit the World Wide Web site for the Census Bureau or use search words such as *employment rate*, *unemployment rate*, and *poverty*.

ANALYZING PRIMARY SOURCES

Read the following excerpt from Thomas Sowell's book *The Economics and Politics of Race*, and answer the questions that follow.

"Historically, there is little question that non-whites have encountered more economic and social barriers than whites in the United States. . . . Yet what is surprising is the cold fact that there has been little correlation [apparent connection] between the degree of discrimination in history and the economic results today. It would be hard to claim that Puerto Ricans have encountered as much discrimination as the Japanese—who have about *double* their incomes. It would even be more difficult to claim that Puerto Ricans have historically encountered a level of discrimination comparable to that of

blacks, who have higher occupational status and 20 percent higher incomes.

"It may seem difficult to reconcile the demonstrable [apparent] color prejudice which has applied to all non-white groups. . . . with the equally demonstrable fact that various non-white groups today equal or exceed the economic level of various white groups. Part of the answer is that the translation of subjective prejudice into overt [open] economic discrimination—or of discrimination into poverty—is by no means automatic. . . .

"One of the most obvious reasons why some groups earn higher incomes than others is often ignored: They work more [hold more jobs]. More than half of all Chinese American families have more than one income earner, while only about one-third of the Puerto Rican families have multiple income earners. . . .

"Another factor of major importance that is often ignored is that groups differ greatly in age, and therefore in work experience. Age has profound effects of its own—independently of race and ethnicity—on incomes, unemployment rates, . . . and a host of other social variables. . . .

"The regional distribution of ethnic groups affects their average income in the nation. . . . The relative economic positions . . . could be misunderstood if regional distribution were not taken into account.

"American ethnic groups have varied widely in their regional distribution patterns, largely for historical reasons going back to the era of mass immigration. But however various ethnic groups came to be located where they are, their economic fate is tied to the fate of the industries and occupations of those regions."

1. According to Sowell, is there a link between the degree of discrimination against non-white groups and poverty? Explain.

2. What factors does Sowell site to explain the difference in incomes among groups?

3. According to Sowell, how would the average incomes of a nonwhite group living in a region of the United States with two large prospering factories and a nonwhite group living in a region with an unemployment rate of 23 percent be expected to differ? Why?

YOUR ASSIGNMENT

Macroeconomic Measures

Imagine that it is early January and you are a city manager who must develop recommendations for promoting economic growth in your town or city. You will soon have to present your recommendations to the city council. To help you put together the recommendations, a local university professor, Dr. Lott O. Pfigurin, and a group of his economics graduate students have prepared some economic reports about the current condition of the national and local economies.

Professor Pfigurin and his students know that measuring economic performance and creating a plan for economic growth requires information. The data they have provided include figures on gross domestic product, economic indicators, unemployment, and the state of inflation. You will find Professor Pfigurin's economic reports on the following pages.

As you review this information, answer the accompanying questions in your Economics Notebook. Then prepare your recommendations for the city council. The recommendations should include specific and general goals for your local economy and will need to reference the information provided by Professor Pfigurin.

Make sure your recommendations are handwritten neatly or typed. You also should create some visual guides to help explain your plan. You might, for example, draw line or bar graphs representing key national and local economic data. Your report should then be presented to the city council (the rest of the class).

CENTER FOR ECONOMIC RESEARCH

City Manager
Anytown, USA

Dear City Manager:

Thank you for your recent request for assistance from the Center for Economic Research. Several graduate students and I have compiled some information to help you prepare recommendations for developing the local economy. If you need any further assistance after reviewing the data provided here, please feel free to contact me.

I have enclosed figures on gross domestic product, economic indicators, and unemployment and inflation rates. The last figure includes additional information that you should consider about the local economy. I hope this information is helpful in designing your plans for economic growth.

Sincerely,

Prof. Lott O. Pfigurin

FIGURE 1: GROSS DOMESTIC PRODUCT
(in billions of dollars)

GDP four years ago	$8,117.3
GDP three years ago	$7,995.8
GDP two years ago	$7,899.5

Key economic data for last year's GDP:
(in billions of dollars)

Personal consumption expenditures	$5,875.5
Gross private domestic investment	$1,251.9
Government purchases of goods and services	$1.564.7
Exports of goods and services	$1,203.5
Imports of goods and services	$1,339.8

CENTER FOR ECONOMIC RESEARCH

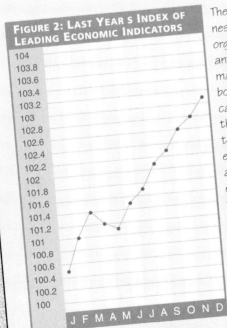

FIGURE 2: LAST YEAR'S INDEX OF LEADING ECONOMIC INDICATORS

The Conference Board is a business membership and research organization. In an effort to anticipate economic performance in future months, the board examines economic indicators. Information from all of these indicators is then used to create an index of leading economic indicators. In general, a rising index of leading economic indicators shows that future economic growth is expected. A declining index shows the opposite. Figure 2 shows the performance of the index of leading economic indicators over the past 12 months.

Economics Lab

CENTER FOR ECONOMIC RESEARCH

In an effort to gauge the strength of the local economy, my graduate students and I estimated the average annual local unemployment rates in recent years. National unemployment figures for the same period are roughly the same.

FIGURE 3: LOCAL UNEMPLOYMENT RATES

4 years ago 6.9%	3 years ago 7.7%	2 years ago 6.4%	Last year 5.3%

WHAT DO YOU THINK?

1. Review the information in Figure 3. When was unemployment highest in the local economy? How much lower was last year's unemployment rate?

2. Using the data in Figure 4, and the formula on page 260, calculate the local consumer price index (CPI) over the last four years. After you have calculated the CPI, use those figures and the formula on page 261 to calculate the rate of inflation over the same period.

3. How would you characterize the local inflation rate over the last four years: non-existent, creeping, moderate, or galloping?

CENTER FOR ECONOMIC RESEARCH

The Center for Economic Research estimated the cost of a list of local market basket items after each of the last several years. These figures can be used to calculate local inflation. In the base year when the market basket was valued at $5,000.

FIGURE 4: LOCAL MARKET BASKET

Four years ago	$5,125
Three years ago	$5,330
Two years ago	$5,450
Last year	$5,550

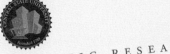

CENTER FOR ECONOMIC RESEARCH

Factors Affecting Local Economic Growth

Now that you have examined the economic data my students and I have provided, please review the following examination of factors important to growth in the local economy.

- The presence of Central State University in our community is significant in regards to worker–training opportunities. The city government might consider working with the university to develop training programs for local workers.

- Current inflation data is encouraging because it indicates that interest rates for bank loans, which can be used for capital investment, will probably be relatively low in the coming months.

- Natural resources in the local area include significant timberland and natural gas deposits. These resources have not yet been developed.

WHAT DO YOU THINK?

1. How can the presence of Central State University and the training and educational opportunities it provides help local economic growth?

2. In what way does current inflation data indicate that bank loans may be made at relatively low interest rates? How does low inflation help consumers?

3. What advantages are provided by the presence of significant and untapped resources, such as timber and natural gas deposits?

THINGS TO DO

1. Review the information provided by Prof. Pfigurin and the results of your calculations from his data. Then illustrate this information in tables, charts, or graphs that can be presented to the city council.

2. Prepare a summary of current economic conditions. The summary should include a review of last year's GDP, an analysis of leading economic indicators, and data concerning local unemployment, inflation, and economic resources. It also should discuss the potential for local economic growth in coming months: i.e., is the outlook for growth poor or good?

3. Keeping in mind the outlook for local economic growth, prepare a list of recommendations for the city council. You might want to rely on Prof. Pfigurin's comments. For example, would you promote the development of untapped resources in your area?

4. Assemble your summary and your recommendations into a report suitable for presentation to the city council (your class).

UNIT
5

CHAPTER 12
ROLE OF GOVERNMENT

CHAPTER 13
MONEY AND THE BANKING SYSTEM

CHAPTER 14
THE FEDERAL RESERVE SYSTEM AND MONETARY POLICY

CHAPTER 15
FISCAL POLICY

Economics Lab

How would you develop the nation's fiscal policy? Find out by reading this unit and taking the Economics Lab challenge on pages 370–373.

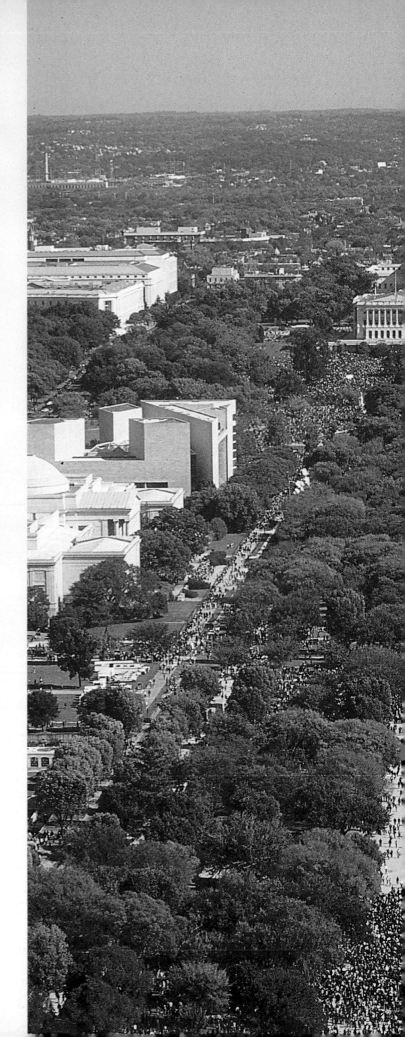

GOVERNMENT AND THE ECONOMY

ROLE OF GOVERNMENT

How do you get to school each day? How do you know the number of calories in your favorite snack food? How is the mail delivered in your neighborhood?

The answers to these questions probably involve the government. In the United States, even though individuals generally own the factors of production, the government's involvement in the economy is widespread. The government provides funds for road building, requires nutrition information on package labels, provides mail delivery, and supplies many other services. As you read this chapter, consider the role of the government in the U.S. economy and how you can have an influence on the government's economic actions.

Economics Notebook

In your Economics Notebook, list five ways the government affects your daily activities. Consider how the government affects your education, employment, and consumption of products.

GROWTH OF GOVERNMENT

Objectives

▶ What factors influence the growth of government?

▶ Why have government expenditures increased over time?

▶ How do federal, state, and local governments spend their money?

What organization employs the greatest number of people in the United States? The answer is the government. In 1997 the federal, state, and local governments employed about 19.5 million workers.

The U.S. government was not always so large. When the United States was established in 1776, it had little government. Unlike older countries that had many professional officials, the United States was developing new institutions that were small and operated on limited funds. For example, when George Washington took office as president in 1789, he had no official staff beyond the members of the cabinet. To help him carry out his duties, he hired one assistant—his nephew—whom he paid at his own expense. Today the White House staff consists of hundreds of government employees who assist and advise the president.

Factors Encouraging Growth

The growth of government has taken place as the result of four key factors:

▶ population growth,
▶ changing public attitudes,
▶ a rising standard of living, and
▶ national emergencies.

Population Growth The United States has grown dramatically over time—from 13 states along the Atlantic coast to 50 states that stretch across North America and into the Pacific. As the nation's territory has increased, so has its population. Meeting the many needs of this expanding population has meant increasing the number of government employees. Why? A larger population requires, for example, more educational facilities, increased road construction and repair, more police protection, and larger national defense forces.

How much has the U.S. population increased? When it was founded, the United States was home to fewer than 4 million people. By 1996 the population had grown to more than 265 million,

POPULATION GROWTH

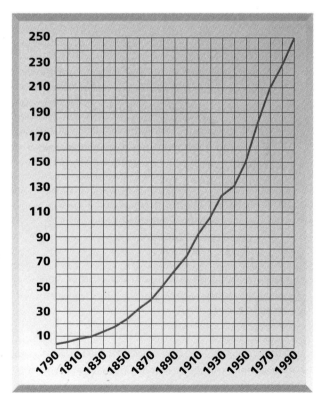

Year

Source: *Statistical Abstract of the United States: 1996*

FIGURE 12.1 The population of the United States has grown dramatically since the nation's founding. **How is population growth related to growth in government?**

Global Exchange

Embargoes

Governments sometimes use embargoes to influence the government of another country. An embargo is an act restricting or prohibiting commerce between countries.

For example, the United States has tried to topple Fidel Castro's communist government in Cuba by prohibiting the sale of U.S. goods to that country and the sale of Cuban products to the United States. Because Cuba previously had depended largely on U.S. trade, this embargo has severely damaged Cuba's economy. Nevertheless, Castro has remained in power for more than 35 years.

Another embargo was put into effect in 1990, when the United Nations ordered international economic penalties against Iraq in response to that country's invasion of its neighbor, Kuwait. This embargo prohibited Iraq from doing business with other countries and banned the international sale of its oil—Iraq's largest source of revenue.

The international community hoped that the embargo would influence the Iraqi government to change its foreign policy and dismantle its weapons of mass destruction. The embargo alone did not succeed, however, and so in 1991 an international force was sent to defeat Iraq's military in Operation Desert Storm.

The combination of economic sanctions and military defeat devastated the Iraqi economy. Inflation rose dramatically, resulting in famine and the collapse of health care services. To lessen the hardships faced by citizens, the United Nations and Iraq agreed to a plan in 1996 that allows Iraq to sell oil in exchange for food and medicine.

ROLE OF GOVERNMENT *Private efforts such as this soup kitchen proved unable to combat the widespread poverty created by the Great Depression.* **How did people's attitudes toward government involvement in the economy change during this period?**

making the United States the third-most-populous nation in the world. (See Figure 12.1.)

Changing Public Attitudes As noted in Chapter 6, laissez-faire economics is based on the belief that the economy does best without government interference. Before the Great Depression of the 1930s, most Americans supported a laissez-faire economic policy. During the depression, however, millions of people lost their jobs and had great difficulty supporting themselves. Homelessness increased dramatically. In cities, people waited in lines for hours to receive a hot meal from "soup kitchens" that sprang up to help the poor.

These relief efforts, however, were not sufficient. Communities and private charities proved unable to ease the hardships of the vast numbers of people hurt by the Great Depression. As a result, many people began to recognize the need for—and accept—government intervention in the economy.

Under President Franklin D. Roosevelt the federal government introduced a number of programs designed to ease the hardships of the Great Depression and to put people back to work. Although these programs—known as the New Deal—did not end the depression, they did contribute to a change in public attitudes about the government's role in the economy. A number of New Deal reform programs remain a central part of the U.S. government today.

Population increases and changing attitudes have led to more assistance for traditionally disadvantaged groups such as minorities and the poor. For example, because the number of people in poverty has risen from more than 25 million in 1971 to about 39 million in 1994, government assistance programs such as Medicaid, foster care, and veterans' pensions also have expanded.

the number of civilian employees of the federal government more than doubled, from just less than 402,000 workers in 1914 to nearly 855,000 workers in 1918. Similarly, the number of federal employees increased during World War II, from about 1 million in 1940 to almost 4 million in 1945. Government spending increased as well. (See Figure 12.2.)

Although the number of federal employees dropped after both wars, the number never fell to prewar levels—and the government continued many of the programs that were introduced during wartime. Why? Even after the wars ended, people wanted the benefits from these programs to continue. For example, in 1944 Congress passed the GI Bill of Rights, which provided funds for veterans to attend college. Members of the armed forces continued to benefit from this

Rising Standard of Living

As was the case during the Great Depression, economic hardship can lead to the growth of government. Economic success, however, also can lead to larger government. How does this happen?

Once people earn enough to meet their basic needs, they then look for ways to fulfill their wants—usually through increased spending. In turn, as people spend more and improve their standard of living, they expect goods and services to improve—which frequently that means new government programs. As a result, the U.S. government has grown in areas such as education, health care, and consumer protection.

National Emergencies A

national emergency such as a war also can cause the government to increase in size. For example, during World War I

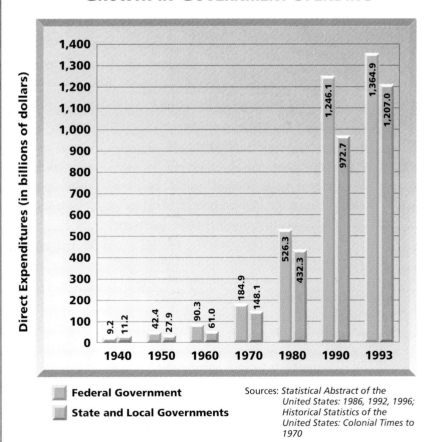

GROWTH IN GOVERNMENT SPENDING

Direct Expenditures (in billions of dollars)

Year	Federal Government	State and Local Governments
1940	9.2	11.2
1950	42.4	27.9
1960	90.3	61.0
1970	184.9	148.1
1980	526.3	432.3
1990	1,246.1	972.7
1993	1,364.9	1,207.0

■ Federal Government
■ State and Local Governments

Sources: *Statistical Abstract of the United States: 1986, 1992, 1996; Historical Statistics of the United States: Colonial Times to 1970*

FIGURE 12.2 Government spending often increases in times of national emergency such as war. **In what decade did federal government spending more than quadruple?**

program—which was later expanded—for decades after World War II had ended.

Growth in Government Spending

Suppose you take up a new hobby, such as competitive skateboarding. You will need to increase your expenditures to buy the required equipment, including a skateboard, pads, and a helmet. Just as your new hobby increases your expenses, new government programs lead to increased government spending. For example, spending by the federal, state, and local governments in the United States in 1950 was about $70 billion. Dramatic increases in the number of government

Careers in Economics

Civil Engineer

Who plans the construction of your city's power plant, sewage system, city hall, stadiums, office buildings, and many other public structures? The answer is a civil engineer. Civil engineers design and oversee the construction of many projects that are important to a healthy economy.

Some civil engineers work for the government. Others work for private businesses or as consultants. Because there are so many kinds of engineering projects, civil engineers typically specialize. Transportation engineers, for instance, design and test roads, bridges, and other transportation structures. Environmental engineers design and construct such things as water purification systems and recycling plants. Civil engineers—of any specialty—are constantly challenged to design and maintain the many public facilities needed by a growing population.

What kinds of people make good civil engineers? Civil engineers must be detail oriented and excellent problem solvers. For instance, they might be asked to determine the best way to construct a canal through rough terrain to link two bodies of water. Or they might have to determine what kinds of materials are best for building a bridge needed to support heavy freight traffic. They must know how much a given material costs,

how strong it is, and how it will stand up under various conditions. Civil engineers also must ensure that their constructions are stable and safe.

Civil engineers undergo extensive study and training. A bachelor's degree in engineering is essential, and many civil engineers earn a master's degree or doctorate. Coursework usually includes mathematics, physics, and computer science. To become a state-registered civil engineer or to obtain a state license, a candidate must have a college degree from a school that is officially approved by the Accreditation Board for Engineering and Technology.

Some civil engineers work for the government, designing public facilities such as this airport terminal.

HOW FEDERAL, STATE, AND LOCAL DOLLARS ARE SPENT

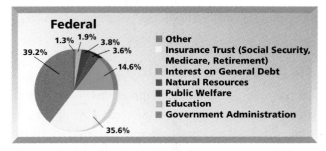

Federal

1.3%   1.9%   3.8%
39.2%   3.6%
              14.6%

35.6%

- ■ Other
- □ Insurance Trust (Social Security, Medicare, Retirement)
- ■ Interest on General Debt
- ■ Natural Resources
- ■ Public Welfare
- ▨ Education
- ▨ Government Administration

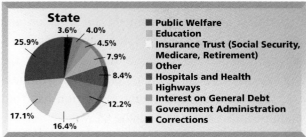

State

3.6%   4.0%
25.9%   4.5%
              7.9%
              8.4%

17.1%   12.2%
      16.4%

- ■ Public Welfare
- ▨ Education
- □ Insurance Trust (Social Security, Medicare, Retirement)
- ■ Other
- ■ Hospitals and Health
- ■ Highways
- ▨ Interest on General Debt
- ▨ Government Administration
- ■ Corrections

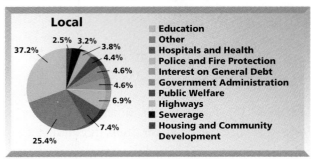

Local

2.5%   3.2%
37.2%   3.8%
              4.4%
              4.6%
              4.6%
              6.9%

              7.4%
25.4%

- ▨ Education
- ■ Other
- ■ Hospitals and Health
- ▨ Police and Fire Protection
- ■ Interest on General Debt
- ▨ Government Administration
- ■ Public Welfare
- ▨ Highways
- ■ Sewerage
- ■ Housing and Community Development

Source: *Statistical Abstract of the United States: 1996*

FIGURE 12.3 Federal, state, and local governments have different spending priorities.

programs meant that by 1993, total government expenditures had risen to more than $2.5 trillion, or almost $9,970 for every man, woman, and child in the United States.

The federal government spends the largest share of this figure—some $1.4 trillion in 1993, for example. About half of federal expenses go toward paying for insurance benefits and interest on debts. Other federal expenses include national defense, education, public hospitals, housing and community development, and law enforcement.

State and local governments also spend large sums of money—an average of more than $3.3 billion a day, or $38,274 a second, in 1993. Spending by state governments, for example, rose from about $15 billion in 1950 to nearly $530 billion in 1993. During the same time, spending by local governments increased from about $17 billion to more than $677 billion.

The largest expenditures in state and local budgets are generally for education, public welfare, and road construction and maintenance. These categories account for just less than 50 percent of all state and local spending. The rest of state and local spending pays for public libraries, hospitals and health care, police and fire protection, public buildings, sanitation services, and government administration. (For a breakdown of government spending, see Figure 12.3.)

SECTION 1 — REVIEW

1. Why has the U.S. government grown in size?

2. Why has U.S. government spending increased over the years?

3. What are the main expenditures of federal budgets? state budgets? local budgets?

4. Thinking and Writing Critically
Many people describe some government programs as a "safety net" for people whose

needs are not met by the private sector. For example, someone who is not able to find a job receives unemployment benefits from the government. Explain the safety net metaphor in your own words. Who does the safety net "catch"?

5. Applying ROLE OF GOVERNMENT Conduct an Internet search for information about your state government's budget. How is your state's money spent?

ECONOMIC GOALS

Economics Dictionary

privatization

transfer payment

Objectives

▶ Why does the government regulate business?

▶ How does the government work to provide public goods?

▶ In what ways does the government promote individuals' well-being?

▶ How does the government work to stabilize the economy?

Think about what government does for you. Does your community have garbage collection? Do you use a public library? What kind of financial aid is available to students who plan to attend college?

Currently, the federal, state, and local governments provide these services—and many others—to you and other citizens. This has not always been the case, however. Throughout much of U.S. history, popular acceptance of laissez-faire economic practices limited the government's economic role. As government grew, however, it took on an increasing number of functions that affected the economy.

Specifically, federal, state, and local governments began to regulate businesses, provide public goods, promote

citizens' economic well-being, and stabilize the economy. Today the governments share the first three of these goals, while economic stabilization is practiced primarily by the federal government.

Regulating Business

In the United States, all governments—federal, state, or local—regulate business through rules and procedures that guide economic activity. (See Figure 12.4 for information about federal regulatory agencies.) Some of these rules and procedures affect the ways that companies interact with individuals, while others address the impact of company policies on the environment and the market. Government regulation has four main purposes:

▶ preventing abuses,

▶ protecting consumers,

▶ limiting negative externalities, and

▶ promoting competition.

Preventing Abuses As noted in Chapter 8, one key purpose of government regulation is to

ROLE OF GOVERNMENT *Most local governments maintain parks for citizens' recreational use.* **What are two other ways that government impacts your life?**

FEDERAL REGULATORY AGENCIES

Agency	Abbreviation	Year	Description
Interstate Commerce Commission	ICC	1887–1995	regulated rates and other aspects of commercial transportation by railroad, highway, and waterway
Federal Trade Commission	FTC	1914	administers antitrust laws forbidding price-fixing, other deceptive or fraudulent practices, and unfair competition
Food and Drug Administration	FDA	1927	enforces laws to ensure purity, effectiveness, and truthful labeling of food, drugs, and cosmetics; inspects production and shipment of these products
Federal Communications Commission	FCC	1934	licenses and regulates radio and television stations; regulates interstate telephone and telegraph rates and services
Securities and Exchange Commission	SEC	1934	regulates and supervises the sale of listed and unlisted securities and the brokers, dealers, and investment bankers who sell them
National Labor Relations Board	NLRB	1935	administers federal labor-management relations laws; settles labor disputes; prevents unfair labor practices
Federal Aviation Administration	FAA	1958	regulates air commerce; sets standards for pilot training, aircraft maintenance, and air traffic control; controls U.S. airspace
Equal Employment Opportunity Commission	EEOC	1964	investigates and rules on charges of discrimination by employers and labor unions
Environmental Protection Agency	EPA	1970	coordinates federal programs to protect public health and to safeguard and improve the natural environment—air, water, and land
National Highway Traffic Safety Administration	NHTSA	1970	enforces laws to promote motor vehicle safety and to protect drivers, passengers, and pedestrians; sets safety and fuel economy standards for new motor vehicles produced or sold in the U.S.
Occupational Safety and Health Administration	OSHA	1970	investigates accidents at the workplace; enforces regulations to protect employees at work
Consumer Product Safety Commission	CPSC	1972	enforces safety standards for consumer products
Federal Energy Regulatory Commission	FERC	1977	fixes rates for and regulates the interstate transportation and sale of electricity, oil, and natural gas

FIGURE 12.4 Federal agencies regulate a wide range of activities. **What are the four main purposes of regulating businesses?**

prevent business from taking unfair advantage of workers. For example, you may have noticed the initials *EEOC* in job advertisements in newspapers. The government, through the Equal Employment Opportunity Commission (EEOC), makes and enforces regulations that protect workers from discrimination in hiring or promo-

tions based on age, sex, race, religion, or national origin.

The government also sets standards for working conditions. Federal agencies such as the Occupational Safety and Health Administration (OSHA) monitor businesses and punish violators. According to government statistics, enforcement of OSHA regulations contributed to a decrease in workplace fatalities—from 18 per 100,000 workers in 1970 to 4 per 100,000 workers in 1993.

Protecting Consumers In addition to regulations that protect workers, the government also passes laws that protect consumers, savers, borrowers, and investors. For example, the Food and Drug Administration (FDA) and Consumer Product Safety Commission (CPSC) protect people from products such as unsafe foods, medicines, and toys. The Federal Trade Commission (FTC) and the Federal Communications Commission (FCC) ensure that advertising and sales practices are ethical, truthful, and fair.

The federal government also insures citizens' checking and savings deposits and oversees insured banks to make sure that they follow banking laws. (This topic is more fully explained in Chapter 13.) Federal credit laws also protect borrowers. The Securities and Exchange Commission (SEC), meanwhile, protects investors against fraud in the securities trade. It sets procedures for the registration and sale of stocks and

the licensing of securities dealers. The SEC has the power to punish any violators.

Many state and local governments have created agencies and developed regulations that further protect consumers and borrowers. These regulations apply to all businesses that operate within the state or local boundaries.

Limiting Negative Externalities Another way in which governments protect workers, consumers, and society is through regulations that minimize the negative side effects of some economic activities. As noted in Chapter 5, these side effects are called externalities. Examples of negative externalities include pollution, traffic congestion, and soil erosion. The Environmental Protection Agency (EPA), Nuclear Regulatory Commission (NRC), and other government agencies establish and enforce regulations intended to limit these negative externalities.

For example, in 1991 the EPA awarded a $350,000 grant to Robert Smee, director of the Pacific Materials Exchange in Spokane, Washington. Smee's company allowed companies and cities to sell their waste products, such as scrap steel and used Freon™ (a coolant used in refrigerators and air conditioners), to organizations using these products as raw materials. The EPA grant enabled Smee to develop a computerized network linking waste exchanges across the United States.

Promoting Competition Another purpose of government regulation is to promote competition. As noted in Chapter 6, government accomplishes this goal through the creation and enforcing of antitrust legislation. This type of regulation prevents the formation of monopolies and breaks up existing ones. The Sherman Antitrust Act of 1890 was the first major antitrust legislation in the United States. Later legislation clarified and strengthened this act.

ROLE OF GOVERNMENT *The Environmental Protection Agency inspects toxic waste sites to protect citizens from negative externalities.* **What are three additional purposes for regulating businesses?**

Providing Public Goods

In addition to regulating businesses and the products they make, governments themselves provide goods and services. These public goods are goods and services made available to—and consumed by—all citizens.

Why does the government provide public goods? As noted in Chapter 6, the price system fails to assign the cost of public goods among all consumers. The government, however, *can* accomplish this goal. It can charge—or tax—all citizens for the cost of public goods, even if some people do not use the goods directly. For example, the government charges Maryann Ellis for the public school attended by Jaime Montez, even though Maryann does not have children enrolled in the school.

Additionally, the government can ensure that public goods are available to all citizens who need them. For example, an education is available for Jaime whether he decides to attend a public school or a private one. Furthermore, government must make public goods available to all citizens, though citizens can decide for themselves whether to use those goods. Jaime's parents may indeed choose to enroll him in a private school, but the government cannot prohibit him from gaining an education at a public school if he so chooses.

How are public goods provided to citizens? Federal, state, and local governments frequently share the responsibility of funding and distributing public goods. Governments have sometimes decided, however, that private industry is capable of providing certain public goods.

Shared Responsibility How do governments share the responsibility for providing public goods? Some goods, such as courts, corrections departments, and law enforcement agencies, are found at each level of government. Other goods are the primary responsibility of one level of government with funding from—and the cooperation of—the other levels. Local government, for

ROLE OF GOVERNMENT *Library collections and services often are government-funded.* **Why do governments provide public goods and services?**

example, manages public education but receives state and federal funding to help pay the costs. An exception to this system of shared responsibility is national defense, which is provided solely by the federal government.

Privatization In recent years some governments have turned to the privatization of public goods. **Privatization** refers either to the sale of government property or to the handling of government services by private businesses. Garbage collection, for example, has been privatized in many cities. Even some hospitals formerly run by the government are now operated by private hospital chains.

Why would a government decide to privatize some of its services? Supporters of privatization justify it in three ways. First, they argue that private firms can operate certain industries more efficiently than the government can. A case in point is mail delivery. The U.S. Postal Service faces considerable competition from private carriers.

Many businesses opt to use Federal Express or United Parcel Service (UPS), for example, for mail or packages that must be delivered quickly.

Second, supporters of privatization argue that the government should not compete with private business. The Federal Housing Administration (FHA), for example, provides housing loans in direct competition with private lenders.

Third, supporters point out that government could reduce its costs and pay off some of its debt through the sale of public properties and services. Great Britain, for instance, has raised more than $20 billion since 1979 through the sale of certain government-run businesses.

Opponents of privatization argue that public goods are provided by the federal government because private industry was unable or unwilling to provide those goods to all consumers in the first place. Opponents also point to the tremendous resources that government has available to meet the special requirements and circumstances of providing public goods.

ROLE OF GOVERNMENT *The U.S. government works to promote citizens' economic well-being.* **How does it pursue this goal?**

Promoting Economic Well-Being

The third major economic role of government is promoting economic well-being. To fulfill this function, the government works to improve people's standard of living and to redistribute income among citizens.

Improving the Standard of Living The standard of living for a nation, state, or region reflects how people live and how many goods and services they consume. Consider your community. Where do you and your neighbors buy food? How many people are likely to own consumer goods such as television sets, computers, and stereo systems? What educational opportunities are available, and how many people take advantage of them?

Diet, product consumption, medical care, and education are four areas that affect people's standard of living and for which the government has shown a high degree of concern. Another is medical care. Programs like Medicare and Medicaid provide health insurance to older Americans and to people with low incomes. The government also helps hospitals cover the cost of treating people who do not have insurance.

How do these programs raise people's standard of living? Obviously, people receiving medical care are helped by this policy as their health improves. At the same time, the general public is helped as regular and preventive health care reduces both the need for expensive long-term care and the likelihood of epidemics—diseases that spread quickly through a population.

Redistributing Income To promote economic well-being, some government programs also are designed to reduce the gap between rich and poor. The government tries to accomplish this through a system of transfer payments. In a **transfer payment**, the government takes money collected from one group of citizens and distributes (transfers) it to another group of citizens.

Transfer payments work by the government establishing specific aid programs that distribute

REDISTRIBUTING INCOME

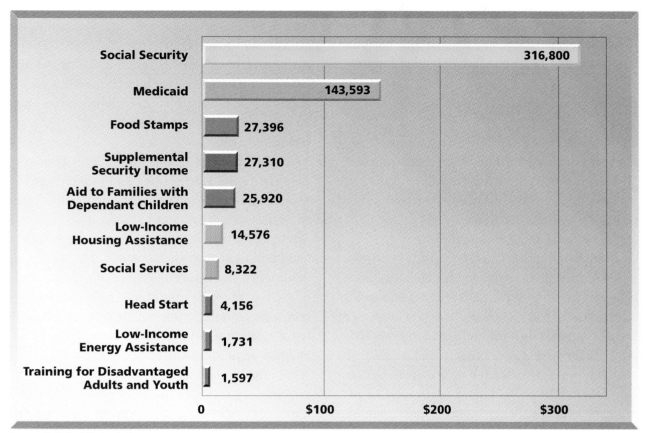

Source: *Statistical Abstract of the United States: 1996*

1994 Federal Government Expenditure (in millions)

FIGURE 12.5 The government tries to reduce the gap between rich and poor through transfer payments. **Which three transfer programs account for the greatest government expenditures?**

income to anyone who meets certain qualifications. Some of these programs provide incomes for households, while others help pay for medical care, higher education, housing, and job training or retraining.

Some programs are wholly financed and administered by the federal government. The federal government, for example, provides monthly Social Security payments to older people and to people with disabilities. In 1994 the federal government also distributed more than $27 billion worth of food stamps to 28.9 million low-income Americans. Other programs are sponsored by state and local governments. These programs include aid to people who are sick, elderly, and poor—for example, food deliveries and reduced prices for transportation. (See Figure 12.5.)

Some private businesses and public agencies also receive transfer payments—usually in the form of grants-in-aid—to ensure the continued service or production of certain goods. The government, for example, assumes some of the costs of subways, bus lines, commuter trains, and other systems of mass transportation. In this way the government ensures that such services are available and affordable for many people.

Stabilizing the Economy

Although federal, state, and local governments all regulate business, provide public goods, and promote economic well-being, the federal government generally works alone to stabilize the economy. The justification for the government's role in stabilizing the economy comes from the Constitution's mandate to promote the general welfare of the people. The government stabilizes the economy primarily by moderating the business cycle and by responding to market failures.

Moderating the Business Cycle

As noted in Chapter 10, the U.S. economy generally follows a pattern, with periods of prosperity followed by periods of economic slowdown, or recession. This pattern of rising and falling of the economy is called the business cycle.

Prior to the Great Depression the government did not attempt to stabilize the business cycle. However, during the 1930s—and increasingly after World War II—the federal government greatly expanded its role in managing the economy. Today the government tries to steer the economy on a middle course that avoids recession and inflation. To achieve this goal, the government today varies its taxing and spending policies and controls the nation's money supply. These government actions are explained more fully in Chapters 14 and 15.

Responding to Market Failures In addition to moderating the business cycle, the government tries to ensure economic stability by limiting the effects of market failures. Market failures include externalities, the inability or unwillingness of private enterprise to produce some public goods, inadequate business competition, and consumers' inadequate knowledge of market conditions.

You learned earlier in this section how government limits externalities and provides public goods. How does government address the other two types of market failures?

As noted in Chapter 6, inadequate business competition occurs when one or a few businesses dominate a field and control the price and supply of a good, as in the case of a monopoly. The government responds to inadequate competition with regulations that prohibit and dissolve monopolies and that open industries to new competitors.

As for the fourth type of market failure, the government responds to consumers' inadequate knowledge of market conditions by ensuring that information is available to the public. You are already familiar with two agencies that act as "friends of consumers": the CPSC and the SEC.

SECTION 2 — REVIEW

1. Define the following terms: privatization, transfer payment.

2. List government's purposes in regulating business.

3. Why does the government provide public goods?

4. Explain how the government works to promote people's economic well-being.

5. How does the government work to stabilize the economy?

6. **Thinking and Writing Critically** How does the government's work in providing public goods affect your community? Consider goods and services such as public libraries and public transportation. Do you think these goods and services would be better provided through privatization? Explain your answer.

7. **Applying** ROLE OF GOVERNMENT Consider your school as an economic system with limited government involvement, like that of the United States. What regulations prevent abuses, protect consumers, limit externalities, and promote competition?

SECTION 3
GOVERNMENT AND THE PUBLIC

Economics Dictionary
interest group
lobbyist

Objectives
▶ How does the government determine the public interest?
▶ What consequences may result from government promotion of the public interest?
▶ How can individuals and interest groups affect government policies?

You have learned that the government develops economic policies to promote the public interest. Determining the public interest—and how best to promote it—is a complicated process, however. Government economic policies and regulations affect all aspects of production and consumption. Even well-intentioned economic policies can fail to achieve their goals.

Fortunately, in a free-enterprise system citizens can act to influence government policies. Individuals can support or protest issues through voting and other forms of political activism. People also can work together in groups to express their interests and concerns. This interaction between the government and citizens ensures that careful attention is paid to the public interest.

Identifying the Public Interest

How do governments identify the public interest? The public interest is based on the collective needs of many people. Sometimes these needs can conflict with personal preferences. Although the government acknowledges the importance of

individual choice in the U.S. economy, public interest can sometimes outweigh the wishes of an individual or a specific group.

For example, as noted in Chapter 8, the government may forbid a group of workers to strike if their doing so would endanger the health or safety of the public. The government recognizes that workers must be able to voice their concerns about business practices or working conditions, but believes that in some cases the specific concerns of a particular group may conflict with the public interest as a whole.

CASE STUDY

AmeriCorps

ROLE OF GOVERNMENT In many cases the government's attempts to act in the public interest can become controversial. For example, many people have opposed AmeriCorps, the national service program introduced by President Bill Clinton in 1994.

AmeriCorps is part of a nonprofit organization funded by the federal government. Each of the 20,000 AmeriCorps participants receives an annual salary of nearly $8,000 and a $4,725 grant to attend college. In return, he or she works full-time for

ROLE OF GOVERNMENT *Believing it would endanger the public interest, President Ronald Reagan outlawed an air traffic controllers' strike in 1981.* **How do governments identify the public interest?**

a public-service group such as the American Red Cross or Habitat for Humanity.

AmeriCorps members may assist teachers in needy school districts, provide help for disaster victims, or work toward improving health education. In 1995, for example, 24 AmeriCorps members organized over 5,000 nonpaid volunteers to build 50 homes for economically disadvantaged people in Miami.

Nonetheless, the program has its critics. Opponents of AmeriCorps believe that the responsibility to help others lies with the individual and not the federal government. They see government involvement as unnecessary and expensive. Some wonder if AmeriCorps members are motivated more by the college scholarship than by a sense of compassion or satisfaction in helping others.

AmeriCorps supporters, on the other hand, argue that the program encourages the spirit of community service. These supporters claim that the program directly benefits two groups by increasing the services available to disadvantaged people and by enabling more students to pursue a college education. Finally, they believe the Americorps program teaches the value of public service to young men and women, making them more likely to continue to volunteer as they grow older.

ROLE OF GOVERNMENT *AmeriCorps is a national service program for young Americans.* **Why is determining the public interest sometimes controversial?**

Effects of Government Regulation

What are the consequences of policies and regulations related to public interest programs such as AmeriCorps? Such government actions affect all aspects of production, distribution, and consumption, including

▶ prices,
▶ services,
▶ profits, and
▶ productivity.

Prices Government regulation often causes prices to increase. For example, if the government determines that taxi rides are in the public interest, it may try to ensure a minimum supply of taxis by setting a price floor to keep prices from falling below a certain level. Even if a lower price would increase quantity demanded and bring a higher profit, suppliers cannot set prices of their own choosing. Prices thus tend to be higher when a price floor is in effect.

Government regulation also may increase prices indirectly by raising production costs. Suppose that the Petro Plenty Chemical factory pumps its waste products into a nearby river. To protect the public's interest in a clean environment, new government rules require Petro Plenty to limit the amount of waste it produces. These regulations require Petro Plenty to introduce new processing techniques that increase the costs of production. The higher costs are passed on to consumers in the form of higher prices.

Services Different types of government regulation can affect services in different ways. In some cases, regulation can encourage greater levels of service. Suppose that the View Now Cable Television Company wants to offer 32 cable channels to subscribers. Local regulations, however, require the cable company to carry 58 channels. In this case, regulations have increased the cable service available to consumers.

Other forms of regulation can reduce service. For example, if regulations force producers to supply services at a lower price than they otherwise would, producers may reduce service to avoid losing money. Suppose that a city council determines that affordable transportation is in the public interest. The council contracts out bus service on the condition that fares cost no more than 25 cents per passenger. The bus company finds, however, that it cannot make a profit at this price—and reduces bus service to some areas.

Profits

Private companies' profits may increase when government regulations result in higher prices and difficult market entry. Generally, however, regulation tends to lower profits. This fact may become most obvious when regulations are lifted.

Consider the airline industry. When the elimination of federal regulations on airline service was concluded in 1984, airlines were able to reorganize their flight patterns. By reducing the number of nonstop flights and requiring many passengers to change planes at central connecting locations, some airlines were able to increase their profits dramatically.

Productivity

In some cases, government regulation causes labor productivity to decline. As workers spend more time meeting government regulations instead of producing goods and services, the number of goods and services produced per worker declines.

Suppose that Eric and Laura Pineda own a fishing boat and employ five workers who catch 750 fish per day. Productivity, therefore, can be measured at 150 fish caught per worker per day ($750 \div 5 = 150$).

The government determines that the public interest is best promoted by limiting current fishing to ensure that fish are available both now and

ROLE OF GOVERNMENT *Government deregulation of the airline industry was designed to lower the cost of air travel.* **According to this cartoon, what are the consequences of deregulation?**

in the future. As a result, new government regulations require fishing-boat workers to throw back any fish under a certain length.

How does the regulation affect productivity? Some of the workers' time now must be spent sorting the fish and throwing back those that do not meet the new size requirement. Either the five workers must spend less time fishing in order to sort the fish, or Eric and Laura must hire additional workers to sort the fish. Either choice reduces the average number of fish caught per worker, and therefore results in decreased levels of productivity.

Influencing Government

You have learned how government tries to promote the public interest through regulation. Suppose, however, that people are opposed these rules. How can individual citizens make their voices heard and try to influence government decisions?

In the United States, government regulations can be changed if the public opposes them. Both individuals working alone and groups of people working together can affect the policies and direction of government.

Role of Individuals One way that individuals may take action is by voting. By electing public officials with an economic philosophy similar to their own, citizens make their economic opinions heard. For example, the victories of President Bill Clinton over his Republican opponents in the 1992 and 1996 elections indicated support for his economic plans. Elected representatives are particularly sensitive to public opinion because they must satisfy voters if they hope to be re-elected.

To ensure that you are using your vote wisely, you must become informed about the economy and the candidates. Identify the issues that concern you and find out how each candidate plans to address your interests. For example, what are the candidates' stands on taxes, the minimum wage, and job training? By paying attention to the words and actions of each person running for office, you can determine which one would best represent your views.

Another way individuals can influence the government's impact on the economy is through political activism. For example, Ralph Nader, one of the most well-known activists in the United States, has worked for more than 30 years to influence government policy and hold corporations accountable for their practices.

During the late 1950s Nader became concerned about the number of fatal car accidents taking place on the nation's highways. As a result, he began to research the connection between legal standards for safety and the way automobiles were designed. Nader believed that many more people would survive car accidents if their vehicles were made crashworthy— equipped with features such as padded dashboards, seat belts, collapsible steering wheels, and stronger door latches. To publicize the results of his research and to improve government safety regulations, Nader testified before state legislatures in 1965 and published the book *Unsafe at Any Speed*.

Nader soon gained national attention. After getting the media interested in the issue, he persuaded members of Congress to hold hearings on regulations for the auto industry. His actions contributed to passage of the National Traffic and Motor Vehicle Safety Act of 1966. Many of the automobile safety features we take for granted today were developed and required by law as a result of Nader's car-safety crusade.

Role of Interest Groups Individuals also may take action collectively as part of interest groups. An **interest group** is an organization of citizens who work together to achieve their common goals, often by influencing government policy. Interest groups frequently achieve results when individuals acting alone could not.

In the United States, interest groups represent diverse ethnic and minority groups, labor unions, farmers, and businesspeople. Some large interest groups, such as those involved with unions, have considerable influence because they represent the votes of millions of members.

How do interest groups try to influence economic policy? Interest groups may give money to political campaigns and encourage group members to vote for a particular candidate.

In addition to his work as an individual activist, Ralph Nader has also led several interests groups. "Nader's Raiders"—as the groups' members often were called—wrote and published many reports on industrial hazards, pollution, unsafe products, and government neglect of safety laws. These groups' efforts encouraged the

ROLE OF GOVERNMENT *In the United States, the public can change government economic policy.* **How does voting exercise this influence?**

ECONOMICS

in Action

Young Lobbyist

Suppose that you believe the government should invest more money in protecting the environment. How would you make your views known?

You might try writing letters to your elected representatives, urging them to propose legislation to raise the level of funding for environmental protection. Before the next election, you also could research the various candidates' positions on the issue and then suggest to people of voting age that they vote for the candidate who supports your position. You could join a pressure group that has lobbyists who urge politicians to support the same goal. The most direct way to voice your opinions, however, would be to become a lobbyist yourself.

At age 21 Dan Stafford became director of the Austin, Texas, field office of the grassroots citizen organization United States Public Interest Research Group (U.S. PIRG). As director, Dan lobbies government officials, urging them to support a variety of political and economic initiatives ranging from environmental issues to consumer protection and campaign finance reform.

Dan began working for PIRG as a canvasser, going door to door through neighborhoods asking people to sign petitions, write letters to their representatives, and donate money to advance the group's goals. He quickly assumed the position of field manager, in charge of coordinating canvassing efforts. Within a year he became director of the Austin field office.

Dan believes PIRG should build "strength through the grassroots and then . . . go and meet with our representatives and do the lobbying." His responsibilities include recruiting canvassers of all ages, lobbying local representatives, and holding press conferences on a variety of topics.

A significant portion of the issues that PIRG confronts involve economics. In addition to his efforts to strengthen environmental protection, Dan's group has defended consumers' rights to sue makers of dangerous or defective products. The group also has forced the recall or modification of dangerous toys through its annual toy safety study. In addition, PIRG recently published reports documenting how fees have skyrocketed for basic banking services such as automated teller machine (ATM) transactions.

Why would someone want to become a lobbyist? Dan points to the influence of his parents. His father—a minister—and his mother—a nurse—were both politically active. "Watching my parents be active in other people's lives and working to help the community . . . instilled that (drive) in me."

Dan believes that young people who work for pressure groups and become lobbyists "actually put themselves to use and have responsibility. You feel like part of a team. I can't stand up and say I single-handedly did something, but I can say I have been part of a team of people across the country that has been influential in making positive changes."

What Do You Think?

1. Do you believe lobbying is an effective way to make your voice heard? Why or why not?
2. What advantages do you think a young lobbyist brings to the job? What are the possible disadvantages of hiring a young person for this job?

US PIRG lobbyist Anna Aurilio discusses the group's concerns with U.S. House Budget Committee Chair Rep. John Kasich of Ohio.

creation of several government regulatory agencies, including the Environmental Protection Agency, the Occupational Safety and Health Commission, and the Consumer Product Safety Commission. Currently Nader works for consumer safety and for the reform of the political system through his interest group Public Citizen.

Most interest groups advance their plans through **lobbyists**—people hired to express a particular point of view to legislators. Lobbyists research issues and provide lawmakers with valuable information about the impact of upcoming legislation. Lobbying groups affect government policies at all levels of government.

How does a lobbyist exert pressure on elected officials? Suppose that Jeff Brenner is a lobbyist for the Small Business Owners League. The league provides grants and low-interest loans to new businesses. Jeff arranges a meeting with Rebecca Lavoie, a candidate for the state legislature, and tells her that the Small Business

ROLE OF GOVERNMENT *Members of an interest group work together to achieve common goals.* **Why might an interest group hire a lobbyist?**

Owners League will officially support her in the election. Jeff outlines the league's goals and proposes a piece of legislation that will lower the taxes paid by small businesses. Jeff and other members of the league hope that Rebecca will promote the league's goals if she is elected to the legislature. Rebecca, however, may choose not to support the league's goals and its proposed tax policy once she is elected.

SECTION 3 —REVIEW

1. Define the following terms: interest group, lobbyist.

2. What factors must the government weigh in trying to determine the public interest? Why might the public interest be difficult for the government to identify?

3. How can government regulation affect prices, services, profits, and productivity?

4. Describe how individuals and interest groups can influence government policy.

5. **Thinking and Writing Critically** Describe a situation in which you have attempted to persuade someone such as an employer to adopt an action or policy that would benefit you or a group to which you belong. Was your attempt successful? Were your methods similar to those used by lobbyists or interest groups?

6. **Applying** ROLE OF GOVERNMENT Conduct an Internet search for information about interest groups. Select an interest group and describe its goals and activities.

SECTION 1   In 1994 more than 19 million people worked for the federal, state, and local governments in the United States. Government has not always been a key employer, however; until the late 1800s the government was very small.

Throughout the 1900s all levels of U.S. government have grown in size and complexity because of various factors. These factors include population growth, changing public attitudes, a rising standard of living, and national emergencies.

The introduction of new government programs has increased government spending at the federal, state, and local levels. Education, public welfare, and interest on debts are among the largest expenditures for governments at all levels.

SECTION 2   In the United States, government has four basic economic goals: to regulate business, provide public goods, promote citizens' economic well-being, and stabilize the economy. The first three goals are shared by the federal, state, and local governments, while the federal government alone works to stabilize the economy.

Government involvement in the U.S. economy has increased dramatically since the abandonment of laissez-faire economic policies in the 1930s. Federal, state, and local governments regulate business to prevent abuses, protect consumers, limit negative externalities, and promote competition.

Governments often share responsibility for providing public goods to their citizens. In some cases, however, privatization has shifted that responsibility from the government to private companies.

The government promotes economic well-being by working to improve the standard of living. In addition, transfer payments allow the government to redistribute wealth.

The federal government acts to stabilize the economy by moderating the business cycle and responding to market failures. These two functions enable the government to minimize the effects of recessions, encourage competition, and promote fair business practices.

SECTION 3   In the free-enterprise economy of the United States, individuals and groups can influence government economic policies. The government often attempts to introduce programs that serve the public interest. At times, however, these programs may conflict with the desires of individual citizens.

Economic policy and regulations can influence all aspects of production and consumption. In particular, regulations affect prices, services, profits, and productivity. By electing people with economic views similar to their own, citizens can influence economic policy as individuals.

Interest groups also can influence both the election and the policy making of public officials. Their methods include providing information to elected representatives, contributing to campaigns, and encouraging their members to vote for a particular candidate. Many interest groups rely on professional lobbyists to promote their goals.

Economics Notebook

Refer to the list you made in your Economics Notebook at the beginning of this chapter. Which of these effects of government might be considered economic? Explain your answer in your Notebook.

CHAPTER 12

REVIEW

REVIEWING CONCEPTS

1. What are the key factors that encourage government expansion?

2. What are the main purposes of government regulation?

3. Why do governments provide public goods?

4. How does the government promote economic well-being?

5. How does government work to promote the public interest?

6. What effects can regulation have on prices, service, profits, and productivity?

THINKING AND WRITING CRITICALLY

1. **ROLE OF GOVERNMENT** Considering the changes that have taken place in American society, do you think that the government has kept pace with society's changing needs over the last 200 years? Explain your answer.

2. **ROLE OF GOVERNMENT** Using the categories listed in Figure 12.3 on page 289, redistribute funds to create a new federal spending plan. Explain your priorities.

3. **ROLE OF GOVERNMENT** What are the advantages and disadvantages of the government's work to stabilize the economy?

4. **ROLE OF GOVERNMENT** Consider your school as a regulated economic system. What effect do regulations have on grades, productivity, services, and individual well-being?

YOUR LOCAL ECONOMY

What businesses in your community are subsidized? Create a chart or table that describes these subsidies and explains how local businesses benefit from government funding.

INDIVIDUAL PORTFOLIO PROJECT

Create a pie chart showing what percentage of your school district's funds comes from federal, state, and local government. Write a caption explaining how these funds are spent.

PRACTICING SKILLS: UNDERSTANDING MEASUREMENT CONCEPTS AND METHODS

Each year, millions of Americans participate in public opinion polls. The results of these polls often are presented in the media. Being able to read polls accurately can help you understand what people think about many issues, including economics. Use the guidelines below to study the information from the poll on page 305, and answer the questions that follow.

Examine the question. Is the question neutral, or does it lead you to respond in a certain way? Is it worded so that it will mean the same thing to everyone who answers the poll?

Examine the answers. Pollsters usually provide a limited set of responses so the results can be more easily compiled.

Examine the results. When the polling is complete, pollsters compute the percentage of people who selected each answer. These figures are the poll's facts. Pollsters use the facts to make generalizations, or broad statements that describe the relationship among the facts.

1. Does the question posed by this poll meet the standards for a well-worded question? Why or why not?

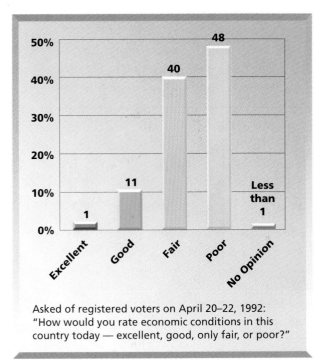

Asked of registered voters on April 20–22, 1992: "How would you rate economic conditions in this country today — excellent, good, only fair, or poor?"

Source: *The Gallup Poll 1992*

2. What are the facts of the poll? Is the generalization "George Bush lost the presidential election in 1992 because many people believed economic conditions were poor" a valid one? Explain your answer.

THE INTERNET: LEARNING ONLINE

Select three government agencies that provide consumer protection, and conduct an Internet search to find each agency's World Wide Web page. Briefly describe the duties, responsibilities, and activities of the organizations you have selected. What other information do the Web pages provide?

ANALYZING PRIMARY SOURCES

President Franklin D. Roosevelt's First Inaugural Address (March 4, 1933)

Franklin D. Roosevelt was first elected to the U.S. presidency in 1932. His inaugural address, delivered in 1933, discussed the problems faced by Americans during the Great Depression. Read the excerpt and answer the questions that follow.

"Values have shrunken to fantastic levels; taxes have risen; our ability to pay has fallen, government of all kinds is faced by serious curtailment [shortening] of income; the means of exchange are frozen in the currents of trade; the withered leaves of industrial enterprise lie on every side; farmers find no markets for their produce; the savings of many years in thousands of families are gone. More important, a host of unemployed citizens face the grim problem of existence, and an equally great number toil with little return. . . .

"Our greatest primary task is to put people to work. This is no unsolvable problem if we face it wisely and courageously. It can be accomplished in part by direct recruiting by the government itself, treating the task as we would treat the emergency of a war, but at the same time, through this employment, accomplishing greatly needed projects to stimulate and reorganize the use of our natural resources. . . .

"Finally, in our progress toward a resumption of work we require two safeguards against a return of the evils of the old order; there must be a strict supervision of all banking and credits and investments; there must be an end to speculation with other people's money, and there must be provision for an adequate but sound currency. . . .

"If I read the temper of our people correctly, we now realize as we have never before, our interdependence on each other; that we cannot merely take, but we must give as well; that if we are to go forward we must move as a trained and loyal army willing to sacrifice for the good of a common discipline. . . .

"I shall ask the Congress for the one remaining instrument to meet the crisis—broad executive power to wage a war against the emergency as great as the power that would be given me if we were in fact invaded by a foreign foe."

1. How does Roosevelt compare the 1933 economy to a national emergency? Does he support an interventionist or laissez-faire economic policy to meet this emergency?

2. How will Roosevelt's plan achieve the four main purposes of regulation?

3. How is Roosevelt's vision of national recovery related to the factors of government growth?

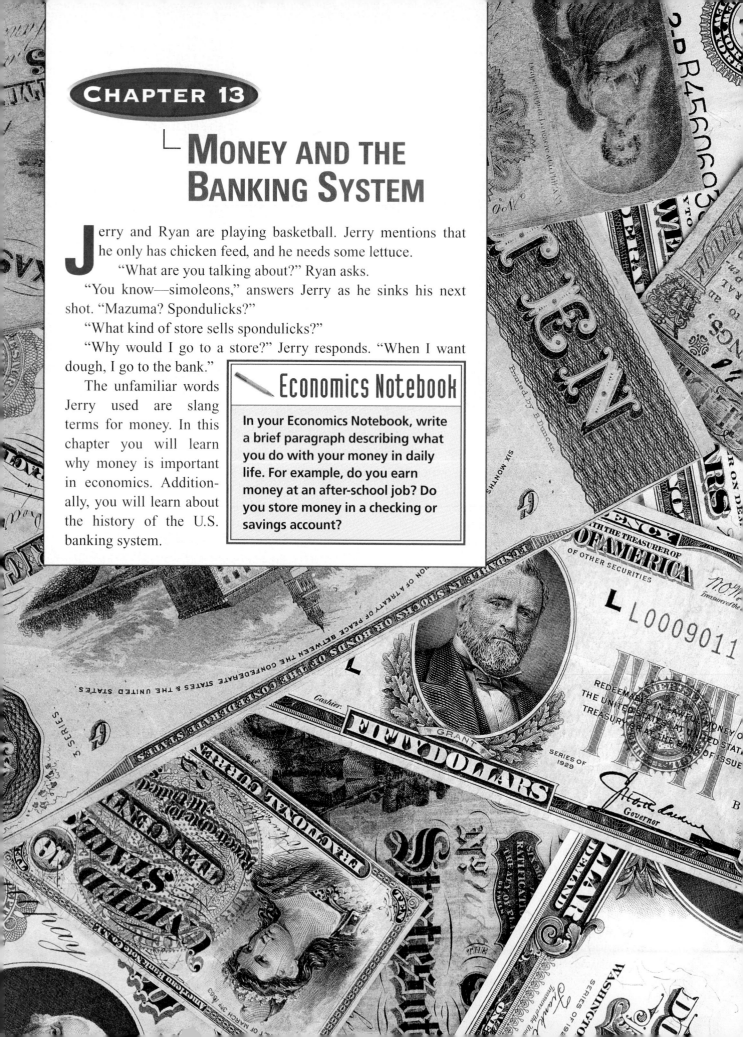

CHAPTER 13

MONEY AND THE BANKING SYSTEM

Jerry and Ryan are playing basketball. Jerry mentions that he only has chicken feed, and he needs some lettuce.

"What are you talking about?" Ryan asks.

"You know—simoleons," answers Jerry as he sinks his next shot. "Mazuma? Spondulicks?"

"What kind of store sells spondulicks?"

"Why would I go to a store?" Jerry responds. "When I want dough, I go to the bank."

The unfamiliar words Jerry used are slang terms for money. In this chapter you will learn why money is important in economics. Additionally, you will learn about the history of the U.S. banking system.

Economics Notebook

In your Economics Notebook, write a brief paragraph describing what you do with your money in daily life. For example, do you earn money at an after-school job? Do you store money in a checking or savings account?

SECTION 1
└ MONEY

Economics Dictionary

medium of exchange
standard of value
store of value
commodity money
representative money
specie
fiat money
currency
near money

Objectives

▶ What functions does money serve?

▶ What characteristics must an item have to be used as money?

▶ What are the sources of money's value?

▶ What types of money are used in the United States?

Suppose that you go shopping and decide to buy a jacket. When you pay for the jacket you hand the clerk a live chicken. The clerk refuses to accept the chicken, so you offer him 12 oranges, a walrus tusk, a picture of your cousin, and a coffee mug. The clerk refuses all of these items as well. Finally you open your wallet and offer the clerk several pieces of paper, each bearing a picture of an 18th-century politician named Alexander Hamilton and the number *10* printed in green. Why does the clerk accept these pieces of paper but not the other items? Both the clerk and you recognize the pieces of paper—a form of money—as a guaranteed standard of value in the United States.

What is money, and what gives it value? In this section you will find the answers to these questions as you learn about the functions and characteristics of money, the sources of money's value, and the various forms of money.

Functions of Money

As noted in Chapter 1, it is possible to barter, or exchange goods and services, without using money. In bartering, no medium of exchange is needed. Bartering still occurs in many parts of the world, particularly in traditional economies. Also, in some highly developed economies, individuals barter by performing services for one another. In the United States, for example, a carpenter might exchange his or her services with an electrician or a plumber rather than pay for the services with money.

How does money differ from barter? Money is anything that people commonly accept in exchange for goods and services. Money was developed to overcome the problems associated with bartering, such as those in the example of buying a jacket.

In the United States, money has three basic functions, each of which makes it a more efficient system than barter. Money serves as a medium of exchange, a standard of value, and a

EXCHANGE, MONEY, & INTERDEPENDENCE *Money is anything that people commonly accept in exchange for goods and services.* **What are the three basic functions of money?**

Money provides a way to judge the relative values of two products. ***How is the standard of value expressed in the United States?***

store of value. Any item that serves any of these three functions is a type of money.

Medium of Exchange

Money primarily is a medium of exchange. A **medium of exchange** is any item that sellers accept as payment for goods and services. As a medium of exchange, money assists in the buying and selling of goods and services, because buyers know that sellers will accept money in payment for products. For example, if you have a part-time job in a restaurant, you will be paid in money rather than in barbecue sauce. You can, of course, use that money to buy barbecue sauce—as well as movie tickets and concert T-shirts—if you so choose.

Standard of Value

Another use of money is as a **standard of value**. That is, money provides people with a way to measure the relative value of goods and services by comparing their prices. In this way, people can compare the worth of items such as a television and a bicycle. They also can use prices to judge the relative values of two different models or brands of the same type of item.

In the United States the standard of value is expressed in dollars and cents. Goods and services for sale are marked with a price that shows their value using these forms of measurement. If an audiocassette costs $10 and a pizza costs $5, a consumer knows that the relative value of the cassette is twice that of the pizza.

In addition to allowing consumers to compare prices, money as a standard of value helps clarify opportunity costs. Suppose that Melanie Chu has $10 to spend. She knows that this amount of money allows her to choose either a cassette or two pizzas. If Melanie chooses to buy two pizzas, she gives up the chance to buy the cassette—the opportunity cost of her decision. Consumers like Melanie make more informed choices when they consider both the price and the opportunity cost of their decisions.

Money's function as a standard of value also is important in record keeping. Whether measured in pounds of salt, sacks of rice, bales of cotton, or dollars and cents, businesses need to determine profits and losses. Similarly, governments must be able to figure tax receipts and the cost of expenditures. Money provides a standard system of measurement for these accounting tasks. That is, it allows businesses and the

Money's function as a store of value is evidenced by this sunken treasure. ***What two conditions must be met for money to serve as a store of value?***

government to calculate their expenses and profits in a recognizable standard of value.

In turn, this system of measurement allows investors to compare two businesses' performance by looking, for example, at how many dollars they made in profit during a specific time period. It would be much more difficult to compare one business's "profit" of 500,000 pounds of salt with another's 300,000 sacks of rice.

Store of Value A third function of money is that it can be saved, or stored for later use. For money to serve as a **store of value**, two conditions must be met. First, the money must be nonperishable. That is, it cannot rot or otherwise deteriorate while being saved. Would steak make a good store of value? Probably not, because the steak would spoil. Second, the money must keep its value over time. In other words, the purchasing power of the money must be fairly constant. Water would be a poor store of value because it evaporates—you would lose purchasing power as quickly as your water supply dried up.

If both of these conditions are met, people can accumulate their wealth for later use. If not, most people would be hesitant about saving money today, for it would be worth little or nothing tomorrow.

Characteristics of Money

Now that you know what money does, how can you determine if a particular item would work well as money? To be used as money, an item must have certain characteristics. The five major characteristics of money are

- durability,
- portability,
- divisibility,
- stability in value, and
- acceptability.

Durability Durability refers to money's ability to be used over and over again. Eggs would be a poor choice for money because they are fragile and perishable. Metals such as gold and silver,

One for All and All for One

Many people around the world hope that decreased trade restrictions will encourage global economic growth. To strengthen their position in the world market, a number of European nations have worked together to reduce trade barriers, forming the European Union (EU). This group of 15 nations has developed a new currency called the euro.

In 1996 the European Monetary Institute concluded a two-year contest to create the design of the new currency, which will consist of seven bills ranging in value from 5 euros to 500. The winning design features architectural details such as windows, bridges, and gateways to symbolize the unification of Europe.

The first printing process will take two years, and the bills are expected to go into circulation in 2002. The EU believes that the euro is necessary to ensure economic stability and growth among its member countries. Supporters feel that a single currency would benefit both the EU and its trading partners by stabilizing profits and eliminating the difficulties in maintaining many exchange rates.

However, many Europeans are still uncertain about changing to a new currency. Some member countries believe monetary unification will threaten their national independence, both politically and culturally. Bill Cash, a leader in Great Britain's Conservative Party, said, "You can't have a single currency without a single European bank, and that would almost certainly be located in Germany. We would end up having our economic policies dictated by foreigners."

SOURCES OF MONEY'S VALUE

Type of Money	Definition	Examples
Commodity Money	an item that has value of its own and is used as money	• precious metals, gems • salt in ancient Rome • tobacco, beaver skins, wampum in early colonial America • cowrie shells in Ashanti society
Representative Money	an item that has value because it can be exchanged for something valuable	• bills of credit in Massachusetts Bay Colony
Fiat Money	an item that has value because a government decree says it does	• U.S. coins and paper money

FIGURE 13.1 Money can be categorized by its source of value. **Which of the three types of money do you use in your everyday transactions?**

however, are ideal because they can withstand wear and tear. In fact, many coins minted thousands of years ago are still in existence. Are U.S. dollars durable? Yes, because they can be used many times. Additionally, a damaged dollar bill can be replaced easily.

Portability Money's usefulness may depend on its portability, or ability to be carried from one place to another and transferred from one person to another. As a medium of exchange, money must be convenient for people to use. Large stones, such as those used for money on the island of Yap in the South Pacific, would be difficult to use in a large region because of the problems of moving them. U.S. paper money, on the other hand, is small and lightweight, making it portable.

Divisibility Divisibility refers to money's ability to be divided into smaller units. The U.S. dollar is divisible into any amount between 1 and 100 cents. By combining the various coins and bills, buyers and sellers are able to make transactions of any amount down to the nearest penny.

Divisibility also enhances money's use as a standard of value, because exact price comparisons between products can be made. For example, many grocery stores display shelf labels that list the price of a good and the price per unit, such as an ounce. One 24-ounce bottle of POWERaDE® may cost $1.29, while a 32-ounce bottle may cost $1.59. Each ounce of POWERaDE in the smaller bottle costs cents ($1.29 ÷ 24), while each ounce in the larger bottle costs about 5.0 cents ($1.59 ÷ 32). The divisibility of the dollar into cents enables consumers to compare prices of various products.

Stability in Value As you know, for money to be useful as a store of value, it must be stable in value. Stability in value encourages saving and maintains money's purchasing power. Most people who save money are confident that it will have approximately the same value when they want to buy something with it as it had when they put it into savings. Suppose that you put $50 in a savings account and withdraw it in one year. Although prices probably will have increased somewhat because of inflation, you still will be able to pay for goods and services with the money you have saved.

Acceptability Acceptability means that people are willing to accept money in exchange for their goods and services. People accept money because they know that they, in turn, can spend it for other products. Tourists from the United States to a Pacific island where shells are used as money, for example, would have trouble buying goods with their dollar bills. Shopkeepers would not accept the paper money because it could not be used to buy more merchandise on the island. If the tourists exchanged their dollars for shells, however, they would be able to make purchases with the local money.

Sources of Money's Value

As you have learned, money must have—and retain—value. But how does money acquire this value? Economists have identified three sources of value for money. In fact, money can be identified by its source of value. The three types of money are commodity money, representative money, and fiat money. (See Figure 13.1.)

Commodity Money An item that has a value of its own (as a commodity) and that also is used as money is called **commodity money**. Throughout history, societies have used many commodities as money. Precious metals such as gold and silver—and gems such as rubies, emeralds, and diamonds—often have been used as money. Today salt is a commonplace commodity, but in ancient Rome salt was so rare and desirable that it was used as money.

Rather than being a rare item, commodity money is in some cases the most convenient type of money available. For example, tobacco was used as money in Virginia in the early 1600s. Why? Tobacco was plentiful because tobacco farming was the major source of income for individuals as well as for the colony.

Representative Money An item that has value because it can be exchanged for something

else of value is **representative money.** Such items have no intrinsic value. That is, their only value is the value they represent.

The first use of representative money in colonial America occurred in the late 1600s. In 1690 the Massachusetts Bay Colony issued bills of credit to help finance King William's War, which was fought against American Indians. Printed on these bills of credit was the amount of money that colonists had loaned to the Massachusetts government. These bills could be redeemed with the colony's treasurer.

Other colonies soon followed the Massachusetts example and issued bills of credit that could be redeemed for **specie**—gold or silver. The amount of specie held by a government "backs," or defines, the worth of representative money. If a government has large reserves of specie and limits the amount of representative money issued, then the money has a high value. This value decreases, however, if a government has a small reserve of specie and issues more representative money.

During the American Revolution the Continental Congress issued representative money, called Continentals, to finance the war for

EXCHANGE, MONEY, & INTERDEPENDENCE *Precious metals such as gold and silver have been used as money.* ***What are some other commodities that have been used as money?***

independence from Great Britain (1775–1783). Few Continentals were redeemed for specie, however, because the government had little of it. The Continentals lost so much of their value that they became nearly worthless, and colonial merchants often refused to accept them.

Fiat Money Value is attached to **fiat money** because a government fiat, or decree, says that it has value. In the United States, coins and paper money are examples of fiat money.

Like representative money, fiat money has little or no value without this government decree. The materials used to produce U.S. coins are, in fact, worth much less than the face value of the coins. The money has value solely because the government says that the paper money and coins must be accepted for all transactions. Thus, unlike representative money, fiat money cannot be redeemed for specie or other items. Its value ultimately stems from citizens' faith in the U.S. government.

The majority of nations in the world today use a form of fiat money called **currency**—coins and paper bills—for money. The Lydians, an ancient people in Asia Minor, minted the world's first coins about 635 B.C. The Chinese developed the first paper currency, perhaps as early as A.D. 650.

EXCHANGE, MONEY, & INTERDEPENDENCE *Paper currency is printed by the Bureau of Engraving and Printing in Washington, D.C.* **How does the U.S. government work to prevent counterfeiting?**

Forms of Money

The United States primarily relies on fiat money. Its money takes the form of coins, paper money, checks, and another type of money known as near money.

Coins and Paper Money Coins and paper money make up U.S. currency. Coins are made by the U.S. Mint, a bureau of the Department of the Treasury. Paper currency is printed by the Bureau of Engraving and Printing in Washington, D.C. Although the government held gold and silver as partial backing for paper money until 1971, today U.S. currency is not redeemable in specie.

C A S E   S T U D Y

Counterfeit Money

EXCHANGE, MONEY, & INTERDEPENDENCE Next time you open your wallet, look at your money. How can you tell whether the bills are genuine or counterfeit?

In the early 1990s counterfeiting became an increasing problem in the U.S. economy. Forgers illegally copied checks, money orders, and even grocery coupons. The amount of counterfeit U.S. currency circulating in the economy also increased.

How is the U.S. government combating this rise in illegally created currency? In 1996 the Treasury Department designed a new $100 bill—the first major currency redesign since 1929. The design incorporated several security features that make it difficult to forge the new bill. These features include a watermark, or design in the paper, of Benjamin Franklin; a multicolored shade of ink for the numeral in the lower front right-hand corner; a synthetic security thread embedded in the paper; and microprinting.

New designs were introduced for the $50 bill in 1997 and for the $20 bill in 1998. Over the next several years, the Treasury Department also plans to redesign the $10, $5, and $1 bills. As criminals take advantage of technological developments, however, the United States and other countries will have to find even more sophisticated ways to stop counterfeiters. Only by stopping the efforts of these forgers can governments maintain control of the amount of their currencies in circulation.

Demand Deposits Checking accounts make up the largest segment of the U.S. money supply. Because checks can be paid "on demand," in other words at any time, checking accounts sometimes are referred to as demand deposits.

Checking accounts are fiat money because they stand for the bank's willingness to pay on demand in currency issued by the government. Checks generally are accepted because banks are willing to pay the amount of the check when it is presented for payment. Checking accounts, therefore, are considered money because they are a medium of exchange, a standard of value, and a store of value.

Near Money Many financial assets are similar to money. These assets, such as savings accounts and time deposits, are referred to as **near money**, and they are not always counted as part of the nation's money supply. Although such assets are easily accessible, these accounts cannot be used directly to buy goods or to pay debts. Depositors, for example, cannot pay their bills with a certificate of deposit (CD). Because funds in these accounts can easily be converted into cash, however, they are considered near money.

SECTION 1 — REVIEW

1. Define the following terms: medium of exchange, standard of value, store of value, commodity money, representative money, specie, fiat money, currency, near money.

2. Describe the three basic functions of money that make it more efficient than barter.

3. Using the five major characteristics of money, explain why popcorn, beads, and oranges would or would not be suitable items to use as money.

4. What are the possible sources of money's value?

5. What forms does money take in the United States?

6. **Thinking and Writing Critically** Suppose that you and the members of your class decide to establish a monetary system for your school's economy. What will you use as money? Explain why you chose that item, how it functions as money, and how it matches the characteristics of money. What is the source of your new money's value? Provide a sketch of your new money.

7. **Applying** EXCHANGE, MONEY, & INTERDEPENDENCE Conduct an Internet search for information about money in different countries. Select five countries around the world and identify their currencies. What are the selected currencies called? How does the value of the selected currencies compare to the value of U.S. currency?

HISTORY OF U.S. BANKING

Economics Dictionary

gold standard

Objectives

▶ What were the views of Federalists and Antifederalists about U.S. banking?

▶ How did the development in the 1860s of nationally-chartered banks affect the power of state-chartered banks?

▶ How did the government reform and regulate the banking system after World War I?

Why might you deposit money in a bank? You probably would do so because you are confident that your money will retain its value and will be available when you want to withdraw it.

Consumers like you have not always been so confident about the security of banks, however. The U.S. banking system has had to earn consumers' confidence as it has developed along with the nation.

Before the American Revolution, the British government discouraged the establishment of banks in the American colonies. Merchants ran unofficial banks by allowing their customers to deposit their money in accounts and take out loans. These banks were only as secure as the individual merchant's business, however. Establishing a stable banking system thus was seen as a key task for the new nation's leaders.

The U.S. monetary and banking systems have gone through three main periods of development. During those periods, banking power has shifted between a centralized, national banking system and independent state and local banks. The result over time has been an increase in stability and public confidence in the nation's money and banking systems.

Before the Civil War

The first period of development, from the 1780s to 1860, was a time of experimentation and debate in U.S. banking. During this period, money and banking were part of a larger political battle over the role of government.

Conflicting Views of Banking The nation's early leaders generally considered themselves to be allied with one of two groups. The Federalists believed that only a powerful central government could keep the United States strong. The Antifederalists opposed a strong central government and favored leaving most power in the hands of state governments. These two groups viewed the young country's monetary problems quite differently. Although the nation's leaders agreed that the United States needed a stable form of money and a stronger banking system, they disagreed about how to reach these goals.

Federalists such as Alexander Hamilton believed that a strong, centralized banking system was necessary to develop U.S. industry and trade. As secretary of the treasury under President George Washington, Hamilton proposed that a national bank have the power to handle the government's funds, to establish and monitor other banks throughout the country, and to issue currency.

Antifederalists such as Thomas Jefferson opposed the creation of a national bank. They feared that the concentration of economic and political power at the national level would weaken the power of individual states. Jefferson supported a decentralized banking system in which the states, rather than the federal government, would establish and regulate the banks within their borders.

First Bank of the United States Hamilton and the Federalists were successful. In 1791 Congress established the First Bank of the United

Alexander Hamilton   *Thomas Jefferson*

States as a private business. Its 20-year charter, or legal permission to operate, outlined the First Bank's responsibilities, which included the issuing of representative money in the form of banknotes. These banknotes were backed by gold and silver specie. Additionally, the First Bank collected fees and made payments for the federal government.

One year later in 1792 Congress established a national coinage system, and the federal government began to mint gold and silver coins. The government also established the dollar as the official unit of currency.

How successful was the First Bank? It did bring some order to the monetary and banking systems in the United States. It also was successful in regulating banks chartered by the states. For example, the First Bank of the United States required state-chartered banks to hold gold and silver that could be exchanged for currency.

Nonetheless, congressional opponents of the First Bank succeeded in voting down the renewal of its 20-year charter in 1811. As a result, the number of state-chartered banks increased almost threefold, from about 90 in 1811 to nearly 250 in 1816. These state-chartered banks adopted many of the powers associated with the national bank. In the absence of government regulation, these state-chartered banks often issued far more currency than they could back with gold and silver. As a result, many of these banks were unable to redeem paper money, causing a loss of confidence in the banks and their money.

Second Bank of the United States The chaos in the nation's banking system after 1811 caused Congress once again to establish a national bank. Chartered in 1816, the Second Bank of the United States slowly restored confidence in the banking system and in the representative money that state-chartered banks issued.

The Second Bank, however, was not without its critics. Opponents argued that the concentration of wealth in the federal banking system gave too much power to those who controlled it. Other critics argued that the Second Bank restricted economic growth by failing to provide enough credit and currency for the needs of the nation. Still others claimed that it issued too much credit and currency, weakening the U.S. money supply.

Dismantling the Bank The Second Bank came under increasing attack after Andrew Jackson, a vocal critic of the Bank, was elected to the presidency in 1828. In 1832, four years before the official end of the Second Bank's charter, President Jackson vetoed legislation that would have extended it for another 20 years. Jackson's withdrawal of federal government funds in 1833 further blocked the Second Bank's effectiveness for the remaining three years of its life. The fall of the Second Bank set off another rise in the number of state-chartered banks. Between 1830 and 1837 the number of state-chartered banks nearly tripled.

Because state-chartered banks often issued their own currency, bills and coins varied widely from state to state. For example, in 1835 the government of New York prohibited banknotes valued at less than $10. Some banks, on the other hand, issued notes with values as low as 5 cents. Although by 1830 most states required banknotes to carry round-dollar values such as $1 or $5, many people continued to use pieces of dollar bills to represent fractional amounts. In other words, if you visited a store in the 1830s and paid for a 25-cent item with a $1 bill, the clerk might cut the bill into four equal pieces and return three of them to you as change.

In addition to issuing their own banknotes, state-chartered banks issued more credit with fewer restrictions. They also kept smaller and smaller reserves of gold and silver to back the growing supply of paper money. By 1837, people found it increasingly difficult to exchange their paper money for gold or silver. Public confidence in the notes issued by state-chartered banks diminished, and many of those banks failed when they were unable to redeem their banknotes in specie.

The resulting economic panic of 1837, however, did not revive public support for another single national bank. Instead, some states coped with the banking crisis by imposing stricter guidelines on state-chartered banks. Most states, for example, adopted the Second Bank's policy requiring state-chartered banks to hold a specie reserve equal to a certain percentage of the notes they issued.

Civil War to World War I

During the second main period of development—between 1860 and 1913—the federal government created a dual banking system made up of state- and nationally chartered banks. The system brought more uniformity and stability to the money supply and U.S. banks. This system also meant that the power of national banking increased, while state-chartered banks became less powerful.

Fragmented Banking The fall of the Second Bank of the United States in 1836—and the lack of uniformity among the nation's state-chartered banks—created a patchwork banking system during the mid-1800s. By 1861 most of the country's 1,601 state-chartered banks were issuing paper money of questionable value.

The Civil War created even more problems for the nation's monetary system. During the war, Congress issued currency to pay the North's war expenses. Called greenbacks or U.S. notes, the new currency was not backed by specie. Instead, greenbacks were fiat money backed only by the federal government's promise to repay the notes' face value at some future date.

The Confederacy also relied on paper currency during the Civil War. These notes were issued by the Confederate government as well as by individual southern states. This money was worthless by the end of the war, and the banking system in the South was virtually destroyed. In early 1861 nine of the southern states had a combined total of 121 chartered banks. By the end of the war, in 1865, no banks existed in North Carolina, Mississippi, or Florida. Only three banks still operated in Georgia, and South Carolina had only one.

Unifying the Banking System

To rebuild and strengthen the country's banking system, Congress passed the National Banking Acts of 1863 and 1864. These acts gave the federal government the power to charter, or officially establish, banks and to require banks to hold gold and silver reserves. The government's power

EXCHANGE, MONEY, & INTERDEPENDENCE *President Andrew Jackson opposed central banking.* ***What was the effect of the fall of the Second Bank of the United States?***

THE ARAB AND THE CAMEL.

An Arab asked the loaded Camel whether he preferred to go up or down hill. *"Pray, Master,"* said the Camel dryly, *"is the straight way across the plain shut up?"*—ÆSOP.

EXCHANGE, MONEY, & INTERDEPENDENCE *Greenbacks were issued by Congress during the Civil War to pay U.S. war expenses. **What does the cartoonist suggest about the government's financial policies?***

to charter banks enabled it to establish a system composed of nationally chartered and state-chartered banks.

Additionally, the federal government issued a single national currency through the nationally-chartered banks. Unlike the greenbacks issued during the war, this national currency was backed by government bonds. The new currency contributed to the elimination of the many different state bank currencies in use. Most of these state bank currencies were good for local purchases only and relied on the strength and reputation of an individual bank for their value. A national currency provided a nationally acceptable medium of exchange and stabilized the supply of money in the United States.

With the passage of the Coinage Act of 1873, Congress began reducing the country's reliance

on silver as specie. The Gold Standard Act of 1900 committed the U.S. government to the **gold standard**—a monetary system in which paper money and coins carry the value of a specified amount of gold. A gold standard allows people to exchange their banknotes for gold and keeps the government from issuing an unlimited number of banknotes.

Suppose that in 1901 you had U.S. banknotes valued at $150. You would know that you could exchange your paper money for $150 in gold. You would probably choose to keep your paper money, however, because it would be much easier to carry. Additionally, the gold standard ensured that the paper money carried an established and recognizable value—so you would feel no need to exchange it for specie.

All of these government decisions increased public confidence in paper currency and in the banking system. The system did not, however, provide for an efficient method of regulating the amount of money circulating in the economy. Also, the system lacked any central organization.

World War I to the Present

The third developmental period in U.S. banking, from 1913 to the present, has been marked by reform and regulation. As noted in Chapter 12, government involvement in the U.S. economy has increased during the 1900s. Specifically, it has focused on regulating the amount of money in the economy in order to stabilize currency values. The banking system has experienced successes as well as failures from this government involvement.

New Deal Banking Reforms

The Great Depression was brought on by financial panic that swept the nation. Thousands of people withdrew their savings, causing many banks to fail. In the years 1930–33, nearly 8,000 banks went under, some 4,000 in 1933 alone.

Franklin D. Roosevelt's election to the presidency in 1932 brought lasting changes to the monetary and banking systems. Promising a "New Deal" to the nation's people, Roosevelt sought to restore public confidence in the economy and the nation's banking system.

First, Roosevelt kept the nation's banks closed for four days in March 1933. The president's order for the "bank holiday" allowed banks to reopen only after federal auditors judged them to be financially sound.

ECONOMIC INSTITUTIONS & INCENTIVES *Thousands of people rushed to withdraw their savings during the Great Depression.* **Why did Franklin D. Roosevelt order a "bank holiday" in 1933?**

Most banks were reopened within two weeks. Certification by the auditors helped restore confidence in the reopened banks, and soon people and businesses began to use them again.

Another New Deal reform, the Banking Act of 1933, separated investments from savings in order to protect deposits. Many people felt that bank officials had persuaded them to invest in overvalued stock, destroying their life savings. For example, in 1933 Edgar Brown testified before Congress that he had lost $125,000, in part because he had been pressured to invest in National City Bank stock. After the crash in 1929, the bank had bought the stock back at only two thirds the price Brown had paid.

The Banking Act of 1933 thus prohibited the Fed's member banks from providing investment services such as selling stocks and bonds. The act also established a temporary Federal Deposit Insurance Corporation (FDIC), which insured each savings account up to $5,000. The Banking Act of 1935 made the FDIC permanent and

Federal Reserve System In 1913 Congress passed the Federal Reserve Act, establishing the Federal Reserve system—now commonly called the "Fed." The Fed became the nation's central bank, and all nationally chartered banks were required to join the Fed. State-chartered banks, however, were free either to join the Fed or to operate as nonmember banks. In 1996 more than 2,760 commercial banks—including about 15 percent of all state-chartered banks—were members of the Federal Reserve.

In its early years the Fed experienced both success and failure. The chief success was its ability to provide the government with enough credit to finance the U.S. military effort during World War I (1914–18). Its major failures were an inability to control credit during the 1920s and a lack of support for the banking system during the 1930s. In fact, the overextension of credit and the resulting borrower defaults contributed to consumer hardships during the early years of the Great Depression.

Shake, Rattle, and Roll

Earthquakes are one of nature's most powerful and destructive forces. Both engineers and earthquake scientists—known as seismologists—work hard to prevent and lessen the damage caused by earthquakes. Their research allows people to make decisions about how to allocate resources and reduce the chances of economic crisis.

Although earthquakes may strike in several regions of the United States, they are most likely to occur in California. California is particularly subject to earthquakes because of its location on several fault lines, or places where tectonic plates — enormous portions of the earth's crust—meet.

In 1994 the "Northridge quake" caused extensive damage to the city of Los Angeles and much of the rest of densely populated southern California. This quake alone left more than 60 people dead, 5,000 injured, and 25,000 without homes. The region's transportation and communications networks were crippled, and property damage was estimated at more than $20 billion.

The economic impact of the earthquake, however, extended far beyond southern California. The quake closed down highways, railroads, and airports that are critical to nationwide distribution of goods and services. A quake of rarely matched intensity—the "Big One" that seismologists predict has a better than 50-50 chance of occurring during the next 20 years—could pose a serious threat to the national economy.

Seismologists know that earthquakes are caused by tectonic plates grinding against each other. Stress builds up between the plates over time, eventually causing the earth's crust to shift—what we experience as an earthquake. By studying these fault lines, seismologists hope to predict future earthquakes.

While the science of earthquake prediction is far from perfect, it provides important information. For instance, emergency planners use scientists' predictions to locate emergency resources where they will most likely be needed.

Predicting the location and intensity of earthquakes also aids structural engineers, who design devices that can lessen the property damage caused by quakes. One device, for example, cradles a building's foundation on a set of steel rollers, enabling it to move with an earthquake rather than staying rigid and breaking apart.

Recent advances in structural engineering have led many people to call for retrofitting existing buildings and structures—that is, adding quake-resistant structural devices. Currently, the California Department of Transportation is in the process of retrofitting more than 2,000 roads and bridges in the state.

What Do You Think?

1. Should the federal government discourage people from building near fault lines in order to reduce the potential costs of disaster relief? Explain your answer.

2. Is the cost of retrofitting buildings and transportation structures worthwhile if scientists can make only vague predictions about the location and likelihood of future earthquakes? Explain your answer.

Scientists use antennae connected to a network of satellites called Global Positioning System (GPS) to measure and predict earthquakes.

ECONOMIC INSTITUTIONS & INCENTIVES *During the 1960s and 1970s a number of banks were established to meet the needs of particular groups.* **How has banking changed since the Great Depression?**

expanded its insurance for each account. Today depositors' money is insured up to $100,000 for each account.

The Gold Reserve Act of 1934 eliminated the gold standard in the United States and allowed the government to purchase all gold held by U.S. banks. Further, Federal Reserve notes were no longer to be backed by gold. The act also prohibited the use of gold coins and the redemption of Federal Reserve notes at banks. Gold held in the Treasury was used to set up a fund designed to help stabilize the value of the dollar.

Expanded Banking Services After the Great Depression, banking practices changed dramatically. Banks began to lend money directly to consumers, as well as to corporations and finance companies. Consumer loans made up less than 1 percent of total bank assets in 1945, but by 1995 more than 12.5 percent of bank assets came from consumer loans. Sales and consumer finance companies, on the other hand, saw their percentage of consumer loans drop from about 40 percent of assets in the early 1940s to less than 23 percent by the late 1980s.

Some consumers felt that their needs were not met by most commercial banks. In response, during the 1960s and 1970s a number of banks were established to serve particular groups. These banks, such as Women's Bank in San Diego and Freedom National Bank in Harlem, focused on providing checking and savings accounts, loans, and other financial services to members of specific gender and ethnic groups. Although many of these banks failed, some expanded to offer services to the general population. For example, Women's Bank soon changed its name in an attempt to gain more business, becoming known instead as California Coastal Bank.

SECTION 2 — REVIEW

1. Define the following term: gold standard.

2. How did conflict over the First and Second Banks of the United States reflect Federalist and Antifederalist views of government?

3. How did the development of a national banking system in the 1860s weaken state banks?

4. Explain how and why the government tried to regulate the banking system after World War I.

5. Thinking and Writing Critically How did the turmoil of the Civil War encourage the development of a national banking system?

6. Applying ECONOMIC INSTITUTIONS & INCENTIVES Conduct an Internet search for information about the gold standard. Do any countries rely on the gold standard today? Are there other commodities that are used as monetary standards?

SECTION 3

U.S. BANKING TODAY

Economics Dictionary

commercial bank

savings and loan association

mutual savings bank

debit card

deregulation

default

Objectives

▶ What are the most common types of U.S. financial institutions?

▶ How has automation affected banking practices?

▶ What were the results of banking deregulation?

▶ What crises did financial institutions face in the late 1980s?

As you have learned, the U.S. banking system has changed dramatically over time. Changes such as home banking and debit cards continue to take place all around you. Recently, the three main trends in banking have been automation, deregulation, and stabilization of the banking industry. Before looking at these trends, however, you must be able to identify the players in the field—the financial institutions.

Types of Financial Institutions

Today you have many banking options. Suppose that you decide to open a savings account. You visit each of the several different financial institutions located near your home to find out what services are offered. Soon your mind is whirling with interest rates, regular savings accounts, money market accounts, and certificates of deposit. How do you choose among financial institutions? What do you want to know about these institutions before handing over your hard-earned money?

Four major types of financial institutions have emerged as the U.S. banking system has evolved. Figure 13.2 on page 316 shows the types of financial institutions in the United States today and how many of each type exist, broken down by the value of their assets. For many years these institutions offered different services and different interest rates. Today, however, they are much more similar in their services and functions. The most common types of financial institutions have included

▶ commercial banks,

▶ savings and loan associations,

▶ mutual savings banks, and

▶ credit unions.

ECONOMIC INSTITUTIONS & INCENTIVES *Commercial banks lend money, accept deposits, and transfer funds.* **What other types of financial institutions are common in the United States?**

Commercial Banks In 1995 nearly 10,000 **commercial banks** existed in the United States. The main functions of commercial banks today are to lend money, accept deposits, and transfer money among businesses, other banks and financial institutions, and individuals. Commercial banks make almost 40 percent of all mortgage loans and almost 50 percent of all other loans.

In the 1800s commercial banks developed as institutions for business and commerce. In the early 1900s, however, commercial banks began to offer services to individuals. Today commercial banks generally offer customers the widest range of services of all financial institutions.

Savings and Loan Associations Like commercial banks, **savings and loan associations** (S&Ls) were established to lend money and accept deposits. Sometimes called "thrifts," these savings and loan associations were begun as "home-building societies" in the mid-1800s. Members deposited money into a large general fund and took turns borrowing it—and paying it back—until each member was able to build a house. Today the nation has nearly 2,000 S&Ls. Individuals and families continue to make up the majority of S&L customers.

Federal regulations and laws allowed S&Ls to expand, enabling them to offer many of the same services available at commercial banks, such as credit cards and insured deposits. Interest rates—both on savings accounts and on loans—vary among savings institutions.

Mutual Savings Banks In the early 1800s institutions called **mutual savings banks** were set up to serve people who wished to make small deposits that large commercial banks did not want to handle. Like an S & L, business for a mutual savings bank traditionally came from personal savings and home mortgage loans. Interest rates for loans at mutual savings banks often were slightly lower than those at commercial banks.

Credit Unions Employees of large businesses and institutions and members of large labor unions often belong to credit unions. Today approximately 11,700 credit unions are in operation in the United States. When credit union members deposit money, they

FINANCIAL INSTITUTIONS, 1995

Assets	FDIC–Insured Commercial Banks	FDIC–Insured Savings Institutions	Credit Unions
Less than $5.0 million			5,874
$5.0 million– $9.9 million	1,756	162	1,799
$10.0 million– $24.9 million			1,830
$25.0 million– $49.9 million	2,369	293	959
$50.0 million– $99.9 million	2,534	454	597
$100.0 million– $499.9 million	2,593	822	568
$500.0 million– $999.9 million	268	137	42
$1.0 billion– $2.9 billion	220	102	16
$3.0 billion or more	201	59	2
TOTALS	**9,941**	**2,029**	**11,687**

Source: Statistical Abstract of the United States: 1996

FIGURE 13.2 There are several types of financial institutions in the United States. **Which type was most common in 1995? Which type had the largest number of institutions with more than $500 million in assets?**

Careers

in Economics

Bank Teller

Are you interested in learning about how a bank works? Do you have good interpersonal skills as well as strong math ability? If so, you might consider a job as a bank teller.

What does a bank teller do? The word *teller* comes from the Dutch word *tellen*, meaning "to count." Tellers do indeed count money—but they also are responsible for many other transactions between the bank and its customers. These duties include cashing checks, providing account information, accepting loan payments and account deposits, paying withdrawals, and selling bank products. To successfully perform these tasks, a teller must be familiar with the bank's policies and procedures and be able to clearly explain them to customers.

Although accurately handling a wide variety of transactions is a key part of their job, tellers' most important role is to represent the bank to its customers. For many clients, the teller is the only form of personal contact they have with their bank. For this reason, banks expect their tellers to be courteous and helpful. "People friendly" tellers are an important part of a bank's public image.

Banks require that tellers have a high school diploma and the ability to operate various types of bank and office equipment such as personal computers and adding machines. Classes in math, business, and secretarial skills are helpful training for this position. Many employers also look for candidates with experience in retail sales.

Technological innovations, such as electronic funds transfers and automated teller machines, are expected to alter significantly the nature of teller positions in the future. However, as long as there is a need for personal contact between clients and their bank, tellers will continue to play an important role in the nation's banking system.

Bank tellers are responsible for most transactions between banks and their customers.

purchase shares that pay interest. Credit unions use this savings pool to supply low-cost loans to their members.

Credit unions usually offer higher interest rates on savings and lower interest rates on loans than do other financial institutions. Personal, automobile, and home improvement loans account for the majority of the loan activity.

Automation

Three main trends have influenced financial institutions in recent years. The first trend is automation, which means reliance on computers to handle transactions. Also called electronic funds transfer (EFT), automated banking increases banks' efficiency by allowing them to execute banking transactions electronically, by

ECONOMIC INSTITUTIONS & INCENTIVES *Many routine banking tasks now are handled by ATMs.* ***What are some advantages of using an ATM?***

computer. This process allows transactions to affect accounts immediately. It saves banks money by decreasing the number of workers needed for banking operations. The four main types of automated banking are

▶ automated teller machines,
▶ automatic clearing house services,
▶ point-of-sale terminals, and
▶ home banking.

Automated Teller Machines Are you among the millions of people who use an automated teller machine (ATM) to deposit or withdraw money from a bank account? If not, you probably know someone who is—in August 1996 more than 217 million ATM cards were in circulation. Those ATM cards, if laid end to end, would stretch across the United States from coast to coast four times.

Many routine banking tasks that had been handled by bank tellers now are handled by

ATMs. Bank customers, for example, make deposits or withdrawals from checking and savings accounts at ATMs. They can also make payments on bank loans or transfer money from one account to another automatically.

What are the advantages of using an ATM? You may not have time to stand in line at the bank, or you may need the money after the bank closes. Most ATMs operate 24 hours a day, making them convenient for customers. ATMs are convenient for the bank, too, because fewer tellers are needed. In fact, some banks now charge a fee to customers who rely on tellers for transactions that can be handled by ATMs.

Automatic Clearing House Services Some banks make it possible for you to pay bills without writing checks. Of course, you still have to supply the money, but your bank will transfer funds automatically. Banks do this through automatic clearing house services (ACH), a system that transfers money from a customer's account to those of his or her creditors. Usually, ACH is used to pay regular monthly bills, such as home mortgage payments and rents, insurance premiums, and utility bills. Why might you decide to pay your bills through automatic clearing house services? You would save time as well as money on postage and would have fewer envelopes to seal—and you would know that your payments will arrive in time.

Point-of-Sale Transactions Have you seen someone pay for gasoline or groceries by running a plastic card through an electronic scanner? Customers are able to purchase items in this way at gas stations, grocery stores, and convenience stores that have point-of-sale terminals. A point-of-sale transaction involves the direct transfer of money from a buyer's bank account to a seller's bank account. A buyer pays for goods at the checkout counter by inserting a plastic card, called a **debit card**, into the terminal. Money then is transferred automatically from the buyer's account to the seller's account. By mid-1995 more than 528,000 point-of-sale terminals were in use across the United States.

How do point-of-sale transactions benefit you? A debit card requires you to use a personal identification number (PIN). Without knowing this PIN, the card is useless, thereby reducing the problems caused by theft. You also can check the amount of money available in your account anytime you want by inserting your card into a point-of-sale terminal.

Some banking experts believe that the use of debit cards soon will replace the use of checks in the U.S. economy. They note that debit cards help merchants by ending the risk of bad checks and eliminating the inconvenience and expense of processing credit card transactions.

The use of debit cards, however, has some drawbacks. For example, debit cards can be used only in stores with the terminals. In addition, consumers are accustomed to the grace period, or lag time, offered by credit cards. When consumers make a credit card purchase, they do not have to pay for the good or service until they are billed for it. This period of credit that allows a purchaser to "buy now and pay later" is the grace period. Consumers lose their grace period with debit cards because a point-of-sale transaction transfers money out of their accounts instantly. Debit cards mean you "buy now and pay now."

Home Banking One of the most dramatic developments in banking involves the Internet. Many banks offer a variety of services to Internet customers. For example, Citizens Bank—headquartered in Indiana—opens accounts over the Internet for customers who are unable to come to one of the bank's branches. Georgia State Bank offers similar services, and Wilber National Bank in New York permits customers to download software for banking transactions and bill payment. In California the Bank of Stockton allows customers to download and reconcile their account statements, transfer funds, and pay bills through the Internet.

Even more popular than Internet banking are telephone and home banking. For example, Bank One offers its customers in Texas the opportunity to check account balances, transfer money, and even apply for loans over the telephone. Elec-

tronic home-banking services link personal computers in homes with the bank's computers. Bank records can be accessed by a customer's computer, enabling the transacting of bank business from home. Home banking provides convenience to customers and helps banks by reducing the time and money spent recording transactions.

Deregulation

The second major trend is **deregulation**, or the reduction of government restrictions. Deregulation has resulted in more competition in banking, as well as the rise of interstate, or regional, banking in the United States.

Increased Competition Banking deregulation began in 1980 when Congress passed the Depository Institutions Deregulation and Monetary Control Act. This act eliminated many of the

ECONOMIC INSTITUTIONS & INCENTIVES *Point-of-sale transactions transfer money directly from the buyer's bank account to the seller's bank account.* ***How do debit cards provide security?***

traditional differences between financial institutions such as commercial banks and S&Ls. In effect, the portions of the act that concern interest rates, checking accounts, and required reserves made banking both more competitive and more uniform in the services offered.

Suppose that you decide to buy a car. Traditionally, you would have arranged a loan from an S&L or a credit union. Deregulation has allowed banks to offer interest rates comparable to those available from other institutions, so you have many more loan offers from which to choose. Similarly, traveler's checks were once issued only at banks. Today, however, vacationers have the convenience of buying traveler's checks at almost any financial institution.

Regional Banking Another major change as a result of deregulation has been the growth of regional banking. Historically, banks and their branches had been limited by law to their home states. In 1985, however, the Supreme Court affirmed that the states—not just the federal government—have a role in regulating regional banking. This ruling allowed banks to merge with other banks and to build branch offices in other states whose state legislatures were agreeable to the expansion.

Would you prefer to do business with a local bank or with one based in a different state? Many banking experts view the trend toward regional banking as beneficial, primarily because larger financial institutions can offer a wider variety of services to consumers. Other experts foresee problems with regional banking—for example, that larger banks from distant regions may be unresponsive to customers' needs. In addition, smaller banks fear that the larger banks' greater size gives them a competitive edge in the market. Small banks also worry that they might be absorbed by larger banks—even when wishing to remain independent.

ECONOMIC INSTITUTIONS & INCENTIVES *Deregulation has encouraged the growth of regional banking and increased the number of bank mergers.* **What are the pros and cons of regional banking?**

BANK FAILURES, 1970–1995

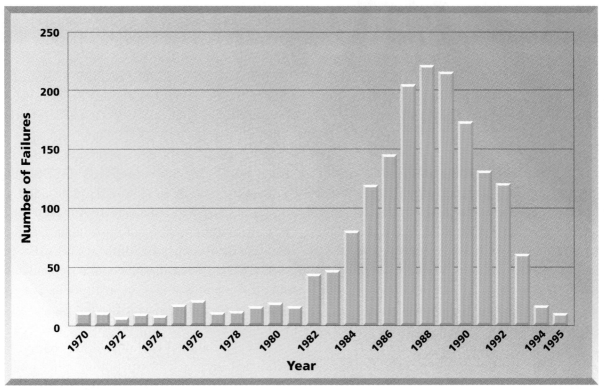

Source: Federal Deposit Insurance Corporation

FIGURE 13.3 More banks failed in the 1980s than in any other decade since the Great Depression. **How is bank failure defined?**

Larger banks generally support the expansion of regional banking to full interstate banking, or nationwide banking. Nationwide banking would allow any bank to open branches and to merge with banks in any state. Supporters argue that national banking would create more competitive markets. Further, they note that "bigness" in the banking industry would allow it to benefit from economies of scale.

Financial Troubles in Banking

The third major banking trend of recent years is the stabilization of financial institutions. The need for increased stability could be seen in three main areas: loan defaults, bank failures, and what became known as the savings and loan crisis.

Loan Defaults During the 1980s many people and businesses relied heavily on borrowed money. In some cases they were unable to repay the funds they had borrowed. This failure to make payments on a loan is called a **default**. Although loan defaults occurred in many parts of the economy, there were a particularly large number of defaults among farmers. The Farm Credit System (FCS), a network of 37 banks that offer loans to farmers nationwide through so-called farm banks, suffered from a wave of loan defaults in the 1980s. Many farmers were unable to make payments on property and equipment that had been purchased with FCS credit. Although the Farm Credit System at that time was the largest farm lender in the United States—with about $61.5 billion in outstanding loans—the organization was on the verge of bankruptcy in 1986.

Bank Failures Loan defaults and other financial worries led to more bank failures in the

1980s than in any decade since the Great Depression. A bank fails when it no longer has enough assets on deposit to cover its accounts. Between 1980 and 1985 the annual number of FDIC–insured banks that failed rose from 11 to more than 100. Added to this total are the numerous near failures and banks in serious financial trouble. The trend in bank failures is shown in Figure 13.3 on page 321.

S&Ls in Crisis Perhaps the most visible sign of instability in U.S. banking during the 1980s involved savings and loan associations. A number of factors contributed to the S&L crisis. First, borrowers failed to make payments on many loans granted by S&Ls in the early 1980s. This situation caused some savings and loan associations to fail and others to be absorbed by larger financial institutions.

Another factor contributing to the S&L crisis was that some S&Ls had only private insurance. About 30 states approved private deposit insurance during the mid-1980s, which allowed state-chartered S&Ls to choose private insurance instead of insurance provided by the Federal Saving and Loan Insurance Corporation (FSLIC). By 1986 nearly 18 percent of the nation's S&Ls had chosen private insurance. In some states, however, private insurance plans lacked the financial resources needed to handle S&L failures.

In response, in 1989 President George Bush signed the Financial Institutions Reform, Recovery, and Enforcement Act. This act addressed several aspects of the banking industry, but focused primarily on S&L reform. The act abolished the FSLIC and established the Resolution Trust Corporation (RTC) to stabilize additional S&Ls in danger of collapse. By August 1994 the RTC had straightened out more than 730 S&Ls and was overseeing 11 additional S&Ls. By 1996 the RTC had been dissolved, and deposit insurance for savings and loan institutions was provided by the FDIC—with the tab picked up by U.S. taxpayers.

In 1996 the total cost of the S&L bailout was estimated at nearly $150 billion, plus interest. One economics reporter pointed out that if the money had not been needed for the bailout, it could conceivably have paid for 57,692 M-1 Abrams tanks—seven times the number used by the U.S. Army.

SECTION 3 — REVIEW

1. Define the following terms: commercial bank, savings and loan association, mutual savings bank, debit card, deregulation, default.

2. Describe the main types of financial institutions. Which of these institutions is present in your community?

3. How have automation and the spread of computers made banking more accessible to consumers?

4. How did deregulation affect banks and other financial institutions?

5. How did the U.S. government work to resolve the S&L crisis?

6. **Thinking and Writing Critically**
Suppose that your classroom is a state, and that you and your classmates decide to establish a bank. What services will your bank offer? Will people in other "states" be able to use your bank?

7. **Applying** ECONOMIC INSTITUTIONS & INCENTIVES
Consider the effects of automated banking. Which form of automatic banking seems most useful? Explain your answer.

CHAPTER 13 — SUMMARY

SECTION 1 Money is a key to the economic process. For centuries people have traded and bartered, but the use of money has made more sophisticated transactions possible.

Money has three basic functions: it serves as a medium of exchange, a standard of value, and a store of value. As a medium of exchange, money is accepted in exchange for products. As a standard of value, money provides a basis for price comparison. As a store of value, money can be saved for later use.

Money has five major characteristics: durability, portability, divisibility, stability in value, and acceptability. Durability means that money can be used repeatedly, and portability means that money is easy to move. Divisibility allows money to be divided into smaller units. Stability in value means that money retains its value over time, and acceptability means that people recognize and accept money in exchange for goods and services.

Societies use different items as money. Some societies rely on commodity money, while others use representative money and fiat money. The United States relies on fiat money in the form of coins, paper money, checks, and near money.

SECTION 2 Like money, banking has evolved to meet the needs of a changing U.S. society. Throughout much of U.S. history, the idea of a central bank has been controversial. In the late 1700s the federal government established the Bank of the United States, which operated from 1791 to 1811. The Second Bank of the United States operated from 1816 to 1836.

Problems with the First and Second Banks led to a period of unregulated state banking. Financial panics and the Civil War, however, persuaded Congress to establish a national banking system.

Further troubles and panics led to the development of the Federal Reserve system and the era of modern banking. Under President Franklin D. Roosevelt, economic reforms gave the federal government a larger role in the banking system.

Banking services expanded during the 1960s and 1970s, as banks began to extend more loans to individuals. Additionally, some people felt that their needs were not met by traditional banking practices, and opened specialized banks.

SECTION 3 Americans' banking choices broadened to include a wide variety of financial institutions: commercial banks, savings and loan associations, mutual savings banks, and credit unions. Technological advances have led to automated banking. Federal deregulation has led to competition and reorganization in the banking industry. Additionally, poor lending practices and uncertain insurance programs contributed to the collapse of many financial institutions during the 1980s. By the 1990s the U.S. government had stabilized the banking industry and resolved—often at taxpayer expense—many of the problems that had caused the crisis.

Economics Notebook

Review what you wrote in your Economics Notebook at the beginning of this chapter about your monetary activities. How do recent trends in banking, such as automation and deregulation, affect your activities? Record your answer in your Notebook.

REVIEW

REVIEWING CONCEPTS

1. What are the major functions of money?

2. Identify the types of money used in the United States.

3. Compare the views of Federalists and Antifederalists on banking.

4. How has the U.S. government worked to regulate the banking industry during the 1900s?

5. How has banking changed as a result of automation?

6. How did the U.S. government respond to the S&L crisis of the 1980s?

THINKING AND WRITING CRITICALLY

1. **EXCHANGE, MONEY, & INTERDEPENDENCE** The U.S. government is considering introducing a one-dollar coin to replace the paper dollar. What do you believe would be the pros and cons of using such a coin?

2. **ECONOMIC INSTITUTIONS & INCENTIVES** What were the long-term consequences of the failures of the First and Second Banks of the United States?

3. **ECONOMIC INSTITUTIONS & INCENTIVES** Where would you choose to do your banking—a commercial bank, savings and loan association, mutual savings bank, or credit union? Explain your answer.

4. **ECONOMIC INSTITUTIONS & INCENTIVES** How has deregulation affected your possible financial transactions, such as buying a car and making withdrawals?

YOUR LOCAL ECONOMY

Create a chart that shows the names of local, regional, and nationally chartered banks in your community. Include their locations, types of services, FDIC affiliation, and assets. Write a paragraph explaining which of these banks you would choose for your banking needs and why.

COOPERATIVE PORTFOLIO PROJECT

As a group, develop a banking institution. Compare the services of commercial banks, savings and loans, mutual savings banks, and credit unions. You may want to assign one group member to collect information about each type of institution. Choose which type you will develop, name your institution, and then create an advertisement—designed either for the Yellow Pages or a Web page—that describes its services.

PRACTICING SKILLS: UNDERSTANDING CHARTS AND GRAPHS

Time lines often are used to provide a visual organization of events. Time lines enable people to quickly grasp the sequence of events by displaying them in chronological order. To read a time line, determine the years covered and the intervals into which the time line is divided. Study the sequence of events, and look for relationships among them.

Study the time line on page 325, which shows important developments that led to changes in money and banking in the United States. Then answer the questions that follow.

EARLY U.S. BANKING HISTORY

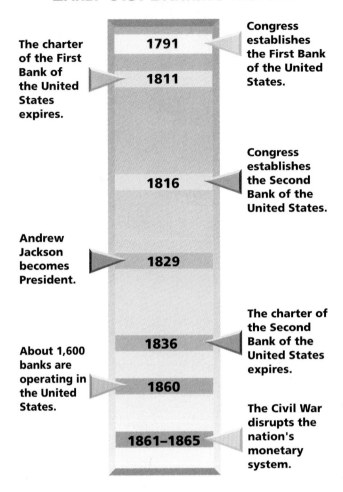

The charter of the First Bank of the United States expires.

1791 — Congress establishes the First Bank of the United States.

1811

1816 — Congress establishes the Second Bank of the United States.

Andrew Jackson becomes President.

1829

The charter of the Second Bank of the United States expires.

About 1,600 banks are operating in the United States.

1836

1860

The Civil War disrupts the nation's monetary system.

1861–1865

1. What period of time does this time line cover?

2. When was the nation's monetary system disrupted?

3. Which happened first—the election of Andrew Jackson to the presidency or the failure of the Second Bank of the United States?

THE INTERNET: LEARNING ONLINE

Conduct an Internet search to gather people's opinions about the European Union's development of the monetary unit known as the euro. You might start by using search words such as *euro* and *European Union*, as well as the names of journals and newspapers such as the *Economist*, the *Washington Post*, the *New York Times*, and the *Wall Street Journal* that would be likely to have editorials on the subject. Write a paragraph explaining why you agree or disagree with the majority of the opinions you read.

ANALYZING PRIMARY SOURCES

Maggie L. Walker

In 1903 Maggie L. Walker founded the St. Luke Penny Savings Bank and became the first female bank president in the United States. When St. Luke's later merged with two other banks to become The Consolidated Bank and Trust Company, Walker served as chair of the new company's board of directors. Today this bank thrives as the oldest continually African American–operated bank in the United States. Read this excerpt from a speech made by Walker in 1901 and answer the questions that follow:

"What do we need to still further develop and prosper us, numerically and financially? First we need a savings bank. . . . Let us put our moneys together; let us use our moneys; let us put our money out at usury [lending with interest charged] among ourselves, and reap the benefit ourselves. . . . Let us have a bank that will take the nickels and turn them into dollars. . . .

"We need to start and operate a factory for the making of clothing for women and children, men's underwear and a millinery [women's hat] store. . . .

"What we need is an organ, a newspaper to herald and proclaim [announce] the work. No business, no enterprise, which has to deal with the public, can be pushed successfully without a newspaper. . . . We have the men, we have the women, we have the brain. Let us form a partnership of heads and brains, and actually do something. . . .

"I have faintly outlined and intimated [hinted at] some of the things we ought to do. . . . We want an executive to run a factory, run a paper, run a bank, that will develop something and give some of the noble women work."

1. Does Walker's vision of a bank most resemble a commercial bank, a savings institution, or a credit union? Explain your answer.

2. Why did Walker plan to establish a newspaper as well as a bank?

3. How were women to benefit from Walker's goal of establishing these businesses?

CHAPTER 14

THE FEDERAL RESERVE AND MONETARY POLICY

E xamine a $1 bill. At the top are the words *Federal Reserve Note*. As discussed in Chapter 13, the Federal Reserve acts as the central bank for the United States. But how exactly does the Federal Reserve system work, and what does it have to do with your money?

In this chapter you will learn about the development and organization of the Federal Reserve system. Additionally, you will learn how the Federal Reserve establishes monetary policy, and what tools are available to the Fed.

✎ Economics Notebook

If you had a checking account containing $100, a savings account containing $250, and a CD worth $500, which would you consider to be "readily available"? Explain your answer in your Economics Notebook.

MARRINER S. ECCLES
FEDERAL RESERVE BOARD BUILDING

1936

THE FEDERAL RESERVE SYSTEM

Economics Dictionary

pyramided reserves

Objectives

▶ How did the Panic of 1907 affect U.S. banking?

▶ What are the purposes and characteristics of the Federal Reserve system?

▶ How is the Fed organized?

When first proposed in 1790, the idea of a central bank was controversial, and it remained so throughout much of U.S. history. Although the First and Second Banks of the United States worked to strengthen and stabilize the national economy, many people felt that a central bank placed far too much economic power in the hands of the federal government.

After the demise of the Second Bank of the United States, the government was not able to charter another central bank during the 1800s. Even a series of recessions during the late 1800s failed to revive public support for a central bank. The Panic of 1907, however, which caused the collapse of many banks and endangered the entire monetary system, broke the historic resistance to central banking.

Panic of 1907

The Panic of 1907 had two causes. First, the nation's monetary system at the time had no mechanism for expanding the amount of money in circulation. This meant that business expansion was restricted because consumers and businesses competed for a fixed supply of loanable funds. As individuals and businesses found themselves unable to borrow money, they began to withdraw their savings. During these "runs" on banks, many depositors withdrew funds from an institution at the same time. As a result, financially stable banks went bankrupt in 1907 because they had nowhere to turn for emergency cash, and a widespread financial panic took hold.

Second, the system of pyramided reserves failed. In a system of **pyramided reserves**, virtually all smaller, local banks deposit some of their reserves at larger city banks. These larger city banks, in turn, deposit some of their own cash reserves in the largest commercial banks in a nation's financial centers, such as New York, Chicago, and San Francisco in the United States. These largest banks use part of these deposits to extend loans and hold the rest as reserves.

During periods of prosperity the larger commercial banks receive more deposits and have more funds to loan. At such times a system of pyramided reserves encourages business expansion. During recessions, however, financial panic runs require smaller banks to withdraw their

FINANCIAL INSTITUTIONS & INCENTIVES *During the Panic of 1907, thousands of people rushed to their banks to withdraw the money in their accounts.* **How did these cash withdrawals cause the collapse of many banks?**

deposits from the larger banks. As happened in the Panic of 1907, the reserves of the larger banks could not cover the sudden demand for cash because they had loaned out too much of the deposits. Thus, many businesses went bankrupt, and many depositors lost their savings.

To keep these two situations from recurring and causing another panic, in 1908 the newly created National Monetary Commission proposed the re-establishment of a central bank. As noted in Chapter 13, Congress recognized the need and responded to the recommendation by passing the Federal Reserve Act in 1913. The act created a central bank called the Federal Reserve system, more commonly referred to as the "Fed." (See Figure 14.1.)

Careers in Economics

Accountant

In the complex worlds of banking, business, and personal finance, perhaps one of the most important jobs is that of accountant. You probably have heard accountants referred to by other names: bean counters, for example, or number crunchers. These names imply that accounting is not a glamorous career. Nevertheless, businesses and banks, like the Federal Reserve system, could not function without accountants.

Accountants perform a variety of vital functions. They collect and analyze data and check the accuracy of financial reports. An accountant may determine, for example, how much profit an auto dealership made last month. The dealership's management would then use that information to make decisions about such things as inventory and the size of the sales staff.

In addition, individuals hire accountants to sort through regulations, calculate tax payments, or advise them on investments. In fact, as tax laws have become more complicated, the demand for services provided by accountants has increased significantly. Banks also rely on accountants to keep track of investments, loans, and other financial transactions.

Accountants make up one of the largest professions in business today. By the 1990s more than 1 million people worked as accountants in the United States. What kind of person makes a good accountant? As you might guess, accountants must have strong math skills and an eye for detail. High ethical standards also are essential, for accountants often work with sensitive, confidential information.

Most accountants have a bachelor's degree in accounting, although large accounting firms sometimes require a master's degree. About one third of accountants become certified public accountants, or CPAs, by passing the Uniform CPA Examination of the American Institute of Certified Public Accountants.

Accountants provide financial analysis and advice to businesses, banks, and individuals.

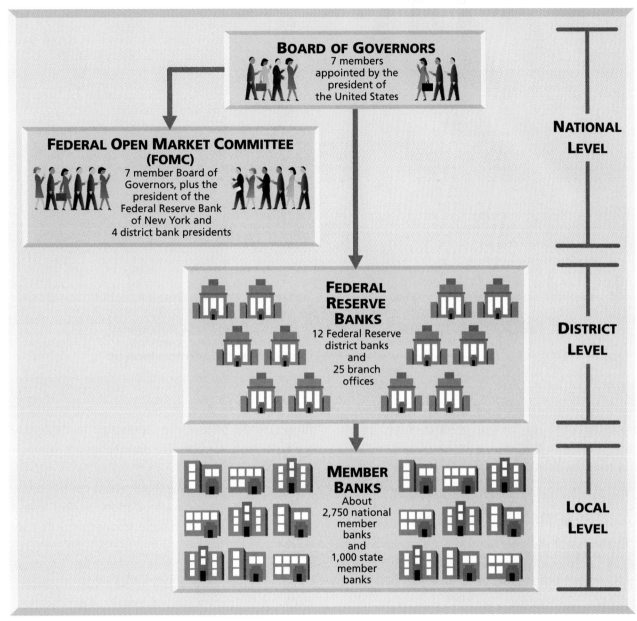

Source: Federal Deposit Insurance Corporation

FIGURE 14.1 The Federal Reserve acts as the central bank for the United States, but is designed in a way that avoids control of the U.S. economy by a limited group of financiers. **How does the Fed stabilize banking on a national level?**

Role of the Fed

The Fed's stated goals were "to furnish an elastic currency, [and] . . . to establish a more effective supervision of banking in the United States." Today the Fed achieves these goals by serving three main purposes.

First, the Fed supervises member banks. Second, it holds cash reserves. These cash reserves represent funds available for short-term borrowing by commercial banks or by the government. The cash reserves guarantee that money is available in the economy when needed. Third, the Fed

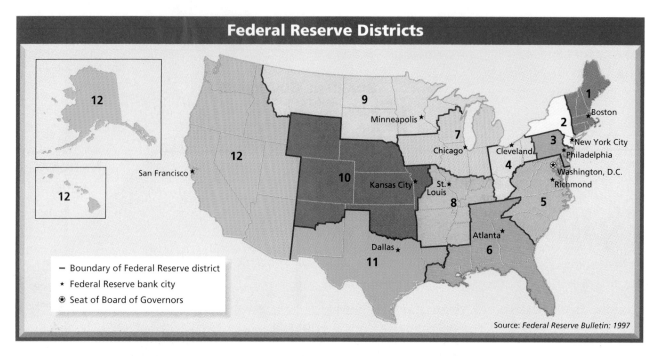

Federal Reserve Districts

Boston
New York City
Philadelphia
Washington, D.C.
Richmond
Minneapolis
Chicago
Cleveland
Kansas City
St. Louis
San Francisco
Atlanta
Dallas

— Boundary of Federal Reserve district
★ Federal Reserve bank city
⊛ Seat of Board of Governors

Source: *Federal Reserve Bulletin: 1997*

FIGURE 14.2 The Federal Reserve system is organized on national and regional levels, with 12 district banks, the Board of Governors, and the FOMC. **Where is the seat of the Board of Governors located?**

moves money into or out of circulation. In so doing, it is able to stabilize the national monetary and banking systems.

Characteristics of the Fed

The Fed is not the only central bank in the world. Many nations around the world, such as the United Kingdom, Japan, and Canada, have central banking systems. The U.S. Federal Reserve system, however, has several features that distinguish it from central banks in other nations. These features include

▶ lack of a single central bank,
▶ ownership and control by the member banks, and
▶ optional membership in the Fed for some banks.

First, in most countries there is a single central bank. The Federal Reserve system, on the other hand, relies on district banks to carry out the banking policies developed at the national level. These district Federal Reserve banks

however, do have some flexibility in designing policies to best meet the unique needs of their districts.

Second, in most countries with a central bank, the government owns all or most of the central bank's stock, allowing tight government control of the central bank. In contrast, the U.S. government does not own stock in the Fed. Instead, member banks own stock in the Federal Reserve banks in their respective districts. In part because this stock is held by member banks rather than by the government, the Fed operates with a high degree of independence from political authorities—although it does ultimately report to Congress.

Third, most nations with a central banking system require all banks within their borders to be members of the central bank. In the United States, all nationally chartered banks are required to join the Fed. For state-chartered banks, however, membership in the Fed is optional. In fact, less than 40 percent of the commercial banks in the United States are members of the Federal Reserve system.

Organization of the Fed

The fact that the Federal Reserve system was designed to oversee banking practices throughout the United States caused many people to be concerned that a single central bank would hold too much power over the nation's economy. To avoid this problem and distribute financial control among different regions, the Fed is organized on two levels: national and district.

National Level The Fed makes its key decisions at the national level. The main decision-making bodies are the Board of Governors and the Federal Open Market Committee (FOMC).

The Board of Governors is the highest policy-making body in the Federal Reserve system. The board supervises the Fed's banking services and issues policies designed to regulate the supply of money in the economy. The president of the United States appoints—and the Senate then confirms—each of the seven members of the Board of Governors.

Each governor is appointed to a 14-year term. These terms are staggered so that one new governor is added to the board every two years. The board's chairperson serves a four-year term. Long terms of office and staggered appointments are designed to free the governors from any political influence by the executive and legislative branches of the federal government, as well as to limit the influence of any one governor.

The seven members of the Board of Governors and the president of the Federal Reserve Bank of New York are permanent members of the FOMC. The remaining four members are district Federal Reserve bank presidents who serve one-year terms on a rotating basis.

District Level The traditional fear of a single bank dominated by a few financiers led to the decision to create 12 separate Federal Reserve banks. Each of these district banks serves a designated geographic region of the United States (see Figure 14.2). In addition, 25 branch offices are located throughout the nation. All commercial banks chartered by the federal government are member banks of the Fed.

The member banks in each Federal Reserve district elect six of the nine directors of their Federal Reserve bank. No more than three of the six directors may be bankers. Other directors often have experience as business owners. The Board of Governors selects the remaining three directors of each bank.

SECTION 1 — REVIEW

1. Define the following term: pyramided reserves.

2. List the major causes of the Panic of 1907, and explain how the government worked to resolve the panic.

3. Explain the role of the Fed. How does the Fed differ from central banks in other countries?

4. Why is the Federal Reserve system organized on national and district levels?

5. **Thinking and Writing Critically** How is the Federal Reserve system designed to be largely independent of the federal government? Why would this separation from elected representatives be desirable?

6. **Applying** ECONOMIC INSTITUTIONS & INCENTIVES Select one of the Federal Reserve district banks and conduct an Internet search to learn more about the Fed. Write a brief paragraph describing the information presented on the bank's Web page.

THE FEDERAL RESERVE AT WORK

Economics Dictionary

check clearing

money supply

Objectives

▶ What services does the Fed provide to banks?

▶ How does the Fed serve the federal government?

▶ How do economists measure the U.S. money supply?

What does the Federal Reserve system do for you? Directly, the Fed does not provide many services to you, for it is not designed to provide services to individuals. Instead, the Fed serves consumers like you *indirectly*—by providing services to commercial banks and to the federal government.

Services to Banks

As you know, one of the Fed's main roles is to supervise and provide services to commercial banks through its 12 Federal Reserve district banks. Although you cannot open a checking or savings account at a Federal Reserve bank, the banking services it provides make transactions at your local commercial bank easier and faster. What Fed activities enable these improvements to commercial banking?

The Fed oversees the flow of money between member banks and its district banks. It does so mainly by clearing checks and by lending reserves to commercial banks.

Clearing Checks Checks are used in millions of financial transactions every day. In fact, Americans write about 40 billion checks every year. The Fed keeps track of these billions of monetary transfers through the service of **check clearing**, which is a method of crediting and debiting banks' reserve accounts—and, in turn, checking accounts.

How does check clearing work? Suppose that you decide to buy a pair of running shoes at Foot Locker. Although the shoes are yours as soon as you write the check, it takes a little longer—and several more steps—to transfer money from your bank account to the store's. Figure 14.3 illustrates check clearing and highlights the Fed's role in the process.

Loans to Banks When you need a loan, you might visit a bank such as Glendale Federal Bank in California or Chevy Chase Bank in Maryland. When a bank or other depository institution needs a loan, it contacts its district Federal Reserve bank. Because their depositors may make large and unexpected withdrawals, banks often need short-term loans to replenish their reserves, or supplies of cash. Federal Reserve banks loan reserves, usually for periods of one day to several weeks.

Most Federal Reserve loans are sought for seasonal factors, natural disasters, and financial emergencies. Seasonal factors are the fairly predictable annual events that deplete reserves in banks. For example, the cash reserves of small rural banks are often reduced during the spring and summer planting and growing seasons when farmers withdraw their cash and apply for loans to pay for farm operations. Similarly, gift purchases during the December holiday season typically involve large withdrawals, and disasters such as floods or hurricanes naturally spur demands for loans. These withdrawals reduce cash reserves in banks. In these cases the Fed often lends money to depository institutions to replenish their reserves. In 1973 the Federal Reserve also established a seasonal credit program to help small banks in particular meet these swings in demand.

In financial emergencies such as a recession, the Fed serves as a "lender of last resort" by making emergency loans to commercial banks. Under special circumstances, a Federal Reserve bank also may extend loans to corporations and individuals who are unable to obtain funding from other financial institutions. To receive a loan from a Federal Reserve bank, financial institutions must meet strict qualifications such as collateral requirements. In deciding whether to make such a loan, the Fed analyzes the effect of the emergency on the national or regional economy. It then makes only those loans considered vital to the economic well-being of the region or

THE FED AND CHECK-CLEARING

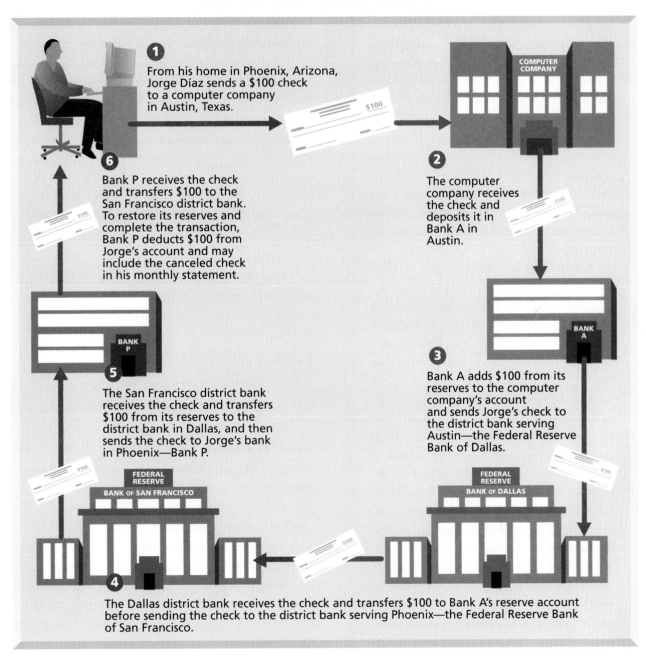

1 From his home in Phoenix, Arizona, Jorge Díaz sends a $100 check to a computer company in Austin, Texas.

2 The computer company receives the check and deposits it in Bank A in Austin.

3 Bank A adds $100 from its reserves to the computer company's account and sends Jorge's check to the district bank serving Austin—the Federal Reserve Bank of Dallas.

4 The Dallas district bank receives the check and transfers $100 to Bank A's reserve account before sending the check to the district bank serving Phoenix—the Federal Reserve Bank of San Francisco.

5 The San Francisco district bank receives the check and transfers $100 from its reserves to the district bank in Dallas, and then sends the check to Jorge's bank in Phoenix—Bank P.

6 Bank P receives the check and transfers $100 to the San Francisco district bank. To restore its reserves and complete the transaction, Bank P deducts $100 from Jorge's account and may include the canceled check in his monthly statement.

FIGURE 14.3 One of the Fed's primary functions is to service commercial banks.
Why must Jorge's check go through both the Dallas and San Francisco district banks?

Global Exchange

Sharing the Wealth

Just as the Federal Reserve system works to stabilize the U.S. economy, the World Bank works on an international level to improve the economies of countries around the globe. The World Bank has been providing funds for economic development since it began operation in 1946.

The World Bank was founded to fund Europe's recovery from World War II. Shortly after its founding, however, the institution broadened its work. Using funds provided by wealthier member countries, the bank has loaned tens of billions of dollars to assist the economies of developing countries around the globe.

When Algeria, for example, needed money in 1997 to increase its farm production and boost employment, its government turned to the World Bank. The World Bank agreed to provide $89 million for programs designed to battle soil erosion and improve the nation's roads. In the process, those projects also created jobs in poor, rural parts of the country.

Among other countries receiving World Bank support is Georgia, a former republic of the Soviet Union. Using World Bank funds, commercial banks in Georgia have made loans to private companies introducing programs designed to improve farm production in rural areas. Additionally, in 1997 the World Bank hosted a meeting at which donors pledged more than $640 million in aid toward the economic recovery of Sierra Leone, a West African country whose economy had been damaged during five years of civil war.

nation. All institutions that borrow often from the Fed become subject to financial review and close supervision by the federal government.

Services to Government

What is your budget? Think about how much money you earn and how much you spend every year. Each year the U.S. government raises and spends more than $1.5 trillion. The Treasury Department and the Fed generally work together to manage this vast sum and the government's complex financial activities.

What role does the Treasury Department play in this task? Think of the Treasury Department as the U.S. government's banker. The secretary of the treasury is the chief financial officer for the government and ensures that the U.S. Treasury pays all the government's bills. Through the Internal Revenue Service (IRS) and the U.S. Customs Service, the Treasury Department collects taxes. Through the U.S. Mint and the Bureau of Engraving and Printing, it produces coins and currency.

How does the Fed work with the Treasury? The Fed's role in managing the government's financial activities consists of providing the following services:

▶ serving as the government's bank
▶ supervising the Fed's member banks
▶ regulating the national money supply

Serving As the Government's Bank If the Treasury Department is the government's banker, then the Fed is the government's bank. That is, the Fed's banking services to government are similar to those that banks provide to individuals.

How does the Federal Reserve act as the government's bank? First, the Fed serves as the depository for federal revenues. Government funds are deposited in Federal Reserve banks by the Treasury. Second, the Fed holds a Treasury checking account on which the Treasury writes checks to cover tax refunds, Social Security payments, and all other government payments. Third, the Fed records the deposits and withdrawals of federal funds and conducts the purchase and sale of government securities such as Treasury bills. Finally, the Fed advises the legislative and executive branches of government on developing a coordinated economic program.

Supervising Member Banks The Fed also functions as the banking system's "watchdog." Each of the 12 Federal Reserve banks has a staff of bank examiners that supervises the financial activities of member banks. These examiners monitor loans and investments and conduct reviews of bank records. All financial depository institutions are required to maintain cash reserves to guarantee that depositors can withdraw their money when needed. The Fed monitors the reserves held by member banks, ensuring that these banks have enough money to meet withdrawal requests. In addition, the Fed regulates bank mergers and the chartering of bank holding companies to ensure that individual commercial banks do not gain too much power over the U.S. economy.

Regulating the Money Supply The Fed's third key function is the regulation of the nation's **money supply**, or the amount of money circulating in the U.S. economy. As noted in Chapter 13, the United States relies on a single form of currency. This money is produced in two forms: Federal Reserve notes—dollars—which are printed by the Treasury Department's Bureau of Engraving and Printing, and coins, which are generated by the U.S. Mint. The 12 Federal Reserve banks distribute this currency.

New currency is put into circulation for two major reasons. One reason is to replace old and worn-out notes, which eventually are destroyed. Banks regularly ship worn-out notes to their district Federal Reserve bank in exchange for new notes. The other reason is to increase the amount of money in circulation by expanding the pool of cash that the Federal Reserve banks can loan.

How does the Fed increase or decrease the U.S money supply? On behalf of the entire system, the Federal Reserve Bank of New York buys and sells U.S. government securities on the open

COMPONENTS OF THE MONEY SUPPLY, 1995

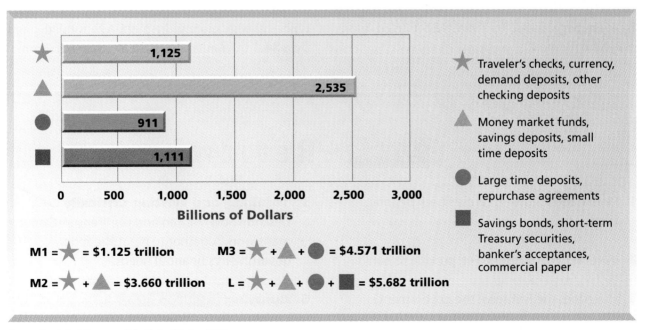

Source: *Statistical Abstract of the United States: 1996*

FIGURE 14.4 The most common measures of the money supply are M1 and M2. **What additional components are included in M3 and L?**

market. Trading in securities allows the Fed both to increase or decrease the money supply and to provide the government with the cash it needs to finance public goods and services. The process by which the Fed trades securities is discussed in greater detail in Section 3.

Money Supply

Before taking action to regulate the money supply, the Fed must determine how much money is circulating in the economy. Economists—those working for the Fed and elsewhere—have determined several ways to measure the nation's money. The two most common measures of the money supply are called M1 and M2. Other measures are called M3 and L.

M1 The narrowest, as well as the simplest, measure of the money supply is M1. Economists who prefer to use M1 believe that the money supply should consist only of funds that are easily accessible and in actual circulation. Thus, M1 counts all the currency in circulation, the value of all traveler's checks, all checking account deposits, and similar accounts in financial institutions. Checking and checking-type accounts represent nearly 63 percent of the M1 total. (See Figure 14.4 on page 335.) In 1995, M1 totaled more than $1 trillion.

M2 A broader measure of the money supply is M2, which totaled more than $3.6 trillion in 1995. Some economists insist that M1 does not include all readily available funds. They consider M2 to be more accurate because in addition to the money counted in M1, M2 includes money market accounts, money market mutual fund shares, and other savings deposits—such as certificates of deposit (CDs) in amounts under $100,000—that allow people easy access to their funds.

M2 also includes money deposited in savings accounts. The development of automated teller machines (ATMs) has allowed savings accounts to serve some of the same purposes as checking accounts. As noted in Chapter 13, ATMs allow depositors instant access to their savings accounts, turning those savings into spendable funds.

M3 and L Other economists believe that even M2 fails to accurately measure the money supply. They rely on either M3 or L, which are broader measures than M2. M3 includes the money in M2 as well as all large time deposits, such as CDs valued at $100,000 or more. L, meanwhile, includes these M3 amounts as well as savings bonds, short-term Treasury securities, and other types of near money. In 1995 M3 totaled more than $4.5 trillion, and L more than $5.6 trillion.

SECTION 2 —REVIEW

1. Define the following terms: check clearing, money supply.

2. What services does the Fed provide to banks?

3. How does the Fed serve the government?

4. What are the four different measurements of the U.S. money supply? Which funds are included in each measurement?

5. **Thinking and Writing Critically**
Describe how the Fed and the Treasury Department work together to meet the federal government's financial needs.

6. **Applying** EXCHANGE, MONEY, & INTERDEPENDENCE
Explain how the development of automated banking has led some economists to consider M1 to be too limited a measure of the nation's money supply.

MONETARY POLICY STRATEGIES

Economics Dictionary

monetary policy
easy-money policy
tight-money policy
discount rate
prime rate
reserve requirement
margin requirement
moral suasion

Objectives

▶ Why does the Fed rely on either an easy-money policy or a tight-money policy?

▶ How does the Fed make monetary policy?

▶ What are the challenges associated with determining monetary policy?

The services provided by the Federal Reserve make the U.S. monetary and banking systems more efficient and sound. The major goal of the Fed, however, is to promote the goals of economic growth and stability. The Fed tries to achieve this goal through the use of monetary policy.

Monetary Policy and Aggregate Demand

Through its monetary policy, the Fed regulates the amount of money and credit available in the economy. **Monetary policy** is the plan to expand or contract the money supply in order to influence the cost and availability of credit. By regulating the money supply and the interest rates charged for credit, the Fed influences aggregate demand. As noted in Chapter 11, aggregate demand is the total demand for all products in the economy. As you also know, demand requires that consumers be willing and able to buy a product. Aggregate demand has the same requirements, but reflects demand for all goods and services in the U.S. economy rather than for a particular product.

The Fed measures both the money supply and aggregate demand in order to develop a monetary policy. Based on the amount of money and the spending habits of people across the United States, the Fed adopts either an easy-money policy or a tight-money policy.

Easy-Money Policy An **easy-money policy** is designed to expand the money supply, increase aggregate demand, create jobs and thus reduce

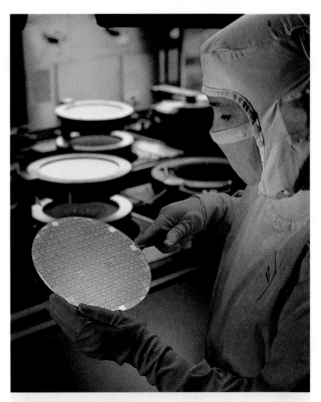

MONETARY POLICY *The popularity of computers has made silicon chips such as these a significant part of aggregate demand.* **How does the Fed influence aggregate demand?**

MONETARY POLICY *In 1997 Fed chairman Alan Greenspan was criticized for over-reacting to fears of inflation.* **What monetary policy did Greenspan support at that time?**

may determine that inflation is likely to develop because too much money is circulating and credit is too accessible. To restrict or contract the money supply and thus limit credit, the Fed adopts a tight-money policy. A **tight-money policy** is characterized by higher interest rates and a contraction of the money supply, both of which are designed to reduce aggregate demand.

Suppose that Jack Hendricks wants to buy a new dishwasher. He discovers that interest rates on loans have increased. Jack decides to delay his purchase until interest rates decline. As other consumers also postpone purchases, aggregate demand declines.

unemployment, and promote economic growth. The Fed usually adopts an easy-money policy during a recession because the economy needs a financial boost. By charging banks a lower interest rate to borrow money, the Fed makes more money available to those banks. When banks pay less in interest on loans from the Fed, they are able to lower the interest rates they charge their customers.

When banks charge lower interest rates, people and businesses borrow more money. Increased borrowing and spending in turn stimulate economic growth as businesses make more products and hire more workers. Businesses then expand by investing new capital.

Suppose that the Fed charges a lower interest rate to banks, and as a result bank interest rates on car loans drop from 8 percent to 6.5 percent. Samantha Shapiro decides that because interest rates are lower, she can afford to borrow money to buy a car. As other consumers make similar decisions, demand for cars increases. Automobile producers hire more workers and provide more cars. These workers have new income and further stimulate aggregate demand.

Tight-Money Policy In contrast to an easy-money policy, a tight-money policy slows business activity and helps stabilize prices. The Fed

CASE STUDY

Alan Greenspan and Tight-Money Policy

MONETARY POLICY Alan Greenspan, chairman of the Federal Reserve's Board of Governors since 1987, is a strong supporter of tight-money policy. He believes that decreasing the amount of money in circulation and reducing the rate of economic growth will maintain price stability.

For example, in February 1995, reports indicated that the U.S. economy was enjoying its highest rate of economic growth in 10 years. Rather than allow this to continue, the Board of Governors—under Greenspan—introduced policies to slow the economy.

Why would the Fed not want the economy to grow even further? Economic growth causes demand for goods and services to rise, and when demand outpaces supply, prices tend to inflate. To prevent inflation, Greenspan raised the interest rate that the Fed charges banks. Banks were less willing to borrow money, so the money supply was tightened.

Continuing this tight-money policy, in 1997 Greenspan warned that stock prices were rising too quickly. Some economists predicted that the Fed would raise interest rates if the market did not stabilize. After warnings over several months, the Fed adopted policies to increase interest rates.

Components of Monetary Policy

How does the Fed put monetary policy to work? There are several ways the Fed can influence the money supply, the availability of credit, and aggregate demand. The key components of the Fed's monetary policy are open-market operations, the discount rate, and the reserve requirement. The Fed also has other formal and informal ways to affect aggregate demand in the economy, including margin requirements, credit regulation, and moral suasion. Figure 14.5 summarizes the Fed's monetary policy tools.

Open-Market Operations The main tool of the Fed is open-market operations, or the buying and selling of government securities. The Federal Open Market Committee (FOMC) makes decisions to buy or sell government securities based on the monetary policy set by the Board of Governors. The Federal Reserve Bank of New York conducts the transactions through private securities dealers, who buy and sell billions of dollars worth of government securities in a single day.

How does the Fed decide whether to buy or to sell government securities? If the Fed wants to contract the money supply, it does so by selling government securities. The cash paid for the securities is ultimately withdrawn from bank reserves, thus shrinking the money supply and decreasing aggregate demand.

When the Fed wants to inject money into the economy, on the other hand, it buys back government securities. The buy-back money paid for these securities ultimately winds up in individuals' and businesses' bank accounts, increasing cash reserves and loan pools. When the government buys securities directly from a bank, the bank's reserves similarly are increased. Either way, the money supply expands. As more money enters circulation, banks make more consumer loans, enabling consumers to purchase more goods and services. To meet this increase in aggregate demand, production rises and the supply of goods and services increases.

Discount Rate A second major component of the Fed's monetary policy is the **discount rate**, the interest rate that the Fed charges member

SUMMARY OF MONETARY POLICY TOOLS

Formal Tool	Fed Action →	Effects on Economy →	Money Supply
Open-Market Securities	buys government securities	bank reserves increase; aggregate demand and production increase	expands
	sells government securities	bank reserves shrink; aggregate demand decreases	contracts
Discount Rate	lowers discount rate	encourages banks to borrow from the Fed; bank reserves increase	expands
	raises discount rate	discourages banks from borrowing from the Fed; bank reserves decrease	contracts
Reserve Requirement	lowers the reserve requirement percentage	banks hold fewer reserves and extend more loans; interest rates fall; aggregate demand and production increase	expands
	raises the reserve requirement percentage	banks hold more reserves and extend fewer loans; interest rates rise; aggregate demand and production decrease	contracts

FIGURE 14.5 The Fed works to promote economic growth and stability through its monetary policy. **Describe how the Fed can use these tools to enact an easy-money policy.**

Building Businesses in the Inner City

Business decisions can be complicated matters, whether one works with the Federal Reserve or sells pastries from a cart on a street corner. In fact, one of the most important resources for business owners is the information they need to make smart decisions about their companies.

The Initiative for a Competitive Inner City (ICIC) was created to meet this need for businesses in inner-city neighborhoods. The national nonprofit organization works to encourage economic development in low-income areas. One ICIC program, for example, matches students in graduate business schools with businesses in inner cities.

Many business owners in inner-city neighborhoods do not have formal business training and often are too busy running their businesses to plan for the future. "Some places are losing money, but they don't know where the holes are," says graduate student Ileana Scheytt. To improve the economic health of these small businesses, students in the ICIC program provide owners with free advice on such things as marketing, borrowing money, and keeping good records.

Scheytt, for example, worked as a consultant to businesses in Harlem while earning a master's degree in business administration (MBA) at Columbia University in the mid-1990s. Harlem, a predominantly African American neighborhood in New York City, has a rich cultural history spanning more than 80 years. Besides being home to the Apollo Theater and a thriving music scene, it has produced many well-known authors. Since World War II, however, overcrowding, racial discrimination, and other factors have made Harlem one of this country's poorest neighborhoods.

Columbia business school students use their knowledge to help bring new vitality to Harlem businesses by conducting market surveys, developing business plans and by providing other such services. Students have worked with institutions such as the Dance Theater of Harlem, the Madame Alexander Company (maker of a line of collectible dolls), and Georgie's Pastries.

Among the most important tasks for the students was helping to make it easier for Harlem businesses to get the capital that they need to grow. To that end, Columbia Business School students designed a small-business loan program for the neighborhood's Carver Federal Savings Bank. In 1996 the bank's first small-business loan helped a local restaurant, the West Indian Eatery, buy needed equipment to expand its operation.

The ICIC has developed similar consulting programs at more than 30 business schools across the country, including the Yale School of Management in New Haven, Connecticut, and the University of Washington in Seattle. All provide consulting services that help business owners in disadvantaged neighborhoods.

What Do You Think?

1. Why is it important that businesses in inner-city neighborhoods get the help they need to be successful and grow?
2. What institutions besides colleges and universities can help businesses in disadvantaged neighborhoods thrive?

Patti Lewis, president of the Alexander Doll Company, received business advice from the Initiative for a Competitive Inner City.

banks for the use of its reserves. It adjusts the discount rate to encourage or discourage borrowing. The Fed extends short-term loans to commercial banks to help them maintain sufficient cash reserves. Banks generally attempt to borrow from the Fed only after they have exhausted all other methods of meeting their temporary cash shortfalls.

Lowering the discount rate encourages banks to borrow, increasing the reserves that banks can in turn loan to businesses and individuals. Conversely, increasing the discount rate discourages banks from borrowing from the Fed.

Changes in the discount rate can directly effect the interest rates charged by banks and other financial institutions. Banks and other lenders often pass on the savings from decreases—or costs from increases—in the Fed's discount rate to their customers by lowering or raising their prime rate. The **prime rate**, the interest rate that commercial banks charge on loans to their most reliable business customers is then used to determine the bank's general interest rate. (See Figure 14.6.) As interest rates fall and consumers and businesses take out more loans, the money supply increases. Why? An interest rate is the "price" of borrowing money. When the Fed lowers the discount rate on loans—charging

commercial banks a lower price for borrowed money—banks then can decrease the interest rates they charge individual borrowers.

Reserve Requirement A third part of the Fed's monetary policy is its reserve requirement. The **reserve requirement** is the money that must be held by banks either in their own vaults or in their accounts at the district Federal Reserve bank. As you have learned, the reserve requirement ensures that banks can meet demand requests.

The reserve requirement is a percentage of each member bank's total net transaction accounts. In other words, the Fed determines how much money is in transaction accounts in each member bank, and requires the bank to hold a percentage of that total in reserve.

In 1997 the reserve requirement was 3 percent on all such funds on deposit up to $49.3 million and 10 percent on funds over that amount. Banks are not required, however, to hold reserves on time deposits and other accounts that are less liquid than checking accounts.

The Fed can increase or decrease the money supply and influence aggregate demand through its control of the reserve-requirement percentages. When the Fed lowers the percentage, banks

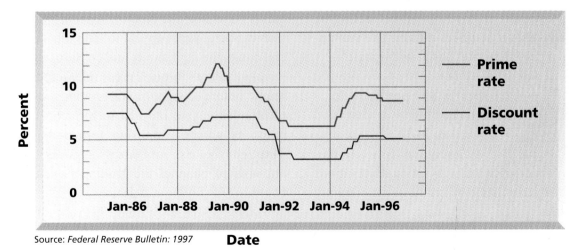

DISCOUNT RATE AND PRIME RATE

Source: *Federal Reserve Bulletin: 1997*

FIGURE 14.6 Changes in the Fed's discount rate can affect the interest rate charged by banks and other lending institutions. **During what period did the prime rate rise despite no change in the discount rate?**

do not need to hold as large a portion of their deposits as reserves. The result is that banks can extend more loans. The combination of more money and easier credit produced by the easy-money policy serves to increase aggregate demand and production in the overall economy.

By raising the percentages of the reserve requirement, on the other hand, the Fed forces banks to hold a larger portion of their deposits as reserves. This enables banks to cut back on their lending, thus contracting the money supply. As the supply of loanable funds shrinks, interest rates rise. As a result, aggregate demand and production slow down. The Fed uses such a tight-money policy to fight inflation.

The percentage requirements change annually according to a formula specified in the Monetary Control Act of 1980. The Fed does not often make frequent or dramatic changes to the reserve requirement, however, because such changes would create uncertainty in the banking system, thus making it more difficult for banks to make long-term loans and investments.

Margin Requirements The Fed also places indirect controls on credit as part of tight-money or easy-money policy. The Securities Exchange Act of 1934 authorizes the Board of Governors to set **margin requirements**, the percentage of cash an investor must have to buy stocks, options, and other investments. If, for example, the margin requirement is set at 60 percent of the stock's value, the investor must put up 60 percent of the investment's purchase price in cash. The remaining 40 percent can be purchased with credit.

Suppose that Elise Donovan wants to buy 100 shares of a stock priced at $10 per share for a total of $1,000. She will need to pay at least $600 in cash, buying no more than $400 of stock with credit. The goal of margin requirements is to prevent the occurrence of wild price fluctuations caused by over-reliance on credit in the purchase of securities.

A high margin requirement discourages investment in the stock market. Low margin requirements, on the other hand, may make stock investing more popular. Since the stock market

crash of 1929, the Fed generally has set relatively high margin requirements.

Credit Regulation A second indirect control is the Fed's power to regulate consumer credit in times of national emergency. During World War II and the Korean War, for example, the Fed required high down payments and shorter repayment schedules for consumer loans. These requirements limited the availability of credit, as many people were unable to meet the requirements. As credit became more expensive, fewer people chose to buy consumer goods. The new, lower level of aggregate demand led producers to reduce supply. The government then was able to encourage many suppliers to produce war-related products.

The Fed coordinated its consumer credit policies with its easy- or tight-money policies. Suppose that Evelyn Ogata decides to borrow money so that she can convert her garage into a spare bedroom. Under an easy-money policy, she is able to arrange for a long loan repayment period. If she borrows money while a tight-money policy is in place, however, she may have to make higher payments over a shorter period of time. The Fed's ability to regulate credit was revoked in 1952.

Moral Suasion In addition to its official tools, the Fed can informally restrict aggregate demand in the U.S. economy. **Moral suasion** refers to the unofficial pressures that Federal Reserve policy makers exert on the banking system. Moral suasion can be a direct appeal to individual commercial banks through letters and conferences, public announcements through press releases, and testimony before congressional committees. These techniques enable the Fed to influence banking practices without imposing formal regulations. Through the use of moral suasion, the Fed attempts to channel the lending policies of all banks in the direction it desires.

Policy Limitations

The enormous size of the U.S. economy presents a number of obstacles that the Federal Reserve

MONETARY POLICY *The difficulty of economic forecasting is one of the main challenges to effective monetary policy.* **Why must the Fed make economic forecasts?**

must deal with in order to carry out its duties. The Fed's main challenges are

▶ economic forecasts,
▶ time lags in developing and carrying out monetary policy,
▶ priorities and trade-offs,
▶ lack of coordination among government agencies in formulating economic policies, and
▶ conflicting opinions about monetary policy.

Economic Forecasting

To develop monetary policy, the Fed first must create an economic forecast, or a prediction of future business activity and consumer spending. Will automobile production increase or decrease? How many laptop computers will be sold? Will consumers buy more gasoline? These economic forecasts provide the assumptions on which the Fed's policies are made. Making these forecasts is a difficult task, however, because the U.S. economy includes millions of economic actors, products, and markets. Incorrect forecasts can lead to inappropriate policies.

Time Lags

Once an economic forecast is developed, time passes before policies go into effect. These time lags are the unavoidable delays that occur before government agencies are able to put their policies into action. Three types of time lags disrupt the effectiveness of the Fed's monetary policy.

First, collecting and studying the tremendous amount of economic data needed for analysis and action by the Federal Reserve can take months. Second, once the data have been studied, time-consuming discussions occur before agreement on an appropriate monetary policy is reached.

Third, additional months may pass before the impact of the monetary policy is felt throughout the economy. Consumers and businesses need time to adjust their buying and selling decisions to tight-money or easy-money policies. Aggregate demand and business activity seldom react instantly to the Fed's actions.

Priorities and Trade-Offs

A third limitation on monetary policy is that it cannot do more than it is designed to do. Monetary policy is designed primarily to fight either inflation or recession. In some cases certain economic policies used to remedy one problem may make another problem worse. For example, an easy-money policy fights the problems of recession but often causes an increase in inflation. Conversely, a tight-money policy is effective in combating inflation, but it tends to decrease business activity and contribute to recession. The Fed must weigh trade-offs and establish priorities for the nation's various economic challenges to develop an effective economic policy.

Lack of Coordination

A fourth limitation on the Fed's actions is that other government agencies sometimes target different economic priorities than those identified by the Fed. This lack of coordination among government agencies can hinder economic stability and often sends mixed signals to the market.

During the early 1980s, for example, some economists believed that both the government's

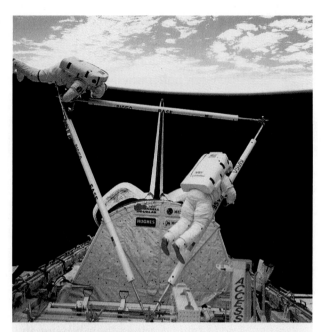

MONETARY POLICY *Lack of coordination among government agencies can send mixed signals to the market.* **How might government spending on programs such as space exploration contradict the Fed's policies?**

monetary policies and its fiscal policies seemed to contradict one another. The Fed's tight-money policy, targeting inflation as the nation's chief economic problem, sought to restrict the money supply and reduce aggregate demand. At the same time, however, Congress and the president approved massive tax reductions and federal spending hikes. These actions increased demand and total spending in the economy.

Conflicting Opinions A final limitation on monetary policy effectiveness is the disagreement some economists have about the Fed's priorities. For example, monetarists are economists who believe economic growth and stability result from regular, long-term alterations to the money supply. Monetarists argue that the Fed's manipulation of the money supply and aggregate demand damages the economy rather than improving it. Monetarists believe that the Fed should increase the money supply by an established amount each year rather than responding to short-term ups and downs in the economy.

The disagreement over the goals of U.S. monetary policy among policy makers underscores the fact that economics is not an exact science like physics or chemistry. Because of this lack of certainty, the Federal Reserve and other government agencies cannot develop policies that consistently solve all of the complex economic issues in the United States.

SECTION 3 — REVIEW

1. Define the following terms: monetary policy, easy-money policy, tight-money policy, discount rate, prime rate, reserve requirement, margin requirement, moral suasion.

2. What are the goals of an easy-money policy by the Fed? of a tight-money policy?

3. What tools does the Fed use to enact monetary policy?

4. What obstacles can hinder the Fed's monetary policy?

5. **Thinking and Writing Critically** How has moral suasion influenced your economic activities or other aspects of your daily life? Explain your answer.

6. **Applying** ECONOMIC INSTITUTIONS & INCENTIVES
   Conduct an Internet search on a topic such as easy-money and tight-money policies, the reserve requirement, the discount rate, or the prime rate. What information is available online about these subjects? Discuss your findings with other members of your class.

SECTION 1 Before 1913 central banking had a stormy history in the United States. Repeated panic runs—notably the Panic of 1907—and other banking problems led to the creation of the Federal Reserve system in 1913.

The Federal Reserve system, or the "Fed," acts as the central bank of the United States. The Fed provides commercial banks and the government a reliable source of cash, holds ready cash reserves to be used for short-term borrowing by these institutions, and makes large loans to these institutions to stabilize the national monetary and banking systems.

Several features distinguish the Fed from central banks in other countries. These include the lack of a single central bank, ownership and control by the member banks, and non-mandatory membership for some banks.

The Fed is organized on district and national levels, and is composed of 12 district Federal Reserve banks. The actions of these district banks are coordinated by a central decision-making authority in Washington, D.C., called the Board of Governors.

SECTION 2 The Federal Reserve system provides a number of banking services in the U.S. economy. The activities of the Federal Reserve can be divided into two categories: services to banks and services to the government.

The Fed oversees the flow of money among member banks and its district banks, mainly by clearing checks and by making loans to commercial banks. The Fed manages the U.S. government's financial activities by serving as the government's bank, supervising member banks, and regulating the money supply.

Economists measure the money supply in different ways. These measures are known as M1, M2, M3, and L. M1 includes the most limited amount of funds, while L includes the widest amount. Each type is distinguished by how it identifies "readily available" money.

SECTION 3 Through its monetary policy, the Fed attempts to promote economic growth and stability as well as to avoid recessions. To reach these goals, the Fed pursues either an easy-money policy or a tight-money policy. Easy-money policy is characterized by low interest rates and is used in times of recession to expand the money supply, increase aggregate demand, create jobs and reduce unemployment, and promote economic growth. A tight-money policy is characterized by higher interest rates and a contracting money supply. It is used during periods of inflation to slow business activity and stabilize prices.

The Fed's three major tools of monetary policy are open-market operations, the discount rate, and reserve requirements. Other methods include margin requirements, credit regulation, and moral suasion. The Fed's actions, however, are limited by several factors, including economic forecasts, time lags in developing and carrying out monetary policy, priorities and trade-offs, lack of coordination among government agencies in forming economic policies, and conflicting opinions about monetary policy.

Economics Notebook

Review what you wrote in your Economics Notebook at the beginning of this chapter. How does your definition of "readily available" compare with the various measurements of the money supply?

REVIEWING CONCEPTS

1. What events led to the development of the Federal Reserve system?

2. How does the organization of the Federal Reserve system avoid placing too much power in a single bank?

3. How does the Fed compare to central banks in other countries?

4. Why is the Fed considered a "lender of last resort"?

5. How does the Fed put monetary policy to work? What are the tools of easy-money and tight-money policies?

6. What are the main difficulties the Federal Reserve encounters when developing monetary policy?

THINKING AND WRITING CRITICALLY

1. **ECONOMIC INSTITUTIONS & INCENTIVES** Why did people in the United States fail to support a central bank for nearly 60 years, despite a civil war and several recessions? Do you think another serious national crisis such as a war or depression might change the way the Federal Reserve system currently works? Explain your answers.

2. **ECONOMIC INSTITUTIONS & INCENTIVES** Do you think the government should control the Fed more directly? Explain your answer.

3. **MONETARY POLICY** If you were responsible for determining the size of the nation's money supply, which measure would you use and why?

4. **MONETARY POLICY** Considering the nation's current economic situation, do you believe the Federal Reserve should rely on an easy-money policy or a tight-money policy? Why?

YOUR LOCAL ECONOMY

Contact a local bank and research its interaction with the Federal Reserve. For example, how do interest rates on loans offered by your bank compare with the discount rate? What is your bank's prime rate? Create a chart or poster that presents your findings.

INDIVIDUAL PORTFOLIO PROJECT

Imagine that you chair the Federal Reserve Board. Write a press release responding to public criticism of the Fed's policy of raising interest rates to slow the growth of the economy. Be sure to address the issue of inflation in your statement.

PRACTICING SKILLS: UNDERSTANDING MEASUREMENT CONCEPTS AND METHODS

Statistics are numerical data. These data often are presented in tables or charts organized into different columns and rows according to topic. Where columns and rows cross, or intersect, the data are related.

Statistical tables allow students of economics to analyze numerical data easily, to recognize relationships, and to make comparisons. Study the table on page 347 and then answer the questions below.

1. What is the subject of the data in the table?

2. What specific information can you learn about the money supply from this table?

GROWTH OF THE MONEY SUPPLY, 1985–1995 (IN BILLIONS)

Year	M1	M2	M3	L
1985	$ 620	$2,498	$3,198	$3,825
1986	724	2,735	3,486	4,122
1987	750	2,834	3,673	4,329
1988	787	2,998	3,912	4,664
1989	794	3,164	4,065	4,894
1990	826	3,282	4,124	4,976
1991	897	3,384	4,178	5,004
1992	1,024	3,439	4,187	5,076
1993	1,129	3,494	4,250	5,165
1994	1,149	3,509	4,320	5,304
1995	1,125	3,660	4,571	5,682

Source: *Statistical Abstract of the United States: 1996*

3. Does the data in the table indicate that from 1985 to 1995 the money supply has (a) increased, (b) decreased, or (c) remained constant?

4. Which measure of the money supply showed the least amount of growth between 1990 and 1995?

THE INTERNET: LEARNING ONLINE

Conduct an Internet search of the Federal Reserve system to learn what publications are available from the Fed and its district banks. Order some of the publications that interest you, and present the contents of one of these publications to the class.

ANALYZING PRIMARY RESOURCES

Federal Reserve Act of 1913 as Amended by the Banking Acts of 1933 and 1934

The Federal Reserve Act of 1913 established and outlined the functions of the Federal Reserve system, with amendments becoming law in 1933 and 1934. Read the following excerpts from the legislation, and answer the questions that follow.

"The Board of Governors of the Federal Reserve System shall annually make a full report of its operations to the Speaker of the House of Representatives, who shall cause the same to be printed for the information of the Congress. . . .

"Federal reserve notes, to be issued at the discretion of the Board of Governors of the Federal Reserve System for the purpose of making advances to Federal Reserve banks through the Federal Reserve agents as hereinafter set forth and for no other purpose, are authorized. The said notes shall be obligations of the United States and shall be receivable by all national and member banks and Federal Reserve banks and for all taxes, customs, and other public dues. They shall be redeemed in lawful money on demand at the Treasury Department of the United States, in the city of Washington, District of Columbia, or at any Federal Reserve bank. . . .

"Federal Reserve notes shall bear upon their faces a distinctive letter and serial number which shall be assigned by the Board of Governors of the Federal Reserve System to each Federal Reserve bank. Federal Reserve notes unfit for circulation shall be canceled, destroyed, and accounted for under procedures prescribed and at locations designated by the Secretary of the Treasury. . . .

"In order to furnish suitable notes for circulation as Federal Reserve notes, the Secretary of the Treasury shall cause plates and dies to be engraved in the best manner to guard against counterfeits and fraudulent alterations. . . . Such notes shall be in form and tenor [meaning] as directed by the Secretary of the Treasury under the provisions of this chapter [the Federal Reserve Act of 1913] and shall bear the distinctive numbers of the several Federal Reserve banks through which they are issued. . . . When such notes have been prepared, the notes shall be delivered to the Board of Governors of the Federal Reserve System subject to the order of the Secretary of the Treasury for the delivery of such notes in accordance with this chapter [the Federal Reserve Act of 1913]."

1. How does the Federal Reserve Act provide for the Fed's accountability to the U.S. Congress?

2. How does the Federal Reserve Act define the purpose and use of Federal Reserve notes?

3. How does the Fed work with the Treasury Department to regulate the issue of Federal Reserve notes?

4. How do Federal Reserve notes reflect the district organization of the Fed?

CHAPTER 15

FISCAL POLICY

Suppose that you work 15 hours a week in a bookstore, earning $5.50 per hour. At the end of the week, you receive a paycheck, which you expect to be worth $82.50. Instead, you find that your check is for quite a bit less money. On your way home you stop at a music store, where you buy two cassettes for $8 each. Although the cost of the cassettes is $16, the clerk says that you must pay $17.12.

Why do you receive less income and pay more for the cassettes than you expect—and where does that money go? The "missing" money goes to the federal, state, and local governments in the form of taxes. The governments use these taxes for programs and policies that serve a wide variety of purposes. In this chapter you will learn how the governments use taxes and fiscal policy to regulate the economy.

Economics Notebook

In your Economics Notebook, list the taxes you have paid during the past month. Have these taxes influenced your spending and saving habits? Write a paragraph explaining your answer.

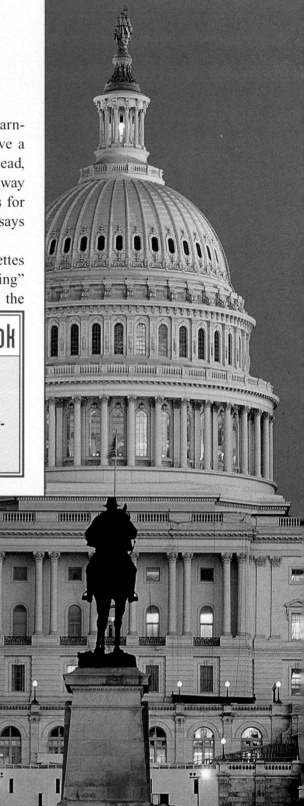

DEFINING FISCAL POLICY

Economics Dictionary
fiscal policy
tax rate
excise tax
estate tax
gift tax
customs duty

Objectives
▶ What role do taxes play in fiscal policy?
▶ What kinds of tax rates do governments set?
▶ Which taxes are the most profitable?

As noted in Chapter 14, the Federal Reserve system uses monetary policy to influence the economy. Another tool the government can use for this is **fiscal policy**—or spending, taxing, and borrowing policies.

The government collects taxes to pay for programs such as road construction, education, and national defense. The government also uses taxes to influence the behavior of individuals. For example, the federal and state governments have placed taxes on products such as tobacco and alcohol in part to discourage people from consuming large quantities of these potentially harmful substances.

Types of Taxes

Taxation is not random. Governments can choose among three basic types of tax rates:

▶ proportional,
▶ progressive, and
▶ regressive.

Whether a tax is proportional, progressive, or regressive depends on the **tax rate**—the percentage of a person's income that goes toward taxes.

Proportional Taxes Some states have proportional taxes, also called "flat rate taxes." A proportional tax takes the same percentage of income from individuals at all income levels.

To understand how this type of tax affects taxpayers, suppose that a state has a 5 percent proportional tax on income. If Nathan Lewis earns $100,000 per year, he pays $5,000 in taxes ($100,000 × 0.05 = $5,000). Stephanie Chisholm earns $10,000 per year and pays the same 5 percent rate, or $500 ($10,000 × 0.05 = $500). Although the tax burden appears to fall equally on all taxpayers, it is probably easier for Nathan to pay the 5 percent tax than it is for Stephanie. Proportional taxes therefore have a greater impact on people with lower incomes.

Progressive Taxes A progressive tax takes a larger percentage of income from a high-income person than from a low-income person. Currently, the main progressive tax in the United States is the federal income tax.

Under current income tax laws, there are different tax rates for people with different levels of income. For example, in 1996 a person with a taxable annual income of $24,000 or less fell into the 15 percent tax bracket, or category. Those individuals who had a taxable income of more than $263,750 were in the highest tax bracket—39.6 percent. These tax brackets cause the burden of the federal income tax to fall more heavily on people with high incomes than on people with low incomes. In addition, income below a certain level is not taxed at all.

Regressive Taxes A regressive tax takes a larger percentage of income from members of low-income groups than from members of high-income groups. Sales taxes are one kind of regressive tax. A sales tax is levied on the sale of some goods or services.

How is a sales tax regressive? Suppose that Dean Hamilton and April Strong each buy a

Global Exchange

Taxes

Since the 1700s Americans have complained about their taxes. Yet how much do they have to complain about compared with other countries?

The tax burden shouldered by Americans is one of the lowest of the advanced industrial countries. In general, all taxes are lower in the United States than in Europe. For example, untaxed gasoline costs about 96 cents a gallon in the United States, while in Britain it costs only 65 cents. When taxes are added to the price, however, British drivers pay about $3.08 for a gallon, while Americans pay only about $1.45. In Sweden, individuals may pay as much as 56 percent of their incomes in national income taxes—compared to a top bracket of 39.6 percent in the United States.

Why do people in other countries pay higher taxes? European governments use tax revenue to fund medical care, mass transportation systems, generous pension plans and unemployment insurance, college educations, and nursing-home care. Europeans tolerate high taxes because they place a high value on having certain goods and services provided by the government.

In every society, citizens and their governments must make decisions about how to use resources. These decisions necessarily involve trade-offs. Obviously, Europeans' trade-offs for extensive social services take the form of high taxes and result in relatively lower personal income. Likewise, Americans' trade-offs for taking home a higher percentage of their earnings are fewer support services for the general public.

paperback book priced at $5.99, with a sales tax of 7 percent. They each will pay $6.41 for the book: $5.99 + ($5.99 × 0.07) = $6.41. The money paid in sales tax, however, is a larger percentage of Dean's $18,000 annual salary than of April's $25,000 salary. With a regressive tax, therefore, the tax burden falls more heavily on people in lower-income groups than on people who earn high incomes.

By 1994, forty-five U.S. states and the District of Columbia had sales taxes, with rates generally ranging from 3 percent to 8 percent. In addition, many cities such as Los Angeles, Chicago, Dallas, New Orleans, and New York City have city sales taxes.

Collecting Taxes

Governments rely on a combination of proportional, progressive, and regressive taxes to collect funds. (See Figure 15.1.) The largest sources of tax revenue are

▶ individual income taxes,
▶ corporate income taxes,
▶ Social Security taxes,
▶ property taxes, and
▶ sales taxes.

Individual Income Taxes The individual income tax is a progressive—and in some cases proportional—tax on a person's income, including wages or salary, interest, dividends, and tips. Individual income taxes are collected by the federal government and most state governments, as well as some local governments. In 1993 individual income taxes provided about 39 percent of federal revenues, about 14 percent of state revenues, and less than 2 percent of local revenues.

Wage earners pay individual income taxes through a payroll withholding system. Employers deduct tax money from employees' paychecks and forward it to the government. Various government agencies—for example, the federal government's Internal Revenue Service (IRS), a branch of the Treasury Department—collect the taxes.

This "pay-as-you-go" system of tax collection also applies to self-employed workers, who pay regular estimated tax payments—approximations of what is owed—to the government.

Corporate Income Taxes

In the United States, governments tax corporate profits. Many corporations pay taxes at reduced rates because they are eligible for tax breaks, such as those designed to promote plant modernization. In 1993, corporate income taxes made up about 9 percent of federal tax revenues, about 3 percent of state tax revenues, and less than one half of one percent of local tax revenues.

Social Security Taxes

Like individual income taxes, Social Security taxes are withheld from workers' paychecks. Withholding of these taxes was authorized by the Federal Insurance Contributions Act (FICA). They are used to finance two social welfare programs. The first is Old-Age, Survivors, and Disability Insurance (OASDI), or Social Security. The second is Medicare, which provides health care to older Americans, regardless of income.

FICA taxes are both proportional and regressive. How can this be true? The FICA tax is proportional because it takes a set percentage of an employee's wages—7.65 percent of incomes up to $57,600 in 1993. Income above that amount is taxed at a lower percentage, making the tax regressive as well as proportional.

For example, suppose that Lily Bell makes $20,000 per year, Matt Levine makes $57,600 per year, and Alicia Fuentes makes $70,000. Lily and Matt will pay the same percentage of their salaries—7.65 percent—in FICA taxes. Alicia will pay 7.65 percent on the first $57,600 of her salary, and a lower percent on the remaining $12,400. The tax burden therefore falls equally on all people making $57,600 or less per year, but less heavily on people making more than $57,600 per year. This means that more of the FICA tax is paid by people who are less able to afford it.

Social Security taxes are the second-largest source of revenue for the federal government. By 1996 they represented 35 percent of the federal government's tax revenue.

Property Taxes

State and local governments also rely on property taxes. Most property taxes apply to houses, factory buildings, condominiums, the land on which these structures are built,

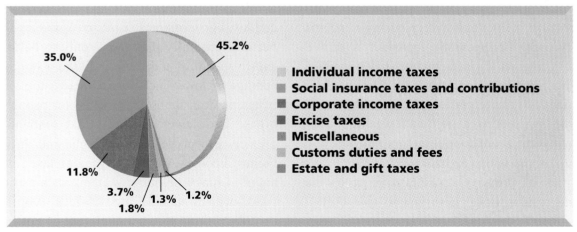

FEDERAL TAX RECEIPTS BY SOURCE, 1996

45.2%
35.0%
11.8%
3.7%
1.8%
1.3%
1.2%

■ Individual income taxes
■ Social insurance taxes and contributions
■ Corporate income taxes
■ Excise taxes
■ Miscellaneous
■ Customs duties and fees
■ Estate and gift taxes

Source: *Economic Report of the President: 1997*

FIGURE 15.1 Governments use proportional, progressive, and regressive taxes to enact fiscal policy. **What are the three largest sources of tax revenue for the federal government?**

State Sales Tax Rates

WA 6.5%
OR 0%
AK 0%
HI 4%
CA 6%
NV 6.5%
ID 5%
UT 4.875%
AZ 5%
MT 0%
WY 4%
CO 3%
NM 5%
ND 5%
SD 4%
NE 5%
KS 4.9%
OK 4.5%
TX 6.25%
MN 6.5%
IA 5%
MO 4.225%
AR 4.5%
LA 4%
WI 5%
IL 6.25%
MS 7%
MI 6%
IN 5%
KY 6%
TN 6%
AL 4%
GA 4%
FL 6%
OH 5%
WV 6%
VA 3.5%
NC 4%
SC 5%
PA 6%
NY 4%
NH 0%
VT 5%
ME 6%
MA 5%
RI 7%
CT 6%
NJ 6%
DE 0%
MD 5%
Washington, D.C. 5.75%

Source: State Services Organization

FIGURE 15.2 Sales tax rates vary considerably among the 50 states. **Why are sales taxes regressive?**

and undeveloped real estate holdings. Some states also collect taxes on personal property such as household furnishings, boats, and jewelry. Local governments rely on property taxes to finance needs such as education, police and fire protection, and sanitation.

Despite its common use by state and local governments, the property tax often is controversial because it does not take a person's income into account. For example, consider a retired couple living on a fixed income and owning a three-bedroom home on a large lot. Despite their fixed income, the retired couple probably would pay more in property taxes than a wealthier couple living in a condominium apartment on a small lot in the same neighborhood.

Critics of property taxes also point to the unequal results. Local governments that collect large amounts of funds through property taxes can provide quality education, recreation facilities, police and fire protection, and other services. Towns and cities that do not raise much money through property taxes, however,

sometimes provide inadequate public goods and services. Although traditionally property taxes make up less than 1 percent of state revenues, they provide more than a quarter of revenues for local governments.

Sales Taxes A sales tax is a regressive tax assigned to certain goods and services by state and local governments. Sales taxes are regressive because generally they apply only to basic consumer spending and therefore take a larger percentage of lower incomes. Although the *amount* of tax paid on items is the same for people with higher and lower incomes, that amount is a greater percentage of a lower income than of a higher income. Additionally, sales taxes do not apply to many higher-cost items such as houses or to services such as attorney fees. People who can afford these products therefore do not experience the same sales tax burden as people with lower incomes.

Some states that have sales taxes do not tax food, medicine, clothing, and other necessities.

Everything Old Is New Again

For many Americans, the suburbs represent an ideal life. Home ownership, quiet neighborhoods, and safe streets have become a pull so strong that New York City's suburbs now reach as far west as Pennsylvania—so that work and home may be separated by nearly 100 miles and the entire state of New Jersey.

This urban sprawl is not limited to the East Coast. Michael Fifield, director of Arizona State University's Joint Urban Design Program, has commented that practically the only thing preventing Phoenix from filling all of Arizona is the city of Tucson.

A number of urban planners and property developers have grown dissatisfied with suburbs. They believe that the familiar elements of suburban development—privacy fences, large lawns, and wide streets—serve as barriers between neighbors. These planners, called New Urbanists, argue that people should be able to live in communities that bring neighbors together, in the style of neighborhoods built before World War II.

How do the New Urbanists want to change the way people live? First, they want to build more homes in less space. Today the typical suburb has between one to three houses per acre. New Urbanism, on the other hand, envisions as many as five or six homes per acre. These homes would involve a mix of architectural styles, such as single-family houses, garage apartments, and apartment complexes.

Living closer to the neighbors means smaller lots. Instead of separately owned stretches of grass, New Urbanist communities generally feature small lawns and gardens—with a large open "common" area within walking distance, so that children have space to play.

Additionally, New Urbanism seeks to prevent the need for long-distance drives to shopping malls and huge discount warehouses. Rather, residents in these communities would be encouraged to walk to nearby local businesses.

The ideas generated by the New Urbanism movement have provided a model for several communities. Seaside, Florida, was built in the 1960s and has influenced other developments such as Kentlands, Maryland, and Laguna West, California. Henry Turley, planner of Harbor Town, Tennessee, wanted to offer a wider range of housing prices to make the community "a slice of the world—the more complete and varied the better." As a result, Harbor Town houses range in price from $114,000 all the way to $425,000.

Not all urban planners believe that New Urbanism will work. Instead, many feel that these communities are more like theme parks than neighborhoods. These people also argue that shops such as corner groceries cannot survive without the brisk business that accompanies population densities like those in Manhattan.

What Do You Think?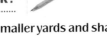

1. Do you think that smaller yards and shared common areas such as town squares would increase contact with neighbors? Explain your answer.

2. Many U.S. cities have strict zoning codes for suburban development. How might this affect potential New Urbanist communities?

Kentlands, Maryland, is one of a growing number of communities designed to promote interaction among neighbors.

FISCAL POLICY *When you bring an item from another country into the United States you generally must pay a tax on that item.* **What is the name of this tax?**

Other Taxes and Revenues Excise taxes, estate and gift taxes, and customs duties represented another 6.2 percent of all federal tax revenues in 1996. An **excise tax** is a tax on the manufacture, sale, or consumption of a particular good or service. The federal government places excise taxes on products such as gasoline, tobacco, firearms, alcohol, telephone services, and tires, as well as various forms of gambling. Excise taxes are regressive taxes because they tend to take a larger percentage of income from members of low-income groups than from members of high-income groups.

Estate and gift taxes are taxes on houses, cars, jewelry, and other personal assets when they are transferred from one owner to another under specific circumstances. An **estate tax** is a tax placed on the assets of a person who has died, and is paid out of the estate rather than by an individual. Federal estate taxes are levied only on estates worth more than $600,000. A **gift tax** is placed on the transfer of certain gifts of value, such as money or other personal property. The gift-giver pays the tax if his or her gifts to an individual exceed $10,000 annually.

A **customs duty** is a tax on imported goods that are brought into the United States from other countries. A customs duty is also referred to as a tariff.

These exemptions soften the economic burden of sales taxes on low- and moderate-income groups. In 1993, sales taxes provided 5 percent of federal revenues, 22 percent of state revenues, and 5 percent of local revenues. (See Figure 15.2 on page 352 for information about state sales tax rates.)

SECTION 1 — REVIEW

1. Define the following terms: fiscal policy, tax rate, excise tax, estate tax, gift tax, customs duty.

2. Explain the importance of taxes to fiscal policy.

3. What are the three types of tax rates?

4. In the United States, what taxes provide the federal, state, and local governments with most of their funds?

5. **Thinking and Writing Critically** Compare proportional, progressive, and regressive taxes. Which seems to be most fair in the way the tax burden is imposed? Explain your answer.

6. **Applying** ROLE OF GOVERNMENT Visit the World Wide Web page maintained by the Internal Revenue Service (IRS). What online services does the IRS provide to taxpayers?

SECTION 2

FISCAL POLICY STRATEGIES

Economics Dictionary

supply-side economics

demand-side economics

tax incentive

investment tax credit

restrictive fiscal policy

expansionary fiscal policy

Objectives

▶ How do supply-side and demand-side theories differ?

▶ What are the chief tools of fiscal policy?

▶ What factors limit the success of fiscal policy?

You know that taxes are an important part of fiscal policy, but how does the government determine that policy? The answer can be found in two schools of economic thought—supply-side economics and demand-side economics.

Supply-Side Economics

What is supply-side economics? **Supply-side economics** focuses on achieving economic stability and growth by increasing the supply of goods and services throughout the economy. Under supply-side economics, the government's role in the economy is limited to providing firms with incentives to increase production. As the supply of goods and services increases, their prices drop. Increased production also requires businesses to hire additional workers, leading to a lower unemployment rate. These workers then spend more money, increasing demand. (See Figure 15.3 on page 356.)

The leading supporter of supply-side thought during its early years was French economist Jean-Baptiste Say (1767–1832). Say is best-known for his statement that supply creates its own demand. According to this theory, producers provide enough goods and services to meet their own needs and produce additional goods and services to exchange for items that meet their wants.

Suppose that Carl Jasper has a computer and a desktop-publishing program. He creates flyers to let people know that he is beginning a desktop-publishing business—in other words, he is advertising the supply of his services. Carl is able to do this because he already has met his own publishing needs. Melissa Hayes sees one of Carl's flyers and decides that she would like him to produce stationery printed with her name and address. Carl's supply, therefore, has created demand for his product.

During the 1980s President Ronald Reagan used many of the ideas of the supply-side economists when formulating his economic policies. Political party conflicts prevented Reagan's supply-side plans from being fully implemented. Instead, tax cuts were accompanied by spending increases.

Elements of Supply-Side Economics What, according to supply-side economists, is the government's role in the economy? Generally, they believe that the government should adopt a laissez-faire approach. In particular, the government should reduce taxes.

Supply-side economists favor tax cuts to encourage individuals and firms to invest in new businesses and products. They argue that tax cuts increase individuals' disposable incomes and corporations' profits, and that some of this "extra" money will be invested. The increased tax revenues from businesses either begun or expanded with the new investment—along with reduced government spending—will offset the loss in revenue from the tax cuts.

Supply-side economists also view many types of government regulation as obstacles to economic growth. They argue that excessive regulations can increase production costs, delay

FISCAL POLICY 〔355〕

FISCAL POLICY MODELS

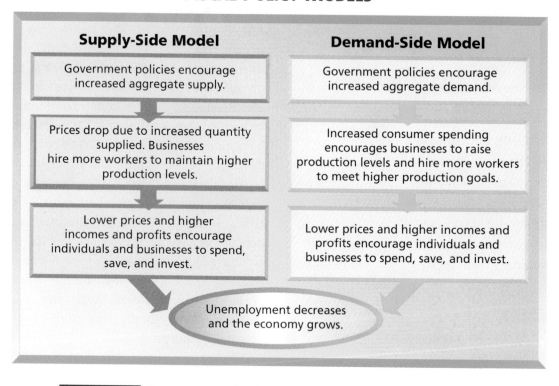

FIGURE 15.3 A government's fiscal policy may be based on either supply-side or demand-side economics. **What goal do these models share?**

construction on public and private projects, and reduce incentives for businesses to develop new products.

Limitations of Supply-Side Economics Why do some people disagree with the ideas of the supply-side economists? Critics of the supply-side model question two major assumptions of supply-side theory.

One assumption of all economic philosophies is that economists can predict the economic behaviors of people. Critics point out the limitations of this assumption. For example, in the 1980s supply-side economists assumed that, for the most part, individuals and firms would *invest* the money they gained through tax cuts. Instead, many people chose to *spend* this money, increasing aggregate demand and inflation.

Second, critics of supply-side economics argue that many of the tax cuts are unfair. During the 1980s, for example, the wealthy benefited more from this tax cut legislation than did the

poor. These critics also point out that spending cuts made along with the tax cuts fell most heavily on social programs for the poor, the unemployed, and other traditionally disadvantaged groups.

Demand-Side Economics

Instead of concentrating on the importance of supply, demand-side economists emphasize the role of demand. **Demand-side economics** focuses on achieving economic growth through the government's influence on aggregate demand.

The "father" of demand-side economics was British economist John Maynard Keynes [KAYNZ]. In 1936 Keynes published *The General Theory of Employment, Interest, and Money*. With this book, he presented a theory that revolutionized economic thinking.

Economists knew that changes in aggregate demand cause fluctuations in the business cycle.

They recognized that when aggregate demand decreases, businesses produce fewer goods and lay off workers, causing a slowdown in economic growth.

Based on his observations of economic activity during the Great Depression, Keynes reasoned that marketplace forces alone were not enough to increase aggregate demand during economic downturns. Instead, he argued that active government involvement was necessary to achieve full employment and improve sluggish business activity.

Demand-side economics received a boost in the United States when Congress passed the Employment Act of 1946. The act pledged to promote "maximum employment, production, and

Careers in Economics

RESEARCHER CD-ROM

Auditor

The mention of an auditor strikes fear into the hearts of many Americans. People often think of auditors solely as Internal Revenue Service (IRS) employees who investigate individuals and businesses to make sure they have complied with the law. In fact, auditors work for private companies as well as the government and their work usually involves routine financial maintenance, rather than pursuing tax evaders.

There are three kinds of auditors. Internal auditors are employed by a company to inspect its financial affairs. Independent auditors work for companies that specialize in auditing. These auditors examine the finances of other companies. Tax auditors are employed by federal and state governments to examine taxpayers' records and assess their tax liabilities.

In general, an auditor's job is to study a business's financial records. They review contracts, business correspondence, and company documents as well as make sure that corporate policies and government regulations are followed. In addition, auditors study ways to improve company operations.

To become an auditor, you must have a bachelor's degree in accounting, although many firms prefer to hire someone with a master's degree in accounting or business administration. Computer and math skills are essential.

The use of computers has increased the need for auditors and changed how they do their job. Computer systems make it easy for companies to gather financial information about their business. Accounting software has eliminated many of the routine mathematical tasks in auditing and made it easier to compile reports. As a result, auditors now spend more time analyzing data, making recommendations on business strategy, and developing better accounting systems.

An auditor reviews a business's financial records to ensure that general accounting practices are followed.

purchasing power" in the U.S. economy. In effect, the act defined economic growth and stability as goals of the federal government. To meet these goals, the government began to use fiscal policy to fight economic downturns, unemployment, and rising prices.

Tools of Fiscal Policy

Although economists may disagree about the relative importance of supply-side or demand-side theories, they rely on the same methods of enacting fiscal policy. The five chief tools of fiscal policy are

- marginal tax rates,
- tax incentives,
- government spending,
- public transfer payments, and
- progressive income taxes.

Tax Rates Congress often uses taxation to regulate aggregate demand in privately owned businesses. Suppose that businesses in many areas of the country begin to lay off workers. For example, if Leena Al-Nasser loses her job with an advertising agency, she probably will reduce her expenses. As other people make similar choices—either because they have been laid off or because they anticipate losing their jobs— aggregate demand declines and the economy moves toward recession. How might Congress respond to this dilemma?

To help reduce unemployment, Congress decreases taxes. This increases people's disposable incomes and allows firms to retain more of their profits. Additional money encourages more total spending, or higher aggregate demand.

To help limit inflation, Congress raises taxes. Higher taxes decrease an individual's disposable income and a corporation's profits. Higher taxes also slow business activity and reduce the chances of "too much money chasing too few goods."

Tax Incentives The second tool of fiscal policy is tax incentives. A **tax incentive** is a special tax break that government extends to businesses to encourage investment in new capital.

One major tax incentive is the **investment tax credit**, which permits firms to deduct from their corporate income taxes a percentage of the money they spend on new capital. To help reduce unemployment, Congress raises the investment tax credit, encouraging businesses to spend more money on expansion and thereby increasing aggregate demand. To help reduce inflation, Congress decreases the investment tax credit, which restricts business activity and thus lowers aggregate demand.

How do tax incentives work? Suppose that Congress sets the investment tax credit at 40 percent in a given year and that Computer Village, an Internet service provider (ISP), invests $1 million in new capital. Under these conditions, Computer Village is able to deduct $400,000 from its income taxes ($1,000,000 $\times$ 0.40 = $400,000). Thus, the real cost of the new capital is only $600,000 because of the $400,000 in tax savings ($1,000,000 − $400,000 = $600,000). On the other hand, if the investment tax credit is

FISCAL POLICY *The Alamodome in San Antonio, Texas, was funded in part by a city tax on public transportation.* **What are the five main fiscal policy tools that governments use?**

Accounting Act. This legislation created the Bureau of the Budget and empowered the president to formulate an annual federal budget and present it for Congress's approval. In 1971 the Office of Management and Budget (OMB), a part of the executive branch, replaced the Bureau of the Budget and was charged with putting together the president's budget proposal. Further budgetary reforms passed in 1974 established a process for the federal government to follow when creating a budget.

The Budget Process Today How is the federal budget created today? First, the budget is developed by the president, who consults with the OMB, the Council of Economic Advisers, the Department of the Treasury, and other presidential advisers. Although the budget may predict revenues and expenditures for several years, it focuses on the next fiscal year. A **fiscal year** is a 12-month financial period that typically does not duplicate the dates of the calendar year.

After the president has prepared the budget, it is analyzed by Congress. Once the budget has been examined and approved by both houses of Congress, it is returned to the president for signing. By the time the budget is returned to the president, many changes may have been introduced. The president may sign the budget if the changes are acceptable, or otherwise may veto it, requiring the process to continue. (See Figure 15.4 for a breakdown of the 1996 federal budget.)

Federal Budget Deficits

In most years since the 1930s, increases in federal spending were not matched by increases in government revenues. In fact, in the years 1990–94 spending exceeded revenues by more than $200 billion annually. When the government spends more money than it collects, a **budget deficit** occurs. A **budget surplus**, on the other hand, occurs when government revenues exceed government expenditures during the fiscal year.

Economists use the term **deficit spending** to refer to the government policy of spending more money for its programs than it is able to cover

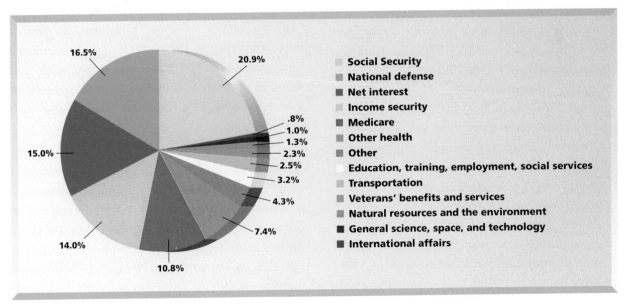

FEDERAL BUDGET, 1996

- Social Security
- National defense
- Net interest
- Income security
- Medicare
- Other health
- Other
- Education, training, employment, social services
- Transportation
- Veterans' benefits and services
- Natural resources and the environment
- General science, space, and technology
- International affairs

16.5% 20.9% .8% 1.0% 1.3% 2.3% 2.5% 3.2% 4.3% 7.4% 10.8% 14.0% 15.0%

Source: *Budget of the United States Government: 1996*

FIGURE 15.4 The federal budget is the federal government's plan for the use of government revenues. **What factors encouraged the U.S. government to institute a formal budget process?**

FEDERAL DEFICIT, 1940–1996

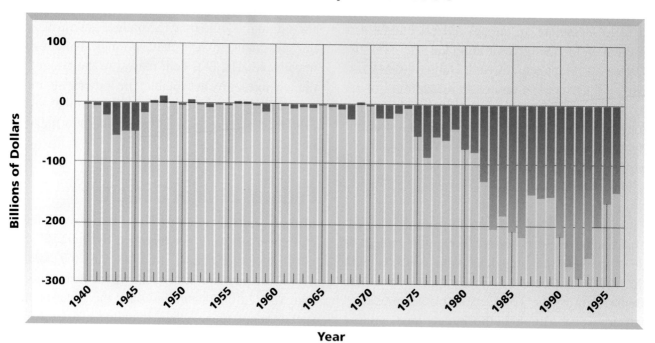

Sources: *World Almanac: 1997; Statistical Abstract of the United States: 1996*

FIGURE 15.5 The U.S. government has spent more money than it has collected—creating a budget deficit—during most years since 1940. **Why does the government rely on deficit spending?**

with its revenues. Figure 15.5 shows that deficit spending has increased dramatically since 1969, the year of the last federal budget surplus. Deficit spending averaged $5.3 billion a year in the 1960s, $36.5 billion a year in the 1970s, and $156.5 billion a year in the 1980s. In 1992 the deficit reached nearly $300 billion.

Why has the government relied on deficit spending? First, national emergencies such as wars frequently have caused an urgent need for vast spending increases. Second, in providing public goods, the federal government has used deficit spending for social programs.

A third reason the federal government has used deficit spending is to stimulate the economy during recessions. During a recession the federal government may decrease taxes and increase spending, thereby putting money into the economy. This process, however, further increases the deficit. The fourth reason for budget deficits has been the federal government's efforts to promote the economic well-being of its citizens.

The National Debt

What happens when you spend more money than you earn? To cover your costs, you probably will need to borrow money. Similarly, to pay for deficit spending, the federal government must borrow money. The **national debt** is the total amount of money that the federal government has borrowed, and includes all deficits from previous years.

Growth of the National Debt Under the U.S. Constitution, the federal government assumed all outstanding debts of the Confederation Congress. In 1790 the national debt was about $75 million. During George Washington's administration the government first decided to sell government securities, a money-raising method that is still used today.

Since Washington's presidency the national debt has risen and fallen. Sometimes federal budget deficits have increased the size of the national debt, and sometimes budget surpluses have reduced it.

The national debt passed the $1 billion mark for the first time during the Civil War. In 1917, the year the United States entered World War I, the national debt was just under $3 billion. Two years later, the debt had climbed to more than $25 billion. Since World War II the national debt has continued to increase steadily. In 1982 it topped the $1 trillion mark and doubled again within four years. By 1996 the national debt had reached more than $5 trillion.

Debt Ceilings Public concern about the size of the national debt has led Congress to approve debt ceilings. A **debt ceiling** legislates a limit on the size of the national debt. The debt ceiling of $11 billion approved during World War I was soon abandoned because of the government's need for additional credit. In 1918 the national debt increased to $12.5 billion, and by 1919 this debt had doubled. The national debt continued to rise, and in 1986 Congress raised the debt ceiling to $2 trillion. By 1996 the debt ceiling had been raised even higher, to $5.5 trillion.

Impact of the National Debt Is the U.S. economy helped or hindered by the national debt? Some economists argue that the benefits achieved from deficit spending—and the resulting rise in the national debt—exceed the costs. They note that government spending on social programs improves the quality of life for many people. Other economists argue that the short-term and long-term economic costs of the debt are severe. For example, in 1995 the federal government paid more than $232 billion in interest on the national debt. These economists argue that annual deficits and the national debt should be reduced so that money used for interest payments could be spent on programs such as national defense, road construction, and education.

Balancing the Federal Budget

The high federal deficits and the rapid rise of the national debt have caused many policy makers to look for ways to balance the federal budget so that expenditures will not exceed revenues. The two ways to balance the budget are to increase revenues and to decrease expenditures. Some policy makers believe that a balanced budget should be required by law.

Increasing Revenues The main tool that the federal government uses to increase revenues is taxation. Many politicians are reluctant to raise taxes because voters rarely want to give more money to the government. In some cases, tax increases may prove unavoidable, however, and Congress passes legislation that changes tax rates and tax brackets. For example, President Bill Clinton signed the 1993 Omnibus Budget Reconciliation Act, which raised individual income tax rates for people in the highest tax bracket. The act also raised taxes on gasoline and provided a number of tax incentives.

FEDERAL DEBT

Dependence Day 1996

FISCAL POLICY *High deficits and the rapid rise of the national debt have caused policy makers to seek ways to balance the federal budget.* **Why are many politicians reluctant to raise taxes?**

Decreasing Expenditures Another way the government can balance the federal budget is by decreasing spending. For example, during the early 1990s a number of U.S. military bases were closed to help reduce spending on national defense. Similarly, of all orders for new aircraft in 1985, about 65 percent were placed by the federal government. By 1993 that number had dropped to 48 percent.

Legislating a Balanced Budget Despite government actions to increase revenues and decrease expenditures, the remedies did not succeed in bringing federal deficits under control during the 1980s and early 1990s. One proposal, the Balanced Budget and Deficit Reduction Act of 1985—also called the Gramm-Rudman-Hollings Act (GRH)—set up a program to balance the budget within five years. This law required automatic cuts to nearly every government program if the budget deficit exceeded a certain amount.

Although the deficits did decline between 1987 and 1989, the GRH deficit targets proved unachievable. A recession in 1990 and 1991 resulted in increased deficits once again. In response, more lawmakers began to call for an amendment to the U.S. Constitution requiring the government to develop and enact balanced budgets.

CASE STUDY

Balanced Budget Amendment

ROLE OF GOVERNMENT In 1995 Congress seemed likely to approve a constitutional amendment that would force lawmakers to balance the federal budget. Beginning in 2002, Congress would be able to rely on deficit spending only in times of war or if three fifths of the members gave their permission.

Although the proposal quickly won approval in the House of Representatives, it was not approved by the Senate. This was not the first time such an amendment had failed. Why do people oppose such amendments?

Opponents of these amendments worry that they would limit the government's ability to maintain many programs or respond to recessions. With a Balanced Budget Amendment in place, the government might be forced to cut spending and raise taxes—even in times of recession. Such actions could make a recession worse. Furthermore, critics argue, a balanced budget amendment would require the government to decrease funding for popular programs. Until Congress can agree on the issues of spending and taxes, it is likely that the debate over this constitutional amendment will be heard again.

SECTION 3 — REVIEW

1. Define the following terms: federal budget, fiscal year, budget deficit, budget surplus, deficit spending, national debt, debt ceiling.

2. Describe the roles played by the president and Congress in developing the federal budget.

3. Why does the government sometimes rely on deficit spending?

4. Why do many policy makers want to balance the federal budget? How might they do this?

5. **Thinking and Writing Critically** Suppose that you have $10 per week to spend on entertainment and $10 to spend on food. What happens if you spend $15 each week on entertainment? How can you balance your personal budget?

6. **Applying** **ROLE OF GOVERNMENT** Visit the World Wide Web page maintained by the White House. What information about the federal budget is available at this Web site?

SECTION 1 In addition to monetary policy, the government uses fiscal policy to influence the economy. Fiscal policy is the use of government income and expenditures to manage the economy.

Federal, state, and local governments in the United States must finance their operations through various kinds of taxes. The federal government raises most of of its revenues through individual income taxes, corporate income taxes, and Social Security taxes. Excise taxes, estate taxes, gift taxes, and customs duties make up a much smaller portion of federal taxes. State and local governments raise revenues primarily through individual income taxes, sales taxes, and property taxes.

SECTION 2 Fiscal policy is influenced by the schools of supply-side economics and demand-side economics, both of which pursue the goal of economic growth. During the 1980s supply-side economics influenced public economic policy in the United States. Supply-side economics concentrates on increasing the nation's aggregate supply. The federal government has often used fiscal policy based upon the demand-side theories of John Maynard Keynes to regulate aggregate demand and promote economic growth and stability in the economy.

The chief tools of fiscal policy are marginal tax rates, tax incentives, government spending, public transfer payments, and the progressive income tax. Fiscal planners use these tools whether they believe in supply-side theory or demand-side theory.

Fiscal policy has several limitations. Timing problems often occur because there are delays in putting policy into effect. Political pressures arise because fiscal policy is developed by elected officials. These officials often are reluctant to introduce unpopular policies such as tax increases and cuts to popular programs. Policies sometimes create undesired effects because economic behavior is often unpredictable. Finally, agencies within the federal government do not always coordinate federal fiscal policies. In addition, state and local governments often have policies that differ from the federal government's fiscal policy.

SECTION 3 Currently, all governments develop budgets to help them plan revenues and the amounts and direction of expenditures. The federal government has full-time executive and legislative offices that work only on the budget.

The budget is developed by the president, in consultation with advisers. This proposal is then analyzed by both houses of Congress. When both houses have approved the budget, it is returned to the president for signing. The president may veto the budget, however, if congressional changes are not acceptable.

Federal spending in particular has grown significantly. Deficit spending since the end of World War II has caused great increases in the annual budget deficits. Some citizens and policy makers believe that an amendment should be added to the U.S. Constitution requiring the federal government to have a balanced budget.

Economics Notebook

Review the taxes you listed in your Economics Notebook at the beginning of this chapter. Now that you have read this chapter, would you change your list in any way? Which governments—federal, state, or local—benefit from the taxes you pay?

REVIEWING CONCEPTS

1. Explain why governments collect taxes, and provide an example of each of the following: proportional tax, progressive tax, regressive tax.

2. How did John Maynard Keynes influence economic thought?

3. What tools do lawmakers use to enact fiscal policy?

4. Why is fiscal policy sometimes difficult to enact?

5. Describe the process of developing and approving the federal budget.

6. What actions might the government take to balance the federal budget?

THINKING AND WRITING CRITICALLY

1. **FISCAL POLICY** How are FICA taxes both proportional and regressive? Considering how the government uses FICA taxes, do you think the tax rate should be changed or remain the same? Explain your answer.

2. **ROLE OF GOVERNMENT** Why is the property tax controversial? Would you prefer to live in a municipality that levies high property taxes or in a municipality that levies low property taxes? Explain your answer.

3. **FISCAL POLICY** Explain the differences between supply-side and demand-side economics. In your opinion, which method works best to create a healthy economy?

4. **ROLE OF GOVERNMENT** Describe the factors that encouraged Congress to pass the Budget and Accounting Act in 1921. What factors might encourage additional budgetary reforms during the twenty-first century?

YOUR LOCAL ECONOMY

What kinds of taxes are levied by your local government? How do you and your family benefit from tax collection? For example, do tax revenues support your education? Explain your answer.

COOPERATIVE PORTFOLIO PROJECT

Develop a "study budget" for your group. Consider your "expenditures"—such as time and the cost of supplies—for homework and other projects during a given week. Then consider your "income" in terms of work completed satisfactorily. Do your group's income and expenditures balance? Explain your answer.

PRACTICING SKILLS: LEARNING FROM VISUALS

Editorial cartoons often are used to influence public opinion about economic, political, and social issues.

Two important techniques that cartoonists use to express their message are caricature—the exaggeration or distortion of physical features—and symbolism—the use of an image to represent an idea, feeling, or object.

Using the guidelines that follow, study the editorial cartoon on page 369 to determine its significance and meaning. Then write a brief paragraph explaining your interpretation of the cartoon.

1. Identify the figures by reading the labels and caption.

2. Identify the symbols and caricatures (for example, the elephant is the symbol of the

Reprinted with permssion, "Star Tribune", Minneapolis

STEVE SACK
Courtesy Minneapolis Star-Tribune

Republican Party and the man beside it is President Bill Clinton).

3. Determine what action is taking place. What is the significance of this action? Why do you think the figures in this particular cartoon are reluctant to open the door labeled "Budget Defict Reduction"?

4. Describe the cartoonist's overall message.

THE INTERNET: LEARNING ONLINE

Some journalists and economists predict that Social Security funds will be used up before younger contributors are scheduled to receive them. Describe how the Social Security Administration's Web page responds to this controversy.

ANALYZING PRIMARY SOURCES

The General Theory of Employment, Interest, and Money

John Maynard Keynes (1883–1946) was one of the most influential economists in world history. His 1936 book, *The General Theory of Employment, Interest, and Money*, founded modern macroeconomics. Read the following excerpt from the book, and answer the questions that follow.

"The task of transmuting [changing] human nature must not be confused with the task of managing it. We must recognise that only experience can show how far the common will, embodied in the policy of the State, ought to be directed to increasing and supplementing the inducement [encouragement] to invest; and how far it is safe to stimulate the average propensity [tendency] to consume, without forgoing [neglecting] our aim of depriving capital of its scarcity-value within one or two generations. It may turn out that the propensity to consume will be so easily strengthened by the effects of a falling rate of interest, that full employment can be reached with a rate of accumulation little greater than at present. . . . For in such matters it is rash to predict how the average man will react to a changed environment.

"The State will have to exercise a guiding influence on the propensity to consume partly through its scheme of taxation, partly by fixing the rate of interest, and partly, perhaps, in other ways. . . . I conceive . . . that a somewhat comprehensive socialization [state ownership] of investment will prove the only means of securing an approximation to full employment; though this need not exclude all manner of compromises and of devices by which public authority will co-operate with private initiative. But beyond this no obvious case is made out for a system of State Socialism which would embrace most of the economic life of the community. It is not the ownership of the instruments of production which it is important for the State to assume. If the State is able to determine the aggregate amount of resources devoted to augmenting [increasing] the instruments and the basic rate of reward to those who own them, it will have accomplished all that is necessary."

1. What is Keynes's opinion about the idea that economists can predict economic behavior?

2. What role would government play in influencing "the propensity to consume"?

3. How does Keynes distinguish between government involvement and State Socialism?

YOUR ASSIGNMENT

A Fiscal Fix

Imagine that you and your classmates have decided to put your recently acquired economic knowledge to work by influencing government policy. Your group has formed a new organization called Citizens for a Good Economy (CGE). The organization's goal is to promote government policies that help strengthen the U.S. economy. In particular, CGE has decided to join the political debate over U.S. fiscal policy.

One of CGE's first tasks will be to decide which fiscal policies to lobby the U.S. government to implement. To make these determinations, the class should work in groups. Each group will prepare fiscal policy recommendations to present to Congress. CGE has hired an expert from the financial and political consulting firm of Bunker, Jefferson, and Stivich, (BJ&S) to help your group study fiscal policy.

The BJ&S consultant has provided you with some background information: fact sheets from the campaigns of two key congresspersons, slides showing recommendations from a leading association of bankers, a review of recent corporate tax revenues, the Fed's current monetary policy, and available fiscal policy tools. This information can be found on the following pages. As you review this information, answer the accompanying questions in your Economics Notebook. Then work with the other members of your group to develop fiscal policy recommendations.

Make sure you back up the recommendations in your report by explaining why you believe your group's suggestions would promote a healthy economy. Your recommendations should be prepared for use in a presentation to other CGE members (your class). The presentation may include handouts, posters, or other visual guides.

YOUR VOTE COUNTS

U.S. REPRESENTATIVE JAN LIPSCY

43 years old
fifth-term congresswoman from Michigan
chair, House Budget Committee

SUPPORTS THE FOLLOWING POLICIES:

instituting a flat tax and cutting taxes
cutting government spending
setting strict limits on public transfer payments
eliminating many tax incentives and regulations
balancing the budget
having the Fed set low interest rates

We Need Your Vote!

U.S. SENATOR ABE JENKINS

56 years old
second-term senator from Arizona
chair, Senate Budget Committee

SUPPORTS THE FOLLOWING POLICIES:

★ maintaining a progressive tax with limited or no tax cuts

★ keeping government spending at its current level

★ using public transfer payments to help the needy

★ maintaining tax incentives, particularly those that would promote investment in poor, inner cities

★ balancing the budget, but without deep cuts in social programs

★ having the Fed set low interest rates

WHAT DO YOU THINK?

1. Which congressperson is more likely to support recommendations that favor supply-side economic policies? Which is more likely to support demand-side policies?

2. The two congresspersons agree that the Fed should encourage low interest rates. Given their differences in other areas, why do you think both congresspersons might support such a policy?

Economics Lab

WHAT DO YOU THINK?

1. In what ways might a reduction in government regulation help the economy? What downsides might there be?

2. Why do you suppose bankers would support a drop in corporate tax rates and an increase in tax incentives?

3. A balanced budget might lower interest rates. In what ways would this benefit banks and the economy in general?

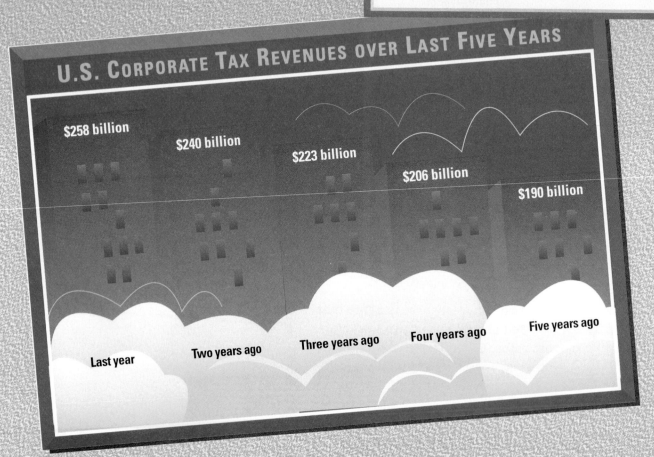

U.S. CORPORATE TAX REVENUES OVER LAST FIVE YEARS

$258 billion

$240 billion

$223 billion

$206 billion

$190 billion

Last year   Two years ago   Three years ago   Four years ago   Five years ago

CURRENT FED MONETARY POLICY

- slowly raising the discount rate
- increasing the margin requirements
- requiring higher down payments on consumer credit purchases

FISCAL POLICY TOOLS

- taxation
- tax incentives
- government spending
- public transfer payments
- progressive income tax

WHAT DO YOU THINK?

1. What kind of overall monetary policy does the Fed appear to be following? What does that policy indicate about the Fed's thinking concerning the current condition of the economy?

2. What kinds of monetary policies might the Fed adopt to speed economic growth?

3. Recall that Representative Lipscy and Senator Jenkins both favor the setting of lower interest rates. The Fed, however, is increasing the discount rate. What kinds of fiscal policies might Congress adopt to keep interest rates from rising higher than it thinks would be good for the economy?

THINGS TO DO

1. As a group, compare notes and ideas about the information presented by Bunker, Jefferson, and Stivich.

2. Discuss the fiscal policies that Citizens for a Good Economy thinks the government should use to promote economic growth. Your group should decide the best ways to approach each of the fiscal policy tools available to Congress.

3. Prepare brief arguments to persuade Lipscy and Jenkins to support your fiscal policy proposals.

4. As a group, prepare a presentation for the rest of the CGE (your class). Your presentation should clearly state your proposals, the reasons for supporting them, and strategies for winning support from key members of Congress. Make sure your proposals are consistent. For example, if you propose increasing government spending and lowering taxes, be prepared to explain how an increasing budget deficit will affect economic growth.

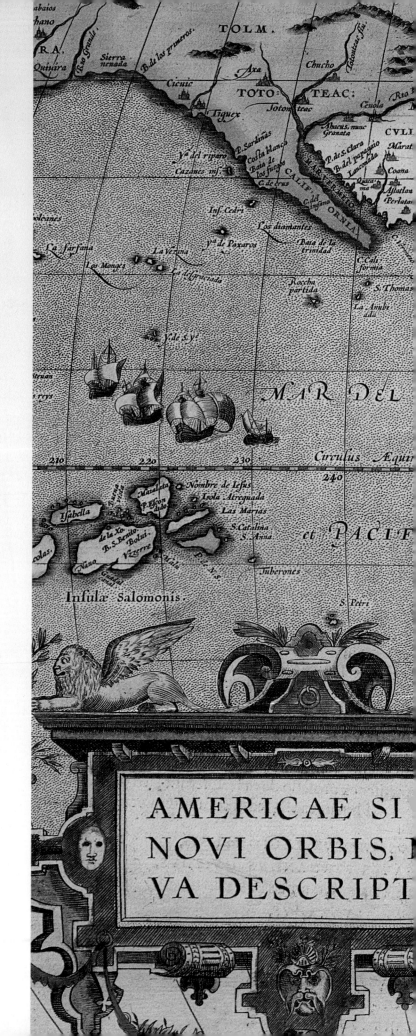

UNIT
└6

Economics Lab

How would you develop an international trade network? Find out by reading this unit and taking the Economics Lab challenge on pages 450–53.

INTERNATIONAL ECONOMICS

CHAPTER 16

COMPARING ECONOMIC SYSTEMS

The 1980s and 1990s saw dramatic changes in the world economy. A number of nations turned to new economic systems or adapted existing methods of answering the questions of what, how, and for whom to produce.

As noted in Chapter 2, most nations have mixed economic systems. Mixed economic systems combine elements of the pure market model with elements of the pure command model. In this chapter you will learn more about the types of economic systems that exist in the world today. These economic systems include market capitalism, command capitalism, market socialism, and command socialism—also referred to as authoritarian socialism or communism.

Economics Notebook

In your Economics Notebook, list five economic decisions you have made in the past month. How have you answered the questions of what, how, and for whom to produce?

SECTION 1

DEVELOPMENT MODELS

Economics Dictionary

market system
command system
market socialism

Objectives

▶ How can ownership of capital be used to identify an economic system?

▶ How do command systems and market systems differ?

Economic systems can be identified in two ways. The first is by ownership of the factors of production capital. An economic system in which most capital is owned by the government is called a socialist economic system. A system in which most capital is privately owned is called a capitalist economic system.

The second way to identify economic systems concerns how decisions about the use of capital and the other factors of production are made. As noted in Chapter 1, all societies must answer three basic economic questions: what to produce, how to produce, and for whom to produce. A system in which these questions primarily are answered by individuals and businesses is called a **market system**. A system in which those decisions are generally made by the government is called a **command system**.

Figure 16.1 shows how these ownership and decision-making characteristics can result in different economic systems. The two columns show public versus private ownership of capital and natural resources. The two rows show public versus private decision-making in the allocation of those resources.

Capitalist Economic Systems

Figure 16.1 describes a market capitalist economy like that of the United States, in which natural, human, capital, and entrepreneurial resources are generally owned or controlled by individuals rather than by the government. Decisions about how these resources are to be used are made primarily by their owners.

The capital and resources used by businesses such as the Walt Disney Company, Kimberly-Clark Corporation, or Time Warner Inc. are owned by the shareholders of those firms; the company's management decides how those resources will be used on a day-to-day basis. Most resources in the market capitalist economy of the United States fit the model of private ownership and private decision making.

Not all decisions are made by individuals and businesses; some are made by federal, state, or local governments. For example, the federal government owns the capital that the military uses

COMPARING ECONOMIC SYSTEMS

Ownership of Natural Resources and Capital		
	Private	Government
Allocation Choices — Private	**Market Capitalism** Examples: United States, Western Europe, Japan	**Market Socialism** Examples: Yugoslavia, China
Allocation Choices — Government	**Command Capitalism** Examples: many nations in Latin America, Africa, and the Middle East	**Command Socialism** Examples: Soviet Union, Cuba, North Korea

FIGURE 16.1 A nation's economic system is defined by who owns most of the capital and who makes decisions about how capital is used. **Who makes allocation choices in a command capitalist system?**

and determines how those resources will be used. The government also regulates many of the choices that firms make on the use of the capital and other resources they own. For example, the Department of Agriculture may tell farmers participating in a price support program how much of a particular crop to plant. The government also regulates such things as food inspection, maintenance of historic structures, length of the workday, and use of wetlands.

Command capitalism is indicated by a greater degree of government involvement. While individuals continue to play an important role, the government makes a wider variety of economic choices and owns a higher percentage of the factors of production.

Careers in Economics

RESEARCHER CD-ROM

Business Geographer

What would be the most profitable location for an ice cream parlor—Alaska or Florida? While the answer may seem obvious, all entrepreneurs must put serious time and effort into finding the best locations for their place of business. One of the best sources of such information comes from the field of geography.

When you think of geography you might think of the names and locations of cities, rivers, mountain ranges, and countries. But geography is more than knowing the location of places on a map. Geography is the study of all the earth's characteristics, be they mountain ranges, human-made places like cities, or the location of populations and natural resources.

Businesspeople seek the services of geographers who specialize in studying the economic aspects of the earth's features. To compete successfully, businesses need to know the most favorable locations for capital investments and market growth. They also must understand the environmental impact of their operations on surrounding areas.

Business geographers, or economic geographers, as they are sometimes called, can provide companies with this information because they study the earth's features as economic resources.

Business geographers analyze the usefulness of natural resources for humans and interpret how the natural and human-made world interrelate. Part of this task is to determine the most profitable location or market for a particular business.

Business geographers have a variety of employment options in manufacturing, retail, and transportation. They typically have undergraduate degrees in geography. Coursework may include various fields of geography—economic, urban, transportation, and population—as well as cartography (mapmaking), and statistics. In addition, classes in marketing, management, and consumer behavior enable business geographers to speak the "language" of business.

Business geographers analyze the earth's features and resources to determine the best locations for businesses.

Socialist Economic Systems

In socialist economies, the society or government owns all or most of the capital and natural resources. Most production is done by state-owned firms. Figure 16.1 shows two versions of socialism: market, also called democratic, and command, also called authoritarian.

Flag of the Soviet Union

The most prominent example of a command socialist economy, which combined state ownership with state decision making, was the Union of Soviet Socialist Republics, known as the Soviet Union. After World War II, the Soviet Union aggressively spread its economic system to nations in Eastern Europe, Central America and the Caribbean, Asia, and Africa.

For decades the Soviet Union represented a political and economic system opposed to the capitalist nations of the West. Economic hardships eventually weakened the Soviet Union, however, and it collapsed in 1991 and dissolved into 15 independent nations. (See Figure 16.2 on page 380.) Most of these nations have rejected socialist economic systems in favor of capitalist economic systems. With the fall of the Soviet Union, former communist nations of Eastern Europe, such as Poland, Romania, and Hungary, also replaced command socialism with market or command forms of capitalism. By 1997, Cuba and North Korea were the only nations that still relied strictly on command socialism as the model for their economic systems.

An alternative to command socialism is market socialism, which emerged in Yugoslavia after World War II. **Market socialism**—or democratic socialism—is identified by government control of major industries, with some decisions made by individuals. Even this form of socialism failed, and Yugoslavia's government and economy collapsed in the 1990s.

Why did these forms of socialism fail? The problem appears to have been fundamentally one of incentives. The "invisible hand" of the market

Marketing Communism

For nearly 30 years the Berlin Wall stood as a symbol of the gulf between capitalism and communism. Built in 1961 to keep East Germans from entering capitalist—and politically democratic—West Berlin, the wall, its concrete guard towers, and barbed wire represented political and economic repression.

Germans on both sides of the wall recognized the power of this historic symbol. When East Germany's communist government collapsed in 1989, East and West Germans worked joyfully together to tear down the wall and reunite the city. The destruction of the Berlin Wall became something of a precelebration for the reunification of all of Germany, which took place a year later. People from all over the country—and around the world—flocked to Berlin to join in the party.

Pieces of the wall were immediately snatched up and sold as souvenirs, turning this symbol of communist rule into a commodity in the global capitalist market. In fact, American entrepreneurs began shipping pieces of the wall to the United States to be sold. One entrepreneur airlifted 20 tons of the rock from Berlin to Chicago.

Meanwhile, price competition among sellers of wall souvenirs became fierce. While the earliest pieces sold for as much as $15, competition quickly brought the price down to $7. In the future, as pieces of the wall become scarce, their value will probably go up. Thanks to the laws of supply and demand, a piece of the wall may one day become a collector's item with significant market value.

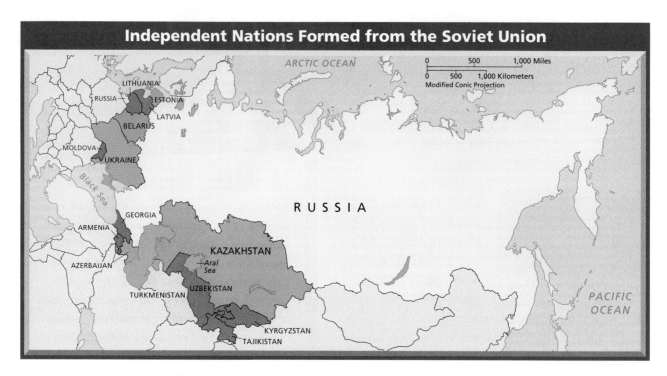

Independent Nations Formed from the Soviet Union

FIGURE 16.2 The Soviet Union was the most prominent example of the command socialist system. In 1991 it dissolved into 15 independent nations.

system was replaced by government orders. These government orders seldom correctly reflected consumer preferences. People who make decisions regarding the use of resources they do not own have no incentive to seek out the most productive use of the resources. In fact the decisions of these socialist economies—both command and market—were usually based on ideology rather than the principal of economic efficiency.

SECTION 1 —REVIEW

1. Define the following terms: market system, command system, market socialism.

2. How do capitalist and socialist economic systems differ?

3. Compare command systems with market systems.

4. What role do incentives play in capitalist and socialist economic systems? Which system relies more heavily on economic efficiency?

5. **Thinking and Writing Critically** What are the reasons for the failure of both command and market socialism in recent years?

6. **Applying** ECONOMIC SYSTEMS Consider your school as an economic system. Who answers the three economic questions of what, how, and for whom to produce? What capital is available, and who owns it? Based on your answers to these questions, what kind of economic system does your school have?

SECTION 2

CAPITALISM

Economics Dictionary

mercantilism

indicative planning

nationalization

Objectives

▶ What factors contributed to the development of capitalism?

▶ How does capitalism in Japan, Germany, France, and South Korea compare with capitalism in the United States?

In a capitalist economic system, the ownership of resources is left to individuals and businesses. However, nations differ in their definitions of the role of government in a capitalist system. This difference is often based on their economic history. In command capitalist economies, the government takes an active role in guiding the allocation of resources. Governments may control prices or regulate how resources are to be used. Governments play a more passive role, however, in market capitalism. They influence the allocation of resources through their taxation, spending, and regulatory policies, but leave the bulk of allocation choices to the private sector.

Origins of Capitalism

Capitalism became the dominant economic system in Europe and the United States in the 1800s. This system emerged as part of a series of economic systems over the last several centuries.

Decline of Manorialism During the Middle Ages, Europe's main economic system was manorialism, with land-owning nobles granting peasants the opportunity to work the land in exchange for fixed payments. By the 1100s new agricultural techniques and technological developments led to increased food production, which in turn supported the growing population.

Prosperity and population growth encouraged the expansion of trade—both within Europe and with other regions. As trade increased, people began to invest money in businesses to make a profit.

Over time, the power of landowners began to decline. Just as merchants gained economic power, kings grew stronger politically and were increasingly able to form centralized governments. The rise of these new nations created a need for national currencies and a banking system, two key institutions of capitalism.

Mercantilism Between 1500 and 1800, the governments of major European nations used the

ECONOMIC SYSTEMS *A gold merchant and his wife work together at their banking business in the 1500s.* **What economic system did European nations use during this time period?**

Japanese semiconductor firms captured most of the market during the 1980s. **How has the Japanese government helped businesses such as this semiconductor producer?**

theory of mercantilism to direct their economies. **Mercantilism** defined a nation's power in terms of its supply of gold and silver. Since these commodities were rare, Europeans generally believed that a nation could grow stronger only by gaining more wealth—and therefore power—than other nations. This accumulation of national wealth took place through a combination of trade and conquest.

Mercantilist power required a steady source of raw materials, encouraging European nations to establish trading posts and colonies around the world. Government leaders then established trade monopolies and introduced trade barriers to maintain control over their supplies of raw materials. Governments thus maintained tight control over national economies.

Adam Smith's Influence

By the mid-1700s, many Europeans believed that mercantilism interfered with economic growth. Reform-minded economists urged governments to grant individuals more economic freedom. One of the most influential of the economists opposed to

mercantilism was Adam Smith. As noted in Chapter 2, Smith's *Wealth of Nations* argued that economies would prosper without government interference. Smith wrote that the profit motive would make a free economic system efficient, and that competition in the marketplace would eliminate inefficient businesses. Later, this type of economic system became known as a free-enterprise, or capitalist, system.

Capitalism Today

Market capitalism currently functions with varying degrees of government involvement. Governments in every capitalist economy play an active role in assisting the poor and in providing such public goods as law enforcement, education, and environmental protection. Although the amount of governmental control varies from nation to nation, it remains much more limited than in a socialist economy. In the United States, for example, the government intervenes in the economy only on a limited basis. In Japan, South Korea, France, and Germany, on the other hand, the government has had a great deal of influence in how the economy is run.

Capitalism in Japan The Japanese government plays a crucial role in the country's economy. The key players are the Ministry of International Trade and Industry (MITI) and the Ministry of Finance. MITI encourages the production of certain goods and discourages the production of others. In the 1970s, for example, when U.S. companies dominated the semiconductor market, MITI imposed tariffs to protect Japanese firms from foreign competition and assisted in joint research efforts by Japanese manufacturers. Such tariffs limited the number—and increased the prices—of foreign goods allowed into the country. Goods produced in their own country therefore were more affordable for Japanese consumers.

By the mid-1980s, Japanese firms commanded an increasing share of the global market for semiconductors. Although U.S. firms have won back much of the market in recent years,

MITI's intervention appears to have helped the Japanese companies.

The Ministry of Finance, which runs the Bank of Japan, Japan's central bank, encourages banks to make more credit available to specific industries. Although the Bank of Japan cannot direct the lending activities of private banks, it can provide guidance to private banks—for example, encouraging them to increase their lending to the desired firms and industries.

Capitalism in Germany

Germany emerged from defeat in World War II to a position as an economic superpower. Its economy is the fourth-largest in the world, now behind that of the United States, China, and Japan. Germany has a long tradition of government involvement in the economy and social welfare programs. Many government social welfare programs considered standard by capitalist economies today—such as social insurance—were originally developed in Germany in the 1880s.

Germany's market capitalist economy was created after the Allies divided the defeated nation into four zones following the war. In 1948 the United States, Great Britain, and France economically united their zones, which became known as West Germany, and established a single currency. The Soviet Union's zone became known as East Germany and operated under a command socialist, or communist, economic system.

The Western Allies imposed a command capitalist economic system with extensive price controls. In 1948, when the Allied generals who ruled the occupied nation were away, Ludwig Erhard—the German leader they had appointed—ordered all price controls repealed. Throughout the West German economy, shortages disappeared rapidly. The resulting economic growth continues, although it has slowed since the 1980s.

Like the United States, Germany relies on the types of monetary and fiscal policies noted in

ECONOMIC SYSTEMS *The unification of East Germany and West Germany in 1990 was symbolized by the dismantling of the Berlin Wall.* **What problems have resulted from the reunification of Germany?**

François Mitterrand—president of France from 1981 to 1995—encouraged nationalization of many French industries. **What other characteristic defines France's strong central government?**

even more independent of elected officials than is the U.S. Federal Reserve system—has helped the nation experience one of the lowest inflation rates in the world over the last two decades.

Privatization of formerly state-owned firms in the former East Germany has moved fairly quickly. Most industrial capacity in the region has been transferred to private ownership. As noted in Chapter 12, privatization is the process in which government-owned firms are transferred to the private sector.

Capitalism in France France has long had a capitalist economy, but it also has a tradition of a strong central government. Perhaps the most striking feature of the French system since World War II was its reliance on a system of **indicative planning**, or providing economic information and setting goals that are not mandatory. Under this system, the General Planning Commission created a series of five-year plans for the French economy. This planning process was not a command system because private firms were not required to base their economic decisions on the growth targets of the plan.

The election of François Mitterrand—a French socialist candidate—as president in 1981 contributed to greater government control over industry through **nationalization**, a policy in which the government purchases and takes over the operation of a private firm. Nationalization efforts in France were concentrated in industries such as iron ore and steel production. The government's ownership share in key industries increased dramatically between 1981 and 1983. At that time the government controlled about one third of the total output of the French economy.

However, by 1993 more conservative leaders had been elected. The French government announced a reversal of the earlier socialist policy through the introduction of privatization. The ownership of 21 state-owned companies, including Renault, were to be shifted to the private sector. This process continued into the 1990s.

Capitalism in South Korea The government-financed Korea Development Institute (KDI),

Chapters 14 and 15. However, German fiscal policy differs from that of the United States in one important respect. In the United States, fiscal policy decisions by state and local governments are largely independent of federal policy. While the federal government may seek to influence state and local spending, it does not regulate their spending and tax choices. Germany, on the other hand, has established two commissions to coordinate the budgets of the federal, state, and local governments in an effort to promote economic stability.

Although Germany has had a history of low inflation and low fiscal deficits, the sudden collapse of East Germany in 1989 and its reunification with West Germany in 1990 created severe economic problems. Low productivity and high unemployment among former East Germans, combined with Germany's generous unemployment benefits, resulted in large deficits. The Bundesbank, Germany's central bank—which is

South Korea's version of MITI, is an economic planning agency in South Korea. The agency brings government planners together with business owners to develop Korea's economic plans.

Like the Japanese, South Koreans have offered incentives to businesses to direct resource allocation as well as production. For example, in the mid-1970s incentives were provided to the automotive, shipbuilding, steel, and other heavy industries. By the early 1990s South Korean shipbuilders were successful global competitors, and automobiles had become a major export industry.

C A S E   S T U D Y

Capitalism, Singapore Style

ROLE OF GOVERNMENT Singapore in Southeast Asia has one of the fastest-growing economies in the world. A former British colony, in 1994 the country had the 18th-highest standard of living in the world. Its economy is one of several East Asian economies known as "tigers" for their aggressive rates of economic growth.

Singapore's miracle economy has its costs, however. Although its economy is capitalist, its government regulates many elements of personal behavior. For instance, the Singapore government imposes fines for failure to flush a public toilet and for chewing gum in public.

According to the leader of modern Singapore, Lee Kwan Yew, the city's rapid economic growth is the direct result of its authoritarian social policies. "We would not have made economic progress if we had not intervened in very personal matters—who your neighbor is, how you live, the noise you make, how you spit, or what language you use."

However, many economists dispute the claim that Singapore's economic growth is a result of its social policies. They point to other factors as the more likely reasons for economic growth—for instance, the country's homogenous population (76 percent ethnic Chinese) and its long history as an international trade center while under British rule.

Nevertheless, some Americans admire Singapore's rigid social policies. For instance, in 1994 an American teenager living in Singapore was convicted of spray painting graffiti on cars and as punishment was whipped with a bamboo cane. While many Americans viewed the caning as excessively harsh and an affront to humanitarian values, others applauded the Singaporean government's tough stand against juvenile delinquency. Still other Americans accept Singapore's authoritarian social policies with a grain of salt, disagreeing in principle but recognizing their policies as a component of a different culture.

An important question, however, is whether authoritarianism enhances a capitalistic country's economic performance. If so, is the trade-off between free choice and economic growth worth it?

SECTION 2 — REVIEW

1. Define the following terms: mercantilism, indicative planning, nationalization.

2. What is the economic role of government in Japan, Germany, France, and South Korea?

3. How has privatization influenced the economies of Germany and France?

4. **Thinking and Writing Critically**
   What economic challenges developed in the early 1990s as a result of German reunification?

5. **Applying** ECONOMIC INSTITUTIONS & INCENTIVES
   How did the ideas of economists such as Adam Smith shift Europe away from mercantilism and toward laissez-faire capitalism?

SOCIALISM

Objectives

▶ What conditions led to the development of socialism?

▶ How has high taxation affected Sweden's economy?

Socialism is a broad term used to describe several types of noncapitalist economic systems. Whereas capitalism is rooted in the concepts of private property and private decision making about the allocation and use of resources, socialism is an economic system rooted in an entire society's ownership of some or all of the means of production.

Socialists believe that public ownership of industries protects workers from harsh working conditions. Furthermore, socialists believe that central planning is necessary to channel resources into socially desirable areas. One of the goals of central planning is to oversee the distribution of wealth in a nation so that no one is too wealthy or too poor.

Economic socialism does not necessarily indicate the level of political freedom in a country. For example, North Korea and Sweden both have practiced government ownership of some resources and industries. Political freedom, however, is very limited in North Korea but was widespread in socialist Sweden.

Origins of Socialism

In the early 1800s, social thinkers such as Robert Owen and Charles Fourier established a number of socialist communities in which members shared the proceeds of their labor and promoted the good of the community rather than their own interests. These socialist experiments were in part a reaction to harsh working conditions during the Industrial Revolution. Long working

ECONOMIC SYSTEMS *Members of experimental socialist communities such as New Harmony, Indiana, shared the proceeds of their labor.* **How, according to socialist beliefs, does public ownership of industries protect workers?**

hours, low pay, child labor, and hazardous working conditions created workplace conditions that were often unpleasant. Overcrowded tenements, industrial pollution, and the lack of adequate sanitation and medical facilities also contributed to a decline in the workers' quality of life.

Largely in response to these conditions, reformers began to question the capitalist system. Some reformers favored an end to capitalism and the establishment of an economic system that would provide a more equal distribution of wealth. Collectively, these reformers were called socialists. Some socialists called for violent revolutions to topple the capitalists and reorganize ownership of the factors of production. Others supported a peaceful, gradual transition from capitalism to socialism.

Market Socialism

Socialists who believed in peaceful change adapted their economic and political ideals to changes in economic and political conditions during the 1900s. One of these adaptations became known as market, or democratic, socialism. By studying the economic history of Sweden, you can better understand how market socialism has worked.

Socialism in Sweden

Under market socialism, the people retain basic human rights and elect government officials, which gives them some control over economic planning. By electing officials whose economic policies they agree with, the people have a say in their country's economy. Great Britain and France have practiced market socialism in the past. In an effort to reverse their economic declines, both Great Britain and France have privatized many industries that had been nationalized and shifted toward the capitalist system. For many years Sweden's combination of private industry and government-directed services made the country appear to be a model of market socialism. From 1986 to 1991, however, Sweden's system underwent dramatic change.

ECONOMIC SYSTEMS *Sweden's combination of government and private business ownership once made it a model of market socialism.* **What industries are controlled by the Swedish government today?**

Industry Ownership Today government ownership of industry stands at approximately 10 percent of the country's industries. Sweden's government has maintained ownership or control of shipbuilding and steel production, as well as part of the national railway network, broadcasting systems, and hydroelectric facilities. Private firms, such as Electrolux and Volvo, own about 90 percent of industry in Sweden.

Workers' Freedoms During Sweden's socialist period, Swedish workers enjoyed many of the economic freedoms commonly associated with capitalist economies. In some respects, the power of workers was greater in Sweden than in the United States or Japan. For example, Sweden's workforce is the most heavily unionized of the world's industrialized nations. More than 80 percent of Swedish workers belong to unions, compared to about 15 percent of U.S. workers and about 26 percent of Japanese workers. Additionally, Swedish workers routinely have been entitled to representation on the boards of directors of major corporations and shared in corporate decision making.

*The Swedish people have enjoyed one of the highest standards of living in the world. **What are some of the social programs the Swedish government has financed?***

private interests. Representatives of the government, labor unions, industry, and agriculture negotiated together to develop annual plans that set production and employment targets.

Taxation Under socialism, taxes in Sweden were among the highest in Europe. The Swedish government used the tax revenues to finance many social programs, including comprehensive health insurance, unemployment insurance, retirement benefits, free education through college, subsidized public housing, and child care. This gave Sweden one of the highest standards of living in the world.

The high taxes that Swedish workers paid were a source of controversy. High taxes forced workers to demand higher wages, which increased the prices of goods produced for domestic and international markets. Moreover, tax revenues did not keep pace with the rising costs of social programs. As a result, the government had to run deficits and borrow heavily to meet its economic and social goals.

In the early 1990s Sweden experienced its worst recession since the Great Depression. Faced with the need to reduce its deficit, the Swedish government launched a program to limit welfare benefits and turn over the production and management of many government services to private firms.

Economic Planning Economic planning in the Swedish socialist economy was the responsibility of people who represent both public and

SECTION 3 — REVIEW

1. How did social thinkers such as Robert Owen and Charles Fourier contribute to the development of socialism?

2. What are the major characteristics of market socialism?

3. What were the advantages and disadvantages of Sweden's tax system during the socialist period? Why were these taxes controversial?

4. **Thinking and Writing Critically**
   Do you believe market socialism could be a successful economic system? Explain your answer.

5. **Applying** ECONOMIC SYSTEMS During the 1800s many utopias, or communities designed to create the ideal society, were established in the United States. Does market socialism seem to be a good basis for an ideal society? Explain your answer.

COMMUNISM

Economics Dictionary

bourgeoisie
proletariat
collectivization
perestroika
Great Leap Forward
people's communes
Cultural Revolution
Four Modernizations
household responsibility system
Tiananmen Square Massacre

Objectives

▶ How did Karl Marx use history to develop the theories of communism?

▶ What economic factors contributed to the fall of the Soviet Union?

▶ How did centralization affect the economy of the People's Republic of China?

German philosophers Karl Marx and Friedrich Engels first outlined the theories of communism, or command socialism, in the *Communist Manifesto* (1848) and *Das Kapital* (1867). From these theories, an economic system—and a way of life—was born.

Communism is a type of socialism in which the government owns and controls the means of production. This economic system is closest to the pure command model. The former Soviet Union and the People's Republic of China before the introduction of market-oriented reforms both represent communism.

Theories of Karl Marx

Karl Marx wrote that economic factors determine political and social change. Marx viewed history as a series of class struggles between the oppressors, who owned the means of production, and the oppressed, who supplied the labor.

Rise of the Bourgeoisie Marx's view of the Middle Ages, for example, focused mainly on the decline of manorialism and the rise of mercantilism described in Section 2. Gradually, with the expansion of trade and the growth of cities, a class of merchants arose. As these "middle class" merchants—whom Marx called the **bourgeoisie** (burzh-wa-ZEE)—became more powerful, they challenged the ruling nobles. Marx noted that the bourgeoisie's triumph over the nobility in this struggle led to the creation of capitalist economic systems in many parts of Europe by the late 1700s.

Rise of the Proletariat Marx did not see the rise of the bourgeoisie as the end of the class struggle. Instead, he saw that during the early

ECONOMIC SYSTEMS *Karl Marx's theories of communism gave rise to the economic system of command socialism.* **What are two prominent examples of communist countries?**

CAPITAL AND LABOUR.

ECONOMIC SYSTEMS *Marx believed that the differences between the bourgeoisie and the proletariat would lead to violent revolution.* **What did Marx believe would happen once capitalism was destroyed?**

Industrial Revolution, the bourgeoisie gained control of the means of production and became the oppressors of the working class. The working class—whom Marx called the **proletariat** (proh-luh-TAYR-ee-uht)—provided the labor needed for the production process in return for very low wages.

Marx saw all of the profits from production going to the bourgeoisie. Their wealth grew while the proletariat continued to work for low wages. In Marx's view, the class struggle would continue to intensify until the proletariat eventually overthrew the bourgeoisie in a violent revolution.

Destruction of Capitalism Marx expected that the working class would organize a government, which he called the "dictatorship of the proletariat," that would oversee the final destruction of capitalism. Marx believed that once capitalism was destroyed, a classless society would develop. Everyone would then be equal and all people would share ownership of the means of production. In his theory, Marx stated that the dictatorship of the proletariat would be temporary. He saw workers in all nations toppling the

bourgeoisie and establishing an ideal worldwide society without government.

Simplification of History

Marx believed that the victory of the proletariat was the inevitable conclusion of capitalism. Marx, however, simplified history and ignored political forces by attributing nearly all events to a class struggle. He also incorrectly predicted that capitalism would lead to deteriorating standards of living for the working class. He did not foresee the rising economic status that workers in industrialized nations such as the United States have enjoyed throughout the 1900s.

Finally, the government of the Soviet Union, which practiced communism from 1917 until its breakup in 1991, did not simply wither away after coming to power. Soviet society also was not the classless society that Marx imagined. Instead, the leaders of the Soviet Communist Party enjoyed special privileges and made up the intellectual, political, and social elite of the nation. The majority of the people had—and still have—standards of living below those of capitalist nations.

Rise of Communism

During the early 1900s many revolutionary groups formed in Russia. The Bolsheviks—later called Communists—were one of these opposition groups. Under the leadership of Vladimir Ilich Lenin, in 1917 the Bolsheviks overthrew the existing government in Russia and proclaimed Russia the world's first communist nation.

War Communism The early years of communism were marked by political and economic experimentation. Lenin's first experiment is known as the period of "war communism"

(1917–21). It was a time of civil war and extreme hardship following Russia's defeat in World War I and the overthrow of Czar Nicholas II. Under Lenin's war communism, the state abolished private property, broke up large estates in rural areas, and nationalized and redistributed land. In cities, the communist government took control of factories and allowed the workers to run them. A forced-labor policy relocated scarce labor resources to important industries.

War communism failed because the peasants had no incentive to produce crops when the government confiscated agricultural products to feed the army and urban workers. Furthermore, untrained industrial workers knew little about managing factories. War communism therefore caused agricultural and industrial output to fall dramatically.

New Economic Policy

In 1921 Lenin introduced the New Economic Policy (NEP), which restored some private incentives. Peasants were allowed to sell surplus crops on the open market for profit, and small private firms were allowed to open in the cities. Under the NEP, thousands of entrepreneurs revived the economy. Larger enterprises, however, remained in the hands of the government.

Stalin's Rule

When Lenin died in 1924, he was succeeded by Joseph Stalin. The new Soviet leader moved toward a more centralized decision-making system. Stalin instituted strict central planning and eliminated private property.

Under Stalin's leadership, a series of Five-Year Plans were established—beginning in 1928—that set long-term economic goals and allocated scarce resources. Under these plans, Stalin and his successors set quotas for increased industrial and agricultural production. Workers who failed to meet quotas were severely punished.

The Soviet government emphasized heavy industries such as steel, concrete, machinery, chemicals, and mining at the expense of many consumer-oriented industries. Shortages of basic necessities such as clothing soon followed.

In agriculture, the government instituted a policy of **collectivization**, under which the state took control of land to form large state-run farms. Many peasants fiercely resisted collectivization, so the government forcibly sent them to work as laborers in factories or in the mines. Exact numbers are not known, but historians estimate that millions of lives were lost in Stalin's centralization of power.

Central Planning

A central planning agency called the Gosplan determined the quantities of output that key Soviet firms would produce each year and the prices that would be charged. Other government agencies set output levels for smaller firms. Long-term goals were outlined in the Five-Year Plans, while annual plans set short-term quotas.

Managers of state-owned firms received rewards if they met annual quotas. However, this

ECONOMIC SYSTEMS *Vladimir Ilich Lenin was the first leader of the Soviet Union (1917–24).* ***With what economic programs did Lenin experiment?***

ECONOMICS
in Action

Brave New World

The collapse of communism in the former Soviet Union has brought many opportunities as well as many challenges for the Russian people. One of the most persistent challenges has been the question of how to distribute economic goods efficiently. Most market capitalist countries rely on the "invisible hand" of the free market to allocate resources in an efficient manner. In the countries formerly governed by the communist Soviet Union, however, distribution was controlled by the government. Thus, when the Soviet command system collapsed, Russia was left without a well-developed distribution network to fill the void.

With virtually no established means of distributing goods, aspiring entrepreneurs had to look for ways to bring products to consumers. Among this group are "shuttle shoppers"—people who travel to other countries to buy goods for resale.

Anchorage, Alaska, is one common stop, where shuttle shoppers visit discount stores such as Costco, Sam's Club, and Kmart. Others frequent bazaars in Turkey. One Russian woman travels from Moscow to Istanbul twice a month, spending at least $10,000 per trip. Profits on Turkish goods—including dolls, clothing, and medical devices—can rise as high as 60 percent.

China is also a center for shuttle shopping. One entrepreneur—the leader of a group of 23 traders—has claimed to sell jogging suits in Moscow for seven times the purchase price in China. Other merchants travel to China in search of consumer electronics and household appliances.

Although the profits can be impressive, these entrepreneurs accept high levels of risk as part of the business. All 23 of the Russian traders traveling to China had been robbed at some point, sometimes repeatedly. Additionally, shuttle shopping involves extensive travel, long hours, and complicated government regulations. For example, Russia imposes a 50 percent tax on imports, which can reduce profits significantly. Documentation requirements may vary as well. Russians entering Turkey can easily obtain multiple entry visas good for five years. On the other hand, when Russia issued new passports for foreign travel, Chinese officials were not aware of the change and turned away travelers carrying the new documents.

Money poses additional problems. Because of the challenges of determining comparative currency values, many traders rely on U.S. dollars for shuttle shopping exchanges.

Shuttle shopping expeditions provide Russian entrepreneurs with the opportunity to import goods that are not available—or are expensive to produce—in their own country. These businesspeople have found a way to earn a profit while participating in Russia's transition from communism to free enterprise.

What Do You Think?

1. Why is a distribution network important in an economy?
2. How has the Russian government influenced the development of free enterprise? How have government actions created challenges for free enterprise?

Russian "shuttle shoppers" can make impressive profits, but must accept high levels of risk as part of their business.

system of quotas and rewards created inefficiency in several ways. First, no central planning agency could incorporate consumer preferences and production costs in its decisions concerning how many goods to produce. Decisions about what to produce were made by Communist Party leaders, rather than in response to the market forces of supply and demand. Further, planners could not select prices that would result in equilibrium. As discussed in Chapter 5, prices in a market economy adjust to changes in supply and demand. Given the ever-changing nature of consumer behavior and production costs, it should be no surprise that the central planners could not select equilibrium prices arbitrarily. Soviet planners typically selected prices below equilibrium, causing shortages to develop throughout the economy.

Production Problems   Under Stalin, Soviet planners emphasized the production of industrial and military goods at the expense of consumer and agricultural goods. After Stalin died in 1953, central economic plans gradually included more consumer goods. While industrial and military products were still the top priority, many Soviet citizens urged the government to produce more consumer goods and services after the people became aware of higher standards of living.

Agriculture was a major problem area for the Soviet planners. Agricultural productivity was low because of shortages of capital, lack of incentives because of the quota system, and an often harsh climate. About one fifth of the Soviet labor force was employed in agriculture, compared to about 3 percent in the United States. Despite the large agricultural labor force, however, the Soviets had to import large quantities of food each year.

The Soviet Union experienced increasing problems with communism by the 1980s. Because Soviet factory managers had no incentives other than meeting their annual production quotas, they often were reluctant to use new technologies. By the late 1970s Soviet production technologies were outdated compared with those of the United States.

ECONOMIC SYSTEMS *Soviet citizens stand in line to buy food in a Moscow butcher shop in 1990.* **Why were shortages a chronic problem in the Soviet Union?**

Beginnings of Reform

The republic of Russia dominated the former Union of Soviet Socialist Republics. It contained more than half of the Soviet people and more than three fourths of the nation's land area. Moscow, Russia's capital, was also the capital and center of power for the entire former Soviet Union. In addition to these strengths, Russia was shifting toward market capitalism as a result of reforms that had been introduced during the final years of the Soviet Union. Because of Russia's position within the Soviet Union, any successful shift to market capitalism had to begin there.

Collapse of the Soviet Union   During the 1970s and 1980s, some Soviet economists began arguing that the old system could never deliver standards of living comparable to those achieved in market-based economies. The first Soviet leader to introduce the necessary reforms was Mikhail Gorbachev, who became general secretary of the Communist Party—the highest political position in the Soviet Union—in 1985.

Gorbachev instituted reforms that called for much greater economic independence for state enterprises and increased worker incentives. The policy, called **perestroika**, or "restructuring," was an effort to move the economy toward market socialism. However, Soviet bureaucrats and military leaders in particular wanted none of the reforms pushed by Gorbachev.

To compromise, Gorbachev chose to leave the communist system in place and seek modest reforms that allowed prices for some output to be negotiated between firms that produced the goods and firms that purchased them. Left in place were state ownership of enterprises and the shortages resulting from bad management of the remaining output. In an effort to deal with the shortages of the price-controlled goods, Gorbachev ordered a number of dramatic price increases in 1991.

Gorbachev's price hikes did little to correct the shortages, in part because the state-owned firms had no reason to respond to the higher prices by increasing output. Both managers and workers in these firms were paid salaries set by the government. Thus, there was no means by which either managers or workers could benefit from the higher prices. A firm in a market economy would be expected to increase its quantity supplied in response to a higher price—something that Soviet state-owned firms failed to do.

FALL OF THE SOVIET UNION

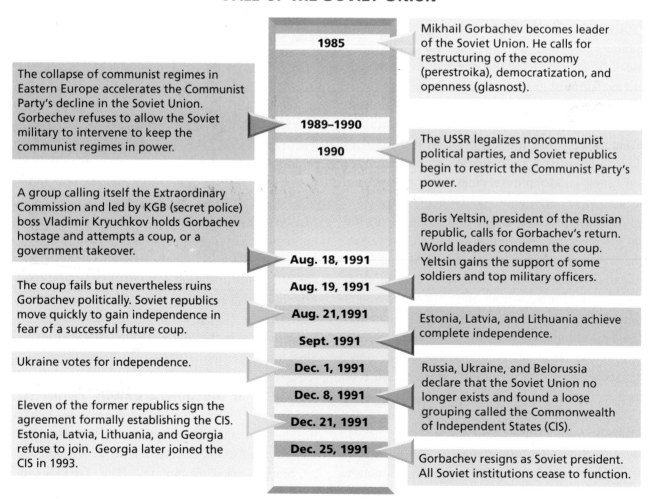

The collapse of communist regimes in Eastern Europe accelerates the Communist Party's decline in the Soviet Union. Gorbechev refuses to allow the Soviet military to intervene to keep the communist regimes in power.

A group calling itself the Extraordinary Commission and led by KGB (secret police) boss Vladimir Kryuchkov holds Gorbachev hostage and attempts a coup, or a government takeover.

The coup fails but nevertheless ruins Gorbachev politically. Soviet republics move quickly to gain independence in fear of a successful future coup.

Ukraine votes for independence.

Eleven of the former republics sign the agreement formally establishing the CIS. Estonia, Latvia, Lithuania, and Georgia refuse to join. Georgia later joined the CIS in 1993.

1985

1989–1990

1990

Aug. 18, 1991

Aug. 19, 1991

Aug. 21,1991

Sept. 1991

Dec. 1, 1991

Dec. 8, 1991

Dec. 21, 1991

Dec. 25, 1991

Mikhail Gorbachev becomes leader of the Soviet Union. He calls for restructuring of the economy (perestroika), democratization, and openness (glasnost).

The USSR legalizes noncommunist political parties, and Soviet republics begin to restrict the Communist Party's power.

Boris Yeltsin, president of the Russian republic, calls for Gorbachev's return. World leaders condemn the coup. Yeltsin gains the support of some soldiers and top military officers.

Estonia, Latvia, and Lithuania achieve complete independence.

Russia, Ukraine, and Belorussia declare that the Soviet Union no longer exists and found a loose grouping called the Commonwealth of Independent States (CIS).

Gorbachev resigns as Soviet president. All Soviet institutions cease to function.

Sources: *Encyclopedia Britannica: 1997* and *Microsoft Encarta*

FIGURE 16.3 Despite Mikhail Gorbachev's attempts at political and economic reform, the Soviet Union collapsed in 1991.

Communism Outside the Soviet Union

The communist nations of the world shared certain characteristics. Each of these nations had a one-party totalitarian political system. The government and the Communist Party controlled the economy.

Since the 1950s communist nations had adapted communism to meet their own needs. Some nations followed a highly centralized command system similar to that in the Soviet Union. Others permitted individuals to make some economic decisions. The most important of these communist nations is the People's Republic of China.

ECONOMIC SYSTEMS *Under Mikhail Gorbachev's leadership Soviet republics began to break away from the Soviet Union.* **What new group did many of the former Soviet republics found?**

In the summer of 1991 communist leaders opposed to economic reform tried to overthrow Gorbachev but failed within a few days. Taking advantage of the resulting chaos within the central government, the republics of the Soviet Union declared their independence. For a summary of the events leading to the dissolution of the Soviet Union, see Figure 16.3.

Russian Reform Boris Yeltsin, president of the newly-formed Russian Federation, had been a leading supporter of market capitalism even before the Soviet Union collapsed. Once Russia became an independent republic, Yeltsin sought a rapid transition to market capitalism. Yeltsin's efforts were slowed by the remaining former communist officials, however.

Despite these hurdles, Russian economic reformers have accomplished a great deal. Prices and production of most goods have been freed from state controls. Thousands of state-owned firms have been privatized, and Russians now are free to start their own businesses.

To privatize state firms, Russian citizens were issued vouchers that could be used to purchase shares in state enterprises. Under this plan, individuals could use their vouchers to bid for ownership in the firms.

Communism in the People's Republic of China

In recent years, the People's Republic of China has moved toward a more market-responsive communism. This move was a direct result of the failure of overcentralized economic planning, and followed decades of government involvement in the economy.

The Chinese communists came to power in 1949 after a long and bloody civil war. Mao Zedong (MOW zuh-DOOHNG), head of the Chinese Communist Party, assumed leadership of the new government. The economic history of the People's Republic of China can be divided into two periods. In the first period, under strict communism, China launched the Great Leap Forward program and the Cultural Revolution. The second period has been characterized by a more market-responsive communism.

Great Leap Forward In 1953 the Chinese Communists launched the first Five-Year Plan, which stressed industrial development. With the aid of the Soviet Union, China enjoyed some economic successes. Impatient with progress in industry and agriculture, however, Mao pushed for more rapid industrial and agricultural development in the second Five-Year Plan. This plan began with what was referred to as the **Great Leap Forward**.

The Great Leap Forward established groups of collective farms called **people's communes** in an attempt to increase the agricultural output of China. Under a system known as the iron rice bowl, farmwork was done in small units called production brigades. Government planners determined what, how, and how much communes produced. All output produced was delivered to the government.

In China's industrial sector, the Great Leap Forward stressed the production of steel and other heavy industries. More than a million small backyard furnaces were built to expand steel production, while light industries were neglected.

These policies caused industrial output to fall dramatically, which spelled economic ruin for China. Misuse of resources also led to low agricultural productivity, which contributed to the deaths of 20 to 30 million Chinese in the worst famine in history. In 1960 China's government abandoned the Great Leap Forward.

Cultural Revolution After a brief economic recovery from 1961 to 1965, China's economy

ECONOMIC SYSTEMS *Production brigade members attend a class at Shuangwang People's Commune.* **What were the economic outcomes of the Great Leap Forward?**

was again plunged into chaos. The chaos lasted from 1966 to 1976 during a period called the **Cultural Revolution**.

The Cultural Revolution was a violent movement aimed at safeguarding the communist system. Leaders of the Cultural Revolution denounced party officials, factory managers, scientists, teachers, college professors, and other professionals as "class enemies." Many factories and schools were closed. Millions of people were forcibly relocated to remote rural areas, where they had to perform manual labor and were "re-educated" to become supporters of Mao and his government.

Four Modernizations In 1976 the death of Mao and the end of the Cultural Revolution marked a shift toward more market-responsive policies. A new program of economic development called the **Four Modernizations** targeted modernization in agriculture, industry, science and technology, and defense.

In the late 1970s Deng Xiaoping (DUHNG SHOW-PING) became China's leader. Deng's brand of Chinese socialism combined state planning with market incentives to achieve the Four Modernizations. Under Deng, the most significant agricultural reform was the establishment of the **household responsibility system**, also called the contract responsibility system. This system permits peasants to lease state-owned land for and to pay their rent by delivering a portion of their crop to the government. The remainder of the crop can then be sold for profit on the open market. The government encourages individuals to build homes on their plots, raise animals, and acquire tractors and other capital that will lead to improved productivity.

Deng also instituted reforms in the industrial sector. In a new Five-Year Plan, Deng redirected production into light industries that manufactured televisions, refrigerators, radios, and other consumer goods. This focus away from heavy industries established a better balance between the production of consumer goods and capital goods and reinforced incentives for individual productivity.

PER CAPITA GDP: CHINA, 1960–1993

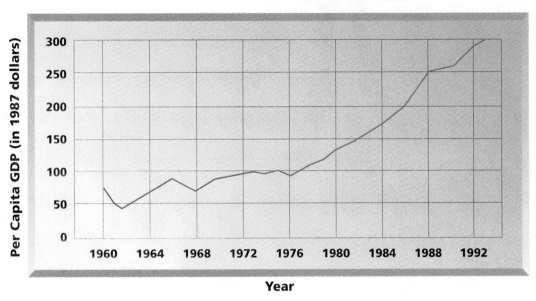

Per Capita GDP (in 1987 dollars)

Year

Source: *Economic Report of the President: 1997*

FIGURE 16.4 China's economy has responded favorably to market-oriented reforms begun in the late 1970s. **During what ten-year period has China's per capita GDP increased most dramatically?**

The government also extended to industry the household responsibility system used in agriculture. Under this arrangement, central planners set broad production goals and some quotas, but plant managers are free to hire and fire workers. Further, managers determine what to produce beyond their quotas. Any additional products can be sold for profit. The government levies a progressive income tax on profits, but plant managers can use after-tax profits for reinvestment or workers' pay raises and bonuses.

The government also created free-trade zones in the region around Shanghai and other east-coast ports and joined in ventures with foreign corporations to encourage investment in these zones. The free-trade zones reflected Deng's belief that foreign capital, technology, and management would strengthen the Chinese economy.

China's economy responded favorably to Deng's market-oriented reforms, and agricultural and industrial output rose substantially. Additionally, China now has a greater variety of consumer goods available. Figure 16.4 shows China's growth in per capita output from 1980 to 1993.

Increasingly, economic reforms were accompanied by calls for greater political freedoms. For example, in 1989 a million demonstrators gathered in Beijing's Tiananmen Square. These protesters hoped to gain the freedom to choose their leaders and to improve conditions in universities. Several thousand students went on a hunger strike. Unable to stop the demonstration peacefully, government leaders ordered tanks and armed troops to remove the unarmed protesters by force. Hundreds of protesters were killed and thousands more were injured in the resulting **Tiananmen Square Massacre**, and the political system remained largely unchanged.

The economic reforms of China's Five-Year Plans continued after Deng's death in 1997. Their goals continue to include the reduction of direct government controls.

Challenges for China In effect, China has a two-tiered economic system, with a central command system and a market system operating at the margin. By leaving the state system in place, the Chinese avoided the disruptions that troubled

ECONOMIC SYSTEMS *Student protesters call for political reforms in Beijing's Tiananmen Square in 1989.* **What was the outcome of this demonstration?**

those countries making the transition to a market economy.

How well has this approach worked? China has one of the fastest-growing economies in the world. Its per capita output increased dramatically. Because of China's huge population, per capita income remains low, but the nation's economy is now the second largest in the world.

SECTION 4 — REVIEW

1. Define the following terms: bourgeoisie, proletariat, collectivization, perestroika, Great Leap Forward, people's communes, Cultural Revolution, Four Modernizations, household responsibility system, Tiananmen Square Massacre.

2. How did Karl Marx view history?

3. What were the drawbacks of central planning in the former Soviet Union?

4. How did the Four Modernizations attempt to shift China away from rigid central planning?

5. **Thinking and Writing Critically**
   Do you think that economic reforms can be successful without political reforms? Explain your answer.

6. **Applying** ECONOMIC INSTITUTIONS & INCENTIVES
   Karl Marx suggested the following principle: "From each according to his abilities, to each according to his needs." Restate this principle in your own words. Would this be a sound philosophy for an economic system? What role do incentives play in this economic and social principle? Explain your answer.

SECTION 1 Economic systems can be classified by ownership of capital and by the process of answering the questions of what, how, and for whom to produce. The four kinds of economic systems arising from this classification are market capitalism, command capitalism, market socialism, and communism. In a market capitalist system, capital is privately owned, and decisions are made primarily by the owners of capital. In a command capitalist system, economic decisions are frequently made by the government. In a market socialist system, capital is generally owned by the government, which makes many economic decisions, although individuals and businesses also have important decision-making roles. In a communist system nearly all capital is owned—and nearly all decisions are made—by the government.

SECTION 2 Capitalism emerged in Europe during the 1700s and 1800s, as nations moved away from mercantilism and governments became less involved in economic decision making. One of the major economic thinkers of the day was Adam Smith, who argued that a market economy was largely self-regulating and did not require government involvement.

Forms of capitalism vary widely around the world. While the United States and Germany are market capitalist systems with relatively limited government involvement, other nations such as Japan follow command capitalism.

SECTION 3 Socialism arose from dissatisfaction with working and living conditions during the early Industrial Revolution. Early socialist thinkers such as Robert Owen and Charles Fourier sought a more equal distribution of wealth.

Market socialism, also called democratic socialism, is characterized by the people having basic human rights and electing government officials, which gives them some control over their country's economic planning. This system has in the past been seen most clearly in Sweden, where the government owned some of the country's industries.

SECTION 4 Command socialism, also called authoritarian socialism or communism, developed primarily from the views of German philosopher Karl Marx. He believed that history was a series of class struggles that would eventually result in collective ownership of all capital.

The Soviet Union was the most influential nation to rely on communism. The leaders of the Soviet Union abolished private property, redistributed land, and developed a rigidly centralized economy. By the 1980s poor economic performance led to a call for reforms. In 1991 the Soviet Union collapsed.

The communist People's Republic of China has moved from strict communism to a more market-oriented form of socialism. For many years China relied on central planning, but low productivity led to economic turmoil. Market reforms have encouraged many in China to call for political reforms, and economic growth has raised China's standard of living.

Economics Notebook

Return to the list of decisions you wrote in your Economics Notebook at the beginning of this chapter. How do these decisions— and your answers to the other questions— reflect a market capitalist economy? Record your answer in your Notebook.

REVIEWING CONCEPTS

1. Describe the similarities between manorialism in the Middle Ages and China's contract responsibility system of the 1970s.

2. How do U.S. and German fiscal policies differ?

3. What is the difference between nationalization and privatization?

4. What problems developed in Russia because of Lenin's "war communism"?

5. How did Mikhail Gorbachev contribute to economic reform in the Soviet Union?

6. What was the Great Leap Forward, and why did it fail?

THINKING AND WRITING CRITICALLY

1. **ECONOMIC INSTITUTIONS & INCENTIVES** Would you be willing to pay as much of your income in taxes as the Swedish people have done in return for free health and education benefits? Explain your answer.

2. **ECONOMIC SYSTEMS** What are some of the advantages and disadvantages of living in a capitalist society?

3. **ECONOMIC SYSTEMS** After the collapse of the Soviet Union in 1991, why do you think the majority of the 15 independent nations chose market systems instead of the communist systems that had been in place?

4. **ECONOMIC SYSTEMS** Why did Swedish workers have more power during Sweden's socialist period than workers have in the capitalist nations of the United States and Japan?

YOUR LOCAL ECONOMY

Incentives increase workers' motivation and productivity. Contact the personnel or human resources department of a company in your area. Ask about incentives provided for the company's employees such as bonus plans, stock-purchase plans, retirement plans, etc. Present your findings to the class.

INDIVIDUAL PORTFOLIO PROJECT

There are advantages and disadvantages to both capitalism and socialism. Design an economic system that combines the advantages of both systems. Who will own and manage the resources? What incentives, if any, will there be for workers? What social programs will be available? What will the tax rate be? Make a presentation to the class about the economic system you have developed.

PRACTICING SKILLS: UNDERSTANDING MAPS

Political maps use colors and lines to illustrate boundaries between countries and to describe information such as territorial changes. To understand a map, read the title and labels to determine the map's subject and geographic area. Then study the legend or key to become familiar with any symbols, lines, colors, and shadings. Using these guidelines, study the map on page 401 and answer the following questions.

1. What countries were formerly satellites of the Soviet Union?

2. What countries were formerly part of the Soviet Union, but are currently not members of the Commonwealth of Independent States?

Eastern Europe

Legend:
- Former Soviet republic
- Former East European satellite of Soviet Union
- Member of Commonwealth of Independent States

FINLAND
ESTONIA
RUSSIA
LATVIA
Baltic Sea
LITHUANIA
RUSSIA
BELARUS
POLAND
GERMANY
UKRAINE
CZECH REPUBLIC
SLOVAKIA
AUSTRIA
MOLDOVA
SLOVENIA
HUNGARY
ROMANIA
CROATIA
ITALY
Black Sea
BOSNIA AND HERZEGOVINA
SERBIA
BULGARIA
MONTENEGRO
ALBANIA
MACEDONIA

0   300 Miles
0   300 Kilometers
Azimuthal Equal-Area Projection

3. Was Germany a satellite of the Soviet Union? Explain your answer.

THE INTERNET: LEARNING ONLINE

The fall of the Soviet Union meant the end of its communist system. Conduct an Internet search using key words such as *Soviet Union*, *Berlin Wall*, and *Russian Federation* to learn about the economic changes that affected Eastern Europe after 1991. What benefits were encountered? What disadvantages were encountered? Draw a wall of bricks to represent the Berlin Wall. Within each brick, describe an economic advantage or disadvantage encountered because of the collapse of the Soviet Union. Present your finished product to the class.

ANALYZING PRIMARY SOURCES

Lou Yumin's Account of a New System

During the 1980s the Chinese government instituted a system of increased personal responsibility for agricultural workers. In the following account, peasant farmer Lou Yumin describes how the system improved her family's standard of living. She, her husband, and their three children grew vegetables for sale in private markets. Read the excerpt below and answer the questions that follow.

"We raise a dozen kinds of vegetables, and every morning we have to pick what's ripe and decide what will sell at the best prices in the market. . . .

"All production matters used to be arranged by our production brigade strictly according to the higher state plan. The state purchased everything we grew, transported it and sold it through retail shops. This had some good and bad points. It did guarantee the vegetable supply and automatically controlled prices. But the complicated procedures often caused delays, so produce got stale and there was a lot of spoilage. City people complained a lot.

"And, under the old policy, good workers and lazy ones were paid the same. . . . The present system's better. Each family in our village contracts land from the brigade (our family has 0.43 hectare [approximately one acre]). This year we have been allowed to sell our vegetables independently if we like, and we're all happy about this. In the past I never bothered to plan my work or figure out how to do it better. I just did whatever our brigade leaders ordered. Now I think about everything—what we should grow, when to apply fertilizer, when to harvest, etc. . . .

"Now, the harder we work, the more money we get. In the first six months of this year we sold 14,000 yuan [about $3,600 in 1986] worth of vegetables to our village's trading center. Deducting our production costs, that gave us a net income of 10,000 yuan, making us one of the best-off families in the village. We also earned a bonus for every 100 yuan of vegetables we sold, for an extra 470 yuan."

1. According to Lou Yumin, how did production and distribution of goods occur in the past?

2. What were the strengths and weaknesses of the control by the production brigades?

3. What reforms have been made in Chinese agriculture in recent years?

4. How has free enterprise encouraged Lou Yumin and her family?

CHAPTER 17

DEVELOPING COUNTRIES

Why are some nations more prosperous than others? How can the allocation and use of resources affect economic activity? How do nations work to expand their economies and improve the standard of living for their citizens? The answers to these questions can provide information about why the economies of two countries may operate in very different ways—even if the countries are close geographically.

In this chapter you will learn how nations are classified by economic development. In addition, you will learn why some countries develop more slowly than others, and how national leaders may help speed economic development.

✎ Economics Notebook

In your Economics Notebook, define "personal economic development." For example, will you consider yourself "economically developed" when you get your first full-time job or when you buy a car?

ECONOMIC DEVELOPMENT

Economics Dictionary

economic development
developed nations
developing nations
arable
subsistence agriculture

Objectives

▶ What characteristics do developing nations have in common?

▶ How can scarcity of resources affect a developing nation?

In the world today there are nearly 200 nations, all at different stages of economic development. **Economic development** is a broad term that includes the size and sophistication of a nation's industrial, service, technical, and agricultural sectors.

The industrialized nations of the world, which economists generally classify as **developed nations**, have a high level of industrial and technical expertise, as well as a variety of economic institutions, such as banking systems, stock markets, and trade networks. The World Bank—an international economic organization—has classified some 25 nations as being "high income" or highly developed. The United States, Canada, Japan, most nations in Europe, and several other nations in Asia and the Middle East are among the developed nations. The combined populations of the developed nations make up about 14 percent of the world's population.

Economists classify the remaining nations of the world as developing nations. The majority of the world's population lives in these developing nations. **Developing nations** are characterized by low per capita gross domestic product (GDP), limited resources or inefficient use of resources, rapid population growth rate, and dependency on agriculture as the main form of production.

Low Per Capita GDP

Per capita GDP, a widely used indicator of the standard of living, is the average dollar value of a nation's annual total output for each person. The per capita GDP is calculated by dividing a nation's total GDP—as discussed in Chapter 10—by its total population.

Economists subdivide developing nations according to income level based on per capita GDP. In the mid-1990s the per capita GDP of low-income developing nations was $700 or less. For lower-middle-income countries, per capita GDP ranged between $701 and $3,000. Upper-middle-income countries' per capita GDP ranged from $3,001 to $12,000. In contrast, the developed nations had per capita GDP of more than $12,000. For a comparison of per capita GDP around the world, see Figure 17.1 on pages 404–405.

Limited Resources

Scarcity and misuse of resources in developing nations are problems that are caused by both natural and historical forces. Natural forces have affected the distribution of resources through climate and the availability of water resources, mineral deposits, and **arable**—or productive—land. For example, in Libya, Mali, Niger, and other countries that lie across the Sahara in Africa, less than 4 percent of the land is arable, mainly because of the lack of rainfall. On the other hand, in much of tropical Africa, where rainfall is plentiful, the soil is drained of its fertility and is unsuitable for most types of agriculture.

Historical forces that have negatively affected the distribution or use of resources include people's decisions and actions. For example, many developing nations were once European colonies. From the 1500s to the mid-1900s, the European powers used colonies to supply agricultural products and raw materials for Europe's industries. In turn, the European powers made only limited investments in colonial economies, transportation networks, and education systems. Colonialism often slowed economic development in much of Asia, Africa, and Latin America.

Rapid Population Growth

The population growth rate, or the annual percentage of increase in a nation's population, is higher in most developing nations than it is in the developed nations. Since 1980 the population growth rate of the many developing nations in Latin America, the Middle East, Africa, and Asia has averaged almost 2 percent, compared to an average of 0.7 percent in developed countries. The population growth rate of developing nations is therefore nearly three times higher than the rate of developed nations.

Some experts argue that many statistics downplay population expansion in developed countries. The United States, for example, increases by some 2.6 million people each year. About one third of this increase is a result of immigration, but the United States has one of the highest birthrates among developed nations.

Other experts point out that population growth is not the result of higher birthrates. In fact, world birthrates declined from 5.3 children per mother in 1950 to 3.4 children per mother by 1994. Instead, advances in health care, hygiene, and sanitation have enabled people to live longer, so that although fewer people are being born to each mother, more are living to adulthood—and consuming more goods and services.

The world's population in 1996 was nearly 5.8 billion and is projected to exceed 7 billion soon after the year 2010. Most of this increase will occur in developing nations. For a comparison of

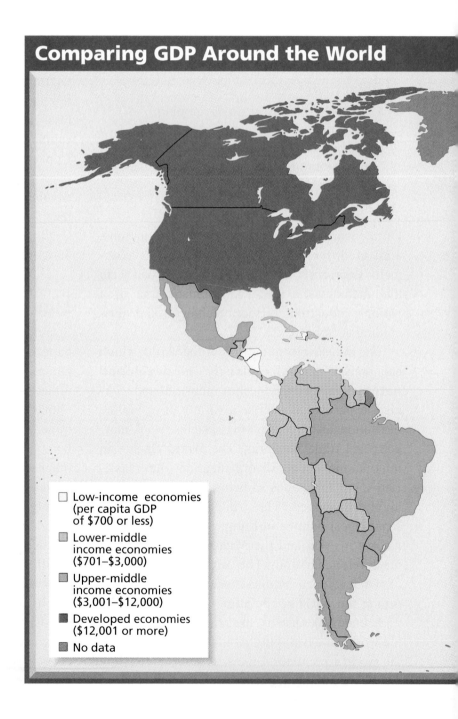

Comparing GDP Around the World

☐ Low-income economies (per capita GDP of $700 or less)

☐ Lower-middle income economies ($701–$3,000)

☐ Upper-middle income economies ($3,001–$12,000)

■ Developed economies ($12,001 or more)

■ No data

FIGURE 17.1 Developed, or industrialized, nations make up about 14 percent of the world's population. **What characteristics do most developing nations share?**

selected national population growth rates, see Figure 17.2 on page 406.

Traditional Agricultural Economies

Many people in developing nations still must produce their own food in order to survive. In **subsistence agriculture**, families grow just enough to meet basic needs and do not produce crop surpluses to trade. Most developing nations, however, have been able to produce surpluses of agricultural products to sell in international markets. These surpluses are usually in commercial plantation crops, such as peanuts from The Gambia, coffee from Colombia and Brazil, bananas from Honduras, cocoa from Ghana and Côte d'Ivoire, and sugar from Cuba and the Dominican Republic. Generally these cash crops are raised solely for export by the producers, who are usually wealthy landowners.

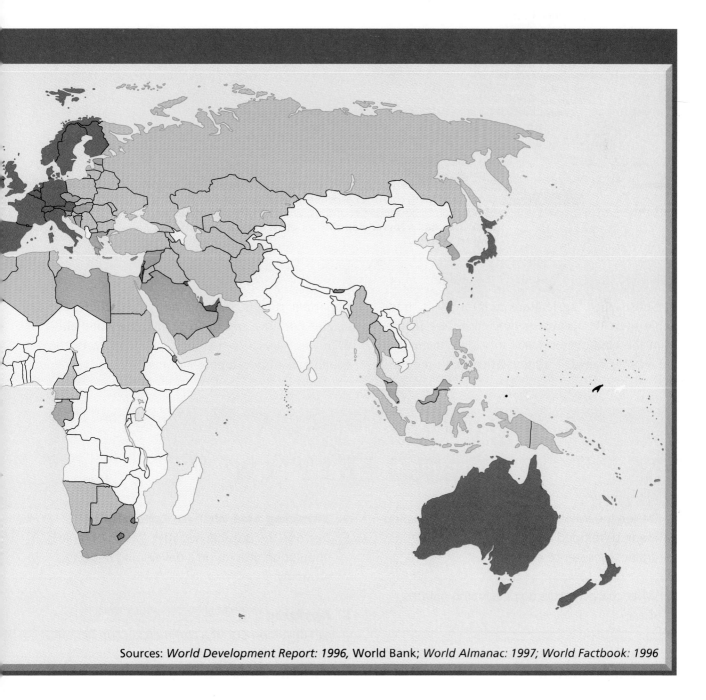

Sources: *World Development Report: 1996,* World Bank; *World Almanac: 1997; World Factbook: 1996*

COMPARING POPULATION GROWTH RATES, 1990–1995

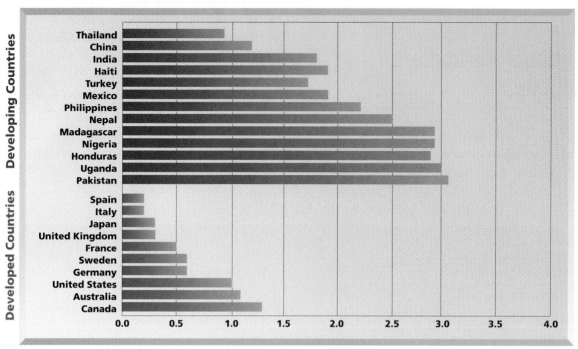

Growth Rate (in percent)

Sources: *World Development Report: 1997,* World Bank

FIGURE 17.2 Most developing countries experience rapid population growth in comparison to developed countries. **Which of these developing countries has a lower population growth rate than the United States?**

Subsistence agriculture reinforces a traditional lifestyle because people earn their income from the land, which tends to isolate them from the outside world. Tradition often plays the most important role in shaping religious beliefs, the size of families, and the role of women and children in society—all of which affect the economies of developing nations.

SECTION 1 —REVIEW

1. Define the following terms: economic development, developed nations, developing nations, arable, subsistence agriculture.

2. What characteristics do developing nations share?

3. What factors contribute to resource scarcity in developing nations?

4. **Thinking and Writing Critically** Describe the possible negative effects of rapid population growth on a developing nation's economy.

5. **Applying** INTERNATIONAL GROWTH & STABILITY How can development of a commercial crop benefit a nation's economy? Who might *not* benefit from such a crop? Explain your answer.

CHALLENGES TO GROWTH

Economics Dictionary

one-crop economy
capital formation
expropriation

Objectives

▶ How do many developing nations respond to scarce factors of production?

▶ How can the status of an economic infrastructure help or hinder a developing nation?

▶ How can political instability challenge a developing nation?

D eveloping nations face great challenges in pursuing economic growth. Decisions about how to use the factors of production are made more difficult by scarcity. While all societies must respond to scarcity, developing nations generally lack the institutions and systems that would enable them to use resources efficiently, which slows economic growth.

Other obstacles may exist that affect economic development. A limited infrastructure can hinder education, commerce, production, and transportation. Political instability can disrupt trade. Social and cultural traditions may cause some people to resist change. In this section you will learn why many developing nations experience slow economic growth.

Scarcity and Resource Use

To achieve economic growth and development, a nation must be able to increase its total per capita output of goods and services. But to increase the output of goods and services, a developing nation must improve the quantity—and quality—of the available factors of production. This improvement, in turn, relies on the effective use of resources. Scarcity and the inefficient use of natural, human, capital, and entrepreneurial resources can limit the potential for growth in developing nations.

Natural Resources Developing nations tend to specialize in the production of one or a few goods, usually agricultural products or raw materials. Although specialization tends to promote international trade, it can also lead to one-crop economies.

A nation that concentrates on the production of a single item has a **one-crop economy**. When referring to one-crop economies, economists use the term *crop* to include many nonagricultural products, such as minerals. One-crop economies often are unstable because the entire economy depends on the world price for a single product.

SCARCITY & CHOICE *Guatemala specializes in the production of coffee. **What are the disadvantages of one-crop economies for developing nations?***

INTERNATIONAL GROWTH & STABILITY *Like most developing nations, India has a large supply of labor.* **What are some reasons that developing nations often experience low worker productivity?**

developing nations is available only to people living in urban areas.

Capital Resources Capital resources and technology are essential to economic growth, but they are in short supply in most developing nations. Capital—when transformed into production plants, machinery, and new equipment—can increase worker productivity. A basic economic goal of many developing nations, therefore, is **capital formation**, the accumulation of the financial resources and capital goods necessary for economic development. Three major obstacles—lack of savings, lack of private investment, and rapid deterioration of existing capital—frequently hinder capital formation in developing nations.

The first obstacle, lack of savings, occurs because people in developing nations find it difficult to put off present consumption. Many people are already living at a subsistence level. After

Environmental factors also may limit growth in a one-crop economy. Suppose that a country specializing in coffee production experiences a severe winter. If a freeze destroys the crop, producers will not be able to supply coffee to the market. Because the country generates few other products that might provide income, its economy will be weakened.

Human Resources Because of their high population growth rates, most developing nations have an ample quantity of workers. However, substandard education and job training, an inadequate diet, and a low level of medical care often result in low worker productivity. In addition, high unemployment and underemployment, each a result of unstable economies, can challenge developing nations.

Most developing nations recognize the importance of long-term investment in human resources. For this reason, many developing nations are spending more money on primary and secondary education. Shortages of funds, however, tend to limit the number of schools and qualified teachers. As a result, education in some

Reprinted by permission from the "Earth Summit Times"

INTERNATIONAL GROWTH & STABILITY *Capital resources and technology are in short supply in most developing nations.* **What are some obstacles to capital formation in developing nations?**

in Economics

Urban and Regional Planner

The hope of economic opportunity brings many people to urban areas. In many developing countries, new city-dwellers may instead find crowded living conditions and extreme poverty, because there are not enough jobs in these cities to support rapid population growth.

Urban growth is also common in developed countries. While cities in these nations do experience overcrowding and poverty, decision makers are generally able to avoid the extreme conditions found in developing nations by consulting with experts called urban and regional planners.

Urban and regional planners study the location and extent of housing, hospitals, businesses, transportation networks, and parks and recreational facilities. After evaluating existing conditions, an urban and regional planner then creates a plan for managing a city's growth.

An urban and regional planner generally has an undergraduate or graduate degree in urban planning. Courses in statistics, economics, architecture, and geography may also be helpful. Internships provide students with on-the-job experience, enabling them to apply classroom studies to real-world situations.

An urban and regional planner may have an area of specialization—for example, commercial development in inner cities or the environmental effects of construction. An urban and regional planner might study transportation patterns in a city to determine how people move between homes and workplaces. Should a bus route be discontinued? Should a new highway be built to accommodate increased traffic?

Most urban and regional planners work for government agencies, but some work as consultants with private businesses. If you are interested in helping communities meet the needs of expanding populations, you might consider a career in urban and regional planning.

Urban planners study a city's characteristics to create plans for managing its growth.

meeting their basic needs for food, shelter, and clothing, they have no money left to save.

If domestic savings cannot fund capital formation, foreign investment is necessary. Many investors, however, are reluctant to invest in the economies of developing nations for several reasons. First, they fear that business leaders' lack of experience could result in mistakes related to what products to produce or what capital should be used in production. Second, there are few incentives to invest in places where the domestic population cannot support markets by purchasing consumer goods. Third, the economic, political, and social environments of many developing nations are unstable. Outside investors generally try to avoid such situations

How Many Worlds?

You may have heard people refer to "Third World countries." Just where is the "Third World"—and which worlds are "First" and "Second"? Although these terms are not widely used today, historically they reflected international tensions.

When World War II ended in 1945, Europe was divided into capitalist nations allied with the United States and communist nations largely controlled by the Soviet Union. During the postwar years, increased tension led to the struggle known as the Cold War. Each side attempted to extend its military, political, and economic power throughout the world.

In 1955, representatives of 29 African and Asian nations met in Bandung, Indonesia, and formed an association of "nonaligned" nations. In doing so, these countries meant to avoid permanent alliances with either the United States or the Soviet Union. The nonaligned nations—soon joined by Yugoslavia—came to be called the Third World. The United States and its allies thus made up the First World, and the Soviet Union and its Eastern European satellite nations were together referred to as the Second World.

Most Third World countries in Africa and Asia were former colonies. Several European nations had controlled empires that included territories from the Mediterranean to Southeast Asia. Many of these colonies gained their independence after World War II.

Economic development in the colonies had focused largely on the exploitation of natural resources for use in industrialized nations. As a result, newly independent nations often lacked their own economic infrastructure. Because they were less prosperous than industrial countries, they were classified as developing nations. The term *Third World* often was extended to any developing nation, even if it was not part of the nonaligned group introduced at the Bandung Conference.

India, one of the most prominent of the nonaligned countries, gained its independence in 1947. Although it has since made some economic progress, its economy is still developing.

India's decision to remain nonaligned was summed up by its first prime minister, Jawaharlal Nehru (juh-WAH-huhr-lal NER-oo), shortly after India became independent. "We do not propose to accept anything that involves in the slightest degree dependence on any other authority," he declared. "Sometimes each country thinks that if you are not completely lined up with it you are its enemy. . . . We have to keep aloof from that and at the same time develop the closest relations with all."

What Do You Think?

1. Many economists, political scientists, and historians agree that the Cold War ended with the fall of the Soviet Union in 1991. In light of this, do you think that the "Third World" still exists? Explain your answer.

2. Why might a nation's leaders decide that their country should be nonaligned? What economic challenges might result from this decision?

Financial assistance from the Soviet Union paid for construction of the Aswan High Dam, but did not change Egypt's nonaligned status.

Many developing nations spend money on national defense rather than economic development. **How does this choice affect entrepreneurship in developing countries?**

Angola, for example, spent 31 percent of its GDP on national defense in 1993. In contrast, military spending accounted for 1.4 percent of Spain's 1995 GDP. Additionally, a lack of consistent education limits the number of people with training in fields such as mathematics, science, and computer programming, as well as management and finance.

Other Obstacles

In developed nations such as the United States and New Zealand, the economic, political, and social environments have contributed to economic growth. In the developing nations, however, these factors have often created obstacles to economic development.

Inadequate Infrastructure In many developing nations, the economic infrastructure has been inadequate to support economic development. As previously noted, a nation's economic infrastructure is its transportation, communications, banking, education, and other institutions and systems that encourage production and promote trade. Developing nations lack well-developed communications networks and roads, railroads, bridges, harbors, and airports. Inadequate schools and a shortage of teachers restrict the number of literate workers, technicians, scientists, and entrepreneurs who are needed to shape economic progress in developing nations.

In addition, the lack of stable monetary and banking systems in some developing nations discourages savings and investments. For example, during recent decades, extremely high inflation rates in Bolivia and Brazil made their currencies nearly worthless.

Nationalization and expropriation of private property also have discouraged savings and investment. As noted in Chapter 16, nationalization takes place when the government assumes

because of the high risk of losing their investments. Finally, a lack of roads, railroads, ports, and utilities generally discourages investment spending. Shortcomings in the economic infrastructure often make the production and distribution of finished products much more difficult.

Capital goods often deteriorate more rapidly in developing nations than in developed nations. Breakdowns in machinery occur from misuse or because workers are unable to read operation and maintenance manuals. Repairs to factories are delayed because there are not enough trained mechanics. Additionally, spare parts often are available only from manufacturers in other nations, further slowing repairs.

Entrepreneurship The forces that account for the gap in capital formation between developing nations and developed nations also account for a gap in entrepreneurship. The lack of savings and private investment in developing nations discourages entrepreneurship, thus slowing the development of new business.

Entrepreneurs also suffer from insufficient financial support from the government. Many developing nations spend money on national defense rather than on economic development.

INTERNATIONAL GROWTH & STABILITY *In the former Soviet Union, privatization of state farmland has been difficult.* **What is one goal of privatization?**

disincentive to savings and investments. Both domestic and foreign investors need to be assured that their investments are secure and that there is a reasonable chance for a return. Revolutions, civil wars, and riots generally cause investors to feel that their funds would not be secure, discouraging economic development.

During the 1980s power struggles in Angola, Nicaragua, El Salvador, Ethiopia, Sri Lanka, Iran, and Iraq disrupted normal business activity. In each of these countries, large sums of money were spent on military goods, and capital investment was destroyed. In 1991, for example, the Persian Gulf War resulted in the destruction of many capital resources in Iraq and Kuwait. To rebuild those countries' economies, new capital goods had to be purchased or developed before consumer goods could be produced.

Social and Cultural Obstacles

In some developing nations, society and culture restrict economic development. A country's traditions,

ownership and control of a business after compensating the former owner. On the other hand, **expropriation** occurs when a nation's government takes control of a firm or industry without compensating the owner. Developing nations have nationalized and expropriated many types of enterprises, such as mines, farms, oil refineries, and factories.

Although many countries have also turned to privatization to improve their economies, this process is not without risk. As noted in Chapter 12, privatization occurs when former public assets such as industry, land, and machinery are sold to individuals or to private businesses. The transition of former communist economies to market economies demonstrates the challenges of privatization. In the former Soviet Union the sale of state-owned farmland and machinery has been difficult. Many factories, for example, were very expensive, making it difficult for individuals or firms to purchase them.

Political Instability

The frequent political instability in some developing nations is another

INTERNATIONAL GROWTH & STABILITY *In 1991 the Persian Gulf War destroyed many capital resources in Iraq and Kuwait.* **In what other ways can political instability affect economic growth?**

class structures, and people's rising expectations may interfere with a nation's economic planning and development.

Strongly rooted customs may lead people to resist changes to traditional production methods. Nations that have primarily agricultural economies generally remain more bound by tradition than nations that are more industrialized and urbanized. In recent decades, however, education, the spread of technology, and increased contact with the developed world have weakened some of the resistance to economic change.

As they begin to experience economic growth, some people in developing nations may expect a rapid increase in the number of goods and services they will be able to consume. These expectations in part come from exposure to the prosperity of developed nations, as shown through the mass media. However, supply is not always able to meet increased demand.

Finally, traditional class structures in some developing nations may limit opportunities for

INTERNATIONAL GROWTH & STABILITY *These Japanese workers are performing traditional group exercises.* **How can society and culture influence economic development?**

individuals. Fewer opportunities to climb the social and economic ladder may reduce incentives to become better educated. Moreover, the ruling elite often opposes change because the present social system guarantees them a privileged position.

SECTION 2 —REVIEW

1. Define the following terms: one-crop economy, capital formation, expropriation.

2. Explain how scarce factors of production can affect developing nations.

3. How do nationalization and expropriation affect economic infrastructures?

4. What are the potential effects of political instability on a nation's economy?

5. Thinking and Writing Critically
How can privatization pose challenges to a developing nation?

6. Applying INTERNATIONAL GROWTH & STABILITY
The spread of television has provided people around the world with a view of life in developed nations. In your opinion, is this view likely to contribute to or become problematic for economic development? Explain your answer.

PATHS TO ECONOMIC DEVELOPMENT

Economics Dictionary
land reform
multinational corporation

Objectives
▶ What are the advantages and disadvantages of the socialist and capitalist models of decision making?

▶ What types of aid do governments of developed countries extend to developing countries?

▶ What are the key public sources of foreign aid?

Not all developing nations have the same type of economic system. Decision makers in each nation set their own goals for development and thus follow varied paths to economic growth.

Decision-Making Models

Leaders of some developing nations follow the socialist model of decision making, while leaders in other nations follow the capitalist model. The choice of which decision-making model to use is not always made solely with economic growth and development in mind.

Socialist Model Decision making in the socialist model, which is associated with communist governments, is centralized in the hands of national leaders. Although many former command socialist economies are making a transition to a market system, there are still a few developing nations—such as Cuba, North Korea,

and Vietnam—using the socialist model of decision making.

The biggest advantage of central planning is the government's ability to direct resources and production toward specific economic goals. This allows the government to change direction quickly. For example, if a government that has traditionally focused on producing military equipment decides that more consumer goods are necessary, it does not need to wait for the forces of supply and demand to take effect. The major disadvantages of central planning are inefficiency, bureaucratic resistance to change, and possible corruption of the bureaucracy that develops and carries out the central plan.

Capitalist Model In a capitalist market economy the decision-making process is decentralized. The government does not control economic decisions; instead, individuals and businesses make most of the decisions through markets. The economic progress of the United States, Japan, and nations in Western Europe has demonstrated

INTERNATIONAL GROWTH & STABILITY *Fidel Castro is the leader of a developing nation—Cuba—that follows the socialist model of decision-making.* **What are the advantages and disadvantages of this model of centralized planning?**

that high levels of economic development are possible through decentralized decision making. Therefore, the economies of many developing nations now follow the capitalist model of economic decision making. Some of the most successful nations in East Asia—such as Singapore, Taiwan, and South Korea—have relied on the capitalist model during their development.

One major advantage of the capitalist model of decision making is the opportunity that individuals have to make economic decisions. In a free-enterprise system, individuals are encouraged to become entrepreneurs. Free enterprise also allows businesses to invest however they choose in new capital and technology. Both owners and workers produce because it is in their self-interest to do so.

Decentralized decision making places few direct controls on how resources are used and which goods are produced. This may present a disadvantage to economic growth if the government wants to direct more investment in capital goods to encourage future growth. Businesses, however, may choose to produce additional consumer goods to meet demand rather than invest in capital goods for future growth and stability. Government influence in the capitalist model is exercised through taxation, subsidies, and regulations that operate through the market system.

Planning for Economic Development

Whether developing nations prefer the capitalist or socialist model of decision making, they must create development plans. A development plan—an outline of how a nation's resources should be used to meet its economic goals—is essential to economic progress. In socialist economies, central planners in the government bureaucracy are responsible for the development plan. In capitalist economies, where the mix of public and private decision making varies from country to country, private businesses and elected representatives in government each plan for the development and control of resources.

Changing of the Guard

At midnight on June 30, 1997, the former British colony of Hong Kong—for nearly 100 years a symbol of free-market economics—became part of the communist People's Republic of China. This dramatic change is sure to have far-reaching effects on both Hong Kong and China.

In 1898 the British government leased Hong Kong from China for a period of 99 years. Hong Kong's strategic location on the Kowloon Peninsula and island of Hong Kong contributed to the development of one of the strongest economies in Asia, with one of the busiest ports in the world.

Across the bay created by the Pearl River delta lies the Portuguese colony of Macao (muh-кow). Even smaller than Hong Kong, the colony has a population of about 500,000 people. For several centuries Macao was a very important port in Asia. Today, however, Macao's main industry is tourism.

China is scheduled to regain control of Macao in 1999. The return of these two territories has caused concern among people in capitalist nations. Both colonies have allowed much greater freedom than China offers its own citizens. The Chinese government, on the other hand, sees the return as a time for national pride.

Some observers wonder whether Hong Kong and Macao will be able to sustain their economic success and individual freedoms, while others wonder if their tradition of free markets and economic power will, instead, change China. Onlookers agree, however, that only time will tell.

Trade-Offs The problem of scarcity prevents any nation from satisfying all of its economic needs and wants. Therefore, a developing nation must make trade-offs. For example, a developing nation may need a new irrigation system for one region of the country and a new road network for another region. Lacking the resources to meet both needs, the government makes a choice. If the irrigation system receives funding, the road network is the trade-off. As noted in Chapter 1, the next-best or alternative use of resources is the first choice's opportunity cost, so in this case the road network becomes the opportunity cost of building the irrigation system.

Production Possibilities To recognize the realities of trade-offs and opportunity costs note the production possibilities curve shown in Figure 17.3. The graph shows one major type of production choice faced by all developing nations—whether to produce more capital goods or more consumer goods.

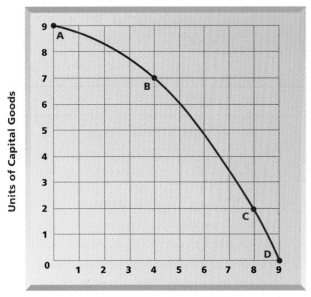

PRODUCTION POSSIBILITIES CURVE FOR DEVELOPING NATIONS

Units Of Consumer Goods

FIGURE 17.3 Production decisions involve opportunity costs and trade-offs. **What is the opportunity cost of producing eight units (point C) as opposed to four units (point B) of consumer goods?**

The horizontal axis shows units of consumer goods, and the vertical axis shows units of capital goods. At point A, nine units of capital goods and zero units of consumer goods are produced, meaning all resources are channeled into the production of capital goods. At point D, nine units of consumer goods and zero units of capital goods are produced, because all resources are devoted to the production of consumer goods.

Decision makers realize that all production decisions have an opportunity cost. For example, suppose a country's development plan focuses largely on the production of capital goods. At point B, seven units of capital goods and four units of consumer goods are produced. Compared to point A, two units of capital goods are given up to gain four units of consumer goods. The opportunity cost of these four units of consumer goods is two units of capital goods.

This curve is a simplified model of the trade-offs and opportunity costs involved in making production decisions. The model assumes that nations can devote all of their resources to just two types of goods—consumer or capital goods. In reality, there are other production choices—such as whether to spend money on military or nonmilitary goods and whether to invest more heavily in agricultural or in industrial capital. The graph also reflects the assumption of a constant level of resources. As a nation's resources or technology increases, the production possibilities curve shifts to the right. The shape of the curve also shows that there are increasing opportunity costs as specialization intensifies.

Expanding Production Possibilities

Developing nations can expand their production possibilities by increasing the quantity or by improving the quality of their factors of production or by improving their production technology. The successes of the "green revolution" illustrate how production possibilities can be expanded.

The green revolution is the use of pest-resistant and high-yielding hybrid seeds, as well as the application of modern technology—advanced machinery, fertilizers, irrigation systems, and pesticides—to agriculture. Since the 1960s the green revolution has expanded agricultural production in many developing nations.

Increasing the amount of land under cultivation and the number of laborers working the land also expands agricultural production. In many developing nations, most of the arable land traditionally has been owned by a small number of wealthy people. **Land reform** is the redistribution of agricultural land from a few major landowners to a larger number of the people who work the land. However, in some command economies the opposite has occurred: small plots have been combined into larger fields to make more efficient use of technology.

INTERNATIONAL GROWTH & STABILITY *Bolivian farmers attend an educational workshop held at an experimental farm.* **How can improved farming techniques expand production possibilities?**

Financing Economic Development

To pay for economic development, developing nations rely on both domestic and international funds. Individuals' and corporate savings generally are the most important source of domestic funds. Foreign funds come from businesses and nonprofit organizations, foreign governments, as well as international development organizations.

Domestic Savings

In some developing nations, domestic savings are the major source of funding for economic development. Developing nations have undertaken infrastructure projects such as roads, railroads, dams, and schools without foreign funding, even though many people in developing nations exist at subsistence level. For example, Paraguay and Brazil have worked together to construct a hydroelectric plant. South Africa is undergoing a domestically funded reconstruction program to reduce unemployment and inequities in health care, education, and other social services. Domestic funds also helped pay for construction of Gabon's Transgabonese Railway, which links the coast with the nation's interior.

In most developing nations, domestic savings alone are insufficient to finance economic development. Therefore, many developing nations seek international capital.

International Private Capital

Several major sources of private capital are available to developing nations. Although nonprofit organizations may provide funding to developing countries, the primary sources of capital are banks—which extend loans to businesses and to governments in developing nations, and earn a profit by collecting interest payments on these loans—and businesses known as multinational corporations (MNCs).

A **multinational corporation** is a firm that owns production facilities in two or more countries and that usually markets its products worldwide. These companies generally sell a wide range of products. For example, Unilever, a Dutch-British MNC, has about 500 subsidiaries that operate in some 75 countries. In the United States alone, Unilever sells products including Lipton Tea®, Promise® margarine, Pepsodent® toothpaste, and Lever 2000® soap, as well as perfumes by designers such as Calvin Klein and Karl Lagerfeld. (See Figure 17.4 on page 418.)

Multinational corporations invest money and technology in developing nations and earn profits in local and international markets. The construction of new plants and the use of advanced machinery funded by MNCs in turn add to the host nation's capital goods.

Political and economic instability, however, often discourage banks and MNCs from extending credit to or investing in developing nations. Banks are careful about loaning money to nations that are already heavily in debt, while MNCs must be cautious to avoid losing capital investments in nations experiencing political turmoil. Nevertheless, banks and MNCs continue to make loans to developing nations.

INTERNATIONAL GROWTH AND STABILITY Multinational corporations are formed in part to increase competitiveness in the global economy. MNCs work to reduce environmental, political, or cultural risks so that they can increase profits and expand their share of their markets.

In the search for higher profits and greater market share, many MNCs attempt to reduce costs. By locating production plants in developing countries, for example, MNCs typically are able to lower labor costs.

Critics of these practices argue that while multinational corporations may rely on inexpensive labor in developing countries, they take profits out of those countries. According to a United Auto Workers report, for example, in 1995 the minimum wage paid to Nike athletic shoe workers in Indonesia was $2.20 per day. Opponents also argue that MNCs use up natural resources, interfere with local businesses, and take job opportunities away from skilled, semi-skilled, and unskilled workers in developed countries.

The supporters of multinational corporations counter these arguments by asserting that MNCs are likely to pay taxes in every country in which they do business, thereby contributing to local economies. Additionally, supporters argue, equating U.S. wages with wages in developing countries is complicated and inaccurate. While an international minimum wage is believed by some people to be necessary, others argue that it would be unfair to require an individual corporation such as Nike to pay U.S. wages in developing countries. In addition, they assert, MNCs provide jobs for people in developing countries, provide training for employees around the world, and increase the capital resources of developing nations by constructing new plants and introducing new resources technology.

International Government Sources of Capital

The governments of many developed countries have special programs to help developing nations. The money, products, and services that are extended through these programs are collectively called foreign aid. Each year the governments of developed nations supply billions of dollars through economic assistance, military

MULTINATIONAL CORPORATION: UNILEVER'S 1996 SALES

FIGURE 17.4 Multinational companies invest money and technology in developing nations. **What is another major source of private capital for developing nations?**

OFFICIAL DEVELOPMENT ASSISTANCE FROM OECD MEMBERS

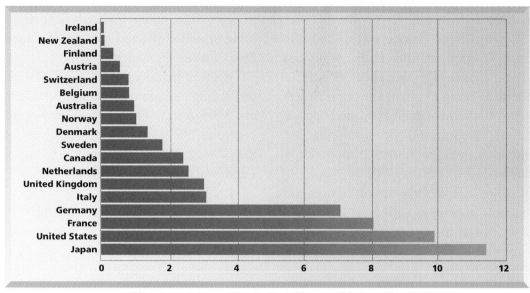

Official Assistance Totals (in billions of U.S. dollars)

Source: *World Development Report: 1995,* World Bank

FIGURE 17.5 The Organization for Economic Cooperation and Development extends aid to developing countries. **What are some of the reasons for extending foreign aid?**

assistance, and emergency assistance to developing nations.

Financial and technical aid, loans, and cash grants that contribute directly to economic development are all types of economic assistance. Supplying the services of specialists such as engineers, scientists, teachers, and physicians is also considered economic assistance.

Military assistance to developing nations takes the form of loans, cash payments, technical expertise, and equipment for military purposes. A developed country is most likely to extend military assistance to its allies, thus making military assistance an important part of the developed nation's foreign policy.

Finally, governments extend emergency aid—food, medical supplies, clothing, and other goods that sustain life—in times of crisis. A major portion of U.S. aid to developing countries is provided in the form of social infrastructure development, such as health care and education. Figure 17.5 shows how much money various governments extend to developing countries around the world.

Reasons for Extending Foreign Aid The United States remains one of the largest sources of foreign aid in the world, even though this aid is a small percentage of the federal budget. Like other developed nations, the United States extends foreign aid for economic, political, military, and humanitarian reasons.

Foreign aid encourages international trade. The economic and social improvements made possible through foreign aid increase the distribution of money throughout the world economy. Foreign aid also can reduce political strife that often disrupts international trade. In addition, foreign aid commonly benefits the supplier because the assisted countries tend to spend money on exports from their donors.

Developed nations sometimes grant foreign aid for political reasons because the aid promotes the donor nation's foreign policy. After World War II, for example, the United States channeled more than $13 billion in military and economic aid to like-minded European nations to stop the spread of communism. By funding economic and physical rebuilding, the Truman Doctrine and the

Marshall Plan improved postwar conditions while helping support democracy and capitalism in allied nations.

In 1961 the United States established the Alliance for Progress to aid Latin American nations. The Alliance was designed in part to improve the well-being of people in Latin America and in part to promote democracy and oppose the spread of communism. Often foreign aid leads to further political and military cooperation among nations.

A final major motive for granting foreign aid is the reduction of human suffering. Nonprofit organizations, governments, and many international organizations have a humanitarian motive for providing foreign aid.

Effectiveness of Foreign Aid Foreign aid has improved the standard of living and quality of life for millions of people in developing nations. Still, experts question whether people in those nations are receiving the maximum benefit from foreign aid.

Some experts, for example, believe that closer supervision by developed nations can improve the effectiveness of aid programs. Such supervision is often strongly opposed by the people and governments of developing nations, who view it as interference with their economic freedom. Nevertheless, governments and international development organizations are now attaching specific conditions to some loans and other forms of assistance to direct the use of economic resources. See Figure 17.6 for information about the debt owed by developing nations.

International Public Sources of Capital

Agencies such as the U.S. Peace Corps—whose goal is to teach skills that increase workers' productivity—provide agriculture experts, engineers, teachers, and other specialists to developing nations. In 1997 the Peace Corps had about 6,500 volunteers working in more than 90 countries around the world.

Many nonprofit organizations also provide aid to developing nations. For example, the International Red Cross and the Save the Children Fund provide food and medical assistance to victims of disasters such as famines.

International organizations are a major source of funding and often serve as a vehicle to distribute foreign aid. The international organizations providing the most significant levels of aid are the World Bank, the International Monetary Fund, and the United Nations.

The World Bank The World Bank was founded at the Bretton Woods Conference in 1944. Its initial purpose was to rebuild European economies after World War II. More recently, the organization has focused on economic progress in developing nations. The World Bank Group consists of the International Bank for Reconstruction and Development (IBRD), the International Development Association (IDA), and the International Finance Corporation (IFC). In 1988 the Multilateral Investment Guarantee Agency was added to the World Bank Group. Since its founding the World Bank has lent more than $300 billion to developing countries.

The IBRD is the largest part of the World Bank and is owned by the governments of 180

INTERNATIONAL GROWTH & STABILITY *The Peace Corps sends teachers, engineers, and other specialists to developing nations. **What international organizations provide the most aid to developing countries?***

EXTERNAL DEBT OF DEVELOPING NATIONS, 1995

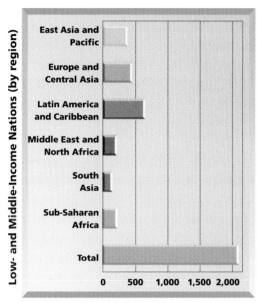

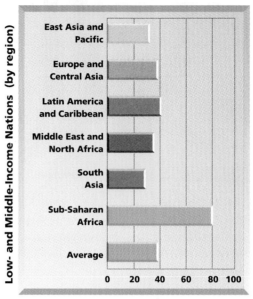

Source: *World Development Report: 1997,* World Bank

FIGURE 17.6 Developing nations use public and private loans to improve their economies. **Which countries have the greatest external debt as a percent of their GNP?**

---

countries. Over the years IBRD loans have been directed at particular types of development. During the 1950s and 1960s, for example, the IBRD granted loans mainly for such internal improvements as roads, railways, and port facilities. During the 1970s the IBRD stressed loans for agricultural development. Since the 1980s loans have focused on economic reorganization rather than building projects.

The International Development Association has 159 members and makes loans only to the lowest-income developing nations. To be eligible for IDA loans, a nation's annual per capita GDP must be in the category of low-income countries.

The 170-member International Finance Corporation encourages private investment in developing nations. To achieve this goal, the IFC works closely with domestic businesses and foreign firms. IFC negotiations and advice help clear the way for direct investment by multinational corporations.

The newest member of the World Bank—the 134-member Multilateral Investment Guarantee

Agency—encourages foreign investment and ensures investors protection from noncommercial risk such as war or nationalization.

International Monetary Fund The International Monetary Fund (IMF) also was founded at the 1944 Bretton Woods Conference. The IMF has made hundreds of short-term loans. For a nation to receive an IMF loan, it must introduce certain economic policies or structural reforms.

In 1997 the IMF pledged to provide $4 billion of a $16 billion aid package designed to strengthen the economy of Thailand. The package was the second-largest economic bailout ever. In exchange for the funds, Thai leaders agreed to increase taxes, reduce spending, and introduce financial reforms.

United Nations The United Nations (UN), established as the world's leading international peacekeeping organization in 1945, also is concerned with economic development. Most of its members are developing nations.

INTERNATIONAL GROWTH & STABILITY *The UN promotes economical development through the United Nations Development Program which works closely with agencies such as the World Health Organization and the Food and Agricultural Organization.* **In what year was the United Nations established?**

officials in El Salvador to help former civil war participants become farmers. This program provided tools and training in efficient agricultural techniques.

The UN has financed thousands of development projects in education, health, agriculture, and industry. UN funding comes from its member nations.

The UN promotes economic development through the programs of its specialized agencies. The United Nations Development Program (UNDP) coordinates its efforts with those of agencies such as the Food and Agriculture Organization (FAO), the World Health Organization (WHO), and the United Nations Industrial Development Organization (UNIDO). During the 1990s, for example, the UNDP worked with

Regional Organizations

Various regional organizations also extend credit to nations within certain geographic locations. Major regional organizations, such as the Inter-American Development Bank, the African Development Bank, and the Asian Development Bank, make loans to developing nations in their respective regions in order to improve local economies.

For example, in the mid-1990s the African Development Bank provided some $430 billion for infrastructure development in southern Africa. The program included such projects as extension and improvement of a toll road, railroad constructions, and upgrades to telecommunications networks. These projects were designed to provide greater access to markets in the region.

SECTION 3 — REVIEW

1. Define the following terms: land reform, multinational corporation.

2. What are the advantages and disadvantages of the socialist and capitalist decision-making models?

3. Why do governments in developed nations extend economic, military, and emergency assistance to other countries?

4. What are the largest international organizations that provide foreign aid to developing countries?

5. **Thinking and Writing Critically**
Imagine that you are the leader of a developing nation and that you want to build paved roads between the capital and other cities in your country. What sources of foreign aid might you seek? Explain your answer.

6. **Applying** ECONOMIC INSTITUTIONS & INCENTIVES
Consider Adam Smith's theory that pursuing individual self-interest can result in benefits for an entire society. When governments, international organizations, and businesses provide foreign aid, do their actions support Smith's theory? Explain your answer.

SECTION 1 Of the nearly 200 nations in the world today, some 25 are classified as developed nations. The others are known as developing nations. Developing nations generally share such characteristics as low per capita GDP, limited resources, rapid population growth rates, and traditional agricultural or one-crop economies.

The lowest-income developing nations have per capita GDP of $700 or less. Other developing nations have per capita GDP of between $701 and $12,000, while developed nations have per capita GDP of $12,001 or more.

Resource limitations in developing nations stem from limited natural resources, such as a lack of arable land, and historic forces, such as European colonization. The inefficient use of resources in developing nations also can hinder economic development.

Population growth in developing nations is much higher than that in developed nations. In fact, developing nations have population-growth rates that are about three times those of developed nations. As a result, most population growth between 1990 and the year 2000 is expected to take place in developing nations.

Most people in developing nations depend on subsistence agriculture, growing just enough to meet basic needs. Some developing nations have been able to produce surpluses in the form of commercial plantation crops. Profits from these crops are most likely to benefit the producers, who tend to be wealthy landowners, rather than a country's general population.

SECTION 2 Developing nations experience scarcity and underutilization of resources. The scarcity and misuse of the factors of production—land, labor, capital, and entrepreneurship—restricts economic growth.

Other obstacles to economic development include an inadequate infrastructure, political instability, and social and cultural issues. A nation that lacks a well-built road system, for example, is likely to have difficulty maintaining reliable markets. Political struggles can disrupt business activity and destroy capital resources, and social and cultural issues may make people reluctant to change traditional methods of production and exchange.

SECTION 3 Leaders of developing nations use either a socialist or a capitalist model of decision making. Regardless of which model the leaders use, however, they must establish development plans to guide the use of their scarce resources. In creating these plans, leaders must consider all the production possibilities and trade-offs related to a proposed course of action.

Developing nations rely on both domestic and foreign funds to finance economic development. Domestic savings is an important source of funds in many nations, but most seek foreign capital as well. Banks, multinational corporations, and nonprofit organizations supply vast amounts of private capital for development. Money and training from foreign governments and international organizations are also crucial to economic development.

Economics Notebook

Review the paragraph that you wrote in your Economics Notebook at the beginning of this chapter. How does your definition correspond to capital formation, economic infrastructure, and other elements of national economic development? Record your answer in your Notebook.

CHAPTER 17

REVIEW

REVIEWING CONCEPTS

1. How is per capita GDP used to classify developing and developed nations?

2. What are developing nations' three major obstacles to capital formation?

3. Why is scarcity a problem for developing nations?

4. How can leaders influence economic growth and development in a nation that uses the capitalist decision-making model?

5. Provide an example of each of the following: economic assistance, military assistance, and emergency assistance.

6. List three sources of foreign capital.

THINKING AND WRITING CRITICALLY

1. INTERNATIONAL GROWTH & STABILITY Explain the difference between developed and developing nations. Select one of the latter and explain how it exemplifies the common characteristics of a developing country.

2. INTERNATIONAL GROWTH & STABILITY How might social and cultural issues interfere with economic progress in developing countries?

3. PRODUCTIVITY How can developing nations expand their production possibilities? What effect does this expansion have on the production possibilities curve?

4. INTERNATIONAL GROWTH & STABILITY What is the "green revolution"? How might it help a country strengthen its economy?

YOUR LOCAL ECONOMY

Contact a nonprofit organization that provides aid to people in your community. Interview a volunteer and a person who has received help to discover the benefits that each receives. Report your findings to the class.

COOPERATIVE PORTFOLIO PROJECT

Imagine that you and your group are owners of a multinational corporation that is interested in opening a business in a developing country. Have members of your group research developing countries around the world. Select the economy that seems best suited for your business, and write a proposal for marketing your product. Some group members should develop an outline and text for the proposal while others create illustrations.

PRACTICING SKILLS: UNDERSTANDING MAPS

Using the political map and information about Central American countries on page 425, create a special-purpose map that illustrates per capita GDP. Organize your map in whatever way you think is most understandable and effective. Consider the use of color, relative size of countries, and symbols. Include a key to explain the information. When you have finished, answer the questions that follow.

1. Which country has the lowest GDP?

2. Explain why per capita GDP is higher in Costa Rica than in Guatemala, even though Guatemala has a higher overall GDP.

3. If you were an investor, in which of these countries would you want your company to be located? Explain your answer.

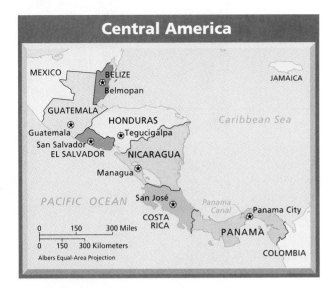

Central America

Country	Pop.	GDP (1994 $)	Per Capita GDP
Belize	219,296	575 mil.	$2,750
Costa Rica	3,463,083	16.9 bil.	$5,050
El Salvador	5,828,987	9.8 bil.	$1,710
Guatemala	11,277,614	33 bil.	$3,080
Honduras	5,605,193	9.7 bil.	$1,820
Nicaragua	4,272,352	6.4 bil.	$1,570
Panama	2,655,094	12.3 bil.	$4,670

Source: *World Almanac: 1997*

THE INTERNET: LEARNING ONLINE

Conduct an Internet search for information about the Peace Corps. How did the organization evolve? What kinds of aid has the organization provided over the years? What types of people volunteer for the organization? Focus on one aspect of the Peace Corps that interests you, and present this information to the class.

ANALYZING PRIMARY SOURCES

"Education and Economic Development"

In 1979 Sir Arthur Lewis, a British economist, shared the Nobel Prize in economics with Theodore Schultz for a study of the economies of developing nations. Lewis wrote this article in 1961. Read the excerpt below and answer the questions that follow.

"Poor countries cannot afford to pay for as much education as richer countries. They have therefore to establish priorities in terms both of quantity and quality. . . .

"From the standpoint of economic development, one may distinguish between types of education which increase productive capacity and types which do not. Teaching an African cook to read may increase his enjoyment of life, but will not necessarily make him a better cook. Education of the former kind I have called 'investment education', while the latter kind is called 'consumption education'. From the standpoint of economic development, investment education has a high priority, but consumption education is on a par with [equal to] other forms of consumption. The money spent on teaching cooks to read might equally be spent on giving them pure water supplies, or radios, or better housing, and must therefore compete in the context of all other possible uses of resources. . . .

". . . The main limitation on the absorption of the educated in poor countries is their high cost, relative to average national output per head. In a country where most people are illiterate, the primary school graduate, whose only skills are reading and writing, commands a wage much higher than a farmer's income. . . . The poor countries may need the educated more than the rich, but they can even less afford to pay for or absorb large numbers of them. . . .

". . . An economy can ultimately absorb any number of educated people. It follows that it is erroneous, when making a survey of the need for skilled manpower, to confine one's calculations to the numbers that could be absorbed at current prices. One ought to produce more educated people than can be absorbed at current prices, because the alteration in current prices which this brings about is a necessary part of the process of economic development."

1. How does Lewis distinguish investment education from consumption education?

2. Why, according to Lewis, is it difficult for developing countries to absorb a large number of educated workers?

3. Why does Lewis suggest that education should not be limited based on current prices?

CHAPTER 18

INTERNATIONAL TRADE

"Free trade, one of the greatest blessings which a government can confer on [grant] a people, is in almost every country unpopular," wrote Lord Macaulay in 1824. Trade has taken place for thousands of years, whether within a city or across national boundaries. How then can a government confer free trade on its people? And if free trade is a blessing, why might it be unpopular?

In this chapter you will learn how international trade works and why it is conducted, as well as how payments are made between trading nations. Additionally, you will learn why free trade sometimes is controversial, and how nations work either to promote or to restrict free trade.

✏ Economics Notebook

In your Economics Notebook, keep track of the items you use during a week, such as clothing and electronic equipment. List the countries in which 10 of these items were produced.

SECTION 1

SPECIALIZATION AND INTERDEPENDENCE

Economic Dictionary

absolute advantage
comparative advantage

Objectives

▶ How does specialization encourage trade?

▶ How can absolute advantages influence economic choices?

▶ How can comparative advantages affect a nation's economy?

Why do nations participate in trade? There are two factors that make international trade possible. First, international trade is voluntary. Nations choose which resources and products they will trade. Second, trade creates wealth. Nations pursue trade in order to increase their wealth in terms of goods, services, or resources.

Specialization and Trade

Specialization and economic interdependence serve as the basis for international trade. As noted in Chapter 1, specialization occurs when producers provide a limited number of goods or services. Such specialization may occur because of a nation's particular resources. For example, much of the world's coffee comes from nations in Central and South America, while countries such as Switzerland—which do not have a climate appropriate for coffee production—must import all their coffee.

Without international trade, a nation can consume only the goods and services it produces.

The development of international trade enables a nation to specialize in the production of goods and services that can be traded for other products. Specialization offers a nation the opportunity to become efficient in the production of a few goods and services and to trade them for whatever goods and services that nation cannot supply to its people.

CASE STUDY

The European Union

INTERNATIONAL GROWTH & STABILITY In the early 1990s many Europeans feared that the elimination of trade barriers among European nations would lead to a single European economy and society. Instead of a group of distinct nations each with its own language and customs, these people argued, free trade would blur populations—and eventually cultures.

So far, these fears have not materialized. Economists have instead noted increasing specialization based on traditional centers of production. For example, before the European Union (EU) was established, Carrara, Italy, was a marble-carving center for centuries, even long after its quarries were depleted. After the EU was formed, Carrara's carving industry was not challenged by new marble-carving centers. In fact, Carrara remains the leading marble-carving center in Europe despite the fact that lowered trade barriers also allow marble to be imported to Naples, Marseilles, or any other location in Europe.

Similarly, moviemakers in Spain have tried to establish a film animation industry in the city of Seville. Film animators continue to flock to London's Soho district, however, where artists and filmmakers have centered their activity for years.

This continued specialization encourages interdependence among European nations. Limited natural, human, capital, and entrepreneurial resources force cities and nations to make choices that result in specialization and interdependence. Simplified trade requirements have not led, for example, to pork production centers all over Europe, but have eased the process of shipping hams and bacon from Denmark to other countries.

Absolute and Comparative Advantage

The factors of production—natural, human, capital, and entrepreneurial resources—are not distributed equally throughout the world. This uneven resource distribution encourages nations to trade in order to improve their citizens' standard of living. For example, Japan has very limited oil reserves. To acquire oil, it must produce other goods and services that can be traded. How a nation decides what to produce is determined by two related economic concepts originally described by the nineteenth-century British political economist David Ricardo—absolute advantage and comparative advantage.

Absolute Advantage A nation has an **absolute advantage** in producing a certain good when it can do so with greater efficiency than can its partner in trade. For example, if Costa Rica and Panama both produce coffee, cocoa, and lumber, and Costa Rica can produce each at a lower cost, then it would be correct to say that Costa Rica holds an absolute advantage over Panama for these items. Similarly, if an attorney can type 120 words per minute while her secretary, who is not an attorney and has no training in the law, can type only 100 words per minute, then it would be correct to say that the attorney has an absolute advantage in both practicing law and typing.

Comparative Advantage The existence of an absolute advantage does not mean that the nation with the absolute advantage will produce everything while the other nation will produce no goods and services at all. The particular items each produces will be determined by identifying its comparative advantage. The **comparative advantage** may be found by determining where the greatest absolute advantage occurs for each nation.

Consider again the attorney and her secretary. While the attorney is absolutely more productive in both practicing law and in typing, the greatest advantage is in practicing law. The secretary may

INTERNATIONAL TRADE *A nation decides what to produce—bananas, for instance—by determining its absolute and its comparative advantages.* **How is a nation's comparative advantage determined?**

not know anything about practicing law, but may be quite skilled at typing. Therefore, the attorney has the comparative advantage in practicing law. On this basis the attorney would be wise to practice law and let her secretary handle the typing. Comparative advantage thus determines how individuals specialize.

In the same manner, comparative advantage influences specialization on a national level. The key to comparative advantage is the concept of trade-offs. As noted in Chapter 1, trade-offs are the items sacrificed, or not selected, when production choices are made. Suppose that if Costa Rica devoted all its resources to producing coffee it could produce 25 million pounds per year, and if it devoted all its resources to growing bananas it could produce 5 million pounds per year. In terms of resources, Costa Rica thus would be producing five pounds of coffee for every pound of bananas. The pound of bananas would be the trade-off for the five pounds of coffee. Costa Rica's exchange ratio between coffee and bananas would be 5:1.

Customs Inspector

Each year nearly a half billion people and billions of dollars of products enter the United States through any one of the country's 300 air, sea, and land ports of entry. The U.S. Customs Service oversees this enormous flow of people and products. Some 19,000 Customs Service employees enforce travel and immigration laws and ensure that incoming products meet the many laws and regulations of the United States.

The customs inspector is the frontline worker in this critical operation. Inspectors are stationed at each national port of entry, where they individually process and inspect each person and shipment of products entering the country. They often work with other government agencies such as the Immigration and Naturalization Service, the Drug Enforcement Administration, and the Department of Agriculture.

To qualify for a position as a customs inspector, applicants must be citizens of the United States and must pass a physical examination, a background check, and a drug test. Inspectors also must have work experience that involves interacting with people and learning and applying a large collection of detailed facts.

In addition, customs inspectors undergo extensive training. Employees begin with 11 weeks of formal law enforcement instruction, including written and physical tests, practical exercises, and firearms classes. This formal training is then supplemented by continual on-the-job training.

The customs inspector's job is not an easy one. Inspectors are expected to work long, irregular hours, often at remote border locations around the country. Their work, however, plays a crucial role in maintaining the economic health of the United States.

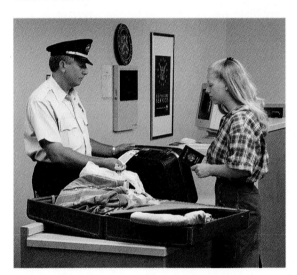

Customs inspectors ensure that products entering the United States comply with U.S. laws and regulations.

Suppose also that if Panama devoted all of its resources to coffee production, it could produce 12 million pounds per year. If Panama devoted all of its resources to banana production, on the other hand, it could produce 4 million pounds per year. In terms of resources, Panama would be producing three pounds of coffee for every pound of bananas. The pound of bananas would be the trade-off for the three pounds of coffee, making Panama's exchange ratio between coffee and bananas 3:1.

Clearly, Costa Rica would be more productive in both coffee and bananas. However, the country would be comparatively—or relatively—more productive in producing coffee. On that basis, it would benefit both nations to specialize, with

ABSOLUTE AND COMPARATIVE ADVANTAGE

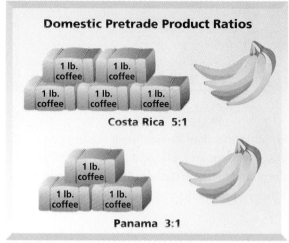

Domestic Pretrade Product Ratios

Costa Rica 5:1

Panama 3:1

Costa Rica–Panama

Trade Ratio 4:1

FIGURE 18.1 Pretrade product ratios describe original production possibilities, while trade ratios reflect comparative advantage. **How do countries benefit from specialization?**

Costa Rica producing coffee and Panama producing bananas. The exact trade ratio will determine just how much each country would benefit by trade, but so long as the trade ratio was between 5:1 and 3:1, both nations would benefit from specialization.

Suppose that the trade ratio was determined to be 4:1. If Costa Rica specialized in coffee, with international trade it would only have to give up—or trade off—four pounds of coffee for one pound of bananas. Without trade it would have to give up five pounds of coffee for a single pound of bananas (see Figure 18.1). Costa Rica therefore would benefit from international trade and specialization.

If Panama specialized in bananas at the 4:1 trade ratio, for every pound of bananas it traded it would receive four pounds of coffee. Without trade it would have to give up—or trade off—a pound of bananas for only three pounds of coffee. Thus, Panama, too, would benefit from trade and specialization. The original domestic pretrade production ratios of 5:1 and 3:1 describe each nation's original production possibilities, while the new production ratio of 4:1 describes the situation once the concept of comparative advantage is applied.

SECTION 1 —REVIEW

1. Define the following terms: absolute advantage, comparative advantage.

2. How does specialization encourage international trade?

3. Why might policy makers choose to concentrate on absolute advantage when making economic choices?

4. Why might policy makers choose to pursue a comparative advantage rather than an absolute advantage?

5. Thinking and Writing Critically How does specialization affect your choices as an individual? Describe a recent specialization-based exchange of products or resources in which you have participated.

6. Applying INTERNATIONAL TRADE Imagine that your economics classroom is a nation and that you and your classmates have the opportunity to engage in a trade of tutoring services with a "mathematics" nation, a "science" nation, and a "government" nation. What are your absolute advantages? comparative advantages?

FOREIGN EXCHANGE AND CURRENCIES

Economics Dictionary

foreign exchange market
foreign exchange rate
adjustable-peg system
devaluation
appreciation
floating exchange rates
balance of payments
balance of trade
trade surplus
trade deficit

Objectives

▶ Why are foreign exchange rates necessary?

▶ How does a nation determine its balance of payments?

▶ What is the significance of the balance of trade?

I n early 1997 there were nearly 200 nations in the world, each with its own government and national currency. National currencies such as dollars, pesos, and rupees generally are accepted in payment for goods and services within a nation's borders. To participate in international trade, however, nations must have a way of determining the values of their currencies in relation to one another.

Markets exist for the buying and selling of national currencies, just as they do for stocks, bonds, and other commodities. These currency markets are known as **foreign exchange markets**.

Foreign Exchange Rates

When a business in one country imports items, it makes payment in the exporting nation's currency. When a business in another country exports items, it also needs to receive payment in its own currency. Foreign exchange markets are designed to resolve these situations. Through the foreign exchange markets, currencies are converted into other currencies. Once the value of one currency is determined in relation to another, a **foreign exchange rate** for the two has been established.

In the United States, foreign exchange rates are expressed in two ways. The first is the number of units of another nation's currency that equal one dollar. In October 1997, for example, one U.S. dollar equaled 120.97 Japanese yen, and 5.96 French francs. The second is the U.S. dollar value for each unit of foreign currency. At that

EXCHANGE, MONEY, & INTERDEPENDENCE *Currencies are converted into other currencies through foreign-exchange markets.* **How are foreign exchange rates expressed in the United States?**

time, the Japanese yen was worth $.0083, and the French franc was worth $.1677.

Since World War II, nations have used one of two foreign exchange rate systems: the adjustable-peg system and the floating, or flexible, system. In an **adjustable-peg system**, the currency of one nation was initially pegged, or established, in relation to U.S. dollars, which had a fixed price in gold. The relationship was not fixed permanently, however. As economic situations changed, nations could change the exchange rate of their currency with currencies of other nations. This new rate would remain intact until one country chose to change the relationship between its currency and that of other nations. The adjustable-peg exchange rate system was used from 1944 to 1971.

Bretton Woods Conference

Adjustable-peg exchange rates were introduced at the Bretton Woods Conference in 1944. At that conference, 44 allied nations agreed that each nation should define its currency in terms of U.S. dollars, with an ounce of gold worth $35. Once set, these rates established base rates with all other currencies. Further, with this exchange rate system, each nation agreed to keep its currency stable in relation to other countries' currencies.

The Bretton Woods Conference established the International Monetary Fund (IMF) to make the system work. This organization, based in Washington, D.C., promotes international monetary cooperation, currency stabilization, and international trade. In 1997 more than 180 countries were members of the IMF.

Eliminating the Adjustable-Peg System

At the heart of this system was the assumption that international trade patterns would remain unchanged. For more than 20 years this system worked relatively well, with few currency changes. As international trade patterns began to change rapidly during the 1960s and 1970s, however, countries found it increasingly difficult to maintain established exchange rates under the adjustable-peg system.

When one nation's currency decreases in value relative to other currencies, **devaluation**, or depreciation, has occurred. When a nation's currency is devalued, its products become cheaper to other nations; at the same time, other nations' products become more expensive to buyers in the nation that has devalued its currency.

On the other hand, when a nation's currency increases in value compared to other currencies, **appreciation** has occurred. Following this appreciation, that nation's products will become

"Sorry, your uncle left nothing of value, only U.S. dollars."

BALANCE OF PAYMENTS *When this cartoon was drawn in 1978, the value of the U.S. dollar was decreasing relative to foreign currencies.* **How did currency devaluation and appreciation contribute to the elimination of the adjustable-peg system?**

more expensive for people who purchase them in other countries. Additionally, other countries' products will become relatively less expensive in the nation with the appreciating currency. Because of the constant changes in international trade patterns, nations were unable to rely on the adjustable-peg system, and in 1971 a new system, based on floating exchange rates, was established.

Floating Exchange Rates
With **floating exchange rates**, the value of a currency is determined by the laws of demand and supply. As a result, currency values can change from one minute to the next.

These constant changes in the exchange value of a nation's currency can have both positive and negative effects. For example, during the mid-1980s the demand for U.S. dollars was high. Foreign investors wanted to buy dollars to invest in U.S. businesses and securities, and the U.S. dollar was viewed as one of the world's most secure currencies because of the strength of the U.S. government and a low U.S. inflation rate. In addition, many people around the world relied on dollars as a medium of exchange and investment. As a result of these factors, the U.S. dollar appreciated in value.

This appreciation led to what economists call a "strong" dollar, which has more purchasing power relative to other currencies. The strong dollar had a negative effect on U.S. exporters, who sold products to other nations, while having a positive effect on U.S. consumers buying foreign goods. In other words, foreign-made goods became less expensive in U.S. markets, and goods made in the United States became more expensive in foreign markets.

To understand how a strong dollar affects exports and imports, consider the following example. Suppose that five French francs equal a single U.S. dollar. At that exchange rate an item priced at $100 would sell in France for 500 francs. However, if the exchange rate changes as a result of the dollar's appreciation so that 8 francs equal a dollar, it would take 800 francs—instead of 500—to buy the U.S. item. Clearly,

INTERNATIONAL TRADE *A strong U.S. dollar works to reduce the price on foreign-made goods such as this Mexican rug.* **How does a strong dollar affect goods made in the United States?**

this change in the exchange rate would reduce the quantity of U.S. goods demanded in France.

The quantity of French goods demanded in the United States would increase, as those goods would decrease in price when the exchange rate changed. A French manufacturer who initially priced his or her products to be sold in the United States at the equivalent of 500 francs each would have required Americans to pay $100 for that item; however, after the change in relative currency values to 8 francs per dollar, Americans could buy the same item for $62.50 each. This price decrease would lead to an increase in the quantity of French goods demanded in the United States.

The previous examples assumed that the forces of demand and supply acted without government involvement. In reality, however, governments do intervene from time to time in foreign exchange markets to keep the value of their own or other nations' currencies from rising either too much or too little. At times, governments have stepped in to influence the value of their currencies.

ECONOMICS
in Action

Global Enterprise

Pacific Rim countries—those bordering the Pacific Ocean—make up one of the fastest-growing trade regions in the world. One might wonder what kind of business might be successful in this region and how such a business could be formed. A group of high school students in Alaska found some creative answers to these very questions.

Edgecumbe Enterprises—founded and run since 1985 by students at Mt. Edgecumbe High School in Sitka—was founded to export smoked salmon. Salmon are plentiful in Alaskan waters, but in Asia low levels of supply result in high prices for this popular fish. The company began as a salmon processing plant, with a grant from the U.S. Department of Health and Human Services that paid for equipment and the development of package and label designs. In the spring of 1989, Mt. Edgecumbe students made four shipments of smoked salmon to Asia.

Using money from the grant, students made marketing trips to Japan and China to meet with marketing and sales experts and to learn about local business practices and culture. For example, students studied Japan's quality-control techniques. They then applied their newfound knowledge, incorporating these methods into their own company. This increased efficiency and helped ensure the high product quality necessary to compete on the international market. The hands-on experience enabled students to negotiate Japan's trade barriers and regulations.

The curriculum at Mt. Edgecumbe High School focuses on the study of the economies and societies of the Pacific Rim. Because trade with Asia is a key part of Alaska's economy, school officials worked to develop a curriculum that would promote trade and entrepreneurship, while establishing high academic standards.

Graduation from Mt. Edgecumbe requires a heavier course load—including several unusual classes—than other Alaska high schools. Students must take at least a year of Japanese or Chinese language classes and a yearlong course on Pacific Rim cultures.

Traditional classes also focus on developing future entrepreneurs. Students and teachers use their exeriences with Edgecumbe Enterprises to frame their learning of basic skills. For example, math classes involve calculating exchange rates, art classes include lessons in brochure design, and computer classes teach students to analyze business expenses and profits using spreadsheets.

What Do You Think?

1. How might studying different cultures help businesses involved in international trade?
2. Briefly discuss the advantages and disadvantages of designing a curriculum around a specific subject like international trade.
3. Considering the characteristics of your own school and local economy, how might your high school curriculum be changed to involve students in real business?

Students at Mt. Edgecumbe High School in Sitka, Alaska, developed a business to sell salmon in Asia.

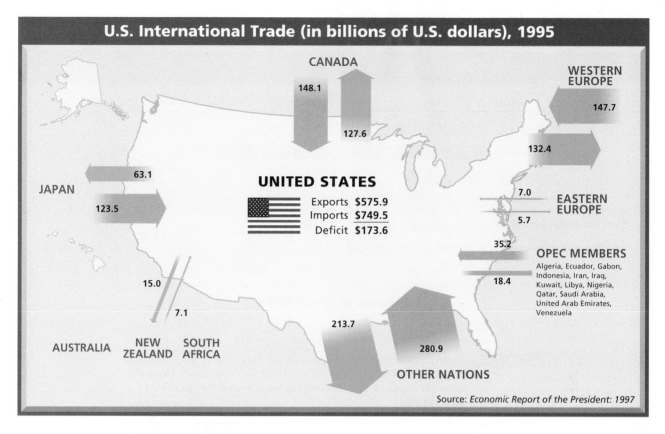

U.S. International Trade (in billions of U.S. dollars), 1995

CANADA
148.1
127.6

WESTERN EUROPE
147.7
132.4

JAPAN
63.1
123.5

UNITED STATES

Exports $575.9
Imports $749.5
Deficit $173.6

EASTERN EUROPE
7.0
5.7

35.2
18.4

OPEC MEMBERS
Algeria, Ecuador, Gabon, Indonesia, Iran, Iraq, Kuwait, Libya, Nigeria, Qatar, Saudi Arabia, United Arab Emirates, Venezuela

15.0
7.1

AUSTRALIA   NEW ZEALAND   SOUTH AFRICA

213.7
280.9

OTHER NATIONS

Source: *Economic Report of the President: 1997*

FIGURE 18.2 Like individuals, nations buy goods on credit, financing the purchase with funds from sales to other nations. **To what single country does the U.S. export the largest dollar value of goods?**

Foreign Exchange Markets

The economies of the world are linked by foreign exchange markets. Traditionally, the most important function of a foreign exchange market has been to convert one currency into an equivalent amount of a second currency. This currency conversion is needed for three types of international transactions: trade, tourism and travel, and investing. Each of these types of international transactions requires a record of payment and exchange.

Balance of Payments and Trade

Understanding a nation's economic health is much like understanding that of an individual. Individuals earn income by supplying labor and other productive services in the market, and in turn they spend their income buying goods and

services in the market. If they earn more than they spend, they have savings. On the other hand, if they spend more than they earn, they accumulate debt. This debt may be financed by various types of borrowing, such as the use of credit cards or loans. However, there are limits to the amount of debt that individuals can accumulate. These limits usually depend on consumers' ability to repay the debt. (Credit is discussed more fully in Chapter 9.)

Nations conduct business in much the same way. For example, the United States buys more than it sells to other nations during certain years and sells more to other nations than it buys in other years. The nations that buy more than they sell must finance those purchases either by borrowing from or selling assets to other nations, or by allowing other nations to hold their currency (see Figure 18.2).

FOREIGN DIRECT INVESTMENT IN THE UNITED STATES, 1993

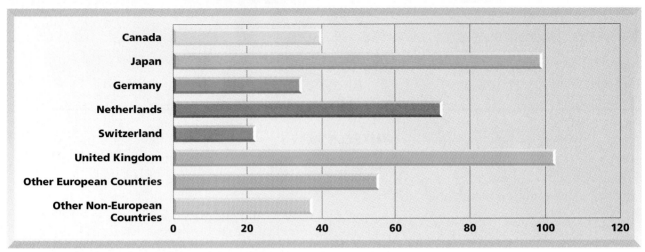

Billions of U.S. Dollars

Source: *Statistical Abstract of the United States: 1996*

FIGURE 18.3 Governments and corporations invest their money and capital in countries that offer the highest potential for earnings. **How do interest rates in the United States affect foreign direct investment?**

Balance of Payments

A nation's **balance of payments** is an annual accounting record of all the payments and receipts occurring between its residents, businesses, and governments and the residents, businesses, and governments of other nations. The U.S. balance of payments provides information about finances and investment between the United States and all its trading partners.

The balance of payments is divided into the current account and the capital account. The current account shows the dollar value of goods and services that U.S. citizens and companies bought from and sold to other countries, the income that Americans and U.S. multinational corporations earned in other countries, and the income that foreign individuals and companies earned in the United States.

The capital-account portion of the balance of payments keeps track of the flow of money or capital between nations. Like individuals, governments and corporations make their investments in places that offer the highest rate of return accompanied by safety and other factors.

For example, relatively higher interest rates in the United States are usually accompanied by an increase of foreign capital flowing to the United States. If interest rates are relatively low in the United States, then foreign capital likely will be invested in other nations.

The international flow of money for investment purposes is nothing new. As of 1995 other nations had more than $560 billion directly invested in the United States (see Figure 18.3). In 1994 Great Britain, the largest foreign investor in the United States, owned more than $100 billion of U.S. assets, including such well-known companies as Burger King and Pillsbury. Japan is the second-largest owner of U.S. assets, including such well-known U.S. businesses as Firestone Tire & Rubber and Columbia Pictures.

When both the current and capital accounts are totaled, rarely will the total expenditures in other nations be balanced exactly with the receipts from other nations. Generally a nation will run a current-account deficit and a capital-account surplus, or a current-account surplus and a capital-account deficit.

Balance of Trade The difference between a nation's imported and exported products is known as its **balance of trade**. This merchandise balance of trade has historically been the most important factor in determining the nation's overall balance of payments.

When the United States exports more than it imports, it has a **trade surplus**. The last year the United States had a trade surplus in goods and services was 1981. When the United States imports more than it exports—as is generally the case—it has a **trade deficit** (see Figure 18.4).

U.S. Trade Deficit The United States has experienced ongoing trade deficits since the early 1970s. When the Organization of Petroleum Exporting Countries (OPEC) dramatically raised the price of oil, the United States had to increase its oil expenditures. That additional spending represented a sharp rise in the dollar value of imports into the United States and resulted in a trade deficit for the United States.

The U.S. trade deficit persisted because of a lag in productivity in the United States compared to other nations such as Japan, Singapore, and South Korea. As productivity increased in these nations, their goods became more competitive in global markets and relatively less expensive in the United States.

This problem was aggravated by the rise in the value of the dollar against other currencies. As this occurred it became even more expensive for people in other nations to buy U.S. goods. As Americans purchased more imported goods such as cars and electronics, and as U.S. exports grew far more slowly, the trade deficit widened. Furthermore, it became less expensive for Americans to buy foreign-made goods. (For a breakdown of U.S. imports and exports, see Figure 18.5 on page 438.)

In the 1990s, however, U.S. productivity began to rise. As a result, in 1995, 1996, and 1997 the United States grew increasingly competitive in the arena of international trade.

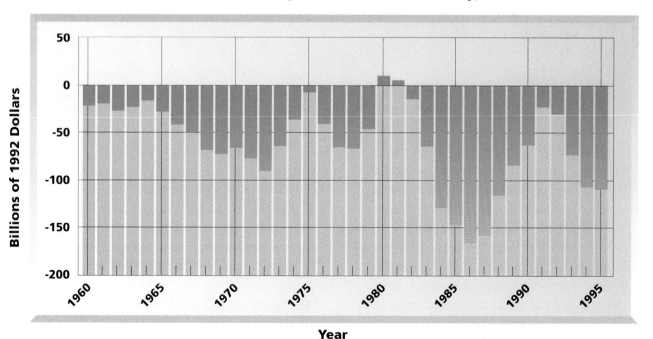

U.S. BALANCE OF TRADE (GOODS AND SERVICES), 1960–1995

Source: *Economic Report of the President: 1997*

FIGURE 18.4 The balance of trade historically has been the most important factor in determining the nation's overall balance of payments. **What factors contribute to ongoing trade deficits in the United States?**

U.S. Imports and Exports, 1995

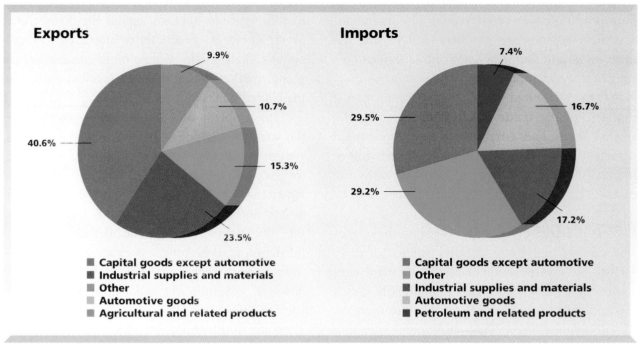

Exports

- 9.9%
- 10.7%
- 40.6%
- 15.3%
- 23.5%

- ■ Capital goods except automotive
- ■ Industrial supplies and materials
- ■ Other
- ■ Automotive goods
- ■ Agricultural and related products

Imports

- 7.4%
- 16.7%
- 29.5%
- 29.2%
- 17.2%

- ■ Capital goods except automotive
- ■ Other
- ■ Industrial supplies and materials
- ■ Automotive goods
- ■ Petroleum and related products

Source: *Economic Report of the President: 1997*

FIGURE 18.5 The kinds of goods imported and exported by the United States affect its balance of trade. **How does the export of agricultural products compare to the import of petroleum? How might prices affect the balance of trade?**

SECTION 2 —REVIEW

1. Define the following terms: foreign exchange market, foreign exchange rate, adjustable-peg system, devaluation, appreciation, floating exchange rate, balance of payments, balance of trade, trade surplus, trade deficit.

2. Contrast adjustable-peg exchange rates with floating exchange rates, and explain why exchange rates are an important factor in international trade.

3. When determining the balance of payments, what is the purpose of the current account? the capital account?

4. What are the causes of the U.S. trade deficit?

5. Thinking and Writing Critically If the value of a currency such as the British pound increases, what is the effect on the value of the U.S. dollar? Explain your answer with an example not described in the text.

6. Applying INTERNATIONAL TRADE Conduct an Internet search to find out how the Commercial Service of the U.S. Department of Commerce promotes international trade. Write a paragraph summarizing the activities of the Commercial Service.

COOPERATION AND TRADE BARRIERS

Economics Dictionary

trade barrier

revenue tariff

protective tariff

import quota

voluntary trade restriction

embargo

free trade

protectionism

Objectives

▶ Why do nations impose trade barriers?

▶ What are the key arguments made in favor of free trade?

▶ What types of agreements indicate that nations are following a policy of cooperation?

International trade allows people and nations to specialize in the production of goods and services. Economically, international trade is a positive force promoting efficiency and growth. Because of a variety of factors, however, nations often restrict the free exchange of goods across national borders.

Trade Barriers

Government actions that are designed to protect domestic industries and jobs from foreign competition are called **trade barriers**. The major types of trade barriers are tariffs, import quotas and voluntary restrictions, and embargoes.

Tariffs Any tax on imports is a tariff. Tariffs are either **revenue tariffs**, which raise money for

government, or **protective tariffs**, which restrict the number of foreign goods sold in a country. Until the early 1900s, revenue tariffs—or customs duties—were a major source of income for the U.S. government. After the U.S. government adopted the income tax in 1913, revenue from tariffs was considerably less important to government finances.

A protective tariff is designed to favor domestic industries over foreign competitors. By increasing the prices of imported goods, protective tariffs tend to reduce the quantity of foreign goods demanded.

Suppose that a Japanese firm sells a motorcycle for $5,000 and that a comparable U.S.-made motorcycle costs $7,000. The $2,000 price difference would cause many buyers in the United States to purchase the Japanese model. If the U.S. government places a 50 percent protective tariff on Japanese motorcycles, the imported motorcycle's price will jump substantially, to

INTERNATIONAL TRADE *Nations often restrict the free exchange of goods across national borders.* **What are three types of trade barriers?**

AVERAGE TARIFF RATES IN THE UNITED STATES, 1825–1995

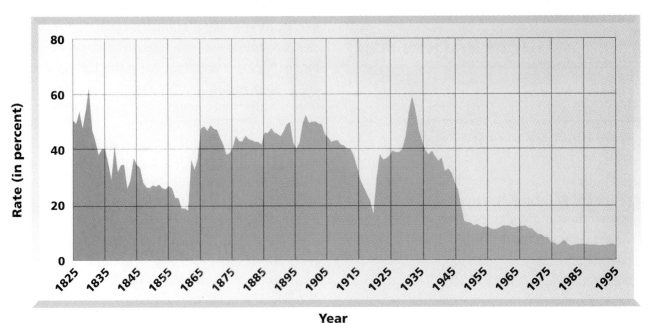

Sources: *Historical Statistics of the United States: Colonial Times to 1970; Statistical Abstract of the United States: 1986, 1996*

FIGURE 18.6 Revenue tariffs were a major source of income for the U.S. government prior to 1913. Since the adoption of the income tax, however, most U.S. tariffs have been protective rather than revenue-generating. **How do protective tariffs work to safeguard U.S. companies from foreign competition?**

$7,500 [(0.5 × $5,000 = $2,500) + $5,000 = $7,500]. The protective tariff increases the price of the Japanese motorcycle, thus making it more expensive than the American motorcycle. This price difference would encourage many consumers in the United States to buy the American model.

The United States has used protective tariffs for much of its history. The McKinley Tariff Act of 1890 set such high tariffs that many foreign competitors were totally excluded from American markets. The Smoot-Hawley Tariff of 1930, which was enacted at the onset of the Great Depression, decreased imports by almost 60 percent and had a negative impact on all international trade.

Since World War II the United States has reduced its use of protective tariffs (see Figure 18.6). Exceptions to this policy continued into the 1990s, however, including heavy tariffs on Japanese motorcycles and trucks.

Import Quotas and Voluntary Restrictions

Governments also can use import quotas and voluntary trade restrictions to decrease imports. Both of these forms of regulation are intended to help domestic businesses sell their products by limiting the quantity of a specific product that can be imported into a country. An **import quota**, which sets a fixed amount of an item that can be imported, is a law. A **voluntary trade restriction** is a binding agreement between two nations that does not require congressional action and legislation.

Import quotas and voluntary trade restrictions occasionally are directed at specific goods from specific nations. In 1981, for example, the U.S. government responded to domestic automakers' requests for industry protection from Japanese competition. In that year, Japan agreed to limit the number of cars exported to the United States to about 1.7 million cars each year. In 1985 this voluntary trade restriction agreement was changed to allow 2.3 million Japanese cars to be imported into the United States annually. Today such voluntary trade restrictions no longer exist on the importation of Japanese cars.

Embargoes A law that cuts off imports from, and exports to, specific countries is called an **embargo**. Historically, embargoes have been enacted for political—rather than economic—reasons. The Embargo Act of 1807, for example, was a politically motivated embargo designed to stop France and Great Britain from raiding ships belonging to U.S. merchants.

More recent embargoes also have been used for political purposes. In 1985, for example, President Ronald Reagan placed a partial embargo on the sale of certain military and computer goods and technology to the Republic of South Africa. This action was intended to pressure the South African government into ending apartheid—an oppressive political, economic, and social system based on racism. Trade restrictions were lifted in 1991 as South Africa moved to end apartheid.

Other Trade Barriers Other trade barriers include licensing requirements and extensive paperwork, which can interrupt the free flow of goods between countries. Some nations require firms to obtain a special license before they can import goods. By restricting the number of licenses, these nations ensure that fewer foreign goods are imported.

In some nations, paperwork delays also interfere with trade. In Japan, for example, imports are subject to extensive testing and inspection, and time-consuming and expensive paperwork must be completed. Many exporters choose not to sell their products in Japan for this reason.

In 1959 Fidel Castro established a communist government in Cuba, expropriating U.S.-owned property. The United States opposed Castro and banned direct trade between the countries. With the passage of the Helms-Burton Act in June 1996, however, companies—even those from nations other than the United States—that do business in Cuba may encounter barriers to trade with the United States. Specifically, the Helms-Burton Act provides various punishments for any companies or their employees who are caught using properties in Cuba that were expropriated from U.S. firms and organizations.

Free Trade Versus Protectionism

Free trade is international trade that is not subject to government regulation. Supporters of free trade believe that exports and imports should flow freely between nations. Not everyone supports free trade, however. Some people believe in **protectionism**—the use of protective tariffs between nations to favor domestic industries. The arguments used by both protectionists and supporters of free trade are based on

▷ infant industries,
▷ job protection,
▷ standard of living,
▷ specialization,
▷ national security, and
▷ fairness.

INTERNATIONAL TRADE *Countries often use trade embargoes to apply political pressure.* **Why did the United States enact a trade embargo against South Africa in 1985?**

Cybertrade

Suppose that you want to buy a stereo system. You visit an electronics store in your neighborhood, but you do not find the system you want. In the past, you might have turned to a mail order catalog or simply waited for your neighborhood store to get the system you want. Today, however, you can order the stereo of your choice through the Internet.

The vast network of computers known as the Internet allows people around the world to collect information, communicate, and buy and sell goods and services. By the year 2000, experts expect that the Internet will generate over $2.6 billion in advertising revenue alone.

The Internet is radically changing the nature of international trade. For example, even the smallest businesses now can have access to customers all over the world by creating a home page on the World Wide Web. Previously, only large companies could afford to reach a global market.

The spread of Internet trade raises some troubling issues for many consumers, however. Concerns about the security of using credit card numbers on the Internet have been raised, for example.

Internet trade also is forcing countries to redesign national and international trade laws. The Internet is a complex network that exists outside of the world of cash purchases and sales clerks. Because trade is conducted in this world of electronic "cyberspace," national boundaries are not a factor. Thus, existing trade laws often are difficult—if not impossible—to apply.

Infant Industries First, protectionists argue that a nation's "infant" industries should be protected from foreign competition until they are able to establish themselves. By restricting imports by the competitors of these new industries, the government allows the "infants" to build up a strong domestic market. Today, many developing nations use this strategy to help kick start their economies.

Those on the side of free trade believe that the decreased competition resulting from trade barriers encourages poor resource use, because the protected businesses have less incentive to be efficient. Free-trade supporters also claim that these temporary protective measures are likely to be extended indefinitely because of the political pressures that businesses exert on government. Once protected, always protected, they argue.

Job Protection A second argument in favor of protectionism is based on the claim that reducing foreign competition allows more businesses to compete in the domestic market and provides more jobs for domestic workers. Free-trade supporters, on the other hand, claim that trade restrictions actually reduce the employment of U.S. workers. They note that trade barriers put up by the United States historically have caused other nations to respond by erecting barriers to U.S. trade. These barriers hurt U.S. businesses in the world market and ultimately reduce the number of American jobs.

Standard of Living Protectionists point out that trade barriers help maintain the high wages and standard of living available in the United States. The trade barriers between nations are needed, they say, because other nations' cheap labor gives them an unfair advantage in world markets.

People who support free trade believe that the high wages and high standard of living in the United States can be maintained without trade barriers. They claim that U.S. businesses can afford to pay high wages and still produce competitively priced products because of U.S. workers' skills and efficiency levels.

INTERNATIONAL TRADE *Protectionists opposed the signing of a free-trade agreement among the United States, Mexico, and Canada in 1993.* **What arguments support the creation of trade barriers?**

Specialization People who favor protectionism argue that free trade encourages businesses to overspecialize. They further claim that overspecialization can cause a nation's economy to be hurt by changes in world demand. These protectionists urge nations to encourage businesses to produce a wide variety of products while protecting businesses that lack an absolute or comparative advantage.

Those who support free trade believe that it benefits the world economy and that competition guarantees the best product at the best price. They recognize that an economy based on a single product is not as strong as a highly diversified economy, like that of the United States.

National Security and Fairness Both protectionists and free-trade supporters agree that some industries must be protected from foreign competition and failure because they are vital to a nation's national security. In the United States, protected industries include steel and other heavy industries, advanced technology businesses, and energy-based industries. This kind of protectionism makes the United States less dependent on foreign firms during times of national emergency. While acknowledging that vital industries must be protected, people who support free trade claim that non-essential industries abuse this argument with false claims.

On the issue of fairness, protectionists argue that few, if any, nations allow truly free trade. Protectionists feel that U.S. barriers should match those of other nations. Free-trade supporters agree that some nations violate the notion of fair trade, but they prefer to dismantle trade barriers.

Rarely is a government's trade policy completely protectionist or completely based on free trade. Instead, most nation's policies reflect a variety of international and domestic factors that can stem from economic or political factors, or both. The government may protect some industries while allowing free trade in others. In the United States, government officials closely watch the nation's trade situation so they can react to policy changes in other nations.

International Cooperation

To reap the economic and political benefits of global trade, many nations have engaged in international cooperation. Some examples of trade cooperation among nations are reciprocal trade agreements, regional trade organizations, and international trade agreements.

Reciprocal Trade Agreements With the election of President Franklin Roosevelt in 1932, the United States began an ambitious plan to restore slumping international trade. The Reciprocal Trade Agreements Act of 1934 identified protective tariffs as the leading obstacles to trade and sought to reduce them in two ways. First, it gave the president the power to reduce tariffs by as much as 50 percent, provided that other nations made similar compromises regarding trade regulations.

Second, it allowed Congress to grant most-favored-nation (MFN) status to U.S. trading partners. Any partner awarded this status pays the same, preferred tariffs as those paid by all such partners. Thus, if the United States lowers the wheat tariff from 20 percent to 10 percent for one MFN, the tariff reduction automatically applies to all other MFNs.

Congress has the final authority to grant and to revoke MFN status. Before the Korean War in the early 1950s, for example, the former Soviet Union enjoyed most-favored-nation status. This privilege was revoked during the Korean War, however, as tensions increased between the two nations. Controversy has also arisen with U.S. trading partners, including China and Iraq.

Regional Trade Organizations Many nations have formed regional trade organizations or alliances to reduce or eliminate trade barriers among member nations. Such benefits, however, usually are limited to the member nations and may have negative consequences on nations that are not a part of the alliance.

Examples of existing regional trade organizations include the European Union (EU)—which includes Austria, Belgium, Denmark, Finland, France, Germany, Greece, Ireland, Italy, Luxembourg, the Netherlands, Portugal, Spain, Sweden, and the United Kingdom and Ireland—and the Caribbean Community and Common Market (CARICOM)—which includes Antigua and Barbuda, the Bahamas, Barbados, Belize, Grenada, Guyana, Jamaica, and several smaller nations. Other organizations are the Central American Common Market, which includes Costa Rica, El Salvador, Guatemala, Honduras, and Nicaragua; the Association of Southeast Asian Nations (ASEAN), including Brunei Darussalam, Indonesia, Malaysia, the Philippines, Singapore,

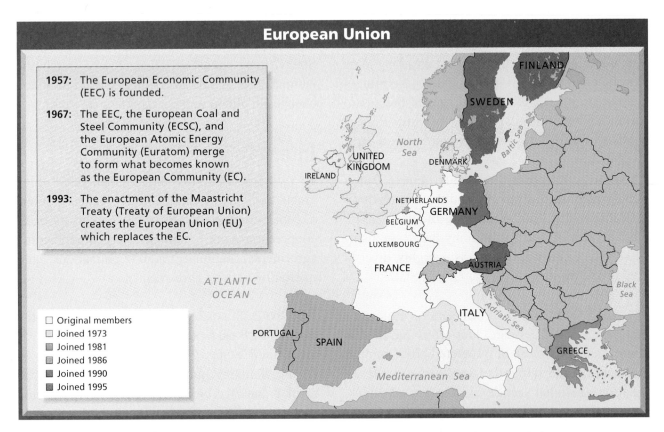

FIGURE 18.7 The European Union is one of the oldest regional trade alliances in the world. **Which countries are the most recent members of this organization?**

North American Free Trade Agreement (highlights)
• established a free-trade zone across the United States, Canada, and Mexico
• provided for the gradual elimination of tariffs on goods traded among NAFTA countries
• required NAFTA countries to improve access to their agricultural markets
• reaffirmed the right of each member to set and enforce its own level of protection of human, animal, and plant life and health through measures that are scientifically based, necessary, and fair
• required each member country to treat other members' investors and their investments as favorably as it treats its own; set up arbitration rules to settle investment disputes
• affirmed a member's right to establish a monopoly, but required them to minimize impairment of free trade
• established rules to govern temporary entrance by citizens of one NAFTA country into other NAFTA countries for business purposes; identified categories of travelers eligible for temporary access to other countries
• required members to protect and enforce intellectual property rights of the other countries — for example copyrights, trademarks, patents, and trade secrets — and to prevent enforcement measures from hindering legitimate trade
• provided for countries to join or withdraw from NAFTA

Source: Organization of American States

FIGURE 18.8 The economic and political benefits of international trade encourage nations to reduce trade barriers. **What three countries participate in NAFTA?**

Thailand, and Vietnam; and the Southern Common Market (MERCOSUR), which includes Argentina, Brazil, Paraguay, and Uruguay.

International Trade Agreements
The most significant international trade agreement of the post–World War II period was the General Agreement on Tariffs and Trade (GATT), a multinational trade agreement. Twenty-three noncommunist nations signed this agreement in 1947.

GATT members met periodically in conferences known as rounds to discuss issues in international trade. Two of the best-known rounds of GATT talks were the Kennedy Round, which

concluded in 1967, and the Tokyo Round, which was completed in 1979. Each round of talks resulted in substantial tariff reductions and opened additional talks on related issues.

In the 1980s growing concern about nontariff barriers such as quotas, voluntary restrictions, export subsidies, and licensing requirements also were included in GATT negotiations. The GATT talks in Geneva, Switzerland (1982), and the Uruguay Round (1986–1993), reaffirmed nations' support for free trade despite increasing pressures from protectionists.

In 1995 GATT was superseded by the World Trade Organization (WTO). Membership in the WTO now includes some 90 nations that have pledged work to reduce tariffs and eliminate quotas.

NAFTA Another significant development in the expansion of international trade was the negotiation of the North American Free Trade Agreement (NAFTA). Signed by the United States, Mexico, and Canada in 1992, this agreement was designed to reduce—and eventually eliminate—tariffs on all goods and services coming into and out of these countries. (For more information on NAFTA, see Figure 18.8.)

Multinational Corporations
In recent years, more global companies have built plants in the countries with which they do business. The decision to build in a foreign nation can benefit both the multinational corporation (MNC) and the host nation. The corporation is able to avoid some shipping fees, protective tariffs, and quotas. The host nation benefits from additional employment opportunities and higher revenues

INTERNATIONAL TRADE *Recently, many multinational corporations (MNCs) have built plants in the countries in which they do business.* **What are the incentives for MNCs to set up production facilities in the countries in which their products are sold?**

from taxes on the corporation's income, profits, and properties.

During the 1980s and 1990s a number of foreign firms located plants in the United States. Nissan, for example, began building cars and trucks in Tennessee, and Honda began making motorcycles and cars in Ohio.

Some companies choose to organize joint ventures. Under joint ownership arrangements, two companies from different nations can agree to build and operate a production plant. The profits are shared by both companies, usually according to a written agreement.

Joint ventures begun during the 1980s and 1990s include the General Motors and Toyota joint venture to produce cars at a new plant in California, Boeing Corporation's teaming with the Japanese Aircraft Corporation to develop more advanced aircraft, and the agreement between RCA and Japan's Sharp Corporation to build satellites together in the United States. These recent changes in international trade have created new trade issues, such as whether goods produced by joint ventures in the United States should be considered "American-made."

Another concern is that MNCs and joint ventures will outproduce and thereby hurt domestic producers in nations in which they build plants. To address this, nations throughout the world have instituted performance standards for multinationals that build plants in their countries. These standards require the corporation to export a certain percentage of its output. The hope is that such requirements will protect domestic industries.

SECTION 3 — REVIEW

1. Define the following terms: trade barrier, revenue tariff, protective tariff, import quota, voluntary trade restriction, embargo, free trade, protectionism.

2. How might a nation hope to benefit from trade barriers? What are the opportunity costs of trade barriers?

3. How do protectionists support their belief that nations should use trade barriers?

4. What evidence supports the claim that free trade is necessary for economic strength?

5. **Thinking and Writing Critically**
Explain how economic cooperation among nations has led to increased international trade.

6. **Applying** **INTERNATIONAL GROWTH & STABILITY**
Conduct an Internet search to find information about trade agreements and organizations. You might use search words such as *free trade*, *NAFTA*, or *WTO*. Select three agreements or organizations and create a chart that summarizes the major elements of each. Write a caption for your chart and display the chart in your classroom.

SECTION 1 The two motivations for international trade are the fact that it is voluntary and that it creates wealth. International trade encourages individuals and businesses to specialize—to produce a limited number of goods and services—and leads to worldwide interdependence. Specialization may occur because of particular human or natural resources unique to a nation.

How a nation decides what to produce is determined by absolute and comparative advantage—two related economic concepts originally described by nineteenth-century economist David Ricardo. A nation has an absolute advantage in producing a certain good when it can do so with greater efficiency than can its trading partner. A nation's comparative advantage is determined by calculating where the largest absolute advantage occurs for each good.

SECTION 2 The money needed to carry on international trade is funneled through foreign exchange markets where one nation's currency is converted into another's. These markets also allow international business transactions. Once the value of one currency is established in relation to another, a foreign exchange rate has been established.

Since World War II, trading nations have used two foreign exchange systems: first, the adjustable-peg system—introduced at the Bretton Woods Conference in 1944—and later the floating, or flexible, system—established in 1971. The floating exchange rate allows the value of a currency to be determined by the laws of demand and supply and to change from one minute to the next.

Nations determine the strength of their international trade by measuring the balance of payments and the balance of trade. A balance of payments is an annual accounting record of transactions, and a balance of trade is a record of imports and exports.

SECTION 3 Economic and political factors sometimes lead nations to restrict international trade. Common trade barriers include tariffs, import quotas, voluntary trade restrictions, and embargoes.

Nations are said to conduct free trade when international trade is not restricted by governments. Trade barriers sometimes are used to protect domestic industries. Arguments for both free trade and protectionism are based on infant industries, job protection, standard of living, specialization, national security, and fairness.

In recent years, many nations have reduced trade barriers to increase international cooperation. Reciprocal trade agreements impose lower tariffs on goods imported from nations that also reduce tariffs. Regional trade organizations are alliances based on the reduction of trade barriers between members of the alliance. Important examples of international cooperation include the World Trade Organization (WTO) and the North American Free Trade Agreement (NAFTA).

Multinational corporations also increase international trade. Additionally, international joint ventures encourage cooperation among companies of different nations.

Economics Notebook

Review the list that you created in your Economics Notebook at the beginning of this chapter. What does this list suggest about international trade? Explain your answer in your Notebook.

REVIEWING CONCEPTS

1. Why might a nation practice specialization?

2. Explain the difference between absolute advantage and comparative advantage.

3. Why was the adjustable-peg system replaced by the floating exchange system to determine foreign exchange rates?

4. What effect does currency depreciation have on a nation's exports and imports?

5. What are three types of trade barriers? Explain how each works to restrict international trade.

6. List three specific examples of trade cooperation among nations.

THINKING AND WRITING CRITICALLY

1. **INTERNATIONAL TRADE** If nation A devoted all its resources to one product, it could produce 30 million pounds of coconuts or 5 million pounds of pineapples each year. Likewise, nation B could produce 16 million pounds of coconuts or 4 million pounds of pineapples. What is the trade ratio for each nation? Which nation has the absolute advantage in coconuts? Pineapples? What would you suggest to these nations in terms of production and trade?

2. **INTERNATIONAL TRADE** Explain how a nation's balance of payments provides information about its trading relationship with other nations. Consider the nation's current account and capital account in your answer.

3. **INTERNATIONAL TRADE** Which policy do you think best serves the economic interests of the United States—free trade or protectionism? Explain your answer.

4. **INTERNATIONAL TRADE** Suppose Japanese car imports are selling better than domestic cars in the United States. Should the United States implement trade barriers to increase domestic car sales? Explain your answer.

YOUR LOCAL ECONOMY

Use the Internet or the Yellow Pages to locate a company in your area that does business in foreign countries. Contact a company representative to find out more about what issues international companies must consider in their day-to-day transactions. What trade barriers do they confront? How do they deal with the exchange of foreign currency? How do current trade agreements affect their business?

INDIVIDUAL PORTFOLIO PROJECT

Suppose that in her last letter, your French pen pal expressed an interest in acquiring some popular music CDs that she cannot get in France. She is willing to send you the money to purchase them for her. Determine the prices in U.S. dollars of five CDs, and research the current exchange rate of francs to dollars. Write your pen pal a letter explaining how you went about finding out the exchange rate, what the exchange rate is, how much each CD costs in U.S. dollars, and how much she would need to send you in French francs for you to be able to make the purchases.

PRACTICING SKILLS: CONDUCTING RESEARCH

As noted in this chapter, South African apartheid was an oppressive political, economic, and social system based on racism. The system was abolished in 1991. Research the topic of apartheid to determine what effect, if any, the United States' embargo had on abolishing the system.

Several sources will aid your research. First you should use your library's on-line catalog to find books about the topic. *The Reader's Guide to Periodical Literature* will help you locate magazine articles pertaining to the subject. You also should search the Internet for information, using the keyword *apartheid*.

As you read, you may find it helpful to take notes on a set of index cards. Use a new card every time you find a fact that supports or refutes the argument that the embargo was effective. When you have enough information to make a decision, organize your note cards and write a one-page essay explaining your decision, supported by facts from your research.

THE INTERNET: LEARNING ONLINE

Use the Internet to research the International Monetary Fund (IMF). Find out which countries belong to the IMF, who runs the IMF, and how the IMF works to keep currency stabilized. Write a brief paragraph summarizing your findings.

ANALYZING PRIMARY SOURCES

Who's Bashing Whom? Trade Conflict in High-Technology Industries

Laura Tyson is an economic expert on international trade who served as President Clinton's National Economic Adviser. Read this excerpt from her 1993 book and answer the questions that follow.

"During the last half century, America defined its priorities in geopolitical terms. . . . We have succeeded beyond our wildest dreams, emerging as the world's only military superpower. But we are no longer the world's only economic superpower. Indeed, in the full flush of geopolitical triumph, we are teetering over the abyss of economic decline.

"The signs are everywhere: anemic [feeble] productivity growth, falling real wages, a woefully inadequate educational system, and

Laura D'Andrea Tyson

declining shares of world markets for many high-technology products. After more than a decade of faltering American economic performance . . . our economic competitiveness . . . is in slow but perceptible decline. . . .

". . . To what extent does responsibility for the nation's competitive decline lie with its trading partners, and to what extent does responsibility lie at home? . . .

". . . The traditional approaches to trade and domestic policy that served the nation so well when American companies had an unrivaled technological lead are no longer adequate. In particular, we can no longer afford to ignore the efforts of Japan and Europe to promote their own high-technology producers. . . . We must devise macroeconomic, trade, and industrial policies that promote our own high-technology industries while continuing to lobby for a more liberal trading system."

1. What signs does Tyson use to support her argument that the U.S. economy is in a state of decline?

2. Why does Tyson think trade and domestic policies are no longer adequate for American companies?

3. Does Tyson lean more toward free trade or protectionism? Explain your answer.

YOUR ASSIGNMENT

Developing an Economy

Imagine that you and other members of your group are on the staff of the Ministry of Economic Development for the country of Lotsaland. The nation operated under a command socialist economy for more than 50 years. Recently, however, a new government—of which you are a part—has been moving the country toward market capitalism. This transition has been difficult, but was deemed necessary because under command socialism the economy grew at a slower rate than the population. Much of the pressure for capitalist reforms came from citizens desiring a higher standard of living.

After seven years of reforms, economic decisions in your country now are made largely by individuals and businesses rather than entirely by the government. The government, however, still influences business decisions through various regulations. As staff members for the Ministry of Economic Development, your group's job is to encourage foreign investment in your country as the economy continues to develop into a market system. On the following pages are documents and other information your group has collected. This information should be used to help you develop a speech encouraging foreign business owners—bankers and the heads of multinational corporations—to invest in your country.

After you have reviewed each of these documents, answer the accompanying questions in your Economics Notebook. Then prepare the speech for the Minister of Economic Development to give at a conference of foreign business owners. The speech should point out reasons why foreign business people should invest in your country.

Legend

○ Capital
◎ Other cities
▤ Farming
🐗 Ranching
▲ Iron Ore
● Aluminium
🎋 Oil
— Highway
— Railroad

Distance Scale

0   40   80 mi

0   40   80   120K

REPUBLIC OF LOTSALAND

People: **Population**: 11,136,777. **Age distribution**: <18: 24%; 65+: 14%. Pop. Density: 352.55 per sq. mi. (136 per sq. km). Urban: 77%. Language: Lotsalandian.

Geography: **Area**: 31,589 sq. mi. (81,815.5 sq. km). **Neighbors**: Ziber on N, Carnegia on E, Richtany on S. **Topography**: mountainous eastern third, flat or low hills elsewhere. **Capital**: Lotsa City. **Major cities**: Lotsa City (1.6 million), Sea City (600,000), Newtown (500,000), Hightown (420,000).

Government: **Form**: Communist state in transition to democratic republic. **Defense spending**: 4.1% of GDP. **Military size**: 200,000.

Economy: **Industries**: Machinery, mining, steel, motor vehicles, oil. **Chief crops**: wheat, corn, potatoes. **Minerals**: iron ore, aluminum, oil. **Livestock**: cattle, pigs, sheep. **Labor force**: 42% industrial, 18% agricultural, 40% service.

Finance: **Monetary unit**: lottabux. **Gross domestic product** (in U.S. dollars): $83.3 billion. **Per capita GDP**: $7,480. **Imports**: $14.2 billion; trading partners: Carnegia 51%, Richtany 30%, Ziber 14%, Other 5%. **Exports**: $22.5 billion; trading partners: Carnegia 54%, Richtany 24%, Ziber 17%, Other 5%. **National budget**: $17.7 billion. **International gold reserves**: 2.1 million oz. **Consumer price change (inflation) over last year**: 10.2%.

Transport: **Railroads**: 5,799 mi. (9,330.6 km). **Motor vehicles**: 1.6 million passenger autos, 420,000 commercial vehicles. **Air transport**: 2 international airports.

Communications: **Television sets**: 1 per 4.1 people. **Radios**: 1 per 2.6 people. **Telephones**: 1 per 4.7 people. **Daily newspaper circulation**: 389 per 1,000 people.

Health: **Life expectancy**: 70, male; 73, female. **Births** (per 1,000 people): 11. **Deaths** (per 1,000 people): 10. **Hospital beds**: 1 per 98 people. **Physicians**: 1 per 344 people. **Literacy rate**: 98%.

–254–

WHAT DO YOU THINK?

1. Would you expect Lotsaland's literacy rate to be an advantage or a disadvantage for its future economic development? Why?

2. What kinds of resources are available for economic development? Where are Lotsaland's aluminum deposits located?

3. Are Lotsaland's cities connected by modern highways and rail lines? How should this affect economic development?

Economics Lab

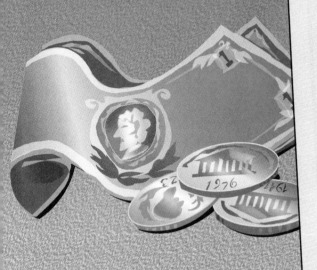

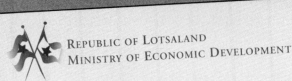

REPUBLIC OF LOTSALAND
MINISTRY OF ECONOMIC DEVELOPMENT

Fact Sheet

- Seven years ago the government of the Republic of Lotsaland began to enact various reforms aimed at moving the country toward market capitalism. These reforms include transferring economic decision making from government officials to individuals and businesses.

- As a result of these economic reforms, the rate of economic growth in Lotsaland has been steadily increasing for six years. This economic growth rate has led to increased prosperity among Lotsalandians. This prosperity, however, has not been felt by all of Lotsaland's citizens.

- The World Bank and the International Monetary Fund have provided billions of dollars in loans to help economic development in Lotsaland. In return for these loans, the government has agreed to allow individuals and businesses to make more economic decisions.

- The government has set a goal of cutting military spending from 4.1 percent of GDP to less than 2 percent within five years. This spending cut will allow more resources to be used to produce nonmilitary goods.

- Because iron ore is plentiful, Lotsaland has a comparative advantage over other countries in the production of steel. On the other hand, the country's aluminum deposits are located in the Lottapeaks Mountains, making mining difficult. As a result, Lotsaland can produce 20 tons of steel for every 4 tons of aluminum products.

WHAT DO YOU THINK?

1. What points on this fact sheet are most likely to encourage foreign investment in Lotsaland?

2. What are some possible outcomes of using fewer resources to produce military goods? Explain your answer by sketching a model of a production possibilities curve.

3. What is the exchange ratio between steel and aluminum products? What ratio would make importing aluminum products more efficient than making them domestically?

Republic of Lotsaland
Ministry of Economic Development

RAFT

A Proposal for the Regional Association of Free Trade (RAFT)

In recent years the Republic of Lotsaland has seen great economic growth as a result of its market reforms. To promote even greater economic growth, the Republic of Lotsaland proposes the creation of a Regional Association of Free Trade (RAFT) that would include itself and neighboring countries seeking improved economies through market reforms.

RAFT would pursue the following goals:
* the gradual elimination of import tariffs and import quotas—or the quantity of goods each country permits to be imported—among member countries,
* the development of a large market in which goods from member countries can be produced and sold freely,
* and cooperation among member countries to promote friendly political and economic relations.

The Republic of Lotsaland proposes that the RAFT agreement—under terms that pursue the above goals—be completely implemented within three years. In addition, Lotsaland invites the following countries to become founding members of RAFT: Richtany, Ziber, and Carnegia.

RAFT does not wish to disrupt free trade among its member countries and non-RAFT members. Therefore, each member country will be permitted to pursue its own trade policies with non-member countries.

WHAT DO YOU THINK?

1. Why might Lotsaland's membership in the Regional Association of Free Trade appeal to foreign investors?

2. How would a free-trade association help each member country market what it produces most efficiently?

3. Why do you suppose that Lotsaland's government does not want the RAFT agreement to interfere with trade among member and nonmember countries?

THINGS TO DO

1. With the other members of your group, review the information and documents in this activity and the notes you have taken about them in your Economics Notebook.

2. As a group, compile a list of reasons why foreign bankers and multinational corporations would want to invest in Lotsaland.

3. Write a speech for the minister of economic development to give to foreign bankers and leaders of multinational corporations. Assign the writing of various parts of the speech to individual group members.

4. All group members should then assist in the preparation of the final speech to be delivered by the minister for economic development. The formal speech should be typed or neatly handwritten on letterhead from the Republic of Lotsaland's Ministry of Economic Development.

H O L T

Economics

REFERENCE SECTION

CONSUMER HANDBOOK

① BUDGETING

Economics is a study of choices—the choices people make in order to satisfy their needs and wants. Such choices are necessary because people's needs and wants often are greater than the economic resources available to satisfy them. For consumers, preparing a personal budget is essential to making wise economic choices.

A budget is a money plan. It identifies the amount of money a consumer can expect to earn and spend during a given period of time. Preparing a personal budget is not a difficult task, but it does take time and careful thought.

Assessing Your Budget Needs

Before preparing a budget, you should assess your budget needs. You can start by studying your income and expenses for a given period of time, such as one month.

In general, consumers plan their personal budgets on a monthly basis because the payments for many expenses—such as housing, electricity, and telephone service—are due each month. Additionally, many people save a portion of their income on a monthly basis. To assess your budget needs, keep detailed records of the money you earn and the money you spend during a one-month period. You may wish to save copies of your bills as well as cash register and credit card receipts to help you.

At the end of the month, record your findings. You may wish to use a computer software program

to assess and organize your budget, or you can prepare a handwritten budget on a sheet of paper. If your budget is handwritten, divide the paper into two columns. Label the first column "Income" and the second column "Expenses." Then list your income and expenses for the month under the proper column. (Note that savings should be entered under the "Expenses" column.) You will begin to see a pattern of earning, spending, and saving money. This pattern reflects your budget needs and can be used as the basis for your personal budget.

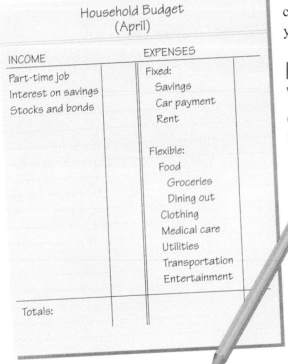

Household Budget
(April)

INCOME	EXPENSES
Part-time job	Fixed:
Interest on savings	Savings
Stocks and bonds	Car payment
	Rent
	Flexible:
	Food
	Groceries
	Dining out
	Clothing
	Medical care
	Utilities
	Transportation
	Entertainment
Totals:	

Estimating Your Income

Once you have assessed your budget needs, you will be equipped to prepare your personal budget. First, write the name of the month that the budget is for at the top of a sheet of paper. Then divide the paper into "Income" and "Expenses" columns, as you did when assessing your budget needs. In the Income column, record your estimated income for the month. Be sure to include whatever money you expect to earn from part-time jobs, as well as any money you expect to receive from interest on savings or other investments.

Estimating Your Expenses

In the Expenses column, identify the costs that you anticipate for the month. It is important to include as many details as possible. List all the expenses that you think you will have, including those for personal items and other small purchases.

When listing expenses, it often is helpful to divide them into two categories—fixed expenses and flexible expenses. Fixed expenses are the same from month to month. Rent and car payments, for example, are fixed expenses. Flexible expenses, on the other hand, change from month to month. They include food, clothing, medical care, and medicines.

Your expenses may not be very high if you live with a parent or guardian. When you live independently, however, you probably will find that your highest monthly expenses will fall into the same general categories as those of other consumers. These categories include housing, food, clothing, and transportation.

Housing Expenses

Housing costs are high, whether you rent an apartment or own a house or condominium. For most people, their largest monthly expense is housing—whether rent or a mortgage payment. When preparing a budget for housing expenses, however, it also is important to list the costs of utilities. Utilities are essential services such as electricity, gas, water, telephone service, and trash removal. Additional housing expenses include home repairs, property insurance, property taxes, furniture, decorating, maintenance equipment, and cleaning supplies.

Food Expenses

Grocery bills usually make up the largest portion of food expenses. Meals and snacks purchased away from home also should be listed under food expenses. If you typically eat dinner in a restaurant twice a month, for example, the money used to pay for these meals should be reflected in your food budget.

Clothing Expenses

Clothing costs involve more than the price of new clothes and shoes. Laundry and dry-cleaning bills, shoe repairs, and mending supplies also should be listed under your clothing expenses.

Transportation Expenses

Transportation costs may range from bus and subway fares to the expenses of automobile ownership—monthly car payments, gasoline and oil, repairs, insurance, car washes, and accessories.

Other Expenses

Most consumers' budgets include expense categories other than housing, food, clothing, and transportation. These categories vary among consumers, depending on their needs, and might include health care, life insurance, education, and entertainment. In addition, some consumers include a category for miscellaneous expenses that are difficult to predict.

Savings

One other category should be listed under monthly expenses in every consumer's budget. This category is savings. The main goal of a

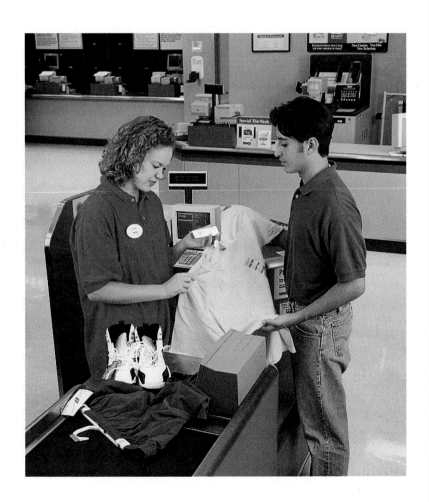

money plan is to help consumers make wise economic decisions. An important part of being a wise consumer is saving money.

Saving money is important because inflation and unforeseen expenses sometimes can ruin even the most carefully planned budget. Many items in your budget, such as medical bills and home and auto repairs, tend to increase in cost over time. In addition, expenses for unexpected developments— such as flood damage or an automobile accident— cannot be anticipated. For these reasons, it is useful to set money aside each month in an emergency fund for use on those occasions when an unplanned expense occurs.

Saving money is important for other reasons too. You might want to save for certain items that you cannot afford to buy right away, but saving money to satisfy short-term goals is not the only reason for saving. For example, many people save for major expenses such as college tuition. It also is important to save—or invest—for the future in order to assure a comfortable standard of living in later years. Known as unearned income, the interest and dividends from savings and investments also can supplement your earned income.

Revising Your Budget

For a budget that accurately predicts your needs, wants, and priorities, periodic revisions are needed. Revision is necessary because your income and expenses will change over time. Income often changes significantly with a new job or promotion. Likewise, expenses will change as your personal circumstances change.

One useful way of assessing the need for budget revision is to make an annual budget. After you have kept a budget for a number of months, prepare a budget listing all expected income and expenses for one year. An annual budget will help you get an overall picture of your financial situation and decide whether you are allocating enough funds for savings and spending as you planned.

Practicing Consumer Skills

1. Why are personal budgets traditionally based on one-month periods?
2. What general expense categories should be included in your personal budget?
3. Why is it important to revise your budget from time to time?

② COMPARISON SHOPPING

Buying and selling goods in a free market is the cornerstone of the U.S. free-enterprise system. It also is the means by which consumers satisfy their needs and wants. To satisfy the greatest number of needs and wants in spite of limitations on the amount of resources available, today's consumers must learn to be smart shoppers.

Preparing to Shop

Smart shoppers plan ahead. Before setting out for the grocery store or heading to the mall, there are several things you can do that will help prepare you to shop as efficiently and affordably as possible.

Defining Your Needs and Wants

One of the most important parts of being a smart shopper is defining the particular need or want that you wish to satisfy by purchasing a product. Suppose that you are in the market for a computer. You may need the computer only to perform simple word processing tasks. Such a computer is quite different from one that has the power and capacity to run CD-ROM programs and allow you to access the Internet. By defining your needs and wants and setting priorities ahead of time, you will be better able to make a wise buying decision.

Setting a Spending Limit

Many of the buying decisions that you make depend on the amount of money that you have available to spend. To make the best decisions on how to use limited income, you may want to determine a spending limit before going shopping. This assessment will better prepare you to buy a product that will not only satisfy your needs and wants but also fit your budget.

Doing Your Homework

Before making a major purchase, you may wish to consult one or more consumer publications. Magazines such as *Consumer Reports* provide useful information on a variety of products, including automobiles, electronic equipment, and appliances. A trip to the library can provide you with information about the features and product histories of items you wish to buy.

Deciding Where to Shop

Choosing the best location to make your purchases is part of being a smart shopper. One way to decide where to shop is to pay attention to advertisements that appear in newspapers or are broadcast on the radio and television. If you know that a product is on sale at a certain store, you may wish to start your shopping trip there. It also may be a good idea to consider shopping at a discount store. Discount stores buy products in large quantities and can thus sell them at reduced prices. Before making a decision about where to shop, however, you may wish to phone several stores to make sure that the item you are looking for is in stock—and to check on its price.

Deciding When to Shop

The time or season when you shop also can affect your buying decisions. Car dealers, for example, often put new cars on sale in the spring or summer to help clear their showrooms for next year's models, which are delivered in the fall. Being aware of such sale patterns can help you save money.

Other, more personal, factors also should be considered in decisions about when to shop. You may want to avoid going shopping when you are tired, because tired shoppers tend to buy products on impulse so that they can get home faster. Similarly, if you go grocery shopping when you are hungry, you may buy more than you planned.

How to Shop Wisely

Making wise buying decisions requires more than advance planning. Once at the store, you must pay careful attention to the products you select.

Reading Food Labels   When shopping for food, it is particularly important that you read labels carefully. One of the first things you should notice is the brand of the product. You probably are familiar with many name brands of foods. The same foods, however, often are available in house brands or generic brands. These products generally have simple package designs and do not carry the advertising costs associated with name brands.

Compare the ingredients that are found in generic and in name-brand products. Some house and generic brands contain the exact same ingredients as the more expensive name brands—but at a lower price—and therefore are the better buys.

Food labels also should be read for information about a product's contents. Federal law requires manufacturers to list the ingredients found in their products, as well as the number of calories and percentage of fat. Additionally, information about vitamins and nutrients is included. These labels can be particularly helpful to people who have allergies or who are on restricted diets. Consumers also should look for the date after which perishable items should not be purchased.

Reading Product Descriptions   Before making a purchase, it also is a good idea to read an item's product description. Most product descriptions contain information about the care of a product. Clothing items, for example, contain information about whether—and how—they should be washed or dry cleaned. Some product descriptions also contain information about a product's proper use and warnings about its misuse. An electrical product such as a space heater, for example, may contain information about how to use the product most efficiently by taking advantage of various settings. It also may contain warnings about placing the heater away from flammable objects.

When reading product descriptions, also be sure to note whether the product must be assembled or if it requires batteries. These factors may affect your buying decision.

Comparing Product Features   Using all of the information available, carefully compare the various features of the product you are considering for purchase. Before purchasing an item, be certain that it will perform all of the tasks you expect of it. You may want to ask the sales clerk to clarify exactly what the product can—and cannot—do. Ask about the product's warranties or guarantees. If practical, ask for a trial use.

Quality Considerations   High-quality items have features that make them more attractive to consumers. Such items may last longer, look nicer, and perform better. Consumers usually are willing to pay more for high-quality products and services.

Quality, however, is often difficult to measure. Certain brand-name products, for example, penetrate the market by appealing to consumer tastes and preferences. Such products become popular to own, but it is important to remember that popularity is not the same as quality. Before buying any product, check the label and product description as well as the overall appearance to get a better, more accurate idea of the product's quality. Again, you also may want to research the product in consumer magazines.

Quantity and Price Considerations
If you use large quantities of an item that can be stored easily and is nonperishable, you often can save money by buying the item in a larger size—one that contains more units. You can tell if you are getting the most for your money by checking the unit prices marked on the product or on the store shelf. A unit price is the price of a product by unit, weight, or volume. The unit price of a certain brand of canned fruit, for example, may be 44 cents an ounce. The unit price of the same brand of fruit in a larger can may be 42 cents an ounce. By checking the unit prices, you can tell that the larger can is the better buy.

Practicing Consumer Skills

1. Why is it important to define specific needs and wants before going shopping?

2. What information can be obtained by reading food labels and product descriptions?

3. What is the unit price of a product?

UNDERSTANDING WARRANTIES

As a smart shopper, you should be sure that the products you buy are durable and in excellent condition. Manufacturers generally are required by law to provide a warranty, or written guarantee, of the condition of their products. A warranty specifies the manufacturer's obligations to the consumer; contains information about the quality and attributes of the product, including its expected lifespan; and explains the manufacturer's plan to assure product performance.

Warranties and the Law
Warranties are subject to both federal and state laws. In many states, warranties are governed by the Uniform Commercial Code, which monitors trade rules and regulations. The Magnuson-Moss Warranty Act, passed by Congress in 1975, states that the seller of a product must explain the terms of the warranty at the time of purchase. The Magnuson-Moss Warranty Act also requires that a manufacturer must specify if and how the warranty is limited.

What Warranties Cover
Most warranties cover the materials from which a product is made, as well as the quality of work used in making it. Should defects be found in the materials or the quality, the product normally will be repaired or replaced.

Be aware, however, that warranty coverage may not include all parts of a product. Specific limitations—also called exemptions—of the warranty often are written in small print. An automobile warranty, for example, may exclude problems stemming from rust. A microwave oven warranty may cover the oven's internal working parts but may exempt its case or its mechanical parts. Be sure to read the entire warranty carefully before you make a major purchase.

Most warranties do not cover repairs that might be necessary because of normal wear, misuse, abuse, negligence, or accidents. In such cases, the warranty may be void.

Most warranties are valid only for a specific time period. After this period expires, the warranty no longer applies. Normally, the longer the warranty period, the better the quality of the product. The warranty period usually starts at the time of purchase. In the case of certain appliances, however, such as those that must be installed in the home, the warranty may start on the first day of actual use.

When a Product Is Defective

If you find that a product covered by a warranty is defective, you have certain rights. The extent of these rights depends on the manufacturer and the terms of the warranty.

Some warranties require that you return the product to the manufacturer for repair or replacement. Others require that you return the item to the place of purchase. Some warranties cover repairs on the defective merchandise, while others will replace it. Still others offer to refund the purchase price.

Generally, warranties require that you present a proof of purchase before any corrective action can be taken. Because of this requirement, it is a good idea to check the warranty when you first purchase a product to see what will be required if it is found to be defective. Label and save any packaging, receipts, or other items required by the manufacturer's or store's warranty.

Practicing Consumer Skills

1. What is a warranty?

2. What do warranties generally cover?

3. What steps can a consumer take when a product covered by a warranty is found to be defective?

 CONSUMER CREDIT

As a consumer, one of the most valuable assets you have is credit. Using credit enables you to make purchases now and—with a finance charge—pay for them over time. Most consumers use credit to buy houses, automobiles, appliances, and other large purchases.

How Credit Is Extended

Credit can be extended to you by a financial institution or by a vendor selling a product. Financial institutions extend credit by issuing loans such as mortgages, short-term notes, and bank cards such as Visa® and Mastercard®. Many vendors such as department stores and oil companies extend credit by issuing credit cards. To apply for most types of credit, you must fill out an application listing such information as your place of employment, income, and outstanding debts. If your application is approved, the institution will assign you a credit limit, indicating the maximum amount you may spend using credit.

Advantages of Credit

One of the most important advantages of credit is its convenience. It allows you to buy what you need when you need it. Suppose, for example, that you need to buy a new refrigerator but do not have enough cash. If you have the ability to pay over time, the use of credit may be a practical and convenient choice.

Disadvantages of Credit

Although credit has many advantages, it also has disadvantages that a smart shopper should consider. The most obvious disadvantage is that credit usually is not free. For this reason, it is very important that consumers understand the terms of any credit arrangement that they make. The 1968 Truth in Lending Act requires that consumers be informed in writing of the finance charge, total transaction cost, and annual percentage rate associated with credit. Even with such requirements, the real cost of using credit can be deceptive. The combination of high interest rates and long term payments can cause the actual cost of credit to increase significantly.

Consumer Credit Ratings

When you first apply for credit, most financial institutions or vendors assign you a credit rating based upon the information that you provide on your credit application. This credit rating is an esti-mation of the probability that you will repay your debts based on your income and monthly expenditures. Even after you are assigned a good credit rating and your credit is approved, businesses continue to rate your credit behavior as you make purchases on credit. If you misuse your credit or are late making payments. lenders report this information to credit bureaus, which keep records of consumer credit ratings. If you fail to make payment on a loan, for example, the lender will report that information to a credit bureau. If you default on several loans, you will have a very poor credit rating and will find it difficult, if not impossible, to obtain credit in the future.

Practicing Consumer Skills

1. How is credit extended?

2. What are the advantages and the disadvantages of credit?

3. Why is it important for you to maintain a good credit rating?

⑤ CHECKING ACCOUNTS

Today one of the easiest and most common ways to pay bills and transfer money to other individuals or businesses is through the use of a personal checking account.

James B. Cauldwell
1234 Back Road
Anywhere, USA 00000

3583
00-0/0000
1

19____

Pay To The Order Of

$

Dollars

Last National Bank
456 Main Street
Anytown, USA

For

Opening a Checking Account

If you have money to deposit, you can open a checking account at most banks, credit unions, or savings institutions. These depository institutions offer various kinds of checking accounts. In most cases, the right account for you depends on the amount of money that you plan to keep in the account.

The traditional checking account has no minimum or monthly balance requirements. For most of these accounts, however, the customer must pay monthly service charges and check-printing fees. Typically, money deposited in the account does not earn interest.

An alternative to the traditional checking account is the NOW (negotiable order of withdrawal) account. The NOW account is an interest-bearing savings and checking account. The customer can write checks on the amount that is deposited and collect interest on the amount remaining. However, the customer usually must keep a minimum monthly balance in the account to receive the interest and free-checking privileges.

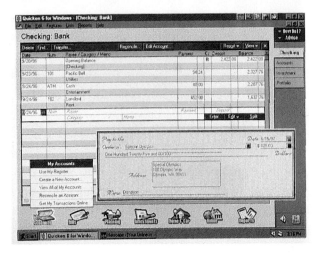

This minimum can nevertheless be quite high. For example, the minimum balance on a special account called a super-NOW account is $2,500.

Writing and Cashing Checks

A signed check represents money. For this reason, it is important that you follow special procedures both in writing and cashing checks.

Writing Checks

Most checks are printed with the account owner's name, address, and telephone number appearing in the upper left corner and the check number in the upper right corner. Checks are numbered consecutively to help people and banks keep track of which ones have been written.

Near the check number is a place for you to write the date. Across the center of the check are the words "Pay to the Order of" and a blank space. In this space, write the name of the person or business to whom you are writing the check. This person or business is known as the payee. To the right of the payee's name is a place to write the amount of the check in numerals. The amount also must be spelled out in words on the next line.

In the lower left corner of the check is a line labeled "Memo." Use this line to record any information that might be helpful to you about the check, such as what was purchased with the check.

In the lower right corner of the check is a space for you to sign your name. Without your signature, the check cannot be cashed. Across the bottom of the check you will see the name of the bank or institution with which you have the account. You also will see a series of numbers. The first series is the bank's identification number. The second series is your checking account number.

Cashing Checks

When someone gives you a personal check, it must be endorsed before it can be cashed. To endorse the check, simply sign your name in the proper space on the back as it appears on the front.

To receive the amount of the check in cash, you must go to a bank in person. There the teller may ask you to write your account number on the check before giving you the cash.

To deposit the check in your checking account, you must fill out a deposit slip. Deposit slips usually are provided to you with your checks. Your name, address, telephone number, and checking-account number are printed on the front of the deposit slip, just as they appear on your checks. The deposit slip also includes spaces in which you must write the date and add up the total amount of the deposit. If you are depositing several checks, these should be listed separately, sometimes on the reverse side of the slip. If you are receiving some of the money you deposit back in cash, you should indicate the amount as "less cash" and sign the deposit slip on the line provided.

You may deposit checks through the mail, at an automated teller machine (ATM), or in person at your bank. If you are sending an endorsed check through the mail or using the ATM machine to make a deposit, however, it is best to write your account number and the words "For Deposit Only" beneath your signature. Taking this precaution could prevent someone else from cashing your check.

Recording Your Transactions

Each time that you write or deposit a check, it is important that you keep a record of the transaction. Some institutions offer checks with carbon copies, and most also provide you with a record book, or register, for this purpose. In the record book, you should note the check number, date, payee, and amount of each transaction. You also should keep track of your current balance: after writing a check, its amount should be deducted from your balance, and after making a deposit, its amount should be added to your balance.

Balancing Your Checking Account

To help you verify the amount of money you have in your checking account, your banking institution will send you an account statement each month. This statement typically includes your balance at the beginning of the month, a list of the transactions made during the month, and your balance at the end of the month. It also includes an explanation of any special charges made against your account during the month, such as service charges or check-printing fees, as well as any monthly interest added to your balance.

Along with the monthly statements, many banks also return the checks that you wrote and that were cashed by the payees. These checks are known as canceled checks. In addition, for occasions when you do not receive receipts when depositing funds into your account, some banks also include your deposit slips with your statement.

When you receive your monthly bank statement, it is important to reconcile, or make sure that the balance you have recorded agrees with the bank's version of your balance. The easiest way to balance your checking account is to follow the directions on the back of the bank's statement. If you find an inconsistency, go back through your record book to verify that you have entered the amounts of all checks correctly. Also, make certain that you have noted which checks have not been cashed. Any time that you cannot reconcile an inconsistency between your records and the bank statement, you should call the bank for assistance.

Practicing Consumer Skills

1. What various kinds of checking accounts are available?

2. What information must be filled in when you write a check?

3. How do you endorse a check?

6 CONDUCTING A JOB SEARCH

When you are looking for a job, the classified section of the newspaper will be invaluable. Also known as the want ads, the classified section contains ads for jobs in businesses in the local area. It may also contain selected ads from businesses across the country.

When searching for the best possible job available, it is helpful to consult more than one newspaper, particularly if you live in a large metropolitan area. In addition to studying the want ads from your city's leading newspapers, you might also study newspapers from nearby suburbs and towns. If you are willing to relocate, it also would be a good idea to consult newspapers from other cities. Most large newsstands or bookstores stock a selection of out-of-town newspapers. Many public libraries also carry a good selection of out-of-town papers. In addition, you can access the classifieds in out-of-town newspapers on the Internet. The Sunday paper usually has the largest help-wanted section.

The Want Ads

Locate the want ads, then refer to the jobs that interest you by checking under the headings that list specific job classifications. Want ads usually are listed in alphabetical order by job classification. Such job classifications might include accounting, administration, bookkeeping, clerical, computer programming, data processing, education, engineering, financial, insurance, marketing, medical, printing, professional, sales, secretarial, and word processing. Concentrate on the listings in which you are most interested and for which you are qualified, but do not limit your search to one particular heading. You should apply for all the jobs that appeal to you, even if you think you may not be fully qualified.

You may find that a job you are looking for is listed under more than one category. Openings for a cook, for example, may be listed under bakers, chefs, and restaurants. By reading through other categories, you also may be able to uncover interesting job openings in related fields. It is helpful to read the want ads thoroughly the first few weeks of a job search to become familiar with the categories that pertain to your qualifications and interests.

The Internet

The Internet is an excellent tool for searching employment opportunities. The Internet provides access to extensive databases, such as college alumni directories and professional organizations, that can provide information that is helpful for networking and contacting potential employers. Many companies have websites that advertise current job openings and some allow you to submit an application over the Internet. In addition, people who are looking for a job can post their resumes on their own home page.

Practicing Consumer Skills

1. How are jobs listed in the classified section of the newspaper?

2. Why should you read several different sections of the want ads when beginning a job search?

3. List three ways that the Internet can be used to find employment information.

7 YOUR RIGHTS AS AN EMPLOYEE

Before you start any new job, you will want to discuss your job description—a written summary of the duties you will actually be responsible for and expected to perform—and the company's benefits with your employer. Ask your employer to explain the responsibilities of the position and the hours you will be expected to work. Your salary is based on the responsibilities of your job, as are employer-provided benefits such as sick leave, vacation pay, and health insurance.

This discussion normally is part of your job interview and provides you with an opportunity to ask questions and understand the terms and conditions of your employment. Be sure to clarify any unclear issues at this time. Most often, you will begin a new job with this type of verbal agreement. Sometimes, employers also will ask you to sign a written contract outlining your duties, responsibilities, and salary. Other conditions of your employment and company procedures will be clarified for you during your first few weeks of work.

Further Clarification of Benefits

Soon after you start your job, you will learn the day-to-day schedule it requires. For example, you may or may not have breaks. You may be enrolled in health insurance, life insurance, dental insurance, and pension programs. Most companies will give you a policy manual outlining your benefits and responsibilities. In addition to clarifying your benefits, it also is important that new employees fully understand the deductions that will be taken from their paychecks on a regular basis.

Payroll Deductions

Employers make payroll deductions for federal and state income taxes, Social Security taxes, insurance plans, and in some cases, pension plans and other optional programs. Your earnings before these deductions are called your gross pay. Your earnings after these deductions are called your net pay.

Federal Income Tax Forms   When you begin a new job, you will be asked to fill out a federal income tax form, or W-4. On the form, you need to indicate the number of dependents you want to claim and whether you are married or single. The amount withheld from your gross pay for federal income taxes will be based on the information you provide on the W-4.

Social Security   Congress passed the Social Security Act in 1935 to provide workers with disability and accident insurance, unemployment compensation, and old-age retirement benefits. Although not all categories of workers are covered by Social Security, most are. If you are covered under Social Security, Federal Insurance Contributions Act (FICA) payments also will be deducted from your gross pay.

U.S. Labor Laws

Historically, your rights as a worker have been defined and preserved by the interaction of employers, employees, labor unions, and the government. Some of these rights as a worker include a guaranteed minimum wage; the right to freedom from employment discrimination because of age, sex, race, or national origin; and the right to work in a safe environment.

National Labor Relations Act   In addition to the Social Security Act, one of the earliest worker-oriented laws passed was the 1935 National Labor Relations Act, or Wagner Act. This law guaranteed employees the right to belong to a union and to engage in collective bargaining. Many states also have passed right-to-work laws, which outlaw closed shops in which workers must join a union to get or keep their jobs.

Fair Labor Standards Act   The 1938 Fair Labor Standards Act grants workers the right to a minimum wage. Not all employers are obligated to pay this minimum wage, but most companies with a relatively large number of employees are required to by the law. The Fair Labor Standards Act also sets the standard workweek at 40 hours and grants employees who are paid on an hourly basis the right to overtime pay.

Civil Rights Act   The Civil Rights Act was signed into law by President Lyndon Johnson in 1964. This law protects a person's freedom to vote, use public facilities, and seek employment. Title VII of this act broadens the scope of employee rights by preventing employers from discriminating against individuals on the basis of race, color, religion, sex, or national origin. Under this law, employees cannot be discriminated against in hiring, pay, employment privileges and opportunities, or union membership. Employers cannot advertise in a discriminatory manner, and employment agencies may not fail to recommend a person for a job for prejudicial reasons.

Equal Employment Opportunity Commission

The Equal Employment Opportunity Commission (EEOC) administers Title VII of the Civil Rights Act. The commission encourages employers and employment agencies to settle discriminatory charges voluntarily. The commission also can help an injured party file a discrimination suit.

Employment Rights for Minorities and Women

In the 1970s the federal government began to pass laws to further assure employment rights for minorities and women. As part of this effort, the government adopted a program called affirmative action. Affirmative action seeks to make up for past discrimination by requiring that certain employers set hiring and fair employment goals for minorities and women.

In recent years, federal courts and the Supreme Court have acted to make sure that affirmative action does not discriminate against people who are *not* members of minority groups. As a result, employers have begun to shift away from using numerical goals, or quotas, for hiring and promoting women and minorities.

Safety Measures

Employees also have the right to work in a safe environment. Federal safety measures are enacted to help eliminate hazards in the workplace. Many of these laws concern the use of protective clothing and glasses, standards for safe equipment, and other matters that affect workers' safety. The Occupational Safety and Health Administration (OSHA), a division of the U.S. Department of Labor, administers these laws and promotes safe and healthful working conditions in all industries.

Practicing Consumer Skills

1. What should you discuss with your employer before starting a new job?
2. What deductions will be made in your paycheck?
3. List four of your rights as a worker in the United States.

8 CONTRACT OBLIGATIONS

A contract is an agreement between two or more parties that is enforceable by law and is used to regulate terms of trade. Both verbal and written agreements are considered to be contracts. A verbal agreement, however, is binding only if it involves a relatively small sum of money over a short period of time and does not involve a real estate purchase.

As a consumer, you probably will enter into a variety of contracts. Some of the more common types of contracts are those involving an installment purchase, the buying and selling of real estate, a personal loan, the purchase of stocks or bonds, the use of a credit card, the purchase of an automobile, a rental agreement, agreements for

such services as appliance maintenance and lawn care, and all types of insurance policies.

Contract Criteria

An agreement qualifies as a contract when it meets four basic criteria. First, an offer and a promise to accept the offer must be made. A credit card company may offer you a $2,000 credit line for a $25 annual fee but it would not be a valid contract unless you accepted the offer, paid the $25, and used the card.

Second, all parties must be competent, or legally qualified, to enter into a contract. Contracts that are signed by minors, people who are mentally

Before You Sign a Contract

Before signing a contract, first read it thoroughly. You may think the document's legal terminology is confusing, or it may be less complicated than you thought. If you find any part of the contract unclear, you can contact a lawyer who will explain the contract's terms.

Second, be sure you agree with the terms of the contract. Identify what the agreement will require of you. Also identify the obligations of the other parties involved in the agreement.

Third, make certain you understand your options for terminating or changing the contract. Unless a contract specifies a trial period, it may be difficult to change it once it has been signed. In some cases, the terms of a contract can change when other conditions change. A real estate contract, for example, may specify that the interest rate on a loan will fluctuate with changes in the market. Be sure that you understand any circumstances under which the agreement could be changed.

Fourth, be sure you know what will happen if you break your promise. Most contractual obligations still stand even if you are unable to pay your debts. In that case, you could lose the title to your house or car, for example. Some contracts also state that if you die during the life of the contract, your heirs are obligated to repay the debt.

impaired, or people under influence of alcohol or drugs are not legal or binding. Third, the terms of the agreement must be legal. For example, you cannot legally collect money on a promise to deliver a stolen automobile. Fourth, an element of "bargain for exchange" must be present. This means that both parties must agree to fulfill certain promises. These can involve money, goods, an action, and or restraint from action. If one person agrees to deliver something and gets nothing in return, there is no contract.

Practicing Consumer Skills

1. What criteria must contracts meet?
2. What should you consider before signing a contract?

⑨ PAYING TAXES

Taxes have a tremendous impact on many aspects of the lives of U.S. consumers. Government at the state, local, and federal levels collects many different kinds of taxes, including sales taxes, property taxes, excise taxes, and income taxes. Money from these taxes pays for a variety of public goods and services. These taxes also pay for many federal programs.

Government and Taxes

The power of the U.S. government to collect taxes dates back to 1788—the year that the Constitution was ratified. The Constitution originally specified that taxes collected by the government had to be divided fully among the states according to population. Responding to an 1894 federal law imposing an income tax, the Supreme Court ruled the tax

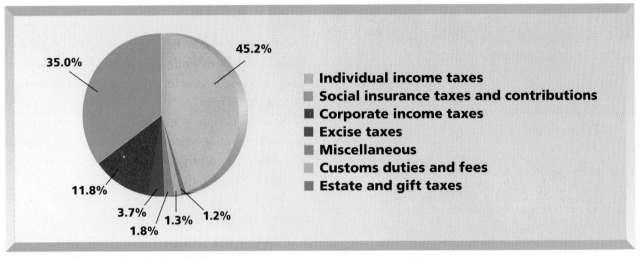

45.2%

35.0%

11.8%

3.7%

1.8%

1.3%

1.2%

- Individual income taxes
- Social insurance taxes and contributions
- Corporate income taxes
- Excise taxes
- Miscellaneous
- Customs duties and fees
- Estate and gift taxes

Source: *Economic Report of the President: 1997*

unconstitutional because it did not meet this requirement.

The increasing costs of government in the growing nation, however, led many to support an income tax. This support eventually resulted in the adoption of the Sixteenth Amendment in 1913. This amendment gave Congress the power to "lay and collect taxes on incomes, from whatever source derived without apportionment among the several States."

Tax Reform Act of 1986

The Sixteenth Amendment provides the basis of the income tax as we know it today. However, many issues concerning taxes have changed in the years following 1913. The primary tax issue of the 1980s was tax reform. Many supporters of reform cited inequities in the tax system, numerous tax loopholes, and overly complicated tax regulations.

The Tax Reform Act of 1986, which resulted from this movement, is the most significant overhaul of the income tax system since 1913. The law restructured the tax code to make it more fair. Among other changes, the new tax law greatly reduced the number of tax brackets. It also changed the tax status of certain tax shelters, real estate investments, and deductions on consumer debts, thereby simplifying the tax code.

IRAs and Other Tax Shelters The Tax Reform Act of 1986 also made significant changes in the status of individual retirement accounts (IRAs) and other tax shelters. A tax shelter is a special investment plan in which the amount invested is not taxed until it is withdrawn from the plan. The IRA, which has been a particularly popular tax shelter, is an account into which people may contribute up to $2,000 of income per year. If the employee's spouse is not employed, the maximum annual contribution is $2,250. Individuals do not pay taxes on this money or on the interest or dividends it earns until the money is withdrawn, usually upon retirement.

Employees who do not have other pension or retirement programs provided by their employer may contribute to an IRA and deduct their contributions from their taxable income. New legislation, in 1997, allowed people who had other pension programs at work to qualify for these IRA investment opportunities only if they had incomes of less than $25,000 for single people or combined incomes of less than $40,000 for married people filing a joint income tax return. Starting with 1998 returns, however, these levels begin to go up. By 2002, the cut-off will be $50,000 for singles and $80,000 for married couples. For those who qualify, their tax deduction is proportionately reduced as taxable income increases.

At these higher income levels, contributions to IRA accounts are no longer tax-deductible. People who do not qualify under these guidelines are still able to set aside money in IRAs. They also can defer taxes on this money until their retirement. However, they are cannot deduct their contributions from their income taxes.

The Roth IRA, first available in 1998, offers a new method of saving. Single people with an income up to $95,000 and married couples with a combined income of $150.000 can contribute $2,000 per year to the Roth IRA. While the contributions are not tax-deductible, the interest on the account is tax-deferred, which means that the IRA–holder does not pay taxes on the interest their savings earns. Furthermore, the proceeds can be withdrawn tax-free after five years if they are withdrawn to pay for a first-time home mortgage or when the IRA–holder reaches the age of 59$\frac{1}{2}$. Another popular tax shelter and retirement plan is the 401(k) program, or the Deferred Income Plan. This plan is one in which an employee and his or her employer make deposits into the employee's retirement program. Taxes are deferred on the money in the account until the employee's retirement.The upper limit on employer contributions is $7,000 per year and is reduced proportionately if the employee has any other retirement plan.

Real Estate Investments   A significant tax break for most people is the fact that home owners are able to deduct mortgage interest—for no more than two home's—from their taxes.

Practicing Consumer Skills

1. Why was the Sixteenth Amendment passed?

2. What problems in the tax codes led to tax reform in the 1980s?

3. How does an IRA function as a tax shelter?

⑩ HOME MORTGAGES

A loan is a transfer of funds that carries with it the legal obligation of repayment. A mortgage is a type of loan. Consumers typically apply to banks or other lenders for mortgages in order to finance purchases of property. In general, mortgages are associated with the purchase of a home.

any special conditions of the sale will be specified in writing in the agreement. Once the agreement is signed, there is a "contract pending" on the house. During this time, the seller of the house may not sell it to anyone else while the buyer awaits mortgage approval.

Real Estate Agreements

Most consumers in the housing market use a real estate agent to help them find a house to buy. Using a realtor has several advantages. For example, a real estate agent help buyers determine how much money they can afford to spend on housing. Then the agent will help find an affordable house that will meet the buyers' needs.

When deciding to purchase a certain house, most buyers will make a bid on the house to the seller. If the seller agrees to the price, both parties sign a real estate agreement. The price of the house and

Lending Institutions

Any bank, savings institution, or other lender may grant a mortgage loan. Wise consumers should shop around for the lowest interest rate before deciding on a lending institution.

When visiting possible lending institutions, prospective buyers should gather information about the various types of mortgages available. The most common mortgage is the conventional, or fixed-rate, mortgage. This type of loan is made for a stated period of time, such as 30 years, at an established rate of interest. The borrower makes a fixed monthly installment payment that includes repayment of both principal and interest.

Today several alternatives to the conventional mortgage exist. One of the most popular is the adjustable rate mortgage—a loan in which flexible interest rates are built into the mortgage. If interest rates drop, the borrower pays less toward interest and more toward principal in his or her fixed installment payments. Interest on mortgages is almost always tax-deductible.

After a consumer decides to apply for a certain kind of mortgage, the lending institution must determine whether to qualify, or approve credit for, the buyer. This process may take several weeks or even months. During this time, the lending institution will verify the borrower's income, employment history, current salary, and credit rating. The lending institution then notifies the borrower to tell them if the mortgage has been denied or approved.

Closing

Soon after a loan has been approved, the buyer, seller, real estate agent, representatives of the lending institution, and other people involved in the purchase of the house meet to sign the legal papers necessary to close the original agreement. This meeting is referred to as the closing. The closing usually is the last step in what can be a long process of buying a house.

Practicing Consumer Skills

1. What is a mortgage?

2. What is specified in a real estate agreement?

3. What does a lending institution verify before approving a loan?

⑪ INSURANCE

Careful financial planning should include plans for the unexpected. As a consumer, you need to know about the various types of insurance that can protect you and your family in times of crisis.

Kinds of Insurance

Today many kinds of insurance are available to meet a variety of needs. Among the most important types of insurance are automobile, homeowner's or renter's, medical and disability, and life.

Automobile Insurance Two basic types of automobile insurance—collision and liability—are available. Collision insurance pays for damages to your car if you are involved in an accident. Most collision policies include a deductible, or specified amount of the repair cost that you must pay before the insurance will pick up the cost. Liability insurance pays for the medical expenses of those injured in an accident and for damages to others' property.

Homeowner's and Renter's Insurance

Like automobile insurance, two kinds of homeowner's or renter's insurance—property and liability—are available. Property insurance will pay for the replacement or repair of a dwelling or other structure on your property, as well as its contents. If you are renting an apartment and do not own the structure, it still is a good idea to buy insurance for the contents of your apartment. Liability insurance pays for the medical expenses of persons who may be injured on your property.

Medical and Disability Insurance

Traditionally, medical insurance was available only as part of a major medical insurance plan, which pays for medical expenses billed by the doctors and hospitals of your choice. Not all medical services are covered, however, and some that are include deductibles.

Today a popular new form of medical insurance—health maintenance organizations (HMOs)—is available. HMOs pay for all or part of medical expenses billed by the doctors and hospitals designated by the organization. Often, these plans cover medical expenses such as yearly examinations and well-baby care in an effort to prevent future medical problems.

Disability insurance provides income assistance to those who become disabled from accident, injury, or illness and can no longer work. This insurance can be either short-term—covering temporary inability to work—or long-term—covering permanent inability to work.

Life Insurance

Life insurance pays benefits to the families of policy holders who die. The two kinds of life insurance available are term insurance and whole life insurance. Term insurance expires after a specified period of time. Individuals who have young children or large mortgages may choose to invest in term insurance because it is relatively inexpensive and will provide a surviving spouse with money to raise children and pay off a mortgage or other large debts. Whole life insurance covers you throughout your life and offers dividends that generally are used to pay for more insurance after the policy has been in effect a certain number of years. In most cases, whole life insurance is more expensive than term insurance.

How to Buy Insurance

Various kinds of insurance—particularly medical, disability, and life—usually are offered as part of an employer's benefits package. When you buy other kinds of insurance individually, be sure that the insurance company from which you buy is an established company with a reputation for paying claims readily and in full. If you need more than one kind of insurance, shop around to find the company that can offer you the best insurance package.

Practicing Consumer Skills

1. What is the purpose of insurance policies?
2. What are the major kinds of insurance?

12 BUYING A NEW CAR

Buying a car can be complicated. To simplify the process and get the most for your money, consider basic factors in advance, such as the and style of the car you want and the amount you can afford to spend.

Size and Style

When you consider the style of the car you want, you will be defining how you plan to use your car and the models that you will consider. A large, comfortable car may be most appropriate for people who do a lot of traveling. Smaller cars usually get better gas mileage and are very practical for driving the short distances. If you use your car to transport several people, like younger siblings or your friends, you will find that some models suit your needs better than others. You can choose from a variety of models including sedans, minivans, hatchbacks, and pickup trucks.

Style typically is a matter of personal preference. Most models will be available in a variety of colors. The basic lines and design of the cars also will vary. In some cases, you may be able to save money if you are flexible about color and detailing because dealers often will accept a lower price for models that they have in stock.

What You Can Afford to Spend

When deciding what you can afford to spend on a car, you must consider the total cost of the car—that is, the base price of the car plus options, initial fees, and maintenance costs.

Options All vehicles are manufactured with standard equipment. The list price of the car is the base price without options. Options are added features that are not necessary for the operation of the car. You will have many options to choose from, but you should know that each increases the price

of the car. Among the options available on many cars are air-conditioning, radios, stereo systems, CD players, leather interiors, rear window defoggers, chrome styling, automatic window controls, whitewall tires, antilock brakes, and more.

After you have identified the base price of the car, consider the options you want, one at a time. It may be a good idea to rank the options in order of priority, listing those most important to you first. Then list the prices of the options. This may help you identify those options that meet your needs and that you can afford, as well as those that you are willing to give up. When budgeting for options, also keep in mind that you will need to consider the costs of initial fees and the continuing costs of owning a car.

Initial Fees and Continuing Costs Initial fees are one-time charges for items such as sales tax, title, and original license plates. These costs usually are not included in the base price of the car.

The amount for sales tax may be more than you expect. Sales taxes are a percentage of a products' cost. Depending on the price of the car, the sales tax on an automobile can add up to hundreds of dollars.

In addition to initial fees, the continuing costs of owning a car must be considered when thinking about your budget. These include insurance premiums, repair and maintenance costs, license plate renewal fees, and the price of gasoline. Information for most models of domestic and foreign cars may be found in publications such as *Consumer Reports*, generally available at your local library or newsstand.

Once you have compared the prices of car models and options, compare the prices offered at different car dealers before making your final selection. You may

From the sales of domestic compact models, the automakers had reason to believe that Americans would not continue to purchase smaller cars when the price of gasoline went down. As a result, many U.S. manufacturers failed to invest in the styling, safety features, and special options that might have made compact cars more desirable to the American buyer. This trend provided increased opportunities for foreign automobile competition in U.S. markets. The strength of the U.S. dollar in foreign-exchange markets also meant that imported cars were relatively less expensive for consumers in the United States than they otherwise might have been. Some of the manufacturers that established a significant hold in the U.S. automobile market as a result were Toyota, Honda, Mitsubishi, and Nissan.

Domestic automakers began to take foreign competition more seriously in the 1980s. A new effort was made to produce stylish cars with down-sized engines, advanced safety features, better gas mileage, and unique high-tech features. In addition, some Japanese car manufacturers began to build their cars in production facilities in the United States, such as the Honda plant in Ohio.

Whether you decide to purchase a domestic car or a foreign car, you have a wide range of choices as a consumer. Keep in mind that your overall goal is to buy a car that suits your needs as well your budget.

find that certain dealers can make a better offer for the basic car that you want than others can. It is a good idea to shop around, talk to salespeople, and compare your choices until you are satisfied that you are buying the car you want at the best possible price.

Foreign Cars

In the 1960s the most popular imported car was the German-made Volkswagen. It was relatively affordable, easy to repair, and because of its good gas mileage, it was less expensive to operate than many domestic cars.

In the years that followed, many other foreign cars began to compete with Volkswagen in the U.S. car market. Over time, foreign cars became more and more popular in the United States. Many consumers came to believe that the smaller, more economical foreign cars had significant advantages over larger American-made cars.

When gasoline prices skyrocketed in the 1970s—further increasing demand for fuel-efficient foreign cars—U.S. manufacturers began an effort to downsize domestic cars. Almost every major U.S. auto company produced what they called a "compact" model to compete with imported vehicles.

Most domestic car manufacturers, however, believed that high gasoline prices would be temporary.

Practicing Consumer Skills

1. What should consumers keep in mind when deciding on the size and style of a car?
2. What costs does the total price of a car include?
3. What impact has foreign competition had on American car manufacturers?

Stocks are popular investments because they offer the potential to earn profits with fairly limited risk. Stocks represent partial ownership of a corporation. This ownership is issued in portions called shares. Stocks can provide a profit either through dividends or when resold at a higher price.

Types of Stock

Shares of stock are divided into two types—common and preferred. The type of stock issued by a corporation depends on the legal organization of the corporation and the decisions made within the corporation as the market changes.

Common Stock   Owners of common stock receive dividends at a variable rate. When the corporation's profits are high, dividends usually are high; when the corporation's profits fall, dividends also fall. If a corporation is operating at a loss, it does not pay any dividends on common stock.

Preferred Stock   Owners of preferred stock receive dividends at a fixed rate, regardless of the level of the corporation's profits. In addition, owners of preferred stock receive their dividends before the owners of common stock do.

Advantages and Disadvantages of Stock Investments

Consumers buy stock as either long-term or short-term investments. As a long-term investment, stocks can

- help protect against inflation,
- serve as a means of increasing financial capital, and
- provide future income.

People who buy and sell stock for short-term gain are called speculators. The object of speculation is to buy low and sell high in order to make a "quick profit." Such investing is extremely risky because prices in the stock market are highly unstable in the short term. While investors hope to sell at a higher price and thus earn a profit, at times they may be forced to sell at the same or a low price and thereby lose money.

UNDERSTANDING STOCK MARKET REPORTS

The annual dividend is 46 cents per share.

Trading volume of the week, in 100-share lots—thus, 19,532,000 shares were traded.

PepsiCo closed at $31.75 per share.

PepsiCo stock price has risen 8.5% this year.

| 52 week | | | | | | Volume | Wkly | | | Charge | | YTD |
Hi	Lo	Name	Div	Yield	PE	Wkly.	Hi	Lo	Last	Fri	Wkly	% Chg
16	7³/8	Kmart			26	238,786	13¹/2	12¹/4	12¹/2	-¹/4		+20.5
53³/4	41	McDnlds	.30	0.7	21	165,646	45¹/8	42¹/2	44¹/2	-¹/4	+1¹/4	-1.9
35⁷/8	28	PepsiCo	.46	1.4	34	195,320	33⁵/8	31⁵/8	31³/4	-¹/8	-1¹/4	+8.5
52⁷/8	26	Reebok	.30	0.6	25	13,269	51³/8	45³/4	50¹/8	+1¹/8	+3³/8	+19.3

$35.875 is the highest and $28.00 is the lowest price of PepsiCo stock in the past 52 weeks, adjusted for splits.

The yield tells what percentage of each share would be returned as dividends, given the current closing price.

The price-to-earnings (PE) ratio is calculated by dividing the stock's last closing price ($31.75) by the company's earnings per share. A higher PE indicates lower earnings, and a lower PE indicates higher earnings.

PepsiCo stock went as high as $33.625 and as low as $31.625 per share during the week.

PepsiCo stock dropped 12.5 cents per share on Friday but dropped $1.25 for the week as a whole.

Influences on Stock Prices

Almost any economic or political event can affect stock prices in the short term. An increase in the unemployment rate or the election of an unpopular foreign leader can cause stock prices to plummet. Or, the passage of a law in Congress to reduce taxes or the announcement of falling interest rates can cause stock prices to rise.

Stock prices also are influenced by news about specific corporations. The announcement that a corporation exceeded its quarterly profit for example, can cause the price of its stock to rise. Likewise, rumors of problems in a corporation, can cause its stock price to fall.

Purchasing Stock

Consumers thinking about purchasing stock should follow these guidelines:

▶ look for stock in a growth industry, as opposed to industries in which growth has peaked.

▶ look for corporations with higher-than-average growth rates.

▶ read business periodicals and newspapers to identify corporations with good overall performances.

▶ avoid corporations with large debts.

▶ look for corporations with consistent dividend increases.

Investing in Stocks

The goal of a stock market investment is to achieve a high rate of return, either as the result of short-term speculation or over the long term. Investments in high-growth stocks represent investments over the long term.

Long-term Investment and Economic Change High-growth stocks are stocks in corporations that have high rates of growth over time, despite changes in the overall economy. The growth rates of such corporations are higher than the growth rates of other corporations, or of the economy as a whole.

When the economy is expanding and businesses are making profits, many stocks can be categorized as growth stocks. When the economy is contracting, or going through a recession, many stocks lose their growth status. High-growth stocks typically maintain their growth even during other economic downturns.

By definition, growth stocks pay no or few dividends at first. Instead, they grow in value over time. Making money in business almost always requires investing money over the long term. Growing businesses typically invest in capital such as facilities and equipment, new marketing and distribution strategies, research and development, and product or service improvement. For this reason, expanding companies normally do not make significant dividend payouts early on. A person investing in a high-growth stock should do so patiently in hopes of increased long-term value.

Buying High-Growth Stocks Finding the right high-growth stock is the most difficult task involved in making this type of investment. It is not difficult to identify stocks and companies that have performed well in the past. Knowing whether growth will continue into the future or if some presently low-growth stock or new stock will "take off" is much more difficult.

Selecting a high-growth company means choosing a company with good earnings. Earnings must be great enough to create profits to reinvest in expansion. In fact, some experts believe the single

most important factor in selecting a high-growth stock is choosing one with a high rate of retained earnings and reinvestment.

Other criteria for selecting a high-growth stock should be the market potential for a company's product or service and the possibilities a company has to benefit from technological change or a restructuring of the economy. You might also consider whether the company has strong managerial leadership and relatively low wage requirements.

No matter how carefully an investor chooses investments, the possibility of losing money always exists. Although companies' annual reports and financial periodicals such as *Money* or *Inc.* help inform consumers, high-growth stocks can be risky. When investing in such stocks, an individual should be in a financial position to sustain a loss.

Practicing Consumer Skills

1. What is the difference between common stock and preferred stock?

2. Why is short-term stock investment especially risky?

3. How can a long-term investment be affected by changes in the economy?

4. Why is it difficult to identify high-growth stocks?

5. What are the criteria for selecting a high-growth stock?

14 MUTUAL FUNDS

One of the most popular investment choices for consumers today is mutual funds. A mutual fund is a fund in which investors' money is pooled to purchase a variety of securities.

As investments, mutual funds have a number of advantages. One of the most important is that, mutual funds are managed by professional financial experts who know market trends, thus freeing investors from the time and effort required to purchase securities on their own. Such management also helps limit the risks of investment. In addition, mutual funds enable investors to buy a variety of securities with a minimal amount of money.

STOCK MARKET PERFORMANCE

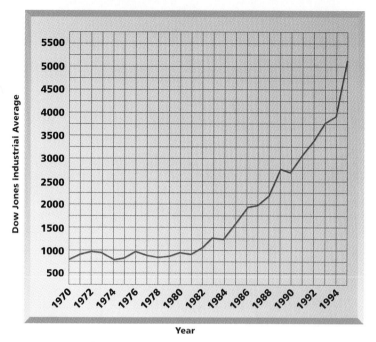

Source: *Statistical Abstract of the United States: 1975,1980,1996*

Because the funds allow investors to pool their capital, an individual investor can own a few shares each of many stocks.

Kinds of Mutual Funds

Stock, money, and bond securities are three types of securities available through a mutual fund.

Stock Market Mutual Funds Buying stocks in a mutual fund provides several advantages. Buying a variety of stock minimizes the risk of loss by spreading the investment out over several possible outcomes—a process known as diversification. For their stock investments, many consumers prefer to pool their money with a number of other people, invest in a number of stocks, and hire a professional to manage their investments.

Money Market Mutual Funds Money markets are markets in which investors lend money on a short-term basis to banks, businesses, and governments. Money market certificates generally pay the current interest rate, called a yield. A money market mutual fund is a mutual fund investing in a variety of short-term money market instruments.

The typical interest rate for such funds often is generally higher than regular savings, but lower than stocks. In addition, because they are for the short term, money market mutual funds enable investors to switch to other investments as market conditions change.

Bond Market Mutual Funds

The bond market is the market in which investors buy, sell, and trade government and corporate bonds. Investors thus lend money to governments and corporations for relatively long periods of time and at fixed rates of interest. Investors generally invest in the bond market when interest rates are high or before an expected drop in rates because a bond's yield is guaranteed. Bond market mutual funds, or bond funds, are funds in which investments are made in a variety of bonds and therefore are similar to other mutual funds.

How to Invest in Mutual Funds

Investors can buy a mutual fund from a stock broker, an insurance salesperson, or on their own. Some mutual funds require consumers to pay a sales commission. By law, this commission cannot be more than 8.5 percent. Other funds, called "no-load" funds, do not charge sales commissions. However, all mutual fund accounts charge consumers a management fee averaging 1.0–1.5 percent.

Investors who want to invest in a mutual fund on their own may subscribe to a mutual fund advisory service or study the publications of such services in the library. Charges for advisory service publications range from $20 to $120 per year.

Practicing Consumer Skills

1. What are the advantages of investing in a mutual fund?

2. What is diversification?

3. Describe three types of mutual fund investments.

United States: Political

To understand the relative locations of Alaska and Hawaii as well as the vast distances separating them from the rest of the United States, see the world map.

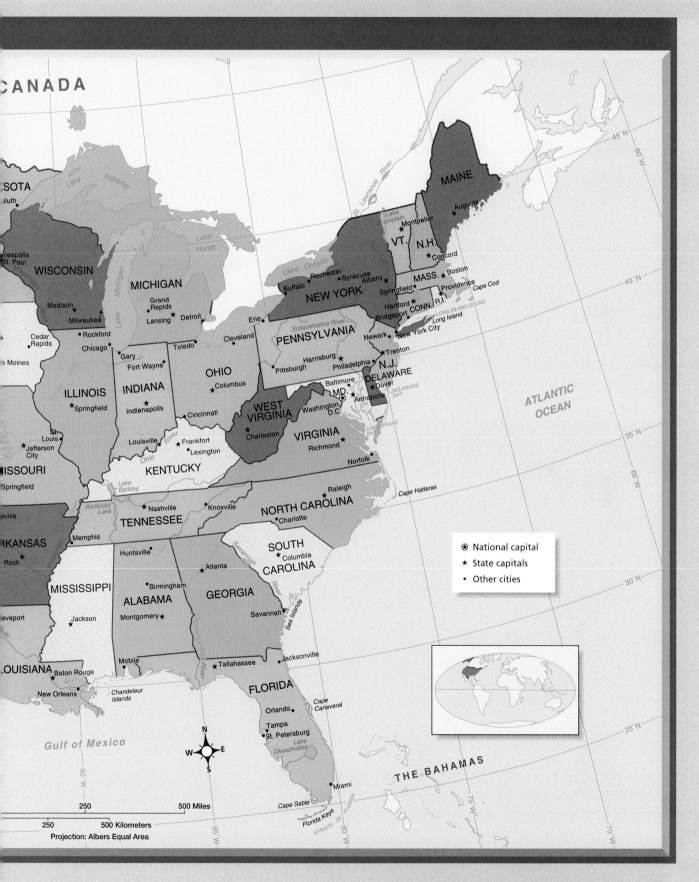

CANADA

SOTA
uluth

WISCONSIN

Madison
Milwaukee

Cedar
Rapids

s Moines

Chicago

Rockford

Gary

Fort Wayne

ILLINOIS

Springfield

INDIANA

Indianapolis

MICHIGAN

Grand
Rapids
Lansing
Detroit

Toledo

Cleveland

Erie

OHIO

Columbus

Cincinnati

Lake Superior

Lake
Huron

Lake Michigan

Lake Ontario

Buffalo
Rochester
Syracuse
Albany

NEW YORK

St. Lawrence River

Lake
Champlain

Montpelier

VT. **N.H.**

Concord

Springfield **MASS.** Boston

Hartford **CONN.** **R.I.** Providence Cape Cod

Bridgeport

LONG ISLAND SOUND

Long Island

Newark New York City

Trenton

PENNSYLVANIA

Susquehanna River

Harrisburg
Pittsburgh
Philadelphia **N.J.**

DELAWARE

Baltimore
Dover

MD.
Washington
D.C.
Annapolis

MAINE

Augusta

ATLANTIC OCEAN

DELAWARE
BAY

St.
Louis
Jefferson
City

MISSOURI

Springfield

eville

RKANSAS

Rock

Louisville

Ohio River

Frankfort
Lexington

KENTUCKY

Lake
Barkley

Kentucky
Lake

Nashville

Memphis

**WEST
VIRGINIA**

Charleston

VIRGINIA

Richmond

CHESAPEAKE
BAY

Norfolk

Cape Hatteras

Raleigh

Knoxville

NORTH CAROLINA

Charlotte

Huntsville

TENNESSEE

**SOUTH
CAROLINA**

Columbia

Birmingham

Atlanta

MISSISSIPPI

ALABAMA

Jackson

Montgomery

GEORGIA

Savannah

Sea Islands

Savannah River

⊛ National capital

★ State capitals

• Other cities

eveport

OUISIANA Baton Rouge

New Orleans

Chandeleur
Islands

Mobile

Tallahassee

Jacksonville

FLORIDA

Orlando

Cape
Canaveral

Tampa
St. Petersburg

Lake
Okeechobee

Gulf of Mexico

N
W E
S

Miami

Cape Sable

Florida Keys

THE BAHAMAS

STRAITS OF FLORIDA

250

500 Miles

250

500 Kilometers

Projection: Albers Equal Area

45° N

60° W

40° N

35° N

65° W

30° N

25° N

75° W

80°

70° W

90° W

85° W

United States Population Density

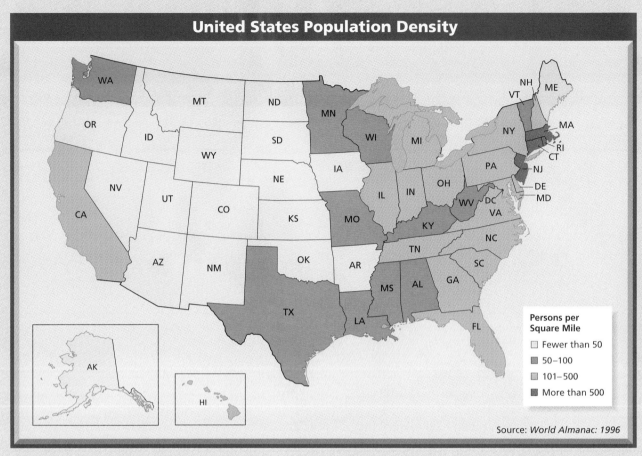

Persons per Square Mile

- ☐ Fewer than 50
- ▨ 50–100
- ▨ 101–500
- ■ More than 500

Source: *World Almanac: 1996*

Per Capita Personal Income in Current Dollars

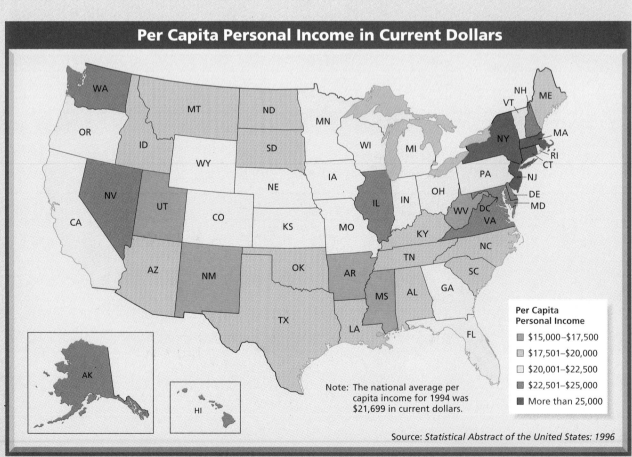

Note: The national average per capita income for 1994 was $21,699 in current dollars.

Per Capita Personal Income

- ▨ $15,000–$17,500
- ▨ $17,501–$20,000
- ☐ $20,001–$22,500
- ▨ $22,501–$25,000
- ■ More than 25,000

Source: *Statistical Abstract of the United States: 1996*

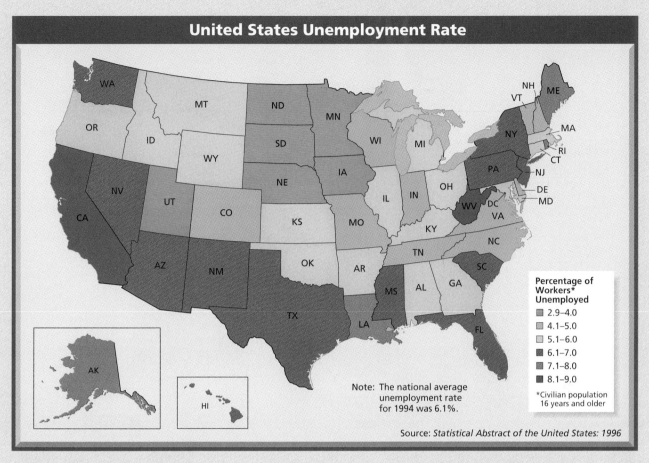

United States Unemployment Rate

Percentage of Workers* Unemployed
- 2.9–4.0
- 4.1–5.0
- 5.1–6.0
- 6.1–7.0
- 7.1–8.0
- 8.1–9.0

*Civilian population 16 years and older

Note: The national average unemployment rate for 1994 was 6.1%.

Source: *Statistical Abstract of the United States: 1996*

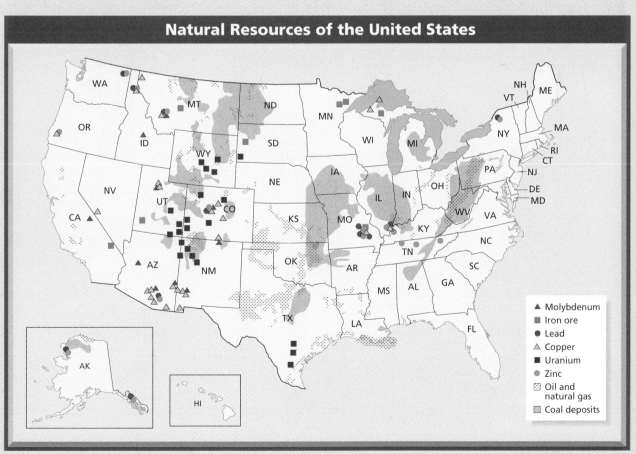

Natural Resources of the United States

- ▲ Molybdenum
- ▪ Iron ore
- ● Lead
- △ Copper
- ■ Uranium
- ● Zinc
- ⊡ Oil and natural gas
- ▨ Coal deposits

The World: Political

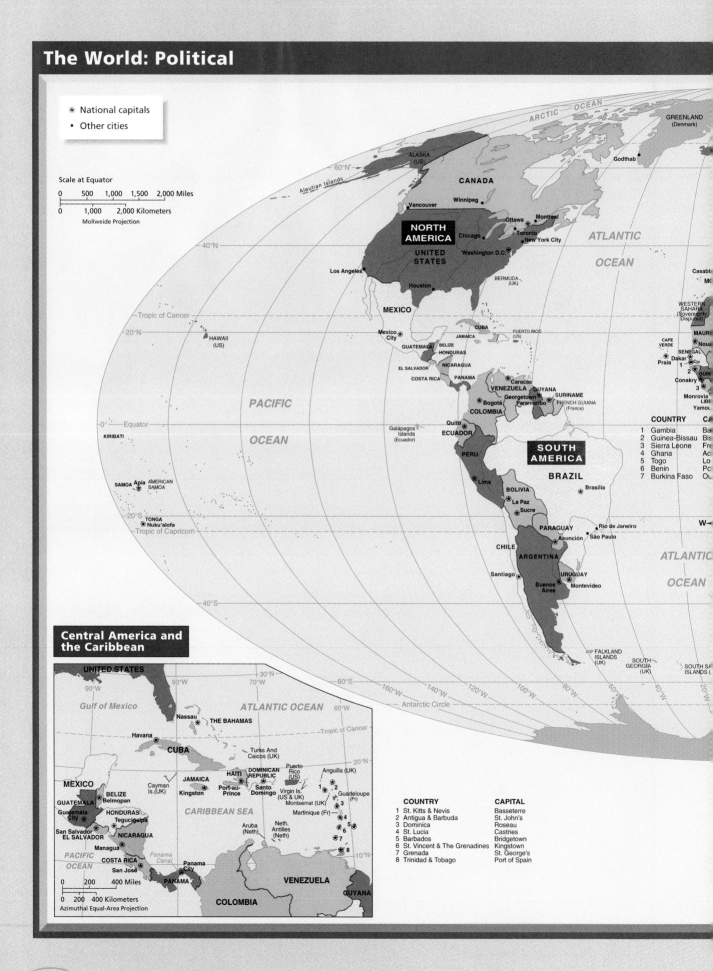

National capitals
Other cities

Scale at Equator
0   500   1,000   1,500   2,000 Miles
0   1,000   2,000 Kilometers
Mollweide Projection

ARCTIC OCEAN

GREENLAND
(Denmark)

ALASKA
(US)

CANADA

Godthab

Winnipeg

Vancouver

NORTH
AMERICA

Ottawa   Montreal
Toronto
Chicago   New York City

ATLANTIC

Washington D.C.

UNITED
STATES

OCEAN

Los Angeles

Houston

BERMUDA
(UK)

Casabla

MO

MEXICO

WESTERN
SAHARA
(Sovereignty
Disputed)

Tropic of Cancer

HAWAII
(US)

Mexico
City

CUBA

JAMAICA

PUERTO RICO
(US)

CAPE
VERDE

Nou

MAURI

SENEGAL

Dakar

GUATEMALA   BELIZE
HONDURAS

Praia   1

2

GUIN

EL SALVADOR   NICARAGUA

Conakry   3

COSTA RICA   PANAMA

Caracas

VENEZUELA   GUYANA

Monrovia   LIBE

SURINAME

Georgetown

Yamou

PACIFIC

Bogotá

Paramaribo

FRENCH GUIANA
(France)

COLOMBIA

COUNTRY   CA

Galápagos
Islands
(Ecuador)

Quito

OCEAN

ECUADOR

1 Gambia   Ba
2 Guinea-Bissau   Bis
3 Sierra Leone   Fre
4 Ghana   Ac
5 Togo   Lo
6 Benin   Po
7 Burkina Faso   Ou

Equator

KIRIBATI

PERU

SOUTH
AMERICA

Lima

BRAZIL

SAMOA   Apia   AMERICAN
SAMOA

BOLIVIA

Brasília

La Paz
Sucre

W

20°S

TONGA
Nuku'alofa

Tropic of Capricorn

PARAGUAY

Rio de Janeiro

CHILE

Asunción   São Paulo

ATLANTIC

ARGENTINA

URUGUAY

OCEAN

Santiago

Buenos
Aires   Montevideo

40°S

FALKLAND
ISLANDS
(UK)

SOUTH
GEORGIA
(UK)

SOUTH SA
ISLANDS
(UK)

60°S

Antarctic Circle

Central America and the Caribbean

UNITED STATES

Gulf of Mexico

ATLANTIC OCEAN

Nassau

THE BAHAMAS

Havana

CUBA

Turks And
Caicos (UK)

Tropic of Cancer

MEXICO

JAMAICA

Cayman
Is.(UK)

HAITI

DOMINICAN
REPUBLIC

Puerto
Rico
(US)

Anguilla (UK)

1   2

Kingston

Port-au-
Prince

Santo
Domingo

Virgin Is.
(US & UK)

3

Guadeloupe
(Fr)

Montserrat (UK)

GUATEMALA

BELIZE

Belmopan

CARIBBEAN SEA

Martinique (Fr)

4

Guatemala
City

HONDURAS

Tegucigalpa

Aruba
(Neth)

Neth.
Antilles
(Neth)

5
6

San Salvador
EL SALVADOR

NICARAGUA

7

Managua

8

PACIFIC
OCEAN

COSTA RICA

Panama
Canal

San José

Panama
City

PANAMA

VENEZUELA

GUYANA

COLOMBIA

0   200   400 Miles
0   200   400 Kilometers
Azimuthal Equal-Area Projection

COUNTRY	CAPITAL
1 St. Kitts & Nevis	Basseterre
2 Antigua & Barbuda	St. John's
3 Dominica	Roseau
4 St. Lucia	Castries
5 Barbados	Bridgetown
6 St. Vincent & The Grenadines	Kingstown
7 Grenada	St. George's
8 Trinidad & Tobago	Port of Spain

United States Balance of Trade with Selected Nations, 1995

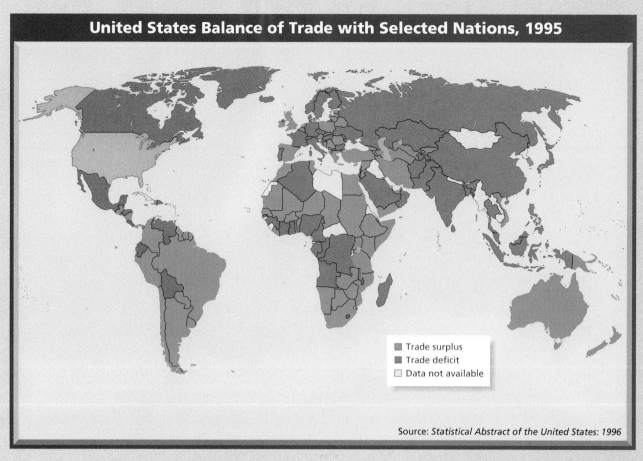

Trade surplus
Trade deficit
Data not available

Source: *Statistical Abstract of the United States: 1996*

World Population Density

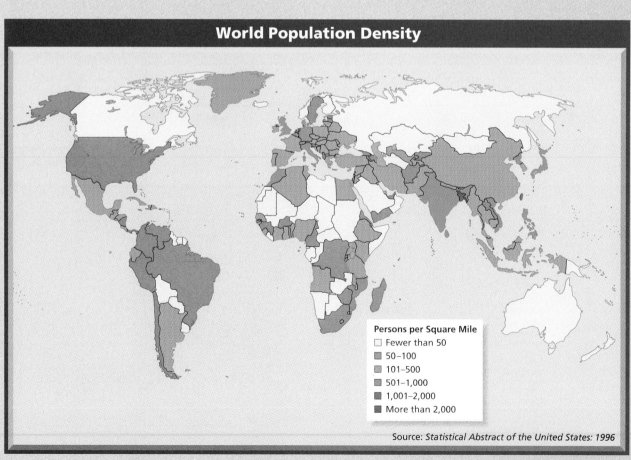

Persons per Square Mile
Fewer than 50
50–100
101–500
501–1,000
1,001–2,000
More than 2,000

Source: *Statistical Abstract of the United States: 1996*

World Labor in Agriculture

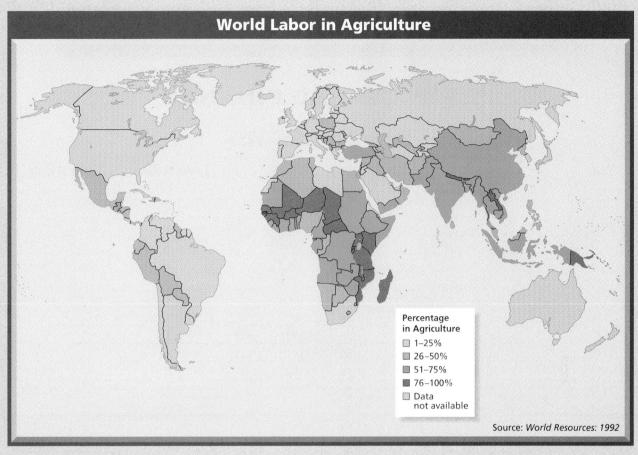

**Percentage
in Agriculture**

- 1–25%
- 26–50%
- 51–75%
- 76–100%
- Data
  not available

Source: *World Resources: 1992*

World Urban Population

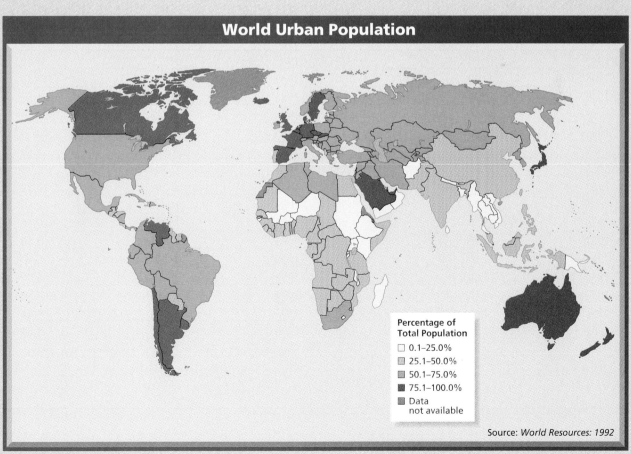

**Percentage of
Total Population**

- 0.1–25.0%
- 25.1–50.0%
- 50.1–75.0%
- 75.1–100.0%
- Data
  not available

Source: *World Resources: 1992*

BANKING AND FINANCE

Prime Rate, 1929–1996

Year	Lowest Rate	Highest Rate	Year	Lowest Rate	Highest Rate
1929	5.50	6.00	1963	4.50	4.50
1930	3.50	6.00	1964	4.50	4.50
1931	2.75	5.00	1965	4.50	5.00
1932	3.25	4.00	1966	5.00	6.00
1933	1.50	4.00	1967	5.50	6.00
1934	1.50	1.50	1968	6.00	6.75
1935	1.50	1.50	1969	6.75	8.50
1936	1.50	1.50	1970	6.75	8.50
1937	1.50	1.50	1971	5.25	6.75
1938	1.50	1.50	1972	5.00	6.00
1939	1.50	1.50	1973	6.00	10.00
1940	1.50	1.50	1974	8.75	12.00
1941	1.50	1.50	1975	7.00	10.50
1942	1.50	1.50	1976	6.25	7.25
1943	1.50	1.50	1977	6.50	7.75
1944	1.50	1.50	1978	8.00	11.75
1945	1.50	1.50	1979	11.50	15.75
1946	1.50	1.50	1980	11.00	21.50
1947	1.50	1.75	1981	15.75	20.50
1948	2.00	2.00	1982	11.50	17.00
1949	2.00	2.00	1983	10.50	11.50
1950	2.00	2.25	1984	10.75	13.00
1951	2.50	3.00	1985	9.50	10.75
1952	3.00	3.00	1986	7.50	9.50
1953	3.00	3.25	1987	7.50	9.75
1954	3.00	3.25	1988	8.50	10.50
1955	3.00	3.50	1989	10.50	11.50
1956	3.50	4.00	1990	10.00	10.50
1957	4.00	4.50	1991	6.50	9.50
1958	3.50	4.50	1992	6.00	6.50
1959	4.00	5.00	1993	6.00	6.00
1960	4.50	5.00	1994	6.00	8.50
1961	4.50	4.50	1995	8.50	9.00
1962	4.50	4.50	1996	8.50	8.25

Source: Federal Reserve Board, *Economic Indicators*

Discount Rate, 1914–1996

Year	Lowest Rate	Highest Rate	Year	Lowest Rate	Highest Rate
1914	5.00	6.00	1956	2.50	3.00
1915	4.00	5.00	1957	3.00	3.50
1916	3.00	4.00	1958	1.75	3.00
1917	3.00	3.50	1959	2.50	4.00
1918	3.50	4.00	1960	3.00	4.00
1919	4.00	4.75	1961	3.00	3.00
1920	4.75	7.00	1962	3.00	3.00
1921	4.50	7.00	1963	3.00	3.50
1922	4.00	4.50	1964	3.50	4.00
1923	4.00	4.50	1965	4.00	4.50
1924	3.00	4.50	1966	4.50	4.50
1925	3.00	3.50	1967	4.00	4.50
1926	3.50	4.00	1968	4.50	5.50
1927	3.50	4.00	1969	5.50	6.00
1928	3.50	5.00	1970	5.50	6.00
1929	4.50	6.00	1971	4.50	5.25
1930	2.00	4.50	1972	4.50	4.50
1931	1.50	3.50	1973	4.50	7.50
1932	2.50	3.50	1974	7.50	8.00
1933	2.00	3.50	1975	6.00	7.25
1934	1.50	2.00	1976	5.50	6.00
1935	1.50	1.50	1977	5.25	6.00
1936	1.50	1.50	1978	6.50	9.50
1937	1.00	1.50	1979	9.50	12.00
1938	1.00	1.00	1980	10.00	13.00
1939	1.00	1.00	1981	12.00	14.00
1940	1.00	1.00	1982	8.50	12.00
1941	1.00	1.00	1983	8.50	8.50
1942	0.50	1.00	1984	8.00	9.00
1943	0.50	1.00	1985	7.50	8.00
1944	0.50	1.00	1986	5.50	7.50
1945	0.50	1.00	1987	5.50	6.00
1946	0.50	1.00	1988	6.00	6.50
1947	1.00	1.00	1989	6.50	7.00
1948	1.00	1.50	1990	6.50	7.00
1949	1.50	1.50	1991	3.50	6.50
1950	1.50	1.75	1992	3.00	3.50
1951	1.75	1.75	1993	3.00	3.00
1952	1.75	1.75	1994	3.00	4.75
1953	1.75	2.00	1995	4.75	5.25
1954	1.50	2.00	1996	5.00	5.25
1955	1.50	2.50			

Source: Federal Reserve Bank of New York

Compound Savings of an Annuity

Years Saved	1%	2%	3%	4%	5%	6%	7%	8%	9%	10%
1	1.000	1.000	1.000	1.000	1.000	1.000	1.000	1.000	1.000	1.000
2	2.010	2.020	2.030	2.040	2.050	2.060	2.070	2.080	2.090	2.100
3	3.030	3.060	3.091	3.122	3.153	3.184	3.215	3.246	3.278	3.310
4	4.060	4.122	4.184	4.246	4.310	4.375	4.440	4.506	4.573	4.641
5	5.101	5.204	5.309	5.416	5.526	5.637	5.751	5.867	5.985	6.105
6	6.152	6.308	6.468	6.633	6.802	6.975	7.153	7.336	7.523	7.716
7	7.214	7.434	7.662	7.898	8.142	8.394	8.654	8.923	9.200	9.487
8	8.286	8.583	8.892	9.214	9.549	9.897	10.260	10.637	11.028	11.436
9	9.369	9.755	10.159	10.583	11.027	11.491	11.978	12.488	13.021	13.579
10	10.462	10.950	11.464	12.006	12.578	13.181	13.816	14.487	15.193	15.937
11	11.567	12.169	12.808	13.486	14.207	14.972	15.784	16.645	17.560	18.531
12	12.683	13.412	14.192	15.026	15.917	16.870	17.888	18.977	20.141	21.384
13	13.809	14.680	15.618	16.627	17.713	18.882	20.141	21.495	22.953	24.523
14	14.947	15.974	17.086	18.292	19.599	21.015	22.550	24.215	26.019	27.975
15	16.097	17.293	18.599	20.024	21.579	23.276	25.129	27.152	29.361	31.772
20	22.019	24.297	26.870	29.778	33.066	36.786	40.995	45.762	51.160	57.275
25	28.243	32.030	36.459	41.646	47.727	54.865	63.249	73.106	84.701	98.347
30	34.785	40.588	47.575	56.085	66.439	79.058	94.461	113.280	136.310	164.490
40	48.886	60.402	75.401	95.026	120.800	154.760	199.640	259.060	337.890	442.590
50	64.463	84.579	112.800	152.670	209.350	290.340	406.530	573.770	815.080	1,163.900

Example: If you invested $1,000 yearly in a retirement plan paying 7 percent a year compounded annually, at the end of the thirtieth year you would have saved $94,461 ($1,000 × 94.461).

ECONOMIC INDICATORS

Consumer Price Index for All Urban Consumers, Annual Average of Change, 1914–1996

1982–84 = 100

Year	% Changed	Year	% Changed
1914	1.0	1956	1.5
1915	1.0	1957	3.3
1916	7.9	1958	2.8
1917	17.4	1959	0.7
1918	18.0	1960	1.7
1919	14.6	1961	1.0
1920	15.6	1962	1.0
1921	-10.5	1963	1.3
1922	-6.1	1964	1.3
1923	1.8	1965	1.6
1924	0	1966	2.9
1925	2.3	1967	3.1
1926	1.1	1968	4.2
1927	-1.7	1969	5.5
1928	-1.7	1970	5.7
1929	0.0	1971	4.4
1930	-2.3	1972	3.2
1931	-9.0	1973	6.2
1932	-9.9	1974	11.0
1933	-5.1	1975	9.1
1934	3.1	1976	5.8
1935	2.2	1977	6.5
1936	1.5	1978	7.6
1937	3.6	1979	11.3
1938	-2.1	1980	13.5
1939	-1.4	1981	10.3
1940	0.7	1982	6.2
1941	5.0	1983	3.2
1942	10.9	1984	4.3
1943	6.1	1985	3.6
1944	1.7	1986	1.9
1945	2.3	1987	3.6
1946	8.3	1988	4.1
1947	14.4	1989	4.8
1948	8.1	1990	5.4
1949	-1.2	1991	4.2
1950	1.3	1992	3.0
1951	7.9	1993	3.0
1952	1.9	1994	2.6
1953	0.8	1995	2.8
1954	0.7	1996	3.0
1955	-0.4		

Source: U.S. Bureau of Labor Statistics

Average Annual Incomes for Selected Occupations, 1900–1990

Year	Average for All Workers	Coal Miners	Farm Workers	Federal Employees	Gas and Electric Workers	Health-Care Providers	Public School Teachers	Salespeople
1900	490	547	247	1,033	620	256	548	508
1910	630	805	336	1,108	622	338	677	630
1920	1,489	2,130	810	1,648	1,432	752	1,817	1,270
1930	1,494	909	444	1,492	1,603	933	1,717	1,569
1940	1,392	1,235	463	1,125	1,795	927	1,906	1,382
1950	3,255	3,245	1,454	3,220	3,571	2,067	3,778	3,034
1960	5,260	5,367	1,848	4,721	6,150	3,414	6,241	5,756
1970	7,747	9,790	3,787	8,040	10,028	6,593	10,110	NR
1980	15,757	24,555	7,434	17,217	21,701	14,728	25,372	18,822
1990	15,641	28,460	NA	NA	26,875	21,653	26,875	18,236

Source: U.S. Bureau of Labor Statistics

NR = Income not reported

NA = Information not available. The Bureau of Labor Statistics did not compile this data in 1990.

Prices of Selected Consumer Products
New York City, 1900–1995

Year	Beef Roast (per pound)	Butter (per pound)	Chicken (per pound)	Eggs (per dozen)	Rice (per pound)
1900	$0.18	$0.27	$0.13	$0.23	$0.07
1905	0.14	0.28	0.17	0.32	0.09
1910	0.19	0.39	0.19	0.36	NR
1915	0.22	0.36	0.22	0.39	0.09
1920	0.41	0.71	0.44	0.78	0.17
1925	0.39	0.55	0.39	0.63	0.11
1930	0.41	0.46	0.37	0.52	0.09
1935	0.34	0.37	0.32	0.44	0.09
1941*	0.41	0.42	0.34	0.45	0.09
1945	0.33	0.51	0.47	0.60	0.14
1950	0.75	0.74	0.44	0.67	0.17
1955	0.70	0.72	0.45	0.70	0.20
1960	0.76	0.74	0.43	0.63	0.19
1965	0.85	0.75	0.42	0.57	0.20
1970	1.02	0.88	0.46	0.67	0.22
1975	1.78	1.06	0.68	0.85	0.50
1980	3.65	1.99	0.77	0.91	0.52
1986*	4.17	NR	0.88	0.92	NR
1990	4.54	1.92	0.86	1.00	0.49
1995	4.81	1.73	0.94	1.16	0.55

Source: U.S. Bureau of Labor Statistics

*Prices for 1940 and 1985 were not recorded.

NR = Prices not recorded

Unemployment in the United States, 1911–1996

Year	Number of Unemployed People (in thousands)	Unemployment Rate (in percent)	Year	Number of Unemployed People (in thousands)	Unemployment Rate (in percent)
1911	2,518	6.7	1954	3,532	5.5
1912	1,759	4.6	1955	2,852	4.4
1913	1,671	4.3	1956	2,750	4.1
1914	3,120	7.9	1957	2,859	4.3
1915	3,377	8.5	1958	4,602	6.8
1916	2,043	5.1	1959	3,740	5.5
1917	1,848	4.6	1960	3,852	5.5
1918	536	1.4	1961	4,714	6.7
1919	546	1.4	1962	3,911	5.5
1920	2,132	5.2	1963	4,070	5.7
1921	4,918	11.7	1964	3,786	5.2
1922	2,859	6.7	1965	3,366	4.5
1923	1,049	2.4	1966	2,875	3.8
1924	2,190	5.0	1967	2,975	3.8
1925	1,453	3.2	1968	2,817	3.6
1926	801	1.8	1969	2,832	3.5
1927	1,519	3.3	1970	4,088	4.9
1928	1,982	4.2	1971	5,016	5.8
1929	1,550	3.2	1972	4,882	5.5
1930	4,340	8.7	1973	4,365	4.8
1931	8,020	15.9	1974	5,156	5.5
1932	12,060	23.6	1975	7,929	8.3
1933	12,830	24.9	1976	7,406	7.6
1934	11,340	21.7	1977	6,991	6.9
1935	10,610	20.1	1978	6,202	6.0
1936	9,030	16.9	1979	6,137	5.8
1937	7,700	14.3	1980	7,637	7.1
1938	10,390	19.0	1981	8,273	7.5
1939	9,480	17.2	1982	10,678	9.5
1940	8,120	14.6	1983	10,717	9.5
1941	5,560	9.9	1984	8,539	7.4
1942	2,660	4.7	1985	8,312	7.2
1943	1,070	1.9	1986	8,237	7.0
1944	670	1.2	1987	7,425	6.2
1945	1,040	1.9	1988	6,701	5.5
1946	2,270	3.9	1989	6,528	5.3
1947	2,311	3.9	1990	6,874	5.5
1948	2,276	3.8	1991	8,426	6.7
1949	3,637	5.9	1992	9,384	7.4
1950	3,288	5.3	1993	8,734	6.8
1951	2,055	3.3	1994	7,996	6.1
1952	1,883	3.0	1995	7,405	5.6
1953	1,834	2.9	1996	7,226	5.4

Note: From 1911 until 1947, figures are for workers aged 14 and older. After 1947, figures are for workers aged 16 and older.
Source: U.S. Bureau of Labor Statistics

FEDERAL BUDGET

Summary of Federal Government Finances, 1789–1997

Year	Total Revenue	Total Expenditures (in mill. of dollars)	Surplus or Deficit (-)	Year	Total Revenue	Total Expenditures (in mill. of dollars)	Surplus or Deficit (-)
1789–91	4	4	*	1833	34	23	11
1792	4	5	-1	1834	22	19	3
1793	5	4	*	1835	35	18	18
1794	5	7	-2	1836	51	31	20
1795	6	8	-1	1837	25	37	-12
1796	8	6	3	1838	26	34	-8
1797	9	6	3	1839	31	27	5
1798	8	8	*	1840	19	24	-5
1799	8	10	-2	1841	17	27	-10
1800	11	11	*	1842	20	25	-5
1801	13	9	4	1843	8	12	-4
1802	15	8	7	1844	29	22	7
1803	11	8	3	1845	30	23	7
1804	12	9	3	1846	30	28	2
1805	14	11	3	1847	26	57	-31
1806	16	10	6	1848	36	45	-10
1807	16	8	8	1849	31	45	-14
1808	17	10	7	1850	44	40	4
1809	8	10	-3	1851	53	48	5
1810	9	8	1	1852	50	44	6
1811	14	8	6	1853	62	48	13
1812	10	20	-10	1854	74	58	16
1813	14	32	-17	1855	65	60	6
1814	11	35	-24	1856	74	70	4
1815	16	33	-17	1857	69	68	1
1816	48	31	17	1858	47	74	-28
1817	33	22	11	1859	53	69	-16
1818	22	20	2	1860	56	63	-7
1819	25	21	3	1861	42	67	-25
1820	18	18	*	1862	52	475	-423
1821	15	16	-1	1863	113	715	-602
1822	20	15	5	1864	265	865	-601
1823	21	15	6	1865	334	1,298	-964
1824	19	20	-1	1866	558	521	37
1825	22	16	6	1867	491	358	133
1826	25	17	8	1868	406	377	28
1827	23	16	7	1869	371	323	48
1828	25	16	8	1870	411	310	102
1829	25	15	10	1871	383	292	91
1830	25	15	10	1872	374	278	97
1831	29	15	13	1873	334	290	43
1832	32	17	15	1874	305	303	2

*$500,000 or less

Year	Total Revenue	Total Expenditures (in mill. of dollars)	Surplus or Deficit (-)	Year	Total Revenue	Total Expenditures (in mill. of dollars)	Surplus or Deficit (-)
1875	288	275	13	1922	4,026	3,289	736
1876	294	265	29	1923	3,853	3,140	713
1877	281	241	40	1924	3,871	2,908	963
1878	258	237	21	1925	3,641	2,924	717
1879	274	267	7	1926	3,795	2,930	865
1880	334	268	66	1927	4,013	2,857	1,155
1881	361	261	100	1928	3,900	2,961	939
1882	404	258	146	1929	3,862	3,127	734
1883	398	265	133	1930	4,058	3,320	738
1884	349	244	104	1931	3,116	3,577	-462
1885	324	260	63	1932	1,924	4,659	-2,735
1886	336	242	94	1933	1,997	4,598	-2,602
1887	371	268	103	1934	2,955	6,541	-3,586
1888	379	268	111	1935	3,609	6,412	-2,803
1889	387	299	88	1936	3,923	8,228	-4,304
1890	403	318	85	1937	5,387	7,580	-2,193
1891	393	366	27	1938	6,751	6,840	-89
1892	355	345	10	1939	6,295	9,141	-2,846
1893	386	383	2	1940	6,548	9,468	-2,920
1894	306	368	-61	1941	8,712	13,653	-4,941
1895	325	356	-31	1942	14,634	35,137	-20,503
1896	338	352	-14	1943	24,001	78,555	-54,554
1897	348	366	-18	1944	43,747	91,304	-47,557
1898	405	443	-38	1945	45,159	92,712	-47,553
1899	516	605	-89	1946	39,296	55,232	-15,936
1900	567	521	46	1947	38,514	34,496	4,018
1901	588	525	63	1948	41,560	29,764	11,796
1902	562	485	77	1949	39,415	38,835	580
1903	562	517	45	1950	39,443	42,562	-3,119
1904	541	584	-43	1951	51,616	45,514	6,102
1905	544	567	-23	1952	66,167	67,686	-1,519
1906	595	570	25	1953	69,608	76,101	-6,493
1907	666	579	87	1954	69,701	70,855	-1,154
1908	602	659	-57	1955	65,451	68,444	-2,993
1909	604	694	-89	1956	74,587	70,640	3,947
1910	676	694	-18	1957	79,990	76,578	3,412
1911	702	691	11	1958	79,636	82,405	-2,769
1912	693	690	3	1959	79,249	92,098	-12,849
1913	714	715	*	1960	92,492	92,191	301
1914	725	726	*	1961	94,388	97,723	-3,335
1915	683	746	-63	1962	99,676	106,821	-7,146
1916	761	713	48	1963	106,560	111,316	-4,756
1917	1,101	1,954	-853	1964	112,613	118,528	-5,915
1918	3,645	12,677	-9,032	1965	116,817	118,228	-1,411
1919	5,130	18,493	-13,363	1966	130,835	134,532	-3,698
1920	6,649	6,358	291	1967	148,822	157,464	-8,643
1921	5,571	5,062	509				

Continued on next page

Summary of Federal Government Finances, 1789–1997

Continued from page 495

Year	Total Revenue	Total Expenditures (in mill. of dollars)	Surplus or Deficit (-)	Year	Total Revenue	Total Expenditures (in mill. of dollars)	Surplus or Deficit (-)
1968	152,973	178,134	-25,161	1986	769,260	990,505	-221,245
1969	186,882	183,640	3,242	1987	854,396	1,004,164	-149,769
1970	192,807	195,649	-2,842	1988	909,303	1,064,489	-155,187
1971	187,139	210,172	-23,033	1989	991,190	1,143,671	-152,481
1972	207,309	230,681	-23,373	1990	1,031,969	1,253,163	-221,194
1973	230,799	245,707	-14,908	1991	1,055,041	1,324,400	-269,359
1974	263,224	269,359	-6,135	1992	1,091,279	1,381,681	-290,402
1975	279,090	332,332	-53,242	1993	1,154,401	1,409,414	-255,013
1976	298,060	371,792	-73,732	1994	1,258,627	1,461,731	-203,104
1977	355,559	409,218	-53,659	1995	1,351,830	1,515,729	-163,899
1978	399,561	458,746	-59,186	1996	1,453,062	1,560,330	-107,268
1979	463,302	504,032	-40,729	1997 est.	1,505,425	1,631,016	-125,591
1980	517,112	590,947	-73,835				
1981	599,272	678,249	-78,976				
1982	617,766	745,755	-127,989				
1983	600,562	808,380	-207,818				
1984	666,499	851,888	-185,388				
1985	734,165	946,499	-212,334				

Note: Due to rounding, the surplus or deficit may not equal exactly the difference between revenues and expenditures.

Sources: U.S. Bureau of the Census, Office of Management and Budget

Public Debt of the Federal Government, 1803–1997

Year	Total Public Debt (in millions)	Year	Total Public Debt (in millions)	Year	Total Public Debt (in millions)
1803	$77.1	1822	$93.5	1841	$5.3
1804	86.4	1823	90.9	1842	13.6
1805	82.3	1824	90.3	1843	32.7
1806	75.7	1825	83.8	1844	23.5
1807	69.2	1826	81.1	1845	15.9
1808	65.2	1827	74.0	1846	15.6
1809	57.0	1828	67.5	1847	38.8
1810	53.2	1829	58.4	1848	47.0
1811	48.0	1830	48.6	1849	63.1
1812	45.2	1831	39.1	1850	63.5
1813	56.0	1832	24.3	1851	68.3
1814	81.5	1833	· 7.0	1852	66.2
1815	99.8	1834	4.8	1853	59.8
1816	127.3	1835	*	1854	42.2
1817	123.5	1836	*	1855	35.6
1818	103.5	1837	0.3	1856	32.0
1819	95.5	1838	3.3	1857	28.7
1820	91.0	1839	10.4	1858	44.9
1821	90.0	1840	3.6	1859	58.5

Year	Total Public Debt (in millions)	Year	Total Public Debt (in millions)	Year	Total Public Debt (in millions)
1860	$64.8	1907	$1,147.2	1954	$271,259.6
1861	90.6	1908	1,177.7	1955	274,374.2
1862	524.2	1909	1,148.3	1956	272,750.8
1863	1,119.8	1910	1,146.9	1957	270,527.2
1864	1,815.8	1911	1,154.0	1958	276,343.2
1865	2,677.9	1912	1,193.8	1959	284,705.9
1866	2,755.8	1913	1,193.0	1960	286,330.8
1867	2,650.2	1914	1,188.2	1961	288,970.9
1868	2,583.4	1915	1,191.3	1962	298,200.8
1869	2,545.1	1916	1,225.1	1963	305,859.6
1870	2,436.5	1917	2,975.6	1964	311,712.9
1871	2,322.1	1918	12,455.2	1965	317,273.9
1872	2,210.0	1919	25,484.5	1966	319,907.1
1873	2,151.2	1920	24,299.3	1967	326,220.9
1874	2,159.9	1921	23,977.5	1968	347,578.4
1875	2,156.3	1922	22,963.4	1969	353,720.3
1876	2,130.8	1923	22,349.7	1970	370,918.7
1877	2,107.8	1924	21,250.8	1971	397,300.0
1878	2,159.4	1925	20,516.2	1972	435,936
1879	2,298.9	1926	19,643.2	1973	466,291
1880	2,090.9	1927	18,511.9	1974	483,893
1881	2,019.3	1928	17,604.3	1975	541,925
1882	1,856.9	1929	16,931.1	1976	628,970
1883	1,722.0	1930	16,185.3	1977	706,398
1884	1,625.3	1931	16,801.3	1978	776,602
1885	1,578.6	1932	19,487.0	1979	829,470
1886	1,555.7	1933	22,538.7	1980	909,050
1887	1,465.5	1934	27,053.1	1981	994,845
1888	1,384.6	1935	28,700.9	1982	1,137,345
1889	1,249.5	1936	33,778.5	1983	1,371,710
1890	1,122.4	1937	36,424.6	1984	1,564,657
1891	1,005.8	1938	37,164.7	1985	1,817,521
1892	968.2	1939	40,439.5	1986	2,120,629
1893	961.4	1940	42,967.5	1987	2,346,125
1894	1,016.8	1941	48,961.4	1988	2,601,307
1895	1,096.9	1942	72,422.4	1989	2,868,039
1896	1,222.7	1943	136,696.1	1990	3,206,564
1897	1,226.8	1944	201,003.4	1991	3,598,498
1898	1,232.7	1945	258,682.2	1992	4,002,136
1899	1,436.7	1946	269,422.1	1993	4,351,416
1900	1,263.4	1947	258,286.4	1994	4,643,711
1901	1,221.6	1948	252,292.2	1995	4,921,018
1902	1,178.0	1949	252,770.4	1996	5,181,930
1903	1,159.4	1950	257,357.4	1997 est.	5,453,677
1904	1,136.3	1951	255,222.0		
1905	1,132.4	1952	259,105.2		
1906	1,142.5	1953	266,071.1		

*less than 0.1

Source: U.S. Department of the Treasury

UNITED STATES POPULATION

Population of the United States, 1790–1990

Year	Population (in thousands)
1790	3,929
1800	5,308
1810	7,240
1820	9,638
1830	12,866
1840	17,069
1850	23,192
1860	31,443
1870	39,818
1880	50,156
1890	62,948
1900	75,995
1910	91,972
1920	105,711
1930	122,775
1940	131,669
1950	150,697
1960	179,323
1970	203,235
1980	226,546
1990	248,718

Source: U.S. Bureau of the Census

Population of the United States by Race and Ethnicity, 1900–1990

(in thousands)

Year	White	African American	Hispanic/ Latino	Total	OTHER American Indian, Inuit, Aleut	Asian, Pacific Islander
1900	66,809	8,834	NA	351	NA	NA
1910	81,732	9,828	NA	413	NA	NA
1920	94,821	10,463	NA	427	NA	NA
1930	110,287	11,891	NA	597	NA	NA
1940	118,215	12,866	NA	589	NA	NA
1950	134,942	15,042	NA	713	NA	NA
1960	158,832	18,872	NA	1,620	NA	NA
1970	178,098	22,581	NA	2,557	NA	NA
1980	194,713	26,683	14,609	5,150	1,420	3,729
1990	208,710	30,486	22,354	9,523	2,065	7,458

NA=This information is not available because it was not reported in the official census.

Source: U.S. Bureau of the Census

Population of the United States by Gender, 1870–1990

(in thousands)

Year	Male	Female
1870	19,494	19,064
1880	25,519	24,637
1890	32,237	30,711
1900	38,816	37,178
1910	47,332	44,640
1920	53,900	51,810
1930	62,137	60,638
1940	66,062	65,608
1950	74,833	75,864
1960	88,331	90,992
1970	98,926	104,309
1980	110,053	116,493
1990	121,244	127,474

Note: Before 1870, population figures reported by gender
are incomplete.

Source: U.S. Bureau of the Census

Immigrants to the United States by Region, 1901–1994

Year	Africa	Asia	Australia and Pacific Islands	Europe	North America	South America	Total
1901–10	7,368	196,501	13,024	8,136,016	336,416	25,472	8,795,386
1911–20	8,443	192,559	13,427	4,375,564	1,084,613	59,058	5,735,811
1921–30	6,286	97,400	8,726	2,477,853	1,458,701	58,015	4,107,209
1931–40	1,750	15,872	2,417	348,289	146,348	12,089	528,431
1941–50	7,367	36,471	14,551	621,704	282,032	72,772	1,035,039
1951–60	14,092	150,681	12,976	1,328,293	800,852	196,090	2,515,479
1961–70	28,954	421,464	25,122	1,129,670	1,337,460	378,914	3,321,677
1971–80	91,500	1,633,800	37,300*	801,300	1,645,000	284,400	4,493,300
1981–90	192,300	2,817,400	41,900*	705,600	3,125,000	455,900	7,338,100
1991–94	117,700	1,366,100	21,000*	599,800	2,168,600	236,600	4,509,800

*Figure includes Australia, New Zealand, and countries listed as "unknown."

Source: U.S. Bureau of the Census, U.S. Immigration and Naturalization Service

GLOSSARY

Glossary

This glossary contains terms you need to understand as you study economics. After each term there is a brief definition or explanation of the term as it is used in *Holt Economics.* The page number refers to the page on which the term is introduced in the textbook.

Phonetic Respelling and Pronunciation Guide

Many of the key terms in this textbook have been respelled to help you pronounce them. The letter combinations used in the respellings throughout the narrative are explained in the following phonetic respelling and pronunciation guide. The guide is adapted from *Webster's Tenth New Collegiate Dictionary, Webster's New Geographical Dictionary,* and *Webster's New Biographical Dictionary.*

MARK	AS IN	RESPELLING	EXAMPLE
a	alphabet	a	*AL-fuh-bet
ā	Asia	ay	AY-zhuh
ä	cart, top	ah	KAHRT, TAHP
e	let, ten	e	LET, TEN
ē	even, leaf	ee	EE-vuhn, LEEF
i	it, tip, British	i	IT, TIP, BRIT-ish
ī	site, buy, Ohio	y	SYT, BY, oh-HY-oh
	iris	eye	EYE-ris
k	card	k	KAHRD
ō	over, rainbow	oh	oh-vuhr, RAYN-boh
ù	book, wood	ooh	BOOHK, WOOHD
ò	all, orchid	aw	AWL, AWR-kid
òi	foil, coin	oy	FOYL, KOYN
àu	out	ow	OWT
ə	cup, butter	uh	KUHP, BUHT-uhr
ü	rule, food	oo	ROOL, FOOD
yü	few	yoo	FYOO
zh	vision	zh	VIZH-uhn

A syllable printed in small capital letters receives heavier emphasis than the other syllable(s) in a word.

absolute advantage the ability of a nation, region, or company to produce a certain good or service more efficiently and cheaply than any other nation, region, or company. **428**

adjustable-peg system a system in which the exchange rates between currencies are fixed at specific values instead of reflecting changing economic conditions. **432**

affirmative action a program, supported by law, requiring U.S. employers, labor unions, and other institutions to eliminate discrimination against women and minorities by increasing hiring, promotion, training, and other opportunities for members of these groups. **174**

aggregate demand the total amount of goods, investments, and services that consumers want to buy during a specific period of time. **257**

aggregate supply the total supply of all goods and services available in an economy. **257**

allocate to distribute scarce resources—such as money, land, equipment, or labor—in order to satisfy the greatest number of needs and wants. **8**

annual percentage rate the total cost of credit expressed as a yearly percentage. **215**

antitrust legislation federal and state laws that regulate big business and labor unions to prevent or dismantle monopolies. **130**

appreciation 1) an increase in the buying power of money 2) an increase in the value of a possession, such as a share of stock, a work or art, or real estate 3) an increase in the value of a nation's money relative to that of another nation. **432**

arable fit for or used for growing crops. **403**

arbitration a process for settling a dispute in which a mutually agreed-upon third party listens to each side and makes a settlement decision. **187**

articles of incorporation an application to form a new corporation. **154**

authoritarian socialism an economic system in which the government owns or controls nearly all factors of production; also known as communism. **27**

B

balance 1) the amount on the credit side of an account 2) the difference between the debits and credits in a series of transactions. **196**

balance of payments the accounting record of what a nation owes to and is owed by foreign countries and international institutions. **436**

balance of trade the difference between the value of a nation's exports and that of its imports. **437**

bankruptcy a legal process in which an individual or business whose debts exceed the value of their assets is forgiven those debts in excess of their assets. **216**

barter the direct exchange of goods and services without the use of money. **15**

bear market a financial market in which in the price of stocks, bonds, or other traded commodities is generally on the decline and in which investors believe that prices will continue to fall. **209**

black market buying and selling of goods in violation of the law, typically at a higher price than has been officially established. **112**

board of directors a panel elected by the stockholders of a corporation to establish its policies and overall direction. **155**

bourgeoisie 1) the middle class, particularly as distinct from the upper class and the poor 2) the people who own the means of production in a capitalist nation. **389**

broker a person who carries out investors' orders to buy and sell stocks and bonds. **206**

budget a plan listing the expenses and income of an individual or organization. **200**

budget deficit the amount that an organization's spending exceeds the revenue it takes in over a designated period. **363**

budget surplus the amount that an organization's income exceeds its spending over a designated period. **363**

bull market a financial market in which the price of stocks, bonds, or other traded commodities is generally on the rise and in which investors believe that prices will continue to rise. **209**

business cycle a recurring pattern in economic activity that is characterized by alternating periods of expansion and contraction. **236**

buyer someone who purchases or consumes a good or service. **117**

C

capital accumulation the expansion of an economy's amount of capital goods. **202**

capital deepening the increasing of capital resources at a faster rate than the increasing of the labor force, causing a rise in the capital-to-labor ratio. **244**

capital formation the accumulation of financial and capital goods that promote increased production and economic development. **408**

capital gain the profit earned through the sale of a capital asset. **205**

capital good a building, structure, machine or tool that is used to produce goods or services. **5**

capital loss a loss that results when a capital asset, such as a home, equipment, or investments, is sold for less than it cost. **205**

capital resource an item that is used in the production of other goods and services. **5**

capital-intensive a condition describing a company, industry, or national economy that depends on machines or capital assets to produce goods. **172**

capitalism a market-based economic system in which individuals own and control the factors of production. **28**

capital-to-labor ratio The amount of capital resources available per worker. **244**

cartel group of producers or sellers of a certain good or service who unite to control prices, output, and market share. **126**

check-clearing the daily process of debiting and crediting banks' reserve accounts and checking accounts. **332**

closed shop a business that hires only labor union members. **178**

coincident indicators a set of economic factors that move up or down with the overall economy, measuring current economic activity. **240**

collateral property pledged by a borrower as security for a loan—for example, real estate, automobiles, or equipment. **149**

collective bargaining the process by which labor union leaders, speaking for the members they represent, and management representatives meet to negotiate labor contracts. **186**

collectivization the Soviet Union's policy of taking privately owned land to form large state-run farms. **391**

collusion an effort by producers or sellers of a particular product to secretly set production levels or prices. **125**

command economy an economy in which a central government authority makes all basic economic decisions and controls the factors of production. **25**

command system an economic system in which basic economic decisions are made by the government. **377**

commercial bank a financial institution whose chief purpose is to accept savings and checking deposits, make loans to businesses and individuals, and tranfer money among businesses, other banks, financial institutions, and individuals. **316**

commodity money a money system that is based on an item (a commodity) that has value to a society. **305**

common stock a share of ownership in a corporation; grants dividends and a voice in corporate management to the shareholder. **155**

communism economic system in which the government owns or controls nearly all factors of production; also known as authoritarian socialism. **27**

comparative advantage the ability of a nation, region, or company to produce a certain good or service more cheaply than any other country. **428**

competition in business, a state of rivalry among sellers of the same or similar products, in which each seller tries to gain a larger share of a market and to increase profits. **32**

complementary good a good that is commonly used with another good and for which demand increases (or decreases) when the demand for the related good increases (or decreases). **62**

conglomerate combination a corporation made up of several companies involved in different industries and markets. **160**

consumer one who buys goods or services for personal use rather than for resale or use in production or manufacturing. **3**

consumer good a finished product that is consumed by an individual. **7**

consumer price index (CPI) a measure of changes in the prices of market basket items, specific goods and services commonly purchased by a typical family. **260**

contract a legally binding agreement, either oral or written, between individuals, such as to buy and sell goods and services. **30**

contraction a period in the business cycle during which business activity slows down and overall economic indicators decline. **236**

cooperative a business that is owned collectively by those who use its goods or services. **163**

coordinated campaigning a strategy in a labor dispute in which workers or a labor union use a variety of tactics, such as picketing, primary boycotts, and secondary boycotts, to force an employer to give in to their demands. **189**

copyright a government-granted right to exclusively duplicate, perform, display, publish, and sell copies of a literary, musical, or artistic work for a specified period of time. **128**

corporate bond a document representing a loan made by an investor to a corporation. **155**

corporate charter a document that a government issues to grant certain rights and impose certain restrictions on a bank or corporation. **154**

corporation a business in which a group of owners, called stockholders, share in the profits and losses. **153**

cost of production the total cost of materials, labor, and other inputs required in the manufacture of a product. **74**

cost-push inflation a general rise in prices that results from a rise in the costs of production. **258**

credit a form of exchange that allows consumers to use items with a promise of repayment over a specified time. **16**

credit bureau a company that collects and reports to its clients information about a person's financial condition and past record in meeting his or her financial obligations. **215**

credit rating an evaluation of a person's or a company's financial condition and reliability, especially concerning its record of meeting financial obligations. **215**

Cultural Revolution   a violent movement in China from 1966 to 1976 that sought to preserve the communist system. **396**

currency   the paper money and coins that are in circulation in a nation and that make up its money supply. **306**

customs duty   a tax on goods brought into the United States. **354**

cyclical unemployment   unemployment that is caused by downturns in the business cycle. **256**

—————————— **D** ——————————

debit card   a plastic card used to make withdrawals at an automatic teller machine or a place of business. **318**

debt ceiling   the maximum limit of debt that a local, state, or national government allows for itself by law. **365**

default   the failure to make payments on a loan. **321**

deficit spending   a government policy of spending more money on its programs than it is able cover with expected revenue. **363**

deflation   a general decrease in the prices of all goods and services. **258**

demand   the amount of a good or service that consumers are willing and able to buy at various prices during a given period. **5**

demand curve   a graphic representation of a demand schedule, showing the relationship between the price of an item and the quantity demanded during a given period, with all other things being equal. **54**

demand schedule   a table that shows the level of demand for a particular item at various prices. **54**

demand-pull inflation   a general rise in prices that occurs when overall demand for goods increases faster than the output of goods. **258**

demand-side economics   an economic theory developed by John Maynard Keynes proposing that government should stimulate the economy through measures that influence the overall demand for goods and services. **356**

democratic socialism   an economic system in which some means of producing and distributing goods are owned or controlled by an elected government. **28**

depreciation   **1)** a decrease in the value of a capital good because of its age, use, or deterioration.

Machinery in a factory, for example, declines in value over time and therefore suffers depreciation. **91** **2)** a decline in the value of one nation's currency relative to that of another nation. **432**

depression   a prolonged and severe recession. **236**

deregulation   a lifting or lessening of government control or restrictions on a company, industry, or profession. **319**

derived demand   the increased demand for resources, such as labor, that results from consumer demand for a particular product. **171**

determinant of demand   a nonprice factor that influences the amount of demand for a good or service. **56**

determinant of supply   a nonprice factor that influences the available supply of a good or a service. **79**

devaluation   a reduction in the value of a nation's currency. **432**

developed nation   a nation with a high level of industrial development and technical expertise, as well as various established economic institutions such as banks and stock markets. **403**

developing nation   a nation with little industry and that has a low standard of living in comparison with developed nations. **403**

differentiate   to point out something that distinguishes an item from similar items; to make distinctions among similar things. **120**

diminishing marginal utility   the natural decreases in the utility of a good or service as more units of it are consumed. **53**

discount rate   the interest rate charged by the Federal Reserve for loans to member banks. **339**

discouraged worker   an unemployed worker who is not seeking employment because of job-related reasons. **252**

disposable income   money that remains after taxes have been paid. **195**

diversification   **1)** the practice of spreading savings among several types of investments, such as gold, real estate, time deposits, or a variety of different stocks and bonds   **2)** the practice of reducing business risk by expanding the variety of goods or services offered or the geographic areas served. **201**

dividend   a stockholder's portion of a corporation's profit. **155**

division of labor   the division of a complex procedure into small tasks, enabling workers to increase output through specialzation. **10**

easy-money policy government methods, such as reduced interest rates, to expand the economy's money supply. **337**

economic development the degree to which a nation has developed its industrial, service, technical, and agricultural sectors. **403**

economics the study of how society chooses to use scarce resources to satisfy its unlimited wants and needs. **3**

economies of scale a condition in which, because of the level of resources needed, the cost of producing each unit of a product declines as the total number of units produced increases. **127**

economist someone who studies economic theory and applies it to the real world. **3**

efficiency the production of goods and services using the smallest amount of resources for the greatest amount of output. **63**

elastic demand the situation that exists when quantity demanded changes greatly in response to a change in price. **63**

elastic supply the situation that exists when quantity supplied changes greatly in response to a change in price. **77**

elasticity of demand the degree to which changes in the price of a good or a service affect quantity demanded. **163**

elasticity of supply the degree to which changes in the price of a good or a service affect quantity supplied. **76**

embargo a government order that forbids importing or exporting goods with a specified nation. **441**

entrepreneur someone who undertakes and develops a new business enterprise or develops a new product, risking failure or loss for the possibility of financial gain. **7**

entrepreneurship the organizational abilities and risk taking involved in starting a new business or introducing a new product to consumers. **7**

estate tax a tax levied on the assets, or property, of a person who has died. **354**

exchange the process by which producers and consumers agree to provide one type of item in return for another. **15**

excise tax a tax placed by the federal government and some state governments on the manufacture, sale, or consumption of certain goods, often those considered to be luxury items or socially undesirable products. **354**

expansion a period of the business cycle during which economic activity is increasing toward a peak. **236**

expansionary fiscal policy a government policy designed to stimulate economic activity by reducing taxes and increasing spending. **360**

expropriation the seizure of private property by a government, either with no payment or only partial payment to its owners. **412**

externality an effect that an economic activity has on people and businesses that are neither producers nor consumers of the good or service being produced. An externality may be either positive (beneficial) or negative (harmful). **101**

factor of production a resource used to produce goods and services. **4**

federal budget the estimate of the revenues and expenses of the federal government for a fiscal year. **362**

fiat money money that is not backed by gold, silver, or other items of value but that has worth because a government requires that it be accepted as a medium of exchange. **306**

finance charge the total cost of credit. **215**

fiscal policy the overall government program that establishes levels of taxing, borrowing, and spending that promote the desired economic goals for the nation. **349**

fiscal year any 12-month period for financial reporting that ends on a date other than December 31. A typical fiscal year may begin on July 1 and run through June 30 of the following calendar year. **363**

fixed cost a cost of doing business that remains constant as production increases or decreases. **91**

fixed expense an expense that does not vary from month to month or with a change in the level of a person's activity or, for a business, in the level of output. **201**

flexible expense an expense that may change from month to month according to an individual's or business's level of activity or output. **201**

floating exchange rate a foreign exchange rate that continuously varies according to supply and demand. **433**

foreign exchange market a market in which the currencies of different nations are bought and sold. **431**

foreign exchange rate the rate at which one nation's currency can be exchanged for another's. **431**

Four Modernizations a program for economic development in China that was announced in 1964. The Four Modernizations focused on improving agriculture, industry, science and technology, and defense. **396**

franchise a business that pays another established business to use the latter's name and product line. **162**

free enterprise system in which private business operates with minimal government involvement. **29**

free trade trade among nations that is not restrained by protective tariffs or other governmental restrictions. **441**

frictional unemployment temporary unemployment caused by factors that are not related to the business cycle. **253**

fringe benefit a nonwage payment that employers make to employees in addition to basic wages. **185**

full employment the lowest possible level of unemployment in an economy. **38**

future a commodity that is bought in order to sell at an agreed-upon price and at an agreed-upon time in anticipation of profits. **212**

general partnership a partnership in which all members have equal authority and share equally in the business's profits and losses. **150**

geographic monopoly a market whose geographic area is so limited that a single seller can control an item's manufacture, sale, distribution, or price. **128**

gift tax a tax by the federal government and some state governments on large transfers of property that are made without something of value being given in return. **354**

Gini Index a mathematical measure of income inequality in an economy. **266**

gold standard a system in which the value of a nation's money is defined by how many units of its currency are redeemable for a specified amount of gold. **311**

good an object or material that can be purchased to satisfy human wants or needs. **4**

government monopoly a market in which a government is the sole producer or seller of a product. **129**

Great Leap Forward an unsuccessful economic development plan for the People's Republic of China that was introduced by communist leaders in 1958. **396**

gross domestic product (GDP) the total value of all final goods and services produced within a country in a given year. **229**

gross investment the total value of private spending in the economy for capital assets—such as new equipment, machinery, and buildings—over a specific period of time, plus total changes in business inventories. **231**

gross national product (GNP) the total value of all final goods and services produced with factors of production owned by citizens of a given country. Unlike the gross domestic product (GDP), the GNP includes the income of the overseas divisions of U.S. companies. **234**

horizontal combination a corporation made up of various businesses that produce the same or similar goods and services. **159**

household responsibility system a government program in rural China enabling farmers to lease state-owned land in exchange for a portion of their crop. **396**

human resource any human activity—mental or physical—used in the production process. **5**

hyperinflation an increase in prices that is so rapid and severe that it disrupts normal economic conditions. **261**

import quota a law limiting the amount of a foreign-produced good that may be imported into a nation during a specified period of time. **440**

incentive something that encourages an action or effort. Expectation of rewards and fear of losses are both incentives. **27**

income 1) money payments that households receive from business firms and the government in exchange for resources 2) funds that a business takes in for supplying goods or services. **34**

income effect the effect that a change in an item's price has on consumers' ability to purchase goods. **52**

indicative planning the development of non-mandatory economic goals by a government in order to coordinate private and public sector investment and production plans. **384**

industrialization the process of mechanizing all major forms of production. **172**

inelastic demand the situation that exists when quantity demanded changes only slightly or not at all in response to a change in price. **64**

inelastic supply the situation that exists when quantity supplied changes only slightly or not at all in response to a change in price. **77**

inflation an increase in overall prices that results from rising wages, an increased money supply, and increased spending relative to the supply of products. **258**

inflation rate the rate at which the overall price level of goods and services in an economy is changing. **260**

infrastructure the basic facilities and services that an economy needs in order to function. **202**

injunction a court order in a labor dispute that forbids specified acts by specified individuals or groups. **190**

installment a repeated partial payment made to a financial institution or other credit-extending organization to repay a loan or to pay for goods or services that have been purchased. **215**

interdependence the relationship of mutual reliance and influence among people, businesses, industries, regions, and nations. **18**

interdependent pricing the setting of prices in a manner responsive to—or dependent on—one's competitors. **125**

interest **1)** the financial return gained by investing or lending capital **2)** the money that a borrower pays to a bank or other lender in return for a loan **3)** the return on a debt security investment, such as a bond **4)** a share in the ownership of property—for example, a 25 percent interest in a business. **155**

interest group a group whose members hold common political beliefs and work to influence government officials, policies, and practices. **294**

intrinsic reward nonmonetary compensation that has no financial worth but is desirable because of the recipient's personal values. **171**

investment **1)** the purchase of something of value with the expectation that over time it will increase in value and produce a profit **2)** in economic theory, the purchase of capital goods. **200**

investment bank a firm that buys large blocks of stocks and bonds issued by companies and then resells those securities to investors at a profit. **206**

investment tax credit a tax incentive that allows businesses to deduct from their taxes part of their investment in new equipment. **358**

labor force all persons in a nation who are at least 16 years old and either working or actively looking for work. **169**

labor productivity a measure of how much each worker produces in a given period of time. **177**

labor union an organization of workers that negotiates with employers for better wages, improved working conditions, and job security. **177**

labor-intensive a term to describe an economy that has a large proportion of labor input relative to capital investment. **172**

lagging indicators a set of economic factors that help economists predict the duration of economic upturns or downturns. **240**

laissez-faire economic philosophy that opposes government intervention in the market. **130**

land reform redistribution, or changes in land ownership, carried out or enforced by the government. **417**

law of demand the principle that, all other factors being equal, consumers will purchase (demand) more of a good at lower prices and less of a good at higher prices. **52**

law of diminishing returns the principle that as more of one input (such as labor) is added to a fixed supply of other resources (such as capital), productivity will increase up to a point, after which the marginal product will diminish. **87**

law of supply the principle that producers will supply more of a product or service at higher prices but less of a product or service at lower prices. **73**

leading indicators a set of economic factors that anticipate the expansions and contractions of the business cycle from one month up to two years before similar changes in overall economic activity occur. **240**

liability **1)** a debt obligation **2)** a person or business's legally enforceable responsibility for unpaid expenses. **147**

limited partnership a form of partnership in which some members, called limited partners, invest money but take no part in management. **150**

liquidity the ease with which an individual or a business can convert assets into cash without suffering a substantial monetary loss. **196**

lobbyist an individual who is paid to influence legislators and government administrators to act in ways that are favorable to the lobbyist's employer. **296**

lockout a shutdown of a business by an employer, or other refusal to let striking employees come to work, in protest of worker or labor union demands. **190**

longevity the duration of a firm's life. **149**

Lorenz curve a graph showing how equally income is distributed in an economy. **265**

M

macroeconomics the study of an entire economy or one of its principal sectors. **3**

margin requirement the percentage of the price an investor must pay in cash to purchase a stock, convertible bond, or other security. **342**

marginal cost the cost of producing one additional unit of output. **92**

marginal product the additional output obtained by employing one more unit of input. **87**

marginally attached worker a worker who once held a productive job but is now unemployed and no longer looking for work. **252**

market the free exchange of goods and services; also called the market place. **25**

market basket a representative sample of about 400 goods and services that the U.S. Department of Labor has identified as common purchases of a typical consumer. **260**

market economy an economy in which the government has little say in what, how, and for whom goods are produced and in which the factors of production are owned by individuals. **25**

market equilibrium the point at which the quantity supplied and quantity demanded for a product are equal at the same price. **103**

market failure a flaw in a price system that occurs when some costs have not been accounted for and therefore are not properly distributed. **101**

market socialism a type of socialism in which the means of production are owned or controlled by the government, but individuals and businesses make some economic decisions. **379**

market system an economic system in which the three basic economic questions are answered by individuals and businesses. **377**

maturity the length of time that money must be deposited in a time deposit. **197**

mediation a process for settling disputes in which a neutral third party listens to each side, asks questions and clarifies issues, and proposes a solution. **186**

medium of exchange anything that a seller will accept as payment for a good or service. **302**

mercantilism an economic theory that defined a nation's power in terms of specie; used to direct most European economies between 1500 and 1800. **382**

merger the joining of two or more businesses under a single ownership. **159**

microeconomics the study of a single factor of an economy—such as individuals, households, businesses, and industries—rather than an economy as a whole. **3**

minimum wage the lowest hourly wage rate that an employer legally can pay a worker, as established by federal law. **109**

mixed economy an economy that combines elements of the traditional, market, and command economic models. **27**

monetary policy a government's plan for regulating a nation's money supply and the availability of credit in order to accomplish certain economic goals. **337**

money any item, typically currency, that is commonly accepted in exchange for goods, services, or the settling of debts. **15**

money supply the total amount of money circulating at any given time in a nation's economy. **335**

monopolistic competition a market in which many producers offer a similar—but not identical—good or service. **120**

monopoly a market in which a single seller exercises exclusive or nearly exclusive control over a particular good or service. **119**

moral suasion unofficial pressure that the Federal Reserve uses to persuade member banks to behave in a certain way. **342**

multinational corporation (MNC) a business that is based in one nation but operates divisions or subsidiaries in other nations. **417**

mutual savings bank a bank that is owned by its depositors, who share in its profits. **316**

N

national debt the total amount of money that a nation owes its creditors. **364**

national income accounting the process used for tracking production, income, and consumption in a nation's economy. **229**

nationalization the government takeover of specific companies or of a major segment of a nation's private industry, such as manufacturing, agriculture, or transportation. **384**

natural monopoly a market in which competition is inconvenient and impractical, and thus efficiency is best achieved by a single seller. **127**

natural resource in economics, any material provided by nature that can be used to produce goods or provide services. **4**

near money an asset that can easily be converted into cash when needed. **307**

nominal GDP the value of a nation's gross domestic product (GDP) at the current prices of the period being measured. **232**

nonprice competition any attempt by a seller to attract customers from its competitors other than by lowering its prices. **120**

nonprofit organization an organization that generates revenue from product sales or donations but does not distribute the profits to any owner or trustee. **163**

O

oligopoly a market in which a few large sellers control most of the production of a good or service. **123**

one-crop economy an economy that is dominated by the production of a single item. **407**

open shop a business where membership in a labor union is not a condition of employment. **178**

opportunity cost the value lost by rejecting one use of resources in favor of another. In other words, an action's opportunity cost is the value of the next-best alternative action that is not taken. **11**

output-expenditure model a method of computing the gross domestic product (GDP) by adding the total value of consumer and government spending on goods and services, total private investment, and the total value of exports, and then subtracting the total value of imports. **230**

overhead the sum of a business's fixed costs except for wages and the material costs. **91**

P

partnership a business owned and controlled by two or more people who share in its profits and are responsible for its losses. **150**

patent a government document granting an inventor the right to produce, use, or sell an invention exclusively for a limited period of time. **128**

peak 1) the point of the business cycle during which employment, production, and wages are at their highest. A peak is also called a turning point. 2) the high point of any phase of economic activity. **236**

people's communes large collective farms established in China beginning in 1958. **396**

perfect competition an ideal market condition that includes a large number of sellers of identical goods and services and in which no one seller controls supply or prices. **117**

personal consumption expenditure total spending by consumers for durable goods, nondurable goods, and services during a specified period of time. **231**

poverty rate the percentage of individuals or families in the total population who are living below the poverty threshold and are thus considered by the government to be poor. **264**

poverty threshold the level of income that the government considers necessary to sustain a family at a minimum standard of living. **264**

preferred stock a share of ownership in a corporation. **155**

price ceiling a government regulation that sets a maximum price for a particular good. **108**

price discrimination the setting of different prices for different buyers under the same circumstances. **132**

price floor a government regulation that sets a minimum price for a particular good. **109**

price index a set of statistics that allows economists to compare prices over time. **232**

price leadership a situation in which one major seller in an industry sets a price and other sellers follow in order to remain competitive. **125**

price stability the condition that exists when overall price levels remain relatively constant over a period of time. **38**

price war a series of price reductions that may become so drastic that each seller involved suffers considerable losses. **125**

primary boycott an organized effort to stop purchases of a firm's products. It is a tactic to express disapproval or to force the other party to take some desired action. Primary boycotts are often part of labor disputes. **189**

prime rate the interest rate for loans that banks charge to their most reliable customers. **341**

principal 1) an amount of money that is borrowed, as in a loan. Principal is distinct from interest and profit **2)** the face amount of a bond. **155**

private property property that is owned by individuals and businesses, rather than the government. **29**

privatization the act of returning property or functions previously owned or performed by government to the private sector. **287**

producer a person, group, or business that makes goods or provides services to satisfy consumers' needs and wants. **3**

producer price index (PPI) a measure of the changes in prices of about 3,200 items bought by producers. **260**

product differentiation an attempt by a seller in monopolistic competition to convince buyers that its product is different from and superior to the nearly identical products of competitors. **120**

product market the market in which producers offer—and consumers purchase—final goods and services. **34**

production possibilities curve a graphic representation showing all of the possible combinations of two goods or services that can be produced in a stated period, assuming that the amount of available resources and technology will not change during the period, and that all of the natural, human, and capital resources involved are being used in the most efficient manner possible. **12**

productivity the level of output that results from a given level of input. **9**

productivity growth an increase in output per worker per hour worked. **244**

profit the difference between the revenue received from the sale of a good or service and the costs of providing that good or service. **74**

proletariat the working class, whose members the radical political theorist Karl Marx believed were oppressed by the bourgeoisie and would eventually overthrow the bourgeoisie in a violent revolution. **390**

prospectus a fact sheet that provides detailed financial information about the company issuing the data. **213**

protectionism the use of trade barriers to protect a nation's industries against foreign competition. **441**

protective tariff a tax or customs duty that a nation's government places on certain imports to restrict their sale. **439**

public good any good or service that is consumed by all members of a group, regardless of who has helped pay for it. **102**

purchasing power the amount of income that people have available to spend on goods and services. **52**

pyramided reserves a system in which smaller banks deposit some of their reserves into larger banks and the larger banks deposit some of their reserves into the largest banks. **327**

quantity demanded the amount of a good or service that consumers are willing and able to purchase at a particular price. **51**

quantity supplied the amount of a good or service that producers are willing and able to sell at a particular price. **73**

quota 1) the minimum number of new hires to be made through an affirmative action program. **2)** a maximum or minimum limit to be achieved in dollars or units of something. **174**

rationing a system by which a government or other institution decides how to distribute a good or service; rationing is usually the result of limited supply. **110**

real GDP the value of a nation's gross domestic product (GDP) after it has been adjusted for inflation. **232**

real GDP per capita the dollar value—adjusted for inflation—of all final goods and services produced per person in an economy in a given year. **241**

real investment an investment that creates a new capital good. **202**

recession a substantial and general decline in overall business activity over a significant period of time. **236**

regulation   a rule that a government establishes and enforces to protect the public or provide equal access to specific goods and services. **82**

representative money   a money system in which an item has value because it can be exchanged for something else that is valuable. **305**

reserve requirement   money the Fed requires a bank to hold either in its own vaults or in a district Federal Reserve bank. **341**

resource   anything used to produce goods or services. **4**

resource market   the market in which households exchange resources with businesses and the government. **34**

restrictive fiscal policy   a government policy designed to reduce economic activity in times of overexpansion by increasing taxes and/or reducing government spending. **360**

revenue tariff   a tax or customs duty that a nation's government places on imports in order to raise money. **439**

S

savings and loan association   a financial institution that lends money and in which depositors maintain savings and checking accounts. **316**

savings rate   the percentage of disposable income that is not consumed by purchasing goods and services. **199**

scarcity   the fundamental condition of economics that results from the combination of limited resources and unlimited wants. **8**

seasonal unemployment   unemployment that results from seasonal variations in the economy. **255**

secondary boycott   a refusal to buy the goods or services of any firm that does business with a company whose employees are on strike. **189**

self-interest   the impulse that encourages people to fulfill their needs and wants. **26**

self-sufficiency   the ability to fullfill all of one's needs without assistance. **17**

seller   the producer of a good or service. **117**

seniority   a ranking of employees based on the number of years a worker has been employed by a firm. **185**

service   any action or activity that is performed for a fee. **4**

share   1) the smallest unit of ownership in a corporation, usually expressed as one share of stock 2) the portion of an owner's interest in a business. **155**

shortage   a situation in which the quantity demanded of a good or resource exceeds the quantity supplied. **105**

sole proprietorship   a business that is owned and managed by one person. **145**

specialization   the focus of a worker on only one or a few aspects of production in order to improve efficiency. **10**

specie   money in the form of coins. Historically, specie was valued for the metal it was made from, typically gold or silver. **305**

standard of living   people's economic well-being as determined by the quantity of goods and services they consume in a given time period. **39**

standard of value   a measure of the relative value of various goods or services. **302**

stock   1) a share of ownership in a corporation 2) the inventory of items held for sale by a manufacturer or other seller of goods. **155**

stock split   an action by a corporation to divide its stock into a larger number of shares. **205**

store of value   a characteristic of a medium of exchange that allows it, and thus value or wealth, to be stored. **303**

strike   a work stoppage by employees or labor union members acting together to bring pressure on their employer to give in to their demands on some job-related dispute. **188**

structural unemployment   unemployment that is caused by changes in technology, government policies, long-term consumer demand for certain products, population trends, and other factors unrelated to the business cycle. **253**

subsidiary   a business that another company either owns or in which it has a controlling interest. **160**

subsidy   a payment made by a government to individuals, businesses, or an industry to encourage certain activities that are considered essential or desirable. **82**

subsistence agriculture   a type of farming in which there are only enough crops and livestock raised to meet a family's basic needs, with no excess left over to sell or trade. **405**

substitute good   a product that purchasers use in place of another product, particularly if the price of the other product rises. **60**

substitution effect consumers' tendency to substitute a lower-priced good for a similar, higher-priced one. **52**

supply the amount of a good or service that producers are willing to sell at various possible prices during a given period. **73**

supply curve a graphic representation of a supply schedule, showing the relationship between the price of an item and the quantity supplied during a given time period, with all other things being equal. **75**

supply schedule a table that lists each quantity of a product that producers are willing to supply at various prices. **75**

supply shock an economic disturbance caused by events outside a nation's economy; increases costs of production for one or more industries and often leads to inflation. **258**

supply-side economics the economic theory that focuses on achieving economic stability and growth by increasing the supply of goods and services throughout the economy. **355**

surplus a situation in which the quantity supplied of an item at a given price exceeds the quantity demanded. **105**

T

tax a required payment to a local, state, or national government, usually made on some regular basis. **81**

tax incentive a provision in a tax law intended to stimulate economic activity by encouraging businesses to invest in new capital. **358**

tax rate the percentage at which income, property, or purchases are taxed. **349**

technological monopoly a market that is dominated by a single producer because of new technology it has developed. **128**

technology scientific and technical techniques used to produce existing products more efficiently or of higher quality. **7**

Tiananmen Square Massacre a 1989 incident in which Chinese demonstrators seeking greater political freedoms were brutally attacked by China's armed forces. **397**

tight-money policy government methods, such as increased interest rates, designed to reduce the economy's money supply. **338**

time deposit a deposit—usually a certificate of deposit or a savings bond—in a bank or other financial institution that earns interest and that must remain on deposit for a specified period of time. **197**

total cost the sum of the fixed and variable costs involved in the production of a good or service. **91**

total product all the goods and services produced by a business during a given period of time with a given amount of input. **86**

total revenue a business's total income; sometimes called total receipts. **66**

trade barrier any limitation on the flow of goods between nations. **439**

trade deficit a condition in international trade in which the value of a nation's imports from another country exceeds the value of its exports to that particular country. **437**

trade surplus a condition in international trade in which the value of a nation's exports to another country exceeds the value of its imports from that particular country. **437**

trade-off the sacrifice of one good in order to purchase or produce another. **11**

traditional economy an economy in which production is based on customs and tradition. **24**

transfer payment a payment made by a government to someone who does not produce a good or service in return. **288**

trough the lowest point of a business cycle, in which demand, production, and employment reach their lowest levels. **236**

trust a group of companies that combine to eliminate competition in an industry and thereby gain a monopoly. **130**

U

underemployed working at a job for which one is overqualified, or working in a part-time job when full-time employment is desired. **252**

underground economy illegal economic activities or unreported legal activities that are not accounted for in national economic measures. **233**

unemployment rate the percentage of people in the civilian workforce who are unemployed. **252**

usury the act of charging borrowers a higher rate of interest than is allowed by law. **216**

utility the usefulness of a good or service that contributes to its value. **17**

value the worth of a good or service for the purposes of exchange, expressed as the amount of money that a consumer is willing to pay for a good or service. **17**

variable cost a cost of doing business that changes directly with a change in the level of output, typically rising and dropping as production increases and decreases. **91**

venture capital individual or corporate funds that are invested in entrepreneurial enterprises to encourage economic growth. **203**

vertical combination a corporation made up of various businesses involved in different stages of the production process of the same good or service. **159**

voluntary trade restriction an agreement—not requiring congressional legislation—between two or more nations to limit or control trade by restricting shipments of certain products to a particular country. **440**

wage the payment that a worker receives for his or her labor. **169**

wage-price spiral a cycle that develops when increased wages raise production costs, which then lead to higher prices for goods or services, encouraging workers to demand still higher wages. **260**

Y

yield **1)** the annual income earned on a stock, bond, or other investment security. It is usually expressed as a percentage of its market price **2)** the total income earned on a loan **3)** the total interest income paid on a bond if the bond is held by the purchaser until its maturity. **209**

Z

zoning law a law governing what types of structures and businesses are allowed in a particular area. **146**

INDEX

automation of, 170, 318–319; bank failures, 321, *g321*, 322; Banking Act of 1933, 312; Banking Act of 1935, 312; banking reforms of the New Deal, 311, 312; certificates of deposit, 197–198; commercial banks, 315–316, *c316*; competition in, 320; credit unions, 315, *c316*, 317–318; debit cards and, 319; deregulation of, 319–321; discount rate, 339–341, *g341*; electronic funds transfer (EFT), 318; farm banks, 321; Federal Deposit Insurance Corporation (FDIC), 312; Federal Reserve system and, 312, 332–334; Federal Saving and Loan Insurance Corporation (FSLIC), 322; Financial Institutions Reform, Recovery, and Enforcement Act, 322; financial troubles in, 321–322; home banking, 319; Internet and, 319; legislation concerning, 311–312, 314, 320, 322; loan defaults and, 321; money market deposit accounts, 196–197; moral suasion and, 342; mutual savings banks, 315, 316–317; National Banking Act of 1863, 311; National Banking Act of 1864, 311; national currency and, 311; point-of-sale transactions and, 318–319; regional banking, 320–321; reserve requirement, 341–342; Resolution Trust Corporation (RTC), 322; savings accounts, 196–197; savings and loan associations (S&Ls), 315, 316, 321, 322; types of financial institutions, 315–318. *See also* banking history

Banking Act of 1933, 312

Banking Act of 1935, 312

banking history: Antifederalists and, 308; before Civil War, 308–310; Civil War to World War I, 310–311; Coinage Act of 1873 and, 311; Confederacy and, 311; confidence in banks, 308–314; conflicting views of, 308; dual banking system, 310; Federalists and, 308; fiat money and, 311; First Bank of the United States, 308–309, 327; fragmented banking, 310–311; Gold Standard Act of 1900, 311; gold standard and, 311, 314; legislation and, 311–312, 314; National Banking Act of 1863, 311; nationally chartered banks, 311; New Deal and, 311–312, 314; panic of 1837 and, 310; Second Bank of the United States, 309–310, 327; state-chartered banks, 210, 308, 309; unifying the banking system, 311; World War I to the present, 311–312, 314

bankruptcy, 216

banks. *See* banking

Barbados, 445

Barbuda, 445

barter, 15, 301

bear market, 209

Belize, 445

Bell Atlantic, 134

Berlin Wall, 379, *p383*

black markets, 112

Black Monday, 211

Black Tuesday, 211

BLS. *See* Bureau of Labor Statistics (BLS)

board of directors, 155

Board of Governors of the Federal Reserve system, *c329*, 331, 338, 339, 360

Bolivia, 412, *p417*

bolsheviks, 390

bonds: corporate bonds, 155, 199; government bonds, 210; municipal bonds, 210, 212; reasons for purchasing, 209–210, 212; Treasury bills, 210, *c210*, 212; Treasury bonds, 210, *c210*; Treasury notes, 210, *c210*; yields on, 209

borrowing: credit, 215–216; definition of, 214; interest rates and, 238; loans, 214–215

bourgeoisie, 389

boycotts, 189

Brazil, 412, 417, 445

Bretton Woods Conference, 420, 421, 432

Britain. *See* Great Britain; United Kingdom

brokers, 206–207

***Brown* v. *Board of Education*,** 175

Brunei, 445

budget, 200; fixed expenses and, 201. *See also* federal budget

Budget and Accounting Act of 1921, 363

budget deficit, 363

budget surplus, 363

bull market, 209

Bundesbank, 384

Bureau of Engraving and Printing, 301, 304, 334, 335

Bureau of Labor Statistics (BLS), 251, 260

Bureau of the Budget, 363

Bureau of the Census, 251, 264

Burger King, 436

Bush, George, 322

business cycles, *g238*; business investment and, 236, 238; coincident indicators of, 240; contraction phase of, 236; credit and, 238; definition of, 236; depression and, 236; expansion phase of, 236; external factors and, 239–240; influences on, 236, 238–240; lagging indicators of, 240; leading indicators of, 240; money and, 238; peak phase of, 236; phases of, 236; political climate and, 239; prediction of, 240; price shocks and, 239; public expectations and, 238–239; recession and, 236;

trough phase of, 236; war and, 239–240; world economics and, 239

business geography, as career, 378

business investment, 238

business organizations: cooperatives, 163; combinations, 159–162; corporations, *g145*, 153–158; franchises, 162–163; nonprofit organizations, 163–164; partnerships, *g145*, 150–152; sole proprietorships, 145–149, *g145*; types of, *g145*

buyer: as career, 76

buyers: competition and, 117, 119; informed buyers and perfect competition, 119; informed decisions of, 119. *See also* consumers

Cable News Network (CNN), 146

Canada, 81, 174, 403, 436, 437, 446

capital: accumulation of, 202; capital formation, 408–409, 411; saving as, 195–199. *See also* headings beginning with capital

capital accumulation, 202

capital deepening, 244–245

capital formation, 408

capital gain, 205

capital goods, 231; capital deepening, 244–245; as capital resource, 7; definition of, 5, 7; economic expansion and, 238; as factor of production, 5

capital-intensive economies, 172

capital loss, 205

capital resources: definition of, 5; developing nations and, 408–409, 411; economic growth, 243; as factor of production, 7

capital-to-labor ratio, 244

capitalism: definition of, 28; examples of, 28; as mixed economy, 28. *See also* capitalist economic system

capitalist economic system: command capitalism, 378; decision-making model of, 414–415; definition of, 377; in France, 384; in Germany, 383–384; government involvement in, 377, 382; in Japan, 382–383; market capitalism, 382–385, 414–415; origins of, 381–382; in Singapore, 385; in South Korea, 385

Caribbean Community and Common Market (CARICOM), 445

CARICOM. *See* Caribbean Community and Common Market (CARICOM)

Carnegie, Andrew, 221

cartel, 126

cash reserves, 329

Castro, Fidel, 280, *p414*

CCC. *See* Civilian Conservation Corps (CCC)

Celler–Kefauver Act of 1950, 132

Census Bureau. *See* Bureau of the Census

central planners, 25

certificates of deposit: maturity of, 197; money supply and, 336; as near money, 307; as savings, 197–198

Chávez, César, 181, 189, *p189*, 193

check-clearing, 332

checks: 307, 318, 319, 332; check-clearing by Federal Reserve system, 332, *c333*

Chicago Board of Trade, 213

China: challenges for, 397–398; "class enemies" in, 396; as command system, 389; communism and, 395–398; Cultural Revolution, 396; currency and, 304; Five-Year Plans and, 396–397; Four Modernizations, 396–397; free-trade zones in, 397; Great Leap Forward, 395–396; Hong Kong and, 415; household responsibility system in, 396–397; international trade and, 434; Mao Zedong and, 395; as most-favored-nation, 444; people's communes in, 395–396; per capita gross domestic product and, *g397*; production brigades in, 396; Tiananmen Square Massacre, 397, *p398*; trade with Russia, 392

choice: price system and, 98; scarcity and, 8–10

Chrysler Corporation, 167

CIO. *See* Congress of Industrial Organizations (CIO)

circular flow model, 34–35, *c34*

civil engineer: as career, 282

Civil Rights Act of 1964, 174, 175, *c182*

Civil Rights Act of 1968, *c217*

Civil War, 310–311, 365

Civilian Conservation Corps (CCC), 254

Clayton Antitrust Act, 131–132, 213

Clinton administration, 148

Clinton, Bill, 291, 294, 365, 455

closed shops, 178

CNN. *See* Cable News Network

CNN Online, 37

Coinage Act of 1873, 311

coincident indicators, 240

coins, 306

COLA. *See* cost-of-living adjustment (COLA)

Cold War, 410

collateral, 149, 214

collectivization, 391

collective bargaining, 186

collusion, 125–126

colonization, 403–404

command capitalism: government involvement and, 378; in West Germany, 383

command economies: central planners in, 25; characteristics of, 25; definition of, 23, 25; economic questions and, 26; Egypt (Old Kingdom) as example of, 25; land reform and, 417; Zhou Dynasty as example of, 25

command socialism, 379

command system, 377, 389

commercial banks, 315–316, *c316*

commercials, 61

commodity money, *c302, c304*, 305

common stock, 155

communism: bourgeoisie and, 389; central planning and, 391–393; China and, 395–398; class struggle and, 390; collectivization and, 391; Five-Year Plans and, 391; historically, 389–398; Industrial Revolution and, 389–390; Karl Marx and, 389–390; New Economic Policy (NEP) and, 391; production problems and, 393; proletariat and, 389–390; rise of, 390–393; Stalin's rule and, 391; war communism, 390–391. *See also* authoritarian socialism

Communist Manifesto, 389

Community College Times, 71

comparable worth: quotas and, 174; wages and, 175

comparative advantage, 428–430, *c430*

competition: creating choice, 98; definition of, 32; free-enterprise system and, 32; market structure and, 119; monopolies and, 120–122, 129; perfect competition, 117, 119–120; supply curve and, 83

complementary goods, 62

computers: in banking, 317–319; in industry, 7; and the Internet, 84, 442; and prices, 99

concentration ratio, 124

Confederacy, 311

conglomerate combinations, 160

Congress of Industrial Organizations (CIO), 179

consumer demand. *See* demand

consumer expectations, demand and, 62

consumer goods, definition of, 7

consumer price index 1940–1996, *g261*

consumer price index (CPI), 260–261, 264

Consumer Product Safety Commission (CPSC), *c285*, 286, 296

consumer purchases, 231

consumers: definition of, 3; as economic actors, 33; economic choices of, 32; expectations and demand, 62; tastes and preferences of, 57. *See also* headings beginning with consumer

Continental Congress, 304

continentals, 305–306

contraction phase, 236, *g238*

contracts: definition of, 30; free-enterprise system and, 29–30; as legally binding, 30

cooperatives: credit unions as, 163; definition of, 163; housing cooperatives, 163; marketing cooperatives, 163; purchasing cooperatives, 163; service cooperatives, 163

coordinated campaign, 189

copyrights, 128–129

corporate bonds, 155, 199

corporate charter, 154, 157

corporate combinations: advantages of, 161; as business organizations, 159–162; competition and, 162; conglomerate combinations, 160–161; costs and, 161; disadvantages of, 161–162; efficiency of, 161; financial capital acquisition and, 161; horizontal combinations, 159; mergers as, 159; subsidiaries of, 160–161; unemployment and, 161–162; vertical combinations, 159

corporate income taxes, 350, 351

corporations: advantages of, 156–157; articles of incorporation, 154; board of directors, 155; as business organizations, 153–158; common stock in, 155; control of, 158; corporate bonds, 155; corporate charter, 154; corporate finances, 155–156; decision-making and, 157–158; definition of, 153; disadvantages of, 157–158; dividends on stock, 155–156; formation of, 153–154, 157; government regulation of, 157–158; limited liability of, 156–157; longevity of, 157; new incorporations and business failures, *m156;* officers of, 155; organization and control, *c154;* preferred stock in, 155; stock in, 155–156; stockholder participation in, 158; structure of, 154–155; subsidiaries of, 160–161; taxes and, 158

cost-of-living adjustment (COLA), 185, 262

cost of production, 74

cost-push inflation, 258–260

Costa Rica, 6, 428–430, 445

costs: corporate combinations and, 161; fixed costs, 91; marginal costs, 92; of production, 74; of rationing, 111–112; resource costs affecting production, 80–81; taxes as, 81; total costs, 91–92; variable costs, 91. *See also* opportunity costs, production costs

costs of production, 74

Council of California Growers, 193

Council of Economic Advisers, 363

counterfeit money, 306

CPSC. *See* Consumer Product Safety Commission (CPSC)

craft unions, 178

credit: abuse of, 216–218; annual percentage rates, 215; business cycles and, 238; buying on, 215–218; charge accounts, 215; credit bureau, 215; credit cards, 215–216, 218; credit ratings, 215; definition of, 16, 215; economy and, 217–218; Federal Reserve regulation of, 312, 342; finance charges, 215; as form of exchange, 16; regulation of, 216; terms of, 215–216; usury and, 216

credit bureau, 215

credit cards, 215–216, 218; incentives and, 216

credit ratings, 215

credit regulation, 342

credit unions, 315, *c316*, 317–318

Cuba, 111, 146, 280, 379, 414; as example of authoritarian socialism, 28; trade barriers and, 441

Cultural Revolution, 396

currency. *See* money

Current Population Survey, 251

customs duty, 354

customs inspector: as career, 429

Customs Service. *See* U.S. Customs Service

cyclical unemployment, 252, 256

D

Das Kapital, 389

De Beers, 126

debit cards, 319

Debs, Eugene V., 183

debt. *See* national debt

debt ceiling, 365

decision-making: corporations and, 157–158; free-enterprise system and, 32; in partnerships, 151; production decisions, 86–87, 89–92; self-interest and, 32; in sole proprietorships, 146–147. *See also* economic decisions

decision-making grid, *c11*

decision-making models, developing nations and, 414–415

default, 321

deficit spending, 363

deflation, 258

Dell Computer Corporation, 7, 104

Dell, Michael, 7

demand, 50–68; changes in, 56–62, 62; commercials and, 61; complementary goods and, 62; consumer expectations and, 62; consumer preferences and, 57; definition of, 51; determinants of, 56–60, 62, 73; elasticity of, 63–68; equilibrium price and, 106, *g122;* floating exchange rates and, 433; foreign exchange rates and, 433; government policy decisions and, 58; income and, 59–60; labor force and, 169–172; law of, 52–54; market size and, 57–59; monopolies' effect on, 129; nature of, 51–55; price of related goods and, 60; shifts in, 56–57, *g57;* substitute goods and, 60. *See also* supply, headings beginning with demand

demand curve, *g55, g57;* definition of, 54; quantity demanded and, 56

demand deposits, 307

demand-pull inflation, 258

demand schedules, 54, *c54, c55, g103*

demand-side economics: aggregate demand and, 356–358; definition of, 356; depression and, 357; Employment Act of 1946 and, 357–358; government's role in, 356–357; Keynes and, 356–357; model of, *c356*

democratic socialism: definition of, 28; examples of, 28; as mixed economy, 28

Deng, Xiaoping, 396–397

Denmark, 282, 427

Department of Agriculture, 429

Department of Commerce, 233

Department of Health and Human Services, 434

Department of Labor, 175, 251

Department of the Treasury, 306, 334, 350, 363

Depository Institutions Deregulation and Monetary Control Act, 320

depreciation, 91

depressions, 236

deregulation, 293, 319–321

derived demand, 171–172

determinants of demand, 56–60

determinants of supply, 79

devaluation, 432

developed nations: Asian Development Bank and, 422; definition of, 403; foreign aid and, 417–420; International Monetary Fund (IMF) and, 420–422. *See also* specific countries

developing nations: African Development Bank and, 422; agricultural economies in, 404–405; arable land and, 403; capital formation and, 408–409, 411; capital resources and, 408–409, 411; capitalist model of decision-making, 414–415; central planning and, 414; colonization and, 403–404; cultural obstacles to growth in, 412–413; decision-making models, 414–415; definition of, 403; domestic savings and, 417; education and, 408; emergency assistance for, 419; entrepreneurship, 411; expropriation and, 412; financing economic development, 417; Food and Agriculture Organization (FAO) and, 422; foreign aid and, 419–422; foreign investment in, 409; growth challenges, 407–413; human resources and, 408; infrastructure and, 411–412; Inter-American Development Bank and, 422; International Bank for Reconstruction and Development (IBRD) and, 420; International Development Association (IDA), 420; International Finance Corporation (IFC), 420–422; International Monetary Fund (IMF) and, 421–422; international public sources of capital, 420–422; International Red Cross and, 420; land reform and, 417; military assistance to, 419; Multilateral Investment Guarantee Agency and, 421; multinational corporations (MNC) and, 417–418; nationalization and, 412; natural resources and, 403–404, 407–408; nonprofit organizations and, 417–418; one-crop economies in, 407–408; Peace Corps and, 420; political instability and, 412, 418; population growth and, 404–405; private capital and, 417–418; privatization and, 412; production possibilities and, 416–417; Save the Children Fund and, 420; scarcity and, 416; socialist model of decision-making and, 414; subsistence agriculture in, 404–405; as Third World countries, 410; trade-offs and, 416; United Nations Development Program (UNDP) and, 422; United Nations Industrial Development Organization (UNIDO) and, 422; World Bank and, 420–421; World Health Organization (WHO) and, 422. *See also* economic development, specific countries

differentiate, 120

diminishing marginal utility: definition of, 53; law of demand and, 53–54

discount rate, 339, *c339,* 341, *g341*

discouraged workers, 252

disposable income, 195, 235

diversification, 201

dividends, 155, 204

division of labor, 10

domestic resources, 242–243

Dow Jones Industrial Average, 209, *g209*

Drug Enforcement Administration, 429

durable goods, 231

earthquakes, 313

Easterbrook, Gregg, 249

easy-money policy, 337–338

economic activity: incentives as regulator, 27; self-interest as regulator, 25–26

economic actors, free-enterprise system and, 33–34

economic decisions, 3–4, 119

economic development: African Development Bank and, 422; arable land and, 403; Asian Development Bank and, 422; capital formation and, 408–409, 411; capital resources and, 408–409, 411; colonization and, 403–404; cultural obstacles to, 412–413; definition of, 403; domestic savings and, 417; economic instability and, 418; education and, 408; entrepreneurship and, 411; expropriation and, 412; financing economic development, 417; Food and Agriculture Organization (FAO), 422; foreign aid and, 417–420; human resources and, 408; infrastructure and, 411–412; Inter-American Development Bank and, 422; International Bank for Reconstruction and Development (IBRD) and, 420; International Development Association (IDA), 420; International Finance Corporation (IFC), 420–421; International Monetary Fund (IMF) and, 421–422; international public sources of capital for, 420–422; International Red Cross and, 420; land reform and, 417; Multilateral Investment Guarantee Agency and, 421; multinational corporations (MNC) and, 417–418; nationalization and, 412; natural resources and, 403–404, 407–408; nonprofit organizations and, 417–418; opportunity costs and, 416; paths to, 414–422; Peace Corps and, 420; per capita gross domestic product, 403; planning for, 415–416; political instability and, 412; population growth and, 404–405; private capital and, 417–418; privatization and, 412; production possibilities and, 416–417; Save the Children Fund and, 420; standard of living and, 403; agriculture, 404–405; trade-offs and, 416; United Nations Development Program (UNDP) and, 422; United Nations Industrial Development Organization (UNIDO) and, 422; World Bank and, 420–421; World Health Organization (WHO) and, 422. *See also* developing nations

economic efficiency, 38

economic equity, 38

economic flows, 34–35

economic forecasting, 359–360; business cycles and, 240; Federal Reserve system and, 343

economic freedom, as goal of U. S. economy, 36

economic goals: and trade-offs, 39–40; of United States, 36

economic growth, 241–246; business cycles and, 236; capital deepening and, 244–245; capital resources and, 243; capital-to-labor ratio, 244; costs and trade-offs, 233; credit affecting, 217–218, c218; definition of, 241; domestic resources and, 242–243; entrepreneurship and, 243–244; expanded tax base and, 242–243; expansion and, 236; global markets and, 242; as goal of U. S. economy, 39; human resources and, 243; importance of, 241–243; income distribution and, 242; labor force retraining and, 245; labor productivity and, 244; natural resources and, 243; productivity and, 244–246; real gross domestic product (GDP) per capita and, 241; requirements for, 243–244; research and development and, 244; savings affecting, c218; standard of living and, 241–242; technological advances and, 244

economic indicators, 240

economic interdependence. See interdependence

economic production: economic growth and, 241; gross domestic product (GDP) and, 229–235; gross national product (GNP) and, 234; measurement of, 229–232; output-expenditure model, 230–232; underground economies and, 233

economic questions: basic three, 23; command economies and, 26; identification of, 8–9; market economies and, 26; traditional economies and, 26

economic resources: classification of, 4–5, 7

economic rivalry. See competition

economic security: definition of, 38; as goal of U. S. economy, 38

economic stability: credit promoting, 218; definition of, 38; employment and, 38; as goal of U. S. economy, 38–39; in market economies, 33

economic systems, 22–40, c26; capitalist economic systems, 377–378; command economies, 25, c26; comparison of, 376–398; identifying, 377; market economies, 23, 25–26, c26; Mbuti as example of, 24–25; mixed economies, 27–28; socialist economic systems, 377, 378–380; traditional economies, 23–25, c26; types of, 23–28, c26, c377

economics: definition of, 3. See also economies; economist; headings beginning with economic

Economics and Politics of Race, 271

economies of scale, 127

economist, 3; as career, 5

ecosystem, 12

ecotourism, 6

Eddie Bauer, 111

Edgecumbe Enterprises, 434

education: in developing nations, 408; and labor force, 173; market economies and, 33; productivity and, 246; salary and, 173, c173

EEOC. *See* Equal Employment Opportunity Commission (EEOC)

efficiency: definition of, 10; price system and, 98, 100

EFT. *See* electronic funds transfer (EFT)

Egypt (Middle Kingdom): as example of command economies, 25

El Salvador, 412, 420, 422, 445

elastic demand, g64; definition of, 63; markets and, 65–66; measuring, 66; properties of goods having, 63–64; total revenue and, 67

elastic supply, 76–78, g77

elasticity of demand, 63–68; definition of, 63; measurement of, 66–68; measuring, 66–68

elasticity of supply, 76–78

electronic funds transfer (EFT), 318

Electronic Numerical Integrator and Computer (ENIAC), 99

Embargo Act of 1807, 441

embargoes, 280, 441

employee stock ownership plans (ESOP), 185

employees. *See* labor force

employment, 251, 252; international, 267

Employment Act of 1946, 357–358

ENIAC. *See* Electronic Numerical Integrator and Computer (ENIAC)

entrepreneur: as career, 146; definition of, 7; example of, 88; young entrepreneurs, 118, 237

entrepreneurship: definition of, 7; developing nations and, 411; economic growth and, 243–244; as factor of production, 7; real investment and, 203; venture capital and, 203

environment: government regulations and, 81; opportunity costs and trade-offs, 12

Environmental Protection Agency (EPA), c285, 286, 296

Equal Credit Opportunity Act, c217

Equal Employment Opportunity Commission (EEOC), 174, 285, c285

Equal Pay Act of 1963, 174

equal pay for equal work, 175

equilibrium: demand and, 106–107, *g122;* equilibrium point, 103; market equilibrium, 103–104; prices and, 103–107; shifts in, 106–107; shortages and, 105; supply and, 106–107; surplus and, 104–105. *See also* market equilibrium

equilibrium point, 103

equilibrium wage, *g170*

Erhard, Ludwig, 383

ESOP. *See* employee stock ownership plans (ESOP)

estate plan, 201

estate tax, 354

Ethiopia, 412

EU. *See* European Union (EU)

euro, 303

European Union (EU), 303, 427, *m444*

exchange: definition of, 15; forms of, 15–16; global exchange, 16; interdependence and, 17–18; value and, 17. *See also* barter, credit, money

Exchange Network Services Inc., 84

exchange rates. *See* foreign exchange rates

exchange ratio, 428–430

excise tax, 354

expansion phase, 236, *g238*

expansionary fiscal policy, 360

expenses: fixed expenses, 201; flexible expenses, 201

exports: definition of, 231; net exports, 231–232

expropriation, 412

externalities, 101, 286, 290

factors of production, 4–5, 7; command economies and, 25; definition of, 4; market economies and, 25; mixed economies and, 27–28

Fair Credit Billing Act, *c217*

Fair Credit Reporting Act, *c217*

Fair Debt Collection Practices Act, *c217*

Fair Labor Standards Act, 176

FAO. *See* Food and Agriculture Organization (FAO)

farm banks, 321

Farm Credit System (FCS), 321

FCC. *See* Federal Communications Commission (FCC)

FCS. *See* Farm Credit System (FCS)

FDA. *See* Food and Drug Administration (FDA)

FDIC. *See* Federal Deposit Insurance Corporation (FDIC)

Federal Aviation Administration, *c285*

federal budget: balanced budget amendment, 366; balancing the federal budget, 365–366; Budget and Accounting Act of 1921 and, 363; budget deficits, 363–364; budget surplus, 363; corruption historically, 362; creation of, 362–363; debt ceilings and, 365; decreasing expenditures and, 365–366; deficit spending and, 363–364; definition of, 362; federal budget 1996, *g363;* federal deficit, *g364;* fiscal year and, 363; increasing revenues, 365; legislating a balanced budget, 366; national debt and, 364–365; Omnibus Budget Reconciliation Act of 1993 and, 365; preparation of, 363; Progressive Movement and, 362; taxation and, 365; wartime spending and, 362

Federal Communications Commission (FCC), *c285,* 286

federal deficit, *g364;* economic growth and, 243

Federal Deposit Insurance Corporation (FDIC), 312, 320

Federal Energy Regulatory Commission, *c285*

Federal Housing Administration (FHA), 287–288

Federal Insurance Contributions Act (FICA), 351

Federal Mediation and Conciliation Service (FMCS), 187

Federal Open Market Committee (FOMC), *c329,* 331, 339

Federal Reserve Act of 1913, 311, 328, 347

Federal Reserve Bank of New York, 336, 339

Federal Reserve system, 278–296; aggregate demand and, 337–339, 341–342; bank supervision, 334, 335; cash reserves and, 329; characteristics of, 330; check clearing, 332, *c333;* credit regulation and, 312, 342; discount rate, 339–341, *c339, g341;* district level, 331; districts of, 330, *c330;* economic forecasting of, 343; establishment of, 311–312; fiscal policy and, 361; government services and, 334–336; as government's bank, 334–335; inflation and, 258, 338, 342; interagency coordination and, 343–344; loans to banks, 332–334; margin requirements and, 342; monetarists and, 344; monetary policy and, 337–344; monetary policy tools, *c339;* money supply regulator, 334, 335–336; moral suasion and, 342; national level, 331; open-market operations, 339, *c339;* organization of, *c329,* 331; policy limitations, 342–344; prime rate and, 341, *g341;* priorities of, 343–344; reserve requirement, 341–342; role of, 329–330; services to banks, 332–334; time lags and, 343; trade-offs, 343

federal revenue, 352, 354. *See also* taxation; taxes

Federal Saving and Loan Insurance Corporation (FSLIC), 322

Federal Securities Act, *c212,* 213

federal tax receipts by source, *g351*

Federal Trade Commission Act, 132

Federal Trade Commission (FTC), 132, 213, *c285,* 286

Federalists, 308

FHA. *See* Federal Housing Administration (FHA)

fiat money, *c304,* 305, 306, 311

FICA. *See* Federal Insurance Contributions Act (FICA)

final product: example of, 229–231

finance charges, 216

financial analyst: as career, 239

Financial Institution Reform, Recovery, and Enforcement Act, 322

financial institutions: automated teller machines (ATM) and, 318; automatic clearing house services (ACH), 318; automation and, 318–319; bank failures, 321, *g321,* 322; commercial banks, 315–316, *c316;* competition among, 320; credit unions, 315, *c316,* 317–318; debit cards and, 319; deregulation and, 319–321; electronic funds transfer (EFT) and, 318; Federal Deposit Insurance Corporation (FDIC), 312; Federal Saving and Loan Insurance Corporation (FSLIC), 322; Financial Institutions Reform, Recovery, and Enforcement Act, 322; home banking and, 319; loan defaults and, 321; mutual savings banks, 315; point-of-sale transactions and, 318–319; regional banking, 320–321; savings and loan associations (S&Ls), 315, 316, 321, 322; types of, 315–318

financial planning: budget, 200–201; diversification, 201; estate plan, 201; flexible expenses and, 201; investment plan, 201; for investments, 200–201; retirement plan, 201; spending and saving plan, 201

First Bank of the United States, 307, 327

fiscal policy, 348–366; Balanced Budget and Deficit Reduction Act of 1985 and, 366; collecting taxes, 350–354, 354; coordination of government agencies and, 361; customs duty, 354; deficit spending and, 363–364; definition of, 349; demand-side economics and, *c356,* 356–358; forecasting and, 359–360; estate tax, 354; excise tax, 354; expansionary fiscal policy, 360; federal budget and, 362–363; Federal Reserve system and, 361; federal tax receipts by source, *g351;* gift tax, 354; government spending, 359; Gramm-Rudman-Hollings Act (GRH) and, 366; income taxes and, 359; Internal Revenue Service and, 350; investment tax credit, 358; limitations on, 359; Medicaid and, 359; Medicare and, 351, 359; national debt and,

364–365; nonproductive actors and, 359; Old-Age, Survivors, and Disability Insurance (OASDI) and, 351; political pressures and, 360; progressive taxes and, 349, 350–351, 359; proportional taxes and, 349, 351; public transfer payments and, 359; regressive taxes and, 349–350, 351, 354; restrictive fiscal policy, 360; sales tax rates by state, *m352;* strategies of, 355–361; supply-side economics, 355–356, *c356;* tariffs and, 354; tax incentives and, 358–359; tax rates and, 349–350; taxation and, 358; timing problems and, 359–360; tools of, 358–359

fiscal year, 363

Five-Year Plans, 391, 396–397

fixed costs, 91

fixed expenses, 201

fixed investment, 231

flat rate taxes, 349

flexible expenses, 201

floating exchange rates, 433

FMCS. *See* Federal Mediation and Conciliation Service (FMCS)

Food and Agriculture Organization (FAO), 422

Food and Drug Administration (FDA), 119, *c285,* 286

Food From the 'Hood, 237

Ford, Henry, 83

foreign aid: as economic assistance, 419; effectiveness of, 420; as emergency assistance, 419; as military assistance, 419; purposes of, 419–420; as source of capital, 418–420

foreign exchange and currencies: adjustable-peg system, 432–433; appreciation and, 432–433; balance of payments, 435–436; and trade, 436–437; Bretton Woods Conference and, 432; devaluation and, 432; floating exchange rates, 433; exchange markets, 431; foreign exchange rates, 431–433; "strong" dollar, 433; trade surplus and, 437; U.S. trade deficit, 437

foreign exchange markets, 431

foreign exchange rates: adjustable-peg system and, 432; definition of, 431; demand and, 433; floating exchange rates, 433; "strong" dollar and, 433; supply and, 433

foreign investment in United States, *g436*

foreign labor, 428

Four Modernizations, 396–397

Fourier, Charles, 386

France: capitalism in, 384; European Union (EU) and, 445

franchises: definition of, 162; terms of, 162–163; types of, 162

free-enterprise system: competition and, 32; contracts and, 29–30; decision-making in, 32; definition of, 29; economic actors and, 33–34; rights of individuals within, 29–33; self-interest and, 32–33; United States as example of, 29–35

free trade: definition of, 441; fairness and, 443; infant industries and, 442; job protection and, 442; national security and, 443; specialization and, 443; standard of living and, 442–443

free-trade zones, 397

freedom of choice, 33–34

frictional unemployment, 252, 253

fringe benefits, 184–185

FTC. *See* Federal Trade Commission (FTC)

Fuji Photo Film, 161

Fuji Xerox, 161

full employment, 252; definition of, 38; as goal of economic stability, 38

futures, 212–213; reasons for investing in, 212–213; trading futures, 212–213

Garcia, Rafael Jr., 181

Garcia v. San Antonio Metropolitan Transit Authority, 176

GATT. *See* General Agreement on Tariffs and Trade (GATT)

GDP. *See* gross domestic product (GDP)

General Agreement on Tariffs and Trade (GATT), 445

General Motors (GM), 161, 446

general partnerships, 150

General Planning Commission, 384

General Theory of Employment, Interest, and Money, 356, 369

generic products: demand and, 53

geographer: as career, 378

geographic monopoly, 128

Germany: capitalism in, 383–384; East Germany and, 384; European Union (EU) and, 445; fiscal policies of, 384; hyperinflation and, 261; research and development expenditures, *g244;* value of German mark, 302

GI Bill of Rights, 281–282

gift tax, 354

Gillette Company, *c160*

Gini Index, 265–266, *g266*

global economy, 268

global markets, 230, 242

global warming, 409

GM. *See* General Motors (GM)

GNP. *See* gross national product

Gold Reserve Act of 1934, 312, 313–314

gold standard, 311, 312

Gold Standard Act of 1900, 311

Gompers, Samuel, 178

goods: capital goods, 5, 7; consumer goods, 7; definition of, 4; elastic demand of, 63; public goods, 286–288; related goods effect on supply curve, 84

Gorbachev, Mikhail, 393–394

Gospel of Wealth, 221

government: business cycle and, 289–290; capitalist economic systems and, 377–378; competition in business and, 286; consumer protection, 286; deregulation, 293, 319–321; as economic actors, 33; economic goals of, 284–290; economic well-being and, 288–290; embargoes and, 280; as employer, 279; federal regulatory agencies, *c285;* government programs, 282–283; government spending, *g281,* 282–283, *g283;* growth of, 279–283; health care programs, 288; interest groups and, 294–296; intergovernmental responsibilities, 287; labor force and, 173–176; labor unions and, 183; laissez-faire economics, 280; lobbyists and, 295–296; emergencies and, 281; negative externalities and, 286; New Deal programs, 281; policy decision affect on demand, 58; population growth and, 279, *g279;* privatization and, 287–288; public attitudes and, 280–281; public goods, 286–288; public influence on, 293–296; public interest and, 291–296; redistribution of income, 288–289, *g289;* as regulator, 82, 129, 130–134, 146, 157–158, *c212,* 216, *c217,* 284–286, 292–293; role in market economies, 33; services of, 292–293; standard of living and, 279, 281, 288; transfer payments, 231, 235, 288. *See also* headings beginning with government

government monopoly, 129

government purchases, 231

government regulation: of corporations, 157–158; credit and, 216, *c217;* federal regulating agencies, *c285;* of markets, 130–134; of monopolies, 129; primary purposes of, 284–286; of production costs, 82; security regulations, *c212;* of sole proprietorship, 145–146; supply and, 82

government securities: types of, 210, *c210*

inventory investment, 231

investments: capital accumulation and, 202; definition of, 200; diversification in, 201; economic growth and, 202–203; entrepreneurship and, 203; estate plan, 201; financial investment, 201–202; financial planning for, 200–201; fixed investments, 231; gross investments, 231; inflation and, 261–266; inventory investment, 231; investment plan, 201; nation's economic infrastructure and, 202; real investments, 202, 231; retirement plan, 201; risks of, 200; spending and saving plan, 200–201; technological change and, 202–203; venture capital and, 203

investment bank, 206

investment tax credit, 358

Iran, 412

Iraq, 280, 412

Ireland, 445

IRS. *See* Internal Revenue Service (IRS)

ISP. *See* Internet service providers

Italy, 427, 445; research and development expenditures, *g244*

ITT. *See* International Telephone and Telegraph Corporation (ITT)

J

Jackson, Andrew, 308

Jamaica, 445

Japan, 428; Bank of Japan, 383; capitalism in, 382–383, 414–415; competition in global markets, 230; as developed nation, 403; global markets and, 230; international trade and, 434; investment in United States, 436; Ministry of Finance role in, 382–383; Ministry of International Trade and Industry (MITI), 382–383, 385; multinational corporations (MNC) and, 446; research and development expenditures, *g244;* tariffs in, 382–383; tourism and, 111; deficit of, 437; trade restrictions and, 230; trade with United States and, *c435;* voluntary trade restrictions and, 440–441

Jefferson, Thomas, 308, *p309*

job protection, 442

job security, 185. *See also* labor force, labor unions, unemployment

Johnson & Johnson, 209

Johnson administration: affirmative action and, 174

joint ventures, 161, 446

Jungle, 177

K

Keynes, John Maynard, 356, 357, 369

King William's War, 305

Knights of Labor, 178

Korea, 384–385

Korea Development Institute (KDI), 385

Korean War, 240, 444

Kuwait, 280, 412

L

labor force: affirmative action and, 175; agriculture and, 172; antidiscrimination laws and, 174–175; capital-intensive economies and, 172; changes in, 172–174; collective bargaining and, 186; contract negotiations and, 186–189; definition of, 169; derived demand for, 171–172; education and, 172–173, 245; employment and, 251, 252; entering the labor force, 169–172; factories in 1800s, 177; global competition, 245; government and, 173–176; income gap and, 267, 268; industrial unions, 178; industrialization and, 172; intrinsic rewards and, 171; labor-intensive economies and, 172; market trends and, 171–172; mediation with, 186–187; productivity and, 244–246, *g245;* quotas and, 175; retraining programs, 245–246; skills and, 170–171, 245; statistics, *g169*, 252; unemployment and, 251–256; women in, 172–173; work location and, 171; working conditions and, 171

Labor Policy Association, 181

labor productivity: definition of, 244, *g245*

labor relations consultant: as career, 187

labor unions: African Americans and, 178; American Federal of Labor (AFL), 178–179; arbitration by, 187; boycotts by, 189; challenges to, 180–182; closed shops, 178; Congress of Industrial Organizations (CIO), 179–180; contract issues, 184–186; coordinated campaigning, 189; cost-of-living adjustments (COLA) and, 185; craft unions, 178; declining membership of, 183; definition of, 177; development of, 177–179; employee stock ownership plans (ESOPs) and, 185; employer opposition to, 180; employment patterns affecting, 180–182; fringe benefits and, 184–185; government and, 183; grievance procedures, 186; of, 177–183; unions, 178; job security and, 185; Knights of Labor, 178; local unions, 179; major labor legislation, *c182;* management and, 183, 184–190; membership demographics, 180; membership

Marshall, Alfred, 21

Marshall Plan, 420

Marx, Karl, 389–390

Massachusetts Bay Colony, *c304, 305*

maturity: definition of, 197; of bonds, 210; of time deposits, 197

Mbuti, as traditional economy, 24–25

McGuiness, Jeffrey, 181

McKinley Tariff Act of 1890, 440

measuring unemployment, 251–255

mediation, 186–187

Medicaid, 281, 359

Medicare, 351, 359

medium of exchange, 301, 302

mercantilism, 381–382, 389

merger, 159

Mexico, 115, 174, 445–446

MFN. *See* most-favored-nation (MFN)

microeconomics, 3

Microsoft, 132–133

Mighty Morphin Power Rangers®, 105–106

migrant workers, 255

minimum wage: historically, *g176;* definition of, 109; legislation and, 175–176; as price floor, 109

Ministry of International Trade and Industry (MITI), 382–383, 385

MITI. *See* Ministry of International Trade and Industry (MITI)

Mitterand, Francois, 384, *p384*

mixed economies: authoritarian socialism as, 27–28; capitalism as, 28; categories of, 27; characteristics of, 27–28; definition of, 27; democratic socialism as, 28

MNC. *See* multinational corporations (MNC)

Monetary Control Act of 1980, 342

monetary policy: aggregate demand and, 337–339, 341–342; components of, 339, 341–342; credit regulation and, 342; definition of, 337; discount rate and, 339, *c339,* 341; easy-money policy, 337–338; Federal Reserve system and, 337–344; inflation and, 258, 338; margin requirements and, 342; monetarists and, 344; moral suasion and, 342; open-market operations and, 339, *c339;* policy limitations, 342–344; reserve requirement and, 339, *c339,* 341–342; tight-money policy, 338; tools of, *c339*

money, 300–307; acceptability of, 304–305; bartering and, 301; business cycles and, 238; characteristics of, 303–305; coins, 306; commodity money, *c304, 305;* counterfeit money, 306; currency as, 306; definition of, 15; demand deposits as, 307; divisibility of, 303, 304; durability of, 303–304; fiat money, *c304, 305,* 306, 311; as form of exchange, 15–16; forms of, 306–307; functions of, 16, 301–303; greenbacks as, 311; history of currency, 308–314; as medium of exchange, 301, 302; national currency, 311; near money, 307; paper money, 304, 306; portability of, 302, 303, 304; purpose of, 299; representative money, *c304,* 305–306; sources of money's value, *c304,* 305–306; specie and, 305; stability in value of, 303, 304; as standard of value, 299, 301, 302; store of value and, 302, 303; U. S. banknotes as, 309

money market deposit accounts, 197

money supply: aggregate demand and, 337; components of, *g335;* definition of, 335; easy-money policy, 337–338; Federal Reserve system as regulator, 334, 335–336; growth of, *c347;* inflation and, 338; L, *g335, 336;* M1, *g335, 336;* M2, *g335, 336;* M3, *g335, 336;* monetary policy and, 337–344; tight-money policy and, 338

monopolies: and anti-trust legislation, 130–133; competition and, 129; concentration ratio and, 124; conditions of, 126; consumer demand and, 129; definition of, 119; effect of, 129; geographic monopolies, 128; government monopolies, 129; government regulation of, 129; market entry and, 127; natural monopolies, 127–128; technological monopolies, 128–129; types of, 127–129

monopolistic competition: definition of, 120; non-price competition and, 120–121; perfect competition compared with, 120; product differentiation and, 120; profits and, 121–122

moral suasion, 342

most-favored-nation (MFN) status, 444

MS–DOS, 133

Multilateral Investment Guarantee Agency, 421

multinational corporations (MNC): definition of, 417; developing nations and, 418; joint ventures and, 446; performance standards for, 446

mutual savings banks, 315, 316–317

Nader, Ralph, 294–295, 296

Nader's Raiders, 296

NAFTA. *See* North American Free Trade Agreement

NASDAQ. *See* National Association of Securities Dealers Automated Quotations (NASDAQ)

————————— **O** —————————

output-expenditure model: 230–232; definition of, 230; government purchases, 230, 231; gross investment, 230, 231; investments, 231; net exports, 230, 231–232; personal consumption on expenditures, 230

overhead, 91

Owen, Robert, 386

—————————— **P** ——————————

Pacific Telesis, 134

Panama, 428–430

Panic of 1837, 308, 310

Panic of 1907, 327–328

paper money, 304, 306

Paraguay, 417, 445

Parens Patriae Act of 1976, 132

partnerships: advantages of, 150–151; business losses and, 151; as business organizations, 150–152; conflict potential in, 152; decision-making in, 151; definition of, 150; disadvantages of, 151–152; general partnerships, 150; limited partnerships, 150; longevity of, 152; specialization in, 151; start up of, 150–151; unlimited liability in, 152

patents, 128

Peace Corps, 420

peak phase, 236, *g238*

pensions, 262

people's communes, 395–396

per capita gross domestic product, 403

perestroika, 393

perfect competition: conditions for, 117, 120; definition of, 117; identical products and, 119; informed buyers and, 119; market entry and, 119; structure and, 119; as model, 119–120

Persian Gulf War, 412, *p412*

personal consumption expenditures, 231

personal identification number (PIN), 319

personal income, *c234, 235*

Philippines, 445

picketing, 188–189

Pillsbury, 436

PIN. *See* personal identification number (PIN)

point-of-sale transactions, 318–319

population: comparison worldwide, *g406;* developing nations and, 404–405; government growth and, 279–280; U.S. population growth, *g279*

Portugal, 445

poverty: definition of, 264; income distribution and, 264–268; poverty rate, 264–265, *c265;* poverty threshold, 264; in the United States, 264–265, 281

poverty rate, 1977–1995, *c265*

poverty rate, 264–265

poverty threshold, 264, 265

PPI. *See* producer price index (PPI)

preferred stock, 155

price ceiling, *g109;* definition of, 108; control as example of, 108–109

price discrimination, 132

price floor: definition of, 109; minimum wage as example of, 109

price index, 232

price leadership, 125

price shocks, 239

price shortages, *g109*

price stability: definition of, 38; as goal of economic stability, 38

price system: benefits of, 97–98, 100–101; choice generated by, 98; efficiency of, 98, 100; externalities and, 101; flexibility in, 100–101; incentives of, 98; information gained from, 97–98; instability of, 102; language of prices, 97; limitations of, 101–102; market failures, 101; public goods and, 101–102. *See also* prices

price wars, 125

prices, 96–112; aggregate demand and, 257–258; aggregate supply and, 257–258; consequences of setting prices, 109–110; determination of, 103–107; equilibrium and, 103–107; government effect on, 292; language of, 97; management of, 108–112; price levels, 257–258; price war, 125; rationing and, 110–112; setting of, 108–110; shortages and, 105; stock prices, 207–209; surpluses and, 104–105; system of, 97–102. *See also* headings beginning with price and prices

prices of related goods: demand and, 60, 62; supply and, 84

prices of resources, 80–81

primary boycott, 189

prime rate, 341

principal: on corporate bonds, 155; on loans, 214

priorities: changing priorities, 40; conflicting priorities, 40; scarcity and, 39–40; solutions for conflict in, 40; trade-offs and, 39–40

private property, 29–30, 156

privatization, definition of, 287; 384, 412

Social Security taxes, 351

socialism: decision-making model, 414; definition of, 386; economic planning and, 387–388, 414; Industrial Revolution and, 386–387; industry ownership and, 387; market socialism, 379–380, 387–388; origins of, 386–387; in Sweden, 386, 387–388; taxation and, 388; workers' freedoms and, 387. *See also* socialist economic systems

socialist economic systems: authoritarian socialism, 379; command socialism, 379; definition of, 377; market socialism, 379–380, 387–388

sole proprietorships: advantages of, 145–147; as business organizations, 145–149; by size of receipts, *c167;* control of, 146–147; definition of, 145; disadvantages of, 147–149; growth potential of, 149; liability for, 147; longevity of, 149; profit and, 147; responsibility for, 149; restrictions on, 146; start up of, 145–146; types of, 145; unlimited liability of, 147, 149; zoning laws affecting, 146

South Africa, 126, 417, 441

South Korea, 385, 415, 437

Southern Common Market (AMERCOSUR), 445

Soviet Union: agricultural production and, 393; central planning and, 391, 393; as command socialist system, 379, 389; East Germany and, 383; economic reform in, 393–395; fall of, *c394;* Gosplan and, 391; Lenin and, 390–391; as most-favored-nation, 444; nations formed from, *m380;* production problems in, 393; Stalin and, 391, 393. *See also* Russia

Sowell, Thomas, 271

Spain, 411, 427, 445

specialization: definition of, 10; economic interdependence and, 427–430; in partnerships, 151; trade and, 427, 443

specie, 305, 311

Sri Lanka, 412

SSA. *See* Social Security Administration (SSA)

St. Luke Penny Savings Bank, 325

stability. *See* economic stability

stability in value, 302

Stalin, Joseph, 391, 393

standard of living: definition of, 39; developing nations and, 442–443; growth and, 241–242; government growth and, 279, 281; gross domestic product and, 403

standard of value, 301, 302

Standard Oil Company, 137

Standard Oil Company of Ohio, 132

Standard Oil of New Jersey, 131

Standard Oil Trust, 131

state-chartered banks, 209, 308, 310

stock markets: American Stock Exchange (AMEX), 207; bear market, 209; bull market, 209; crashes, 211; Mexican stock market, 209; National Association of Securities Dealers Automated Quotations (NASDAQ), 207; New York Stock Exchange (NYSE), 207; over-the-counter market, 207; regulation of, *c212*

stockbrokers, 206–207; as career, 206

stockholders: benefits for, 156; capitalist economic systems and, 377; control of corporation, 158; and corporate taxes, 158; limited liability of, 205; participation in corporation management, 158, 205

stocks: bear market, 209; blue chip stocks, 208; brokers of, 206–207; bull market, 209; capital gains and, 205; capital losses and, 205; common stock, 155; corporate finances and, 209; corporate stock, 155; definition of, 155; dividends on, 155–156, 204; Dow Jones Industrial Average, 209, *g209;* employee stock ownership plans (ESOPs), 185; external forces and, 209; growth stocks, 204; income stocks, 204; investment banks and, 206–207; investor expectations and, 209; of, 213; limited risk of, 205; over-the-counter market, 207; ownership of, 205–206; preferred stock, 155; price determinants of, 207–209; profit potential of, 204–205; prospectus for, 195, 213; reasons for investing in, 204–206; stock exchanges, 207; stock splits, 205, *c205;* trading of, 206–208

store of value, 302, 303

strikes: boycotts and, 189; coordinated campaigning and, 189; definition of, 188; injunctions against, 190; and lockouts, 190; management responses to, 189–190; picketing and, 188–189; primary boycotts and, 189; reasons for, 188; replacement workers for, 189–190; secondary boycotts and, 189; Taft-Hartley Act applied to, 189, 190

"strong" dollar, 433

structural unemployment, 252, 253, 255

subsidiaries, 160–161

subsidies, 82

subsistence agriculture, 404–405

substitute goods: definition of, 60; monopoly and, 127

substitution effect: definition of, 52; law of demand and, 52–53

suburbs, 353

Superstation TBS, 147

supply, 72–93; changes in, 79–85; competition and, 83; decrease in, *c90;* definition of, 73; determinants of, 79–80; elasticity of, 76–78; equilibrium and, 103, 106–107; foreign exchange rates and, 433; government regulations and, 82; labor force and, 169–171; law of, 73–75; nature of, 73–78; subsidies and, 82; supply-side economics and, 355–356; taxes and, 81–82. *See also* demand; and headings beginning with supply

supply curve: competition and, 83; definition of, 75; examples of, *g74, g80;* price of resources affecting, 80; producer expectations and, 84–85; technology and, 82–83

supply schedule, *g74,* 75, *g103*

supply shifts, 74–75, 79–80

supply shock, 258

supply-side economics: definition of, 355; elements of, 355–356; government's role in, 355; laissez-faire approach, 355; limitations of, 356; model of, *c356;* taxes and, 355

surplus: definition of, 105; equilibrium and, 104–105; price floors and, 110

Sweden: socialism in, 386, 387–388; trade and, 445

Switzerland, 445

T

Taft, William Howard, 130, 362

Taft-Hartley Act of 1947, 186–187, 189, 190

Taiwan, 415

tariffs, 354, 439, *g440*

tax incentives, 358–359

tax rates: definition of, 349; state sales tax rates, *m352*

taxation: federal budget and, 365; fiscal policy and, 358; inflation and, 358; socialism and, 388; unemployment and, 358. *See also* taxes

taxes: collecting taxes, 350–354; corporate income taxes, 158, 351; customs duty, 354; definition of, 81; direct taxes, 235; economic growth and, 242–243; estate tax, 354; excise tax, 354; expansionary fiscal policy and, 360; Federal Insurance Contributions Act (FICA) and, 351; federal tax receipts by source, *g351;* gift tax, 354; indirect taxes, 235; individual income taxes, 350–351; internationally, 350; investment tax credit, 358; Medicare and, 351; Old-Age, Survivors, and Disability Insurance (OASDI) and, 351; progressive income taxes and, 359; progressive taxes, 349, 350–351; property taxes, 351–352; proportional taxes, 349, 351; regressive taxes, 349–350, 351, 354; sales taxes, 352, *m352,* 354; self-employed workers and, 351; Social Security and, 351; supply

and, 81–82; supply-side economics and, 355; tax incentives, 358–359; tax rates, 349; types of, 349–350. *See also* taxation

Teamsters Union, 188

technological monopoly: definition of, 128; examples of, 128

technology: definition of, 7; developing nations and, 408; economic development and, 408; economic growth and, 244; income gap and, 267, 268; investments and, 202–203; new markets and, 59; new products and, 59; production costs and, 82–83; productivity and, 244; supply curve and, 82–83; unemployment and, 253

telemarketing, 88

Thailand, 421–422, 445

"Third World countries," 410

thrifts, 316

Tiananmen Square Massacre, 397

tight-money policy, 338

time deposits: certificates of deposit, 197–198; savings bonds as, 198–199

total cost, 91

total product, 86

total revenue: definition of, 66; elastic demand and, 67; inelastic demand and, 67–68; maximizing total receipts, 68; as measurement of elasticity, 66–68

Toyota, 446

Toys "R" Us, 230

trade: Internet and, 442; specialization and, 427. *See also* international trade, headings beginning trade

trade barriers: definition of, 439; import quotas and, 440–441; licensing requirements as, 441; and, 439–440; trade restrictions and, 440–441

trade deficit, 437

trade-offs: comparative advantage and, 428–430; definition of, 11; economic goals and, 39–40; Federal Reserve system and, 343; international trade and, 428–430; opportunity costs and, 11–12; priorities and, 39–40

trade ratio, 428–430

trade surplus, 437

traditional economies: characteristics of, 24–25; definition of, 24; economic questions and, 26, Mbuti as, 24–25

transfer payments, 231, 235, 288

Treasury bills, 210, *c210*

Treasury bonds, 210, *c210*

Treasury Department. *See* Department of the Treasury

Treasury notes, 210, *c210*

Triangle Shirtwaist Company, 177

trough phase, 236, *g238*

Truman Doctrine, 420

trusts: anti-trust legislation, 130–133; definition of, 130

Truth-in-Lending Act, *c217*

Truth-in-Securities Act, 213

Turner, Ted, 147

21st Century, 37

Tyson, Laura, 455

UAW. *See* United Autoworker (UAW)

UFCW. *See* United Food and Commercial Workers (UFCW)

UFW. *See* United Farm Workers (UFW)

UMW. *See* United Mine Workers (UMW)

underemployed, 252

underground economies, 232, 233

UNDP. *See* United Nations Development Program (UNDP)

unemployment, 251–256; age and, *g253;* decline of industries and, 253; definition, 251–252; demand-side economics and, *c356,* 357–358; discouraged workers, 252; frictional unemployment, 252, 253; full employment and, 252; government spending and, 359; marginally attached workers, 252; measuring unemployment, 251–252; migrant workers and, 255; public transfer payments and, 359; sex and, *g253;* supply-side economics and, 355, *c356;* taxation and, 358; technological change and, 253; types of, 252–253, 255, 256; underemployed workers, 252; unemployment compensation, 359

unemployment rate, 252, 255, 256

Unilever, 417, *m418*

Union of Soviet Socialist Republics. *See* Soviet Union

Union Summer, 181

unions. *See* labor unions

United Auto Workers (UAW), 418

United Autoworker (UAW), 179

United Farm Workers (UFW), 181, 189

United Food and Commercial Workers (UFCW), 189

United Kingdom, 318, 330, *g436,* 437, 445. *See also* Great Britain

United Mine Workers (UMW), 179

United Nations, 280, 420, 422

United Nations Development Program (UNDP), 422

United Nations Industrial Development Organization (UNIDO), 422

United Parcel Service (UPS), 188

United States: economic features of, 29–35; economic goals of, 36–39, 284–290; features of U. S. economy, 29–35; foreign investment in, *g436;* as free-enterprise system, 29–35; imports and exports, *g438;* income distribution in, 265–268; income gap and, 267; inflation rate 1940–1996, *g262;* international trade, *m435;* natural resources of, 243; poverty in, 264–265; productivity and, *g245,* 246; research and development expenditures, *g244;* trade deficit of, 437; unemployment in 1995, *g253. See also* government

United States Airline Deregulation Act of 1978, 133

U.S. banknotes, 311

U.S. Customs Service, 334

U.S. Mint, 306, 334, 335

U.S. PIRG. *See* United States Public Interest Research Group (U.S. PIRG)

United States Public Interest Research Group (U.S. PIRG), 295

United Steel Workers (USW), 179

University of Texas, 175, 181

unlimited liability: in partnerships, 152; in sole proprietorships, 147, 149

Unsafe at Any Speed, 294

UPS. *See* United Parcel Service (UPS)

urban and regional planner: as career, 409

Uruguay, 445

USA Today, 37

usury, 216

USW. *See* United Steel Workers (USW)

utility, 17, 53

value, 16–17

variable costs, 91

venture capital, 203

vertical combinations, 159–160

Vietnam, 240, 414, 445

Vietnam War, 240

voluntary trade restrictions, 440–441

voting, 294

VOX, 37

ACKNOWLEDGMENTS

For permission to reprint copyrighted material, grateful acknowledgment is made to the following sources:

American Association of Community Colleges: From "Summertime Blues" by Bill Reinhard from *Community College Times,* June 29, 1993. Copyright © 1993 by American Association of Community Colleges.

American Management Association, New York: From quotes by Bill Cunningham from "Upstarts Stand Tall" by Patti Watts from *Management Review,* vol. 78, no. 1, January 1989. Copyright © 1989 by American Management Association. All rights reserved.

Bantam Books, a division of Bantam Doubleday Dell Publishing Group, Inc.: From *Iacocca: An Autobiography* by Lee Iacocca with William Novak. Copyright © 1984 by Lee Iacocca.

César E. Chávez Foundation, P.O. Box 62, La Paz, Keene, CA 93531; Tel. (805) 822-5571, Ext. 230; Fax (805) 822-6103: From a speech by César E. Chávez given on January 19, 1974. Copyright © 1974 by the César E. Chávez Foundation.

China Today: From "Vegetables for City People" (retitled "Lou Yumin's Account of a New System") by Lou Yumin from *China Reconstructs,* vol. XXXV, no. 1, January 1986, pp. 11–12 (North American Edition). Copyright © 1986 by China Today.

Don Curlee: From a letter by Don Curlee to the *Los Angeles Times,* January 1974. Copyright © 1974 by Don Curlee.

Gregg Easterbrook: From "The Sky Is Always Falling" by Gregg Easterbrook from *The New Republic,* vol. 201, no. 8, August 21, 1989. Copyright © 1989 by Gregg Easterbrook.

Jeremy Elson: From quotes by Jeremy Elson from "College Entrepreneurs Help High Schoolers Make a Match" by Peter Behr from *The Washington Post,* vol. 119, February 12, 1996. Copyright © 1996 by Jeremy Elson.

Harcourt Brace & Company: From *The General Theory of Employment, Interest, and Money* by John Maynard Keynes. Copyright 1936 and renewed © 1964 by Harcourt Brace & Company.

Institute for International Economics: From "America's High-Technology Trade Challenge: The Perspective of a Cautious Activist" from *Who's Bashing Whom?: Trade Conflict in High-Technology Industries* by Laura D'Andrea Tyson. Copyright © 1993 by the Institute for International Economics. All rights reserved.

Los Angeles Times Syndicate: From "Youthful Drive: AFL-CIO Hopes Union Summer Will Inspire New Generation" by Stuart Silverstein and Robert A. Rosenblatt from the *Los Angeles Times,* vol. 115, May 2, 1996. Copyright © 1996 by Los Angeles Times Syndicate.

William Morrow & Company, Inc.: From "Economic Differences" from *The Economics and Politics of Race* by Thomas Sowell. Copyright © 1983 by Thomas Sowell, Inc.

The New York Times Company: From "As Piracy Grows in Mexico, U.S. Companies Shout Foul" (retitled "Fighting a Formidable Force") by Julia Preston from *The New York Times,* April 28, 1996. Copyright © 1996 by The New York Times Company.

New York University Press: From *Selected Economic Writings of W. Arthur Lewis,* edited by Mark Gersovitz. Copyright © 1983 by New York University.

W. W. Norton & Company, Inc.: From "The Balance of Resources" from *Only One Earth: The Care and Maintenance of a Small Planet* by Barbara Ward and René Dubos. Copyright © 1972 by Report on the Environment, Inc.

Janet Prindle: From "Adam Smith, Social Investor" by Janet Prindle and Farha-Joyce Haboucha from *The Christian Science Monitor,* December 10, 1996. Copyright © 1996 by Janet Prindle.

21st Century, Box 30, Newton, MA 02161: Quote by John and Stephanie Meyer, quote by David Anable, quote by an anonymous teenager about American art, and quote by an anonymous teenager about problems associated with television as printed in *The Christian Science Monitor,* May 13, 1996. Copyright © 1996 by 21st Century.

SOURCES CITED:

Quotes by Jennifer Hill and Roya Rastegar from "Teens on the Scene: Cub Reporters Cover the Olympics" by Kristine Anderson from *The Christian Science Monitor,* July 30, 1996. Published by The Christian Science Publishing Society.

Quotes by Barbara Duvoisin and Dennis Raphael from "Many Seek American Dream—Outside America" by Warren Richey et al., from *The Christian Science Monitor,* March 19, 1997. Published by The Christian Science Publishing Society.

PHOTO CREDITS

Abbreviations used: (t) top, (c) center, (b) bottom, (l) left, (r) right.

All money borders throughout book: HRW photo.

FRONT COVER, Comstock,Inc.; **TITLE PAGE,** Page iii, Comstock, Inc.;

TABLE OF CONTENTS, Page: vi(t), HRW photo by Peter Van Steen; vi(b), HRW photo; vii(all), viii, ix(all), HRW photo by Peter Van Steen, x(t), R. Crandall/The Image Works; x(b), David Ball/The Stock Market; xi(t), Lars Sward/Pica Pressfoto, xi(b), Forrest Anderson/Gamma-Liaison; xii, xiii, HRW photo by Peter Van Steen; xiv(t), Courtesy of Union Summer, AFL-CIO; xiv(b), John Madere/The Stock Market; xv, HRW photo by Peter Van Steen;

SKILLS HANDBOOK, Page: xx, R. Berenholtz/The Stock Market; xxi, HRW photo by Scott Van Osdol; xxii, Courtesy of Union Summer, AFL-CIO; xxiii, Jay Mallin; xxiii(bdr), HRW photo; xxiv, Courtesy of Oxford University Press, HRW photo by Sam Dudgeon; xxvii(t), Courtesy of Harcourt Brace/Harvest Books, HRW photo by Sam Dudgeon; xxvii(b), courtesy of Library of Congress; xxix, HRW photo by Peter Van Steen; xxxvii, Southern Oregon Historical Society, image #8217

UNIT ONE, Page: xxxviii–1, HRW photo by Peter Van Steen; **Chapter One,** Page: 2, HRW photo by Peter Van Steen; 4(t), HRW photo; 4(b), David Young-Wolff/Tony Stone Images; 5, Larry Downing/Sygma; 6, Gary Braasch/Woodfin Camp & Associates; 8, HRW photo by Peter Van Steen; 10, Sergio Dorantes/Sygma; 12, Paul E. Johnson/Gamma-Liaison; 15, Novosti/R.I.A./Gamma-Liaison; 16, HRW photo by Sam Dudgeon; 17, J.L. Atlan/Sygma; 18, Chris Sorensen; **Chapter Two,** Page 22, HRW photo by Peter Van Steen; 23, N. Rowan/The Image Works; 24, Nick Robinson/Panos Pictures; 25, Giraudon/Art Resource, NY; 26, Corbis-Bettmann Archives; 27(t), Rolando Pujol/Woodfin Camp & Associates; 27(c), Najlan Feanny/SABA; 27(b), Poincet/Sygma; 29, Joan Slatkin/Archive Photos; 30, Don Mason/The Stock Market; 31, S. Gazin/The Image Works; 32, HRW photo by Peter Van Steen; 33, Laurence Parent; 35, 37, HRW photo by Peter Van Steen; 38(t), R Lord/The Image Works; 38(b), Julie Marcotte/Tony Stone World Wide; 40, 42, HRW photo by Peter Van Steen; 45, NASA; 47, HRW photo by Sam Dudgeon;

UNIT TWO, Page: 48–49, HRW photo by Peter Van Steen; **Chapter Three,** Page 50, 51, 53, 56, 58, HRW photo by Peter Van Steen; 59, Courtesy of Proctor & Gamble; 60(both), HRW photo by Peter Van Steen; 61, Spencer Grant/Gamma Liaison; 63,64, 65, 68, HRW photo by Peter Van Steen; **Chapter Four,** Page 72, 73, 76, 77, HRW photo by Peter Van Steen; 81, Brian Atkinson/Tony Stone Images; 82, Courtesy of the Ford Archives, Henry Ford Museum, Dearborn, Michigan; 83, 84, 85, HRW photo by Peter Van Steen; 88, HRW photo by Michael Lyon; 89, HRW photo by Peter Van Steen; 91, Charles Gupton/The Stock Market; 92, HRW photo by Sam Dudgeon; **Chapter Five,** Page 96, HRW photo by Peter Van Steen; 99, UPI/Corbis-Bettmann; 100(t), HRW photo by Peter Van Steen; 100(b), Chuck Pefley/Tony Stone Images; 101, 102, HRW photo by Peter Van Steen; 104, Joseph Pobereskin/Tony Stone Images; 105, HRW photo by Peter Van Steen; 107, HRW photo by Sam Dudgeon; 108, Bernard Boutrit/Woodfin Camp & Associates; 109, HRW photo by Peter Van Steen; 110, Jim Anderson/Woodfin Camp & Associates; 112, Paul Merideth/Tony Stone Images-Click/Chicago Ltd.; **Chapter Six,** Page 116, 117, 118, HRW photo by Peter Van Steen; 120, Ralf-Finn Hestoft/Saba; 121, HRW photo by Peter Van Steen; 126, Gerald Cubitt; 128(t), Baron Wolman/Tony Stone Images; 128(b), HRW photo by Peter Van Steen; 130(l), 130(r), Bureau of Engraving and Printing; 131(tc), Culver Pictures; 132, Archive Photos; 134, 137, HRW photo by Sam Dudgeon;

UNIT THREE, Page: 142–143, Seth Resnick/Gamma Liaison; **Chapter Seven,** Page 144, HRW photo by Peter Van Steen; 146, Rick Stewart/Allsport; 147(t), HRW photo by Peter Van Steen; 147(b), Courtesy of Ninfa's; 148, ©Houston Chronicle; 150, Courtesy of Ben and Jerry's Homemade; 157, 162(t), 162(b), 163(t), HRW photo by Peter Van Steen; 164, Todd Rosenberg/Allsport; **Chapter Eight,** Page 168, HRW photo by Peter Van Steen; 171, Geoffrey Orth/Alaska Stock Images; 172, Print Collection, Miriam and Ira D. Wallach Division of Art, Print and Photographs, The New York Public Library, Astor, Lenox and Tilden Foundations; 175, Archive Photos; 177, 178, Culver Pictures; 181, Courtesy of Union Summer, AFL-CIO; 184, HRW photo by Peter Van Steen; 185, Shelly Katz/Gamma Liaison; 186, HRW photo by Peter Van Steen; 187, 188, AP/Wide World Photos; 189, UPI/Corbis-Bettmann; 190, David H. Wells/The Image Works; **Chapter Nine,** Page 194, HRW photo by Peter Van Steen; 195, Tom & Deann McCarthy/The Stock Market; 198, U.S. Treasury Department, drawn by Dawn Larson, a 6th grade student from Ute, Iowa. Her poster was awarded first place in the 1996 U.S. Savings Bonds National Student Poster Contest; 200, HRW photo by Peter Van Steen; 201, Michael Keller/The Stock Market; 202, Vince Streano/Tony Stone Images; 203, HRW photo by Peter Van Steen; 204, Bryan F. Peterson/The Stock Market; 206, HRW photo by Peter Van Steen; 207, Joan Menschenfreund/The Stock Market; 211, Bettmann Archives; 214, HRW photo by Peter Van Steen; 223, 224, HRW photo by Sam Dudgeon;

UNIT FOUR, Page: 226–227, R. Berenholtz/The Stock Market; Chapter Ten, Page 233, HRW photo by Peter Van Steen; 237, HRW photo by Sam Dudgeon; 239, HRW photo by Peter Van Steen; 241, Forrest Anderson/Gamma Liaison; 243, HRW photo by Peter Van Steen; **Chapter Eleven,** Page 250, Mark Houston/Adventure Photos; 251, HRW photo by Peter Van Steen; 254, Culver Pictures; 256, Bruce Forster/Tony Stone Images, Inc.; 257, 259, HRW photo by Peter Van Steen; 264, Paul Fusco/Magnum Photos Inc.;

UNIT FIVE, Page: 276–277, A. Tannenbaum/Sygma; **Chapter Twelve,** Page 278, HRW photo by Peter Van Steen; 280, Brown Brothers; 282, HRW photo by Peter Van Steen; 284, David Young Wolff/Tony Stone Images, Inc.; 286, Jeffrey D. Smith/Woodfin Camp & Associates; 287, 288, HRW photo by Peter Van Steen; 291, Paul Chesley/Tony Stone Images; 292, 294, HRW photo by Peter Van Steen; 295, Courtesy of United States Public Interest Research Group; 296, AP/Wide World Photo; **Chapter Thirteen,** Page 300,

301, 302(t), HRW photo by Peter Van Steen; 302(b), Mark Greenberg/Gamma-Liaison; 305, Superstock; 306, R. Crandall/The Image Works; 307, HRW photo by Sam Dudgeon; 309(l), National Portrait Gallery, Smithsonian Institution/Art Resource, NY; 309(r), National Portrait Gallery, Smithsonian Institution; gift of the Regents of the Smithsonian Institution, the Thomas Jefferson Memorial Foundation/Art Resource, NY; 310, Courtesy, American Antiquarian Society; 311, Culver Pictures; 312, Brown Brothers; 313, HRW photo by Peter Van Steen; 314, John Van Hasselt/Sygma; 315, 317,318, 319, HRW photo by Peter Van Steen; **Chapter Fourteen**, Page 326, Comstock; 327, HRW photo by Sam Dudgeon; 328, HRW photo by Peter Van Steen; 337, John Madere/The Stock Market; 340, AP/Wide World Photo; 344, NASA; **Chapter Fifteen**, Page 348, Wally McNamee/Sygma; 353, Merrick Advertising; 354, 357, 358, HRW photo by Peter Van Steen; 360, John Ficara/Sygma; 371(l), 371(r), HRW photo by Sam Dudgeon;

UNIT SIX, Page: 374–375, Courtesy, Special Collections Division, The University of Texas at Arlington Libraries, Arlington, Texas.; **Chapter Sixteen**, Page 376, Mike McQueen/Tony Stone Images; 378, HRW photo by Peter Van Steen; 381, AKG London; 382, Karen Kasmauski/ Woodfin Camp & Associates, Inc.; 383, Anthony Suau/Gamma-Liaison; 384, Gilles Bouquillon/Gamma-Liaison; 386, Corbis-Bettmann; 387, Lars Sward/Pica Pressfoto; 388, Blaine Harrington III; 389, AKG London; 390, HRW photo by Sam Dudgeon; 391, AKG London; 392, Dennis Cox/ChinaStock; 393, Filip Horvat/Saba; 396, New China Pictures/Eastfoto/Sovfoto; 398, Charlesworth/Saba; **Chapter Seventeen**, Page 402, Arabella Cecil/Panos Pictures; 407, B. Zaunders/The Stock Market; 408, Robert Frerck/Woodfin Camp & Associates, Inc.; 409, HRW photo by Peter Van Steen; 410, T. Pierce/SABA; 411, W. Campbell/ Sygma; 412(t), Patrick Morrow; 412(b), A. Tannenbaum/Sygma; 413, Diego Goldberg/Sygma; 414, Goitia/Saba; 417, Rhodri Jones/Panos Pictures; 420, Courtesy of Peace Corps; 422, Frank Fournier/Contact/The Stock Market; **Chapter Eighteen**, Page 426, David Ball/The Stock Market; 428, John F. Mason/The Stock Market; 429, HRW photo by Peter Van Steen; 431, Frederick Charles/Gamma-Liaison; 433, Everton/The Image Works; 434, Courtesy of Mt. Edgecumbe High School in Sitka, Alaska; 439, Paul Howell/Gamma-Liaison; 441, Tony Savino/The Image Works; 446, HRW photo by Peter Van Steen; 449, University of California;

REFERENCE SECTION, Page: 454–455, Seth Resnick/Gamma-Liaison; **Consumer Handbook**, Page 457, 458, 459, 460, HRW photo by Peter Van Steen; 461, courtesy of Dunlop Tires; 462, HRW photo by Peter Van Steen; 464, Courtesy of Intuit; 465, R. Lord/The Image Works; 466, Vince Streano/Tony Stone Images; 467, Archive Photos; 469, HRW photo by Peter Van Steen; 471, S. Gazin/The Image Works; 472, AP/Wide World Photo; 474, 475, HRW photo by Peter Van Steen; 476, Joan Menschenfreund/The Stock Market; 478, HRW photo by Peter Van Steen;

ART CREDITS